Business Fluctuations, Growth, and Economic Stabilization: A Reader

BUSINESS FLUCTUATIONS, GROWTH, *and* ECONOMIC STABILIZATION

A Reader

Edited by

JOHN J. CLARK
St. John's University, New York

&

MORRIS COHEN
Fortune Magazine AND St. John's University, New York

Random House   New York

Preface

Recognizing the seriousness of Soviet economic rivalry, Americans have been moved to take stock of their own economic system, to assess its advantages and limitations. They have generally agreed that the United States must achieve a rate of growth which will enable it to maintain its present margin of superiority. But from the lessons of past experience we have come to realize that under the institutional arrangements of private enterprise, growth does not proceed at an even pace; rather, varying rates of growth among the several parts of the economy produce alternating periods of expansion and contraction of the whole. The forces which make for growth make also for changes in the rate of economic progress. Herein lies the challenge to a system of private enterprise: to contain business fluctuations within reasonable limits without destroying the incentives which stimulate economic growth. The readings presented in this volume attest that it is a challenge which, since the middle of the nineteenth century, has provoked from economists an impressive array of professional literature.

Initially, it was our purpose to edit a book of readings in business fluctuations and economic stabilization for use in graduate classes. However, notwithstanding the affectations of economists, their technical jargon and semantic dueling, and their propensity to drop an archaic Latin term* or two into an already unintelligible paragraph, the book should arouse the interest not only of students but of laymen. The latter will discover not literary enchantment, but a sense of proportion and a better insight into the economic issues which today stir the body politic.

The articles and excerpts chosen for inclusion in the book blend the best of classic and contemporary literature, with a view to portraying the evolution of thinking on the business cycle. Thus the table of contents lists some old favorites—articles by Kitchin, Kondratieff, and Schum-

* We sin in this respect ourselves.

peter—along with the prognosis of the pundits of the "new frontier"—
the now famous May and August 1961 issues of the *Morgan Guaranty
Survey*. The bulk, however, consists of literature of the 1940's and 1950's,
decades which saw the fruition of many lines of investigation. This set
of choices, of course, clearly represents a value judgment not necessarily
congenial to all economists and for which we may pay dearly, post-
publication.

We have further organized the essays to achieve a logical and orderly
presentation of the subject matter by adopting the following classification:

I. *Varieties of Business Fluctuations*. This Part deals with the different
kinds of fluctuation to which business activity is subject and provides
necessary background for the empirical analysis and theoretical treatment
of the business cycle phenomenon.

II. *Empirical Analysis of Business Cycles*. The articles in this group
are devoted to descriptions of the business cycle and measurements of
its duration and amplitude.

III. *Business Cycle Theory*. Commencing with three articles treating
the topic in general terms, this Part describes the principal approaches
which economists have taken in seeking the causes of cyclical fluctuations:
Underconsumption, Multiplier and Accelerator Models, Nonmonetary
Investment Theories, Monetary Theories, and Psychological Factors.

IV. *Economic Stabilization, Growth, and Inflation*. In choosing articles
for this classification, we hoped to underscore the questions raised by
policies already adopted to achieve economic stability and further proposals for reform and to place all in the context of world competition
between the private enterprise economy of the United States and the
directed economy of the U.S.S.R.

Discontinuity and fragmentation often characterize books of readings.
It is our hope that the general framework and the introductions to each
of the principal Parts and to each article will impart a continuity to the
whole and permit the reading of the book as a comprehensive treatment
of the subject. Like considerations impelled us to include, in almost all
cases, the complete article or chapter chosen rather than excerpts from
it. This seemed the fairest procedure to assume both toward the author,
who is entitled to offer his hypothesis with suitable qualifications and
nuances, and toward the reader, who is entitled to review the full logic
of the argument.

The task of choosing specific articles and authors was not an easy one,
and doubtless many readers will recall writings they consider more
worthy of inclusion in the volume. The present articles were selected,
however, not only for their intrinsic merit but also because the author's
treatment of the subject matter worked felicitously into our system of
classification. The editors will be well satisfied if the articles stimulate
further investigation by the reader into this vital and timely area of
economic thought.

The reader may be interested in the personal achievements of our contributors, some of whom are, or have been, quite prominent in national affairs. We have endeavored therefore to present in the introductions to the articles a brief biographical sketch of each author. This material appears either in the body of the text or in a footnote.

Any single volume on this subject must, in a sense, be introductory. Graduate students ought to go further into this or that aspect of the subject, and many laymen, responding to the stimulus of a particular author or idea, may wish to do so. Therefore, we have incorporated some suggestions "For Further Reading" at the conclusion of each Part and section and have rounded off the volume with an extensive Bibliography. The latter, although it embodies some items of an earlier era, primarily stresses the literature of the period since World War II. Together with those given by the individual authors, these citations make the book a good starting point for the professional economist, the thesis writer, or the layman striving to formulate a personal hypothesis or judgment on business fluctuations and economic stabilization.

The editors should like to express their appreciation to Mr. Norman Rickard, graduate assistant at the College of Business Administration, St. John's University, for his valued assistance in the preparation of the Bibliography, and to Miss Carol Cerar, secretary to the Graduate Division, who, although involved in the details of forthcoming marriage, found time to complete the preparation of the manuscript. Both served beyond the call of duty.

JOHN J. CLARK
MORRIS COHEN

Contents

PART I

Varieties of Business Fluctuations

❊❊❊

INTRODUCTION

~~~~~~

A major part of any science is simply useful classification. Business fluctuations extend far beyond "the business cycle." Over the past century or so, economists have discovered three main divisions of business fluctuations: seasonal, cyclical, and long-run. (There are, besides, irregular or random fluctuations which represent singular events, such as famines, wars, earthquakes, and tidal waves.) Although none of the articles below deals exclusively with seasonal fluctuations, the authors by no means consider them irrelevant. In point of fact, seasonal fluctuations are important in their own right, and have to be corrected before the cyclical component can be studied. It is perfectly plain that short-term developments are greatly affected by seasonal fluctuations, and serious errors can result if the seasonal factor is ignored.

The business cycle, in Mitchell's sense, is a congeries of fluctuations in a wide variety of economic phenomena. There is no such thing as "the" business cycle; rather, there are subcycles in almost every phase of economic activity. This is not to say that the approach to business fluctuations is to seek and find mechanical relationships which can be reduced to mathematical form and extrapolated. Whatever history has shown, it has made clear that cycles do differ widely, and averages of past cyclical experience can sometimes be misleading.

Some sectors of the economy are more susceptible to fluctuations than others. Cycles in home-building and inventories are leading examples. Cycles in fixed investment, plant and equipment expenditures, and consumer durable outlays are others. Each must be studied separately as individual units as well as in terms of component parts, such as cycles in building of apartments and of single-family homes. The search is continually at a disaggregated level, and the ideal would be thousands of individual components that could be analyzed on high-speed computers.

Not only are there all kinds of seasonal and cyclical patterns; there are also all kinds of long cycles, or long waves. These latter are more controversial; indeed, many economists do not recognize their existence. Over a century, one can measure a large number of business cycles, but one can count only two long waves, if each is assumed to last fifty years—a fact which obviously makes long waves much more difficult to study than business cycles. Yet the concept of the long wave is an intriguing one, and it offers opportunity for a longer perspective. There is always danger that the short-term fluctuations, which are readily observable and highly exciting as they occur, will overwhelm the longer-run tendencies which may, in the end, be even more important.

It should be clear from a reading of the articles in Part I that whereas there are many types of business fluctuations, each interesting and significant in its own right, there exists as yet no general theoretical framework encompassing the whole field. Nonetheless, an appreciation of the theoretical advances already made can only serve to improve the empirical research that remains to be done. Perhaps the last word has not yet been written on the types of business fluctuations. Perhaps we can look forward to the study of fluctuations in those countries where the state directs economic activity. Surely, if we had all the facts, we would discover that economic fluctuations also characterize the Soviet and other communist economies.

[1]

Mitchell on What Happens During Business Cycles[*]

ARTHUR F. BURNS[†]

Editors' Note

Wesley C. Mitchell (1874–1948), considered by many to be the leading American authority on business cycles, coined the term itself in 1913. A founder of the National Bureau of Economic Research and its first and long-time Director of Research, Mitchell was not primarily a theorist, though his goal was a better theory of business cycles based upon the sifting and digesting of a multitude of economic statistics. He died before his work was completed, and Arthur F. Burns, his protégé and friend, who worked closely with him for many years, has carried on.

In this article, which introduced Mitchell's last study, Burns points out that business cycles are widely diffused through a free enterprise, profit-

* Arthur F. Burns' introduction to Wesley C. Mitchell's *What Happens during Business Cycles: A Progress Report*, National Bureau of Economic Research. Studies in Business Cycles 5 (1951), pp. vii-xxi. Reprinted by permission of the National Bureau of Economic Research.

† Born in Austria in 1904, Burns completed his graduate studies at Columbia University, receiving his Ph.D. in 1934. He subsequently served with the faculties of Rutgers University and Columbia. Following a term as Director of Research of the National Bureau of Economic Research from 1946 to 1952, he was appointed Chairman of the Council of Economic Advisors, a post which he held until 1956. Since then, Burns has been President of the National Bureau and Professor of Economics at Columbia. In addition to numerous articles in professional and other media, Burns has written several books: *Production Trends in the United States, Since 1870* (1934); *Measuring Business Cycles* (1946, with Wesley Mitchell); *New Factors on Business Cycles* (1950); *The Instability of Consumer Spending* (1952); *Business Cycle Research and the Needs of Our Times* (1953); *The Frontiers of Economic Research* (1954); and *Prosperity Without Inflation* (1957).

seeking economy. Cycles cannot be considered in terms of a few broad aggregates, but must be viewed in terms of hundreds of time series (Mitchell examined over eight hundred). Each stage of the cycle flows into the next one and sets up the preconditions for it. As a result, each stage is inextricably linked with the succeeding one. Mitchell sets up a "normal" business cycle and describes what takes place. Since the phenomenon is so complex, many factors must be considered. Although the end result is extremely helpful for understanding cyclical fluctuations, it is fair to say that Mitchell never quite succeeded in developing a widely accepted theory of the business cycle. Yet it is also fair to say that Mitchell's contribution to the study of business cycles ranks at the very pinnacle.

❦ Shortly before his death Wesley Mitchell put in my care the completed parts of the "progress report" he was preparing on his long and elaborate investigation of "what happens during business cycles." This book is substantially the document he left behind. I have felt free to make numerous changes of detail, but I have not interfered with the design, nor attempted to complete the narrative. The work of a major scientist, even if not half done, deserves a life of its own, unencumbered by the hand or voice of another. So it is especially when, as in the present case, the fragment has well-defined contours, balance, and direction. But for the guidance of students who may take up the book for the first time, I shall put down a few remarks about Mitchell's objectives and what he accomplished.

I

Business cycles are not merely fluctuations in aggregate economic activity. The critical feature that distinguishes them from the commercial convulsions of earlier centuries or from the seasonal and other short-term variations of our own age is that the fluctuations are widely diffused over the economy—its industry, its commercial dealings, and its tangles of finance. The economy of the Western world is a system of closely inter-related parts. He who would understand business cycles must master the workings of an economic system organized largely in a network of free enterprises searching for profit. The problem of how business cycles come about is therefore inseparable from the problem of how a capitalist economy functions.

This conception governs Mitchell's posthumous book, as it does his earlier writings. Mitchell was not content to focus analysis on the fluctuations of one or two great variables, such as production or employment.

His concern was with *business* cycles and he therefore sought to interpret the system of business as a whole—the formation of firms and their disappearance, prices as well as output, the employment of labor and other resources, the flow of incomes to and from the public, costs and profits, savings and investments, the merchandising of securities as well as commodities, the money supply, its turnover, and the fiscal operations of government. Not only that, but he sought to penetrate the façade of business aggregates and trace the detailed processes—psychological, institutional, and technological—by which they are fashioned and linked together.

Thus Mitchell took as his scientific province a terrain as farflung and intricate as Walras's and Marshall's. But he explored more fully than his predecessors the obstacles to the mutual adjustment of economic quantities in a disturbed environment. "Time . . . is the centre of the chief difficulty of almost every economic problem."[1] Pursuing this Marshallian theme through uncharted jungles of statistics, Mitchell detected systematic differences in the rates of movement of economic variables, and arrived at an early stage of his scientific work at the conception that our economic system of interdependent parts generates a cyclical path instead of moving towards an equilibrium position. This fateful twist aside, Mitchell's economic outlook was thoroughly Marshallian. Had he lived to finish this book, he would have inscribed on its title page Marshall's motto: "The many in the one, the one in the many."

The hypothesis that each stage of the business situation tends to develop out of the preceding stage and to grow into the next in a cyclical pattern poses two major questions: Does economic life actually proceed in recurrent fluctuations having similar characteristics? If so, by what processes are continuous and repetitive movements of this character brought about? In a search for definite and dependable answers, Mitchell examined "facts on a wholesale scale," as had Darwin before him in a related field, and Lyell before Darwin. "My success as a man of science," wrote Darwin, "has been determined . . . by complex and diversified mental qualities and conditions. Of these, the most important have been—the love of science—unbounded patience in long reflecting over any subject— industry in observing and collecting facts—and a fair share of invention as well as of common sense."[2] These, too, were the sources of Mitchell's scientific strength. In his quarto on *Business Cycles*, published in 1913, he anchored a theory of fluctuations to an array of empirical observations unprecedentedly full for its time. But Mitchell was not content with this achievement. World War I had ushered in a new era of economic statistics, able theorists were elaborating new hypotheses, and statistical analysts were rapidly fashioning new devices for disentangling economic

---

[1] Alfred Marshall, Preface to the first edition of his *Principles of Economics* (Macmillan).

[2] Charles Darwin, "Autobiography," in *Life and Letters*, ed. Francis Darwin (Appleton, 1888), Vol. 1, pp. 68, 85-86.

movements. Eager to exploit the new materials for research, Mitchell launched in 1922 a fresh investigation of business cycles.

II

The science of economic fluctuations is only beginning to pass into an inductive stage. Even today the descriptions of business cycles by economists often resemble the descriptions of plant life by writers of antiquity, who commonly relied on "casual observations, no experiments and much speculative thinking."[3] If later botanists often "could not identify the plants by the descriptions," so it has also been in economics. As long as investigators worked by themselves, they could not very well "collect the masses of raw data pertinent to the study of cyclical behavior, segregate the cyclical components from movements of other sorts, and assemble the findings to form a realistic model of business cycles by which explanations could be judged."[4] In recent decades the organization of scientific institutes has greatly enlarged the possibilities of empirical research in economics. Mitchell made the most of the opportunity afforded by the resources of the National Bureau. Taking his own and others' explanations of business cycles as "guides to research, not objects of research" (p. 5), he delved deeply into the facts of cyclical behavior and the relationships among them. The wish to contribute to economic policy was strong in Mitchell. Stronger still was his conviction that intelligent control of business cycles depends upon sound theoretical understanding, which requires tolerably full and accurate knowledge of what the business cycles of experience have been like.

Business Cycles: The Problem and Its Setting, the first major instalment of Mitchell's investigation, was published in 1927. The second appeared in 1946 under the title *Measuring Business Cycles*. In the meantime numerous studies of special aspects of cyclical fluctuations were prepared by the Bureau's staff, and a small group was steadily engaged in analyzing the cyclical behavior of economic processes.[5] It was Mitchell's hope to integrate the findings of his collaborators with his own and other investigators' results; that is, to develop a model of business cycles from carefully screened observations, to use it in explaining how the cycles of experience are typically propagated, and then press on to account for the outstanding differences among them.[6] But he would have fallen short of the goal even if he had lived to complete the present book. Many of the needed materials —especially for foreign countries—were not in shape for use, and the subject of business cycle differences required systematic investigations yet to be undertaken. As it stands, Mitchell's report barely covers the first

---

[3] William Crocker, "Botany of the Future," *Science*, October 28, 1938, pp. 387, 388.

[4] Mitchell, *What Happens during Business Cycles: A Progress Report*, p. 4. All other page references, unless otherwise indicated, are to the text of Mitchell's report.

[5] See the list of publications on business cycles at the end of Mitchell's report.

[6] For a fuller account, see "Wesley Mitchell and the National Bureau," in the Bureau's *Twenty-ninth Annual Report*.

three of the seven parts he had planned. Part I sets out his aims, methods, and materials. Part II deals with the great variety of cyclical movements characteristic of individual economic activities. Part III, not fully completed, shows how the cyclical movements of different parts of the American economy fit together into business cycles, and paves the way for analyzing the processes of expansion, recession, contraction, and revival, to which the last four parts were to be devoted.

Thus the book is a 'progress report,' both in the sense in which Mitchell intended the phrase and in the poignant sense forced by his death. Yet no existing publication elucidates so fully or so authoritatively what happens during business cycles as Mitchell's fragment. The accent of the book is on characteristic behavior, formalized in the concept of a 'typical cycle.' "The only normal condition" of business, as Mitchell once expressed it, "is a state of change";[7] but some states of change are 'normal' and others 'abnormal,' and Mitchell's 'typical cycle' is designed to take account of such differences. Hence, this concept is similar in some respects to the classicists' 'normal.' The role of each is to segregate the effects of complex causes: both are devices of abstraction: both are tools for analyzing new, concrete situations. Mitchell was keenly concerned about the wide variations among the business cycles of experience and eager to press investigations of them. But he deemed it essential, as a first step, to lay bare the typical characteristics of the alternating waves of prosperity and depression that have swept the economic world in modern times. In this emphasis he conformed to the usual practice of business cycle theorists. He broke with tradition, however, by extracting what is 'typical' or 'aberrant' from mass observations, and thus substituting fact and measure, as well as may be, for the impressionistic judgments that have ruled business cycle literature.

III

Mitchell begins his survey of what happens during business cycles by illustrating the varieties of behavior characteristic of economic activities in the United States. Some of the figures in his introductory chart merely confirm common knowledge. For example, commodity prices generally rise and fall with the tides in production; business failures increase during contractions of aggregate economic activity and diminish during expansions; the output of durables fluctuates more widely than the output of perishables; and prices are more stable at retail than at wholesale. It is less generally known, however, that crop production moves rather independently of business cycles, or that production typically fluctuates over a much wider range than prices, that the liabilities of business failures usually turn down months before economic recovery becomes general and turn up months before recession, that both durables and perishables experience their most vigorous decline well before the end of contraction, and that

---

[7] *Business Cycles: The Problem and Its Setting*, p. 376.

retail prices characteristically move later as well as less than wholesale prices.

Students who will take the trouble to ponder these facts are not likely to leave Mitchell's chart quickly. They will notice that orders for investment goods tend to lead the tides in aggregate activity; that private construction is more closely related to business cycles than public construction; that call money rates or even commercial paper rates greatly overstate the fluctuations in the rates of interest at which bank customers ordinarily borrow; that interest rates in New York tend to move before, and more widely than, those in the interior; that the number of business failures lags behind the liabilities; that bond prices tend to lead stock prices, which themselves lead the turns in aggregate activity; that bank deposits appear to be comparatively steady during depressions; that imports conform closely to business cycles while exports do not; that grocery sales fail to show the regular response to business cycles characteristic of retail trade at large; etc. And if the reader looks beyond the large processes that have dominated theoretical literature, he will see how peculiar the cyclical behavior of smaller sectors of activity can be. For example, cattle slaughter tends to move with the tides in aggregate activity while hog slaughter moves inversely; the dollar volume of residential construction contracts fluctuates less, not more, than the physical volume; cotton stocks held at mills run parallel with mill production, while stocks in public storage move inversely.

Thus business cycles are complex phenomena—far more so than has been commonly supposed. The sales of a large firm may be dominated by the tides in aggregate activity; the fortunes of a small firm are rather at the mercy of personal factors and conditions peculiar to the trade or locality. Some activities, like local transit or net gold movements between the United States and Great Britain, are apparently free from cyclical fluctuations. Others, notably farming, undergo cyclical movements, but they have little or no relation in time to business cycles. And these irregular responses, passed over lightly by theoretical writers, accord with reason: "We cannot expect any activity to respond regularly to business cycles unless it is subject to man's control within the periods occupied by cyclical phases, and unless this control is swayed, consciously or not, by short-period economic considerations. The domination of harvests by weather, the 'migratory property' of petroleum underground, the mixed motives of governments in undertaking construction work, the long-range planning that weighs with many men in a position to set 'administered prices,' the time-consuming negotiations that prevent prompt adjustments of certain other prices and many wage rates, the existence of long-term contracts, the years required to complete some large undertakings—these are concrete examples of the multifarious obstacles that interfere with prompt and regular response to the cyclical tides" (p. 95).

The processes that fail to bear the imprint of business cycles are nevertheless a minority. Almost nine-tenths of Mitchell's basic sample of ap-

proximately 800 time series fluctuate in sympathy with the tides in aggregate activity, but the movements of this imposing majority are far
from uniform. Between the cyclical recalcitrants, like farming, and the
cyclical regulars, like factory employment, there is a continuous gradation.
Coal and iron production conform more closely to the tides in aggregate
activity than the production of textiles or gasoline. The prices of industrial
commodities do not conform as well as their production, while the opposite relation rules in farming. Employment conforms better than wage
rates, bank loans than investments, open-market interest rates than cus-
tomer rates, stock prices than bond prices, etc. Some conforming processes
move early in the cyclical procession; for example, orders for investment
goods. Others, like interest rates, are laggards.

Of course, most processes respond to the tides in aggregate activity by
rising during expansions and declining during contractions, though they
may do so with a lead or lag. But business cycles also generate countercyclical movements: "Brisk business increases the domestic demand for
textile goods and so diminishes the exports of raw cotton; it increases the
sale of fresh milk and so restricts the production of butter; it increases the
volume of coin and paper money held by the public and stimulates borrowing from the banks, thereby enlarging demand liabilities and tending
to impair reserve ratios; it leads department stores to carry larger stocks
of merchandise and lowers the piles of iron ore at blast furnaces; it activates
share transactions on stock exchanges and discourages transactions in
bonds. The declines in this list, and many others, are as characteristic a
feature of business cycles as the advances" (p. 66). However, the processes
that run counter to business cycles do so, by and large, with less regularity
than those that respond positively. An expansion of money incomes stimulates a general increase in buying, and this influence may obscure the
concomitant impulse to shift demand away from inferior articles to
goods of higher quality. As it turns out, purchases of staples such as pork,
flour, coffee, and potatoes frequently decline during expansion, but their
inverted response is less regular than the positive response of more costly
articles. "In general, influences that tend to repress an activity in expansion encounter more opposition than influences favoring an increase, and
when repressing influences win out, their victories are less regular from
cycle to cycle than the victories won by influences that push forward.
Mutatis mutandis, the like holds true in contraction" (p. 96).

Large as are the variations in the cyclical timing of economic processes,
the differences in amplitude of fluctuation are more impressive still. In
high grade bond yields, for example, the cyclical wanderings are confined
to a narrow range; the total rise and fall is typically only about 10 per cent
of their average value during a business cycle. The amplitude of the over-all
index of wholesale prices, excluding war episodes, is nearly twice as large;
the amplitude of factory employment four or five times as large, of private
construction contracts over ten times and of machine tool orders over
twenty times as large. On the other hand, stocks of industrial equipment

are remarkably steady, expanding usually during contractions as well as expansions of business cycles. The proportions among economic quantities keep changing so systematically over a business cycle that the "very essence of the phenomenon is omitted unless the chart of business cycles contains numerous lines that indicate the wide differences among the rates at which, and also some of the differences in the times at which, various elements in the economy expand and contract. For, unless these divergencies in cyclical behavior are pictured by fit symbols, we have no suggestion of the basic business-cycle problem: how an economic system of interrelated parts develops internal stresses during expansions, stresses that bring on recessions, and how the uneven contractions of its varied parts pave the way for revivals" (p. 295).

IV

So much for the varieties of cyclical behavior that come to the surface once the lid is lifted from aggregate activity. What sort of whole do the parts make up? When the individual pieces are put together it appears that every month some activities reach cyclical peaks and others decline to their troughs; so that expansion and contraction run side by side all the time. But the peaks tend to come in bunches and likewise the troughs. Hence, when troughs gain on the peaks, expansions grow more numerous and in time dominate the economy. Their supremacy is short-lived, however, and gradually gives way to the encroachments of contraction. The business cycle of experience is the alternating succession of these sustained majorities: first, individual expansions; next, contractions; then expansions once again; and so on. "Business cycles consist not only of roughly synchronous expansions in many activities, followed by roughly synchronous contractions in a slightly smaller number; they consist also of numerous contractions while expansion is dominant, and numerous expansions while contraction is dominant" (p. 79). According as the expansions or contractions of individual activities dominate, the aggregate activity of the economy surges forward or recedes. And when economic crosscurrents are at or near their maximum, the direction of aggregate activity is reversed: it begins to rise if it has been falling, or to fall if it has been rising.

The turmoil that goes on within the cycles in aggregate activity has a systematic core. A highly simplified picture of the system is afforded by the accompanying table,[8] which condenses Mitchell's analysis of "comprehensive series" in Chapter 10. The table shows directions of movement during a typical business cycle—here divided into eight segments, four each for expansion and contraction. Of course, each segment includes several months, and the table is therefore insensitive to minor differences in timing, such as the short lag in income payments. Further, it hides many cross currents that would appear in less comprehensive series, and

---

[8] [Omitted here. See page xvi of Mitchell's report.]

omits certain business factors of which we should take account—especially wage rates, inventories, banking, and governmental finance. But with all its faults, the table gives an effective glimpse of the typical round of developments that constitute a business cycle.[9]

Let us then take our stand at the bottom of a depression and watch events as they unfold. Production characteristically rises in the first segment of expansion; so do employment and money income; and so do commodity prices, imports, domestic trade, security transactions. Indeed, every series moves upward except bond yields and bankruptcies. In the second stage the broad advance continues, though it is checked at one point— the bond market, where trading begins to decline. Bond prices join bond sales in the next stage; in other words, long-term interest rates—which fell during the first half of expansion—begin to rise. In the final stretch of expansion, declines become fairly general in the financial sector. Share trading and stock prices move downward; the liabilities of business failures, which hitherto have been receding, move up again; security issues and construction contracts drop; the turnover of bank deposits slackens; and bank debits in New York City, though not as yet in the interior, become smaller.

These adverse developments soon engulf the economic system as a whole, and the next stage of the business cycle is the first stage of contraction. Production, employment, commodity prices, personal incomes, business profits—indeed, practically all processes represented in the table —decline. Of course, the liabilities of business failures continue to rise, which merely attests the sweep of depression. Long-term interest rates also maintain their rise. But in the next stage the downward drift of bond prices ceases; that is, the rise in long-term interest rates is arrested. By the middle of contraction, bond sales join the upward movement of bond prices. More important still, the liabilities of business failures begin declining, which signifies that the liquidation of distressed business firms has passed its worst phase. These favorable developments are reinforced in the following stage. Share trading and prices revive; business incorporations, security issues, and construction contracts move upward; money begins to turn over more rapidly; even total money payments expand. Before long the expansion spreads to production, employment, prices, money incomes, and domestic trade. But this is already the initial stage of general expansion— the point at which our hurried observation of the business cycle started.

Of course, this recital delineates characteristic movements during business cycles, not invariant sequences. That the description fits individual business cycles imperfectly is apparent from the conformity percentages in the table. Yet these percentages also suggest that the deviations from type are not so numerous as to destroy the value of a generalized sketch. And if this much is accepted, an important conclusion immediately

---

[9] This and the three following paragraphs are adapted from the National Bureau's *Thirtieth Annual Report.*

follows, notwithstanding the omissions of the table; namely, that the check to the dominant movement of business activity, whether it be expansion or contraction, is typically felt especially early in financial processes and activities preparatory to investment expenditure.

The contraction phase of business cycles is not, however, the precise counterpart of expansion. This is clear from the table and becomes clearer still when numerical values are attached to its signs and intervals. The arrays of individual turning points at business cycle troughs "are more dispersed and skewed toward leads" than are the arrays at peaks. Expansions of aggregate activity average longer than contractions. They are also more vigorous, so that the trough from which a given expansion starts is ordinarily above the level from which the preceding expansion started. In the first segment of expansion the rate of improvement "is more rapid than at any other stage of the cycle." A "sharp and general retardation" of the advance occurs in the next segment. In the third, while "reacceleration is the rule," the advance "does not regain the speed" it had at the beginning of expansion. In the final stage of expansion "the business tide . . . becomes fuller of eddies." Contractions follow a different pattern. "The fall accelerates somewhat in the second segment of contraction, whereas the rise is much retarded in the second segment of expansion." The next stage "brings a moderate retardation" of the decline, whereas it "brought a moderate reacceleration" of the advance. The closing stages of expansion and contraction are similar "in that the rate of change becomes slower; but this retardation is much more marked at the end of contraction than at the end of expansion. . . ." "Thus the notions often suggested by the picturesque phrasing beloved of writers upon 'booms and busts'—that prosperity grows at a dizzier pace the longer it lasts, and that slumps gather momentum as they proceed—are wrong if our measures are right. Scarcely less misleading are the implications of the mathematical constructions often used to represent business cycles. A set of straight lines sloping upward to represent expansion, connected at a sharp peak with downward sloping straight lines to represent contraction, misrepresents the facts. . . . Sine curves are not less objectionable. . . . What our observations suggest is that the shapes of business cycles are phenomena *sui generis*."

V

These, then, are some of the broad results that emerge from Mitchell's examination of the cyclical process of the American economy. The full range of the book, its suggestions for further research, and its exemplary scientific care await the reader. Economists anxious to wield a simple formula of the causes of business cycles or the means of controlling them will not find Mitchell's fragment to their liking. Those willing to take conclusions on faith may chafe at its patient elaboration of evidence. But men who seek so earnestly to understand how our economic organization works that they insist on judging evidence for themselves are more likely to lament that too much detail has been suppressed. Scholars will respect Mitchell's pronouncement that his report on findings, after many years of research, is "ill proportioned, tentative, and subject to change as the investigation proceeds" (p. 5).

This book is not easy and everyone will save time by a careful reading of Part I, which, beside outlining aims and methods, provides the modicum of technical vocabulary required for comprehending what follows. Economic theorists are likely to find especially suggestive Chapter 7, which sets out the facts and inquires into the causes of the changing proportions among economic quantities in the course of a business cycle; also Part III, which centers on the consensus of fluctuations in leading sectors of the economy. Chapter 8 is a useful reminder to all that, despite their persistent traits, business cycles are changing phenomena; and that just as each new member of a group has traits of his own, which cannot be inferred from knowledge of the 'average man,' so each business situation must be judged in the light of its own circumstances as well as according to historical patterns. The bulk of this chapter is devoted to technical problems in the decomposition of time series, and only specialists will want to study it fully. Readers pressed for time might move lightly through Chapters 5 and 6 also—except for the closing sections, which will repay careful reading.

The modern theory of employment, which for a time pushed aside both value theory and business cycle theory, is now slowly being fitted into older economic knowledge. The younger economists are rediscovering that cost-price relations play a significant role in shaping the national income and its movements, that the 'consumption function' itself moves cyclically, that investment is not an autonomous variable, that price inflation does not wait for full employment, and that both investment and consumption are heterogeneous aggregates that cannot be understood without separate analysis of their parts. If our harassed generation can win the opportunity to pursue the arts of peace, the fruit and example of Mitchell's work will have their quiet but decisive part over the years in bringing the theory of fluctuations into ever closer contact with the ebb and flow of experience.

2

Cycles and Trends
in Economic Factors[*]

JOSEPH KITCHIN[†]

Editors' Note

This article had an important place in the evolution of the business cycle
concept. Not only did it serve as a precursor of the later and much more
sophisticated approach used by the National Bureau of Economic Research, but it was the first to make a distinction among different types of
cycles—a distinction which is useful to this day. We now realize that
fluctuations can take many forms, and among these are the forty-month
or so-called "minor" cycles first analyzed in this article. The major cycle
is, in Kitchin's view, a combination of two or three minor cycles. In addition, there is the trend or secular change, which Kitchin treated as close
to a straight line. Although today there is little support for the combination of forty-month cycles representing a separate phenomenon, there
seems to be a great deal of evidence for the forty-month cycle first observed
by Kitchin, as witness the successive business downturns in 1953–54, 1957–
58, and 1960–61. Although the statistics Kitchin used to reach his conclusions would now be considered quaint, with the whole emphasis on commodity prices, bank clearings, and interest rates, his main conclusion about
the existence of the minor cycle seems to have gathered support in the
four decades since it was first proposed.

---

[*] Reprinted by permission of the publishers from *Review of Economics and Statistics*,
Vol. V, No. 1 (January, 1923), pp. 10-16; Cambridge, Mass.: Harvard University Press,
Copyright, 1923, by The President and Fellows of Harvard College.
[†] Joseph Kitchin (1871-1932) was a British statistician and corporation director.

❧ The movements of economic factors—whether made up of price or volume—are, it is suggested, mainly composed of:

1. (*a*) *Minor cycles* averaging 3⅓ years (40 months) in length;
   (*b*) *Major cycles*, or so-called trade cycles, which are merely aggregates usually of two, and less seldom of three, minor cycles; and
2. *Fundamental movements* or *trends* which are largely straight line movements.

This generalization is supported by a wide range of annual statistics for Great Britain and the United States, and especially by monthly statistics of clearings, commodity prices, and interest rates for the two countries. The argument based upon the three factors just named is outlined in the following paragraphs:

1. (*a*) MINOR CYCLES *averaging* 3⅓ years (40 months) in length. Though single cycles may vary considerably from this average, an under-average cycle is often followed by an overaverage cycle, and vice versa, so that the average of two or three consecutive cycles is closer than the single cycle to the general average length.

LENGTHS PER CYCLE IN YEARS, RECKONED
FROM MAXIMUM TO MAXIMUM

		1890–1913: Range		1890–1922
		Single cycles	Av. of 3 cycles	Av. of all
Clearings,	U.S.	2.67 to 4.25	2.94 to 3.75	3.29
"	G.B.	2.50 to 4.00	3.00 to 3.75	3.30
Prices,	U.S.	2.41 to 4.67	3.19 to 4.00	3.31
"	G.B.	2.33 to 4.87	3.22 to 3.90	3.28
Interest,	U.S.	2.67 to 4.25	3.03 to 3.72	3.32
"	G.B.	2.83 to 4.16	3.03 to 3.69	3.37

The figures of the first two columns would practically hold good for the longer period 1890–1922, except as regards the last factor—interest. These cycles, equally prominent in the United States and Great Britain, show no material change in their average length with the course of time, judging by studies of a period of a century back. They persisted through war periods with some irregularity, especially in interest during and after the Great War when maxima for the United States and Great Britain were as far apart as 1916.57 and 1918.71—the decimals indicating the time in the calendar year.

The dates of the maxima of these cycles from 1890 onwards have been:

DATES OF MAXIMA OF CYCLES

General Maxima of Clearings, Prices and Interest			Difference from Ideal (months)	
U.S.	G.B.	Ideal	U.S.	G.B.
1890.62	1890.73	1890.00	+ 7½	+ 9
1893.23	1893.34	1893.33	− 1	0
1896.12	1896.11	1896.67	− 6	− 6½
1899.79	1900.01	1900.00	− 2½	0
1903.21	1903.35	1903.33	− 1½	0
1907.60	1907.45	1906.67	+ 11	+ 9½
1910.34	1910.46	1910.00	+ 4	+ 5½
1913.35	1913.29	1913.33	0	− ½
1917.76	1917.06	1916.67	+ 13	+ 4½
1920.37	1920.56	1920.00	+ 4½	+ 6½
Average difference			+ 2¾	+ 2¾

Close agreement of these general maxima with the ideal dates is not to be expected, as the latter come alternately on January 1, May 1, and September 1 of the years concerned, while seasonal variation affects interest strongly, its maxima all falling practically from July to November and averaging September in both countries. The ideal dates suggested represent a sort of general average for factors, some of which normally show an advance on an average date and others a lag. If the ideal date—e. g., for interest allowing for its lag—were say 1900.30 it would tend, on account of the seasonal increase in the autumn, to come to a maximum either towards the end of 1899 or, failing that, towards the end of 1900. Obviously the ideal dates would fit a little better if postponed say 3 months to fit the average of these three particular factors—clearings, prices, and interest—but it is convenient to retain them as shown for the sake of comparison.

These minor cycles are apparently the result of a rhythmical movement due to psychological causes, though, through prices of vegetable foods, they may be influenced by excess or deficiency in crops which fall out of tune with the normal cycle. Such food prices, however, are affected both by crops (deficiencies meaning higher prices and vice versa) and by cyclical fluctuations. There seems to be a general correspondence, however, between minima in crops and maxima in general economic conditions. On the matter of the cause of the cyclical movement, the writer (subject to what has just been written) would be inclined to agree with Mr. Philip Green Wright when he suggests: "Business and price cycles are due to cyclical recurrences in mass psychology reacting through capitalistic production. The rough periodicity of business cycles suggests the elastic recurrence of human functioning rather than the mathematical precision of cosmic phenomena."

(*b*) MAJOR CYCLES, or so-called trade cycles, which are merely aggregates usually of two, and less seldom of three, minor cycles, the limit of each being distinguished by a maximum of exceptional height, by a high bank rate, and sometimes by a panic, though panics seem to be disappearing. The facts that they average about 8 years, and that they usually come at 7- or 10-year intervals, are due merely to the circumstance that they are composed either of two minor cycles (ideally 6⅔ years) or three

DATES OF MAJOR CRISES

General Maxima of Clearings, Prices and Interest			Difference from Ideal (months)	
U.S.	G.B.	Ideal	U.S.	G.B.
	1847.66	1846.67		+ 12
	1857.66	1856.67		+ 12
	1866.43	1866.67		− 3
1872.96	1873.62	1873.33	− 4½	+ 3½
1882.87	1882.00	1883.33	− 5½	− 16
	1890.73	1890.00		+ 9
1893.21		1893.33	− 1½	0
1899.79	1900.01	1900.00	− 2½	0
1907.60	1907.45	1906.67	+ 11	+ 9½
1913.35	1913.29	1913.33	0	− ½
1920.37	1920.56	1920.00	+ 4½	+ 6½
	Average difference		+ ¼	+ 3¼

minor cycles (ideally 10 years). They have occurred in recent times at the dates given above (the figures before 1890 are approximate and based wholly or partly on annual instead of monthly figures). It will be seen that the United States missed the major maximum of 1890 witnessed in Great Britain, and erected the next minor maximum into a major one, but generally the conditions in the two countries swing well together. It will also be noted that the Great Britain maximum of 1882 came 16 months too soon, i. e., it came about a year before its due time, as is shown by the fact that the United States average date was 10½ months earlier. It is generally admitted also that the 1907 maximum was a delayed one.

Minor maxima show themselves in the monthly figures of most factors, but frequently they are not sufficiently prominent to show in yearly averages, though interest is a marked exception to this. They have therefore to be studied in monthly figures only. Taking a number of factors together, intermediate minor maxima have an intensity of, say, 40 per cent of those

Schedule of Maxima and Minima, 1890–1922

The ideal dates have their origin at the beginning of 1890, the maxima being placed 3·33 years apart and the minima midway between. Dates of minima are placed in italics. The dates of maxima and minima are years and fractions of years, representing monthly averages, except for Great Britain's prices and interest, which are end-monthly. Where virtual instead of actual monthly maxima or minima are selected, they are indicated by *.

The figures below each date are index numbers on the basis of 1900–13 = 100 for the following factors for the United States and Great Britain, respectively.

United States bank clearings—1900–13 monthly average, $11,750,000,000. Charted in units of $100,000,000.
Wholesale prices of commodities—Bureau of Labour 1900–22 as revised from 1913 (index 90 for 1900–13 on present basis of 1913 = 100), and 10 commodities 1890–99, as given in REVIEW OF ECONOMIC STATISTICS, vol. 3, p. 369, but condensed to agree approximately with Bureau of Labour annual figures.
Interest rate on 60-to-90 day commercial paper, New York—1900–13 average 4.82 per cent.
London bankers' clearing house returns—1900–13 monthly average, £1,037,000,000. Charted in units of £10,000,000.
Wholesale prices of commodities—Sauerbeck-Statist. 1900–13 average of 75.5 charted as 100.
Market rate of interest on three months' bills, London—1900–13 average, 3.26 per cent.

Ideal dates	United States			Great Britain		
	Clearings	Prices	Interest	Clearings	Prices	Interest
1890.00	1890.37 49	1890.62 90	1890.87 170	1890.54 69	1890.83 96	1890.83 177
1891.67	*1891.62 35	1892.37 82	1892.45 61	1891.62 49	1892.75 88	1892.49 27
1893.33	1893.04 51	1893.12 89	1893.54 202	1893.20 56	1893.16 91	1893.66 96
1895.00	1894.71 30	1895.20 74	1895.45 55	1894.71 44	1895.08 79	1895.57 17
1896.67	1895.79 45	1895.79 82	1896.79 178	1895.79 71	*1895.71 84	*1896.83 100
1898.33	1897.12 31	*1898.96 77	*1898.45 67	*1897.45 56	*1898.83 84	*1898.49 31

Intervals in Years Between Maxima and Minima Respectively

United States			Great Britain		
Clearings	Prices	Interest	Clearings	Prices	Interest
2.67	2.50	2.67	2.66	2.33	2.83
3.09	2.83	3.00	3.09	2.25	3.08
2.75	2.67	3.25	2.59	2.55	3.17
2.41	3.76	3.00	2.74	3.75	2.92
3.41	4.41	3.17	3.75	4.87	3.08

							Intervals					
1900.00	1899.20 74	1900.20 93	1899.96 122	*1899.54 80	1900.58 101	1899.91 173	3.59	2.49	3.67	3.26	3.17	4.00
1901.67	1900.71 49	1901.45 88	*1902.12 83	1900.71 64	1902.00 91	*1902.49 75	3.59	2.92	3.75	3.50	2.67	3.84
1903.33	*1902.79 96	1903.12 96	1903.71 124	1903.04 89	1903.25 93	1903.75 121	3.91	3.34	3.33	4.00	2.49	3.08
1905.00	*1904.62 68	1904.79 92	1905.45 78	1900.17 75	1904.49 92	1905.57 56	4.25	4.67	4.25	4.00	4.16	4.16
1906.67	*1907.04 128	1907.79 108	1907.96 166	1907.04 116	1907.41 109	1907.91 188	3.50	3.83	4.00	3.91	4.67	3.92
1908.33	1908.12 75	1908.62 100	1909.45 67	1908.62 87	1909.16 95	1909.49 37	3.00	2.41	2.83	3.25	2.84	2.92
1910.00	1910.04 146	1910.20 110	1910.79 115	1910.29 132	1910.25 105	*1910.83 134	3.59	2.75	2.67	3.00	2.41	3.00
1911.67	*1911.71 107	1911.37 105	*1912.12 78	1911.62 109	*1911.57 104	*1912.49 73	2.75	3.51	2.75	2.50	3.00	3.00
1913.33	1912.79 146	1913.71 113	*1913.54 126	1912.79 145	1913.25 115	1913.83 152	2.91	4.08	3.75	3.00	3.92	2.59
1915.00	1914.62 84	*1915.45 110	1915.87 62	1914.62 65	*1915.49 141	1915.08 46	4.17	3.91	5.17	4.33	4.24	2.74
1916.67	*1916.96 233	1917.62 210	1918.71 124	1917.12 171	*1917.49 239	1916.57 172	4.50	3.67	3.25	4.67	3.84	4.41
1918.33	*1919.12 220	*1919.12 214	1919.12 108	*1919.29 182	1919.33 244	1919.49 97	3.00	2.75	2.08	3.08	2.84	4.59
1920.00	1919.96 360	1920.37 274	1920.79 166	1920.20 353	1920.33 352	1921.16 208	2.00	2.92	3.50	2.42	2.83	3.08
1921.67	1921.12 227	1922.04 153	1922.62 81	1921.71 254	*1922.16 175	1922.57 55						

Average interval between successive maxima 1890–1922 .... 3.29 3.31 3.32 3.30 3.28 3.37
" " " minima " 3.28 3.30 3.35 3.34 3.27 3.34
Average interval between successive maxima 1890–1913 " 3.20 3.30 3.24 3.19 3.20 3.29
" " " minima " 3.35 3.17 3.28 3.33 3.14 3.33

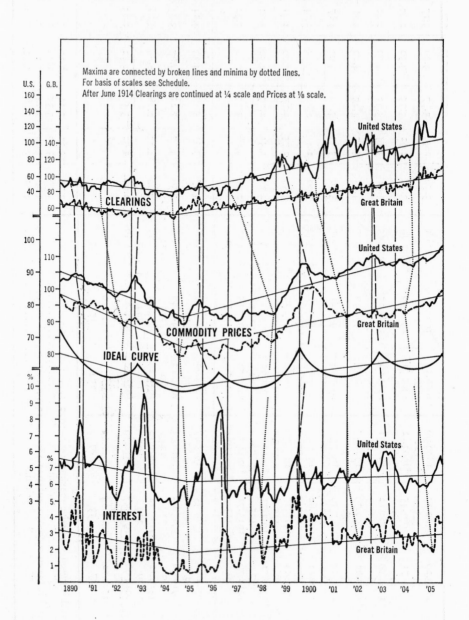

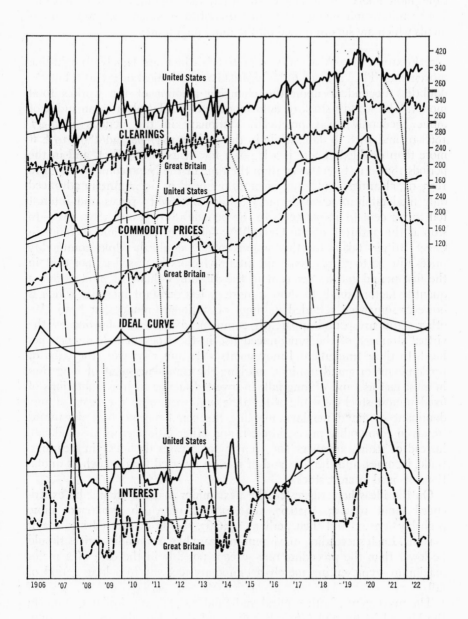

which become erected into major maxima, i.e., major maxima are 2½ times more above the average or trend line than the intermediate maxima.

The minor and major cycles just described represent the wave movements which are superimposed on the more important:

2. FUNDAMENTAL MOVEMENTS, or *trends* which are largely straight-line movements. They are not to be regarded as rhythmical or cyclical, but are doubtless dependent upon the changing amount of the world's total money. The world's stock of gold money per head (taken as an index of money generally) was practically stationary in the periods 1800–47, 1868–91 and 1918 to date, while in the periods 1847–68 and 1891–1918 it more than doubled. There is a lag of a few years in its effect, and in the periods 1825–51 (to get away from the time of the Napoleonic Wars) and 1873–95, clearings, trade, and incomes per head in Great Britain advanced only moderately or even declined, while commodity prices and interest fell 30 per cent to 45 per cent. In the periods 1851–73 and 1895–1913—to stop at the outbreak of the Great War—clearings, trade, and incomes in Great Britain taken together approximately doubled, while commodity prices rose 40 to 50 per cent and interest factors increased 20 per cent in the first period and 80 per cent in the second. Volume of production (a quantity factor) tends to show a more or less constant increase, which is however somewhat retarded in times of stationary money per head. Another stationary period apparently commenced in 1920, following on the virtual stoppage of the pronounced rise in the stock of gold money per head. In these fundamental movements 1851 and 1895 were the years of predominant or grand minima, marking the commencement of long rises in most factors (and of long falls in inverted factors such as quotations of fixed-interest stocks), while 1810, 1873 and 1920 were the years of predominant or grand maxima, marking the commencement of downward trends in commodity prices, interest, and other ratio factors, of moderate instead of strong advances (or even in some cases declines) in clearings, trade, incomes, and the like, and of rises in inverted factors such as quotations of fixed-interest stocks.

On the ideas here suggested the next minor maxima should be experienced about 1923.33, 1926.67, 1930.00, etc., of which 1926.67 or more probably 1930.00 and then perhaps 1936.67, should be erected into major maxima. Each succeeding maximum in a case like commodity prices should be lower than the preceding one—except possibly in the case of a major maximum—representing merely a temporary recovery in a long period of fall.

The movements, both cyclical and fundamental, are similar in time in the United States and Great Britain (and doubtless also in other countries), but with a tendency for the United States to be slightly, say one to two months on an average, in advance of Great Britain.

The accompanying schedule and chart deal further with the theory put forward, and give an opportunity of testing how far it is in accordance with fact. For the United States data the writer is greatly indebted to the REVIEW OF ECONOMIC STATISTICS for its compilations and charts of United States factors. No attempt has been made to correct the figures for seasonal variations or secular trend, but this is done in many charts published in the REVIEW, and in these the minor cycles often show themselves much more markedly than in the accompanying chart. Occasionally virtual or corresponding maxima and minima are taken in preference to actual (and possibly accidental) ones, but rather with the intention of coupling sympathetic movements and certainly without any intentional bias in favor of the theory. The positions of the ideal minima have been placed midway between the maxima for convenience—thus ignoring the tendency for minima to be nearer to the lower of two succeeding maxima—but no particular importance is attached to the relative positions of the minima, which are often rather indefinite in the factors illustrated.

Judging by the figures in the schedule, clearings tend to be 6 months in advance of commodity prices (Bureau of Labour and *Statist* indices), while interest lags 4 or 5 months after them.

ADVANCE OR LAG OF INTEREST AND CLEARINGS ON PRICES: 1890–1913

		Times later	Advance (−) or Lag (+) in Months	
			Extremes	Average
Clearings on prices (U.S.) ...	At Maxima	0 out of 8	−12 to 0	−5¼
	At Minima	1 " " 7	−22 to + 4	−7
	Both	1 " " 15		−6
Clearings on prices (G.B.) ...	At Maxima	2 out of 8	−12½ to − ½	−3½
	At Minima	2 " " 7	−16½ to + 2½	−7½
	Both	4 " " 15		−5½
Interest on prices (U.S.) ...	At Maxima	6 out of 8	− 3 to +12	+4
	At Minima	6 " " 7	− 6 to +10	+4½
	Both	12 " " 15		+4¼
Interest on prices (G.B.) ...	At Maxima	6 out of 8	− 8 to +13	+4½
	At Minima	5 " " 7	− 4 to +13	+4½
	Both	11 " " 15		+4½

As is generally known, movements in the United States tend to be in advance of those in Great Britain. The figures in the schedule yield the following results:

GREAT BRITAIN COMPARED WITH THE UNITED STATES: 1890–1913

		Number of times later	Advance (−) or Lag (+) (months)	
			Extremes	Aver.
Clearings	At maxima	5 out of 8	0 to +4	+2
	At minima	3 " " 7	0 to +6	+1½
	Both	8 " " 15		+1½
Commodity prices	At maxima	5 out of 8	−5½ to +4½	0
	At minima	4 " " 7	−3½ to +6½	+2
	Both	9 " " 15		+1
Interest	At maxima	5 out of 8	− ½ to +3½	+ ½
	At minima	7 " " 7	− ½ to +4½	+2
	Both	12 " " 15		+1¼

If Bradstreet's prices were taken instead of those of the Bureau of Labor the average lag shown by *Statist* prices would be 4 months. The whole period 1890–1922 would show practically the same figures, except in the case of interest. Putting these figures together one gets the following average sequence at maxima and minima on the basis of 1890–1913:

Bank Clearings (United States) 0
    "   " (Great Britain) .... 1½ months
Commodity Prices (Bradstreet's) 3   "
    "   " (Bureau of Labor) 6   "
    "   " (Sauerbeck-Statist) 7   "
Interest (New York, 60 to 90 days) .... 10¼   "
    " (London, 3 months bills) .... 11½   "

It is not of course suggested that the business cycle is of invariable duration. The contrary is shown by the facts which are nakedly given in this statement. But it is suggested that business cycles average 3⅓ years in length, that a shortened cycle is often largely compensated by a lengthened one following it, and that the average, when reinforced by the known lags which occur between various factors, can be made a valuable aid in forecasting. Still more important is the part of the theory dealing with fundamental movements, and especially for present purposes the suggestion that 1920 witnessed the end of a long trend in one direction (upward in most factors) and the commencement of another long but largely opposite trend, so that factors which strongly advanced from 1895 to 1920 may be expected to greatly modify their upward movement (apart from the effects of the war), while others which advanced moderately may move downward, and others still, of which a good example is the quotations of fixed-interest stocks (an inverted factor), may have a rising instead of a falling trend.

This statement is the result of a study, by no means confined to clearings, prices, and interest, which has covered a wide range of Great Britain and United States factors extending back to 1810 and 1860, respectively, and covering prices of commodities, trade, incomes, wages, interest, banking, quotations of stock exchange securities, and quantity or volume figures in considerable variety, based partly on monthly data, but mainly, from the necessities of the case, on annual averages. This work has been sufficient to convince the writer that the theory can be demonstrated in the great majority of cases. The matter now seems to be in a form in which it can be presented for criticism.

3

The Long Waves in Economic Life*

NIKOLAI D. KONDRATIEFF†

Editors' Note

Nikolai Kondratieff worked in the 1920's in Soviet Russia. His article on long waves is an example of the original mind at work. Although many economists do not accept the existence of long waves, the concept has received growing recognition; in recent years, scholars have taken up the long-wave hypothesis and are subjecting it to further testing. The Kondratieff long wave, the duration of which he set at about fifty years, emerged from his studies of data for England and France in the nineteenth and twentieth centuries. His materials covered prices, interest rates, wages, foreign trade, coal, pig iron, and lead. After eliminating the long-term trend, and using a moving average analysis, he discovered long waves in these series, and comparability among countries. If long waves do in fact exist, they would be of the greatest significance. For example, Kondratieff noted that in the period of upswing in the long cycle, prosperity years were predominant. Conversely, in the long downswing, years of depression were the most frequent. Using more recent experience as a further test, one could argue that the years of the Great Depression in the 1930's came in a long-wave downswing, while the prosperous years since World War II have been in a major long-wave upswing. Looking ahead, could the period of the 1970's

* Reprinted by permission of the publishers from *Review of Economics and Statistics*, Vol. XVII, No. 6 (November, 1935), pp. 105-115; Cambridge, Mass.: Harvard University Press, Copyright, 1935, by The President and Fellows of Harvard College.

† Kondratieff formulated the long-wave hypothesis while Director of the Conjuncture Institute of Moscow.

see the beginning of a new long-wave downward trend? Clearly, anyone interested in the broad sweep of economic change should be familiar with the Kondratieff hypothesis and this article.

※※※※※※※※※※※※※※※※※

I. *Introduction*

❧ The idea that the dynamics of economic life in the capitalistic social order is not of a simple and linear but rather of a complex and cyclical character is nowadays generally recognized. Science, however, has fallen far short of clarifying the nature and the types of these cyclical, wave-like movements.

When in economics we speak of cycles, we generally mean seven to eleven year business cycles. But these seven to eleven year movements are obviously not the only type of economic cycles. The dynamics of economic life is in reality more complicated. In addition to the above-mentioned cycles, which we shall agree to call "intermediate," the existence of still shorter waves of about three and one-half years' length has recently been shown to be probable.[1]

But that is not all. There is, indeed, reason to assume the existence of long waves of an average length of about 50 years in the capitalistic economy, a fact which still further complicates the problem of economic dynamics.

II–III. *Method*

[Sections II and III of Kondratieff's exposition may be summarized as follows:

The succeeding study is to be confined solely to an inquiry into various problems connected with these long waves. Investigation here is made difficult by the fact that a very long period of observation is presupposed. We have, however, no data before the end of the eighteenth century and even the data we do have are too scanty and not entirely reliable. Since the material relating to England and France is the most complete, it has formed the chief basis of this inquiry. The statistical methods used were simple when no secular trend was present in the series. If the series displayed a secular trend, as was the case among physical series, the first step was to divide the annual figures by the population, whenever this was logically possible, in order to allow for changes in territory. Then the secu-

---

[1] Cf. J. Kitchin, "Cycles and Trends in Economic Factors," *Review of Economic Statistics*, v (1923), pp. 10-16.

lar trend was eliminated by the usual statistical methods applied to each series as a whole; and Kondratieff refers specifically to the methods presented by Dr. Warren M. Persons in THE REVIEW OF ECONOMIC STATISTICS in 1919 and 1920. The deviations from the secular trend were then smoothed by a nine-year moving average, in order to eliminate the seven to eleven year business cycles, the short cycles, and random fluctuations possibly present.]

IV. *The Wholesale Price Level*

While the index of French prices goes back only to the end of the 1850's, the English and American indices date back to the close of the eighteenth century. In order not to overburden this study with figures, the statistical data are presented exclusively in the form of charts.[2]

The index numbers of prices plotted on Chart 1 have been neither smoothed nor treated in any other way. Nevertheless, a mere glance at the chart shows that the price level, despite all deviations and irregularities, exhibits a succession of long waves.

The upswing of the first long wave embraces the period from 1789 to 1814, i.e., 25 years; its decline begins in 1814 and ends in 1849, a period of 35 years. The cycle is, therefore, completed in 60 years.[3]

The rise of the second wave begins in 1849 and ends in 1873, lasting 24 years. The turning point, however, is not the same in the United States as in England and France; in the United States the peak occurs in the year 1866, but this is to be explained by the Civil War and casts no doubt on the unity of the picture which the course of the wave exhibits in the two continents. The decline of the second wave begins in 1873 and ends in 1896, a period of 23 years. The length of the second wave is 47 years.

The upward movement of the third wave begins in 1896 and ends in 1920, its duration being 24 years. The decline of the wave, according to all data, begins in 1920.

It is easily seen that the French prices after the close of the 1850's move generally parallel to the English and American prices. It is, therefore, very probable that this parallelism existed in the preceding period as well.

We conclude, therefore, that three great cycles are present in the movement of the price level during the period since the end of the 1780's, the last of which is only half completed. The waves are not of exactly the same

---

[2] [Ten pages of tabular material were given by Kondratieff at the end of his article. The charts presented in this translation are not merely reproductions of those in the original article but have been drawn anew from the data given in his tabular appendix. A few slight discrepancies between the new charts and those of Kondratieff were discovered, but in no case were the discrepancies significant.—Editors of *The Review of Economic Statistics*.]

[3] In the upswing, the English index exhibits several peaks, which fall in the years 1799, 1805, 1810, and 1814; but since after the year 1814 a distinctly downward tendency can be observed, we regard this year as the turning point.

CHART 1.—INDEX NUMBERS OF COMMODITY PRICES*
(1901–10 = 100)

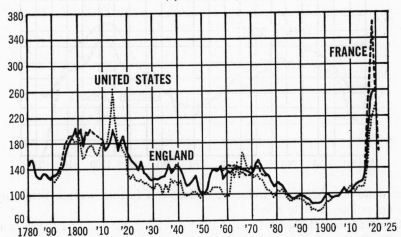

* The *French* data are taken from the *Annuaire Statistique* [Statistique Générale de la France], 1922, p. 341; the index number has been recalculated on a gold basis through use of dollar-franc exchange rates.

For *England*, there is for 1782–1865 the index of Jevons; for 1779–1850, a new index number, computed by Silberling and published in this REVIEW, v (1923); for the period after 1846, we have Sauerbeck's index, which at present is carried on by the *Statist*. Since Silberling's index is based upon more complete data of the prices of individual commodities than that of Jevons, we have used the former for the period 1780–1846. From 1846 on we use Sauerbeck's index number. Both indices have been tied together on the basis of their relation during 1846–50, for which period they are both available; after this procedure, we have shifted the series to a new base, 1901–10. For the period 1801–20 and since 1914, in which periods England was on a paper standard, the index numbers have been recalculated on a gold basis.

For the *United States*, we use the following series, which have been tied together: for 1791–1801, H. V. Roelse (*Quarterly Publications of the American Statistical Association*, December, 1917); 1801–25, A. H. Hansen (*ibid.*, December, 1915); 1825–39, C. H. Juergens (*ibid.*, June, 1911); 1840–90, Falkner (Report from the Committee on Finance of the United States Senate on *Wholesale Prices, Wages, and Transportation*, 52d Congress, 2d session, Report No. 1394, Part 1 [Washington: Government Printing Office, March 3, 1893]); since 1890, the B. L. S. index. All index numbers are on the base 1901–10. For the Greenback period (1862–78), they have been recalculated on a gold basis. All data [except Silberling's index] are taken from the *Annuaire Statistique*, 1922 [which utilizes the sources above cited].

length, their duration varying between 47 and 60 years. The first wave is the longest.

v. *The Rate of Interest*

The course of the interest rate can be seen most conveniently from the movement of the discount rate and the quotations of interest-bearing securities. Because the latter depend less on random fluctuations and re-

CHART 2.—QUOTATIONS OF INTEREST-BEARING SECURITIES

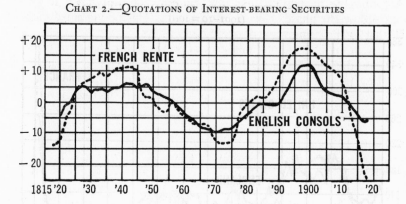

flect more accurately the influence of long-run factors, we use here only the quotations of state bonds.

Chart 2 shows the quotations of the French Rente[4] and of English consols.[5] Both have a secular trend during the period of observation. The chart shows the deviations from the secular trend smoothed by means of a nine-year moving average.

The quotations of interest-bearing securities manifest, as is well known, a movement opposite to that of general business activity and of the interest rate. Therefore, if long waves are operative in the fluctuations of the interest rate, the movement of bond quotations must run in a direction counter to that of commodity prices. Just this is shown in our chart, which exhibits clearly the long waves in the movement of the quotations and consequently of the interest rate.

The chart starts only after the Napoleonic Wars, i.e., about the time that the first long wave of commodity prices had reached its peak; it does not cover the period of the upswing of the latter. Considering the data at hand, however, we may suppose that the quotations of state bonds took part in this movement also.

English consols actually manifest a decidedly downward tendency between 1792 and 1813. Their quotation in 1792 is 90.04; in 1813, on the other hand, it is 58.81. Although they drop most rapidly in the years 1797 and 1798, yet this steep decline is only an episode, and the general downward tendency from 1792 to 1813 stands out quite clearly.[6]

---

[4] Until 1825 the quotations of the five-per-cent Rente, after this the quotations of the three-per-cent Rente. In order to connect both series, we have first computed relatives with the base 1825–30 for both series. Then we shifted the base of the combined series to 1901–10, in order to make them comparable with the price curve. The original data are taken from the *Annuaire Statistique* [Statistique Générale de la France], 1922.

[5] According to the data in William Page, ed., *Commerce and Industry*, Vol. 2 (London, 1919), statistical tables, pp. 224-25. Relatives have been calculated from the figures, with the base 1901–10.

[6] Cf. N. J. Silberling, "British Financial Experience, 1790–1830," THE REVIEW OF ECONOMIC STATISTICS, 1 (1919), p. 289.

Accordingly, the period from the beginning of the 1790's up to 1813 appears to be the phase of rising interest rates. This period agrees perfectly with that of the rising wave of commodity prices.

The wave of bond quotations rises after 1813[7]—or the wave of the interest rate declines—even till the middle of the forties. (See the chart.) According to the unsmoothed data, consols reached their peak in 1844; the Rente, in 1845. With this, the first great cycle in the movement of the interest rate is completed.

The downward movement of bond quotations (or the rise of the interest rate) during the second cycle lasts from 1844–45 to 1870–74.[8] From this time onward until 1897, the market price of interest-bearing securities rises again, and consequently the interest rate goes down. With this, the second great cycle is completed.

The new decline of the quotations (rise in the rate of interest) lasts from 1897 to 1921. Thus the existence of great cycles in the movement of the interest rate appears very clearly.[9] The periods of these cycles agree rather closely with the corresponding periods in the movement of wholesale commodity prices.

VI–VII. *Wages and Foreign Trade*

[In Section VI, Kondratieff examines the course of weekly wages of workers in the English cotton-textile industry since 1806 and of English agricultural laborers since 1789.[10] The original wage data are reduced to a gold basis and then expressed in the form of index numbers with 1892 as the base year. Chart 3 presents these wage figures as deviations from trend, smoothed by use of a nine-year moving average. Kondratieff devotes the remainder of this section to a description of the series presented in Chart 3, from which analysis he concludes that, despite the scantiness of the

---

[7] The first years have disappeared from our chart because of the use of the nine-year moving average.

[8] According to the original data, consols actually reach their lowest point in 1866, but the general tendency continues to be one of decline until 1874. The slump of quotations in 1866 is connected with the increase in the interest rate just preceding the money-market crisis of that year, and with the Austro-Prussian War.

[9] The existence of these cycles is also confirmed by several other studies: P. Wallich, "Beiträge zur Geschichte des Zinsfusses von 1800 bis zur Gegenwart." *Jahrbücher für Nationalökonomie und Statistik*, III. Folge, Vol. 42, pp. 289-312; J. Lescure, "Hausses et Baisses Générales des Prix," *Revue d'Economie Politique*, Nr. 4 (1912); R. A. Macdonald, "The Rate of Interest Since 1844," *Journal of the Royal Statistical Society*, LXXV (1912), pp. 361-79; T. T. Williams, "The Rate of Discount and the Price of Consols," *ibid.*, pp. 380-400. Also, *ibid.*, pp. 401-11, the discussion of the last-mentioned studies, especially the speech of E. L. Hartley, pp. 404-06.

[10] [Earnings of cotton-textile workers for 1806–1906 are taken from G. H. Wood, *The History of Wages in the Cotton Trade* (London, 1910), p. 127; beginning with 1906, they are from the *Abstract of Labour Statistics*.

For agricultural laborers, wage data for 1789–1896 are from A. L. Bowley, "The Statistics of Wages in the United Kingdom During the Last Hundred Years: Part IV, Agricultural Wages," *Journal of the Royal Statistical Society*, LXII (1899), pp. 555 ff. Thereafter, the figures are from Page, *op. cit.* The data refer to England and Wales.]

CHART 3.—WAGES IN ENGLAND

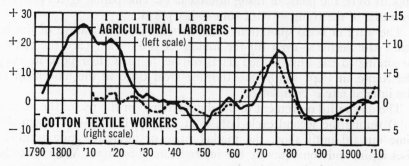

available data, "long waves are undoubtedly present in the movement of wages, the periods of which correspond fairly well with those in commodity prices and the interest rate."

For his foreign-trade series presented in Section VII, Kondratieff takes the sum of French exports and imports. The figures were first corrected for population changes, and thereafter the secular trend (in the form of a second-degree parabola) was eliminated. The resulting deviations, smoothed by use of a nine-year moving average, are presented in Chart 4. After an examination of the chart, the author concludes that the data on foreign trade also show the existence of two great cycles, the periods of which coincide with those observed in the other data.]

VIII. *The Production and Consumption of Coal and Pig Iron, and the Production of Lead*

So far we have examined the movements only of such magnitudes, sensitive to changes in business conditions, as possess either a purely value character, e.g., commodity prices, interest rates, and wages, or at least a mixed character such as the data on foreign trade. Our study, however, would lose much of its force if we did not also analyze the behavior of purely physical series.

For this purpose we choose English coal production,[11] and French con-

CHART 4.—FRENCH FOREIGN TRADE

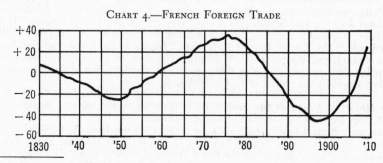

---

[11] According to the data of W. Page, *op. cit.*

sumption of coal,[12] as well as the English production of pig iron and of lead.[13] We divided the original figures by the population, and eliminated from the resulting series the secular trends. The deviations from the lines of trend, after being smoothed by use of a nine-year moving average, were then analyzed. The results are shown in Chart 5.

Continuous data are available, unfortunately, only for the period after the 1830's, in part even only after the 1850's. Consequently, only one and one-half to two great cycles can be shown, but these appear with striking clarity in both charts.

There is a retardation in the increase of coal consumption [in France] until the end of the 1840's, then the advance becomes more rapid and reaches its peak in 1865, according to the smoothed curve (on the chart), and in 1873, according to the unsmoothed curve. In the latter year, English coal production also reaches a maximum, according to the unsmoothed curve. Then follows the decline, which comes to an end in 1890–94, giving way to a new long upswing. So we observe in the data relative to the rapidity in the increase of coal production and coal consumption nearly the whole of two large cycles, the periods of which correspond closely to the periods we have already found when considering other series.

Similarly, English production of pig iron and lead indicates sufficiently clearly the existence of one and one-half large cycles.

IX. *Other Series*

For the sake of brevity, we break off here the systematic analysis of the long waves in the behavior of individual series. We have also examined other data, some of which likewise showed the same periods as those mentioned above, although several other series did not show the cycles with the same clarity. Value series which show long waves are the deposits and the portfolio of the Bank of France, and deposits at the French savings banks; series of a mixed (quantity x price) character are French imports and English imports, and total English foreign trade. As regards the movement of indices of a physical character, the existence of long waves has been established in the coal production of the United States, of Germany, and of the whole world; in the pig-iron production of the United States and of Germany and of the whole world; in the lead and coal production of the United States; in the number of spindles of the cotton industry in the United States; in the cotton acreage in the United States and the oat acreage in France, etc.

It was absolutely impossible, on the other hand, to establish long waves in French cotton consumption; in the wool and sugar production of the United States; and in the movement of several other series.

---

[12] *Annuaire Statistique,* 1908 and 1922.

[13] According to *British and Foreign Trade and Industry,* and the *Statistical Abstract [for the United Kingdom].*

CHART 5.—CONSUMPTION OF COAL IN FRANCE AND PRODUCTION OF COAL, PIG IRON
AND LEAD IN ENGLAND

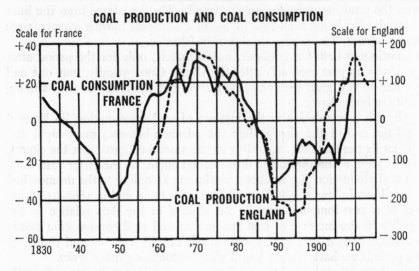

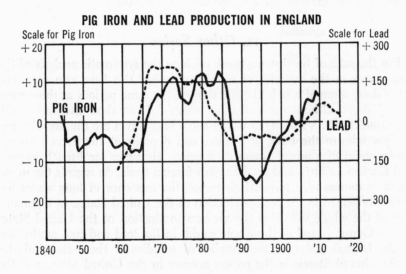

x. *Statistical Findings*

The evidence we have presented thus far permits some conclusions.

(1) The movements of the series which we have examined running from the end of the eighteenth century to the present time show long cycles. Although the statistical-mathematical treatment of the series selected is rather complicated, the cycles discovered cannot be regarded as the accidental result of the methods employed. Against such an interpretation

TABLE 1

Country and series	First cycle		Second cycle		Third cycle	
	Begin-ning of rise	Begin-ning of decline	Begin-ning of rise	Begin-ning of decline	Begin-ning of rise	Prob-able begin-ning of decline
France						
1. Prices	....	....	....	1873	1896	1920
2. Interest rate	....	1816*	1844	1872	1894	1921
3. Portfolio of the Bank of France	....	1810*	1851	1873	1902	1914
4. Deposits at the savings banks	....	....	1844	1874	1892	....
5. Wages of coal miners ..	....	....	1849	1874	1895	....
6. Imports	....	....	1848	1880	1896	1914
7. Exports	....	....	1848	1872	1894	1914
8. Total foreign trade	....	....	1848	1872	1896	1914
9. Coal consumption	....	....	1849	1873	1896	1914
10. Oat acreage[1]	....	....	1850*	1875	1892	1915
England						
1. Prices	1789	1814	1849	1873	1896	1920
2. Interest rate	1790	1816	1844	1874	1897	1921
3. Wages of agricultural laborers	1790	1812–17	1844	1875	1889	....
4. Wages of textile workers	....	1810*	1850†	1874	1890	....
5. Foreign trade	....	1810*	1842‡	1873	1894	1914
6. Coal production	....	....	1850*	1873	1893	1914
7. Pig iron production ...	....	....	....	1871§	1891	1914
8. Lead production	....	....	....	1870	1892	1914
United States						
1. Prices	1790	1814	1849	1866	1896	1920
2. Pig iron production ..	....	....	....	1875–80	1900	1920
3. Coal production	....	....	....	1893	1896	1918
4. Cotton acreage	....	....	....	1874–81	1892–95	1915
Germany						
Coal production	....	....	....	1873‖	1895	1915
Whole world[2]						
1. Pig iron production ..	....	....	....	1872¶	1894	1914
2. Coal production	....	....	....	1873	1896	1914

[1] Reversed cycles.

[2] The data which refer to the whole world have not been corrected for population changes.

* Approximate dates.

† Another minimum falls in the year 1835.

‡ Other minima lie in the years 1837 and 1855.

§ Another maximum falls in the year 1881.

‖ Another maximum falls in the year 1883.

¶ Another maximum falls in the year 1882.

is to be set the fact that these waves have been shown with about the same timing in all the more important of the series examined.

(2) In those series which do not exhibit any marked secular trend—e.g., prices—the long cycles appear as a wave-like movement about the average level. In the series, on the other hand, the movement of which shows such a trend, the cycles accelerate or retard the rate of growth.

(3) In the several series examined, the turning points of the long waves correspond more or less accurately. This is shown clearly by Table 1, which combines the results of the investigation not only of the data considered above but also of several other series.[14]

It is easy to see from this table that there is a very close correspondence in the timing of the wave movements of the series in the individual countries, in spite of the difficulties present in the treatment of these data. Deviations from the general rule that prevails in the sequence of the cycles are very rare. It seems to us that the absence of such exceptions is more remarkable than would be their presence.

(4) Although for the time being we consider it to be impossible to fix exactly upon the years that marked the turning points of the long cycles, and although the method according to which the statistical data have been analyzed permits an error of 5–7 years in the determination of the years of such turnings, the following limits of these cycles can nevertheless be presented as being those most probable:

First long wave
{
1. The rise lasted from the end of the 1780's or beginning of the 1790's until 1810–17.
2. The decline lasted from 1810–17 until 1844–51.
}

Second long wave
{
1. The rise lasted from 1844–51 until 1870–75.
2. The decline lasted from 1870–75 until 1890–96.
}

Third long wave
{
1. The rise lasted from 1890–96 until 1914–20.
2. The decline probably begins in the years 1914–20.
}

(5) Naturally, the fact that the movement of the series examined runs in long cycles does not yet prove that such cycles also dominate the movement of all other series. A later examination with this point especially in mind will have to be made to show which ones of these share the described wave-like movement. As already pointed out, our investigation has also extended to series in which no such waves were evident. On the other hand, it is by no means essential that the long waves embrace all series.

(6) The long waves that we have established above relative to the series most important in economic life are international; and the timing of these cycles corresponds fairly well for European capitalistic countries. On the basis of the data that we have adduced, we can venture the statement that the same timing holds also for the United States. The dynamics in the

---

[14] Table 1 enumerates the maxima and minima according to the original data. The problem of the most accurate method for the determination of the maxima and minima would deserve a special analysis; at present we leave this question open. We believe only that the indicated turning points are the most probable ones.

development of capitalism, however, and especially the timing of the fluctuations in the latter country may have peculiarities.

xi. *Empirical Characteristics*

We were led to these conclusions by the study of statistical series characterizing the movement of the capitalist economy. From another point of view, the historical material relating to the development of economic and social life as a whole confirms the hypothesis of long waves. We neither can nor shall undertake here an analysis of this material. Nevertheless, several general propositions which we have arrived at concerning the existence and importance of long waves may be presented.

(1) The long waves belong really to the same complex dynamic process in which the intermediate cycles of the capitalistic economy with their principal phases of upswing and depression run their course. These intermediate cycles, however, secure a certain stamp from the very existence of the long waves. Our investigation demonstrates that during the rise of the long waves, years of prosperity are more numerous, whereas years of depression predominate during the downswing.[15]

(2) During the recession of the long waves, agriculture, as a rule, suffers an especially pronounced and long depression. This was what happened after the Napoleonic Wars; it happened again from the beginning of the 1870's onward; and the same can be observed in the years after the World War.[16]

(3) During the recession of the long waves, an especially large number of important discoveries and inventions in the technique of production and communication are made, which, however, are usually applied on a large scale only at the beginning of the next long upswing.

(4) At the beginning of a long upswing, gold production increases as a rule, and the world market [for goods] is generally enlarged by the assimilation of new and especially of colonial countries.

(5) It is during the period of the rise of the long waves, i.e., during the period of high tension in the expansion of economic forces, that, as a rule, the most disastrous and extensive wars and revolutions occur.

It is to be emphasized that we attribute to these recurring relationships an empirical character only, and that we do not by any means hold that they contain the explanation of the long waves.

xii. *The Nature of Long Waves*

Is it possible to maintain that the existence of long cycles in the dynamics of the capitalist economy is proved on the basis of the preceding statements? The relevant data which we were able to quote cover about

---

[15] Cf. A. Spiethoff, "Krisen," (*Handwörterbuch der Stattswissenschaften*, 4th edition).
[16] Cf. Ernle, *English Farming Past and Present* (London, 1922), and G. F. Warren and F. A. Pearson, *The Agricultural Situation* (New York, 1924).

140 years. This period comprises two and one-half cycles only. Although the period embraced by the data is sufficient to decide the question of the existence of long waves, it is not enough to enable us to assert beyond doubt the cyclical character of those waves. Nevertheless we believe that the available data are sufficient to declare this cyclical character to be very probable.

We are led to this conclusion not only by the consideration of the factual material, but also because the objections to the assumption of long cyclical waves are very weak.

It has been objected that long waves lack the regularity which business cycles display. But this is wrong. If one defines "regularity" as repetition in regular time-intervals, then long waves possess this characteristic as much as the intermediate ones. A strict periodicity in social and economic phenomena does not exist at all—neither in the long nor in the intermediate waves. The length of the latter fluctuates at least between 7 and 11 years, i.e., 57 per cent. The length of the long cycles fluctuates between 48 and 60 years, i.e., 25 per cent only.

If regularity is understood to be the similarity and simultaneity of the fluctuations of different series, then it is present to the same degree in the long as in the intermediate waves.

If, finally, regularity is understood to consist in the fact that the intermediate waves are an international phenomenon, then the long waves do not differ from the latter in this respect either.

Consequently, there is no less regularity in the long waves than in the intermediate ones, and if we want to designate the latter as cyclical, we are bound not to deny this characterization to the former.

It has been pointed out [by other critics] that the long waves—as distinct from the intermediate ones which come from causes within the capitalistic system—are conditioned by casual, extra-economic circumstances and events, such as (1) changes in technique, (2) wars and revolutions, (3) the assimilation of new countries into the world economy, and (4) fluctuations in gold production.

These considerations are important. But they, too, are not valid. Their weakness lies in the fact that they reverse the causal connections and take the consequence to be the cause, or see an accident where we have really to deal with a law governing the events. In the preceding paragraphs, we have deliberately, though briefly, considered the establishment of some empirical rules for the movement of long waves. These regularities help us now to evaluate correctly the objections just mentioned.

1. *Changes in technique* have without doubt a very potent influence on the course of capitalistic development. But nobody has proved them to have an accidental and external origin.

Changes in the technique of production presume (1) that the relevant scientific-technical discoveries and inventions have been made, and (2) that it is *economically* possible to use them. It would be an obvious mistake to deny the creative element in scientific-technical discoveries and inventions. But from an objective viewpoint, a still greater error would occur if one believed that the direction and intensity of those discoveries and inventions were entirely accidental; it is much more probable that such direction and intensity are a function of the necessities of real life and of the preceding development of science and technique.[17]

Scientific-technical inventions in themselves, however, are insufficient to bring about a real change in the technique of production. They can remain ineffective so long as economic conditions favorable to their application are absent. This is shown by the example of the scientific-technical inventions of the seventeenth and eighteenth centuries which were used on a large scale only during the industrial revolution at the close of the eighteenth century. If this be true, then the assumption that changes in technique are of a random character and do not in fact spring from economic necessities loses much of its weight. We have seen before that the development of technique itself is part of the rhythm of the long waves.

2. *Wars and revolutions* also influence the course of economic development very strongly. But wars and revolutions do not come out of a clear sky, and they are not caused by arbitrary acts of individual personalities. They originate from real, especially economic, circumstances. The assumption that wars and revolutions acting from the outside cause long waves evokes the question as to why they themselves follow each other with regularity and solely during the upswing of long waves. Much more probable is the assumption that wars originate in the acceleration of the pace and the increased tension of economic life, in the heightened economic struggle for markets and raw materials, and that social shocks happen most easily under the pressure of new economic forces.

Wars and revolutions, therefore, can also be fitted into the rhythm of the long waves and do not prove to be the forces from which these movements originate, but rather to be one of their symptoms. But once they have occurred, they naturally exercise a potent influence on the pace and direction of economic dynamics.

3. As regards the *opening-up of new countries for the world economy,* it seems to be quite obvious that this cannot be considered an outside factor which will satisfactorily explain the origin of long waves. The United States have been known for a relatively very long time; for some reason or other they begin to be entangled in the world economy on a major scale only from the middle of the nineteenth century. Likewise, the Argentine and Canada, Australia and New Zealand, were discovered long before the end of the nineteenth century, although they begin to be entwined in the world economy to a significant extent only with the coming of the

[17] One of the best and most compelling arguments for the assumption that scientific and technical inventions and discoveries are not made accidentally but are intimately connected with the needs of practical life is given by the numerous cases in which the same inventions and discoveries are made at the same time at different places and entirely independently of one another. Cf. the long list of such cases in W. F. Ogburn, *Social Change* (New York, 1924), p. 90. Cf. also Dannemann, *Die Naturwissenschaften in ihrer Entwickelung und in ihrem Zusammenhange* (Leipzig, 1923).

1890's. It is perfectly clear historically that, in the capitalistic economic system, new regions are opened for commerce during those periods in which the desire of old countries for new markets and new sources of raw materials becomes more urgent than theretofore. It is equally apparent that the limits of this expansion of the world economy are determined by the degree of this urgency. If this be true, then the opening of new countries does not provoke the upswing of a long wave. On the contrary, a new upswing makes the exploitation of new countries, new markets, and new sources of raw materials necessary and possible, in that it accelerates the pace of capitalistic economic development.

4. There remains the question whether the *discovery of new gold mines*, the *increase in gold production*, and a consequent *increase in the gold stock* can be regarded as a casual, outside factor causing the long waves.

An increase in gold production leads ultimately to a rise in prices and to a quickening in the tempo of economic life. But this does not mean that the changes in gold production are of a casual, outside character and that the waves in prices and in economic life are likewise caused by chance. We consider this to be not only unproved but positively wrong. This contention originates from the belief, first, that the discovery of gold mines and the perfection of the technique of gold production are accidental and, secondly, that every discovery of new gold mines and of technical inventions in the sphere of gold production brings about an increase in the latter. However great may be the creative element in these technical inventions and the significance of chance in these discoveries, yet they are not entirely accidental. Still less accidental—and this is the main point —are the fluctuations in gold production itself. These fluctuations are by no means simply a function of the activity of inventors and of the discoveries of new gold mines. On the contrary, the intensity of inventors' and explorers' activity and the application of technical improvement in the sphere of gold production, as well as the resulting increase of the latter, depend upon other, more general causes. The dependence of gold production upon technical inventions and discoveries of new gold mines is only secondary and derived.

Although gold is a generally recognized embodiment of value and, therefore, is generally desired, it is only a commodity. And like every commodity it has a cost of production. But if this be true, then gold production —even in newly discovered mines—can increase significantly only if it becomes more profitable, i.e., if the relation of the value of the gold itself to its cost of production (and this is ultimately the prices of other commodities) becomes more favorable. If this relation is unfavorable, even gold mines the richness of which is by no means yet exhausted may be shut down; if it is favorable, on the other hand, even relatively poor mines will be exploited.

When is the relation of the value of gold to that of other commodities most favorable for gold production? We know that commodity prices reach their lowest level toward the end of a long wave. This means that at this time gold has its highest purchasing power, and gold production becomes most favorable. This can be illustrated by the figures in Table 2.

Gold production, as can be seen from these figures, becomes more profitable as we approach a low point in the price level and a high point in the purchasing power of gold (1895 and the following years).

TABLE 2.—SELECTED STATISTICS OF GOLD MINING IN THE TRANSVAAL, 1890–1913*

Year	Cost of production	Profit
	Per ton of gold ore	
1890	42 *sh.* 2 *d.*	7 *sh.* 2 *d.*
1895	33 *sh.* 5 *d.*	11 *sh.* 11 *d.*
1899	28 *sh.* 0 *d.*	14 *sh.* 3 *d.*
1903	24 *sh.* 9 *d.*	14 *sh.* 11 *d.*
1906	22 *sh.* 2 *d.*	11 *sh.* 6 *d.*
1913	17 *sh.* 11 *d.*	9 *sh.* 10 *d.*

* Cf. W. A. Berridge, "The World's Gold Supply," THE REVIEW OF ECONOMIC STATISTICS, 11 (1920), p. 184.

It is clear, furthermore, that the stimulus to increased gold production necessarily becomes stronger the further a long wave declines. We, therefore, can suppose theoretically that gold production must in general increase most markedly when the wave falls most sharply, and vice versa.

In reality, however, the connection is not as simple as this but becomes more complicated, mainly just because of the effect of the changes in the technique of gold production and the discovery of new mines. It seems to us, indeed, that even improvements in technique and new gold discoveries obey the same fundamental law as does gold production itself, with more or less regularity in timing. Improvements in the technique of gold production and the discovery of new gold mines actually do bring about a lowering in the cost of production of gold; they influence the relation of these costs to the value of gold, and consequently the extent of gold production. But then it is obvious that exactly at the time when the relation of the value of gold to its cost becomes more unfavorable than theretofore, the need for technical improvements in gold mining and for the discovery of new mines necessarily becomes more urgent and thus stimulates research in this field. There is, of course, a time-lag, until this urgent necessity, though already recognized, leads to positive success. In reality, therefore, gold discoveries and technical improvements in gold mining will reach their peak only when the long wave has already passed its peak, i.e., perhaps in the middle of the downswing. The available facts confirm this supposition.[18] In the period after the 1870's, the following gold discoveries were made: 1881 in Alaska, 1884 in the Transvaal, 1887

---

[18] Berridge, *loc. cit.*, p. 181.

in West Australia, 1890 in Colorado, 1894 in Mexico, 1896 in the Klondike. The inventions in the field of gold-mining technique, and especially the most important ones of this period (the inventions for the treatment of ore), were also made during the 1880's, as is well known.

Gold discoveries and technical improvements, if they occur, will naturally influence gold production. They can have the effect that the increase in gold production takes place somewhat earlier than at the end of the downswing of the long wave. They also can assist the expansion of gold production, once that limit is reached. This is precisely what happens in reality. Especially after the decline in the 1870's, a persistent, though admittedly slender, increase in gold production begins about the year 1883;[19] whereas, in spite of the disturbing influences of discoveries and inventions, the upswing really begins only after gold has reached its greatest purchasing power; and the increased production is due not only to the newly discovered gold fields but in a considerable degree also to the old ones. This is illustrated by the figures in Table 3.

TABLE 3.—GOLD PRODUCTION, 1890–1900
(*Unit: thousand ounces*)

	World total	Trans- vaal	United States	Aus- tralia	Russia	Canada	Mexico	India
1890 ...	5,749	440	1,589	1,588	1,135	65	737	9
1895 ...	9,615	2,017	2,255	2,356	1,388	101	290	230
1900 ...	14,838	3,638	3,437	4,461	1,072	1,029	411	412

Source: Berridge, *loc. cit.*, p. 182.

From the foregoing one may conclude, it seems to us, that gold production, even though its increase can be a condition for an advance in commodity prices and for a general upswing in economic activity, is yet subordinate to the rhythm of the long waves and consequently cannot be regarded as a causal and random factor that brings about these movements from the outside.

XIII. *Conclusions*

The objections to the regular cyclical character of the long waves, therefore, seem to us to be unconvincing.

In view of this circumstance and considering also the positive reasons developed above, we think that, *on the basis of the available data, the existence of long waves of cyclical character is very probable.*

At the same time, we believe ourselves justified in saying that the long waves, if existent at all, are a very important and essential factor in eco-

---

[19] Cf. *Statistical Abstract of the United States*, 1922, pp. 708-09.

nomic development, a factor the effects of which can be found in all the principal fields of social and economic life.

Even granting the existence of long waves, one is, of course, not justified in believing that economic dynamics consists only in fluctuations around a certain level. The course of economic activity represents beyond doubt a process of development, but this development obviously proceeds not only through intermediate waves but also through long ones. The problem of economic development *in toto* cannot be discussed here.

In asserting the existence of long waves and in denying that they arise out of random causes, we are also of the opinion that the long waves arise out of causes which are inherent in the essence of the capitalistic economy. This naturally leads to the question as to the nature of these causes. We are fully aware of the difficulty and great importance of this question; but in the preceding sketch we had no intention of laying the foundations for an appropriate theory of long waves.[20]

---

[20] I arrived at the hypothesis concerning the existence of long waves in the years 1919–21. Without going into a special analysis, I formulated my general thesis for the first time shortly thereafter in my study, *The World Economy and Economic Fluctuations in the War and Post-War Period* (*Mirovoje chozjajstvo i jego konjunktury vo vremja i posle vojny* [Moscow, 1922]). During the winter and spring of 1925, I wrote a special study on "Long Waves in Economic Life" ("Bol'schije cykly konjunktury"), which was published in the volume of the Institute for Business Cycle Research, *Problems of Economic Fluctuations* (*Voprosy konjunktury*, Vol. 1). Only at the beginning of 1926 did I become acquainted with S. de Wolff's article "Prosperitäts- und Depressionsperioden," *Der lebendige Marxismus, Festgabe zum 70. Geburtstage von Karl Kautsky*. De Wolff in many points reaches the same result as I do. The works of J. van Gelderns, which de Wolff cites and which have evidently been published only in Dutch, are unknown to me.

4

The Analysis of Economic Change*

JOSEPH A. SCHUMPETER†

Editors' Note

Each scientific discipline is fortunate to have a few thinkers whose ideas influence the whole profession. Joseph Schumpeter was one of these. He had a distinguished career in Europe, both academically and in business, and spent the last twenty years of his life at Harvard University. One of his main interests was business cycles and his contributions to that subject are major ones. To Schumpeter, innovations were a chief moving force in a capitalist economy. This article highlights the role of innovations as the main source of cyclical fluctuations.

Not all scholars would agree that innovation is the key to the business cycle, but thinking of the problem as the consequence of injecting new products or techniques into the economy will be helpful to the student. Schumpeter's three-cycle schema, though not generally accepted, is also a useful approach. He distinguishes (1) the long-wave or Kondratieff cycle, of about fifty to sixty years; (2) the intermediate or Juglar cycle, of about nine to ten years; and (3) the short or Kitchin cycle, of roughly forty months. While the Juglar cycle has been neglected in more recent years,

* Reprinted by permission of the publishers from *Review of Economics and Statistics*, Vol. XVII, No. 4 (May, 1935), pp. 2-10; Cambridge, Mass.: Harvard University Press, Copyright, 1935, by The President and Fellows of Harvard College.

† Joseph Alois Schumpeter (1883–1950) studied law and economics at the University of Vienna. In 1925, following a miscellany of assignments as teacher, cabinet minister, banker, and jurist, he joined the faculty of the University of Bonn. The advent of Nazism in Germany, however, forced him to migrate to the United States and Harvard University. There he served as Professor of Economics until his death. Schumpeter was a most prolific author both in German and English on a wide range of economic topics. These include: *The Theory of Economic Development* (1911); *Epochen der Dogmen und Methodengeschichte* (a history of economic thought published in 1914); *Business Cycles* (1939); and *Capitalism, Socialism, and Democracy* (1942).

the long waves and short cycles have received renewed interest and are discussed in articles in this volume.

- -

❧ Ever since, in the sixties of the past century, Clement Juglar definitely established the existence of wave-like movements which pervade economic life within the institutional framework of capitalist society, the work of finding, linking-up, measuring relevant fact, has been steadily progressing. Although much hampered by needless controversy and inadequate technique, this work has yielded results which, it is believed, need only be properly coördinated and developed in order to enable economics to offer a substantially satisfactory and reasonably exhaustive picture of the phenomenon, and thus to make what would certainly be its most immediately practical contribution to human welfare. Coördination is particularly necessary of the historical, statistical and analytical modes of approach which are each of them thwarted by that reluctance to coöperation incident to the differences in training, tastes and horizons of individual workers. The purpose of this paper is to explain the main features of an analytic apparatus which may be of some use in marshaling the information we have and in framing programs for further research.

Outside Factors

If we survey, for instance, the course of economic events in England from the beginning of the French Wars in 1792, through the suspension of specie payments, the Peace of Amiens, the trade war with America, up to the crisis in 1809–1810, it becomes obvious that we could without any glaring absurdity account by political "disturbances" for all the fluctuations we observe in our material. Or if we follow the course of the world crisis through the spring of 1931, we may trace the breakdown of the distinct upward movement observable at the beginning of that year to a string of events arising out of the flutter caused by the reopening of the question of the union of Austria to Germany and the movements of short balances incident thereto.[1] Common sense immediately suggests that here

---

[1] If we further ask how it was that that particularly sensitive short-balance situation arose in Germany, we find, following events from 1924 to 1929, that the steadily increasing public expenditure, and the methods by which it was financed, amounted to taxing away what would otherwise have been an annual average increase of working capital of about one billion marks. If we deduct from the figure of foreign short-term indebtedness as it stood in 1930 not only the four billions of counterclaims of German banks on short capital account, and the four to five billions which simply were revolving credits financing Germany's foreign trade and which, therefore, were not dangerous, but also the, roughly, five to six billions, which could and would have been accumulated but for that fiscal policy, it is easily seen that the interest rate would have

we have discovered an obviously important source of economic fluctuations. From the ubiquity of such events it follows that practically every economic fluctuation must be a historic individual and cannot be made amenable to explanation but by minute historical analysis of the innumerable factors actually at work in each case. In other words, in order to understand business cycles we must first of all acquire what may be termed historical experience of the way in which economic life reacts to such disturbances, and this is one of the reasons why every conquest of past fact is of paramount practical importance, in some respects of greater importance than additions to our stock of contemporaneous fact which can increase our knowledge over time only by infinitesimal steps. The statistical and analytical description of the various mechanisms of reaction (with a hope in our minds that we may ultimately get as far as to be able to measure the effects attributable to every such disturbance) seems thus to be the most urgent task before us. It should be observed in passing that for various reasons any influence acting on the economic process is practically sure to produce not a single dent but a wave-like motion extending over a longer time than it takes to reach the next disturbance, as well as, if it impinges on a particular spot, a vibration throughout the whole system. Moreover, with adaptation proceeding almost always with a lag and very often with reference to the rate of change of prices rather than to their absolute magnitude, our attempts at exact description are more than likely to result in expressions admitting of periodic integrals.

This being so, the question arises whether there are any fluctuations at all which arise out of the behavior of business communities as such and would be observable even if the institutional and natural framework of society remained absolutely invariable. Although disturbance of the kind glanced at and reaction thereto may in individual cases be much more important, yet the presence or absence of a fluctuation *inherent* to the economic process in time is practically and scientifically the fundamental problem and the only one to be considered here. In order to make headway with it, we shall proceed as physical sciences do in those cases in which it is impossible actually to isolate a phenomenon by producing it in a laboratory: from our historic and everyday knowledge of economic behavior we shall construct a "model" of the economic process over time, see whether it is likely to work in a wave-like way, and compare the result with observed fact. Henceforth, therefore, we shall disregard not only wars, revolutions, natural catastrophes, institutional changes, but also changes in commercial policy, in banking and currency legislation and habits of payment, variations of crops as far as due to weather conditions or diseases,

---

been lower and that that part of foreign short indebtedness, the proceeds of which replaced the formation of domestic working capital, would have been so small as to be no major factor in the situation. We are thus enabled to account for some of the darkest hues of the situation of 1931–1932 by what was not only on the surface, but also in a more fundamental sense, a political cause. Cf. the last two sentences of this section for a defense of this way of reasoning.

changes in gold production as far as due to chance discoveries, and so on. These we shall call *outside factors*. It will be seen that in some cases it is not easy to distinguish them from features of business behavior. All we can do about this here is to recommend to the reader to hold tight to the common sense of the distinction and to consider that every business man knows quite well that he is doing one kind of thing when ordering a new machine and another kind of thing when lobbying for an increase of the import duty on his product. It will also be seen that many of the things we list as outside factors are, when considered on a higher plane and for a wider purpose, the direct outcome of the working of the capitalist machine and hence no independent agencies.[2] This is surely so but does not reduce the practical value of the distinction on our plane and for our purpose.

Cycles, Trends, Equilibria, Growth, Innovation

For shortness' sake, we assemble in this section a few necessary definitions and propositions, which are really quite simple, although we cannot help adding here and there somewhat pedantic formulations which are necessary in order to make our meaning perfectly precise to the specialist.

Statistically, the term "cycle" means two things: first, that sequences of values of economic quantities in historic time (as distinguished from theoretic time) do not display monotonic increase or decrease, but (irregular) recurrence of either these values themselves or their first or their second time-derivatives; and secondly, that these "fluctuations" do not occur independently in every such time series, but always display either instantaneous or lagged association with each other.

Statistically, we mean by the word "trend" the fact that in many, although not in all, such time series it is possible to divide the whole interval covered by our material into sub-intervals such that the mean values of the

---

[2] Professor W. C. Mitchell, in his review of Professor L. Robbins' recent book (*Quarterly Journal of Economics*, May, 1935), objects to the latter's attributing part of the phenomena of the depression 1929–1934 to "politics." Sociologically, he is of course quite right not only for this case, but generally. The action, e.g., of Sir Robert Peel's administration in repealing the corn laws in 1846 undoubtedly arose out of, and is to be accounted for by the economic pattern of the time and place, itself created by the working of the *whole* social system, of which the capitalist mechanism was a part. But this is relevant only for *some* purposes, for instance, if we wish to *judge* the action of politicians. As far as this is done on predilections of the scientist for certain types of social institutions, it is certainly extra-scientific as well as extra-economic. We should, in this case, have to disagree with *both* the eminent authors mentioned, as they both of them display such predilections. The argument is, however, not relevant if the question is merely what of observable effects may have been due to the Peel policy: for an investigation of the course of English cycles in the 1840's that policy is as much of an outside factor as an earthquake would have been. For the sake of clearness it is essential to keep both standpoints strictly separate. The same reasoning applies, of course, to the distinction of an economic process and its institutional setting in general. The distinction is, in a sense, quite unrealistic. But if we do not make it, we shall never be able to say more than that everything depends upon everything.

time integrals over these sub-intervals are monotonically increasing or decreasing as we go along in time, or that they display recurrence only once.

If we study, say, the economic state of things in all countries in 1872 and behold the wild excesses of that boom, we shall have no difficulty in assigning very realistic meaning to the terms "want of balance" or "disequilibrium." Nor is it difficult, if we look at things one year after, to recognize that however much the then situation differed from that of 1872 it was similar to it in that it was about equally unbalanced. Again, if we analyze the course of events in, say, 1897, we may well sum up the result by speaking of a comparatively equilibrated state of things. This common sense distinction between comparatively balanced and comparatively unbalanced states of the economic system is of utmost importance for the description and measurement of cyclical phenomena. In order to bring out the exact skeleton of such observations we define: (Marshallian) *particular equilibrium* exists in an individual industry if this industry as a whole displays no tendency either to increase or decrease its output or to alter the combination of the productive factors it employs. *Aggregative equilibrium* exists if the sum total of receipts of business as a whole, expressed in current dollars, equals the sum total of costs similarly expressed and including as much profit as will induce everybody to keep on doing what he is actually doing. This kind of thing, which is compatible with plenty of disequilibrium as between industries and within industries, is the basic concept in Mr. Keynes' analysis of the monetary process. *General equilibrium* exists if every household and every firm in the domain under research is individually in a state of equilibrium in the sense of Léon Walras. It is only this last concept that matters for us. To give it statistical meaning, we must link it up with certain points on the graphs of our time series. These we call "normal points." As in reality such states can never be perfectly realized we can be concerned only with states which are nearer to, or farther from, them than other states. Hence we further define: *neighborhoods of equilibrium* are time intervals in which normal points occur in the graphs of our time series excepting those which in that interval are deflected by a definite and provable individual circumstance. (The word "neighborhood" is therefore not used here in its strict mathematical sense.) Discussion of the question how we are to locate these neighborhoods cannot be entered upon in this article.

By "growth" we mean changes in economic data which occur continuously in the sense that the increment or decrement per unit of time can be currently absorbed by the system without perceptible disturbance. Increase of population, resulting in an increase of the supply of labor of at most a few per cent per year (historically an increase of three per cent per year is already high), is the outstanding example. If the factors which enter into this category were the only ones at work, there would be obvious economic meaning to the concept of trend and to its determination by least squares or other methods resting on similar assumptions. In what follows we shall, however, not deal with the problems arising out of mere growth, nor with the very complicated questions of their relation to the other types of factors involved in economic change. In fact we shall, for clearness' sake, disregard it altogether, which, as in the case of outside factors, does not imply any view about its importance.

It stands to reason, finally, that outside factors and growth factors do not exhaust the list of the influences which produce and shape economic change. Obviously the face of the earth would look very different if people, besides having their economic life changed by natural events and changing it themselves by extra-economic action, had done nothing else except multiply and save. If it looks as it does, this is just as obviously due to the unremitting efforts of people to improve according to their lights upon their productive and commercial methods, i.e., to the changes in technique of production, the conquest of new markets, the insertion of new commodities, and so on. This historic and irreversible change in the way of doing things we call "innovation" and we define: innovations are changes in production functions which cannot be decomposed into infinitesimal steps. Add as many mail-coaches as you please, you will never get a railroad by so doing.

It is a question of some interest why the old type of economist, Marshall included, should, while recognizing this element and taking account of it in special cases, yet have persistently refused to face it squarely and to build an analytic apparatus fully descriptive of its mechanism and consequences. For our purpose it is both necessary and sufficient to list innovation, however much it may be linked to the other two, as a third and logically distinct factor in economic change, and to submit the propositions: The kind of wave-like movement, which we call the business cycle, is incident to industrial change and would be impossible in an economic world displaying nothing except unchanging repetition of the productive and consumptive process. Industrial change is due to the effect of outside factors, to the non-cyclical element of growth, and to innovation. If there be a purely economic cycle at all, it can only come from the way in which new things are, in the institutional conditions of capitalist society, inserted into the economic process and absorbed by it. In fact, the cycle seems to be the statistical and historical form in which what is usually referred to as "economic progress" comes about. This is why any serious attempt at analytic and even at practical control of the business cycle must be an historical one in the sense that the key to the solution of its fundamental problems can only be found in the facts of industrial and commercial history.

Prosperity and Depression

To simplify argument we will in this section make the hypothesis, presently to be discarded, that there is sense in speaking of only *one* "cyclical movement" in our material.

We can of course never expect to discover a definite date when the first cycle arose out of a state of perfect equilibrium, but it is essential, in order to avoid circular reasoning, to make our model describe such an event and, as far as historical and statistical description goes, to make it start from what has first to be identified as a neighborhood of equilibrium. We then get the picture of the system of economic quantities drawing away from this equilibrium or neighborhood under the impact of innovations which would supply, barring outside factors, the only possible "force." Let us visualize this by thinking of any of those booms in this country or in England which everyone would label as railroad booms. The new thing in this case takes years to get into working order and still longer to exert its full effects on the location of industry and agriculture, agglomerations of population, the evolution of accessories and subsidiaries, and so on. During this time there would, in strict logic and if the preceding equilibrium had been a perfect one, be little or no increase in the stream of commodities and services (there may in fact be a *decrease* in the output of consumers' goods), while producers' and consumers' expenditures would increase in consequence of credit creation and in other ways. The realistic complement of this is that, during this period, expenditure regularly expands more than output and that the non-innovating sectors of the economic system adapt themselves to this state of things. It is not possible to show here by the historical interpretation of the behavior of time series (neither should it be necessary to show, for it must be obvious to everyone who has ever, e.g., studied the charts published in THE REVIEW OF ECONOMIC STATISTICS) how perfectly this accounts for everything we mean when identifying a given interval as a time of business prosperity. After a period of gestation, which of course must be distinguished from what we may also designate by this term in the case of an individual firm, the products or services of the new business structures reach their markets, displacing either other such products and services, or methods of production and enterprises linked to them which have now become obsolete, and enforcing a process of liquidation, readjustment, and absorption. This would be so even if nobody ever made any errors and nobody ever misbehaved, although there is no difficulty whatever in understanding that the consequences of error and misbehavior will show up during this period in which the system struggles back to a new neighborhood of equilibrium. On the side of money and credit, the fundamental element which induces all others is the fact that as soon as the receipts stream in from the sale of the new products and as far as they are used to pay back bank loans, deposits will have to contract, in strict logic, down to the point of the previous neighborhood and, in reality, some way towards it. Again, there is no difficulty in inserting into this picture, as understandable consequences of this fundamental chain of events, all the accidental phenomena which experience tells us are usually associated with it. This not only gives a truer picture of the nature and the organic functions of cyclical down-swings, but also accords satisfactorily with statistical evidence.

Whatever starts a deviation of the system from equilibrium always, although not with logical necessity, gives rise to secondary phenomena which are mainly due to the fact that business men will act on the rates of change they observe. The sum total of these induced phenomena which are the center of the mass psychology of cycles and greatly intensify their amplitudes, we call "secondary waves." The expression, first used in 1911, is misleading and is kept only because Mr. Keynes has taken it up. But the thing is very important, so much so that the majority of students of the business cycle see nothing else. Whilst this accounts for many errors in diagnosis and remedial policy, it also helps to explain and partly to justify a large group of "theories" which, though missing the essential phenomenon, are yet perfectly satisfactory when viewed as descriptions of part of the mechanism of the secondary waves superimposed on the primary ones.

The units of the cyclical movements, then, lie necessarily between neighborhoods of equilibrium. In the simplest form of the model of economic change they have only two phases. But because of the fact that depressive forces gather momentum on the way back from the prosperity-excursion of the system, notably owing to the phenomena incident to the breakdown of the secondary wave, the system outruns usually the first neighborhood of equilibrium it strikes on its way back, and embarks upon a depression-excursion, from which it is forced up by the action of the equilibrium *ligamina* which bring it up again to another neighborhood from which the prosperity of the next cycle starts. Hence we have as a rule four phases: prosperity, recession, depression, and revival. This is almost generally recognized, but it is important to note that for purposes of fundamental analysis we are not free to count cycles from any point or phase we please; for instance, from peak to peak or trough to trough, but must always begin after the revival and at the beginning of a prosperity. It is, moreover, essential to distinguish these two, although it may be difficult to do so owing to the fact that they are both positive. The failure to do so, and especially to recognize that the "forces" at work in revival are entirely different from the "forces" at work in prosperity, is one of the main sources of faulty analysis.

The fundamental question still remains unanswered. Why should the carrying into effect of innovations (as distinguished from "invention" or experimentation which are quite another matter and do not in themselves exert any influence on business life at all—which is the reason why so little has come out of the Marshallian recognition of the element of invention) *cluster* at certain times, and not be distributed in so continuous a way as to be capable of being just as continuously absorbed as the current increase in the supply of labor is? One answer suggests itself immediately: as soon as the various kinds of social resistance to something that is fundamentally new and untried have been overcome, it is much easier not only to do the same thing again but also to do *similar* things in different directions, so that a first success will always produce a cluster. (See, e.g., the emergence of the motor-car industry.) This is indeed the method of *competitive* capitalism which has not as yet died out in *trustified* capitalism, to spread an improvement and to reap the social harvest—in the succeeding depression. But to carry full persuasion it would be necessary to go much deeper into this phenomenon, the roots of which stretch far beyond the economic field, than is here possible. However, as it has been the unfortunate experience of the present writer that even a very elaborate exposition has failed at times to convey to critics the picture he desired to convey, he prefers to ask the reader to consider the clustering of innovations as a postulate or hypothesis made to fit the facts in the same way as hypotheses are made in physics, irrespective of what might be adduced for or against their objective truth. Yet he feels entitled to say to anyone who doubts this proposition: Look around you in industrial life and see for yourself whether it is not so. Other writers have quite independently stressed the fact that it is possible to associate historically every business cycle with a distinct industry, or a few industries, which led in it and, as it were, applied the torch to what after becomes a flare-up covering a much wider surface.[3] The well established fact that fluctuations in investment goods are so much more marked than fluctuations elsewhere points, by virtue of its being explainable on the postulate mentioned, in the same direction.

It should be added that the above analytic model supplies an interpretation of economic trends which also bears on the technique of their determination. It follows, e.g., that barring the element of growth the trends of our time series are not due to influences distinct from those that create the cyclical fluctuations but simply embody the results of the latter. To these "result-trends," as the writer calls them in his workshop, it is entirely unwarranted to apply formal methods of the type of least squares. For extrapolation there is, of course, no warrant in any case. But there are certain general characteristics which may be used in developing formal methods as more or less rough approximations. No general proposition is possible as to the relative or absolute lengths of the four phases, even apart from the fact that they will be influenced by outside factors. Partly but not wholly for the latter reason no great significance attaches to the mere height or depth of a peak or a trough, although we shall presently find a reason for expecting that certain depressions will be much more severe than others.

The Three-Cycle Schema

The above analysis not only accounts for the fact that waves of prosperity always do arise whenever a neighborhood of equilibrium is reached "from below," and that they always do taper off into a new neighborhood of equilibrium, but, as far as the present writer is able to make out, also accounts for every single fact or characteristic ever proved to be associated with either up-swings or down-swings not provably due to the action of outside

---

[3] The first author to do this consciously was, as far as the present writer knows, Mr. D. H. Robertson (A *Study of Industrial Fluctuations*, published in 1915, and an earlier paper in the *Journal of the Royal Statistical Society*), who, equally independently, also developed a schema of the working of the credit mechanism, similar in many respects to the one implied above and developed in 1911, in his *Banking Policy and the Price Level* (1926).

factors. The reader is invited to make the experiment of testing this assertion by drawing up a list of what he considers these characteristics to be and observing whether they fit into the model offered. But there is no ground to believe that there should be just *one* wave-like movement pervading economic life. On the contrary, it stands to reason that some processes covered by our concept of innovation must take much longer time than others to have full effect. The railroadization or electrification of a country, for instance, may take between one-half and the whole of a century and involve fundamental transformations of its economic and cultural patterns, changing everything in the lives of its people up to their spiritual ambitions, while other innovations or groups of innovations may arise and disappear within a very few years. Moreover, the former will generally be carried out in distinct steps and thus give rise both to shorter fluctuations and longer underlying swells. Under these circumstances it is not the most natural thing to assume the existence of a single cycle and to postulate that it will display any very marked regularities. This is in fact a very bold hypothesis which could be justified only if clearly imposed upon us by our material. But as this is not the case, even apart from what we may reasonably attribute to the outside disturbances to which our material is subject, it seems much more realistic (and also likely to do away with some spurious irregularities, that is to say, irregularities which are only due to the single-cycle hypothesis) to admit that there are *many* cycles rolling on simultaneously, and to face squarely the problem of analyzing their interference with each other. As, however, it is necessary for the purpose of handling our time series to settle on a moderate number of distinct movements which may be thought of as superimposed on each other and as passing their normals or neighborhoods of equilibrium *near* the points where they cross the path of the next higher cycle underlying them, the three-cycle schema is here suggested as a fairly useful working hypothesis. Nothing more than descriptive merits are claimed for it, but manifestly it fulfills the one condition which a device of this kind may reasonably be required to fulfill, the condition of carrying historical meaning, which—with material as exposed as ours is to disturbances by outside factors which are not small, independent, or "numerous" in the probability sense—is much more important than fulfillment of any formal criterion.

Historical knowledge of what actually happened at any time in the industrial organism, and of the way in which it happened, reveals first the existence of what is often referred to as the "Long Wave" of a period of between fifty-four and sixty years. Occasionally recognized and even measured before, especially by Spiethoff, it has been worked out in more detail by Kondratieff, and may therefore be called the Kondratieff Cycle. Economic historians of the nineteenth century have unconsciously and independently testified to the reality of the first of these waves our material allows us to observe, viz., the cycle from about 1783 to 1842, and they have also borne out in advance our interpretation of the phenomenon by coining the phrase of the "industrial revolution," which really implies everything we mean. The phrase is infelicitous and justly considered obsolete by now, but it pictures well how the happenings of the period struck entirely unprejudiced observers. The years 1842–1897 are readily interpreted as the age of steam and steel, particularly as the age of the railroadization of the world. This may sound superficial, but it can be shown in detail that railroad construction and work incident to it, connected with it, or consequential upon it, is the dominant feature both of economic change and of economic fluctuations during that time, and of every one of the four phases into which it is possible to divide it. Future historians finally will find no difficulty in recognizing the initiating importance of electricity, chemistry and motor cars for both the up-swing and the down-swing of the third Long Wave, which rose about 1897. Of course, if we prefer a more usual way of expressing the same thing, we may put these processes also into terms of "investment" and the expansion and contraction of credit: this is certainly a very important part of the mechanism. Unfortunately, this description is not only more usual but also more superficial, and opens the door to all the crudities and errors of the various monetary theories of the cycle. Any satisfactory analysis of causes must start with what induces that credit expansion, as every satisfactory analysis of effects must start by investigating what is done with the increased monetary resources—after which we immediately cease to wonder why the mere increase of credit facilities in or before a depression proves as ineffectual as we know it does. If, however, we stop at the process of investment and postulate that it has a mechanism of its own, we not only fail to get at the core of the matter but we also find it difficult to avoid such desperate logic as is implied in the conclusion that because increase of investment and expansion of credit are associated with a prosperity phase, we therefore can produce prosperity by expanding credit.

The majority of students of the business cycle does not consider the evidence alluded to sufficient to establish this particular cycle. But what does that mean? The term Kondratieff Cycle is for us but a name for a certain set of facts (a certain long-time behavior of the price level, the interest rate, employment, and so on), none of which is open to doubt. It is true that the term also implies an interpretation to the effect that this behavior of our series is amenable to interpretation on the same lines as their behavior in shorter cycles. But this again is merely an inference from historical facts, which have not so far been called in question either. Of course, experience of about two and three-fourths units of a phenomenon does not warrant much generalization, and still less prediction.

It is therefore *only as a statement of fact* that we venture to say that the two complete Kondratieff units within our range of statistical vision contain each of them six cycles of from nine to ten years' duration, equally well established by industrial history, though less clearly marked in our time series, which correspond as a matter of fact roughly to that cyclical movement which was the first to be discovered. Following the same procedure as in the earlier case, we may call them Juglar Cycles. As pointed out by

D. H. Robertson,[4] it is possible in every instance to indicate the particular industry and the particular innovations which are responsible for the up-swing and the process of readjustment.

Finally, every Juglar so far observed (those of the present Kondratieff included) is readily, in most cases and in this country already by inspection, divisible into three cycles of a period of roughly forty months. The existence of this shorter cycle has been pointed out repeatedly these hundred years or more, and still oftener has it been felt and recognized implicitly, but one may remark that it was the two studies by Mr. Kitchin and Professor Crum in THE REVIEW OF ECONOMIC STATISTICS that were chiefly instrumental in establishing it.[5] Evidence about the commercial paper rate, this series being the most purely cyclical of all, is of course particularly important. That this cycle, as well as the others, is more clearly marked in this country than in any other and notably more marked than in England, is easily accounted for by the fact that cycles in most series will tend to be toned down or even ironed out the more a country's economic life is interwoven with interna-tional influences and the more its policy approaches Free Trade. The question of the statistical methods which arise out of this analysis (for statistical methods must arise out of our understanding of the phenomenon they are to be applied to) will be taken up at another time. It is, of course, admitted not only that non-cyclical changes also create wave-like movements but that besides the three just mentioned there are other cyclical waves.[6] It is held, however, that the three-cycle schema works sufficiently well for the purposes of the stage of rough approximations in which we are, and are likely to remain for a considerable time.

A Research Program

If we coördinate available information, statistical and historical, in the light of the principles sketched out, we get not so much a picture as indi-cations which give us an idea of what the real picture would be like. These principles do enable us to link up in a general way the behavior of those of our series which are most symptomatic of the pulse of economic life as a whole. These "systematic" series may be either "synthetic," as, for instance, series of price levels or of physical volume of production, or "natural," as, for instance, series of interest rates, clearing-debits, unemployment, pig-iron consumption, at least for the pre-war time, or the sum total of deposits. They all, also in a general way, behave as they would have to if the view outlined above were true to life. In the case of what, by way of distinction from "systematic," we may call "individual" series, such as the prices and quantities of individual commodities, our analysis becomes more compli-cated and perfect knowledge is necessary of the particular conditions in every branch of industry and commerce, of its lags, frictions and inertias,

---

[4] Cf. previous note, p. 54.
[5] THE REVIEW OF ECONOMIC STATISTICS, vol. v (1923), pp. 10-16 and 17-29.
[6] As pointed out by Wardwell, Kuznets and others.

of the mentality of its men, of the particular random influences to which it is exposed, and especially of its active or passive rôle in any given cycle. As the outside factors impinge upon some phase of a process consisting of a number of superimposed wave-like movements, and as every one of these movements itself impinges upon a particular phase of some other movement underlying it, so all of this impinges on a particular resonator in the case of every individual industry or firm, *which responds according to its own structure*. This is perhaps the best way of stating the problem in its full complexity. It also helps us to understand the many "special cycles" which some students have found or think they have found in various individual industries.

Now first, as regards a research program, it may be suggested that not a single one of the "systematic" series above spoken of represents adequately what it is meant to represent. And in no case is our historical or contemporaneous information adequate to account quantitatively for the fluctuations of the systematic series. It is only one side of the problem that this makes convincing verification of the result of any analysis impossible, and that all we can do at present is to say that the testimony of such facts as we have is compatible or incompatible with it. The other side is that many questions are not questions of principle and analysis at all, but simply of relative quantitative importance. The statement, e.g., that in the down-grade of any cycle inertia of wages counts for something in determining the amount of unemployment, is too obvious to require proof; but not only for practical but also for scientific purposes this is entirely irrelevant as long as we are unable to say whether this element accounts for one per cent or for ninety per cent of the unemployment figure observed in a given place at a given time. No wonder, therefore, that, if we are unable to be more precise than this, economics is considered as entirely useless by the practical man. Yet our analytic apparatus would turn out a definite answer all right, provided the necessary factual information were inserted into it, the assembling of which is, of course, much beyond the means of any individual worker or private group of workers.

Secondly, there is no reliable information at all on a number of subjects which are obviously of primary significance. Two examples must suffice. Waiving our objection to the present tendency to overstress the importance of price levels and monetary magnitudes in general, we may say that the stream of expenditure by households on consumers' goods is one of the most indispensable elements in the analysis of the business cycle. We have acceptable though far from satisfactory indicators for the post-war time but, owing to the exceptional circumstances present in this period, these are almost valueless for a fundamental understanding. And for the pre-war time we have to be content with pay-roll figures and the like, which might easily mislead even if they went further back than they do. Yet there is plenty of stray information stretching over centuries, which, if it could be brought together, would definitely clear up many pressing practical problems such as this one.

Again the process of investment and the corresponding process of credit contraction in down-grades can never, whatever the theorist may say, be fully grasped in its importance and consequences until we know more about the relative importance of its sources and the actual behavior of borrowers and lenders. The decisive figure here is the sum actually spent on the production of durable producers' goods *for new purposes*. It is in these last three words that our chief difficulty lies, which has so far been overcome only in a very few cases: we can follow up, for instance, how much was spent on railroad construction in England in the 'forties. It is difficult enough to find out how great the sum total is that newly enters industry and trade every year. It is still more difficult to find how much of this is spent on equipment. And even this would not be enough. However, an investigation lighting up this very important side of the past and present of capitalist society would be perfectly feasible.

Although, thirdly, the phenomenon of the cycle cannot be defined and understood as a sort of average between independent changes in individual industries, yet the behavior of individual industries, on the one hand causing and on the other hand responding to the sweep of changing business situations, requires a special study for each of them. Plenty of work has been done in this direction, but, as the decisive questions have hardly ever been in the minds of the writers to whom we owe that literature of industrial monographs, the evidence is incomplete and inconclusive. There is hardly any event, or peculiarity of structural pattern, in any industry which would be irrelevant to the question why the business cycle is what it is. Besides, if it be true that industrial change is at the bottom of the cyclical phenomenon, its mechanism can be established only by covering in detail all recorded cases of such change. To the thoughtful observer, for instance, a striking similarity reveals itself immediately between such different processes as the development of the English iron industry from the sixteenth to the end of the eighteenth century, and the rise of the motor-car industry in our time. In these, as in many other cases, we have even now advanced much beyond general impressions. There is, however, a long way between this and the goal of establishing the validity of the schema of innovation and showing how innovation produces, together with its monetary complement, the particular kind of waves inherent to the economic life of capitalist society and paralleled by similar phenomena in other fields of human activity.

5

Long Cycles in Residential Construction*

ARTHUR F. BURNS†

Editors' Note

A home, whether an apartment or a single-family dwelling, differs from other necessities in that it is frequently the biggest purchase a family makes. Buildings usually have a long life and, unless they are trailers, are permanently fixed to the land. It is not surprising, therefore, that residential building is characterized by cycles, for the housing supply, in the whole country as well as in a particular locality, cannot quickly respond to changes in demand. In fact, fluctuations in housing expenditures represent one of the major sources of instability in the economy. That much is clear to all. What is more controversial, however, is the existence of long cycles in residential construction. In this article, Burns explains the reasons why these long cycles exist. His presentation is theoretical rather than empirical. He considers the role of population changes, which have long been recognized as a prime mover in economic events. He also highlights the adjustment mechanism between the supply of housing and demand. A careful review of his argument will suggest that it has wider applicability. Any fixed asset that is long-lived could be subject to long periodic fluctuations. Clearly, the field of long cycles is ripe for further development.

---

* Reprinted from *Economic Essays in Honor of Wesley Clair Mitchell* (New York: Columbia University Press, 1955), pp. 63-104, by permission of Columbia University Press.

† See p. 5.

1. *The Problem*

❦ When we examine monthly figures we find that construction activity has cyclical fluctuations that correspond fairly closely to the cycles in general business, but when we examine annual figures these fluctuations tend to vanish before the eye, while cycles lasting from fifteen to twenty years obtrude themselves. These longer cycles consist of actual rises and declines, not merely of variations in the rate of growth such as are found in the secular trends of all industries. Long cycles of large amplitude characterize railroad construction as well as building construction, and appear to be a feature of investment in fixed capital wherever economic life is organized on a business basis.

The long cycles in building construction have recently received considerable attention in this country. Numerous historical studies for individual localities have been published. The results are remarkably uniform: they show that in one locality and the next there are long cycles of large amplitude in the construction of buildings, and that similar cycles are found in subdivision activity and real-estate trading—so that the cycles in construction are but one phase of the long cycles that characterize real-estate 'activity.' The most painstaking and scholarly of the local studies is Homer Hoyt's *One Hundred Years of Land Values in Chicago*, recently published by the University of Chicago Press.

While the local cycles diverge considerably, they also show a fair degree of similarity in their timing. Hence, it is to be expected that clearly defined long cycles will be found in national construction. This problem has been investigated by Dr. John R. Riggleman, and in June 1933 he published in the *Journal of the American Statistical Association* a preliminary index of building construction in the United States, based on building-permits data, for the period 1875 to 1932. The index has lately been revised and extended. In its present form it begins in 1830 with three cities, includes twenty cities by 1875, and sixty-five cities by 1900, this number being retained through 1933. Dr. Riggleman's index shows long cycles of large amplitude across a century of American experience. The following quotation from an unpublished manuscript by Dr. Riggleman on "Building Cycles in the United States" indicates their duration and amplitude: "The curve moved up from 49 per cent below normal in 1830 to 81 per cent above normal in 1836, down to 57 below in 1843, up to 74 above in 1853, down to 58 below in 1864, up to 19 above in 1869, down to 45 below in 1878, up to 58 above in 1890, down to 30 below in 1900, up to 33 above in 1909, down to 75 below in 1918, up to 66 above in 1925, and down to 87 below in 1933." Dr. Riggleman has tested his national index by constructing separate indexes for seven geographic regions for the period since 1875. The regional indexes show a fair degree of synchronism.[1]

---

[1] The writer is sincerely indebted to Dr. Riggleman for permission to quote from his manuscript.

Dr. Riggleman's index does not segregate residential buildings from other types of buildings. The same is true of most of the long-range studies for localities. But it is to be expected that if there are long cycles in the total construction of buildings there will also be long cycles in the construction of residential buildings, first, because residential construction is a substantial part of the total,[2] and second, because much other building is closely correlated with it. Such figures as we have confirm this expectation. Data for St. Louis since 1880, for New York City since 1902, and for Chicago since 1912 show that the long cycles in the total construction of buildings represent fairly well, except for a dampening of the amplitude, the long cycles in the construction of residential buildings. The short series of broad coverage—the Dodge figures since 1919 and the Bureau of Labor Statistics figures since 1921—reveal the same tendency.

The indications are, then, that there are long cycles in residential construction, that these cycles attain enormous amplitudes, and that they synchronize roughly in the various regions of the country. We attempt in this paper to explore the rational basis of the long cycles in residential construction. Other types of building and alterations are left out of account. But the major forces that impinge on residential construction are not peculiar to it alone. Much of our analysis, though with qualifications that we do not make, applies also to other types of construction.

II. *The Governing Hypothesis and Method of Approach*

The long cycles in residential construction are a result of certain characteristics of dwellings and of men. Normally, our dwellings have a long life; they provide accommodations for their occupants that admit of some shrinkage; they are not subject to transportation; and they are standardized only to a moderate extent. Normally, the inhabitants of this country move more freely from one district of a town to another than from one town to another; they move more freely from dwellings of one class to dwellings of the same general class than to dwellings of another class; they grow in numbers at a rate that varies considerably from year to year whether we consider a hamlet or the country as a whole; and the wisest among them are unable accurately to forecast the future state of the residential market. These characteristics of dwellings and of men are the "basic" factors in the long cycles of residential construction. We can say more simply that they consist of variability in the rate of population increase, durability of

---

[2] The Bureau of Labor Statistics figures on estimated expenditures for new buildings, covering from 257 to 364 cities, indicate that residential construction accounted for 61 per cent of the total during 1921–1933. The F. W. Dodge Corporation figures on contracts awarded, covering from twenty-seven to thirty-seven states, indicate that residential construction during 1919–1933 accounted for 55 per cent of the floor space and for 49 per cent of the dollar value represented by all contracts exclusive of public works and utilities.

dwellings, immobility of dwellings and men, inconstancy of the housing standard, and the uncertainty of men.

These basic factors provide a peculiarly apt setting, even when not worked upon by pecuniary institutions, for the formation of long cycles in residential construction. Their cyclical power will be clearly exposed if we analyze an imaginary economy that aims to provide residential facilities on some standard of need. We shall assume, therefore, that the Planning Council of a collectivist state sets a standard of one residential unit per person, that the Council ordinarily fixes building programs in the light of this standard, and that the construction scheduled for a year is fully executed in that year. It is perhaps necessary to stress that we shall use collectivism merely as a vehicle for expressing the basic factors in the residential cycles of our business economy, which is the sole object of our inquiry and to which we return explicitly in the last section of the paper.

Let us first dispose of some matters of definition. We shall understand by a residential district the area over which the physical distribution of dwellings exercises an important influence on the shifts of persons from one residence to another. If a surplus of residential units in A affects the movements of the population of B and a surplus in B affects the population of A, but neither the one nor the other exercises any appreciable influence on the population of C, then A and B belong to one residential district and C belongs to another. We shall assume that the country consists of a large number of residential districts whose boundaries remain unchanged over the period which concerns us. We do not exclude migration across the boundary lines; all that we assume is that such migration is not influenced perceptibly by housing conditions.

We shall consider the population of a residential district to be composed of several communities, each community to consist of members of a residential class who normally dwell in a distinct type of residential unit. The Council might classify persons for residential purposes according to their industrial grade, marital status, age, or all these and others; so that persons may or may not be permanently attached to the same residential class. But whatever the principle of classification, the members of a residential class will shift freely, as occasion requires, among the residential units corresponding to their class, but reluctantly—if at all—among other residential units. In view of our definitions of a residential district and a community, any surplus of residential units in one community will be of no more use to any other community in the same district than to any of the communities in any other district. The community, therefore, will be the fundamental unit for the accounts of construction.

Residential units we shall consider as durable over time and immobile over space. The residential units intended for the various communities will differ in design, but the units intended for a particular residential class will always be of the same construction. We shall assume that residential units of various types call for an equal expenditure of productive effort. It will therefore be permissible to add the various types of residential units to obtain totals of construction. However, comparisons of the demand for the use of residential units with the supply will still be ambiguous if the totals embrace more than a single community.

The Council cannot hope that the number of residential units in each community will invariably equal the size of its population, but under normal conditions it will use one means or another of approximating this end. The Council might set annual quotas for communities on the basis of estimates of population change and of replacement needs, taking due account of any surplus or shortage that is known to exist. Or else the Council might follow the convenient mechanical rule of basing the building quota for a year on the change in population during the preceding year, plus the number of residential units retired by nature or the state during the preceding year. The first method proceeds partly on known demand and partly on estimated demand. The second method proceeds entirely on an artificial conception of known demand. Let us suppose that the Council uses this method.

III. *Construction in a Single Community under Collectivism*

We begin with a single community. If the community is new, but established upon a sound basis, it will tend to grow in numbers year in and year out. There will be no need to replace residential units except when fire or tornado cause destruction. We assume that we have a new community which escapes destructive visitations by nature. The volume of construction will then vary to the extent that increases in population vary. Suppose that the community numbers successively, as of the first of the year, 10,000, 10,140, 10,230, 10,290, and 10,400 persons. The annual increases are then, 140, 90, 60, and 110. The number of residential units constructed annually will correspond exactly to these increases of population, but it will lag by one year. While the percentage changes in the population are small and positive ($+1.4$, $+0.9$, $+0.6$, and $+1.1$), the percentage changes in the increases of the population and in the volume of building are large and oscillatory (-36, -33, and $+83$). To be sure, the violent fluctuations in building reproduce the increases of what are merely hypothetical figures of population. But the fluctuations in the increases of our imaginary community are as nothing compared to what will frequently happen in small areas.[3] Should the increases in population have a rising tendency for a half dozen years or so, and then a declining tendency, the construction industry would trace out long cycles; and, since

---

[3] It may be of interest to note that the relative fluctuations of the increases in the entire population of the United States have at times been greater; though this is of dubious relevance in the present connection, since pecuniary forces have played an important role in these fluctuations.

the relative fluctuations of the increases in population tend to be large, the cycles in construction would also tend to show large amplitudes.

While the variability of population increases will introduce a violent rhythm in building activity, it will have no such effect on the output of a relatively perishable commodity such as shoes.[4] Suppose that the Council sets a standard of one pair of shoes per person per year and that the production quota for a year is set at the level of the population at the beginning of the year. The annual output of shoes intended for the community will then rise successively by 1.4, 0.9, 0.6, and 1.1 per cent. There will be no cyclical fluctuations in production; there will be fluctuations only in the rate of increase in production. Our buildings and shoes can therefore be viewed as rough instances of a general principle: If real income is to bear a fixed ratio to population, the output of a commodity admitting of only a single use will vary with the size of population, while the output of a commodity admitting of perpetual use will vary with the increases in population. The fluctuations of an empirical population series are virtually always much smaller than the fluctuations of the increases in the series. Hence the fluctuations in the production of residential units will be much greater than in shoes. The reader may, if he so chooses, consider the fluctuations in shoes as the standard of comparison when reference is made in this paper to 'large' fluctuations in construction. In this sense the fluctuations in construction will be 'large' even if the fluctuation of the increases in population are regarded as 'small.'

Our preceding example assumes an uninterrupted rise in population. Let us next consider a decline in population. The community has, let us say, entered the phase when decreases in population take place occasionally, but it has not yet reached the age when residential units must be retired because of physical depreciation. Continuing with the last figure in the example, the population numbers may run 10,400, 10,360, 10,350, 10,350, 10,360, 10,400, 10,450. The volume of construction required on account of population change will then be −40, −10, 0, +10, +40, +50. Since the volume of construction cannot drop below zero, it will remain at zero until the earlier peak in total population has been passed. This means that when an upward trend in population is intermittently marked by declines, the amplitude of construction will be smaller both absolutely and relatively than that of changes in population;[5] that if the level and amplitude of changes in population are on the average the same in the present 'stage' as in the 'stage' of steady growth, the amplitude of construction in this 'stage' will be smaller both absolutely and relatively than in the preceding 'stage'; that the volume of construction may lag by more than one year after changes in population; that a minor cycle following upon

---

[4] Cf. J. M. Clark, *Strategic Factors in Business Cycles* (National Bureau of Economic Research, 1934), pp. 27-44.

[5] In this paper we consider the standard deviation (σ) as the measure of absolute amplitude and the ratio of the standard deviation to the mean as the measure of relative amplitude.

a negative population change may not appear at all in the construction curve; and, finally, that whenever the population remains below a peak figure for some years and then rises above that figure a temporal skeleton of a long cycle in construction may be formed.

Let us now take account of replacements. They will become an appreciable factor in construction when the age of the community has outgrown the useful life of residential units. But first we must indicate more exactly the procedure of the Council in arriving at building quotas. The quota for each year measures the actual construction during the year. The quota is set at the beginning of the year according to the difference which then exists between the size of population and the number of residential units available for residential use. If the former is larger than the latter—that is, if the difference is positive—the quota for the coming year will equal the size of the difference. If the difference is negative or zero, the quota will be zero. Thus the difference always measures the 'required construction' in a year, but it is a theoretical quantity when negative. Were the difference invariably positive the Council could reach the same quota by taking the algebraic sum of the following preceding-year quantities: change in population, number of residential units destroyed by natural elements, and number retired from use as living quarters by state order. The sum of the last two items gives the 'required replacements.' The sum of all three items gives what may be called the 'presumptive construction.' If the required construction is negative or zero the actual construction will be zero; if the presumptive construction is negative or zero the actual construction will also be zero; if the presumptive construction is positive the actual construction may still be zero, for the required construction may be negative or zero. The actual construction would be the same as the presumptive construction only if the negative construction required in any year could actually be realized in that year. We shall therefore need to pay as much attention to presumptive construction as to actual construction when we come to consider the influence of immobility on the amplitude of construction cycles.

We can gain some idea of the role of replacements in total construction by making simple assumptions. Suppose that residential units are retired by order of the Council when they reach a fixed age but are not retired in any other way. Let R stand for the ratio of replacements to total construction in a year, the subscript n for the year, k for the age at retirement, and a for the largest whole number obtained by dividing k into $(n-1)$. Then, if population increases annually by a constant amount,

$$R_n = \frac{a}{a+1}$$

Assume that $k = 50$; R will then be zero from the first through the fiftieth year of the community, 0.5 from the fifty-first through the one hundredth year, 0.67 from the one hundred-first through the one hundred-fiftieth year, and so on. But if the population increases annually by a constant percentage,[6]

$$R_n = \frac{r^{ak} - 1}{r^{ak+k} - 1}$$

where r is the ratio of the population of any year to that of the preceding year, and where n is not equal to $(ak+1)$. The replacement ratio will now approach $1/r^k$ as a limit, instead of 1. Suppose that $r=1.02$ and $k=50$; then, $R_{52}=0.27$, $R_{102}=0.34$, $R_{152}=0.36$, and $R_{n\to\infty}=0.37+$. In general, R increases as a increases, decreases as r increases, and decreases as k increases.

The fluctuations in the number of residential units destroyed by the elements are likely to be uncorrelated with the fluctuations of population changes. The same remark applies to voluntary retirements—at least if we assume that the retirements are based on a standard of fitness, that there is no periodic cycle in changes of population, and that replacements on account of natural destruction are not a negligible portion of total replacements. Hence, if the required construction is at no time negative the absolute amplitude of construction will on the average tend to be larger than that of population changes.[7] This means, of course, that if population conditions are similar, the construction of a community advanced in age will tend to be of larger amplitude than the construction of a community requiring no replacements. However, population decreases may counteract this tendency. If the decline in population is numerically larger than the volume of required replacements, construction will drop to zero and remain at zero until after equality between the number of residential units in existence and the number of persons has been restored by the movement of either or both variables. Under such conditions the amplitude of construction may be smaller than that of changes in population. Irrespective of the sign of population changes, the timing of building fluctuations in the replacement stage will no longer be regularly related to the timing of population changes; there will now be leads and lags of varying duration and occasional coincidences.

Population changes and required replacements will form all sorts of combinations. This is of great importance, for out of these combinations long cycles may be formed in construction even when there are no such cycles in population changes. While required replacements and population changes will tend to be uncorrelated over long periods, they will nevertheless be correlated over short periods—now positively, then inversely. Although the fluctuations of required replacements will ordinarily be smaller than those of population changes, for a time they may be larger. The peaks

---

[6] The writer is indebted to Mr. Arthur Stein and to Mr. Milton Friedman for this expression.

[7] See G. U. Yule, *An Introduction to the Theory of Statistics* (8th ed., Charles Griffin and Company, 1927), Chap. XI, paragraph 2.

or troughs of the two variables may at some turns be approximately coincident. At others the peak of one variable may be coincident with the trough of the other. In the neighborhood of such turning points both variables may undergo especially violent movements, those in required replacements perhaps being the more violent. Chance alternations in the character of the short-time correlation between the two variables are thus likely to promote to some extent the formation of long cycles in construction. This tendency will gain in strength if such declines as occur in population occasionally exceed the volume of required replacements, so that the presumptive construction is negative. The actual construction curve will now be apt to skip completely some minor cycles in the curve of presumptive construction. And if this curve remains below the zero line for several years the curve of actual construction will form a zero trough over a longer period; a temporal base for a long cycle will thus be fashioned, which the construction contributed by other communities may transform into an actual long cycle for the residential district.

IV. *National Construction under Collectivism*

Let us now abandon the community for a larger area. If the population of each of the communities that compose a residential district increases every year and replacements are not needed, the construction of the district will reproduce with a one-year lag the annual fluctuations of the increases in the population of the district. Under similar conditions the residential construction of the country will reproduce with a one-year lag the increases in the national population. The relative fluctuations of increases in population will be smaller in the country taken as a whole than in the generality of communities. Hence the relative fluctuations of construction will be smaller; but they are still apt to be large, since the fluctuations of the increases in national population are likely to be large. The volume of national construction will trace out long cycles only if there are such cycles in the increases of national population; but long cycles may characterize the increases of national population even if there are no such cycles in the generality of residential districts or communities. Under the simple assumptions we have made, the fluctuations in the construction of a residential district or of the country as a whole, no less than of a single community, reflect the force of only two factors: variability of population increases and durability of residential units.

But variability of population increases would have little cyclical power if the longevity of buildings were no greater than of shoes. Suppose that there are long waves in the increases of national population. They will not suffice to generate long cycles in the production of shoes. With a footwear standard of one pair of shoes per person per year and quotas based on the population at the beginning of the year, the output of shoes will simply reproduce the curve of national population. There will be no cycles of any sort in this curve. Hence there will be no cycles of any sort in the output of shoes, though there will be long cycles in the rate of increase in output. Only the immobility of shoes in use could disturb the rigid relation between their production and total population; but for this to happen a net decline would have to take place in the national population of some 'footwear class.' Given a constant standard of housing and footwear, there will need to be long cycles in the population of the country if there are to be long cycles in the production of a perishable good such as shoes, while long cycles in the increases of the population will suffice to generate long cycles in the production of a lasting good such as dwellings.

Residential units, however, do not have everlasting life and in growing communities will sooner or later need to be replaced. If the presumptive construction is at no time negative in any of the communities—that is, if there are no declines in population, or if declines in population are smaller than required replacements—the actual volume of national construction, no less than that of a single community, will be the same as the presumptive construction. We have previously argued that the fluctuations of required replacements will tend to be uncorrelated with the fluctuations of population changes. Under present assumptions, therefore, the absolute amplitude of construction, whatever the area, will tend to be larger than the amplitude of changes in population. The timing relationship between construction and changes in population will tend to be irregular. And, just as the combination of required replacements and population changes may produce long cycles in the construction of a community even when there are no such cycles in its population changes, so the combination of required replacements and population changes may produce long cycles in the total construction of the country even when there are no long cycles in changes of population in either the component areas or the country as a whole.

Let us next consider the possibility that the presumptive construction is at times negative in some of the communities. This will be the case if there are occasional declines in population but no replacements, or if in certain communities at certain dates the volume of required replacements is smaller than the decline of population. If residential units or men were perfectly mobile, the theoretical requirement of negative construction could be satisfied by diverting the surplus of some communities to others. Hence the actual construction of the country would exactly reproduce the presumptive construction—that is, the algebraic sum of the presumptive construction in the individual communities. The theoretical requirement of negative construction in some of the communities would influence neither the correspondence of actual construction to presumptive construction nor the relation of construction to changes in national population; both would be the same as in the case when presumptive construction is invariably positive. Only if the presumptive construction for the country occasionally fell below zero would the curve of actual construction differ from the curve of presumptive construction; and even this could not happen if the mobility of residential units extended to nonresidential uses.

Under conditions of immobility, however, the theoretical requirement of negative construction in any year can be satisfied only through failure to build in later years; and if the negative construction required is much larger than the average annual volume of construction, a surplus of residential units may continue for some years. Immobility is therefore likely to exert an influence on the character of the cycles in national construction whenever the presumptive construction is negative in any of the communities. Suppose that the population throughout the country has been stationary for some time, that there are as many residential units in each of the various communities as there are persons, and that replacements are unnecessary. Suddenly, in district 1 the population increases by 100 in community A and decreases by 100 in B, and in district 2 the population decreases by 100 in A and increases by 100 in B. There are three possible ways of restoring equilibrium without new construction. First, the surplus population of A in district 1 could move to residences of type A in district 2, and the surplus population of B in district 2 to residences of type B in district 1. Second, residential units of type A could be moved to district 1 and of type B to district 2. Third, in district 1 the surplus population of A could move to quarters of type B and in district 2 the surplus population of B to quarters of type A. But each of these possibilities is closed by the assumption of immobility contained in our original definitions of a residential district, a residential unit, and a community. Although the total population has remained unchanged in districts 1 and 2 and in the country as a whole, 100 residential units will have to be built in each of these districts.

In this example immobility has led to a fluctuation in construction when there was none in the changes of total population. Under conditions of mobility the movements of the two variables would be inexorably linked. It is clear, then, that immobility may serve to confuse the relation between national construction and changes of national population. However, we must not infer from the example that immobility will intensify the fluctuations of national construction whenever the presumptive construction is negative in any of the communities. Suppose, for instance, that there are two distinct groups of communities in the country and that replacements are nowhere required. Group I consists of communities that gain in numbers each year; the volume of construction of this group will therefore vary as the increases of its population vary. Group II consists of communities that experience periodic fluctuations in population but along horizontal or declining trends; the construction of this group will therefore be zero. The curve of national construction will reproduce with a one-year lag the curve of population changes in Group I. But the amplitude of population changes in Group I may be smaller or larger than the amplitude of population changes in the entire country, depending—roughly speaking—on whether the population-change curves of Groups I and II are positively or inversely correlated. Hence, immobility may dampen the fluctuations of national construction, magnify them, or leave them uninfluenced.

We may now take replacements into account and formulate more exactly the influence of immobility. Each year we can distribute the presumptive construction for the country between two groups. Let us define Group I as a quantity which equals each year the volume of national construction. By subtracting this quantity from the presumptive construction for the country we shall obtain Group II. The communities having a positive requirement for construction contribute to Group I. The communities having a negative or zero required construction contribute to Group II, as do those having a positive requirement for construction lower than the presumptive construction. There is some overlap between the communities in the two groups, but it will be negligible in a growing country. The composition of both groups will change from year to year.

Inasmuch as national construction reproduces the curve of Group I rather than the curve of presumptive construction for the entire country, immobility may result in an amplitude of construction that is larger or smaller than what would occur under conditions of mobility. The crucial factor is the character of the correlation between Groups I and II.[8] Let r represent the coefficient of correlation between Groups I and II, σ_I the amplitude of Group I, σ_{II} the amplitude of Group II, and σ_N the amplitude of the presumptive construction for the country.[9] Then, if $r = +1$,

$$\sigma_N = \sigma_I + \sigma_{II}$$

and if $r = 0$,

$$\sigma^2_N = \sigma^2_I + \sigma^2_{II}$$

In either case $\sigma_I < \sigma_N$; that is to say, immobility will dampen the amplitude of construction whether Groups I and II are uncorrelated or positively correlated. But if the two groups are inversely correlated immobility may intensify the amplitude of construction. Thus if $r = -1$, the amplitude will be intensified provided $\sigma_{II} < 2\sigma_I$. If $r = -0.8$, the amplitude will be intensified provided $\sigma_{II} < 1.6\sigma_I$. In general, $\sigma_I > \sigma_N$ if $\sigma_{II} < |2r\sigma_I|$. But the two groups may have both major and minor cycles, the major cycles being correlated in one manner and the minor cycles in another. If the major cycles are correlated positively and the minor ones inversely, immobility will dampen the major cycles in construction and may magnify the minor cycles; while if the major cycles are correlated inversely and the minor cycles positively, it may magnify the major cycles and will dampen the minor ones. The influence of immobility on the amplitude of national

---

[8] In this argument we assume implicitly that changes in the presumptive construction of the country are independent of immobility. We do not assume, however, that the presumptive construction of Groups I and II is independent of immobility. The reasonableness of the first assumption can hardly be questioned—particularly if it is observed that required replacements are determined by physical criteria, so that the assumption is simply that changes in national population are independent of immobility.

[9] Supra, notes 5 and 7.

construction cannot therefore be known unless the data of Groups I and II are known.

The most we can do is to rely on reasoned expectations. We may anticipate that the communities of a growing country will tend to be subject to common influences on the side of natural increase and to random influences on the side of required replacements. But we may also expect that the rate of natural increase of some communities will depart from the national pattern; that net immigration will impinge chiefly on growing areas; and that internal migration will tend to produce an inverse relation between the population changes of the gaining and losing communities. Bearing in mind the composition of Groups I and II, it therefore seems probable that if the country experiences extensive internal migration the two groups will be inversely correlated. Immigration will tend to make the amplitude of Group I larger than that of Group II. Even if the amplitude of Group II were the same as that of Group I, a negative coefficient of correlation just greater than 0.5 would suffice to indicate that immobility had intensified the amplitude of national construction. All in all, therefore, it seems more reasonable to anticipate that immobility will magnify the building fluctuations of a progressive country than that it will dampen them.

We have proceeded on the assumption that the Council invariably adheres to the theoretical housing standard of one residential unit per person. Let us now drop this assumption. In practice the Council may occasionally find it desirable to suspend the standard. It will then make use of an instrument that has even greater cyclical power than fluctuations in the rate of population change. Suppose that there are 1,000 persons and 990 residential units in each community. To maintain the theoretical standard ten residential units will need to be built in each community. But if the standard is lowered by 0.5 per cent, only five units will be required; if it is lowered by 1 per cent, no construction at all will be required; if it is lowered by 5 per cent, a negative volume of forty units will be required. Thus, if the housing standard is reduced by a small percentage, the volume of building will be reduced by a much larger percentage from the level that would have been realized under a constant housing standard; the decline in building may readily reach 100 per cent and even then leave a surplus so large that all construction will need to cease for several years. In our example a 1 per cent drop in the housing standard has as much cyclical effect as would a 100 per cent drop in the sum of population change and required replacements. In other cases the disparity between the cyclical effects of the two factors may be larger or smaller; but it is nevertheless to be expected that occasional variations in the housing standard will tend to increase enormously the cyclical fluctuations in construction—even if the variations in the standard are correlated inversely with fluctuations in population changes. The great cyclical power of a fluctuating housing standard might, of course, be harnessed by the Council to counteract the impulses making for instability in construction that derive from a fluctuating rate of population change and of required replacements; but we must repeat that we "use collectivism merely as a vehicle for expressing the basic factors in the residential cycles of our business economy."

If the housing standard is at times reduced the occasions when negative construction is theoretically required will be multiplied. The cyclical role of immobility will therefore be larger; but it is difficult to say whether the role will be to dampen or to magnify the amplitude of construction. Much will depend on the frequency of the changes, their magnitude, and the degree of their uniformity in the various communities. We previously reached the conclusion that immobility is likely to magnify the building fluctuations of a growing country operating on a constant housing standard. This conclusion will still hold if the changes in housing conditions are infrequent but uniform over the country, while their influence on the volume of building is smaller than that of population changes. It will also hold under a variety of other conditions; but there can be little advantage from endowing our imaginary economy with special characteristics beyond the point that we have already gone. We need merely to recall that once the data of Groups I and II are known, the influence of immobility can be deduced from them.

Just as the cyclical power of fluctuations in the rate of population change derives from the durability of residential units, so does the cyclical power of inconstancy in the housing standard derive from the same source. A given reduction in the footwear standard, as previously defined, will produce merely a proportionate reduction in the output of shoes from the level that would have been attained under an unchanged standard. Thus, if the population of each community is 1,000 and the footwear standard is maintained the output of shoes will be 1,000 pairs for each community; otherwise it will be 995, 990, or 950, according as the standard is lowered by 0.5, 1, or 5 per cent. We may therefore say that durability is a necessary condition of the full release of the cyclical power of fluctuations in the housing standard; though durability can release only what is at its disposal —so that the cyclical power of durability will be zero if both the housing standard and population changes are constant. It is also true that the cyclical power of immobility derives from the durability of residential units. But we can no more say that durability—rather than inconstancy of the housing standard, or a fluctuating rate of population change, or immobility—is *the* basic factor in the fluctuations of residential construction, than we can say that "it is the upper" rather than "the under blade of a pair of scissors that cuts a piece of paper:"[10] they are all basic.

The large cyclical power of the basic factors in residential construction creates a presumption that long cycles will be produced through their joint action. The composition of the national construction curve changes.

---

[10] Alfred Marshall, *Principles of Economics* (8th edn., Macmillan, 1925), p. 348.

The incomers emerge from troughs of zero construction, the outgoers enter zero troughs. Any concentration of incomers or outgoers at certain dates will not fail to impress itself on the curve of construction. Temporary suspensions of the theoretical housing standard will also tend to produce sharp movements in the construction curve. If the housing standard is constant that curve, speaking roughly, is a composite of population changes and required replacements; but these variables may move in similar or in opposite directions. Over some years required replacements and population changes may tend upward quite generally, the movements of required replacements may be more violent than those of population changes, the housing standard may move towards parity, and the incomers from zero troughs may greatly outnumber the outgoers. In other years other combinations will emerge. The combination of factors determining the volume of national construction will change over time; and the changing combination of factors of large cyclical power may easily produce long cycles in residential construction—all the more readily, of course, if there be long cycles in the increases of national population. In the absence of long cycles in population changes in the country as a whole, or in the areas gaining through internal migration, the minor cycles in construction may at times obscure the major cycles.

v. *Intensifying Power of Uncertainty under Collectivism*

Our analysis must now be extended to include the factor of uncertainty. We have abstracted from this factor by assuming that the Council sets building quotas according to known demand. But under this scheme there will rarely be a nice adjustment of the supply of residential units to the demand implied by the ruling housing standard. With the standard constant there will be a permanent undersupply of residential units in case the population increases steadily, and shortages will dominate over surpluses in case the population fluctuates but along a rising trend. Let us suppose that the Council normally seeks to attain a closer approximation to the theoretical standard of one residential unit per person. It will then be necessary to set the building quota for a year by estimating the new demand that will arise during the year and adjusting this estimate for any surplus or shortage that is known to exist. By assuming that the Council sets building quotas on the basis of only partial knowledge of demand, we shall take account of the factor of uncertainty and therefore approach more closely the conditions underlying the residential cycles of our business economy.

At the outset let us revert to a single community which gains in population each year and escapes the need for replacements. In this case the Council will need to estimate only the increases in population. Let P stand for the actual increase in population during a year, K for the estimated increase during the year, B for both the building quota and the number of residential units built during the year, S for the surplus (or shortage) of residential units at the beginning of the year, M for the size of population at the beginning of the year, H for the number of units available for residential use at the beginning of the year; and let subscripts refer to successive years. Then we have

$$B_n = K_n - S_n = K_n - H_n + M_n$$

when this quantity is positive; otherwise $B_n = 0$. If the negative construction required in any year could be realized in that year, the following relations would hold:

$$B_n = K_n - S_n = K_n - H_n + M_n = K_n - K_{n-1} + P_{n-1}$$

Actually, however, B_n may be zero when $(K_n - K_{n-1} + P_{n-1})$ is positive, because $(K_n - H_n + M_n)$ may be negative or zero. In conformity to earlier usage, $(K_n - H_n + M_n)$ measures the 'required construction' and $(K_n - K_{n-1} + P_{n-1})$ the 'presumptive construction.' Both are estimated quantities; $(K_n - P_n)$ measures the error of each. Since the increases of population will tend to fluctuate considerably, the estimates will be in error nearly always to some extent and at times to a great extent. These errors may serve to magnify the fluctuations in building; to make them larger than they would be if they were governed by population increases alone. We shall simplify the analysis by restricting it at first to the case where $(K_n - S_n)$ is invariably positive.

The Council will be faced with the task of forecasting population. Suppose that a constant is chosen in some fashion as the estimate of population increase. Assuming equilibrium between population and residences at the start, we have $B_1 = K_1$. Subsequently, however, we have $B_n = P_{n-1}$, since $K_n - K_{n-1} = 0$. Hence, no matter how large the errors of estimate may be, the building curve will be the same as if each year's output had been mechanically set at the level of increase in population during the preceding year. Unfortunately, the assumption of a constant estimate is likely to be inconsistent with the controlling assumption that the Council will attempt to approximate as closely as possible the theoretical housing standard. If an appreciable shortage or surplus continues for several years, the estimated constant will be abandoned. Given the purpose of the Council, the variable nature of population increase will almost certainly lead to inconstancy in the estimates of increase. In any case we shall assume that the estimates are of this character.

Suppose, next, that the Council resorts to 'rational' forecasts, making the best use it can of the knowledge at hand. In that case $(B_n - P_n)$ is likely to be uncorrelated with P_n. Hence the amplitude of B will tend to be larger than that of P; that is to say, the fluctuations of construction will tend to be magnified through errors of estimate.[11] Or else the Council may resort to 'mechanical' forecasts, using some simple formula that appears logical. It might, for example, take as an estimate of population increase in

---

[11] Yule, *op. cit.*, Chap. XI, paragraph 3.

a given year, the actual increase during the preceding year; in this case,

$$B_n = 2P_{n-1} - P_{n-2}$$

Or it might estimate the population increase in a given year at the average increase during the two preceding years; in this case,

$$B_n = \frac{1}{2}(3P_{n-1} - P_{n-3})$$

In general, if the estimate is equal to the arithmetic mean of the actual increases during s preceding years,

$$B_n = 1/s[(s+1)P_{n-1} - P_{n-1-s}]$$

Clearly, any two-year combination of a large and small increase in population will produce an accentuated fluctuation in the curve of building; but the intensification will be largest when $s=1$. As s increases in size the tendency will be for the fluctuations in building to approach the fluctuations in increases of population;[12] the smaller, therefore, will be the intensification of amplitude produced by errors of estimate.

Let us assume, for illustrative purposes, that the increase in population for a given year is estimated at the level of the preceding year; that is to say, that $s=1$. The increases in population trace out fluctuations which, let us say, are irregular but clearly defined. The year following upon a cyclical peak in population increases will then witness a volume of building equal to twice the increase in population during the peak year minus the increase in population during the year preceding the peak. Hence, the peak in building will be sharper than the peak in population increases and is likely to follow it by one year. Similarly, the trough in building will be lower than the trough in population increases and is likely to lag by one year. During a cyclical rise in population increases the estimates are continually too low, which results in a shortage of residential units. To be sure, the shortage at the beginning of one year is corrected in that year, but underestimates of growth in population continue as long as the cyclical rise continues; a shortage therefore continues. Once a peak in population increases has been reached, the volume of construction in the following year not only corrects the shortage but also creates a surplus. The corrective movement in construction during the next year is therefore particularly pronounced, the recession being sharper than could be expected merely from a knowledge of the amplitude of population change. Similarly, there is a surplus of residential units during a cyclical decline in population increases; this becomes converted into a shortage after the trough in population has been passed; and the revivals in construction are peculiarly vigorous.

The intensification of cyclical fluctuations in construction will be more pronounced if we assume a somewhat different method of forecasting. Let

---

[12] If there is a strictly periodic cycle in the increases of population, the amplitudes of P and B will be the same whenever s is a multiple of the period of the cycle.

us suppose that the estimate of population increase for a given year is fixed at the level of the actual population increase during the preceding year plus the excess of the actual increase during the preceding year over the increase during the next preceding year; that is,

$$K_n = 2\,P_{n-1} - P_{n-2}$$

The estimates of population increase will now bear exactly the same relation to the actual increases as the volume of building bears to the actual increases when the estimate for each year is fixed at the level of the actual increase during the preceding year. The estimates, therefore, now undergo fluctuations larger than those of the actual increases of population. They will tend to err on the side of 'optimism' or 'pessimism' according as the second differences of the curve of population increases happen to be negative or positive. The magnified fluctuations of the estimates will lead to still more magnified fluctuations in construction, so that the cycles in construction will be much more violent than in increases of population. How large the opportunities for magnification become, particularly just after the cyclical turning points in population increases are passed, is apparent from the construction formula which expresses the present method of making estimates:

$$B_n = 3P_{n-1} - 3P_{n-2} + P_{n-3}$$

The preceding description of the intensifying mechanism that may be contained in the technique of estimation is limited by the condition that the fluctuations in population increases are never so large as to make S_n exceed K_n. When this occurs a negative volume of construction is theoretically required. Since construction can drop to zero but not lower, it will be impossible to correct the surplus in one year and construction activity may therefore need to be suspended for some time. If the fluctuations in population increases are so large that $(K_n - S_n)$ is frequently negative, there may be little similarity between the cycles in construction and the cycles in population increases. Out of such conditions, however, temporal skeletons of long cycles in construction may be produced.

Let us illustrate by a numerical example the principle of magnification through errors of estimate, without reference to any specific method of estimation. We start with 10,000 persons and 10,000 residential units; that is, with equilibrium between the demand for the use of residential units and their supply. On the basis of recent experience and current prospects the Council anticipates an increase in population of 100; it therefore orders that 100 residential units be built during the year. If the increase in population is 10 instead of 100, there will be a surplus of 90 units. Let us suppose that the Council considers this year abnormal and again plans for an anticipated increase in population of 100. Since there is a surplus of 90 residential units, only 10 will be ordered built. But the population may again increase by only 10, and the surplus will therefore remain 90. It is likely that the Council will now lower drastically its estimate of population increase in the coming year. Suppose that the estimate is 10; in this case the surplus of residential units will be nine times as large as the number required by anticipated growth during the year. All construction will therefore cease; and, if the annual increases in population vary subsequently between 5 and 15, ten years may elapse before construction is again undertaken.

In this example errors of estimate reinforce variability of population increase, the original impulse making for fluctuations in construction. The amplitude of fluctuations is increased and a temporal framework for a long cycle is created. Quasi-cyclical forces are set in motion, in the sense that a given error leads to a corrective adjustment; but these forces have limited scope—the process of adjustment does not of itself breed fresh errors. The volume of building no longer lags passively after population increases, but anticipates them; it may therefore trace out fluctuations even when there are none in population increases. Thus, we could recast the preceding example by assuming that population actually grows at a stable rate, and that errors of estimate originating in inaccurate statistics lead to excessive construction, the errors being later detected through the improved data that accompany the introduction of building quotas.

But the most striking and significant feature of the example is that the magnified fluctuations in construction result from small errors in the forecasts of total population; or, what is the same thing for our purpose, from small errors in the forecasts of total demand for the use of residential units. The estimate of population for the end of the first year is 10,100, the second year 10,110, the third year 10,030. The actual population at the end of the first year is 10,010, the second 10,020, and the third anywhere from 10,025 to 10,035. Hence, there is an overestimate of only 0.9 per cent in the first and second years, and a maximum overestimate or underestimate of 0.05 per cent in the third year. But these small errors in the estimates of total demand mean enormous errors in the estimates of increase in demand: in each of the first two years the increase is overestimated by 900 per cent, and in the third year there is a maximum overestimate of 100 per cent or underestimate of 33 per cent. Under our assumptions the volume of construction in a year would equal the actual increase in demand if there were no errors in the estimates of demand. However, since small errors in estimates of demand mean large errors in estimates of increase in demand, they may produce fluctuations in construction that are vastly larger than the fluctuations in the increases of demand. Even a small overestimate of demand may result, as in the example, in a volume of construction that far exceeds the actual increase in demand; so that many years of inactivity in the construction industry will need to elapse before the error can be corrected.

This will be the case only when the commodity produced is highly durable. Let us suppose again that the theoretical footwear standard is one pair of shoes per person per year. Provision will now be made for the year-end population, so that estimates of this quantity will be identical with estimates of the total demand for shoes. The errors of the estimates of population assumed in the above example will lead also to errors in the production of shoes. But these errors are negligible in size; and, since the unadjusted quotas for the production of shoes vary as the estimates of population, not as the estimates of the increases in population, the errors in the actual production of shoes will also be negligible in size. Hence they will be subject to quick correction and their power to produce fluctuations will be insignificant. Thus the output of shoes in the first year will be 10,100, which is only 0.9 per cent in excess of what is actually required in that year; assuming, of course, that the population is homogeneous from the standpoint of footwear as well as residences. But the output of residential units will leave a surplus equal to 900 per cent of the actual need for new residential units in the year. In the second year the output of shoes will be 10,020, a decline of 0.8 per cent from the preceding year; and the surplus at the end of the year will be 0.9 per cent in excess of true demand. The output of residential units will decline by as much as 90 per cent; but the surplus will nevertheless continue to be nine times as large as the actual demand for new residential units during the year. In the third year the output of shoes will be 9,940, a decline of 0.8 per cent from the preceding year; this will mean a maximum surplus or shortage of 5 pairs of shoes, depending on whether the population is 10,025 or 10,035. However, although the output of residential units will decline by 100 per cent, the surplus of residential units will not be less than five times and may be seventeen times as large as the demand for new units during the year.

The contrast between dwellings and shoes will be even more pronounced if we posit that errors of estimate can cumulate. All along we have assumed that the volume of construction projected at the beginning of each year will correct fully for any error of estimate that may have been made at the beginning of the preceding year, provided, of course, that the correction does not require a negative quantity of construction. We have therefore proceeded on the assumption that errors cannot cumulate. Once the possibility of cumulation is admitted, the opportunities for magnifying building fluctuations through errors of forecast are indefinitely increased. We might assume, for example, that what is known when quotas are set is the surplus or shortage at the beginning of the preceding year rather than of the given year; that is to say, that B_n will be governed by $(K_n - H_{n-1} + M_{n-1})$. Thus, to return to the above example, if $H_0 = M_0$ and $P_0 = B_0$, B_1 will be 100 and B_2 will also be 100. The consequence of delay in the discovery of errors will be a larger surplus of residential units and therefore a longer cessation of building activity. But the effect on the production of shoes will again be negligible.

The preceding analysis is restricted to a community that experiences uninterrupted growth, requires no replacements, and attempts to adhere closely to a standard of one residential unit per person. These restrictions can be removed by writing the equation for B_n in more general form. In addition to the symbols already defined, let R_n be the number of residential units retired during any year, L_n the estimate of this quantity, and C_n the housing standard during the year. If we assume again that errors cannot cumulate, then

$$B_n = C_n K_n + L_n - H_n + C_n M_n$$

when this quantity is positive; otherwise $B_n = 0$. The preceding analysis, therefore, requires little elaboration. Since population changes may now be negative, there may be zero troughs of construction even when there are no errors of estimate. The task of estimation will consist of two parts, one estimate being of population change and the other of required replacements. The errors of these estimates will at times be cumulative, at others compensatory. When they are cumulative and positive, a larger surplus will arise than if the zone of errors had been confined to population change. The larger surpluses will tend to promote longer cessations of building activity; but this tendency will be counteracted by the decline in the useful stock of residential units through failure to make replacements. However, if even a slight reduction of the housing standard should be concurrent with, or follow shortly, a sizable overestimate of required construction, building might need to be suspended for many years.

Errors of estimate are likely to magnify the fluctuations of national construction as well as of the construction of a single community. This would tend to be the case even under conditions of mobility, since the errors for individual communities will not be entirely self-canceling. Immobility, however, may reinforce the amplifying stimulus of errors of estimate; for the errors will tend powerfully to multiply the occasions when negative construction is theoretically required, and in this way to enlarge the zone within which immobility can exercise its cyclical influence. If the housing standard is constant our earlier conclusion that immobility is likely to intensify the amplitude of national construction will probably still be valid—particularly if estimates for the various communities are made by the same mechanical formula. But if there are occasional departures from the standard of one residential unit per person the outcome is more uncertain. In any case once the data of Groups I and II are known, the influence of immobility can be deduced from them. Group I is now the sum for each year of the quantities $(C_n K_n + L_n - H_n + C_n M_n)$ wherever they are positive; while Group II is the quantity we get for each year by subtracting Group I from the algebraic sum of the quantities $[C_n(K_n + M_n) + L_n - C_{n-1}(K_{n-1} + M_{n-1}) - L_{n-1} + R_{n-1}]$ for all communities[13]—this being the construction that would take place under conditions of mobility.

With uncertainty at free play the cyclical power of the several basic factors in residential construction will be at a maximum. The troughs will last longer and be more numerous than when quotas were set by the method of known demand. Some tendency towards direct correlation of

---

[13] This expression is derived from the preceding expression by substituting for H_n the following quantity: $C_{n-1}(M_{n-1} + K_{n-1}) + L_{n-1} - R_{n-1}$.

errors will arise if the same forecasting method is applied to the communities of a country whose population growth is fairly well diffused geographically. This will promote a clustering of zero troughs, which in turn will promote the formation of long cycles. But chance alone will be almost certain to produce some degree of clustering; thus the errors will be generally positive if some unexpected factor acts to diminish the growth of communities throughout the country. Hence the presumption is that when uncertainty reinforces the cyclical power of the other basic factors, the curve of actual construction will show long cycles with clearly defined contours.

vi. *Long Construction Cycles in a Business Economy*

We have shown that long cycles in residential construction may easily come into existence in a collectivist economy that adumbrates our business economy. But these long cycles are mechanical in character; and the process of their formation differs in important respects from that of the long cycles in our business economy. We must now extend and adapt the analysis, so that it may apply to the pecuniary organization of our economy. For our purpose the essence of pecuniary organization is economic freedom, which resolves itself into independent action on the part of individuals or groups with a view, mainly, to private advantage.

The touch of rigor in the preceding pages has exposed the power of the basic factors in the cycles of residential construction. But it is important to note that under collectivism, as we have sketched it, these factors are related only in the sense that a certain state of some factor or factors is a necessary condition of the expression of the cyclical power of other factors. In the actual economy, these integrative ties are maintained, but in addition strong geographic and temporal ties are established through the impact of pecuniary forces. Thus pecuniary forces tend to exercise similar sway over the various regions of the country, which leads to a fair degree of correlation in the fluctuations of construction of the various regions. Further, the common impress of pecuniary forces on the basic factors results in a sharp increase in their effective cyclical power—particularly during periods of extreme expansion or depression in general business. For example, a vigorous and sustained improvement in business conditions will ordinarily stimulate immigration, increase the demand for housing on the part of the average person or family, hasten the retirement of obsolete residential units, and lead to exaggerated forecasts of the real-estate market. In our analysis of collectivism we showed that such changes have large cyclical power in the case of the construction industry. Now, they will tend cumulatively to increase the volume of building once vacancies are at a relatively low level; and the impossibility of transferring dwellings from places or uses of declining demand to places or uses of rising demand, without incurring heavy sacrifices, will promote exaggerated forecasts and therefore work in the same direction. Sooner or later a condition of overbuilding will be discovered; and, as our previous analysis suggests, the durability of dwellings may enforce many years of comparative idleness on the construction industry.

Uncertainty is but one factor in the mechanism of long residential cycles. However, given durable dwellings and the institutional framework of the building and real-estate industries, it is a strategic factor in the prolongation of construction cycles. Let us therefore consider how pecuniary organization, by creating uncertainty at almost every turn, increases the difficulty of adjusting the supply of dwellings to the demand for their use. The current state of the residential market is never a matter of exact knowledge, because dwellings are heterogeneous and realized rentals cannot be ascertained precisely. The volume of current construction is influenced by prospective demand as well as by current demand. Prospective demand may be interpreted in the sense of gross income. This depends on the level of rentals, the size of population, and its housing standard; but these factors are interrelated, and the future state of each is uncertain—partly because it depends to some extent on the volume of future construction. The volume of current construction is governed also by conditions of cost; but land values and construction costs in the present or in the proximate future are only less uncertain than maintenance costs in the distant future. A speculative builder cannot appraise the prospective net income from a certain class of dwellings without taking account of the prospective supply of all classes of dwellings in the same residential district. He must therefore make due allowance for the actions of his fellow builders, who are not in the habit of consulting with him; many of whom, he knows, are more deficient than he in balancing nicely estimates of future income against estimates of present and future costs; and some of whom, he anticipates, have as yet not 'discovered' that deed-searching and house-painting are less profitable than house-building.

The opportunities for producing maladjustment between supply and demand in the market for dwellings are clearly ample. They are enhanced by lax methods of financing construction and by the existence of a double market for dwellings—one for the use of dwellings, another for the dwellings themselves. Excessive liberality in the extension of credit promotes speculation; for it may enable a builder to put up houses without risking much of his own capital. The double market for dwellings also promotes speculation; for, in the first place, it permits the investing public to participate with building operatives in appraising the future state of the rental market, and in the second place, it permits both builders and the public to devote their energies for a time to traffic in real estate with little heed to the rate of interest at which prospective incomes are being capitalized in prices. If a building operative put up houses with a view to rental rather than sale and if he could borrow only a small fraction of his outlays on construction, he would curtail his operations in case he considered the prospects of the rental market unfavorable. But this will not happen if he firmly believes that the outlook of the generality of real-estate traders, or the public who have turned traders, is genuinely optimistic. Nor will it happen if he firmly believes that traders have only a vague notion, if any, concerning the prospective market for the use of dwellings, but nevertheless entertain extremely optimistic notions concerning the prospective market for dwellings. In either case, if costs are not prohibitive, he will build more energetically than ever in the hope of making quick sales. And he will act in the same way, no matter what others may think about real estate, if only his banker is optimistic enough, or expects the public that buys real-estate bonds to be gullible enough, to be willing to lend on the security of what is proposed to be built as much as or more than it will cost to build it.[14] If the disaster envisaged by the building operative actually eventuates, but not before he has succeeded in closing his operations at a profit, his private rationality will have contributed to the collapse of the real-estate market largely produced by mass irrationality.

With disequilibrium between demand and supply as the normal condition in the market for dwellings, corrective forces are constantly being set in motion by the profit motive. But the progress of corrective forces is slow in the case of dwellings, partly because of their durability, partly because of methods of financing and of transferring title, and partly because the profit motive often works blindly. Once a corrective adjustment gets firmly under way, it tends to be carried too far, so that errors are produced which in turn require correction. Hence long cycles operating on the reaction principle are likely to occur in residential construction, no matter what the period of the cycles in the changes in the demand for the use of dwellings may be; though the fluctuations of changes in demand will in actual fact be influenced by the long cycles in construction.[15]

Let us assume that after construction activity has been declining some eight or ten years, a vigorous revival in general business gets under way.[16] There will then be a sharp increase in the demand for the use of dwellings. Families that have 'doubled up' will seek separate quarters; marriages that

[14] See F. F. French, *Financing Private Construction*, an address at the Fifteenth Convention of the Associated General Contractors of America, January 30, 1934.

[15] The statistical indications are that annual increases in the population of the United States have traced out long cycles; that these cycles are largely, but not entirely, attributable to long cycles in immigration; that major depressions in this country have been followed by sharp and protracted declines in immigration and that this factor has played a dominant role in the formation of long cycles in immigration; and, finally, that the long cycles in the increases of national population have corresponded fairly closely, except for the eighties, to the long cycles in the construction of buildings.

[16] Some aspects of the mechanism of long cycles in construction are discussed ably and documented statistically by H. Hoyt in his *One Hundred Years of Land Values in Chicago* (University of Chicago Press, 1933), particularly in Chap. VII. A few suggestive hints are given by Clark, *op. cit.*, passim. For an elaborate statistical inquiry into the major factors in the long cycles of real-estate 'activity,' as exemplified by St. Louis, see R. Wenzlick, "The Problem of Analyzing Local Real Estate Cycles," *Proceedings of the American Statistical Association*, March 1933, and D. S. Wenzlick, "What about Rents," *Journal of the American Institute of Real Estate Appraisers*, January 1933. For illustrative data on fluctuations of real-estate prices, see J. G. Clark, "The Real Estate Cycle in San Diego, California, 1900 to 1932," *ibid.*, April 1933.

have been postponed will be consummated; urban families that have sought refuge on farms will return to the cities; the normal flow of rural population to the cities will be resumed; and immigration will again set in. The number of vacancies will therefore diminish quickly, and rentals may move slowly upward. Hence the gross income from real estate will rise; and the net income will rise faster, since the costs of maintenance are not likely to change appreciably. The pressure on owners of real estate will diminish; foreclosures will decline rapidly; and while there may as yet be little trading in real estate, prices will be higher than in the days when foreclosures were rampant. Conditions in the loan market for both new and old buildings will be improved. Construction costs are likely to be higher; but rising costs will be no bar to construction if the present value of the prospective income from dwellings is reckoned to be larger than their cost. As trading in real estate is revived, and the speculative public again enters the market, the prices of real estate will advance faster than costs of construction. Hence the incentive to new building will be increased.

Once the level of rentals and the rate of occupancy have reached a stage that is generally recognized as profitable, new capital will be increasingly attracted into building. For some time, however, as the demand for the use of dwellings increases, the stock of usable dwellings will increase more slowly. Builders proceed cautiously, fearing that the increase in demand may prove evanescent; much time needs to be expended in choosing sites, formulating plans, arranging loans, letting contracts, and so on; the process of physical construction requires a few months or longer; and the increase in the stock of dwellings is smaller than the volume of new construction, chiefly because of the replacement of obsolete units. But as vacancies tend to disappear, the incentive to build grows stronger; and within a few years the volume of construction will be perhaps several times as large as at the trough of the construction cycle.

There may now occur a depression in general business. This will be reflected in a reduced volume of residential construction. But the level of building activity will continue to be high, since a considerable volume of construction is in process and the condition of the rental market is still sufficiently favorable to stimulate a goodly number of new projects. The continuance of residential construction at a relatively high level will tend to check both the severity and the duration of the depression, while the close of the depression will give a new fillip to both the rental market and the market for houses. Easy credit and speculative zeal will now sharply advance the prices of real estate, and with little regard to the rate of interest at which prospective incomes are being capitalized. As the margin between construction costs and comparable real-estate prices continues to be wide, the volume of building will rise swiftly, particularly since the ranks of builders, no less than of traders, will be swollen by accessions from the public. With speculation rife the adjustment of the supply of dwellings to the increase in demand will be carried too far; and it is only a matter of time before a condition of overbuilding will be generally recognized to exist. At this stage much real estate, both old and new, will be in the hands of owners who have but a thin equity in their property and who will therefore find themselves in difficulty as soon as any decline takes place in rentals or in other sources of income.

A condition of overbuilding is slowly and reluctantly admitted; for what is merely the rising wave of a long cycle is generally mistaken for the underlying trend. The true state of the rental market is screened by the high rate of mobility of occupants of dwellings and by the double demand exercised for some months by families contemplating to vacate rented premises as soon as their new homes are completed. But two sets of forces gather momentum and conspire to bring the boom in residential construction to a halt. In the first place, the rental market becomes strained. It is more and more difficult to rent new dwellings at prices the expectation of which evoked the construction. Renting conditions are still worse in older houses which are also burdened by fairly numerous vacancies. Should a decline in general business occur at this stage, it will sharply intensify the tension in the rental market. In the second place, construction costs creep up on prices of comparable real estate. The competition among builders tends to raise the prices of labor and materials, and the frantic activity tends to diminish the efficiency of labor and management. Hence construction costs rise more sharply than the familiar index numbers may suggest. What is perhaps of even greater importance is that the rise in costs is very uneven, being highest for the inexperienced builders, who have only recently entered the trade. The pressure of rising costs, particularly on inexperienced builders, and of rentals that are barely maintained if not actually declining, will eventually be precipitated in a recognition that a state of overbuilding exists.

A condition of overbuilding cannot be corrected quickly. For a time, the difficulties on the supply side are even likely to increase. Some builders, or else their bankers, may find that the type of dwelling which they construct or the district which they serve still enjoys a favorable market; and this type of construction may continue unabated. Some building projects have been carried too far to be abandoned, and will add to the volume of construction activity for many months. And a demand for specially designed dwellings to be erected on certain preferred sites keeps recurring. Hence, although the volume of building declines, it lingers at a relatively high level at a time when a complete cessation of new construction for several years might be no more than sufficient to bring the supply of dwellings into adjustment with even an increased demand. As the new buildings are completed they enter into competition with the older stock and therefore help to depress rentals.

Therefore, the incentives to new construction progressively diminish. Owners find that their net income from real estate drops much faster than rentals, since costs of maintenance do not decline appreciably and may even rise. Cash sales of real estate are few; and while there may be a semblance of stable values, in actual fact real estate can now be sold at only sharply reduced prices. For a time owners make all sorts of sacrifices to preserve their equities, by drawing upon their savings and business incomes to meet interest on mortgages, amortization payments, and taxes. But if a decline in general business did not set in contemporaneously with the decline in residential construction, it will make its appearance not more than two or three years later. A reduction of the housing standard will take place; and we have already seen that a slight reduction of the housing standard may dispense with the need for new construction even in the face of an increasing population. Nominal rentals will fall considerably and realized rentals even more, at a time when the ability of owners of real estate to draw upon outside sources of income is declining. Hence the transfer of property from owners to creditors will commence on a large scale. The process of liquidation will extend over several years, partly because the period elapsing between the time of default and the end of foreclosure proceedings is normally a half year or longer, partly because mortgages have a term of several years and expire in but small quantities at any one time, and partly because some owners continue to resist stubbornly the loss of their equities at a time when they would do better financially to cut themselves loose from their heavily indebted property. As mortgagees acquire real estate, they are frequently glad to dispose of it for the face value of the mortgage or less, if only because they do not relish the function of real-estate management. There are also distress sales by persons seeking to realize some cash to protect other investments or to meet urgent household needs. Buyers bid cautiously, and many are excluded from the market because transfers cannot be adequately financed. The prices of real estate therefore drop precipitously, and since construction costs do not decline nearly so much, the prices at which dwellings only recently built change hands are considerably lower than it would now cost to build them. Hence the volume of residential construction is negligible, most of it being attributable to demand of a specialized character.

The severe drop in residential construction may help to bring about a deep and protracted depression in general business—one lasting from four to six years, such as that from 1837 to 1842, from 1873 to 1879, or from 1929 to 1933. But if conditions other than the state of the residential market are favorable, the depression will be short-lived. Improvement in general business will be accompanied by improvement in renting conditions. There will also be a revival in residential construction, though most of it will be in regions that have gained by population shifts and much of the rest will be initiated by owners, scattered through the country, who contemplate occupancy. But in spite of the revival the absolute volume of construction will continue at a low level, and will therefore promote an early recession in general business. For, with foreclosures at a high rate and vacancies in most places still numerous, the liquidation in the real-estate market will be uncompleted. So long as foreclosures are active and financial institutions hold title to property that they do not care to manage or to exhibit in their statements, the prices of real estate will continue at levels that imply high capitalization rates of even current incomes. The trend of residential construction will therefore be downward; though its course may be marked by two or three minor waves corresponding to the business cycles that are in the meantime undergoing their swing. We must note that the downward 'trend' of construction is but the declining phase of a long cycle.

Gradually, secular and cyclical forces change the face of the residential market. While the volume of construction has been declining, the trend of population in most cities has been rising; so that the condition of the rental market is bettered. New transportation facilities have become available, or old ones extended; so that residence in the suburbs has become more feasible. At the same time the technique of construction has been improving, and promising innovations in residential facilities have been multiplying. The prices of materials and of labor have, in all likelihood, fallen; and, what is of equal importance on the side of costs, the contractors now bidding for jobs are the more efficient builders who have survived the long depression in residential construction and they can command efficient labor. Finally, foreclosures and distress sales eventually turn downward. The gap between construction costs and comparable real-estate prices will therefore be narrowed, especially in the case of those types of dwellings that have won special favor. For a time, however, little money will be available for financing construction, lenders now tending to be as timorous as some eight or ten years ago they were venturesome.

Nevertheless, the volume of building will slowly rise. Of the many who have long postponed building a home, some will decide that it is not worth risking further hesitation. Some speculative builders, well equipped with capital, will build on a modest scale in anticipation of demand, devoting their resources primarily to houses of the sort that have lately gained most in esteem, but which are better, or more conspicuously, equipped. The revival in building may be one of the agencies that will usher in a revival in general business. Or, what is more likely, the revival in construction will reinforce the revival in other branches of industry, which occurred earlier and itself stimulated the improvement in construction; and it is only as readjustments spread from industry to industry that a general revival in business will get under way. But no matter what the sequence of factors may be, and whatever the role of the ever-disturbing random forces—from which we have abstracted completely in our brief and schematic description—a vigorous revival in business will sooner or later get under way. From this point the long construction cycle will repeat itself. It will not, of course, be a replica of its predecessor; but its general features will be the same and it will belong to the same class of economic movements.

The secular, cyclical, and random forces that combine to terminate the downward movement in the long construction cycle do not appear in exactly the same guise throughout the country. Hence the revival in construction is not synchronous in the various regions of the country, and some districts may entirely escape it. The timing of recessions is no more uniform than the timing of revivals. Only a moderate degree of synchronism in the long construction cycles of the various residential districts is to be expected, and just this is to be found. Since the differences among residential districts are less prominent than the similarities, we can justifiably speak of a long cycle in national construction. But the differences among the districts cannot be set aside, especially if our view extends beyond urban areas. We must therefore revert to the question of the influence of immobility on the amplitude of fluctuations in the national construction of dwellings.

We have already suggested that immobility is one of the channels through which pecuniary forces breed errors and thereby help to bring about, as the case may be, a condition of overbuilding or underbuilding. This might be interpreted as creating a presumption that immobility serves to intensify the fluctuations in national construction, but it does not prove the point. Nor can an analysis of Groups I and II, along the lines earlier suggested, yield a strict proof in the case of a business economy. For, quite apart from the considerations that the unit is now the owner of a dwelling instead of a community and that the data on presumptive construction for Group II are psychic facts, we may no longer assume that the presumptive construction of the country is independent of immobility. Only rough methods and correspondingly uncertain results seem possible. For the period since 1920 we have annual estimates of the increases of the urban and farm population of the United States. If we accepted the increases in urban population as a rough index of Group I and the increases in national population as an index of the presumptive construction of the country, we would infer from their amplitudes that immobility has definitely served to increase the amplitude of national construction. This conclusion is plausible; but it rests on so many dubious assumptions that even the figures involved in the comparison are not worth presenting.

6

The Short Cycle in Residential
Construction, 1946-59*

JACK M. GUTTENTAG†

Editors' Note

Home-building seems to be characterized not only by long cycles, but by
short ones as well. This article, one of the best analyses of residential
building cycles of the past decade, traces the statistics of the postwar period
using the guidelines of the National Bureau of Economic Research terminology. Yet, in what represents a major advance in empirical research on
individual sectors, the cycles are considered in terms not of one particular
series, but of three: nonfarm housing starts, mortgage recordings, and residential contract awards. Even more important, however, is the relationship
Guttentag posits between fluctuations in home-building activity and in
mortgage credit, both its supply and the terms on which it is offered. This
analysis focuses on the significance of new institutional developments, en-
gendered by government intervention, which nevertheless have not obliter-
ated the building cycle, but may have shortened it. What is most striking
is the explanation of why home-building cycles since the end of World
War II have moved out of phase with the general business cycle. These
countercyclical fluctuations have fascinated business cycle students, since
formerly the building cycle itself was a major determinant of the general
cycle. At least for the period studied, 1946 to 1959, the demand for housing
seems to have played a passive role, and mortgage credit has been the
active agent. How corporate and government finance helped this process
is another significant finding. Altogether, this article by a younger writer
is a fine example of contemporary business cycle research. What remains to
be seen is whether the mechanism explained will continue to operate in

* From *The American Economic Review*, Vol. LI, No. 3 (June, 1961), pp. 275-298.
Reprinted by permission of *The American Economic Review* and the author.
† The author, formerly chief, Domestic Research Division, Federal Reserve Bank of
New York, is an Associate Professor of Finance at the University of Pennsylvania.

the 1960's or whether the short home-building cycle will once again contribute to, rather than blunt, over-all fluctuations.

❧ Many of the important issues of housing policy that have arisen over the last decade focus on short-run instability in residential construction. Yet compared to the extensive literature on the long cycle in residential construction, the short cycle has been relatively neglected.[1] The purpose of this paper is to examine the determinants of short-run fluctuations in residential construction during the 1946–59 period.[2]

Part I explains how the short cycles are measured and describes some of their characteristics. Part II considers the relationship between fluctuations in residential construction and changes in the supply of mortgage credit. Many observers have noted that residential construction appears to be quite sensitive to credit conditions in the short run but little evidence for this relationship has yet been produced. In Part III the analysis is broadened to show the relationship between fluctuations in residential construction and in aggregate economic activity. Again, it has been widely noted that residential construction has had a generally stabilizing or countercyclical influence on the economy but no very adequate or complete explanation of this tendency has been provided.

I. *Short Cycles in Residential Construction*

A. STATISTICAL IDENTIFICATION

The procedure used to identify "cycles" in residential construction activity is similar to that used by the National Bureau of Economic Research, except in one respect. Cycles in residential construction are defined here in terms of movements in three related series rather than only one; a movement is not recognized as "real" unless it is found in each of the series. In effect, this rule supplants the amplitude criterion used by the NBER to identify specific cycles.[3] The three series are private nonfarm housing

---

[1] An early investigator of the short cycle was W. H. Newman [15]. More recently L. Grebler [6] [8] has intensively examined a relatively short period, and touched upon some of the issues raised in this paper.

[2] Space limitations preclude my bringing the findings of this paper to bear on housing policy issues.

[3] Burns and Mitchell describe their rule as follows [2, p. 58]: "The lower limit of the range of amplitudes of all fluctuations that we class confidently as specific cycles is our rough guide in deciding whether any doubtful fluctuation . . . is well enough defined to be accepted as a specific cycle." This rule is modified under certain conditions [2, pp. 138-39]. Reflecting the different procedure employed in this study, I have a contraction in 1953 which the NBER has not marked off in the residential awards series, while the dates of my turning points in this series diverge appreciably in a few instances from theirs.

starts, nonfarm mortgage recordings of $20,000 or less, and residential contract awards. In addition, for the period since late 1950 a series is available on FHA applications and VA appraisal requests.[4] Each of these series, although covering an activity common to the other two (residential construction), is derived from an independent source and corrected independently for seasonal variation. This approach provides considerable assurance that the cycles identified are not the result of the erratic nature of the data or of faulty seasonal adjustment, but are ultimately explainable in terms of basic economic forces.

The most important activity not covered by all three series is the mortgaging of existing houses, which is included only in the mortgage recordings series. This activity generally accounts for more than half of the total volume of mortgage recordings. Nevertheless, there is a presumption that the volume of residential construction activity and the volume of mortgage activity will move in the same direction.[5] As indicated later, this presumption appears justified for the postwar period, at least after 1948.

The first clearly identifiable turning point in the three series is in late 1947 to early 1948 (Chart 1). Prior to that time, during 1946–47, the brevity and varying duration of movements in the several series make it impossible to relate them to one another with any degree of certainty. These statistical difficulties probably reflect the rather abnormal market conditions of these years. The construction industry was being reconstituted and materials shortages introduced an erratic element into construction activities. The several short movements hardly register in the recordings series, which was dominated during this period by an unusually active market for existing houses.[6]

During the period 1948 through 1959 there are four distinct periods of both expansion and decline in each of the three principal series (Chart 1). The turning points in each of the series can be related to one another with little difficulty since in most cases the timing discrepancies are small. The four complete cycles, measured peak to peak, have an average duration of 31 months in the awards series, 33 months in the starts series, and 35 months in the recordings series. None of the cycles, whether measured from peak to peak or trough to trough, is shorter than 16 months.

---

[4] With one exception these series measure physical volume. The recordings series measures value and is the only one adjusted for trend. Data on residential awards are published through the courtesy of F. W. Dodge Corp. The author will be happy to provide a complete description of these series, including coverage, turning points, and sources, to interested readers.

[5] This is evident where the principal dynamic factor in the market is a change in the supply of mortgage credit. It is likely also to be the case when market changes originate on the demand side because (a) the relationship between the incremental demand for housing and the credit demand with which it is associated is very close in the short run, and (b) the mortgage credit demand that arises from sources independent of housing demand is relatively small, and part of it at least apparently is quite stable.

[6] This was itself partly a reflection of the fact that new construction was limited.

CHART 1. SELECTED SERIES ON RESIDENTIAL CONSTRUCTION AND MORTGAGE ACTIVITY, 1946–59

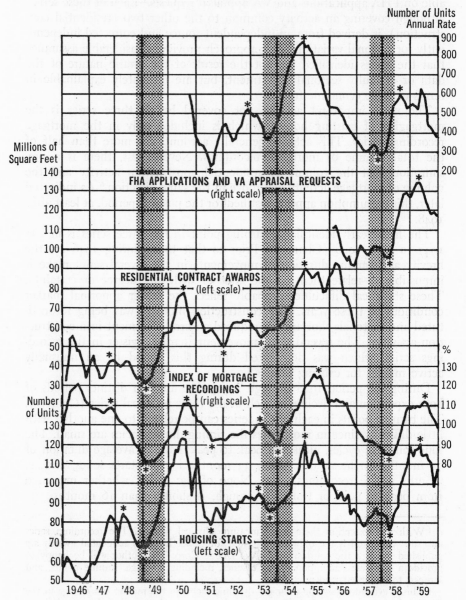

Number of Units
Annual Rate

Millions of
Square Feet

FHA APPLICATIONS AND VA APPRAISAL REQUESTS
(right scale)

RESIDENTIAL CONTRACT AWARDS
(left scale)

Number
of Units

INDEX OF MORTGAGE
RECORDINGS
(right scale)

HOUSING STARTS
(left scale)

1946 '47 '48 '49 '50 '51 '52 '53 '54 '55 '56 '57 '58 '59

Note: Shaded areas represent reference contractions in general business as established by the National Bureau of Economic Research. Series are three-month averages except for housing starts. All series are seasonally adjusted.

CHART 2. AVERAGE REFERENCE CYCLE PATTERNS

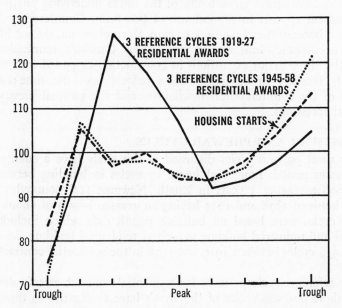

B. EVIDENCE OF A COUNTERCYCLICAL TENDENCY

A broad countercyclical tendency of residential construction during the 1948–59 period is evident in Chart 1. Construction declined during the late stages of the expansions in general business that ended in late 1948 and mid-1953, and throughout most of the expansion running from late 1954 to late 1957. It rose throughout most of the two brief recessions in 1948–49 and 1953–54, and was a stabilizing influence during the 1957-58 recession.

Employing the familiar reference-cycle technique of the National Bureau of Economic Research, the countercyclical tendency is quite prominent (Chart 2). The average pattern for the three complete business cycles during 1945–58 is bowl-shaped after the stage of early recovery.[7] This could be described, of course, as a tendency for residential construction to "lead" general business at turning points. The lead and lag terminology leaves open the question of whether the phenomenon described is purely statistical—the residential construction series, for example, might "lead" general business because they record construction at a relatively early stage in the construction process—or whether it is a reflection of how certain economic processes work themselves out over time.[8]

---

[7] The rise in construction during early recovery is considerably smaller when the 1945–49 cycle is omitted. Such omission could be justified in light of the abnormal situation in the construction market prior to 1948.

[8] One hypothesis (other than the one presented in this paper) which can be used to explain fluctuations in construction and which would attribute causal significance to the

The behavior of the residential sector is here termed countercyclical because the explanation given below of the forces underlying fluctuations in construction appears to support use of this term. Countercyclical forces, however, because they take time to work themselves out, do not invariably produce countercyclical results (to employ Grebler's terminology [8]). That the three major expansions in construction extended into the stage of early recovery in general business reflects both the time-consuming nature of the countercyclical mechanism and the unusual brevity of the postwar recessions.

C. POSTWAR AND PREWAR CYCLES

The short postwar cycles discussed in this study have a counterpart in the prewar period. Long [13] found 17 cycles in building between 1870 and 1938 averaging 4 years in length. Newman [15] counted 11 minor cycles between 1878 and 1933 having an average length of about 5 years. These cycles were based on building permit data which included commercial and industrial building as well as residential building. Moore [14] found 5½ cycles between 1919 and 1938 in the residential contract awards data.

The reference-cycle patterns for residential contract awards during the three short business cycles of the 1920's have similarities to those of the postwar period (Chart 2). As in the postwar period construction declined during the later stages of expansions in general business and began to rise some time during the recessions. During the 1920's, however, there was a much more pronounced procyclical rise during the recovery phase of the business cycle, while the rise during recessions was much weaker. Whether the pattern for the 1920's is countercyclical on balance is problematical, but such tendencies clearly were much less pronounced relative to procyclical tendencies than in the postwar period.[9]

Altogether different patterns show up during the two major business cycles covering the period 1927–38, as residential construction declined rather steadily during the entire 1927–33 cycle and fluctuated with unusual sharpness, largely in procyclical fashion, during 1933–38.

The performance of the residential sector in the postwar period has thus been substantially better than in the 1920's and 1930's. We cannot be sure of all the reasons for this because data are not available for a rigorous study of the causes of the prewar cycles. Nevertheless, some obvious points of difference between the prewar and postwar periods—the relatively more stable economy and the existence of the federal under-

---

"lead" is the familiar acceleration principle. The acceleration hypothesis does not however, for a number of reasons, provide an acceptable explanation for the observed tendency of residential construction to lead general business at turning points. One reason is that it is inconsistent with the evidence presented below that changes in demand were not strategic in the short construction cycles.

[9] Also, the dispersion in the reference-cycle patterns of individual cycles was somewhat greater for the cycles of the 1920's than for the postwar cycles.

writing programs during the later period—must evidently have been of some importance. These structural differences will receive further comment below.

D. SHORT CYCLES AND LONG WAVES

The postwar cycles in residential construction may be placed in perspective by comparing them to the long waves in residential construction, which have been the subject of many investigations.[10] First, and most conspicuously, the postwar cycles differ from the long cycles in their shorter duration. Measured from peak to peak in the starts series the four postwar cycles cover 20 months, 28 months, 32 months, and 52 months. The long cycles vary in length depending on the unit of measurement used and on the investigator, but their minimum length appears to be about 9 years and they may extend for as long as 25 years.

Second, the postwar cycles have a much smaller amplitude. The average amplitude of three long cycles during 1892–1950, as identified by Grebler, Blank and Winnick [9], was about four times that of the four short postwar cycles. The amplitude of the mildest long cycle was roughly twice that of the most severe short cycle.[11] These relative orders of magnitude fully justify a characterization of the short postwar cycles as "ripples on the long waves."

Third, the short cycles differ from long cycles in their basic causes. Most of the standard explanations of long cycles in residential construction run in terms of fluctuations in the *demand*[12] for housing arising primarily out of changing rates of population growth. The influence of factors affecting the supply of mortgage credit may enter into the explanation but only as a secondary factor, intensifying the force of the movements of both expansion and contraction. In contrast, the short cycles appear to be related mainly to changes originating in the mortgage market. This has been true, at least, during the postwar period. In the prewar period income changes probably played an important role, particularly during major business cycles when such changes were especially large.

---

[10] See: [1] [4] [12, Ch. 3] [3, Appendix N] [9, pp. 37-43] [5, Ch. 7] [13] [15] and [18].

[11] Both the short and the long cycles in this comparison are measured in terms of private housing starts. The method of measuring amplitude is the same in each case except that yearly values are used for measuring the amplitude of long cycles and seasonally adjusted monthly values are used in the case of the short cycles. The method is that of the National Bureau, described in [9, p. 40].

[12] In this paper demand will be understood to refer to demand under given mortgage credit conditions, that is under given mortgage interest rates, discounts (when they are paid by the borrower), down payments, maturities, etc. This is sometimes called "basic demand." In a few places the broader concept is used where in mortgage credit conditions are also variable, as when speaking of the "sensitivity of demand" to changes in mortgage terms. Where this meaning is intended it will be obvious from the context.

II. *The Short Cycle and Fluctuations in the Supply of Mortgage Credit*

The evidence on the central role of mortgage credit is indirect. Inferences are drawn about the principal factor underlying an observed movement in construction from the behavior of three market indicators, which will be discussed in turn. Each of these indicators is shown on Chart 3 along with the recordings series, which can be used to represent the movement of residential construction and mortgage activity.

A. CONSTRUCTION AND MORTGAGE YIELDS

Where changes in demand are the chief determinant of changes in construction, we would expect mortgage yields and construction to move in the same direction; where changes in the supply of mortgage credit are the chief determinant, we would expect yields and construction to move in opposite directions.

It is clear from Chart 3 that mortgage yields[13] and residential construction tended to move inversely to each other during the period 1948–59. The timing divergences at most of the turning points (peaks in one case and troughs in the other) are very small. An important exception is the 1950 peak in construction, the one turning point during the period that was caused (initially, at least) by "exogenous" developments—mainly the introduction of credit controls (Regulation X—see pp. 102-103).

The significance of changes in mortgage yields (relative to changes in construction) as an *indicator* of whether supply or demand is the chief influence in the market should be distinguished from the *function* performed by yield changes in maintaining market equilibrium. Of course, changes in yields would not serve as an indicator unless such changes also helped to equilibrate the market. It is not necessarily the case, however, that yield changes will bear the brunt of the equilibrating process, especially in influencing the demand for credit. In rationing funds to borrowers, changes in other lending terms, and particularly in the down-payment requirement, probably are as important as, and possibly more important than, changes in rates.

---

[13] The series on mortgage yields shown on Chart 3, which was constructed especially for this study, is based on the prices at which completed FHA home mortgages are traded in the secondary market. For several reasons the series does not measure very precisely the rate of return that can be earned by investors at any given time, or the rate that borrowers must pay for credit; neither does this series represent the average yield over the entire mortgage market, since secondary market transactions, the volume of which is very small relative to the total volume of mortgages written, are atypical. Hence, little significance can be attached to the yield *levels* indicated by the series. However the series does constitute a fairly sensitive indicator of *changes* in borrower costs and investor returns over the entire market.

CHART 3. SELECTED MORTGAGE MARKET INDICATORS, 1946–59

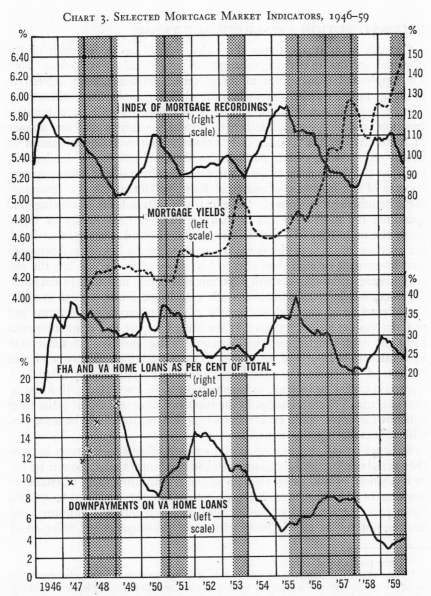

Note: Shaded areas represent contractions in mortgage recordings. Series are three-month averages except for mortgage yields.

---

* Seasonally adjusted.

B. CONSTRUCTION AND MORTGAGE TERMS

Changes in mortgage terms themselves constitute an indicator of the principal factors underlying changes in residential construction. Both the supply and demand for mortgage credit are functionally related to mortgage terms. Furthermore, when the supply of credit is a positive function of a given condition of the loan, the demand will be a negative function, and vice versa. The general reason for this is that any change in terms that makes it easier for borrowers with given qualifications to obtain more credit, *ceteris paribus* also increases risk to the lender. For example, the demand for credit is a negative function of the down payment because of the existence of marginal borrowers for whom the down-payment requirement represents an effective constraint on borrowing and spending; the more they can borrow on their existing equity or liquid assets the more they will spend. The supply of credit, on the other hand, is a positive function of the down payment, since the larger the borrower's own investment or equity relative to his borrowed funds, the less the risk that adverse circumstances will wipe out this equity and lead to default.[14]

Hence, within certain institutionally established limits, we can consider the interaction of demand and supply as determining a set of terms just as it determines an interest rate; at the same time, we can draw inferences as to the nature of the principal dynamic factor underlying a movement in construction from the associated changes in terms. Where a change in demand constitutes the chief factor underlying a change in construction, we would expect an increase in construction to be associated with a restriction of terms. Where a change in the supply of mortgage credit is the chief dynamic factor we would expect an increase in construction to be associated with a liberalization in terms.[15]

Statistics on mortgage terms are sometimes difficult to interpret because they may be influenced by changes in the maximum terms allowed by law or regulation, as well as by changes in the demand or supply of credit. In the case of VA mortgages, however, except for the period 1950–53, the down payment required by law or regulation was either a uniform 2 per cent or nothing at all.[16] Changes in actual down payments reflected al-

---

[14] These points are discussed further in [10].

[15] Note that these implications follow only if it can be assumed that changes in demand or supply are not associated with a marked re-evaluation of lenders' attitudes toward the riskiness of mortgages. Ordinarily, for example, a decline in demand would lead to a liberalization of terms (as well as a decline in interest rates). However, if the decline in demand suggests to lenders that borrowers are not as good credit risks as before or that property values may decline, the result may be a restriction of terms rather than a liberalization; this is the paradox where "money gets easy but lenders get tight." It is doubtful that any sharp revision of attitudes occurred during the period covered by this study, since fluctuations in general business were mild and the mortgage repayment experience of lenders was generally very favorable.

[16] A 2 per cent down-payment requirement was imposed in July 1955 and removed in April 1958.

most entirely the influence of market forces and there was ample scope for the play of such forces. A series on actual VA down payments on new houses is shown on Chart 3.

The chart shows that VA down payments tended to move in the direction opposite to recordings during the declines in residential construction of 1948–49 and 1955–57, as well as during the expansions of 1949–50, 1954–55, and 1958–59. (During 1950–53, the series is influenced by the imposition and subsequent relaxation of credit controls.) This evidence supports the thesis that changes in the supply of mortgage credit were the principal dynamic factor underlying the changes in activity. It also suggests, when considered in conjunction with the evidence on mortgage yields, that there may well be considerable variation as between different cycles or phases of cycles, in the relative importance of yield changes and down-payment changes in rationing credit. Thus, the sharp rise in construction that began early in 1949 was associated in the early stages with only a leveling off of yields and with only a very modest decline (less than one-fifth of a percentage point) over the entire period of expansion. However, down payments declined sharply throughout 1949, and when the 1950 peak in construction was reached the average had fallen to 8 per cent, from about 17 per cent in early 1949.[17] On the other hand, during the 1955–57 period of decline, VA down payments increased only modestly but yields increased by more than 1¼ percentage points.

C. CONSTRUCTION AND THE RELATIVE IMPORTANCE
OF THE FEDERALLY UNDERWRITTEN SECTOR

Another important clue as to the nature of the forces underlying fluctuations in the level of residential construction is provided by the relationship between such fluctuations and changes in the relative importance of the federally underwritten sector of the market. Where supply-of-credit factors are the chief dynamic influence in the market, we expect changes in residential construction and in the relative importance of federally underwritten mortgages to be in the same direction. There are two broadly different reasons for this.

First, to some extent the federally underwritten and conventional sectors of the market overlap, in the sense that borrowers' demands can be met under either form of financing. Where this is the case, switching occurs between the two sectors in response to market changes. For example, assuming an increase in demand occurs, it is profitable for lenders to switch from federally underwritten to conventional financing. Higher rates can now be obtained on conventional mortgages, whereas the maximum interest rate which can be charged on federally underwritten mortgages is fixed by law or regulation (we are assuming, what was generally the case, that this interest rate ceiling is an effective constraint on the rate charged). In addition, with a stronger demand, lending terms can be

---

[17] In the case of existing houses the decline was somewhat smaller.

tightened so that less risky mortgages are obtained, with the result that the insurance or guarantee feature is less valuable than it had been.

Second, the federally underwritten sector is partially segmented from the conventional sector, in the sense that the credit demands of some borrowers can be satisfied only at the more liberal terms available under the federal programs. The ebb and flow of these "marginal" borrowers into and out of the market is controlled mainly by changes in the market terms on FHA and VA mortgages.[18] Thus when the supply of funds that lenders wish to invest in mortgages increases, terms on FHA and particularly on VA mortgages are eased and the relative importance of these programs in the total rises.[19]

As indicated in Chart 3, the relative importance of the federal programs (as measured by the ratio of federally underwritten home loans to total recordings) varied generally in the same direction as residential construction, although the correspondence between the series is somewhat disrupted by credit controls during the period 1950–53. The same general correspondence appears in the housing starts data beginning in 1951 (when monthly data for federally underwritten starts first became available), and in the nonfarm mortgage acquisitions of life insurance companies. Changes in legislation affecting the federal programs as well as in the regulations of the federal agencies played some role, but with the exception of the 1950–53 period, movements in this indicator appear to reflect the overriding influence of swings in the supply of mortgage credit.

D. WHY THE SUPPLY OF MORTGAGE CREDIT IS STRATEGIC

The reason for the strategic role of mortgage credit in the short cycle is not far to seek. Demographic factors and the relative price of housing, which must be crucially important determinants of housing demand and construction in the long run, ordinarily do not change very much in the short run. The demand for housing, moreover, apparently is not very sensitive to short-run changes in income, so long as such changes are fairly moderate and do not generate sharp swings in consumers' expectations. Decisions to vary housing expenditures are not made lightly since they involve a commitment of substantial magnitude generally extending well into

---

[18] The VA program is particularly important in this connection because, as already suggested, during most of the period covered by this study no down payment was required of veteran borrowers by law or regulation. This provided ample scope for lenders to adjust the down payment they required on these mortgages in accordance with their changing appetite for mortgages relative to other investments. This has been one important factor underlying the great volatility of VA mortgage lending.

[19] The relationship between changes in the supply and demand for credit and changes in the relative importance of the federally underwritten sector holds irrespective of whether or not a change in demand is associated with a change in lenders' attitudes toward the riskiness of mortgages. In the case where demand increases, for example, if lenders are encouraged by this development to believe that mortgages are less risky than they had been, this will have the effect of further encouraging them to shift out of federally underwritten mortgages.

the future. Such decisions are likely to be related to what home buyers consider will be their income over a fairly long period.[20]

At the same time housing demand is extremely sensitive to changes in the supply of mortgage credit. It is estimated that on the average about three-fourths of total expenditures on residential construction during the 1948–59 period was financed with mortgage loans. It is this greater sensitivity of housing demand to changes in the supply of mortgage credit than to changes in the flow of current income, and the considerable short-run volatility in the former, that underlie the countercyclical tendency of residential construction. Before analyzing the process in more detail, however, several factors are noted in addition to the supply of credit that exercised a marginal influence on the short construction cycle during the period covered by this study.

E. OTHER INFLUENCES ON CONSTRUCTION IN THE SHORT RUN

Demand. It is unlikely that the volume of new construction demanded per month under given credit conditions did not change over the 1948–59 period, but in the short run such changes were apparently small relative to changes that resulted from swings in the supply of mortgage credit. I have not been able to find any significant relationships between the short cycles and such factors as house prices, income and employment, marriages, household formation, etc., which it is reasonable to assume are related to housing demand.[21] These factors, of course, must have been important determinants of the general level of construction around which the short cycles took place.

Changes in Maximum Allowable Lending Terms on FHA and VA Mortgages. Liberalization of maximum lending terms (down payments and maturities) can be effective in expanding the volume of mortgage lending and construction if the supply of mortgage credit exceeds the demand at existing maximum terms. Terms were liberalized on a number of occasions during the 1948–59 period, but since most of these changes came during periods of relative tightness in the mortgage market they had little immediate effect.[22] This was true, for example, of the liberalization of mortgage terms on FHA mortgages in 1948, on both FHA and VA mortgages in 1951 and 1952 (the relaxation of Regulation X), and on FHA mortgages in 1957. On each of these occasions the new more liberal maximum terms did become effective at a later time when an increase in the supply of mortgage credit caused an easing in the market, but the

---

[20] Calculated estimates of the income elasticity of housing demand that I have seen range quite widely, from .3 to 2.0 and even higher. Margaret Reid [17] suggests that the coefficient relevant to "permanent" income is close to the higher figure, while the much lower coefficients sometimes found reflect the influence of transitory changes in income on the income concept employed.

[21] In itself, this cannot be considered conclusive because of inadequacies in the basic data. Indeed, this was why recourse was had to market indicators.

[22] This was not altogether fortuitous, since the pressure to "do something for housing" usually was greatest during such periods.

change in supply during such periods was the more important factor in the easing of actual terms to borrowers.[23] On the other hand, liberalizations during the years 1946 and 1947 (which lie outside the bounds of our cyclical analysis) were an altogether different matter. The supply of mortgage credit in those years was substantially in excess of the demand at existing maximum terms, partly because of the superfluity of liquidity possessed by lending institutions and partly because of certain restrictive aspects of the federal programs at that time. When these restrictions were removed, it was as if a dam had burst, although because of capacity limitations, the impact was more on prices than on output.[24]

Maximum allowable lending terms on federally underwritten mortgages were restricted on only two occasions during 1948–59.[25] In late 1955 there was a minor restriction which had little or no impact because the market had already tightened beyond it. The other restriction occurred in 1950, first in July on FHA and VA mortgages only, and then with even greater severity in October under Regulation X, which applied to conventional

---

[23] This may be illustrated as follows: Assume that the supply of mortgage credit is an increasing function of the down payment (measured as a per cent of value), and that the interest rate is fixed. Initially, when the market is tight, the down payment prevailing in the market is DP_a, or higher than the minimum of DP_m. Under these conditions, a reduction in the minimum to DP'_m has no effect on the market. When S shifts to S_y, however, the new lower minimum becomes effective. If the minimum had not been reduced, the down payment would have fallen only to the old minimum DP_m, where there would have been an excess supply. Even so, the supply of mortgage credit rather than the change in the minimum down payment is the more important factor in the situation pictured, since only a relatively small part of the total increase in credit ($Q'_m - Q_m$ of $Q'_m - Q_a$) can be attributed to the change in the minimum.

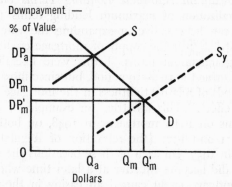

[24] This can be illustrated in the diagram above by assuming that initially the supply function is S_y while DP_a is the minimum down payment so that the minimum is the strategic restraint on mortgage lending. When this minimum is reduced to DP_m, the volume of credit increases substantially (by $Q_m - Q_a$). For a further discussion of the tremendous impact of the early postwar changes in the FHA and VA programs see [7].

[25] Over the entire period, these restrictions were more than offset by liberalizations. In early 1960, therefore, average down payments on FHA and VA mortgages were lower, and maturities were longer than they had ever been before. Some observers were drawing pessimistic inferences concerning the prospects for a continuation of housing's countercyclical role from this fact (see my concluding remarks below).

mortgages as well. Regulation X and its companion restrictions appear to have been largely responsible for the 1950 downturn in residential construction, and hence represent the one exogenous development during the 1948–59 period that was a strategic factor in a short cycle.[26] Even in this case, during the later stages of the decline the effects of the restriction became inextricably intertwined with the effect of the declining supply of mortgage credit that followed the March 1951 accord between the Federal Reserve System and the Treasury. Hence, Regulation X was only partly responsible for the 1950–51 contraction in residential construction.

The Federal National Mortgage Association (FNMA). The tendency inherent in FNMA's secondary mortgage market operations (consisting of the purchase and sale of FHA and VA mortgages) during the 1948–59 period was to mitigate fluctuations in residential construction activity. The basic reason for this was the Association maintained fixed or "sticky" mortgage purchase prices.[27] Hence, FNMA's mortgage holdings rose most rapidly during periods of declining construction and falling mortgage prices and least rapidly during periods of rising construction and mortgage prices. Since construction tended to move inversely to general business, this meant that FNMA made the residential construction sector less of a stabilizing influence on the economy as a whole than it would have been otherwise.

FNMA's "natural" tendency to stabilize the mortgage market was, however, disrupted on several occasions by changes in the framework of law and regulations within which it operated. Thus special legislation, which became effective during the expansion of 1949–50 when construction and mortgage credit from private sources were rising rapidly, provided an added

---

[26] There has been some reluctance to attribute any great efficacy to Regulation X because of the known heavy volume of forward commitments on pre-Regulation X terms that was built up prior to the effective date of the regulation. It has been generally assumed [16] that because of these commitments the impact of the regulation must have been both delayed and diluted. But this view overlooks the following: (a) the fact that there is a stock of outstanding commitments which will permit, say, x months of construction to go forward without being subject to the regulation does not mean (as many observers imply) that there must be a delay of x months before construction is affected. Such a view is unrealistic in assuming that builders will maintain their operations at existing levels until their commitments run out, and then will reduce volume sharply. One of the main problems of builders is finding and holding a cadre of skilled workers, and they usually will go to great lengths to maintain continuity of employment for these workers. A more realistic view of builders' response to controls, therefore, is that they will curtail construction immediately by laying off the most recent additions to the work crew and by reducing overtime; in this way they can husband their commitments and stretch out employment for their basic work force. (b) The July 1950 regulation, a sort of prelude to the more comprehensive restriction imposed in October, must have had considerable impact on the market. This restriction came without any warning and hence without any prior build-up of commitments. Furthermore, by eliminating no-down-payment loans under the VA program, this restriction struck a most sensitive nerve, since these loans had come to account for about three-fifths of all VA primary home loans on new homes at the peak of the 1949–50 housing boom.

[27] Until late 1954 it was FNMA's policy to purchase all mortgages at par. The Housing Act of 1954, effective late that year, stipulated that mortgages acquired under FNMA's principal program be purchased at market prices. Even so, in subsequent years the Association tended to lag well behind the market in adjusting prices.

fillip to FNMA's purchases. Similarly, special legislation enacted during the 1958 recession resulted in $1 billion of purchases at above-market prices as a form of "special assistance," more than offsetting sales that were being made (as a result of the general decline in interest rates) under FNMA's regular secondary market operations.

FNMA's influence on the market was of some marginal importance on several occasions. When FNMA's expansionary stimulus was at its peak (in 1949, 1957 and 1959), the Association accounted for about one-tenth of the total net flow into residential mortgages; in most other years, however, its share was considerably smaller.

Rigid Interest Rates on FHA and VA Mortgages. The existence of fixed maximum interest rates on federally underwritten mortgages (set by law or by the federal credit agencies within the authority granted by law), which were usually at or below the market equilibrium rate, probably intensified somewhat the countercyclical tendency of the residential sector. As general interest rates rose during a period of expansion, the inability of lenders to obtain a higher contract rate on federally underwritten mortgages caused the diversion of credit to other sectors to be greater than it would have been otherwise. This tendency was only partly offset by the practice of "discounting" federally underwritten mortgages. And, of course, during a period of contraction the reverse process occurred. The writer's view, however, is that the rate maxima have been emphasized far out of proportion to their real importance. The countercyclical process can be explained quite well, as we shall see, without any reference to them at all.

That the "dial settings" for maximum allowable interest rates or lending terms under the federal underwriting programs were not, in general, strategic in influencing the short construction cycles does not mean that the programs were unimportant. On the contrary, the general availability of FHA insurance or guarantees to lenders when they needed them was an important factor making countercyclical variations in mortgage lending feasible without undue changes in risk exposure.

III. *The Countercyclical Tendency of Residential Construction*

Returning now to our main theme, that changes in the level of residential construction resulted principally from fluctuations in the supply of mortgage credit, what was the cause of these changes in supply? The thesis advanced here is that changes in the supply of mortgage credit were related in large part to changes in the level of general economic activity, so that fluctuations in residential construction resulted from fluctuations in general economic activity.

Thus, the residential sector in the short run assumed a largely passive role in economic fluctuations as opposed to its more autonomous role in the long run. But precisely because the relationship between the residential sector and the general economy was mediated chiefly by the supply of mortgage credit rather than by the flow of current income, this passivity was of an "inverse" sort. The usual picture of a cyclical expansion or contraction is one of a cumulative process with expansion in one sector leading to expansion in other sectors. In the case we are considering, changes in general business activity set in motion forces leading to movements in the *reverse* direction in construction. Consider the following schematic illustration.

Assume that an expansion in general business occurs, initiated we may suppose by an upsurge in corporate investment. In the early stages of the expansion, the additional demands made upon the capital markets may be small since the corporations have excess liquidity and retained profits are likely to be large. If the expansion follows a period of recession, credit demands will be met with no difficulty and little, if any, increase in interest rates. As expansion develops and spreads, however, the demands upon the capital markets are enlarged, liquidity positions generally are eroded and as capacity ceilings are approached Federal Reserve policy shifts from ease to restraint; interest rates rise and borrowing terms tighten.

Of course, the expansion in general economic activity leads to an increase in disposable income, but the demand for housing is expanded only slightly as a result. At the same time the demand for housing is extremely sensitive to the terms on which mortgage credit is available. After a certain stage of tightness is reached in the capital market, therefore, the reduction in housing demand consequent upon the tightening of credit more than offsets the expansion in demand resulting from the increasing flow of income. While most sectors continue to expand, residential construction turns down.

During a contraction the reverse process occurs. After some point, the easing of credit terms consequent upon a decline in the demand for credit from other sectors (and the easing of monetary policy) has an expansionary effect on housing demand sufficient to offset the effect of the decline in income. Hence, residential construction turns up while other sectors continue to decline. In this way does the residential construction sector act as a sort of countercyclical buffer.

A. DYNAMIC ROLE OF THE CORPORATIONS

It would appear that there are two basic considerations involved in the process. The first, already discussed, is the unusual sensitivity of the residential sector in the short run to changes in the supply of credit. The second is that the tendency towards economic expansion or contraction is initiated outside of the residential construction sector. This deserves further comment.

In the schematic illustration offered above, the dynamic impetus to economic fluctuations is provided by the corporations. This is a prima facie plausible hypothesis since corporations account for a large proportion of investment spending, generally considered to be the key factor in economic fluctuations. During the 1948–59 period, corporations accounted for about three-fifths of gross private domestic investment (excluding non-farm residential construction).

The hypothesis implies that corporate investment has quite different characteristics than spending on residential construction (these differences are associated in part with the characteristics of the spenders). The key differences are that corporate investment is (a) more volatile, and (b) less sensitive to changes in the interest rate and less subject to noninterest rate rationing. Thus, when corporate investment demands increase, the associated demands on the capital markets raise interest rates and tighten credit, but the rebound effect of this tightening on the corporations themselves is slight. Potential home buyers, on the other hand, faced with the need to pay higher rates and to make larger down payments, are forced to curtail their expenditures on housing and their mortgage borrowing. Putting the matter crudely, the volume of mortgage credit is a sort of residual, in that home buyers can obtain only that volume of credit which remains after the more volatile and persistent demands of corporations have been satisfied. Although this conclusion must be qualified in several respects, it appears to be basically correct and provides a reasonable explanation for the observed behavior of the residential construction sector during the postwar period.

Some support for this explanation is provided by Chart 4, which shows movements in the net increment to mortgage debt and to corporate securities (including equities) outstanding. The two series shown are virtually mirror images of each other. We can reject out of hand the possibility that demands for investable funds by corporations and by mortgage borrowers are subject to independent influences which happen to be opposite in their effects. The chart suggests instead an organic interconnection between the processes of financing corporations through security issues and financing home purchasers through the creation of mortgage debt. Moreover, the possible causal relations underlying this interconnection are not unlimited. Possibly one type of demand was more volatile than the other; a second possibility is that the demands were equally volatile but that there were sharp differences in the respective interest rate elasticities (or in the degree to which they were subject to noninterest rate rationing). As already indicated, I believe that both were the case.

B. ROLE OF THE FEDERAL GOVERNMENT AND THE BANKING SYSTEM

How does the federal government fit into this explanation? The characteristics of corporations noted above, which were said to underlie the dynamic character of corporate spending (as compared to the passive character of residential spending) seem to apply even more to the federal government. The credit demands of the government appear to be more volatile than those of the corporations, for example, while the government's credit demands are interest-rate inelastic in the extreme and not to be put off by noninterest rate credit rationing.

As soon as the government is added to our model, it becomes necessary to take into account as well the third dynamic or volatile sector of the economy, namely, the commercial banking system. Broadly, it appears that fluctuations in bank credit tend to offset fluctuations in government borrowing, leaving corporate demands as a sort of residual prime mover in the capital markets. This is not because the monetary authorities are at the beck and call of the Treasury. Rather it reflects the manner in which

CHART 4. NET CHANGE IN NONFARM MORTGAGE DEBT AND IN TOTAL CORPORATE SECURITIES OUTSTANDING, 1949–59

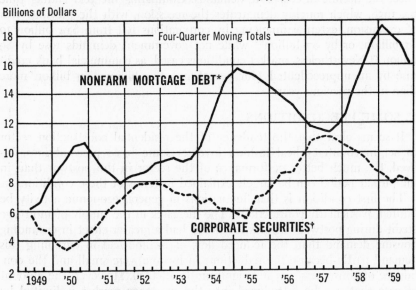

* Centered at second quarter.
† Centered at third quarter.

both government borrowing and Federal Reserve policy are related to the business cycle. During a recession, for example, borrowing by the government increases as receipts from tax payments fall off and expenditures rise. The monetary authorities, following a policy of credit ease designed to cushion the force of the recession and pave the way for recovery, do not allow these heavier borrowing needs by the government to tighten the market. The expansion of bank credit thus offsets the government's increased credit demands. The process may be quite direct, as when the Treasury floats a large cash offering and the Federal Reserve provides the banks with the reserves needed to acquire the new securities without any tightening in their reserve positions. The result is that the recession-induced relaxation of credit demands by corporations has the desired effect of releasing funds for mortgages, as explained above.

During an expansion the reverse process occurs. As government revenues increase, its borrowing requirements tend to fall but because of the policy of restraint followed by the Federal Reserve System this does not have the effect of easing the capital markets. The increasing credit demands of the corporations are thus allowed to tighten the market and draw funds from the mortgage market. Thus, the usual adaptation of monetary policies to the business cycle has the effect of allowing the normal interaction between the corporate and residential construction sectors to proceed without interference from the fluctuating credit demands of the Treasury.

The recession of 1957–58 is a particularly striking example of this because the credit demands of the government rose so sharply as to completely offset the decline in corporate demands. Comparing the year ending June 30, 1958, which roughly demarcates the recession, with the previous year of expansion, external financing by corporations fell from $14 billion to $7 billion, or by $7 billion[28] while net government demands rose by $9 billion.[29] Nevertheless, market conditions eased, as commercial bank credit rose by an unprecedented (for peacetime) $14 billion—$9 billion more than in the previous year.

C. SOME PRECONDITIONS

It seems clear that the tendency of the residential construction sector to act in countercyclical fashion involves some basic preconditions. Indeed, the much better performance of the sector in the postwar than in the prewar period can be largely explained in terms of these conditions.

The first condition is that fluctuations in general economic activity be limited, particularly contractions. The increases in the supply of mortgage credit during postwar business recessions had a greater effect in expanding housing demand than the reduced flow of income had in curtailing this demand partly because the reductions in income were small and the confidence of consumers was not significantly affected. However, the amount of ease that can be introduced into the mortgage market is limited by legal and institutional factors; the expansionary effect of easy credit, at the limit, can be largely offset or even swamped by substantial declines in income, such as those experienced in major prewar contractions.

Moreover, when the level of general economic activity declines beyond some point, the supply of mortgage credit may actually begin to tighten rather than easing further, as lenders become apprehensive with respect to the future economic status of borrowers and mortgage loans begin to appear more risky than before. Although lenders under such conditions might have more loanable funds than previously, they would be less inclined to lend. This would be reflected in a greater restrictiveness in lend-

---

[28] External financing is defined as the net increase in stocks and bonds, mortgage debt, bank loans and federal income tax liabilities plus net reduction in government securities holdings. If income tax liabilities are excluded, external financing declined by less than $5 billion.

[29] From debt redemption of about $3 billion to an increase in debt of about $6 billion,

ing terms, although interest rates on prime securities probably would continue to decline.[30]

This leads to a second precondition, namely, that lenders are able to make sharp countercyclical variations in their mortgage lending without undergoing large changes in risk exposure. Two possible sources of a change in risk exposure have been noted in this paper. Reference has just been made to a shift in lenders' evaluations of the risks associated with loans of given characteristics (given type of security, lending terms, etc.). Such changes probably are quite small in a relatively stable economic environment such as we have had in the postwar period. The impact of any re-evaluations of risk that have occurred has been minimized by the federal underwriting programs, although undoubtedly, from this standpoint, these programs have not been very badly needed in the postwar period.

Risk exposure can also change as a result of a shift in the loan mix, for example, toward loans with smaller down payments. Such changes are, indeed, an integral part of countercyclical shifts in mortgage lending. If lenders are to push out more credit during a recession, for example, when basic housing demand is, if anything, weakening, they must stimulate demand by standing ready to make more liberal loans. Here the importance of the federal underwriting programs becomes evident. Credit terms can be liberalized and demand stimulated, without any appreciable increase in risk exposure, by shifting into federally under-written loans. In the absence of such programs credit liberalization may be hampered, either because lenders are unwilling to court the added risk exposure, or are unwilling to do so without a compensating rise in rate (which can be quite large), or are unable to do so because they are already making most loans at the conservative maximum limits established by law for conventional loans. Thus the federal underwriting programs have been an important structural factor facilitating the countercyclical tendency of the residential sector during the postwar period.

D. TIGHT MONEY BEFORE THE ACCORD?

It may appear surprising that a decline in the supply of mortgage credit could have been responsible for the 1948-49 decline in residential construction. Since lending institutions at that time held very substantial amounts of government securities and the Federal Reserve System was supporting the government bond market, how could there have been a contraction of mortgage credit?

The celebrated accord between the Federal Reserve System and the Treasury in March 1951 has tended to overshadow certain important developments in prior years. These developments, which in themselves constituted partial steps back to an effective monetary policy, in a sense prepared the way for the accord, and influenced the mortgage market as early as the second half of 1947. During that period and again in the

---

[30] This is the paradox referred to above where "money gets easy but lenders get tight."

latter part of 1948, short-term interest rates were allowed by the Federal Reserve System to rise substantially from unusually low wartime levels. The banks appeared to be the only type of financial institution significantly affected by these moves, and their main response to rising short-term yields was to withdraw temporarily from the mortgage market. Between 1947 and 1949 net mortgage acquisitions by commercial banks fell by two-thirds.[31] Since the banks had helped create a climate of extreme ease in the mortgage market in 1946 and early 1947 by aggressively competing for mortgages, their sudden withdrawal from the market had a considerable impact.

The 1948 decline in mortgage credit and residential construction thus resulted from the earliest and mildest of the measures designed to restore the central bank's control over the money supply. This was an unusual instance of developments in the market for short-term instruments of high liquidity directly and seriously influencing the market for long-term instruments of relatively low liquidity. The connecting link, of course, was the portfolio adjustment of the commercial banks, and the fact that the banks had been unusually active in the mortgage market in prior years.

IV. *Future Prospects*

Will the countercyclical mechanism described above continue to operate in the future? It is not the case, as some have argued, that the process will necessarily come to an end as a result of the gradual weakening of basic housing demand relative to the total housing stock—a result of unfavorable demographic factors over the 1950-60 decade, conjoined with the very substantial additions to the stock during this period. Even if this development presages a decline in the average level of construction, which is by no means certain, credit-induced fluctuations (possibly of reduced absolute magnitude, to be sure) might well occur around this lower level.

Nor does the upward ratcheting of mortgage credit terms on FHA and VA mortgages over the period since the second world war, referred to earlier, limit the scope for easing of credit in the future. Liberalization of credit involves not only a relaxation of terms on FHA and VA mortgages but, possibly of more importance, a greater availability of these mortgages. Each period of credit ease has been accompanied by a rise in the relative importance of FHA and VA mortgages in the total. There has not, however, been an upward trend in this ratio over the 1948-59 period as a whole, and in early 1960 the ratio was lower than during most of the period (see Chart 3).

More germane to future prospects is our assessment of the possibility that fluctuations in general business will be more severe in the future than

---

[31] Subsequently, the banks re-entered the mortgage market to help spark the 1949–50 expansion.

they were in the 1948-59 period. To be sure the federal underwriting programs will continue to minimize any disruptive swings in risk exposure that could otherwise result from more severe fluctuations in general business. But large procyclical swings in income could still swamp the effects of countercyclical variations in the supply of mortgage credit.

As a further possibility, the intricate mechanism through which business fluctuations generate countercyclical swings in the supply of mortgage credit might develop kinks at one point or another. The time series in Chart 1, for example, suggest the hypothesis that the response of housing to easy credit may be coming progressively later during recessions. This hypothesis warrants careful study, directed at the portfolio responses at crucial junctures of the major types of mortgage lenders (has this response been influenced by the secular erosion of their liquidity positions during the postwar period?); at the timing of governmental policy actions relative to the business cycle; and at the changing structure of housing demand.

References

1. A. F. BURNS, "Long Cycles in Residential Construction," *Economic Essays in Honor of Wesley C. Mitchell.* New York 1935.
2. A. F. BURNS AND W. C. MITCHELL, *Measuring Business Cycles.* Nat. Bur. Econ. Research, New York 1947.
3. M. L. COLEAN AND R. NEWCOMB, *Stabilizing Construction: The Record and Potential.* New York 1952.
4. J. B. D. DERKSEN, "Long Cycles in Residential Building," *Econometrica,* 1940, 8, 97-116.
5. J. DUESENBERRY, *Business Cycles and Economic Growth.* New York 1958.
6. L. GREBLER, *Housing Issues in Economic Stabilization Policy.* Nat. Bur. Econ. Res. Occas. Paper 72, New York 1960.
7. ———, "Stabilizing Residential Construction—A Review of the Postwar Test," *Am. Econ. Rev.,* Sept. 1949, 39, 898-910.
8. ———, "The Role of Residential Capital Formation in Postwar Business Cycles," *Conference on Savings and Residential Financing,* 1959 Proc., U. S. Savings and Loan League, pp. 57-85.
9. L. GREBLER, D. M. BLANK, AND L. WINNICK, *Capital Formation in Residential Real Estate: Trends and Prospects.* Princeton 1956.
10. J. M. GUTTENTAG, "Credit Availability, Interest Rates and Monetary Policy," *So. Econ. Jour.,* Jan. 1960, 26, 219-28.
11. ———, *Some Studies of the Post-World War II Residential Construction and Mortgage Markets.* Unpublished Ph.D. dissertation, Columbia University 1958.
12. A. H. HANSEN, *Business Cycles and National Income.* New York 1951.
13. C. D. LONG, *Building Cycles and the Theory of Investment.* Princeton 1940.
14. G. H. MOORE, *Statistical Indicators of Cylical Revivals and Recessions.* Nat. Bur. Econ. Res., Occas. Paper 31, New York 1950.
15. W. H. NEWMAN, *The Building Industry and Building Cycles.* Chicago 1935.

16. J. J. O'LEARY, "The Effects of Monetary Policies on the Mortgage Market," *Jour. Finance*, May 1958, 13, 176-87.
17. M. REID, "Capital Formation in Residential Real Estate," *Jour. Pol. Econ.*, Apr. 1958, 46, 131-53.
18. J. R. RIGGLEMAN, "Building Cycles in the United States 1875-1932," *Jour. Am. Stat. Assoc.*, June 1933, 28, 174-83.

7

The Nature and Stability of
Inventory Cycles*

LLOYD A. METZLER†

Editors' Note

Fluctuations in inventories have long been considered a major source of business fluctuations. In fact, many observers maintain that the four postwar business cycles can all be called inventory cycles, though we would take exception. In our view, inventory fluctuations frequently are the *result* of other developments and hence represent the reaction of the economy to other changes. In any event, explaining why inventories expand and contract in a cyclical pattern goes a long way toward explaining the actual nature of the cycles in the past decade or two. This article, though written only twenty years ago, has become a classic. It is theoretical without being highly mathematical; simple charts and numerical examples trace out the argument. The inventory problem is seen as one of dynamics, so time sequences have to be considered. Entrepreneurs' expectations play a critical role. This article has changed the nature of empirical research in inventories. Today, inventory surveys are taken by, among others, the Depart-

* Reprinted by permission of the publishers from *Review of Economics and Statistics*, Vol. XXII, No. 3 (August, 1941), pp. 113-129; Cambridge, Mass.: Harvard University Press, Copyright, 1941, by The President and Fellows of Harvard College.

† Since the completion of his graduate work at Harvard University, Metzler has undertaken a variety of academic and governmental assignments. The former include teaching at Harvard, Yale, and the University of Chicago, where in 1949 he became full professor. Among the latter, we may note: Economist, O.S.S., 1943–44; Economist, Board of Governors, Federal Reserve System, 1944–46; and Consultant, U.S. Department of State, 1950–53. Professor Metzler is a frequent contributor to economic and social science publications, and in 1949 coedited (with Howard S. Ellis) *Readings in the Theory of International Trade*.

ment of Commerce and *Fortune* magazine, and these are framed in terms of businessmen's inventory plans and sales expectations.

❦ Business cycle explanations may conveniently be classified, for the purpose of comparison, according to their implicit stability assumptions. On this basis there are two principal groups, one in which the economy is assumed to be in unstable equilibrium and one in which market relations are assumed to be stable. Proponents of the first group envisage cyclical movements as the consequence of (1) an initial disturbance that sets in motion a cumulative process, and (2) certain limiting stabilizers which reverse the direction of the cumulative movement but which are not operative except in extreme positions, such as full employment, etc. Wicksell's analysis of prices and interest rates provides a good example of this type of theory. In the second group, on the other hand, movements of output and employment represent a process of adaptation to cyclical changes in the parameters of a system that would otherwise be stable. The idea of a determinate relation between changes in the level of non-induced investment and changes in total income, for example, belongs to this group.

Corresponding to either type of cycle theory are two sets of relations, a series of sequences defining time-paths for the variables of the system, and a set of simultaneous equations expressing equilibrium or stationary values of the variables.[1] From this point of view, the distinction between the unstable- and the stable-economy theories is largely one of emphasis. No tendency exists, according to the former, for the economy to approach an equilibrium; consequently, the dynamic system receives most attention. And since an unstable economy obviously does not move steadily upward or downward, the analysis of "turning points" is highly important.[2] The stable-economy theories, on the other hand, emphasize the character of the static system; for this system is regarded as a norm toward which the economy is moving, and which would ultimately be attained except for disturbances in the parameters of the system. Dynamic sequences are relevant for this type of theory only in so far as they indicate the manner in which the economy moves from one equilibrium to another. Indeed, if the period of adjustment is relatively short, the dynamic system may be neglected entirely and time-movements attributed simply to changes in the parameters of the static system.

---

[1] Cf. P. A. Samuelson, "The Stability of Equilibrium: Comparative Statics and Dynamics," *Econometrica*, IX (1941), pp. 97-120.

[2] See Gottfried Haberler, *Prosperity and Depression* (Geneva, 1940), *passim*, but especially Chapter 11.

I

These relations of comparative statics to economic dynamics are presented in an interesting and important form in recent discussions of the determinants of total output. Use of the Multiplier in analyzing income and investment, as noted above, obviously constitutes static analysis of a system that is assumed to be *stable* in equilibrium. That is, an equilibrium level of income is assumed to correspond to any given level of non-induced investment, and the system is assumed to move toward this equilibrium. And yet the implications of such a stability assumption have never been fully explored. From early formulations of the investment-income relation it is not apparent exactly *how* the system moves from one equilibrium to another and *why* it tends to approach equilibrium at all.[3] In the *General Theory* of Mr. Keynes, for example, one searches in vain for a description of the time sequence of events by which an increase of net investment produces a rise of income. Thus, although static relations are worked out in some detail, the dynamic equivalent of the income equation is not fully specified.

Needless to say, an infinite number of dynamic sequences having the Keynes income-investment equation as an equilibrium limit could be formulated. In the group of possible models, however, two types of time relation seem most important. The first of these is the lag in the expenditure of income behind its receipt. This receipts-expenditure period, associated as it is with the income velocity of circulation of money, has much to do with the rate at which a system moves from one equilibrium of income to another.[4] The second important lag is the period required for a change in revenue from sales to produce a change in total output. This period determines the time rate at which an alteration in money demand is converted into a change in income paid out.

Shortly after publication of the *General Theory*, both types of lag were utilized in the formulation of dynamic systems of which the Keynes scheme was a static limit. Mr. D. H. Robertson developed a sequence in which the first type was utilized,[5] while Mr. Erik Lundberg examined the consequences of a system containing the second.[6] Briefly, the Robertson se-

---

[3] See R. F. Kahn, "The Relation of Home Investment to Unemployment," *Economic Journal*, XLI (1931), pp. 173-98; Colin Clark, *National Income and Outlay* (London, 1936), Chapter 12; J. M. Keynes, *The General Theory of Employment, Interest, and Money* (New York, 1936), *passim*. The geometric series which Kahn uses in developing his employment multiplier suggests a dynamic sequence, but the exact character of the lag is never fully explained.

[4] I do not wish to imply that the lag of expenditure behind receipt of income is identical with the inverse of income velocity, but only that, *ceteris paribus*, a reduction of the receipt-expenditure lag increases income velocity. See A. H. Hansen, *Fiscal Policy and Business Cycles* (New York, 1941), pp. 268-70.

[5] D. H. Robertson, "Some Notes on Mr. Keynes' General Theory of Employment," *Quarterly Journal of Economics*, LI (1936), pp. 168-91.

[6] Erik Lundberg, *Studies in the Theory of Economic Expansion* (London, 1937), Chapter 9.

quence was built upon the following assumptions:[7] (1) The expenditure of income was assumed to occur one period after its receipt. (2) Business men were assumed to respond to an increase in money demand with an immediate increase of output, so that income produced in a particular period could be measured by the sum of consumption plus net investment. Mr. Robertson assumed, in other words, a length of unity for the receipts-expenditure period and a zero lag in the response of output to a change in consumer demand.

Mr. Lundberg, on the other hand, built his models upon the following assumptions: (1) Consumers' demand was assumed to respond immediately to a change of income (i.e. the receipts-expenditure period was assumed to be zero). (2) A lag of one period was assumed in the output of consumers' goods behind a change in revenue from sales. In other words, business men were assumed to base their production in period t upon sales in period $t-1$. Thus a discrepancy between *total output* and *total sales* might arise. This discrepancy was assumed to be balanced by a change of inventories.

The foregoing summaries of the Robertson and Lundberg dynamic sequences should indicate clearly that the latter is in most respects the converse of the former. The Robertson model assumes a period of unity for the first type of lag (expenditure behind receipt of income) and a period of zero for the second (output behind revenue from sales), while Mr. Lundberg assumes a zero period for the first and a unit period for the second. For relatively simple sequences, both systems lead to substantially the same results, i.e., a given increase of investment causes total income to approach steadily a new level determined by the Multiplier and the amount of added investment. Both systems, in this case, are stable when the marginal propensity to consume is less than unity, and otherwise unstable. But when more complex sequences are considered, and particularly when allowance is made for the possibility of induced investment, the behavior of the two systems may differ even with the same values of the marginal propensity to consume and the accelerator. Hence it is important to know (a) which scheme more accurately describes the existing state of affairs, and (b) in what respects the two lead to different results.

No doubt some lag exists, in the real world, both in expenditure of income behind its receipt and in the output decisions of business men behind changes of monetary demand. Indeed, the mere fact of inventory fluctuations is adequate demonstration of the latter lag, while the periodic character of income payments lends support to the argument for the former. Logically, of course, there is no reason why a system including both types could not be devised. But as a practical matter, the solutions of such hybrid systems are quite complex, and useful results from them are difficult to derive. Moreover, if the length of one of the lag periods is quite short

---

[7] In addition to the enumerated assumptions, both the Robertson and Lundberg sequences, as well as those developed in this paper, assume the existence of unemployed resources, so that output may be expanded without a rise of prices.

compared with the other, either the Robertson or the Lundberg sequence will give a close approximation to the true situation, the selection depending upon which lag is the shorter. If, for example, business men make production plans on a yearly basis, while the average interval between receipt and expenditure of income is only one-half month, the assumptions of a zero length for the receipts-expenditure lag and a unit period for the sales-output lag will not be seriously unreal. Error will arise only on account of the half-month period at the end of the production year. In other words, except for this half-month interval, the assumption that income paid out within a given production period is spent (or saved) in the same production period is correct. In this case the Lundberg sequence is appropriate. Conversely, if business men revise their plans from day to day, so that the sales-output lag is short compared with the receipts-expenditure period, the Robertson sequence best fits the facts.

Which of the two lags is likely, in fact, to be the shorter? If we measure the receipts-expenditure period by one-half the average interval between income payments, this period is quite short. For wages are paid on a weekly or bi-weekly basis, while salaries are paid monthly, and dividends and interest, which are paid out over longer intervals, represent a smaller proportion of the national income. From this point of view, the Lundberg sequence would seem more realistic. It must be remembered, however, that the length of the receipts-expenditure period is conditioned not only by the average interval between income payments, but also by the nature of consumer habits. In most cases, a rise of income will not lead to an immediate increase of consumption even with a very short payment interval, for some time is essential to adapt oneself to a higher standard of living. Likewise, a fall of income will usually take time to bring about a reduction of consumer demand.[8] Such consumer inertia makes an appraisal of the average lag between income receipt and expenditure extremely difficult. And even if this average could be determined empirically, the length of the second lag (sales-output) would still remain to be determined.

Because of uncertainty regarding the comparative lengths of the two periods, a contrast of the behavior of an economy subject to the Robertson lag with that of an economy where the Lundberg lag is assumed to be most important seems desirable. Since the Robertson model has been elaborated by Professors Hansen[9] and Samuelson,[10] through the introduction of induced investment, I shall confine myself to variants of the Lundberg sequence.

II

Consider, first, a dynamic model based upon the following assumptions: (1) Entrepreneurs have adequate inventories so that any discrepancy be-

---

[8] Mr. Colin Clark finds a lag of about two years for changes in consumption of the British well-to-do behind changes in their incomes (*op. cit.*, p. 254).

[9] *Op. cit.*, Chapter 12.

[10] P. A. Samuelson, "Interactions Between the Multiplier Analysis and the Principle of Acceleration," *Review of Economic Statistics*, xxi (1939), pp. 75-78.

tween output and consumer demand may be met by inventory fluctuations rather than price changes.

(2) Output in a given period is based upon sales of the preceding period.

(3) Consumers' goods are produced entirely in anticipation of sales with no attempt to replenish inventory losses or to get rid of accumulated stocks.

(4) Income is equal to the production of consumers' goods plus net investment.

(5) Consumption within the sales-output period depends upon income of the same period.

(6) All income produced is paid out, i.e., there are no business savings.

These assumptions will be recognized as those of the Lundberg first sequence, except that I have excluded business savings. I make this change because it simplifies the numerical examples while retaining all of the essential features of the Lundberg models. In any case, if business savings represent permanent additions to (private) capital which never enter into the stream of income paid out, they may be considered in our models simply by changing the marginal propensity to consume. This amounts to assuming that corporations pay out income to themselves and that the community marginal propensity is computed by including such corporations as "persons" whose marginal propensity to consume is zero. For example, a community in which 75 per cent of all income produced is paid out, and in which consumers spend all of the income they receive, will have a marginal propensity to consume of 75 per cent, related to income produced. Likewise, a community whose corporations pay out 80 per cent of income produced, and whose citizens spend 90 per cent of income received, will have a marginal propensity to consume of $(.90)\ (.80) = .72$, again related to income produced. Thus, so long as business savings are *permanent* their effect may be summarized in the marginal propensity to consume, and explicit recognition of them in our model sequence is unnecessary.[11]

If v_0 represents the amount of non-induced net investment, while $y(t)$ and $u(t)$ represent total income produced and consumers' goods produced, respectively (in period t), we know that[12]

$$y(t) = u(t) + v_0.$$

This relationship simply expresses the fact that income produced is equal to the output of consumers' goods plus net investment. But output of

---

[11] If undistributed profits are not permanently invested, but simply retained for a period longer than our "unit period," the dynamic sequence becomes quite complex. In this case, simply to change the marginal propensity to consume does not suffice, since business savings of a given period are likely to be balanced by subsequent disbursements in excess of earnings.

[12] To compare net investment with consumption, we must specify a unit of measurement common to both. We may assume either that all magnitudes are in wage units, or, alternatively, that they are in currency units which, because of unemployed resources and constant costs, do not change in value.

consumers' goods in a given period, t, is equal to sales of the preceding period, by assumption (2). Hence if β is the marginal propensity to consume, related to income produced, $u(t) = \beta y(t-1)$ and

$$y(t) = \beta y(t-1) + v_0. \tag{1}$$

Equation (1) shows how income of a given period is related to income of the preceding period and to the amount of net investment. It depicts a sequence identical with the Robertson model. Thus for simple dynamic systems, the behavior of a model is not changed by substituting a sales-output lag for a receipts-expenditure lag.

A numerical example of the way the system approaches equilibrium is given in Table 1. I assume there that the marginal propensity to consume is .6, that net investment (v_0) is 400, and that the economy is initially in equilibrium with a total income of 1000, 600 of which represent consumers' goods. I assume, also, that inventories of consumers' goods amount to 500. Equilibrium is disturbed, in the second period, by an increase of net investment to 500. Production of consumers' goods being 600, total income in period 2 is 1100. Hence consumption is 660, of which 600 represent current production and 60 a reduction of inventories. In the third period, entrepreneurs produce 660 units (last period's sales), and, assuming investment to be maintained at 500 per period, income of this period is 1160, so that sales amount to 696. Again, sales represent partly current production (660) and partly a reduction of inventories (36).

The sequence continues in this manner, with the increase of output and income of each period being smaller than that of the preceding period. Ultimately a new equilibrium of 1250 units of income is approached, and,

TABLE 1.—BEHAVIOR OF A SYSTEM WITH PASSIVE
INVENTORY ADJUSTMENTS
($\beta = .6$)

(1) Production of consumers' goods for sale	(2) Net non-induced investment	(3) Income produced (1)+(2)	(4) Sales	(5) Inventories at close of period
600	400	1000	600	500
600	500	1100	660	440
660	500	1160	696	404
696	500	1196	718	382
718	500	1218	731	369
731	500	1231	739	361
739	500	1239	743	357
743	500	1243	746	354
746	500	1246	748	352
748	500	1248	749	351
..	..	..	..	..
..	..	..	..	..
..	..	..	..	..
750	500	1250	750	350

as long as net investment remains at 500, this level of income will be maintained.

Changes of income and inventories are depicted in Chart 1. For the moment, we need only note that (1) income approaches its new equilibrium steadily; (2) inventories decline by the exact amount of the increase in sales per period; and (3) the income equilibrium is not affected by the inventory reduction, since this represents only a temporary source of disinvestment. None of the conclusions based upon Table 1 is novel. All of them may be found in Mr. Lundberg's first sequence, and part of them in the Robertson analysis. I have, nevertheless, included the table and figure in order to facilitate comparison with more complex sequences to follow.

CHART 1.—BEHAVIOR OF A SYSTEM WITH PASSIVE INVENTORY ADJUSTMENTS:
THE BASIC LUNDBERG SEQUENCE

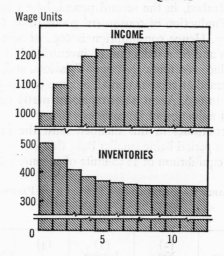

The passive nature of inventory changes in Table 1 makes the sequence rather unrealistic. Business men will ordinarily attempt to replenish inventories depleted by an unforeseen rise in demand, or to reduce inventory accumulations resulting from unpredicted depressions. We ought, therefore, to consider a dynamic model in which allowance is made for such adjustments. We may retain all of the assumptions of the first sequence except No. 3. Rather than assuming inventories to be completely passive (No. 3 of the first sequence), we shall now assume that an attempt is made to maintain them at a constant, "normal" level, s_o. Otherwise, we shall assume as before that production for sale in a given period (as distinguished from production for stocks) is based upon sales of the preceding period. Thus we have the following value for income produced in period t:

$$y(t) = u(t) + s(t) + v_o$$

where $u(t)$ represents production for sale, $s(t)$ production for inventory purposes, and v_0 net non-induced investment.

We wish to know how production for sale, $u(t)$, and production for inventories, $s(t)$, are related to income and sales of preceding periods. As before, production for sale is assumed equal to sales of the preceding period so that $u(t) = \beta y(t-1)$.

The second item, $s(t)$, may be either positive or negative. If stocks exceed the normal level, s_0, which business wishes to maintain, business men will produce fewer consumers' goods than they expect to sell in the hope that by so doing they can reduce inventories. In this case $s(t)$ is negative. On the other hand, if stocks are lower than the normal level, s_0, an attempt will be made to replenish inventories so that $s(t)$ will be positive. Whether positive or negative, however, production for inventories in period t will equal the difference between the normal level, s_0, and the actual level of stocks at the *close* of period $t-1$. But in period $t-1$, entrepreneurs *intended* to produce enough so that stocks at the close of that period would equal the normal level, s_0; i.e., they produced an amount sufficient to cover expected sales plus whatever was needed (positive or negative) to make stocks equal s_0. If actual sales exceeded those anticipated, entrepreneurs were forced to sell goods they had intended for inventories. Conversely, if actual sales fell short of expected sales, entrepreneurs were forced to hold goods they had intended for sale. In either case, the difference between the normal level, s_0, and the actual level at the close of period $t-1$ is simply the difference between actual and anticipated sales of that period.

It follows immediately that production for inventories in period t is equal to the difference between actual and anticipated sales of period $t-1$. In common-sense terms, we say that production for stocks in a given period is equal to the unintended inventory loss of the preceding period. But anticipated sales of $t-1$ were $\beta y(t-2)$, while actual sales were $\beta y(t-1)$. Hence

$$s(t) = \beta y(t-1) - \beta y(t-2).$$

Combining the expressions for $u(t)$ and $s(t)$, we find

$$y(t) = 2\beta y(t-1) - \beta y(t-2). \tag{2}$$

The behavior of this system may be illustrated by another numerical example. In Table 2, I assume, as before, that the marginal propensity to consume is .6, and that we start from a position of equilibrium in which net non-induced investment is equal to 400, income is 1000, total sales 600, production for sale 600, and production for inventories zero. These figures are in the first line of the table. In the second period, I assume that equilibrium is disturbed by an increase of non-induced investment to 500, an increase which is subsequently maintained. Total income thus rises to 1100, and sales to 660, causing an inventory reduction of 60, since anticipated sales (and hence output) in period 2 were only 600. Suppose, now, that entrepreneurs attempt to maintain their inventories at a level of 500. Then in period 3 they will produce 660 units for sale plus 60 units for inventory. Adding to this the 500 units of non-induced investment, we get a total income produced in period 3 of 1220, with sales of 732. Thus actual sales have once again exceeded anticipated sales, so that inventories remain below the normal level of 500.

This is characteristic of the early prosperity phase of a pure inventory cycle. For a time, added income generated by production for inventories plus the secondary effects of increased investment will cause sales to exceed those anticipated by more than production for inventory purposes. Hence

TABLE 2.—RESULT OF ATTEMPTING TO MAINTAIN INVENTORIES:
THE PURE INVENTORY CYCLE
$(\beta = .6)$

(1) Production of consumers' goods for sale	(2) Production of consumers' goods for stocks	(3) Net non-induced investment	(4) Income produced $(1)+(2)+(3)$	(5) Sales	(6) Inventories at close of period
600	0	400	1000	600	500
600	0	500	1100	660	440
660	60	500	1220	732	428
732	72	500	1304	782	450
782	50	500	1332	799	483
799	17	500	1316	790	509
790	− 9	500	1281	769	521
769	− 21	500	1248	749	520
749	− 20	500	1229	737	512
737	− 12	500	1225	735	502
735	− 2	500	1233	740	495
740	5	500	1245	747	493
747	7	500	1254	752	495
752	5	500	1257	754	498
754	2	500	1256	754	500
754	0	500	1254	752	502
752	− 2	500	1250	750	502

inventories actually decline despite attempts to increase them. Sales, however, cannot continue to rise as rapidly as income because of the dampening influence of savings. As a result, the excess of actual sales over anticipated sales declines, and inventories begin slowly to accumulate. But this causes income to rise at a still slower rate, since less is produced each period for inventory purposes. In turn, the decline of the *rate of growth* of income and sales accelerates the increase of stocks. Ultimately (period 6 of the table) actual sales fall short of those expected, and inventories rise above the normal level. Thereafter, attempts of entrepreneurs to reduce stocks lead to a cumulative decline of income because (1) less is produced than is expected to be sold, and (2) the initial decline reduces expectations and hence production for sale in subsequent periods. Moreover, once income begins to decline actual sales fall short of those anti-cipated so that attempts to reduce stocks are abortive.

Once again, however, the stabilizing influence of savings prevents a continuous movement in one direction. With a marginal propensity to consume less than unity, the decline of sales is less than the decline of total income, which means that the depression cannot continue to "feed upon itself." In other words, actual sales cannot continue to fall short of expected sales by as much as the inventory surplus. Eventually, therefore, attempts at inventory reduction will succeed, so that inventories are brought down slowly to the normal level. At this point income begins to rise by reason of the fact that entrepreneurs are no longer attempting to produce less than they sell. Thus the cycle repeats itself, but each time with a smaller amplitude.

This is the simplest form of inventory cycle. I have discussed it in some detail because it contains many features common to more complex se-quences. The nature of the cycle is more clearly seen in Chart 2. The fol-lowing points may be noted:

(1) The cycles are damped, so that income eventually approaches a new equilibrium of 1250, determined by the Multiplier and the increase of non-induced investment.

(2) Induced investment for purposes of inventory accumulation does not affect the income equilibrium.

(3) Inventories lag behind the movement of income. So long as inven-tories remain below the normal level, income rises; whenever they are above normal, income falls. Income reaches a maximum at the point where inventories have finally accumulated to the normal level, and a minimum at the point where they have *fallen* to this norm.

The cycle pictured in Chart 2 is a pure inventory cycle in the sense that it is produced entirely by investment (or disinvestment) for inventory purposes. It may be shown that *any disturbance in a dynamic system such as* (2) *will produce cyclical oscillations about a new level of income pro-vided the marginal propensity to consume is less than unity.* Thus the results of Table 2 do not depend upon any special values of our coefficients. If the marginal propensity to consume were greater than unity, the system would not oscillate when disturbed by an increase of non-induced invest-ment, but would diverge steadily.

III

The dynamic models of Tables 1 and 2 introduce a somewhat artificial assumption about business expectations. In both cases entrepreneurs are assumed to base their expectations of sales in a given period upon sales of the preceding period. It is natural to object that expectations of future sales may depend not only upon the past *level* of sales, but also upon the *direction of change* of such sales. Thus a level of sales of 500 in period $t-1$ which was reached from a level of 400 in $t-2$ might give rise to expectations in period t entirely different from what they would have been had the sales of 500 been approached from a level of 600 in $t-2$. In the former case, sales would normally be expected to exceed 500 in period t, whereas in the latter they would probably be expected to fall short of 500.

To discuss the role of expectations, I shall make use of a coefficient of expectation (η) defined as the ratio between the expected change of sales between periods t and $t-1$ and the observed change of sales between periods $t-1$ and $t-2$. To see what this means, let us consider some ex-

CHART 2.—THE PURE INVENTORY CYCLE
(Income and Inventory Figures from Table 2)

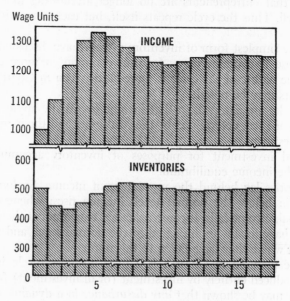

amples. Suppose observed sales in periods $t-1$ and $t-2$ were 500 and 400 respectively. Then the expected change of sales between $t-1$ and t would be the product of the coefficient of expectation by the observed change of sales between $t-2$ and $t-1$ (100 units). If the coefficient were one-half, e.g., sales would be expected to increase by 50 between $t-1$ and t; in other words, expected sales would be 550. Likewise, if the coefficient were zero, no change at all would be expected, so that anticipated sales in t would equal actual sales in $t-1$. Other results for this same example may be tabulated as follows:

Coefficient of Expectation	Anticipated Sales
-1	400
$-.5$	450
0	500
.5	550
1	600

Remembering that actual sales in $t-1$ and $t-2$ were 500 and 400 respectively, we may make the following observations: (1) If the coefficient of expectation is unity, a given rate of change is expected to continue undiminished. (2) If the coefficient of expectation is zero, a given level of sales is expected to continue. (3) If the coefficient is -1, any change between $t-2$ and $t-1$ is expected to be only temporary, so that sales in period t are expected to return to the level of period $t-2$.

In the sequences to follow, the coefficient of expectation will be assumed to lie between the limits $-1 \leq \eta \leq 1$. Although the argument might easily be extended to other values, I believe that this range is sufficiently wide to include most actual cases.[13]

Again we may suppose, as in the first two sequences, that income is spent (or saved) in the period in which it is received. But rather than assuming production for sale to be determined by sales of the past period, we shall now suppose it is related to sales of the *two* preceding periods by the coefficient of expectation, in the following manner:

$$u(t) = \beta y(t-1) + \eta[\beta y(t-1) - \beta y(t-2)]$$

or
$$u(t) = (1+\eta)\beta y(t-1) - \eta \beta y(t-2).$$

If no attempt is made to adjust inventories, total income produced is equal to the output of consumers' goods for sale plus net non-induced investment. Hence

$$y(t) = (1+\eta)\beta y(t-1) - \eta \beta y(t-2) + v_0. \tag{3}$$

Equation (3) is simply an extension of the Lundberg first sequence obtained by introducing a coefficient of expectation. In fact, the Lundberg sequence is the special case of (3) in which $\eta = 0$. It is therefore important to know how the behavior of this basic sequence changes with an alteration of the coefficient of expectation.

Numerical examples of sequence (3) are presented in Table 3. In each example the marginal propensity to consume is .6. Hence any differences between the three cases presented may be attributed to the coefficient of expectation. The initial disturbance, as before, is a rise of 100 in the level of non-induced net investment.

---

[13] It is useful to compare this coefficient with Hicks' "elasticity of expectation" (J. R. Hicks, *Value and Capital*, London, 1939, p. 205). In my terminology, the Hicks elasticity concept is defined as the ratio of the expected relative change between $t-2$ and t to the *actual* relative change between $t-2$ and $t-1$. If a parameter has the values π_2 and π_1 in periods $t-2$ and $t-1$, and if these values lead to an expectation of π_0 in period t, the elasticity of expectation is $\dfrac{\pi_0 - \pi_2}{\pi_2} \div \dfrac{\pi_1 - \pi_2}{\pi_2}$, whereas my coefficient of expectation is $\dfrac{\pi_0 - \pi_1}{\pi_1 - \pi_2}$. If e represents the elasticity of expectation while η, as above, represents the *coefficient* of expectation, it is easily shown that $\eta = e - 1$. Thus a range of variation for e between zero and unity (the range which Hicks considers) corresponds to a range for η between -1 and zero.

An explanation of Table 3, Part A will suffice, since all three parts of the table are constructed according to the same principles. We begin from a position of equilibrium, with sales per period of 600, non-induced investment of 400, and total income of 1000, and we suppose this equilibrium disturbed by an increase in net non-induced investment per period to 500. Income rises in the first period of added investment to 1100, and sales to 660, so that inventories decline to 440. Thus far the results are the same as in Table 1. The coefficient of expectation being positive, however, the rise of sales creates an expectation of a further rise. The coefficient assumed in Table 3A is .2. Thus expected sales in period 3 (and hence production of consumers' goods) are $660 + .2(660 - 600) = 672$. With

TABLE 3.—EFFECT OF EXPECTATIONS UPON THE BASIC
LUNDBERG SEQUENCE

Part A: $\beta = .6$; $\eta = .2$

(1) Production of consumers' goods for sale	(2) Net non-induced investment	(3) Income produced (1) + (2)	(4) Sales	(5) Inventories at close of period
600	400	1000	600	500
600	500	1100	660	440
672	500	1172	703	409
712	500	1212	727	394
732	500	1232	739	387
741	500	1241	745	383
746	500	1246	748	381
747	500	1247	748	380
748	500	1248	749	379
749	500	1249	749	379
..	..	..	..	..
..	..	..	..	..
..	..	..	..	..
750	500	1250	750	380

Part B: $\beta = .6$; $\eta = .5$

600	400	1000	600	500
600	500	1100	660	440
690	500	1190	714	416
741	500	1241	745	412
760	500	1260	756	416
762	500	1262	757	421
757	500	1257	754	424
752	500	1252	751	425
749	500	1249	749	425
748	500	1248	749	424
..	..	..	..	..
..	..	..	..	..
..	..	..	..	..
750	500	1250	750	425

Part C: $\beta=.6$; $\eta=1$

600	400	1000	600	500
600	500	1100	660	440
720	500	1220	732	428
804	500	1304	782	450
832	500	1332	799	483
816	500	1316	790	509
781	500	1281	769	521
748	500	1248	749	520
729	500	1229	737	512
725	500	1225	735	502
733	500	1233	740	495
745	500	1245	747	493
754	500	1254	752	495
757	500	1257	754	498
756	500	1256	754	500
754	500	1254	752	502
750	500	1250	750	502
..	..	..	..	..
..	..	..	..	..
..	..	..	..	..
750	500	1250	750	500

production of consumers' goods of 672 and net non-induced investment of 500, total income produced in the third period is 1172, and sales are 703. These sales in turn create an expectation that revenue in the next period will be $703+.2(703-660)=712$, and so on. The following features of the table may be noted: (1) Income approaches steadily a new equilibrium determined by the Multiplier and the amount of net non-induced investment. (2) For the values of the coefficient of expectation and the marginal propensity to consume of Table 3A, dependence of output upon the rate of change of sales does not change the mode of approaching a new equilibrium, but merely accelerates the speed with which the new level is approached. Thus with a positive coefficient of expectation, income moves more rapidly from the old equilibrium to the new than with a zero coefficient. (3) While sales advance by 150 per period in the new equilibrium, inventories decline only by 120 even though no attempt is made to maintain them.

The second and third parts of Table 3 differ from Table 3A only in the value of the coefficient of expectation. In 3B, η has a value of .5, while in 3C, the coefficient is unity. Comparison of 3B and 3C with 3A suggests the following points: (1) All three sequences are stable, for income approaches a new equilibrium in each case. (2) The income equilibrium is independent of the coefficient of expectation; it depends only upon the propensity to consume and the amount of non-induced investment. (3) For large values of the coefficient of expectation, income does not approach its new equilibrium steadily, but tends to oscillate about this new level in a series of damped cycles.

Explanation of these cycles may be found in the relation of η to the marginal propensity to consume. The initial rise of income leads to expectations of a further rise. And the combined influence of high expectations with the secondary effects of higher non-induced investment may create a level of income above the level justified by the amount of non-induced investment. When this happens, income must necessarily decline. For, with a marginal propensity to consume less than unity, an expansion of production in anticipation of a rise in sales cannot *by itself* create an increase of sales as great as the increase in consumers' goods output. Hence expectations are disappointed, which leads to lower expectations in subsequent periods, with a slowing down in the rate of growth of incomes and further unrealized expectations. The process continues until income actually begins to decline.

Once the decline is started, a further decline is inevitable since business men restrict output in expectation of fewer sales. Again, however, savings act as a stabilizer and reverse the direction of change. With a marginal propensity to consume less than unity, the mere expectation of a decline cannot in itself lead to a reduction of sales as great as the reduction of output. Eventually, therefore, expectations become less pessimistic, owing to the fact that they have not been fully realized in the past. When this occurs, output, although still lower than sales of the previous period, may exceed *output* of the previous period so that income again begins to rise. And thus the cycle repeats itself, each time with a smaller amplitude, as indicated in Parts B and C of Table 3.

We have seen that a positive coefficient of expectation may lead to (1) a steady approach to equilibrium of the same type as in the Lundberg first sequence, only more rapid, or (2) cyclical oscillations about the new equilibrium. Whether the system behaves in the first manner or the second depends upon the relation of the marginal propensity to consume to the coefficient of expectation. The nature of this relation is indicated in Chart 3. A sequence of the type (3) will approach equilibrium steadily for any values of β and η in the region S, while it will oscillate about the new equilibrium if its β and η lie in the region S_o.[14] Thus a positive coefficient of expectation is more likely to lead to cyclical movements the smaller is the marginal propensity to consume. In other words, a smaller coefficient of expectation is required to "overstep the mark" if the system is damped by large savings than if most income is consumed.

With a negative coefficient of expectation, behavior of the system is quite different. The cycle is replaced by a cobweb movement. To show how this cobweb arises, suppose that an economy has a marginal propensity to consume of unity and a coefficient of expectation of -1. And suppose that, because of a change in non-induced investment, income and sales rise from 1000 to 1100 units. Since $\eta = -1$, we know that any change of

---

[14] The region S_o is separated from S by the line $\beta(1+\eta)^2=4\eta$. The inequality $\beta(1+\eta)^2<4\eta$ is simply the condition that the roots of the "characteristic equation" $\rho^2-(1+\eta)\beta\rho+\eta\beta=0$ shall be imaginary.

sales is expected to be temporary, so that entrepreneurs anticipate sales of 1000 in the next period after the change. Consequently, they produce only 1000 units, and if the burst of non-induced investment is not maintained, actual income and sales are 1000. The drop in sales from 1100 to 1000, in turn, leads to sales expectations of 1100 for the next succeeding period; as a result, actual production and sales are 1100. In this manner an initial burst of investment produces an undamped cobweb with income and sales alternating between 1000 and 1100. The system is in *neutral* equilibrium. Had the marginal propensity to consume been less than unity, however, the cobwebs would have been damped, and equilibrium stable. More generally, any model whose β and η lie within the region

CHART 3.—INFLUENCE OF EXPECTATIONS UPON A SYSTEM
WITH PASSIVE INVENTORY ADJUSTMENTS

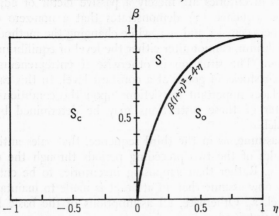

S_o of Chart 3 represents a stable system which approaches equilibrium through a combination of (1) a damped cobweb and (2) a steady change at an exponential rate.

Although expectations may temporarily be negative, the kind of alternate periods of optimism and pessimism depicted in a literal interpretation of a negative coefficient of expectation is probably seldom found in the actual world. Analysis of the case is included, nevertheless, to show that negative expectations do not change the condition of stability (i.e., $\beta < 1$).

An interesting parallel is found between our third sequence and the Hansen-Samuelson extension of Robertson's dynamic model. Without attempting a detailed discussion of the Hansen-Samuelson case, its essential features may be enumerated as follows: (1) A lag of one period is assumed in the expenditure of income behind its receipt. (2) Entrepreneurs are assumed to produce, in a given period, whatever amounts of consumers' goods are demanded in that period (the sales-output lag is zero). (3) Aside from non-induced investment, a part of the production of capital goods in a particular period is assumed to be a linear function of the rate of change of sales in the same period (the acceleration principle). With these assumptions, a dynamic model is constructed which is found to (1) converge steadily, (2) converge cyclically, (3) diverge cyclically, or (4) diverge steadily according to the values of the marginal propensity to consume and the accelerator.

Comparison of equation (3) with the Samuelson equation reveals that the two are identical except that the coefficient of expectation (η) has replaced the accelerator (a in Samuelson's notation). Thus the coefficient of expectation apparently bears the same relation to the basic Lundberg sequence that the acceleration principle bears to the Robertson sequence. Indeed, the right half of my Chart 3 is the same as Samuelson's figure (with η substituted for a) except that I have excluded values of η greater than unity.

So long as inventories are merely a passive factor of adjustment, our discussion of sequence (3) demonstrates that a non-zero coefficient of expectation between -1 and $+1$, while changing the method of approach toward equilibrium, cannot alter either the level of equilibrium or stability of the system. The situation is otherwise if entrepreneurs attempt to maintain their stocks of goods at a constant level. In this case, a positive coefficient places important restrictions upon the conditions of stability. The character of these restrictions may be determined by developing another model.

We may assume, as in the third sequence, that sales anticipations are related to sales of the two preceding periods through the coefficient of expectation, η. Rather than supposing inventories to be entirely passive, however, we now assume that an attempt is made to maintain them at a constant level, s_0. Otherwise, all assumptions of the basic Lundberg sequence are maintained.

We have seen above that income produced in the consumers' goods industries may be divided into two parts: (1) an amount $u(t)$ produced in anticipation of sales; and (2) an amount $s(t)$ produced for stocks. The first item, production for sale, is related to past sales through the coefficient of expectation, exactly as in our third sequence, so that

$$u(t) = (1+\eta)\beta y(t-1) - \eta\beta y(t-1).$$

To complete the sequence, production for stocks, $s(t)$, must be related to income (or sales) of preceding periods. In developing our second sequence, we found that attempting to maintain inventories is equivalent to producing for stocks in each period an amount equal to unintended inventory reductions of the preceding period, and that unintended inventory reductions of a given period are simply the difference between actual and anticipated sales of that period. In other words, production for stocks in period t was found equal to the difference between actual and anticipated sales of period $t-1$. So it is here. Only, now, anticipated sales of period $t-1$ are no longer equal to sales of $t-2$, but are related to sales of the *two* preceding periods through the coefficient of expectation, as follows: expected sales in period $t-1 = (1+\eta)\beta y(t-2) - \eta\beta y(t-3)$. Hence $s(t)$, the difference between actual and anticipated sales of period $t-1$, is

$$s(t) = \beta y(t-1) - (1+\eta)\beta y(t-2) + \eta\beta y(t-3).$$

Remembering that income produced in period t is equal to total production of consumers' goods for all purposes plus net non-induced investment, we have

$$y(t) = (2+\eta)\beta y(t-1) - (1+2\eta)\beta y(t-2) + \eta\beta y(t-3) + v_o. \qquad (4)$$

In Table 4 behavior of sequence (4) is illustrated by two numerical examples. The two examples differ only in the value of the coefficient of expectation; in Part A, η has a value of unity, while in Part B it is one-half. The marginal propensity to consume is .6 in both cases. Let us consider Part A of Table 4. We begin, as always, from a position of equilibrium, with non-induced investment of 400, income of 1000, sales of 600, production for sale of 600, and production for inventory of zero. Equilibrium is disturbed in the second period by a rise of non-induced investment to 500. This increases sales to 660 and reduces inventories to 440. In the third period, production for sale is related to sales of the two preceding periods, just as in Table 3, by the coefficient of expectation. Since this coefficient is unity in Table 4A, sales of 600 and 660 in the first two periods create an expectation that sales of the third period will be 720. In addition to this amount produced for sale, 60 units are produced to make good the unintended inventory reduction of the previous period. Adding to these items the 500 units of non-induced investment, we obtain a total income produced of 1280 units for the third period. In this manner the entire sequence may be built up. Table 4B is constructed in exactly the same manner except that a coefficient of expectation of one-half is used in computing the column, "production of consumers' goods for sale."

Income and inventory figures from the two parts of the table are plotted in Charts 4 and 5. Both charts exhibit the characteristic inventory cycle, with changes in the level of stocks lagging one-fourth cycle behind changes of income. The two charts differ, however, in an important respect. In Chart 4, the amplitude of the cycles grows larger as the sequence develops, whereas in Chart 5 the fluctuations are damped. In other words, the sequence in Table 4B represents a stable system while 4A is essentially unstable. The de-stabilizer in 4A is obviously the coefficient of expectation, for the two parts of the table differ from each other only in the value of this coefficient. Thus, apparently, whenever entrepreneurs attempt to maintain inventories at a constant level, a high coefficient of expectation may create an unstable situation even with a marginal propensity to consume less than unity.

Exactly how large η must be to produce instability is indicated in Chart 6. A system of the type (4) is stable for any values of η and β contained in region S_o; disturbances of equilibrium in such cases produce damped in-

TABLE 4.—EFFECT OF EXPECTATIONS WHEN ENTREPRENEURS
ATTEMPT TO MAINTAIN INVENTORIES

Part A: Unstable Case; $\beta = .6$; $\eta = 1$

(1) Production of consumers' goods for sale	(2) Production of consumers' goods for stocks	(3) Net non-induced investment	(4) Income produced (1) + (2) + (3)	(5) Sales	(6) Inventories at close of period
600	0	400	1000	600	500
600	0	500	1100	660	440
720	60	500	1280	768	452
876	48	500	1424	854	522
940	−22	500	1418	851	589
848	−89	500	1259	755	593
659	−93	500	1066	640	519
525	−19	500	1006	604	421
568	79	500	1147	688	380
772	120	500	1392	835	437
982	63	500	1545	927	555
1019	−55	500	1464	878	641
829	−141	500	1188	713	616
548	−116	500	932	559	489
405	11	500	916	550	355
541	145	500	1186	712	329
874	171	500	1545	927	447

Part B: Stable Case; $\beta = .6$; $\eta = .5$

600	0	400	1000	600	500
600	0	500	1100	660	440
690	60	500	1250	750	440
795	60	500	1355	813	482
845	18	500	1363	818	527
820	−27	500	1293	776	544
755	−44	500	1211	727	528
702	−28	500	1174	704	498
693	2	500	1195	717	476
724	24	500	1248	749	475
765	25	500	1290	774	491
786	9	500	1295	777	509
779	−9	500	1270	762	517
754	−17	500	1237	742	512
732	−12	500	1220	732	500
727	0	500	1227	736	491
738	9	500	1247	748	490

CHART 4.—INCOME AND INVENTORY MOVEMENTS AS DESCRIBED BY DATA IN TABLE 4, PART A

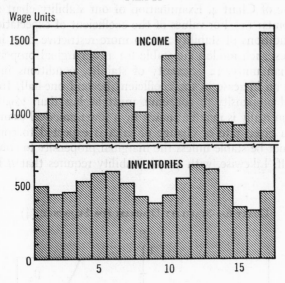

CHART 5.—INCOME AND INVENTORY MOVEMENTS AS DESCRIBED BY DATA IN TABLE 4, PART B

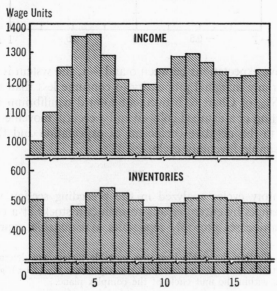

ventory cycles.[15] A system with values of η and β in region U_o, on the other hand, is unstable; disturbances of equilibrium here produce explosive cycles such as those of Chart 4. Examination of our stability chart suggests the following points: (1) For values of the coefficient of expectation less than one-half, conditions of stability are no more restrictive than in our previous sequences; such models are stable for any marginal propensity to consume less than unity. (2) Severity of stability conditions increases very rapidly with an increase in the coefficient beyond one-half. In general, β, the marginal propensity to consume, must be less than $\frac{1}{2}\eta$. How severe this condition really is may be shown by a few numerical examples. If η is unity (i.e., a given rate of change of sales is expected to continue), the system will not be stable unless the marginal propensity to consume is less than one-half. Likewise, with $\eta = \frac{3}{4}$, stability requires that β be less than two-thirds.

CHART 6.—STABILITY DIAGRAM FOR SEQUENCE (4)

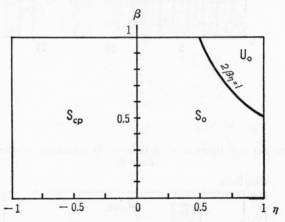

For negative expectations between o and -1, the system is stable, in our sequence, for any marginal propensity to consume less than unity. This is the region, $S_{c,o}$, of Chart 6. Movement toward equilibrium in such cases is a combination of a damped cobweb and a cyclical movement, the former attributable to the negative coefficient of expectation and the latter representing a simple inventory cycle.

IV

The inventory cycles analyzed in the preceding section were a direct result of attempts by entrepreneurs to maintain stocks at a constant level, which in many cases probably represents a reasonable approximation to

---

[15] The lines dividing the stable from the unstable regions are determined from the conditions that the roots of the characteristic equation, $\rho^3 - (2+\eta)\beta\rho^2 + (1+2\eta)\beta\rho - \eta\beta = 0$, shall lie within the unit circle of the complex plane.

the actual situation, particularly if one considers only short-run adjustments. In other cases, however, the assumption that the desirable level of stocks is somehow related to the expected level of sales may be more accurate. In general, the amount of inventories which entrepreneurs regard as "normal" will vary directly with the expected volume of business. Thus, the economy may be subject to the influence of an accelerator as well as a coefficient of expectation, for inventory production will then be related to the rate of change of sales. A complete examination of dynamic systems having a sales-output lag therefore requires analysis of the relations between the inventory accelerator and our coefficient of expectation.

We may begin with the inventory accelerator alone. Suppose that entrepreneurs attempt to maintain inventories at a constant proportion, a, of expected sales. Suppose, further, that sales in a given period (say t) are expected to equal sales of the preceding period (i.e., $\eta=0$). Income produced, as before, is equal to production for sale, $[u(t)]$, plus production for stocks, $[s(t)]$, plus non-induced investment. Anticipated sales being equal to sales of the preceding period, we know that

$$u(t)=\beta y(t-1).$$

Production for inventory purposes, on the other hand, is equal to the difference between the desired level of inventories, $a\beta y(t-1)$, and actual stocks on hand at the close of the previous period, $k(t-1)$; i.e.,

$$s(t)=a\beta y(t-1)-k(t-1).$$

But $k(t-1)$ would have been equal to $a\beta y(t-2)$ except for unintended reductions or increases in stocks during the period $t-1$. And, just as in the previous section, these unintended changes of inventories are the difference between actual sales, $\beta y(t-1)$, and expected sales, $\beta y(t-2)$. Hence $k(t-1)$ $=a\beta y(t-2)-\beta y(t-1)+\beta y(t-2)$ so that

$$s(t)=(1+a)\beta y(t-1)-(1+a)\beta y(t-2).$$

Adding the amounts of production for sale, $u(t)$, and production for inventory, $s(t)$, to non-induced investment, v_0, we obtain the following expression for income of the period t:

$$y(t)=(2+a)\beta y(t-1)-(1+a)\beta y(t-2)+v_0. \tag{5}$$

This equation, except for minor changes, is Mr. Lundberg's second sequence.

Two numerical examples of the model are given in Table 5. In Part A the assumption is made that $\beta=.5$ and $a=.5$, while Part B is constructed upon the assumptions that $\beta=.6$ and $a=1$. The only feature of the tables requiring explanation is the second column, "production of consumers' goods for stocks." Amounts in this column are those needed to bring stocks up to the given proportion, a, of expected sales. In the third line of Part A, for example, expected sales are 550 and inventories of the previous period only 200. Since $a = .5$, sales expectations of 550 should be accompanied by total inventories of 275. Consequently, production for stocks in the third period is 75.

Both parts of Table 5 reveal the usual inventory cycles. In Part A, however, the cycles are damped, while in Part B they are explosive. The inventory accelerator thus appears to act as a de-stabilizer in much the same manner as a positive coefficient of expectation. Stability of the economy cannot be discussed without knowing what combinations of a and β will produce damped cycles, as in Part A, and what combinations will lead to explosive cycles, as in Part B. Solution of this problem is depicted in Chart 7. Any economy whose marginal propensity to consume and in-

CHART 7.—STABILITY DIAGRAM FOR SEQUENCE (5)

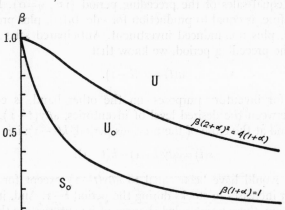

ventory accelerator lie in the region S_o is a stable economy that approaches equilibrium through a series of damped cycles. Both U_o and U, on the other hand, are regions of instability. No economy whose a and β lie in these regions has any tendency at all to approach equilibrium. Systems with a and β in U_o oscillate in explosive cycles when disturbed, as in Part B, while those with a and β in U diverge steadily.[16]

Introduction of the accelerator imposes severe limitations upon stability of the system, particularly if entrepreneurs attempt to maintain inventories at a large multiple of sales. If, for example, a is unity (i.e., entrepreneurs attempt to maintain stocks equal to sales), the economy will not be stable unless the marginal propensity to consume is less than one-half. Likewise,

---

[16] Separation of the stable region from the unstable regions is determined from the conditions that the roots of $\rho^2 - (2+a)\beta\rho + (1+a)\beta = 0$ shall lie within the unit circle of the complex plane. Separation of U_o from U, on the other hand, is determined from the conditions that the roots of the above equation shall be real.

TABLE 5.—THE INVENTORY ACCELERATOR

Part A: Stable Case; $a = .5$; $\beta = .5$

(1) Production of consumers' goods for sale	(2) Production of consumers' goods for stocks	(3) Net non-induced investment	(4) Income produced (1) + (2) + (3)	(5) Sales	(6) Inventories at close of period
500	0	500	1000	500	250
500	0	600	1100	550	200
550	75	600	1225	612	213
612	93	600	1305	652	266
652	60	600	1312	656	322
656	6	600	1262	631	353
631	−38	600	1193	596	350
596	−52	600	1144	572	322
572	−36	600	1136	568	290
568	−6	600	1162	581	271
581	19	600	1200	600	271
600	29	600	1229	614	286
614	21	600	1235	617	304
617	4	600	1221	610	315
610	−10	600	1200	600	315
600	−15	600	1185	592	308
592	−12	600	1180	590	298

Part B: Unstable Case; $a = 1$; $\beta = .6$

(1) Production of consumers' goods for sale	(2) Production of consumers' goods for stocks	(3) Net non-induced investment	(4) Income produced (1) + (2) + (3)	(5) Sales	(6) Inventories at close of period
600	0	400	1000	600	600
600	0	500	1100	660	540
660	120	500	1280	768	552
768	216	500	1484	890	646
890	244	500	1634	980	800
980	180	500	1660	996	964
996	32	500	1528	917	1075
917	−158	500	1259	755	1079
755	−324	500	931	559	951
559	−392	500	667	400	718
400	−318	500	582	349	451
349	−102	500	747	448	250
448	198	500	1146	688	208
688	480	500	1668	1001	375
1001	626	500	2127	1276	726
1276	550	500	2326	1396	1156
1396	240	500	2136	1282	1510

if a is 2, stability requires a marginal propensity to consume less than one-third.[17]

In Chart 8, stability conditions for our fifth sequence are compared with those of its analogue, the Hansen-Samuelson model. The region S represents values of a and β which yield stable results for either model. Similarly, values of a and β in the region U produce instability in both sequences. Any pairs of the two parameters found in S', however, will yield

CHART 8.—STABILITY OF THE HANSEN-SAMUELSON MODEL COMPARED WITH THAT OF SEQUENCE (5)

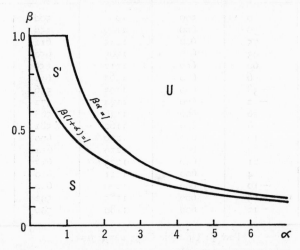

stable results if applied to the Hansen-Samuelson model, but will represent an unstable system in the present case. If a is equal to unity, for example, the Hansen-Samuelson model will be stable for any β less than unity, whereas stability of sequence (5), as noted above, requires a β less than one-half. Thus an inventory accelerator places much more severe restric-

---

[17] Mr. Lundberg's failure to solve his difference equations has led him to draw an incorrect conclusion from one of his models. In his second sequence, which is the same as sequence (5) above, he assumes that 80 per cent of all income produced is paid out, and that 90 per cent of all income paid out is consumed. This amounts to assuming that our β, the marginal propensity to consume related to income produced, is (.8) (.9) = .72. He also assumes that entrepreneurs attempt to maintain stocks at 50 per cent of sales (i.e., $a=.5$). From Chart 7 it is evident that the point $\beta=.72$, $a=.5$ lies in the region U_0. In other words, for these values of the marginal propensity to consume and the inventory accelerator, the economy is unstable; any disturbance produces a series of explosive cycles. And yet Mr. Lundberg concludes from his numerical example that the system approaches *asymptotically* a new equilibrium determined by the Multiplier and the amount of non-induced investment. As a matter of fact, a sequence such as this one never behaves in this manner, although it may approach a new equilibrium through a series of damped inventory cycles.

The Lundberg error provides a good illustration of the treacherous nature of numerical examples. It is unsafe to draw general conclusions from them, for one never knows to what extent the conclusions depend upon special characteristics of the examples chosen.

tions upon stability conditions of the basic Lundberg sequence than does the ordinary accelerator upon the Robertson sequence.

The explanation of this difference is simple. The acceleration principle is usually developed from the assumption that either technological or economic factors require a constant ratio between output of consumers' goods and certain types of capital goods. And then it is shown that, *ignoring changes in replacement demand,* the demand for capital goods is a linear function of the rate of change in demand for consumers' goods. This is the *a* of the Hansen-Samuelson model. If the capital goods in question are extremely durable, ignoring changes of replacement demand will not vitiate the results of a short-run analysis. In the present case, however, the capital goods subject to the acceleration principle are inventories, perhaps the least durable of all. Hence replacement demand should not be neglected.

The manner of considering such replacement is clearly seen in equation (5). In formulating this equation, production in period *t* of goods for stock was put equal to $(1+a)\beta y(t-1) - (1+a)\beta y(t-2)$. Now this expression may be divided into two parts. The first, $a[\beta y(t-1) - \beta y(t-2)]$, is the simplified accelerator, which ignores replacement demand. The second, $\beta y(t-1) - \beta y(t-2)$, is the amount produced to replace unintended inventory reductions of the preceding period. Such unintended changes of stock occur, of course, because actual sales differ from those expected. Without this second item (production for replacement) the Lundberg second sequence would require exactly the same conditions for stability as the Hansen-Samuelson model. When unintended inventory changes are adjusted, however, the inventory accelerator becomes a destabilizer with the same force that is possessed by an ordinary accelerator, one unit larger. An inventory accelerator of unity, for example, imparts as much instability to a system as an ordinary accelerator of two.

The sequence summarized in equation (5) was developed from the assumption of a positive inventory accelerator and a zero coefficient of expectation. Development of sequence (4), on the other hand, required a positive coefficient of expectation and a zero inventory accelerator. A dynamic system more general than either (4) or (5) may be obtained by assuming both the coefficient of expectation and the inventory accelerator to be positive.

Let η and a, as above, represent these two parameters. Production of consumers' goods in a given period may now be divided into three parts: (1) production for anticipated sales; (2) production to replace unintended inventory losses; and (3) production to bring output up to the given proportion, a, of expected sales. Call these three items $u(t)$, $s_r(t)$, and $s_a(t)$, respectively. We have seen above that $u(t)$, production for sale, is related to sales of the two preceding periods in the following manner:

$$u(t) = (1+\eta)\beta y(t-1) - \eta\beta y(t-2).$$

Likewise, unintended inventory reductions (or accumulations) in period $t-1$ are equal to the difference between actual and anticipated sales in that period, so that

$$s_r(t) = \beta y(t-1) - (1+\eta)\beta y(t-2) + \eta\beta y(t-3).$$

Finally, $s_a(t)$, production on account of the "pure accelerator," is equal to the difference between anticipated sales in period t and in period $t-1$ multiplied by the accelerator; i.e.,

$$s_a(t) = a[(1+\eta)\beta y(t-1) - (1+2\eta)\beta y(t-2) + \eta\beta y(t-3)].$$

Since total income produced equals production of consumers' goods for all purposes plus non-induced net investment, we have, upon adding the expressions for $u(t)$, $s_r(t)$, and $s_a(t)$,

$$y(t) = [(1+\eta)(1+a)+1]\beta y(t-1) - (1+2\eta)(1+a)\beta y(t-2) \\ + (1+a)\eta\beta y(t-3) + v_0. \tag{6}$$

The difference equation (6) is the most general dynamic system to be considered. Many of our other sequences are simply special cases of this model. Thus by putting $\eta=0$ we obtain equation (5), while equation (4) is the special case in which $a=0$. Likewise, equation (3) may be obtained by setting both η and a equal to zero in (6).

Behavior of an economy subject to both an inventory accelerator and a coefficient of expectation might be illustrated, as in previous cases, by numerical examples. Both the method of constructing such examples and the character of inventory movements, however, should by now be thoroughly familiar. And inventory cycles corresponding to this more general model are not different, in principle, from those of the special cases. Consequently, I leave it to the reader to construct any examples which seem appropriate to verify the conclusions set out below.

Although income and inventory movements are much the same for the general case (6) as for (4) and (5), the range of values of the parameters a, β, and η within which an economy is stable requires further consideration. For stability of this general system, the marginal propensity to consume, the inventory accelerator, and the coefficient of expectation must satisfy the following inequalities:[18]

$$\left. \begin{array}{r} (1+a)(2+a)\eta\beta^2 - (1+a)(1+2\eta)\beta + 1 > 0 \\ 3 - \beta(2a+3) \quad\quad > 0 \end{array} \right\} \tag{7}$$

In order clearly to grasp just what this means, we may consider some special cases. Let us suppose, as before, that η may have any values between zero and unity; and let us consider only these limiting values. If $\eta=0$, the system will be stable, as in (5), provided only that $\beta < \dfrac{1}{1+a}$. If $\eta=1$, on

---

[18] Again, stability of the system is determined from the condition that the roots of $f(\rho)=0$ shall lie within the unit circle, where $f(\rho)=0$ is the characteristic equation of (6).

the other hand, stability requires that $(1+a)(2+a)\beta^2-3(1+a)\beta+1>0$ where, because of the second of the inequalities (7), the relevant root of the quadratic in β is the lowest positive root.

The nature of these restrictions is best understood by referring to Chart 9. All values of the marginal propensity to consume and the inventory accelerator below the line marked "$\eta=0$" yield stable results when the coefficient of expectation is zero. This is simply case (5). If the coefficient of expectation is unity, however, the economy will not be stable unless β and a lie below the line "$\eta=1$." The chart shows clearly that the coefficient of expectation places very severe restrictions upon our stability conditions —so severe, indeed, that an economy with a unitary coefficient must almost certainly be unstable. Suppose, for example, that business men at-

CHART 9.—INFLUENCE OF EXPECTATIONS UPON THE STABILITY OF A SYSTEM CONTAINING AN INVENTORY ACCELERATOR [SEQUENCE (6)]

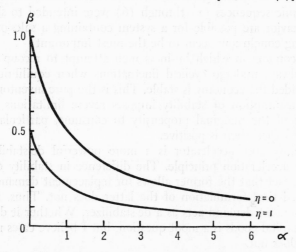

tempt to keep inventories equal to one-half of sales (i.e., $a=.5$). If $\eta=1$, Chart 9 shows that the economy will not be stable unless the marginal propensity to consume is less than (approximately) three-tenths. Even with $a=0$ (no inventory accelerator), stability of a system with a unitary coefficient of expectation requires a marginal propensity to consume less than one-half. It is doubtful whether propensities as low as these could be found, even in the most wealthy countries. We may conclude either (a) that the coefficient of expectation cannot conceivably be as large as unity, or (b) that the economy is essentially unstable except for the operation of certain limiting stabilizers.

If we accept conclusion (a), we place ourselves with the group who envisage cyclical fluctuations as a result of variations in the parameters of an otherwise stable economy. In this case, discussions of an income equilibrium corresponding to a given level of non-induced investment are rele-

vant. The Multiplier, in other words, becomes an important if not a dominant factor in the determination of income. Acceptance of conclusion (b),
on the other hand, makes necessary an explanation of why the economy
exhibits any stability at all. The level of income and employment must be
explained, not by the Multiplier and the amount of non-induced net investment, but by the operation of limiting stabilizers. A comprehensive
discussion of such stabilizers is beyond the scope of this paper. An enumeration of them, however, would certainly include flexible interest rates,
full employment, credit restrictions (other than interest rate changes),
and cyclical changes in the coefficient of expectation, to mention only a
few. How important these stabilizers are, and at what points they begin
to operate, are questions for empirical investigation. Probably no very
useful generalizations may be made about them.

V

The dynamic sequences (1) through (6) were intended to show what
types of behavior are possible for a system containing a sales-output lag.
The following conclusions seem to be the most important:

(1) An economy in which business men attempt to recoup inventory
losses will always undergo cyclical fluctuations when equilibrium is disturbed, provided the economy is stable. This is the pure inventory cycle.

(2) The assumption of stability imposes severe limitations upon the
possible size of the marginal propensity to consume, particularly if the
coefficient of expectation is positive.

(3) The inventory accelerator is a more powerful de-stabilizer than
the ordinary acceleration principle. The difference in stability conditions
is due to the fact that the former allows for replacement demand whereas
the usual analytical formulation of the latter does not. Thus, for inventories, replacement demand acts as a de-stabilizer. Whether it does so for
all types of capital goods is a moot question, but I believe cases may occur
in which it does not.

(4) Investment for inventory purposes cannot alter the equilibrium of
income, which depends only upon the propensity to consume and the
amount of non-induced investment.

(5) The apparent instability of a system containing both an accelerator
and a coefficient of expectation makes further investigation of possible
stabilizers highly desirable.

[8]

The Cobweb Theorem*

MORDECAI EZEKIEL†

Editors' Note

Agriculture is usually considered to be the pure example of perfect competition, and classical economics tells us that in a competitive market equilibrium in price and output will be gradually restored if it is disturbed in any
way. This article, another classic, explains why equilibrium need not result.
Using the familiar supply and demand diagrams, the favorite of elementary
economics courses, the author explains how successive production and price
readjustments may lead away from equilibrium. This process helps to explain the long cycles in many farm commodities. The theoretical explanation of these swings enlists support in the political community for major
government intervention in agriculture. Yet even this intervention has not
removed the "cobweb" effect from agriculture in recent years.

* Reprinted by permission of the publishers from *The Quarterly Journal of Economics*, Vol. LII, No. 1 (February, 1938), pp. 255-280; Cambridge, Mass.: Harvard
University Press, Copyright, 1938, by The President and Fellows of Harvard College.

† Dr. Ezekiel (1899–   ) has earned an international reputation in agricultural
economics. From his first assignment as Statistical Assistant in Agriculture, U. S. Census
Bureau, in 1919, he progressed successively to the posts of Assistant Chief Economist,
Federal Farm Board (1930–33); Economic Adviser to the Secretary of Agriculture
(1933–44); Economic Adviser to the Bureau of Agricultural Economics, U.S. Department of Agriculture (1944–46); and Economist, United Nations Food and
Agricultural Organization (1947–50). A pioneer in curvilinear multiple correlation and
in price forecasting for farm products, he is the author of numerous articles and books,
including: *Methods of Correlation Analysis* (1930); *Jobs for All* (1939); *Toward
World Prosperity* (1947); *Use of Agricultural Surplus to Finance Economic Development in the Underdeveloped Countries—A Pilot Study in India* (coauthor and editor,
1955).

History of the "Cobweb Theorem"

❧ Regularly recurring cycles in the production and prices of particular commodities have been recognized by students of prices for more than fifty years.[1] Many economists have been disturbed by the apparent inconsistency between the persistence of these observed cycles and the tendency towards an equilibrium posited by economic theory. Descriptions of the mechanism of these self-perpetuating commodity cycles were well developed a decade or more ago, but despite various partial explanations, a definite theoretical explanation for them had not been established. Finally three economists, in Italy, Holland, and the United States, apparently independently, worked out the theoretical explanation which has since come to be known as the "cobweb theorem."[2] As it happened, all three papers were published in German, two in the same issue of the same publication. Only recently has the theory begun to be generally recognized in English-speaking countries.

All three originators of the theory followed the same basic idea of carrying successive production, price, and production readjustments back and forth between the supply and demand curves. Schultz's demonstration[3] was the simplest, presenting merely one example, of the convergent type; but also plotting the resulting time-series of prices and quantities. Tinbergen's analysis was more complete, presenting both the convergent and divergent types,[4] and referring to Hanau's statistical analysis of hog prices in Germany[5] as a realistic illustration. Ricci's analysis, published in the same issue with Tinbergen's, presented diagrams of all three basic types, convergent, divergent, and continuous.[6] In each case, these first statements of the cobweb analysis were introduced only incidentally. Schultz used it as an illustration of the difference between simultaneous readjustment of supply to demand and lagging readjustment; Tinbergen as showing that where the production response lags behind the price change "instead of equilibrium being reached . . . a continuing movement of price and production is pos-

---

[1] S. Benner, Benner's Prophecies of Future Ups and Downs in Prices, Cincinnati, 1876.

For a bibliography of other early studies of the corn-hog price cycle, see "Factors Affecting the Price of Hogs," by G. C. Haas and Mordecai Ezekiel, U. S. Dept. Agr. Bul. 1440, 1926, pp. 67-68.

[2] This name was apparently first suggested by Nicholas Kaldor in his article "A Classificatory Note on the Determinateness of Equilibrium," Rev. of Econ. Studies, Vol. 1, p. 122. February 1934.

[3] Henry Schultz, Der Sinn der Statistischen Nachfragen, Heft 10, Veröffentlichungen der Frankfurter Gesellschaft für Konjunkturforschung, Kurt Schroeder Verlag, Bonn, 1930. See especially page 34.

[4] J. Tinbergen, Bestimmung und Deutung von Angebotskurven, Ein Beispiel, Zeitschrift für Nationalökonomie, Wien, Band 1, Heft 5, 1930, p. 671.

[5] Arthur Hanau, Die Prognose der Schweinepreise, Sonderheft 7 and 18, Vierteljahrshefte zur Konjunkturforschung, Institut für Konjunkturforschung, Berlin, 1928 and 1930.

[6] Umberto Ricci, Die "Synthetische Ökonomie" von Henry Ludwell Moore, Zeitschrift für Nationalökonomie, Wien, Band 1, Heft 5, 1930, p. 656.

sible"; and Ricci as a basis for showing (in a review of Moore's work) how important were the precise values of the elasticities of supply and demand, since such greatly different economic consequences might follow from slight differences in their numerical values. No one of the three, however, considered the broader significance of the cobweb theory in its relation to economic theory as such.

Subsequently, in the article cited above, Kaldor called attention to the cobweb analysis as bearing on the determinateness of equilibrium in those cases "where the adjustments are completely discontinuous"; and Leontief showed that where the supply or demand curves are of an erratic shape, the same set of curves might produce either a convergent or a divergent series.[7] The cobweb theory has also been discussed as a theoretical explanation for the hog cycle in England.[8] More recently, it has been incorporated in an American elementary text on economic theory.[9] Despite this increasing attention to it, however, the theory has remained substantially in the form first stated by its originators. This article attempts to develop the theory more generally, and to clarify its relation both to neo-classical economic theory and to statistical price analysis.

Restatement of the Theory of Market Price

The price on a current market, under conditions of pure competition,[10] over a given limited period of time tends to be determined by the interaction of the supply and demand on that market. Demand (indicated by the curve DD' in section A of Figure 1) represents the schedule of the number of units of the commodity (Q), which purchasers stand willing to buy within the period specified at varying prices (P); supply (indicated by the curve SS') represents the number of units of the commodity which holders (or producers) of the product stand willing to sell within the specified period at varying prices. Since for every purchase there must be a sale, the quantity sold must equal the quantity bought. Under pure competition the equilibrium price for the market is indicated by the intersection of the two curves, with the coördinates P_0 and Q_0.

For a commodity where the production process occupies a definite interval of time, the period considered may be taken as so short that the total supply available cannot be changed within the period (as, for example, the

---

[7] Wassily Leontief, Verzögerte Angebotsanpassung und Partielles Gleichgewicht, Zeitschrift für Nationalökonomie, 1934.

[8] R. H. Coase and R. F. Fowler, Bacon Production and the Pig-Cycle in Great Britain, Economica, Vol. II, No. 6, p. 143; also reply by Ruth Cohen and J. D. Barker, and rejoinder by Coase and Fowler, in Vol. II, No. 8, pp. 408-428. 1935.

[9] Archibald MacDonald McIsaac and James G. Smith, Introduction to Economic Analysis, pp. 430-435. 1936.

[10] Here "pure" is used in the same sense as that given by Chamberlin; the market may be imperfect, but if competition is pure, i.e., not monopolistic, the supply and demand curves define the condition of equilibrium. See Edward Chamberlin, The Theory of Monopolistic Competition, pp. 12-29. 1936.

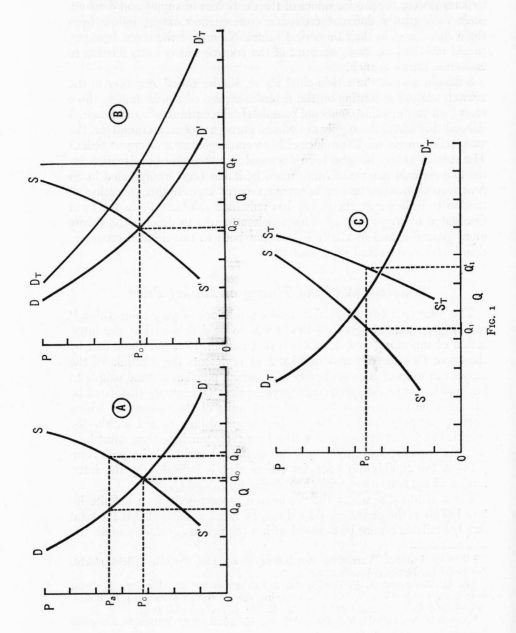

Fig. 1

supply of cotton or potatoes once the year's crop is harvested). The situation under which the current market price is determined for such a commodity is shown in section B of Figure 1. Here the total supply (OQ_t) is represented by the vertical line with its abscissa at Q_t. The demand is represented as before by DD'. As has been shown earlier,[11] under such conditions the reservation demands of holders of the supply may be stated either as a supply curve, SS' of section B of Figure 1, or as part of the total demand curve, $D_tD'_t$; and the equilibrium price is then given either by the intersection of DD' and SS', or of $D_tD'_t$ and Q_t. This method of expressing the current supply curve as part of the demand curve was first suggested by Wicksteed,[12] and was followed by Holbrook Working[13] and other pioneers of price analysis.

When statistical price analysts relate the total supplies on the market in a succession of periods to the prices prevailing in each of those periods, and determine a curve describing that relationship, it is thus the curve of total demand, $D_tD'_t$, which they obtain, rather than the traditional demand curve of economic theory, DD'. If the total supply of the commodity cannot be changed within each period with which they are dealing, in response to the prices of that period, and if they have made adequate statistical allowance for price level, population growth, changes in consumers' income, and other factors which may tend to shift the level or slope of the total demand curve, then their analyses will reveal quite accurately the slope and position of the curve $D_tD'_t$. It is possible to measure the curve DD' separately, or the curve SS', but the determination of each requires a separate study, with a different series of quantity data instead of the total quantity. In the subsequent portions of this paper, the term "demand curve" will be used to refer to the total demand curve, $D_tD'_t$, rather than to the purchasers' demand curve, DD'.

Where a commodity is non-perishable (such as cotton or wheat), a large part of the reservation demand may be for storage rather than for other disposition. In such cases, a low price will tend to reduce the supply for sale in the current period, but to increase the total supply on hand in the next period. At the same time, the price paid in one period may influence the quantity that will be produced in the next succeeding period. These two relations are shown in section C of Figure 1. Here $D_tD'_t$ is the demand curve for the current period, as before. SS', however, is the supply curve for quantity produced in the *next succeeding* period in response to price in the previous period. The horizontal distance from SS' to $S_tS'_t$ represents the carryover of stored supply from the current period to the succeeding period,

---

[11] Mordecai Ezekiel, Statistical Analyses and Laws of Price, Quarterly Journal of Economics, 43, pp. 199-214. 1928.

[12] Philip H. Wicksteed, The Common Sense of Political Economy, pp. 498-544. 1910.

[13] Holbrook Working, Factors Determining the Price of Potatoes in St. Paul and Minneapolis, University of Minnesota, Agricultural Experiment Station, Tech. Bul. 10, p. 17. 1922.

in response to the price of the current period. Thus, for a price of OP_0, new production will supply the quantity OQ_1 in the next period, while the quantity $Q_1Q'_1$ will be carried over in storage, giving a total supply of OQ'_1. This total supply in the subsequent season, in response to the prevailing price in the current season, is given by the total supply curve $S_tS'_t$. Where the negative variation in carryover in response to price is larger than the positive variation in production in response to price, the total supply curve may even be negative in slope, rather than positive as usually assumed. Even when this occurs, however, the total demand curve, composed of the two negative elements of buyers' demand and sellers' reservation demands, will always be more elastic than the total supply curve, composed of the negative element of carryover and the positive element of newly-produced supply. When the term "supply curve" is used hereafter in this paper, it will be the curve of total supply, $S_tS'_t$, which is thus designated.

Restatement of the Theory of Normal Price

The normal price is that price at which the market price would tend to settle over a period of time long enough to bring quantities demanded (by purchasers) and quantities produced into an equilibrium. Traditional theory assumes that under static conditions (and under pure competition) this equilibrium would tend to be reëstablished, following any accidental disturbance. For those commodities where there is an appreciable time interval between a change in price and the change in production in response to that change in price, the cobweb theorem shows that the series of reactions may be quite complex.

The upper portion of Fig. 2 shows the relations between demand and subsequent supply for the special case of a commodity where a change in price in one period does not affect production until the next period but does completely determine supply in that period. The (total) demand curve is represented by $D_tD'_t$; it shows the schedule of prices received in period 1 for varying supplies available in period 1. The (total) supply curve is represented by $S_tS'_t$; it shows the schedule of quantities available in period 2 for varying prices paid in period 1.

Altho this figure is drawn in two dimensions—prices and quantities—it sets forth the relations of three variables. In the case of a current market, quantity bought must equal the quantity sold, for both quantities relate to the same period and are identical. In Figure 2, however, this identity no longer holds. OQ_1 is the quantity which sets the price in period 1; OQ_2 is the quantity (in period 2) called forth by that price. Altho only one price—P_1—is involved, two distinct and different quantities are represented—OQ_1 and OQ_2—and there is no *mathematical* reason why they must be identical. Instead, the cobweb theory reveals the series of reactions which may result from such situations, and demonstrates how and under what conditions equilibrium may be established. Since the two curves of Figure

2 exist in different time dimensions, they are not drawn intersecting, but rather lapping over one another without real contact.

The "Cobweb Theory"

The phases of the cobweb theory which have already been stated by others may first be briefly summarized:

CASE 1, CONTINUOUS FLUCTUATION

In the lower portion of Figure 2, the series of reactions is portrayed for the curves shown in the upper portion of the figure. The quantity in the initial period (Q_1) is large, producing a relatively low price where it intersects the demand curve, at P_1. This low price, intersecting the supply curve, calls forth in the next period a relatively short supply, Q_2. This short supply gives a high price, P_2, where it intersects the supply curve. This high price calls forth a corresponding increased production, Q_3, in the third period, with a corresponding low price, P_3. Since this low price in the third period is identical with that in the first, the production and price in the fourth, fifth, and subsequent periods will continue to rotate around the path Q_2, P_2, Q_3, P_3, etc. As long as price is completely determined by the current supply, and supply is completely determined by the preceding price, fluctuation in price and production will continue in this unchanging pattern indefinitely, without an equilibrium being approached or reached. This is true in this particular case because the demand curve is the exact reverse of the supply curve, so that at their overlap each has the same elasticity. This case has been designated the "case of continuous fluctuations."

CASE 2, DIVERGENT FLUCTUATION

Where the elasticity of supply is greater than the elasticity of demand, the series of reactions works out as shown in the upper portion of Fig. 3. Starting with the moderately large supply, Q_1, and the corresponding price, P_1, the series of reactions is traced by the dotted line. In the second period, there is a moderately reduced supply, Q_2, with the corresponding higher price, P_2. This high price calls forth a considerable increase in supply, Q_3, in the third period, with a resulting material reduction in price, to P_3. This is followed by a sharp reduction in quantity produced in the next period to Q_4, with a corresponding very high price, P_4. The fifth period sees a still greater expansion in supply to Q_5, etc. Under these conditions the situation might continue to grow more and more unstable, until price fell to absolute zero, or production was completely abandoned, or a limit was reached to available resources (where the elasticity of supply would change) so that production could no longer expand. The case has been designated the "case of divergent fluctuation."

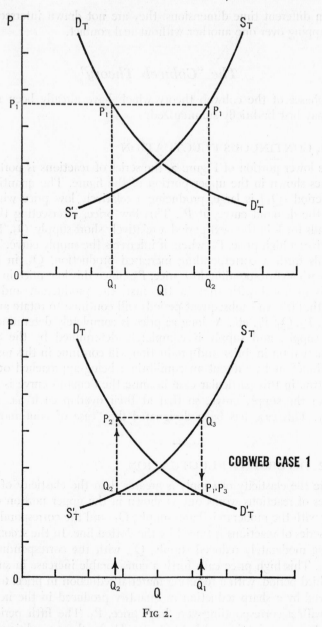

COBWEB CASE 1

FIG 2.

CASE 3, CONVERGENT FLUCTUATION

The reverse situation, with supply less elastic than demand, is shown in the lower portion of Figure 3. Starting with a large supply and low price in the first period, P_1, there would be a very short supply and high price, Q_2 and P_2, in the second period. Production would expand

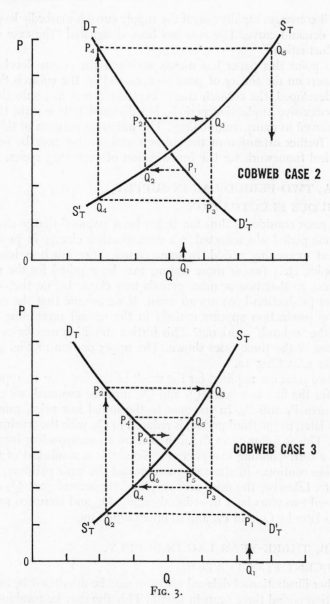

FIG. 3.

again in the third period, to Q_3, but to a smaller production than that in the first period. This would set a moderately low price, P_3, in the third period, with a moderate reduction to Q_4 in the fourth period; and a moderately high price, P_4. Continuing through Q_5, P_5, and Q_6 and P_6, production and price approach more and more closely to the equilibrium condition where no further changes would occur. Of the three cases considered thus far, only this one behaves in the manner assumed by equilibrium theory;

and even it converges rapidly only if the supply curve is markedly less elastic than the demand curve. The case has been designated "the case of convergent fluctuation."

To this point this paper has merely reviewed the points developed in earlier papers on the theory of price analysis and on the cobweb theory.[14] As thus developed, the cobweb theory explains swings in production and price in successive production periods, but does not fully explain the long cycles observed in many commodities. The following portions of this paper present a further extension of the cobweb analysis that may be useful as a theoretical framework for the investigation of such long cycles.

CASE 1A, TWO-PERIOD LAG IN SUPPLY, CONTINUOUS FLUCTUATION

In the cases considered thus far, it has been assumed that a change of price in one period was reflected in a corresponding change in production in the next succeeding period. In some commodities (such as hogs, beef cattle, apples, etc.) two or more seasons may be required for the production process, so that two or more periods may elapse before the effect of price upon production becomes apparent. If we assume that the effect of price upon production appears entirely in the second succeeding period, how will the "cobweb" work out? This further condition may be examined for any one of the three cases shown. The upper portion of Fig. 4 shows it for Case 1, as Case 1a.

Since two years are required for the result of the first year to appear, the supplies for the first two years, Q_1 and Q_2, must be assumed, with the resulting prices P_1 and P_2. In response to the initial low price, production two years later, in the third period, is reduced to Q_3, with the resulting high price, P_3. This is followed in the fifth year by a corresponding increase to Q_5, with a corresponding low price, P_5. Since this is a subclass of Case 1, the reaction continues in alternate years around the same pathway, P_5, Q_7; P_7, Q_9; etc. Likewise, the price and supply of the second year, Q_2 and P_2, are followed two years later by reduced supply, Q_4, and increased price, P_4; four years later by Q_6 and P_6, and so on *ad infinitum*.

CASE 3B, THREE-YEAR LAG IN SUPPLY, CONVERGENT FLUCTUATION

A further illustration of delayed response may be developed by assuming a production period three years in length. This also may be combined with any of the three original cases. Applying it to the third case, results are secured as shown in the lower portion of Figure 4, as Case 3b.

Here three initial supplies are assumed: Q_1, very small; Q_2, moderately

---

[14] Leontief, loc. cit., has shown that in cases where the supply curve and the demand curve are of erratic shape, with marked changes in elasticity along one or both curves, the cobweb reaction may be convergent at some points on the curves, and divergent at others. Such cases are a mixture of the three simple types summarized here.

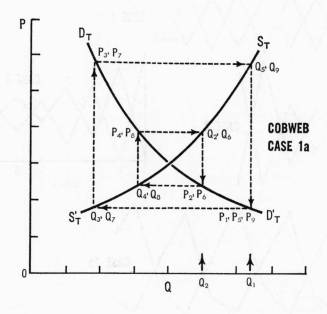

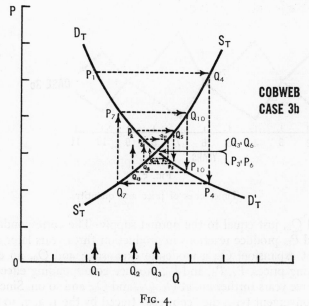

FIG. 4.

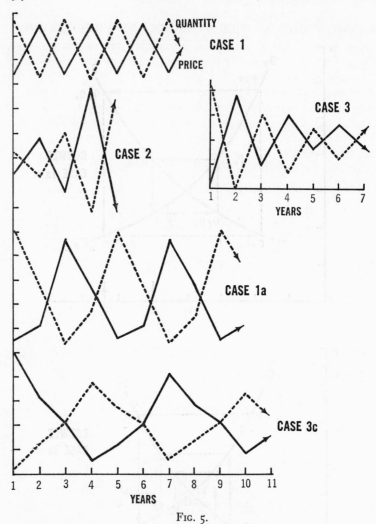

Time series of price and quantity.

small; and Q_3, just equal to the normal supply. The corresponding prices, P_1, P_2, and P_3, produce reactions in production three years later as shown: Q_4, a great expansion; Q_5, a moderate expansion; and Q_6, no expansion. The resulting prices, P_4, P_5, and P_6, produce corresponding effects on production three years further on, at Q_7, Q_8, and Q_9; and so on. Since the case is of the convergent type, the "cobwebs" traced by the 1, 4, 7, 10 series and the 2, 5, 8, 11 series converge slowly, while the 3, 6, 9 series, starting at equilibrium, remains there.

Various other combinations could be developed by assuming even longer periods of response, or by making other combinations with the three basic cases.

THE TIME SERIES TRACED BY PRICE AND PRODUCTION

A time-series chart of prices and production in the successive periods shown in Figs. 2 to 4 reveals more clearly the cyclical character of the resulting processes, as shown in Fig. 5. Cases 1, 2, and 3, with a one-year lag in response, all produce two-year cycles. The continuous, divergent, and convergent character of the three cases is clearly evident, both in production and in price. Case 1a, with a two-year lag in production, has a four-year period from peak to peak; and Case 3c, with a three-year lag, a six-year period. The continuous character of the cycle in Case 1a, and the slow convergence of the cycle in Case 3c, are also apparent.

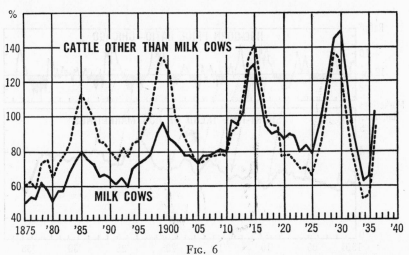

FIG. 6

Purchasing power per head of milk cows and cattle other than milk cows, 1875 to date. (Index numbers [1910–14 = 100].)

While it is evident that these synthetic time series have been constructed under highly rigid assumptions, it is interesting to compare them with some actual price and production cycles, as shown in Fig. [6 and] 7. [Fig. 6 shows the prices of cows and cattle corrected for changes in wholesale prices;] Fig. 7, hog prices stated as a ratio to the price of corn, that is, the number of bushels of corn that can be bought with a hundred pounds of hogs. The changes in the adjusted prices of cattle and milk cows both reflect the underlying cycle in cattle numbers. The similarities are evident; it is also apparent that the actual cycles are more irregular, both in length and in shape, than are the cycles based upon the fixed periods of the theory.

Limitations of the Cobweb Theory

The cobweb theory can apply exactly only to commodities which fulfill three conditions: (1) where production is completely determined by the producers' response to price, under conditions of pure competition (where the producer bases plans for future production on the assumption present prices will continue, and that his own production plans will not affect the market); (2) where the time needed for production requires at least one full period before production can be changed, once the plans are made; and (3) where the price is set by the supply available. Obviously commodities where either price or production is set by administrative decisions (i.e., where monopolistic competition prevails), or where production can respond almost immediately to changed demands, cannot be expected to show the cobweb reaction.

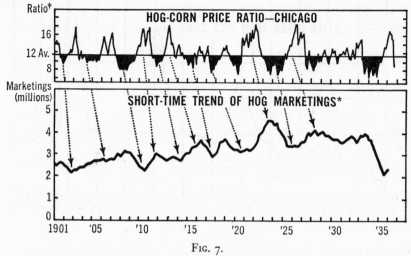

FIG. 7.

Hog-corn price ratios and hog marketings.

Even for the commodities which approximately fulfill the assumptions, however, the theory must be limited. In many commodities farmers can do little to increase their future production, once they have made their initial commitment in acres seeded or in animals bred. But altho they cannot increase, they can reduce at any time until the product is finally marketed, by plowing up portions of the crop or letting it go unharvested, by slaughtering breeding stock, or by slaughtering pigs young instead of fattening them. There is thus in practice some elasticity of response left, on the downward side at least.

A further difficulty arises from the fact that few commodities show clearly marked one-period, two-period, or three-period supply reactions. In many farm commodities, changes in acreage are partly influenced by prices of the preceding year, and partly by those of two years before. In other commodities, such as hogs, not only the price of the commodity itself, but the price of raw materials for its production, such as corn, may be equally important.[15]

An even more serious limitation is that imposed by natural conditions affecting production. Crop production is dependent upon yield per acre as well as acreage; and yields are greatly influenced by the weather. In the past, yields and acreage have been about equally important in influencing cotton production, but yield changes have been far more important than acreage changes in corn. In other crops, such as tobacco, acreage varies much more than yield.[16] Variability in yield may result in a very large crop when acreage has been sharply reduced, or vice versa.

Unusual weather may occasionally change what would otherwise be a large crop to a normal one, and so restore prices to a point where subsequent variation will be slight—until another abnormal yield is secured. Most of the time, however, natural variations may tend to result in unduly high or unduly low production, and thus set a new cycle of response in reaction. Even in commodities which follow the convergent pattern, the actual cycles may be quite similar to those of either of the other types, if abnormally large or small crops occur frequently enough to cause a marked departure from normal and to start again a long series of convergent cycles before stability is again approached. The combination of "cobweb" reactions with occasional crop disasters or gluts may be sufficient to produce recurring cyclical changes in production and prices, rather than stability, as the normal situation over a considerable number of commodities.

Another difficulty arises from the fact that actually production may not swing from very high to very low, even with a one-year response. Analyses of acreage response for various crops show that there is a limit to the per cent farmers will increase their acreage in any single year, so that even with a one-year response period, several years of successive increase in acreage may be required before very high prices are reflected in very high production. A very large contraction in acreage can be made in a single year, however, so that on the down side a single year of very low prices may be followed by a great contraction in acreage. Similarly, in industries producing products with a long life, such as ships or houses, price is not set by the current production, but by current production added to the existing stock, and the current production may be quite small compared to that existing supply. In such cases price affects subsequent *additions to* supply, but *total supply* affects the price. The cobweb theory would need to be further extended and modified to apply to such cases.

Finally, there is no commodity for which the third condition—that the supply alone sets the price—is completely fulfilled. There are many

---

[15] Louis H. Bean, "The Farmers' Response to Price," Jour. Farm Econ., XI, pp. 368-385, especially page 385. July, 1929.

[16] Louis H. Bean, "Some Limitations to the Control of Agricultural Production in the United States," American Coöperation, American Institute of Coöperation, 1932, pp. 461-465.

commodities, especially farm products, whose prices ordinarily show larger variations due to changes in supply than to all other influences combined; yet their prices are also influenced by changes in the supply of competing products, changes in the prosperity or income of consumers, and changes in institutional factors affecting their market, such as tariff quotas, freight rates, weather conditions, and even style changes. Under unusual conditions, as during the years from 1931 to 1934, these forces which shift the position of the demand curve may far outweigh changes in supply as determinants of commodity prices, even for articles such as potatoes where a slight change in supply produces a disproportionately large change in price. In between periods of great economic upheaval, as from 1900 to 1913, or from 1922 to 1929, these shifts in demand may be relatively slight or regular, and it is during such periods that any underlying tendencies to cyclical reactions in individual products would be most clearly revealed.

Not All Commodity Cycles Are "Cobwebs"

Not all cyclical phenomena in individual industries are traceable to the "cobweb reaction." In durable or semidurable goods, the average length of service of the equipment, and the bunching of replacements in recurring periods, may give rise to a separate cyclical phenomenon which has been called "the replacement cycle." In producers' goods, especially in producers' goods several steps removed from the final product, such as in machine tools or die making, the demand for the producers' goods may appear only when production of consumers' goods is increasing, and may disappear entirely when demand for the final product is stable. Similarly, demand for machinery to make the machines to make the final product may appear only when the demand for the final product is increasing at an increasing rate.[17] The derived character of the demand for producers' goods may thus give rise to cyclical phenomena in producers' goods' industries of a quite different character. Many recurring cycles in commodity prices may thus be found to be due to causes other than the cobweb reaction. The cobweb theorem as summarized here should be used as an hypothesis in studying the interactions of supply and demand only for those commodities whose conditions of pricing and production satisfy the special assumptions on which it is based, not as a blanket explanation of all industrial cycles.

Equilibrium Economics in the Light of the Cobweb Theory

The limitations just discussed apply not to the cobweb theory as theory, but to the range within which it is a valid hypothesis. If we assume that, despite these limitations, the cobweb explanation will prove to be

---

[17] J. M. Clark, "Business Acceleration and the Law of Demand; a technical factor in economic cycles," Journal of Political Economy, March 1917; Ragnar Frisch, "The Inter-relation between Capital Production and Consumer-Taking," Jour. of Pol. Econ., October 1931, also replies by J. M. Clark in December 1931 and October 1932 issues.

significant for many commodities, we may then ask how this theory affects economic theory as a whole.

Classical economic theory rests upon the assumption that price and production, if disturbed from their equilibrium, tend to gravitate back toward that normal. The cobweb theory demonstrates that, even under static conditions, this result will not necessarily follow. On the contrary, prices and production of some commodities might tend to fluctuate indefinitely, or even to diverge further and further from equilibrium.

The equilibrium concept lies at the heart of classic theory. If prices and production do not converge rapidly to an equilibrium, then each industry may recurringly attract to it more labor and investment than it can use to advantage, and may leave that labor and equipment only partly utilized much of the time. In a series of industries, all showing individual cycles of the "cobweb" type, at any one time some will be operating at full capacity, or above the equilibrium point; others will be operating below the equilibrium point, at far below capacity; while others will be operating near the equilibrium point, but below the capacity installed at their recurring periods of over-expansion. For the whole series of industries combined, the installed capacity will materially exceed the portion that is in use at any one time; and the workers, trained for service in individual industries and prevented by various frictions from shifting readily into other industries, will always be partly unemployed. If many industries thus tend to develop —for occasional use—more labor and equipment than they need for normal output, labor and capital as a whole will never be fully utilized. If many commodities are chronically varying *above* and *below* their individual equilibria, then the economic system will never organize all its resources for the most effective use, but will always be operating below the total installed capacity and with more or less unemployment. Even under the conditions of pure competition and static demand and supply, there is thus no "automatic self-regulating mechanism," which can provide full utilization of resources. Unemployment, excess capacity, and the wasteful use of resources may occur even when all the competitive assumptions are fulfilled. If enough commodities follow the cobweb form of reaction, competitive readjustments may fail notably to reach the most productive employment of resources.[18]

In seeking to explain the persistent existence of unemployment and excess capacities, modern economists have laid increasing emphasis on the failure of our economic society to provide the competition assumed in traditional theory, and have turned to the new theory of imperfect or monopolistic competition, or to examination of the balance between savings and the need for new investment,[19] as theoretical explanations of the existing situation. From the foregoing discussion, however, it appears that

---

[18] For a different approach to under-utilization of resources, note Alvin H. Hansen, Mr. Keynes on Underemployment Equilibrium, Jour. Pol. Econ., XLIV, p. 667, 1936.

[19] John Maynard Keynes, General Theory of Employment, Interest and Money.

even in those areas of the economic system where reasonably effective pure competition still prevails, cobweb cycles may prevent the system from reaching its most effective utilization of resources. Where competition is absent or monopolistic, we must study the other ways in which production and price are controlled; where pure competition is present, we must examine the mechanism and sequence of price and production reactions to determine whether they do work effectively toward an optimum adjustment.

✕ ❁ ✕

FOR FURTHER READING

▄▄▄

Since Wesley Mitchell is considered by all as the father of the business cycle concept, the reader should examine his first book on the subject, written in 1913: *Business Cycles* (Berkeley, Calif.: University of California Press). He should undoubtedly read the classic *Business Cycles: The Problem and Its Setting* (New York: National Bureau of Economic Research, 1927), which to this day remains one of the most important books ever written on the subject. The concept of long cycles promulgated by Kondratieff has more recently been sharply challenged by George Garvey in his "Kondratieff's Theory of Long Cycles," published in *The Review of Economic Statistics*, XVI (November, 1943). However, the Kondratieff philosophy is being carried forward in the postwar era by Moses Abramovitz of Stanford University and the NBER, who, unfortunately, has not yet published his long awaited book on the subject. However, some preliminary findings are contained in his testimony before the Joint Economic Committee in their major study of *Employment, Growth and Price Levels* (86th Congress, 1st Session, 1959). Close attention should also be given to the classic study by Edwin Frickey on *Economic Fluctuations in the United States* (Cambridge: Harvard University Press, 1942), which raises a number of penetrating questions about the validity of long-run economic changes as statistically measured. Another major contribution to the study of long-term economic change is the prewar work of Arthur Burns on *Production Trends in the United States Since 1870* (New York: National Bureau of Economic Research, 1934). Joseph Schumpeter's monumental work on *Business Cycles* (New York: McGraw-Hill, 1939) is a work too long neglected by students of the subject. The construction trend has been considered also by Clarence D. Long in his *Building Cycles and the Theory of Investment* (Princeton: Princeton University Press, 1940). The most important book on residential construction written in the postwar period is that by Leo Grebler, David M. Blank, and Louis Winnick, *Capital Formation in Residential Real Estate* (Princeton: Princeton University Press, 1956). This study contrasts postwar home-building fluctuations against the background of a longer perspective based upon a major breakthrough in empirical research. No student of inventories can overlook the first important empirical study by Moses Abramovitz on *Inventories and Business Cycles* (New York: National Bureau of Economic Research, 1950). More recently, the Joint Economic Committee has done an important service to the economics profession by publishing three volumes on inventories which summarize the current state of theory and statistical evidence. The series includes *Postwar Fluctuations in Business Inventories; Causative Factors in Movements of Business Inventories;* and *Inventory Fluctuations and Economic Instability.* All the important contributions, including an updating of Abramovitz' work, are included. Finally, the subject of seasonal fluctuations, usually neglected by most students of the subject of business fluctuations, is still best covered in a book written almost thirty years ago and very much worth reading today, namely, Simon Kuznets' *Seasonal Variations in Industry and Trade* (New York: National Bureau of Economic Research, 1933).

PART
II

Empirical Analysis of

Business Cycles

INTRODUCTION

Since the end of World War I, there have been nine depressions or recessions: three in the 1920's, one large one in the 1930's ("officially," i.e., according to the widely accepted dates promulgated by the National Bureau of Economic Research, the leading organization studying business cycles, the 1937–38 cycle is a separate phenomenon), and four since the end of World War II—1948–49, 1953–54, 1957–58, and 1960–61. Of course, cycles occurred prior to World War I, and a comprehension of cyclical experience in the nineteenth century contributes immeasurably to an understanding of today's world. We learn from the economic historian that almost all of the problems we face in the 1960's had their counterpart in earlier times. The script is mostly the same; only the actors have changed their names and costumes.

The National Bureau of Economic Research has directly or indirectly promoted a vast outpouring of statistical studies on the business cycle. The general "reference cycle," established by the National Bureau, and the comparisons of specific cycles in a multitude of economic series, such as prices, wages, costs, output, finance and credit, inventories, orders, employment, sales, and profits, comprise the building blocks of empirical business cycle analysis. The United States Government itself has officially recognized the work of the National Bureau in the Commerce Department's monthly publication, *Business Cycle Developments*, started in October 1961. The reader, with the aid of this publication, can now make contemporaneous judgments as to the state of the business cycle and compare current cycle movements with the historical record.

Nonetheless, empirical analysis of the business cycle must proceed beyond the measurement of cycles in a wide variety of time series. Thus, the development of the social accounts, national income and output in particular, has proved essential in bettering our understanding of the ups and downs in the national economy. By distinguishing the important agents of economic change, namely, consumers, businessmen, foreign traders, and government, the national accounts have added a new dimension to the study of business cycles. This important advancement permits the researcher, by structuring the economy into its basic components, to concentrate on strategic factors and thereby avoid being overwhelmed by a multiplicity of facts. Rather than study a thousand or more time series and combine them into a diffusion index, the national accounts focus attention on the key elements which generate cyclical oscillations.

Furthermore, interrelationships among the expenditure agents may be better appraised in the context of business cycle theory with the aid of the rich body of data now available in the national accounts. For example, cycles in personal income now have a major place in business cycle thinking, as do cycles in consumer spending, which include the relative insensitivity of spending for services and differences in the timing and amplitude of fluctuations in consumer outlays for durables and nondurables. Numerous studies have considered the cyclical relation of income and saving and its difference from the secular or longer-run relationship. The analysis of inventory cycles, over-all and in specific sectors, has enriched our understanding of the general business cycle. Government outlays can dampen or, perhaps, even amplify business fluctuations, so that the government sector itself has an important role in cycle analysis.

In a word, the study of cycles now goes forward far beyond the earlier framework set by Mitchell and Burns at the National Bureau. The linking of facts to theory will provide the major breakthroughs, rather than the mere counting up of a multitude of individual cyclical phenomena. Obviously, the traditional work of the National Bureau will continue apace and will still retain its validity as a foundation for further study. All agree with their dating of business cycles, both historically and in current business analysis, and most economists accept their general scheme for classifying the various stages of the cycle. Clearly, the Bureau continues to advance our knowledge of the indicator approach to cycle measurement. The next step, long overdue, involves the study of the basic forces which make for cyclical change, as well as those which make for economic growth and progress. Further, these studies may highlight the possible conflict between cycle movements and growth. For example, has the dampening of the postwar business cycle resulted in slowing the growth rate? Do we have to experience major cyclical swings in order to obtain a substantial net addition to economic betterment?

Despite the enormous increase in our knowledge of the business cycle, much more empirical work remains to be done. The articles presented below are representative of the various approaches now being used—historical, quantitative-historical, statistical, and that of the National Bureau. They also highlight the gaps in our knowledge: in particular, the role of investment both public and private, and the role of government budgetary policy, as they affect the business cycle.

American Business Cycles,
1865-79[*]

RENDIGS FELS[†]

~~~~~~

Editors' Note

This article traces a series of business cycles in the second half of the nineteenth century and proves once again that there is nothing new under the sun. The mammoth wartime government deficits of the twentieth century had their predecessors during the Civil War; but the aftermath —speculative price booms and postwar depressions—suggests that we have, indeed, learned from history. The value of studying earlier cycles, therefore, lies in the comparison with more recent trends. What was different after World War II from what was the case after the Civil War? For those whose memory of the Great Depression of the 1930's has dimmed or is nonexistent, it may be comforting to learn that there were also great depressions in the nineteenth century, in the 1830's, 1870's, and 1890's. (Perhaps then, too, there were voices explaining depression in terms of secular stagnation.) A century ago, bank panics played a central role in the cycle, agriculture was the major industry, and fluctuations in the railroad industry were critical. Nevertheless, although the terminology and the industrial actors may have changed, a consideration of former cycles cannot fail to improve our understanding of the general phenomenon. It can, for example, help us to appreciate the impact of the new major industries, the changes in the regulation of bank credit, and the role of government intervention. How do the more recent cycles differ from earlier ones? How much have we, in fact, learned with the additions of

[*] From *The American Economic Review*, Vol. XLI, No. 3 (June, 1951), pp. 325-349. Reprinted by permission of *The American Economic Review* and the author.

[†] Professor of Economics, Vanderbilt University. Dr. Fels has written *American Business Cycles, 1865-1897*. Chapel Hill: University of North Carolina Press (1959) and *A Challenge to the American Economy*. Boston: Allyn and Bacon, Inc. (1961).

successive experiences? Obviously, the more cycles we can add to the base of our knowledge, the better can we comprehend the significance and interrelationships among them all.

▰▰▰▰▰▰▰▰▰▰▰▰▰▰▰▰▰▰▰▰▰▰▰▰▰▰▰▰▰▰▰▰▰▰▰▰▰▰▰

❧ The American depression of the 1870's is famous in the minds of economists, being the longest cyclical contraction in American history; yet nowhere in print is there a satisfactory history of this depression and the events leading up to it. The *Review of Economic Statistics* published a lengthy factual account in 1920, but it is devoid of cyclical analysis and rendered out-of-date by recent statistical research.[1] Schumpeter has given his interpretation of the period but not a connected history.[2] Arthur Auble has dealt with the depression of the 1870's in his doctoral thesis, which was not published.[3] Mitchell's *Gold, Prices and Wages* is primarily a collection of statistics; he never completed the analysis for which the statistics were intended.[4] Save for isolated references and studies of particular problems, this completes the roster of noteworthy attempts to deal with this chapter of cyclical history.

1. *General Characteristics of the Period*

The period 1865–79 forms a natural unit for study. It roughly encompasses both a major business cycle and what Isard calls a transport-business cycle. Moreover, because it comprises the era, exclusive of the Civil War, in which the United States had an inconvertible paper currency, cyclical influences from international trade were different from those in the years before and after.

Gordon has defined major cycles as consisting of (1) upswings in which long-term investment opportunities are favorable so that downward spirals are minor and (2) downswings in which long-term investment opportunities have become seriously impaired so that cumulative expansions are weak and rare. In contrast, minor cycles are dominated by inventories, short-term credit conditions, short-run price-cost maladjustments, etc.[5]

[1] Warren M. Persons, Pierson M. Tuttle, and Edwin Frickey, "Business and Financial Conditions Following the Civil War in the United States," *Review of Economic Statistics, Supplement,* July, 1920.

[2] Joseph A. Schumpeter, *Business Cycles* (New York, 1939), Vol. I, pp. 335-40.

[3] Arthur G. Auble, *The Depressions of 1873 and 1882 in the United States* (Harvard University Library, 1949). Another dissertation, this one mimeoprinted, is Ernest R. McCartney, *Crisis of 1873* (Minneapolis, 1935).

[4] Wesley C. Mitchell, *Gold, Prices and Wages Under the Greenback Standard* (Berkeley, Calif.), 1908.

[5] Robert A. Gordon, "Cyclical Experience in the Interwar Period: The Investment Boom of the 'Twenties," unpublished paper presented to the Universities-National Bureau Conference on Business Cycle Research, November 25-27, 1949, pp. 3-10.

Let us make the hypothesis that long-term investment opportunities were favorable from 1865 to 1873 and that they became seriously impaired in the latter year and did not recover until about 1879. If the hypothesis is true, the period 1865-79 forms a major cycle.[6] This sounds reasonable inasmuch as business was generally prosperous from the end of the Civil War through the boom of the early 'seventies (except for two recessions), and was decidedly depressed from the panic of 1873 until 1879. To some extent, the hypothesis will be on trial throughout this article, but some evidence of a general nature is best discussed at once.

In 1865 the stage was set for one of the bursts of innovating activity such as Schumpeter described. During the latter half of the nineteenth century, railroad building was one of the most important forms of investment activity. Yet, on account of depression and strife, by the close of the Civil War it had been nearly a decade since any considerable railroad building had been done. Meanwhile, population was growing rapidly. The area west of the Mississippi, hitherto virtually untouched by the railroads, was ripe for development. A modern investor might have shuddered at the risks involved in building through the sparsely populated West, but in those days of rampant free enterprise, bonds could generally be sold at home or abroad provided the interest rate was high enough. In many cases, the government subsidized railroad building. In addition, the networks east of the Mississippi needed to be filled in. In such favorable conditions, a burst of innovating activity rose to a climax in the early 'seventies, then collapsed.

Conditions were also favorable for investment in housing. There is evidence of a housing shortage at the end of the Civil War,[7] and the close of hostilities greatly accelerated immigration. Hence it is hardly surprising that the building cycle also rose to a peak in the early 'seventies.

We may conclude that the long-term outlook for investment was favorable in the fields of railroad and housing construction (and very likely in other kinds of construction too). But Terborgh has discounted the importance of single great industries, pointing out that steam railroads accounted for only one-eighth of total investment in the decade of the 1870's; and Burns and Mitchell reached negative conclusions on

---

[6] This formulation differs only in detail from the findings of Hansen, Schumpeter, and Isard. Hansen dates major depressions 1864, 1873, and 1883 (presumably the years mentioned are the peaks of the preceding prosperities), which implies a major cycle, counting from trough to trough, from sometime after the Civil War, say 1867, until the end of the depression of the 'seventies, say 1878 or 1879. (Alvin H. Hansen, *Fiscal Policy and Business Cycles* [New York, 1941], pp. 23-24.) Schumpeter dated a "Juglar Cycle" from the beginning of 1870 to the middle of 1879 (*op. cit.*, p. 396). Isard found troughs in the seven series that interested him scattered in the early 1860's and again in the years 1875-79. (Walter Isard, "A Neglected Cycle: The Transport-Building Cycle," *Review of Economic Statistics*, November, 1942, pp. 149-158.)

[7] David A. Wells, *Report of the U. S. Special Commissioner of Revenue*, 41st Congress, 2nd Session, House Ex. Doc. No. 27, Dec., 1869, pp. xxiii-xxiv.

TABLE 1—PRODUCTION AND MONETARY STATISTICS FOR THE UNITED STATES, 1865–1879

(Calendar years except as otherwise noted)

	1865	1866	1867	1868	1869	1870	1871	1872	1873	1874	1875	1876	1877	1878	1879
Production Series															
1. Manufacturing	17	21	22	23	25	25	26	31	30	29	28	28	30	32	36
2. Transportation and Communication	16	16	17	18	20	21	23	25	27	28	27	27	27	28	32
3. Mining						5.5	6.7	7.5	8.7	8.4	8.4	8.3	9.8	10.1	11.5
4. Railroad Miles Built															
a. ICC	1,177	1,716	2,249	3,179	4,615	6,078	7,379	5,870	4,097	2,117	1,711	2,712	2,274	2,665	4,809
b. 10th Census	819	1,404	2,541	2,468	4,103	5,658	6,660	7,439	5,217	2,584	1,606	2,575	2,280	2,428	5,006
5. Building Construction	22	29	38	47	54	52	62	52	47	30	29	25	26	19	19
6. Crop Production		25.5	28.0	30.5	31.5	35.0	35.0	39.0	36.0	37.0	45.5	44.5	49.0	51.5	54.5
Monetary Series															
7. Wholesale Prices	132	116	105	98	94	87	83	85	84	81	78	72	68	62	59
8. Surplus of Federal Government ($000,000, fiscal years)	964	37	133	28	48	102	91	97	43	2	13	29	40	21	7
9. Liabilities of Business Failures ($000,000)	18	54	97	64	75	88	85	121	228	155	201	191	191	234	98
10. Gold Premium (per cent)	57.3	40.9	38.2	39.7	33.0	14.9	11.7	12.4	13.8	11.2	14.9	11.5	4.8	0.8	0.0
11. Net Capital Imports ($000,000, fiscal years)	75	70	74	76	122	130	100	112	145	51	20	−50	−100	−150	
12. Increase in RR Capital ($000,000)				697	172	436	188	495	625	437	436	−190	338	−34	100
13. Currency in Circulation ($000,000, June 30)	1,084	940	859	772	741	775	794	829	838	864	834	807	814	820	819

Sources:

1. *Manufacturing:* Edwin Frickey, *Production in the United States, 1860–1914* (Cambridge, Mass., 1947), p. 54. (1899=100)

2. *Transportation and Communication: Ibid.,* p. 117. (1899=100)

3. *Mining:* Warren M. Persons, *Forecasting Business Cycles* (New York, 1931), pp. 170–71. (1909–13=100)

4. *Railroad Miles Built:*

a. *ICC:* U. S. Bureau of the Census, *Historical Statistics of the United States, 1789–1945* (Washington, 1949), p. 200, first differences of Column 1. (The figures thus obtained are net of abandonments.) The Bureau of the Census took its figures from Interstate Commerce Commission, Statement No. 32151, *Railway Statistics Before 1890* (Washington, 1932) mimeographed. The ICC's source was the various annual issues of *Poor's Manual of Railroads* from 1869.

b. *10th Census: Tenth Census of the United States* (1883), Vol. IV, p. 290. It is not clear to what extent these figures are net of abandonments. In the source document, "Total Miles [in existence?] on December 31," for each year differs from the preceding year by the exact number (to the second decimal place) of miles built. This seems to imply that "Miles Built" are net of abandonments. However, the total miles in existence on June 30, 1880 are broken down, *ibid.,* p. 292, into 87,569 miles in operation and 232 miles on which operations had been suspended. The latter figure is so small that it is clear the difference between the figures of the ICC (which are net of abandonments; see above) and those of the *Tenth Census* must be ascribed not to a different treatment of abandonments but to a questionnaire sent in 1880 to all railroads then in existence. Presumably the figures are more reliable for later than for earlier years.

5. *Building Construction:* Clarence D. Long, Jr., *Building Cycles and the Theory of Investment* (Princeton, 1940), p. 228. (1920–30=100) The index represents number of new buildings (both residential and non-residential). The number of cities entering into the index varies, so that the figures are not always strictly comparable. For 1865–72 the number of cities is 2; for 1873, 3; for 1874, 4; for 1875–77, 5; for 1878, 6; for 1879, 7.

6. *Crop Production:* C. M. Purves, "New Index of Crop Production in the United States," *The Agricultural Situation,* January 1, 1935, p. 4. (1910–14=100)

7. *Wholesale Prices:* U. S. Bureau of the Census, *Historical Statistics of the United States 1789–1945* (Washington, 1945), p. 234. (1926=100)

8. *Surplus of Federal Gov't: Ibid.,* pp. 296–97.

9. *Liabilities of Business Failures:* U. S. Bureau of Statistics, *Statistical Abstract of the United States, 1907* (Washington, 1908), p. 725.

10. *Gold Premium:* Wesley C. Mitchell, *Gold, Prices and Wages Under the Greenback Standard* (Berkeley, 1908), p. 4. Averages based on the opening, highest, lowest, and closing quotations on each business day.

11. *Net Capital Imports:* Frank D. Graham, "International Trade Under Depreciated Paper. The United States, 1862–79," *Quarterly Journal of Economics,* February, 1922, p. 231. Figures are in gold values. They include long term capital movements only and are "estimates computed from unofficial sources such as the Commercial and Financial Chronicle, Bankers Magazine, London Economist."

12. *Increase in RR Capital: Historical Statistics of the United States, 1789–1945,* p. 201, first differences of column 19. Figures include elevated railways, which, however, were probably less than 1% of the total. "Capital" includes stock, mortgage bonds, equipment obligations, etc.

13. *Currency in Circulation: Ibid.,* p. 274.

the effect of long building cycles on business cycles.[8] We must seek stronger support for our hypothesis.

Hansen has replied to Terborgh that the latter has neglected "the leverage effect of the multiplier and the acceleration principle."[9] The railroads in their expansion may have stimulated investment in the higher stages of production, *e.g.*, steel.

More important still, transportation costs were reduced not only by the building of the new roads but also by the consolidation of the old. The formation of such networks as the Pennsylvania, the New York Central, the Philadelphia and Reading, the Chicago, Burlington and Quincy, the Chicago and Northwestern, and the Milwaukee and St. Paul reduced the inconveniences of frequent tieups and delays, the cost of numerous interchanges of freight in long hauls, the diversity of railroad practices, and irresponsibility of carriers.[10] Such reductions in transportation costs both in the new territories opened up in the West and in the areas already served by railroads in the East presumably stimulated investments not related to railroads. This was particularly the case for housing, for the railroads may be regarded as instrumental in sucking a great wave of immigrants into the country (immigration rose from 180,000 in 1865 to 460,000 in 1873)[11] and relocating the existing population. But it is difficult to believe that it was not also true for manufacturing, which now found new advantageous sites and the opportunity of producing for wider markets.[12] We may tentatively conclude that the long-term investment outlook was generally favorable in the latter 'sixties.

The effect of international trade on business cycles in this period is not clear. The inconvertible paper standard in effect allowed exchange rates to fluctuate freely. The Civil War had partly been financed by printing several hundred million dollars worth of paper money popularly called greenbacks. This forced the government to abandon the gold standard since it could not maintain convertibility between gold and dollars. Nevertheless, it continued to require that import duties be paid in gold, and such gold as the banks held could continue to be counted as part of their reserves. Moreover, the Pacific Coast never abandoned the gold standard. About $25 millions of gold remained in active circulation there. Officially, the exchange rate between the dollar and foreign gold currencies such as the English pound sterling remained unchanged, but as gold could be bought for greenbacks only at premium which varied

---

[8] George Terborgh, *The Bogey of Economic Maturity* (Chicago, 1945), p. 84; Arthur F. Burns and Wesley C. Mitchell, *Measuring Business Cycles* (New York, 1946), pp. 418-27.

[9] Alvin H. Hansen, *Economic Policy and Full Employment* (New York, 1947), p. 303.

[10] Walter Isard, *The Economic Dynamics of Transport Technology*, unpublished doctoral dissertation (Harvard University Library, 1943), pp. 61-63.

[11] Harry Jerome, *Migration and Business Cycles* (New York, 1926), p. 35.

[12] Isard, *Dynamics*, pp. 65-67. See also pp. 22-27. This kind of argument is part of Schumpeter's theory of the cycle.

from one transaction to the next, the exchange rate in reality fluctuated freely.

An increased demand for the exports of a gold standard country— say because harvests are poor abroad—tends to increase prices and incomes both because prices and incomes in the export trades go up, with multiplier effects, and because gold imports are increased (or exports decreased), thus increasing the money supply and bank reserves.[13] Eventually, increased incomes and prices mean more imports and less exports, thus bringing trade back into balance; but in the meantime, an expansive impulse has been imparted which will accelerate a concomitant cyclical expansion or retard a cyclical contraction.

Under freely fluctuating exchanges, however, an increased demand for exports merely increases the exchange rate or, in this case, lowers the gold premium. There is no significant way in which the domestic money supply or aggregate income can be affected. Except for capital transactions, the business cycles of the domestic economy are largely isolated from international trade. This conclusion must be qualified, however, because the United States retained the use of gold for some purposes during the greenback era, particularly for international trade. To the extent that Americans were willing to absorb gold, increased exports could be expansionary; and to the extent that they were willing to give up gold, increased imports could be deflationary. However, annual fluctuations in the U. S. gold stock were small.[14] It seems safe to conclude that the paper currency greatly blunted the effect of international trade in goods and services on business cycles.

Capital transactions are a different matter.[15] With freely fluctuating exchanges, capital imports are deflationary. The supply of goods in the domestic economy is increased, either because the capital imports are spent abroad or because they lower the gold premium, thus increasing imports of goods and services and decreasing exports. At the same time, the supply of money is unchanged. Therefore, there is downward pressure on prices. In a similar manner, it can be shown that capital exports are inflationary.

No figures are available on short-term capital movements. Between 1865 and 1873, the United States imported long-term capital. With the onset of depression, capital imports ceased and repayments began. It seems, however, that the deflationary effects in the first period were largely

[13] The gold flow part of the gold standard mechanism is now out of favor. See Lloyd A. Metzler, "The Theory of International Trade," in Howard S. Ellis, ed., *A Survey of Contemporary Economics* (Philadelphia, 1948), pp. 216 and 220. I shall not here repeat my defense of gold flows, which has been published as a note, "Gold and International Equilibrium," in the *American Economic Review*, December, 1949, pp. 1281-83.

[14] U. S. Bureau of the Census, *Statistical Abstract of the United States, 1922* (Washington, 1923), p. 512. As the figures do not include bullion outside the vaults of the Treasury, they do not necessarily tell the whole story.

[15] This paragraph summarizes the theoretical discussion in Gottfried Haberler, *Prosperity and Depression*, 3rd ed. (Lake Success, 1946), pp. 446-51.

postponed, because the capital imports were used mainly to finance railroad building. As the capital market in the United States was still in an embryonic stage, it is reasonable to assume that without capital imports railroad construction would have been cut down by a corresponding amount, so that the imported capital for the time being increased demand as well as supply. In the longer run, the railroads could have been financed out of domestic funds. By using up investment opportunities so fast, the capital movement accentuated the depression of the 'seventies. By then, however, repayments had become substantial. Accordingly, no large net cyclical influence need be ascribed to long-term international capital transactions.

Largely cut off from foreign influences, wholesale prices fell every year except one between 1865 and 1879, the total decline amounting to 55% (or to get away from the precipitate decline immediately after the Civil War, they fell 45% from 1867 to 1879). For agricultural products, the chief reason is not far to seek. Under the influence of a population increase of 32%, the opening up of new areas by the railroads, release of a million soldiers from the Civil War, reconstruction of the South, and a certain amount of mechanization, agricultural output doubled between 1866 and 1878. Had the United States been on the gold standard, international trade would have put a floor under farm prices. With a paper currency, most of the impact of this enormous increase of output fell on the domestic economy. The two-fold result was a fall of domestic prices and a fall in the gold premium as foreigners sought to buy cheap American products. In fact, the gold premium, which was 103% in 1864 and 41% in 1866, disappeared entirely by the end of 1878.

While the steady increase in output indicated that low prices were profitable to many farmers who could obtain cheap land, hardship for some was inevitable. Farms that were marginal in 1865 became submarginal as time went on. Those with heavy debt loads were hard hit; the liquidation wringer they were forced through added to the depression of the 'seventies. Even before the depression, farm troubles were expressing themselves in agitation against the railroads; and there is even evidence of a fall in farm wage rates in the face of a tendency for other wages to show the normal cyclical rise.[16] In the 'seventies, the rapid growth of the grangers was a further expression of agricultural troubles.

The fall of agricultural prices dominated the wholesale price index because (1) farm products enter directly into computation of the index, (2) they serve as raw materials for other industries (for instance, cotton textile prices fell because the price of cotton fell), and (3) falling agricultural prices depressed the gold premium, making imports cheaper. But

---

[16] Frank D. Graham, "International Trade Under Depreciated Paper. The United States, 1862–79," *Quarterly Journal of Economics*, February, 1922, p. 271. The statistics for farm wages are even more unreliable than the general run of statistics for this era. Presumably they indicate not necessarily that farm wages in general fell but only that they fell in certain localities.

there were other reasons why non-agricultural prices fell. Chief among these was the cyclical cumulative contraction following 1873, which reduced wage rates as well as demand. Moreover, between 1865 and 1869, the currency supply contracted. There were also important technological improvements. Reduction of transport costs has already been mentioned. The iron and steel industry, which among other advances started using the Bessemer process at the end of the war, made gains at the expense of England in spite of the appreciation of the greenback.

II. *The Post-Civil War Recession*

At the end of the Civil War, the American economy faced a great problem of readjustment. A federal budget deficit of almost one billion dollars in the fiscal year 1865—perhaps one-seventh of national income—dropped to less than zero in 1866.[17] The wartime speculative boom in wholesale prices collapsed early in 1865 in anticipation of sound finance, and the change necessitated a shift of economic resources which by itself might have been expected to impose a severe strain on the economy. Pig-iron production, for instance, fell from 1,014 thousand long tons in 1864 to 832 in 1865.[18] Another important shift was the release to the working force of one and a half million men who had been directly or indirectly engaged in prosecuting the war.[19] In addition, the working force had to absorb a stream of 300 thousand immigrants in each of the fiscal years 1866 and 1867, compared to 180 thousand in 1865.[20] For one reason or another, the currency supply contracted 30% between 1865 and 1869. As if that were not enough, the South for the time being was economically prostrate. Not until 1878 was the cotton crop to be as large as the 1860 crop.[21]

Great as the needed readjustments were, they are no more impressive than those which were so easily made in the American economy following World War II. But 1945 had three advantages which 1865 lacked—shortages of such modern consumer durables as automobiles and refrigerators, a suppressed inflation that was about to come into the open, and an inflationary export surplus to Europe.[22] Under the circumstances, it is not

[17] For the federal deficit, see Table I. For national income, see Robert F. Martin, *National Income in the United States, 1799–1938* (New York, 1939), p. 6. According to Martin, realized national income in 1869 (the nearest date to 1865 for which estimates can be made) was $6,827 million.

[18] Persons, Tuttle, and Frickey, *op. cit.*, p. 27.

[19] David A. Wells, "The Recent Financial, Industrial and Commercial Experience of the United States: A Curious Chapter in Politico-Economic History," in *Cobden Club Essays, Second Series, 1871–2*, 2nd ed. (London, 1872), p. 491.

[20] Jerome, *Migration and Business Cycles*, p. 35.

[21] *Statistical Abstract of the United States, 1882*, p. 123.

[22] The South in 1865 occupied a position analogous to Western Europe in 1945 (or more accurately, to Germany), but it is doubtful if there was any significant net movement of capital into the South such as might have supported an interregional export surplus for the North. See E. Merton Coulter, *The South During Reconstruction, 1865-1877* (Louisiana State University Press, 1947), *passim*, esp. pp. 10, 20, 148-51, 154, 190-2 and 197.

surprising that instead of a postwar boom, the National Bureau of Economic Research records a cyclical contraction from April 1865 to December 1867.[23] Rather, it is surprising that the reaction was mild. The chief indication of depression was a more rapid fall in wholesale prices than in succeeding years.[24] In only one year, 1867, was the process of cumulative cyclical contraction, as described in business cycle theory, clearly evident.[25] Liabilities of business failures reached $97 million in that year, a figure which, though moderately heavy, was 20% less than in the boom of 1872; New York clearings, which had risen 20% in 1866, in the following year fell below 1865, probably reflecting a decline in the stock market; and Frickey's index of manufacturing production rose less than trend.[26] Here is one more piece of evidence that reconversion adjustments are made easily.

Why was the reaction mild? Balancing the federal budget had nothing like the adverse effect a similar balancing had in 1937, in spite of the relatively greater gap closed. In 1937, the level of activity had become dependent on continued deficit financing. In fiscal 1866, however, disappearance of the deficit merely removed inflationary pressure on prices, allowing them to fall, first because the basis for speculation collapsed and second because output increased. The price decline meant hardship and even liquidation for some, but as long as the existing money supply continued to circulate there was no cause for general contraction.

Another reason for the mild reaction was that investment in building and railroad construction was increasing. According to one estimate, railroad construction increased from 1177 miles in 1865 to 1716 in 1866 and 2249 in 1867. In the latter year, railroad construction was only one-third the mileage of the peak year, 1871, but indirect effects must also be taken into account (see Section I above). Moreover, in the field of building construction, indirect effects from railroad investment were re-enforced by a postwar shortage, so that activity rose in spite of the recession.

And it must be remembered that many of those added to the working force did not seek jobs in industry but went into agriculture, making use of the Homestead Act of 1862 or otherwise acquiring cheap land.

It is more difficult to explain why the 30% contraction of the currency supply between 1865 and 1869 neither caused a severe depression nor pre-

---

[23] Burns and Mitchell, *op. cit.*, p. 78. The dates given in the text above are the peak and trough respectively.

[24] More precisely, the fall was more rapid than that of a straight-line trend fitted to wholesale price data for 1866–1880. Persons, Tuttle and Frickey, *op. cit.*, p. 28.

[25] In fact, Donald W. Gilbert held that there was a "minor revival" in 1866 ("Business Cycles and Municipal Expenditures," *Review of Economic Statistics*, August, 1933, p. 140); and Isaiah Frank thought that an expansion phase began in August 1865 which he was not sure did not continue without interruption until 1869 (Burns and Mitchell, *op. cit.*, p. 111, note 67).

[26] Persons, Tuttle and Frickey, *op. cit.*, p. 39; Edwin Frickey, *Production in the United States, 1860–1914* (Cambridge, Mass.), pp. 54 and 60. The index of manufacturing rose more than trend in 1866.

vented the cyclical expansion of 1868–69. The currency contraction was concentrated primarily on interest-bearing legal-tender notes of the government. These did not circulate significantly, but they added to bank reserves.[27] Absence of trustworthy statistics on state bank deposits makes it impossible to trace the effects of contraction of interest-bearing legal-tenders, but it is significant that the total of state plus national bank notes was a little higher in 1869 than in 1865. Since contraction of bank reserves would affect notes and deposits equally and since the secular trend was to replace notes with deposits rather than the other way round, we may infer that total bank deposits probably did not decline. (This is plausible inasmuch as the banks had large excess reserves at the end of the Civil War;[28] moreover, part of the notes were presumably held by individuals as investments and did not affect bank reserves.) If so, the total money supply (not counting interest-bearing legal tenders as money since they did not circulate) fell perhaps 10% or less over the four years instead of 30%. Even so, currency contraction must have exerted more than a negligible effect.

III. *1867-73*

Under the influence of railroad and building construction, cyclical expansion commenced at the beginning of 1868 and continued, according to the National Bureau, until June of 1869. After that, a mild contraction began. What started recession in the face of a 50% increase in railroad miles built must be a matter of speculation. One possibility is that it originated in financial difficulties. In June, there was a marked money stringency, the call loan rate reaching 44% and never falling below 16%. This was no worse a showing than in November of the preceding year, but inasmuch as call loan money financed the stock market, stock prices declined. Thus the economy had become somewhat vulnerable to contractive forces.

In September, there was a short-lived panic when Jay Gould and Jim

---

[27] *Historical Statistics of the United States*, p. 276; *Banker's Magazine* (New York) August, 1879, pp. 148-150. There was also a great reduction of state bank notes, but it was fully compensated by a rise in national bank notes.

[28] As evidence, although lawful money reserves of national banks declined from $207 millions at the beginning of 1866 to $149 millions in the middle of 1869, loans and discounts rose in the same period from $501 to $686 millions, deposits from $522 to $574 millions, and national bank notes from $276 in 1866 to $292 millions in 1869. (Persons, Tuttle and Frickey, *op. cit.*, pp. 51 and 53; *Historical Statistics of the United States*, p. 276.)

Moreover, the retirement of interest-bearing legal tenders overstates the loss of potential bank reserves. "When the compound-interest notes were finally paid off in 1867, the Banks had influence enough with Congress to procure the passage of a law creating, for their special benefit, 50 millions of temporary loan certificates, payable on demand, but bearing 3 per cent interest, the statute providing that their reserve fund might consist of such certificates." Francis Bowen, *American Political Economy* (New York, 1870), pp. 384-85.

Fisk attempted to corner the gold market. They failed, but they temporarily ran the price of gold up from 132 to 162, demoralizing import and export markets and throwing the commercial world into confusion.[29] Although the *Commercial and Financial Chronicle* observed no lasting damage to business, such a panic could have contributed to the mild recession that followed by discouraging inventory accumulation. This is made clear by the minor business cycles of the 1920's in which fluctuations in inventory investment played a large rôle. According to Kuznets, inventory accumulation was relatively more than twice as large in the decade 1869–78 as in 1919–28.[30] While these figures do not gauge the relative importance for cycles of inventory changes in the two periods, they do indicate that actual decumulation of inventories would not have been necessary to start a contraction of business activity in 1869. Cessation of accumulation would shut off an important avenue for the use of funds. With a declining stock market, the funds might be hoarded long enough to initiate contraction. The fact that the panic came after the cyclical peak does not damage the above hypothesis, for business is subject to many inconsequential ups and downs which do not count as business cycles.

Contraction was necessarily mild as it was bucking against expansion in construction. In fact, the acceleration in additions to railroad miles in operation was greatest in 1869 and 1870. The housing index, however, declined in 1870, though it was to reach a peak in 1871. Professor Frickey's annual index of manufacturing did not increase in 1870, but neither did it decline. The sharp increase in railroad earnings came to a temporary halt. Imports declined for a time. By the beginning of 1871, the *Chronicle* was casually saying, "business is stagnant" but with no implication that anything was seriously awry.[31]

The trough, according to the National Bureau, came in December, 1870, and by the second quarter of 1871, expansion was plainly under way again. Business flourished until the fall of 1873. Frickey's index of manufacturing rose 20% between 1870 and 1873, and his production index for transportation and communication increased even more. Wholesale prices, reversing their downward trend, rose sharply from August 1871 until the spring of 1873. Oddly enough, wage rates, which hitherto had been rising in spite of falling prices, now tended to level off.[32] Railroad earnings rose spectacularly.

Investment in building apparently went into a decline before the panic

---

[29] Davis R. Dewey, *Financial History of the United States*, 10th ed. (New York, 1928), pp. 369-70; Warren F. Hickernell, *Financial and Business Forcasting*, Alexander Hamilton Institute, Vol. I, pp. 311-14; *Commercial and Financial Chronicle*, Vol. IX, (1869), pp. 406, 437, 453-55.

[30] Simon S. Kuznets, *National Product Since 1869* (New York, 1946), pp. 118-19. Net changes in inventories averaged $380 millions in 1869–78, or 5.4% of gross national product, which was $7,033 million. For 1919–28, the figure was $1,756, or 2.2% of GNP ($81,199).

[31] *Commercial and Financial Chronicle*, January 14, 1871, p. 37.

[32] George F. Warren and Frank A. Pearson, *Prices* (New York, 1933), p. 197.

of September 1873. The indexes of both Long and Riggleman show that the peak of *physical* construction came in 1871. The evidence is not clear as to how soon railroad investment began to decline. One estimate gives the peak in miles built as 1871, the other, as 1872. Orders for rails began to fall off only in the spring of 1872, and "apparent consumption" of rails reached its peak in that calendar year. Orders for locomotives also show 1872 as the best year, while orders for cars boomed until the second quarter of 1873.[33] These peaks relate to physical volume only. As steel prices rose sharply in 1872, the peak in expenditures may have come later than the peak in physical expansion. Moreover, in so far as the data relate to orders, physical peaks themselves may have lagged behind the dates given. Annual figures for the increase of railroad capital confirm these misgivings, showing a decided peak in 1873. We may conclude that even if the value of railroad investment did not decline prior to the panic, the transport-building cycle gave every evidence of being at the peak or beyond.

iv. *The Panic of 1873*

The National Bureau dates the cyclical peak as October 1873, the month following the outbreak of the banking panic. If we accept the Bureau's dating, we shall have no alternative but to conclude (as we shall see below) that the panic was the proximate cause of the business downturn. Now in principle there are many reasons for not accepting the Bureau's dates in blind faith. Not the least of such reasons is the scarcity of monthly data for the 1870's. Moreover, the intentionally vague definition of the business cycle employed by the National Bureau, however well suited to their research methods, does not seem precise enough for present purposes. Nevertheless, in spite of the fact that Ayres dated the peak long before the panic,[34] I have not discovered substantial reason for differing with the National Bureau; and in any event an outsider could hardly expect to challenge their results successfully in view of the amount of careful labor they have put into them. I shall, therefore, assume that business activity did not go into a cyclical decline prior to the panic.

This is not to say that a downturn would not have occurred had there been no banking difficulties. But if a patient with malignant cancer dies in a hospital fire, the coroner's report ignores the pathological processes which would have done away with him the next day and records the accidental nature of his death. So will it be here, inasmuch as my purpose is to narrate what did happen, not what might have happened.

---

[33] John E. Partington, *Railroad Purchasing and the Business Cycle* (Washington, 1929), pp. 37-47.

[34] Leonard P. Ayres, *Turning Points in Business Cycles* (New York, 1939), p. 35. Ayres' dating was based on a hybrid index of business conditions obtained by combining 10 series relating to production, consumption and freight movements. Since he used deviations of the series from their norms, he gave his index a bias in favor of early dating of peaks.

The event which made a banking panic inevitable was the failure of Jay Cooke & Co.[35] Cooke, as the man who had financed the Civil War, enjoyed an extraordinary reputation. His downfall did far more damage than the failure of a financial pirate could have. He had taken on the risky job of financing the Northern Pacific Railroad. By May 1873, this road had spent over $15 millions, had little more than 500 miles in operation through a sparsely populated region, and the two portions of its lines were still more than 1,000 miles apart. More than once Cooke had been on the verge of finding customers for his $100 millions of bonds, but each time the deal fell through. Now, to keep the road going, he was advancing money obtained from depositors at short-term in expectation that an European market would develop.

But the market for railroad bonds turned worse in 1873 rather than better. Tight money was perhaps the principal cause,[36] but there were several others. Twenty-five railroads defaulted on interest on their bonds between January 1 and August 31,[37] a circumstance which affected the market unfavorably.[38] The Granger movement, though still in its infancy, prejudiced capitalists against the railroads.[39] The *Chronicle* was consistently optimistic about the safety of railroad bonds and even after the panic admitted only reluctantly that railroad building had been too rapid and that "some roads have been built in sections of the country where they were not yet needed, and could not have had any reasonable prospect of making sufficient net earnings to pay their annual interest";[40] but the *Nation* the previous year published an article claiming that "railroad securities in America are not more profitable on the whole, while decidedly less secure, than the bonds of the United States" and that in western states more roads had been built than the population could support.[41] Some investors abroad, as well as at home, evidently thought along the same lines as the *Nation*. In the summer of 1873, the *Chronicle* reported that foreign purchasers of bonds were favoring governments over railroads.[42] Moreover, despite the fact that Graham's figures (see Table I) show more net long-term capital imports in 1873 than any other year, the *Chronicle* further reported that foreigners were shunning new issues of railroad securities.[43] Although the money stringency had a good deal to do with drying up the market for bonds, the evidence indicates not only that investors

---

[35] The account of the panic which follows is based, except as otherwise indicated, on Oliver M. W. Sprague, *History of Crises Under the National Banking System*, 61st Congress, 2d. Session. Senate Doc. No. 538 (Washington, 1910), pp. 1-89. See also Henrietta M. Larson, *Jay Cooke, Private Banker* (Cambridge, Mass., 1936), Chap. 19.

[36] *Chronicle*, January 10, 1874, p. 28.

[37] *Ibid.*, p. 36.

[38] *Ibid.*, August 2, 1873, p. 150.

[39] *Ibid.*, January 10, 1874, p. 28.

[40] *Ibid.*, November 15, 1873, p. 647.

[41] August 15, 1872, pp. 102-3.

[42] August 9, 1873, p. 173.

[43] March 29, 1873, pp. 407 and 408. See also December 21, 1872, p. 822.

in 1873 were turning away from newly issued railroad bonds but also that they had good reason to do so.

Jay Cooke was not the only one engaged in the dangerous practice of advancing short-term funds for long-term use. The New York banks had loaned money to railroads who expected to raise funds for repayment by selling bonds before the notes fell due.[44] The usual midsummer ease in the money market in 1873 induced the New York banks to increase their loans further with the intention of recalling them before money became tight in the fall.

Such unsound banking practices impinged on a situation made vulnerable by the downturn of railroad and building construction. Imports had reached their peak in 1872. Stock prices and New York clearings declined sharply in the first half of 1873. Wholesale prices resumed their downward trend after reaching a peak in the first quarter. Clearings in Philadelphia reached their maximum in the second quarter.

Cyclic weakness, however, was less important than structural banking weakness. Under the National Banking System, there was no effective central bank to act as lender of last resort and thus shield business and the stock market from panicky calling of loans in time of crisis. In addition, banking troubles were likely to spread from New York throughout the country inasmuch as bank reserves were concentrated in that city. The law permitted country banks to keep three-fifths of their required reserves on deposit in any of fifteen reserve cities. In 1873, New York banks were obligated to other banks for more than their total reserves, and seventy to eighty per cent of bankers' deposits were held by seven of New York's sixty banks. Trouble in New York might lead to hasty withdrawal of bankers' deposits, undermining the position of banks both in New York and the hinterland, encouraging runs, and leading quickly to contraction of loans.

Trouble was more likely to come in autumn than at any other time. Moving of crops regularly necessitated a drain of money from New York to the interior. As the currency supply was highly inelastic, if the New York bank reserves were low (as they were in 1873), failures would be precipitated then if ever. So it was not surprising that unsound railroad financing was exposed in September. On the eighth, the New York Warehouse and Security Co., which had financed the Missouri, Kansas and Texas Railroad, was forced to suspend. On the thirteenth, the important banking house of Kenyon, Cox & Co., in which Daniel Drew was a partner, failed on account of indorsements of paper of the Canada Southern Railroad. These disasters wreaked havoc on the stock market but nothing more.

On Thursday, September 18, Jay Cooke & Co. failed on account of its advances to the Northern Pacific Railroad plus a heavy drain by depositors on its cash resources. This caused general distrust and a rapid calling in of loans, precipitating failure of Fisk and Hatch the next day.

---

[44] *Chronicle*, November 15, 1873, p. 647 and January 10, 1874, p. 28.

Stocks plummeted, and failures followed thick and fast. On September 20, two trust companies suspended. Though they later were able to resume business, immediate consequences were far reaching. One, the Fourth National, held $15 millions of bankers' deposits; hence, the suspension hurt outside banks, and led to runs and the recall of funds from New York.

The panic was handled well. On September 20, the New York Clearing House Association arranged for its members to deposit approved securities with a committee of five, which then issued certificates of deposit ("clearing house certificates") up to 75% of the value of the securities. The certificates could then be used to settle clearing house balances. Thus the policy of every bank recalling loans, thereby ruining each other and business too, was avoided. Unfortunately, mounting calls for cash from the interior forced partial suspension of cash payments. On September 24th, the clearing house banks passed a resolution that all checks issued would be stamped "Payable through the Clearing House," thus concentrating control of reserves in the committee's hands. Partial suspension in New York necessarily caused partial suspension throughout the country, except in California, which was on a gold basis. But the committee controlling the New York reserves restored confidence by using them freely. Panic was over by September 29, eleven days after it had begun. After October 18, New York bank reserves began to increase, and by mid-November the reserve ratio once again exceeded the legal minimum.

What effect did the banking panic have on business? In the first place, there was a brief paralysis of the crop movement. Secondly, on September 20, foreign exchange became blocked. However, the issue of clearing house certificates on September 24 enabled the banks to resume purchasing foreign bills. Towards the end of the week, England began to ship gold, enabling exports to move. Thirdly, the panic caused considerable hoarding, e.g., because businesses kept their cash receipts in their own vaults instead of depositing them in banks. The national banks lost 23% of their holdings of legal tender notes between September 12 and October 13, a symptom of the hoarding. But the New York banks used their reserves so freely that the desire to hoard stopped. In the meantime, however, the hoarding aggravated the effects of partial suspension (which lasted nearly three weeks), and numerous firms had difficulty meeting payrolls. These had to reduce employment because they could neither get the cash to which they were entitled nor negotiate loans. Fourthly, after the middle of October, although there was no longer any difficulty meeting payrolls, businessmen had to cut production because demand had fallen. Contributing to the decline of orders was the decline of railroad and building construction. But it is difficult not to believe that the most important immediate factor was the interruption of business during the panic. To the extent that payrolls could not be met, consumer demand was cut. More significant, it can be assumed that businessmen during the panic either cancelled orders or curtailed making new ones. Once the purely monetary troubles were over, the decline of spending and ordering curtailed output, which in turn reduced spending, and so on in the familiar process. Even without a decline of long-term investment prospects to reenforce it, the panic by itself could have started a cumulative cyclical decline.

v. *Theory of the Downturn*

If we regard theories as tools for understanding reality, we have been able to get along with very few tools in accounting for the downturn of 1873. We have not had to mention any of the theories of the upper turning-point. Nevertheless, it is useful to discuss them at this point, because they can give us a more penetrating understanding. Moreover, theories can be considered as generalizations of reality as well as tools; and we now have an opportunity to test their generality with a case in which the essential processes stand out in unusual clarity. Besides, the discussion may throw some light on the history of business cycle theory, for the facts (some of which have always been widely known) are consistent with several different theories.

1. *Hawtrey.* According to Hawtrey's purely monetary theory, cyclical expansion leads to a drain of currency out of banks and into circulation as wages and incomes rise. Sooner or later the banks reach the end of their reserves and must stop expanding credit, but as the rise in wages and incomes lags behind credit, the drain of currency continues. This forces the banks to contract, initiating depression.

That is roughly what happened in 1873. The banks expanded to the limit during the summer. The autumnal drain of cash into the interior helped set off a violent process of monetary contraction. But this is a superficial interpretation. It leaves too much out of the picture. For instance, it ignores the likelihood that greater elasticity of credit would not have saved the situation but would have permitted the multiplication of unsound financial practices, leading in the end to still greater difficulties;[45] only revival in the securities markets could have saved Jay Cooke and his ilk. Nor do the facts bear out Hawtrey's theory in detail. But the case illustrates how the monetary theory in one form or another could be so popular prior to the 1930's. The facts do not contradict it.

2. *Cassel.*[46] According to Cassel, shortage of capital causes the downturn. At the beginning of the upswing, or high conjuncture, the rate of interest is low. This induces businessmen to take advantage of the opportunities provided by technical progress (*e.g.*, railways), the opening up

---

[45] Schumpeter, *op. cit.*, Vol. I, p. 316.

[46] Gustav Cassel, *The Theory of Social Economy*, translated by Joseph McCabe (New York, 1924), Fourth Book, esp. pp. 596-628. I take Cassel as an example to represent the shortage-of-capital school primarily because he meant his theory to explain the conjunctures of the period 1870–1914. Similar remarks to those that follow in the text above could be made about Hayek's monetary overinvestment theory as summarized by Haberler, *op. cit.*, pp. 33-72.

of new countries, and the increase of population to launch ambitious investment programs. In the upswing, production of fixed capital grows more rapidly than production of consumers' goods. For four reasons, the supply of money capital does not grow as rapidly as the output of capital goods: (1) if savings were a constant proportion of income, the relative growth of output of fixed capital would create a disparity; (2) in fact, savings are not a constant proportion of income but are relatively large at the first part of an upswing when profits are high but towards the end ("in the high conjuncture proper") fall off relatively as wages rise and profits decline, so that the interest rate rises towards the end of the upswing; (3) this is accentuated by the increased returns from fixed capital at the earlier part, which rise more rapidly than the prices of capital goods and therefore tend to raise the interest rate; and (4) in the earlier period, banks create new purchasing power at low interest rates, diverting production to capital goods, and hiding the increasing stringency of capital; but "when the banks afterward find it necessary in their own interest to cut down this excessive supply of media of payment, the real scarcity of capital is suddenly and acutely felt."[47] The high rate of interest at the end of the upswing cuts down the demand for capital goods, frequently forcing the abandonment of projects already begun. Workers in the capital goods industries lose their jobs. Usually, a crisis marks the onset of depression. Cassel defines crisis "as a time of general inability to meet obligations which fall due."[48] It is caused by "an overestimate of the supply of capital, or the amount of savings available for taking over the real capital produced."[49]

In so far as they can be ascertained, the facts of 1865–73 fit Cassel's theory well. After a considerable period of easy money and expanding credit, money conditions became tight in 1872. Meantime, the Northern Pacific and some other roads made grandiose plans based on an overestimate of the supply of capital that would be forthcoming. When the elasticity of the credit system ceased to hide the shortage of capital, the inability of a few to meet their obligations became translated through runs into a panic and a partial breakdown of the banking system. After the crisis, the shortage of capital was accentuated because foreign investors stopped buying American securities.

There is much to commend this interpretation. It turns on a fact other explanations are apt to ignore, namely that the decline of railway investment was due to lack of investors more than lack of projects. On the other hand, one cannot help feeling that investors were chary not (or not only) because they did not have enough funds but because they recognized a change in the profits prospects of new investments. Although Cassel's theory accounts for much more of what happened than Hawtrey's, it still does not cover the whole ground.

3. *Haberler.* As Haberler's *Prosperity and Depression* is now the standard

---

[47] *Ibid.*, p. 628.
[48] *Ibid.*, p. 509.
[49] *Ibid.*, p. 626.

theoretical work on cycles, it is interesting to apply his eclectic theory of the downturn to 1873.[50] I shall omit all reference to monetary contraction because it plays only a small part in Haberler's synthesis and has already been discussed above in connection with Hawtrey.

First, Harberler discusses how a partial breakdown, say in a particular industry, can develop into general contraction. This need not detain us here. Second, he shows how, as the upswing progresses, the economy becomes more and more vulnerable to deflationary shocks. The upswing requires an elastic supply of both money and factors of production. As the banks become loaned up and the available workers all find jobs, the force of the expansion diminishes. Now, in the early 1870's inelasticity of the money supply had a braking influence, but the supply of labor was unusually elastic for boom times due to immigration.

Third, Harberler discusses two endogenous causes of the downturn: the acceleration principle, and a drop of investment because of insufficient demand. If expansion slows down or stops because the money supply becomes inelastic, the acceleration principle makes it extremely likely that workers must shift from capital goods industries where output has been geared to a rate of increase in demand for consumers' goods which can no longer be maintained. Even if aggregate demand for the time being does not decline, it is unlikely that the shifts can be accomplished quickly enough. The result is unemployment in certain capital goods industries followed by cumulative contraction. For 1873, there is no evidence of such a mechanism.

Declining investment on account of insufficient demand, the other endogenous cause Haberler discusses, has a number of variants, chief of which is exhaustion of investment opportunities. If the industries directly concerned are taken by surprise—if they have been overly optimistic, for instance—"the boom will explode with a more or less strong 'detonation' of bankruptcy, to use an expression of Professor Pigou."[51] This explanation is applicable to 1873, and is a major element of Schumpeter's interpretation, as we shall see in a moment. But like Cassel's, Haberler's theory does not cover the whole ground.

4. *Schumpeter*. The theories of Hawtrey, Cassel and Haberler could be summarized briefly without doing undue violence to their substance, but Schumpeter's theory is so elaborate that I shall have to assume the reader is familiar with it and content myself with the comments he has specifically directed to the cycle under consideration here. Discussing the spurt in railroad building during 1869–71, he says,

> Two things are perfectly clear. First, that development . . . was a typical downgrade development within the meaning of our model. It was a Juglar prosperity superimposed on a Kondratieff recession,[52] a new step in what was no longer fundamentally new, but a process of carrying out what had

[50] *Op. cit.*, pp. 347-77.
[51] *Ibid.*, p. 375.
[52] Undoubtedly a slip. It is clear from Professor Schumpeter's model, his chronology on page 396, and his statement on page 338 that he meant Kondratieff *depression*.

PART II: *Empirical Analysis of Business Cycles*

previously been initiated. . . . This left plenty of problems for the individual case, but they were comparatively easy to solve, further eased by the growth of the environment, and of the type which is characteristic of "exploiting investment opportunity" and "pushing into new economic space." Moreover, the general features of the period support this interpretation. There was a great building boom. The well-being of all classes in the years 1869 to 1873 . . . is obviously due to the expansion of production which our schema leads us to expect in every Kondratieff recession. But it is not less clear, in the second place, that that method of financing which so well illustrates our theory, was handled with such carelessness as to make it an additional cause of the situation of 1873. It not only induced but really also presupposed abnormal speculative activity and could not without it have gone to anything like the lengths it did. The phenomena of the Secondary Wave were developed to an unusual degree thereby, and errors and cases of misconduct became possible which our model does not account for per se . . . and it becomes understandable that even as regards the railroad business these things were more obviously in evidence than the underlying process and that it seemed as if construction had been brought to a stop and the success of existing lines had been jeopardized by them rather than by any 'logic of evolution.' But even so, nobody can deny . . . that railroad construction had temporarily exhausted possibilities—a formulation which is more correct than the more common phrase of things having been overdone—and it should be easy to see that this, together with the dislocating consequences immediate and ulterior, for the economic system, of new construction was what created the situation in which the Secondary Wave broke, and with it untenable credit situations and speculative bubbles all over the field of industry and commerce.

. . . It is not astonishing that the impact was primarily on the new, instead of on those elements that progress had made obsolete. For, as was pointed out in our theoretical chapters, this will always happen if the new things stand on a slender and the old things on a safe financial basis. Thus, the role played in the drama by the Northern Pacific failure does not any more contradict expectation from our model than does the fact that, in general, danger signals first became visible in the railroad field.[53]

The passage quoted is a brilliant synthesis of the monetary and "real" forces at work. It brings out the underlying importance of entrepreneurial activity in railroads and shows how it gave rise to the excesses of the boom and the ultimate collapse. Banking panics for Schumpeter are always partly accidental, and so it was in this case; but given the institutional arrangements of the time, his theory shows how at certain times—including this one—events make a panic if not probable at least understandable. That his interpretation does not make use of the shortage of capital which was manifest in 1873 is a source of strength rather than weakness, for he emphasizes a more significant fact, namely, that the railroads were ceasing

---

[53] *Op. cit.*, Vol. I, pp. 335-36.

to be attractive to investors. Although Schumpeter's work as a whole has been subject to important criticisms, for this particular episode it offers a more convincing explanation than any other.

VI. *The Depression of the 1870's*

The cyclical contraction which followed the panic of 1873 was the longest in the history of American business cycles. According to the National Bureau, it lasted until March 1879, a span of five years and five months. In monetary statistics, it was second in severity only to the contraction of 1929-33 among post-Civil War cycles. Hubbard has measured the severity of depressions in terms of the decline in bank clearings or debits. The records begin only with 1875; yet the decline for 1875–78 was greater than for any other except 1893–97 and 1929–33. It was virtually as great as 1893–97 and undoubtedly would have been greater if statistics were available from the peak of 1873.[54] Eckler used six series to measure the severity of depressions. He found that 1873–78 was second only to 1929–32, and this result was mainly due to the three monetary series used.[55]

Nevertheless, in terms of output the contraction of the 'seventies was singularly mild. Frickey's indexes of production for manufacturing and for transportation and communication declined markedly less than in 1893–94 and 1907–8 even though the latter contractions were much shorter; and manufacturing did not decline after 1875 but actually increased 14% in the last two years of the depression.[56] Martin's figures show that in spite of the long depression, real income in 1879 was two-thirds greater than in 1869. Even on a per capita basis, the increase was one-third.[57] In June 1878, which was presumably as bad a time as any, Carroll Wright took a kind of census which showed only 28,500 people unemployed in Massachusetts out of a normal working force in "mechanical industries" of 318,000.[58]

---

[54] Joseph B. Hubbard, "Business Declines and Recoveries," *Review of Economic Statistics*, February, 1936, pp. 18-19.

[55] A. Ross Eckler, "A Measure of the Severity of Depressions, 1873–1932," *Review of Economic Statistics*, May 15, 1933, p. 79. 1929–32 was the deepest depression in all six series. The contraction of the 'seventies was second in two monetary series (clearings and railway revenues) and third in the other (imports). It was second in one of the physical series (coal production), fifth and sixth in the other two (pig iron production and cotton consumption; however, Eckler does not make it quite clear whether cotton consumption was a physical or a monetary series).

[56] The coverage of the indexes is rather meager, so that too much confidence cannot be placed in inferences drawn from them. One need not necessarily conclude that manufacturing output as a whole increased in 1877 and 1878. Nevertheless, the figures are comparable over the whole period, 1865–1914, so that comparisons among different cycles of this period should be reasonably trustworthy.

[57] Martin, *op. cit.*, p. 6. It should not be necessary to stress that national income figures for this period are subject to a wide margin of error.

[58] *Tenth Annual Report of the Bureau of Statistics of Labor*, Massachusetts Public Doc. No. 31, January, 1879, pp. 6-13. Applying the ratio of unemployed in Massachusetts to the whole country, Wright estimated total unemployment in the United States at 570,000.

Although comparison with modern figures is not reliable, this looks no worse than 1930.[59]

The panic of 1873, the disillusionment of investors about the railroads, the indirect effects of the decline in railroad investment, and the position of the 'seventies in the downswing of a building cycle are fully sufficient to account for events through 1876. What needs to be explained is (1) why the depression lasted so long and (2) why it was so mild in terms of output, particularly in the last two years.[60]

If the United States had been on the gold standard in 1873 at the exchange rate which then actually prevailed, cyclical contraction might have come to an end two years sooner than it did. Under gold standard conditions, a small country undergoing depression reduces imports as national income drops, but its exports are maintained. Moreover, if its prices fall, both domestic and foreign buyers shift to its products and away from foreign commodities. For both reasons, depression generates a favorable balance of payments which helps arrest cyclical contraction. The greenback appreciated a small amount between 1873 and 1876 and in the following year appreciated almost seven per cent more. The forces which under paper standard conditions caused this appreciation would under gold standard conditions have been largely channeled into stimulating the domestic economy, or rather, into arresting the fall of prices. In 1877, moreover, there is evidence of an upturn in railroad invest-ment, building construction, manufacturing, and mining. This indicates that under gold standard conditions deflation might well have been ended by 1877, other circumstances being favorable to cyclical revival.

Since the United States was not on the gold standard, we must inquire what effect price flexibility had on the course of contraction.[61] It is safe to assume that prices (including wages) were more flexible in the 1870's than in the 1930's. Wholesale farm prices generally are highly flexible. Inasmuch as they fell somewhat more sluggishly in the 1870's than non-farm prices[62] (whereas they fell much more rapidly than other prices be-tween 1929 and 1933), other wholesale prices must have been highly flexible also.

The effect of price flexibility on cyclical contraction can be brought out

---

[59] In 1930, out of a *total* labor force of 48.7 million, there were 4.2 million unem-ployed. Civil non-agricultural employment was 31.1 million. *Twenty-Sixth Annual Report of the National Bureau of Economic Research* (New York, 1946), p. 31.

[60] I have dealt with Schumpeter's explanation of the depression of the 1870's else-where and shall not repeat myself here. See my article, "The Long-Wave Depression, 1873–97," *Review of Economics and Statistics*, Feb., 1949, pp. 71-72. For a criticism of that article, see Richard V. Clemence and Francis S. Doody, *The Schumpeterian System* (Cambridge, 1950), pp. 80, 90 and 91.

[61] The discussion of price flexibility in the text draws on an article by the present writer, which has been published in the *Quarterly Journal of Economics* for November 1950. On account of space limitations, no more than a summary of the results of that article can be given.

[62] Mitchell, *op. cit.*, p. 54.

by contrasting two situations. First, assume that the economy momentarily rests in Keynesian underemployment equilibrium but wages and prices begin to fall. So long as they continue to fall—and there is no necessary reason why they should not fall forever—statistical series will exhibit many of the characteristics of cyclical contraction; and even if circumstances now become favorable to cyclical expansion, revival will be postponed or hindered by the general deflation. This seems to be more or less what happened in 1877 and 1878.

Second, assume that a cyclical contraction is under way. If price changes do not alter the course of aggregate spending, price flexibility increases output above what it otherwise would have been (with a given amount of spending, output is an inverse function of the price level). Of course, the fall of prices will not leave the course of aggregate spending unchanged, but its effects work in both directions.

In the 1870's, price flexibility probably reduced aggregate spending below what it otherwise would have been but not by so much as to reverse the tendency for flexibility to mitigate the decline of output. I have no direct evidence about the state of expectations, but it is probable that flexibility induced expectations that prices would fall further. As a matter of fact, prices had been falling, with one interruption, ever since 1865; yet until 1878 they were still above the pre-Civil War normal. In addition, in the lame-duck session of early 1875, Congress passed a law providing for resumption of specie payments on January 1, 1879; and in the spring of 1877 the Secretary of the Treasury began to make effective preparations to implement the law. It should have been evident that if resumption was to be carried through, American prices would have to fall relative to foreign prices (which were also falling). The government did not in fact put effective pressure on the price level, but that would not keep the prospect of resumption from affecting expectations unfavorably. Offsetting in part the factors adverse to spending was the rise in the value of currency and publicly held government debt. Because retail prices fell more slowly than wholesale prices, government obligations increased in value only a little over ten per cent. We may conclude, therefore, that price and wage flexibility probably intensified the contraction of spending, mitigated the decline of output, and prolonged the contraction phase of the cycle.[63]

There is one other important circumstance which must be considered. On account of the large amount of investment in railroads prior to 1873, we might expect that several years would pass before the revival of railroad building. On the other hand, there was no shortage of railroads to be

---

[63] It might be inquired why flexibility did not also make the contractions of 1893–94 and 1907–8 mild with respect to output. The answer, I think, lies in the greater violence of the panics with which those contractions began.

The statement that price flexibility mitigated the decline of output but prolonged the contraction phase of the cycle sounds inconsistent. The explanation lies in the fact that the decline in output apparently ended around 1877 whereas the contraction (according to NBER) continued until March 1879.

built. Construction of many roads had had to be abandoned during the depression before their main lines were completed, and the steady growth of population and agricultural output continually increased the inducement for the roads to expand. In view of the experience of the 1880's (the 1885 trough in railroad investment came only three or four years after the peak and was followed by a vigorous expansion), we might reasonably expect railroad activity to revive about 1876 or 1877. And in fact, the evidence indicates that it did so, though it is conflicting as to the exact time. The number of miles built reached its trough in 1875 and then increased substantially in the following year. The increase in railroad capital shows a trough in 1876 with a substantial revival in 1877. Orders for most types of railroad equipment revived in 1876 or 1877.[64] But all the evidence points to an early relapse of railroad investment. Why?

No doubt the continuance of deflation elsewhere in the economy provides part of the answer. Had deflation stopped, the railroads could have sparked a revival. But part of the answer must be sought within the railroad industry itself. There were three specific factors which discouraged investment in railroads: freight rate wars were acute in 1876; railroad strikes, which had to be quelled by military force, occurred in 1877; and federal, state, and local aid to railroad companies was replaced during the depression by efforts, occasionally successful, to pass legislation regulating railroads and railroad rates.

By 1879 conditions were ripe for recovery. Specie payments were successfully resumed on January 1, a step that (if we can believe the *Chronicle*) had favorable effects on business confidence. By that time, prices were well below even the pre-Civil War normal. Not only was there no need to expect prices to fall farther but in fact they stopped falling. In addition, investment in railroads revived strongly in response to the new business furnished by a 50% increase in crop production since 1873 and the sales of railroad land grants to new settlers. During the summer it became apparent that the United States was to enjoy unusually bountiful crops, Europe unusually poor ones, a combination which for a predominantly agricultural country on the gold standard was a powerful stimulant. Thereafter, the expansion phase of the cycle was in full sway.

VII. *Conclusion*

When warfare ended in 1865, long-term investment prospects became favorable, particularly in railroads. Nevertheless, readjustment to peacetime conditions brought on a recession which lasted until the end of 1867. There was another recession in 1869–70, the causes of which are obscure. But the expansion of railroad investment went on, climaxing in a boom in 1872–73. By that time long-term investment prospects, from the point of view of the man who puts up the money, appear to have taken a turn for

---

[64] Partington, *op. cit.*, p. 53.

the worse. Nevertheless, a banking panic, the origins of which lay in the excesses of the railroad boom, was the immediate cause of the cyclical downturn. The theories of Schumpeter and Cassel both fit the facts of the downturn. Of the two, I prefer Schumpeter's, though available evidence is not sufficient to settle the issue. The depression that followed is the longest of which we have record, lasting until early 1879. Though exceedingly severe in monetary terms, it was mild in real terms, partly as a result of price flexibility. The unfavorable long-term investment situation accounts for the depression lasting through 1876 or 1877, but about that time the outlook appears to have improved. However, a number of short-run influences—the fact that the United States was off the gold standard; a high degree of price flexibility; unfavorable price expectations; rate wars, strikes and adverse legislation in the railroad industry—delayed recovery. In 1879, the return to the gold standard put a floor under prices and increased confidence; and poor crops abroad combined with bumper crops in the United States gave a powerful stimulus, so that short-run as well as long-run prospects became propitious.

The hypothesis of a major cycle from 1865 to 1879 (with the peak in 1873) requires a minor qualification. Long-term investment prospects, though the evidence is not altogether certain, apparently changed before the business cycle peak of 1873 and trough of 1879. Strictly speaking, we should perhaps date our major cycle accordingly. But simplicity and convenience dictate that we date the peaks and troughs of major cycles to coincide with peaks and troughs of business cycles. Otherwise, the hypothesis stands up.

[10]

What Caused the Great Depression?*

GILBERT BURCK AND CHARLES SILBERMAN†

Editors' Note

Can it happen again? That question has been asked over and over in the past twenty years and refers, of course, to the Great Depression which lasted from 1929 until the outbreak of World War II. This economic debacle, all agree, was the worst ever suffered in this country, and the consequences are naturally etched in the consciousness of the republic—the business community, intellectuals, writers, professors, artists, and government officials of all political denominations. Although the definitive economic study of the 1930's remains to be written, Burck and Silberman properly highlight the stock market boom and its credit base, explain how production raced ahead of demand, and perhaps more important still, suggest that the 1920's marked a turning point in American history.

We must judge in the context of the 1929 experience the ominous, nagging concern about the economic future of the nation which accompanies the realization that the postwar backlogs of demand may no longer cushion cyclical shocks. Almost every current argument that "it can't happen again" refers to the changes in private and public institutional arrangements that had not occurred when the "new era" of the 1920's came to its inglorious climax. For one thing, we have now a degree of sophistication about economic data that was undreamed of in earlier times. Today we would know a lot sooner whether or not a serious depression was in the making. For another, the role of government has increased greatly, as a

* Reprinted by special permission from the February, 1955, issue of *Fortune Magazine*; © 1955 by Time, Inc.

† Mr. Burck and Mr. Silberman are editors of *Fortune*.

consequence of the Great Depression and of national security requirements; this too, many hold, provides a firm base of demand to dampen future depressions. In addition, government budgets are now used here and elsewhere to stabilize the economy. Can it happen again? The mere fact that the question can be seriously raised suggests the possibility that it can.

❧ When General Motors, on January 3, 1955, jumped nine points in a single hour, one small stockholder spoke the minds of many people, shareholders and non-shareholders alike. "In just an hour," he said, "the value of twenty shares went up by $180. Wonderful! But is *it* going to happen again?" By "it," of course, he meant the disaster of 1929, the Eniwetok of all busts, the crash that rocked the very foundations of the Western world. And his question, which Americans had been asking for ten years with slowly declining concern, was now being asked with renewed anxiety.

Yet even the most anxious often have only the sketchiest idea as to what really went wrong in the 1920's. And many have forgotten exactly what a cataclysm 1929 turned out to be. It precipitated America from the greatest decade of material well-being any nation had until then enjoyed into a decade of despond and doubt and frustration such as few nations have ever endured. The great depression, much more severe in the U.S. than in other Western countries, has been described as second only to the Civil War in its effects on the country, but in most ways it was much worse. It split the nation not geographically but mentally. It robbed otherwise rational men of their ability to be rational about economics. It degraded and stultified American capitalism, and turned some of the country's most creative—and also some of its most practical—minds to the facile promises of fascism, technocracy, social credit, socialism, and Communism. It brought despair and even hunger to millions of ordinary people, and planted blind resentment in their hearts. It wasted a total of nearly 200 *billion* man-hours. It did something that no foreign enemy, national disaster, or old-fashioned "panic" had ever done: it paralyzed, for years, American growth.

And just what *did* cause the depression? Was it simply unrestrained stock-market speculation? Or was it some basic, obscure defect in the economy? It is amazing how many well-informed people, well aware of the overwhelming pertinence of the subject today, have only the vaguest and most confused notion of what actually happened in the Twenties. Their confusion, it is true, is easily pardoned. Nearly all the critical examination of the Twenties was done in the Thirties, when the basic problem was still how to get out of the depression, or in the war years, when the big problem seemed to be to avoid a postwar depression. Although dozens of eminent economists have expounded the reasons for the great depression and although they agree on most basic facts, they disagee considerably on which facts are the most important.

Alvin Hansen, leading American disciple of Lord Keynes, believes that the 1929 debacle *was the result of the fact that several major investment booms came to an end at the same time that the economy's "maturity" was resulting in too much saving and in a general decline in investment opportunities.* Lionel Robbins of the London School of Economics, however, argues that there was too little "real" saving, and that investment expanded unduly and then collapsed because it was financed by a volatile supply of bank credit rather than by stable saving habits. But Sumner Slichter of Harvard, heading a committee to study the depression, found no shortage of real saving in the 1920's, and argued that the rabid speculation of the day made businessmen fear a stock-market collapse and business recession, and so led them to cut back inventory and capital outlays. And the late Joseph Schumpeter of Vienna and Harvard believed that the transportation and agricultural revolutions fomented by the Fords and McCormicks, like all such waves of innovations, could not sustain themselves indefinitely and were bound to end in depression regardless of the stock-market boom.

This article tries to synthesize the important theories and facts about the causes of the depression, including new data prepared for *Fortune* by Dr. Paul Boschan, expert on national income, as well as material from a still unfinished treatise on the interwar period by Professor Robert A. Gordon of the University of California. As the second in *Fortune's* Twenty-fifth Anniversary series on the development and direction of the "New Economy," this article also examines the 1920's as the portentous decade whose evolving mass markets prepared the way for today's Great Breakthrough into the new mass markets of the 1950's. Next month's article in the New Economy series will discuss the 1930's—why the depression dug itself in so deeply and lasted as long as it did.

The Fermenting Twenties

And what was the matter with the economy of the 1920's? Looked at as a collection of aggregate figures, that economy seemed and still seems a model of stability, a fitting opening for the New Era of perennial, prosperous "normalcy" that Waddill Catchings and other prophets of the Roaring Twenties plausibly thought was just beginning. Early in 1929 the President's Committee on Recent Economic Changes, headed by Herbert Hoover while Commerce Secretary, published in two large volumes what is still the most thorough analysis of the 1920's. Its eminent contributors, not having the advantage of hindsight, could find no grievous defects in the economy.

On the contrary, they were full of enthusiasm for the nation's rising income, growing mass markets, rising productivity, high employment, economic balance, managerial prudence—for many of the very virtues, let us note well, that seem to endow today's economy with so much power and stability. Even that great student of the business cycle, Wesley Mitchell, in a wary, yes-but summary of the committee's analysis, agreed that the stability of employment in a period of great technological advance (and hence technological displacement) was, in the last half of the decade, something to rejoice about. Alas, even the decade's most eminent and careful analysts overestimated the stability of this expanding economy.

Let us define a stable, expanding economy as one whose major components, such as production, consumption, employment, and investment, are advancing in a kind of dynamic harmony. When one of the components advances too fast or fails to advance fast enough, dislocations may occur. The trouble with the 1920's, as things turned out, was that, in the last half of the decade, over-all stability concealed the fact that rising components were offset by declining ones. The balance was precarious because the rising components, being in the last analysis dependent upon the others, could not rise indefinitely.

This cyclical trend downward, which will be discussed in detail later, was neither so great nor so growing that it might not have been reversed as all business cycles hitherto had been reversed—at worst by a classic depression (but certainly not one as bad as that of the 1930's), or at best by a short, mild adjustment. What finally occurred was the most severe depression in history; and it occurred, in the main, because the nation's rational enthusiasm for sharing in the splendid future of American business degenerated into the exuberant excesses of unrestrained stock-market and real-estate inflation, manipulated on a scale never before practiced, and spiraled faster and faster in by people who had let their avarice get the better of their common sense. For the stock-market inflation put a false front of prosperity on the economy, postponed the inevitable reckoning, and converted what might have been a routine recession into a cataclysm.

Some of the dislocations of the 1920's were the result of new products and new processes. Oil began to replace coal, rayon began to compete with cotton. Some of the dislocations were inherited from World War I. When American agriculture was called on to feed Europe, for example, farm prices doubled and farmland values and mortgage debt shot up. Then in the deflation of 1921 these prices and values fell almost as far as they had advanced, while farm debt increased. Agricultural prices recovered somewhat, but what with excess farm capacity and a declining world market, they turned down again after 1925.

And some of the dislocations of the 1920's were hidden, so to speak, in the very temper of the people. Americans, then as now (and now as a hundred years ago), were dynamic and restless, bursting with ambition and self-assertiveness, casting old habits to the winds, bristling with new ideas and new developments. The U.S. in the 1920's was, indeed, in a state of unusually violent ferment, politically, socially, morally, intellectually, *and* economically. One extreme generated another. No sooner had the country washed its hands of the idealism of World War I and declared allegiance to the ideal of "normalcy" than its new normalcy became a state of continuous abnormalcy. No sooner had it given itself over to the high-minded hypocrisy of prohibition than it proceeded to disregard not only prohibition but a whole inheritance of customs and morals. Its variety and energy enabled it to try everything with unflagging enthusiasm.

Above all, there was the old frontier delight in gambling for big stakes. Partly because people wanted to get rich quick, partly because they were congenitally optimistic, they debauched themselves not only in the Florida land boom but in a dozen other minor booms whose busts did no harm on a national scale. And who would have guessed that the stock-market boom would be different?

Situations of Strength

All this zymotic energy was, up to a point, a wonderful thing. Because American productivity or output per man-hour grew at a near-record pace, production expanded much faster than population. Henry Ford, who had raised his production from 19,000 cars in 1909 to 785,000 in 1916, had in his intuitive but immensely impressive way shown how rising productivity means lower prices and higher wages. Thanks to a shortage of workers in World War I, labor had demanded and got a large share of rising productivity, and its real wages had risen 30 per cent between 1914 and 1923. Thus labor both created the beginnings of a mass market and prodded management into higher efficiency. So mass production was the talisman of the day. Machinery output increased 50 per cent between 1923 and 1929—while industrial production itself was rising 25 per cent.

As industries "rationalized" and consolidated, modern salesmanship and advertising bloomed in all their early glory. Bruce Barton expounded Jesus Christ in terms of His executive and organizing talents. Mass production was followed by mass distribution—though, as we shall see later, perhaps not soon enough. Chain stores began to spring up; Sears, Roebuck began to build stores in the suburbs.

And so, between 1920 and 1929, industrial production rose 45 per cent, and gross national product 43 per cent, while employment rose only 17 per cent. Unemployment, large by today's standards, showed no increase when expressed as a percentage of the labor force. So the aggregates looked just fine.

To see how the economy really shaped up, let us look closely at the major trends—first at the components that rose steadily throughout the decade and gave it so much stability. For one thing, there were government expenditures (15 per cent on roads), which even in those "unregimented" days were considerable, rising from $6.2 billion in 1920 to $8.2 billion in 1929 (in 1929 dollars). More important were the consumer non-durables and services. Their sales, taken together, rose steadily from $46.5 billion in 1920 to $70.1 billion in 1929, or 50 per cent.

Sales of non-durables alone, in the same period, rose from $25 billion to $37.8 billion or 51 per cent, but consumption of food, which accounts for a major part of non-durable consumption, rose only 27 per cent. Remember that food, in those days, was merchandised as food, more often than not in bulk, and in much plainer and simpler forms than are common today. Out-of-season fruits, precooked and exotic comestibles that are part of every plumber's diet today were then either nonexistent or rarities consumed only by the well-to-do.

The consumption of other non-durables, however, nearly doubled, rising from $9.7 billion in 1920 to $18.3 billion in 1929. Not only did mass markets develop for cigarettes, gasoline, and other "luxuries," but the American standard of clothing was rising. As American Woolen Co. was already learning, even workmen wanted something other than blue serge for their Sunday suits. Silk stockings, usually made of fibers from Japan, were astonishingly expensive by today's standard—the cheaper ones cost about $1.50 a pair—but even the poorest high-school girls found it *de rigueur* to clothe their limbs in silk.

Consumer services, which include rent, recreation, utilities, cleaning, public transportation, financial and legal expenses, and so on, did very well, too. Their sales rose from $21.5 billion in 1920 to $32.3 billion in 1929 (in 1929 dollars), or 50 per cent. Here, too, was the beginning of a great new mass market. Consumption of gas and electricity doubled between 1919 and 1929. The number of wired homes increased from 8,700,000 in 1920 to more than 20 million in 1929, while expenditures on telephones more than doubled. And expenditures on personal care nearly doubled between 1920 and 1929, reflecting no doubt the rise of the now ubiquitous beauty shoppe.

Much of the increase in services, of course, was accounted for by the top income group, which received twice as large a percentage of the national income as it does today. Expenditures on domestic service increased by more than 50 per cent between 1919 and 1929, and brokerage charges and interest, generated by the stock-market boom, increased nearly ten times in the same years. But taking everything together, the growth of non-durables and services was impressively broad. As Hoover's *Recent Economic Changes* rejoiced, it was the timely development of the mass services, which in effect absorbed the population increase, that saved the nation from a critical unemployment problem in the late 1920's.

The Weak Trends

The record of consumer durables and residential construction, however, was not so consistently good. These two had been the economy's major source of strength in the early years of the decade, stimulating immensely, in turn, consumption of non-durables and the establishment of new services like gas stations and garages. Durables rose 38 per cent between 1920 and 1923, and home construction a phenomenal 165 per cent. But both were also responsible for the economy's later weakness. They not only stopped growing, they declined between 1926 and 1929—consumer durables by 5 per cent, house construction by no less than 37 per cent.

Sales of most durables, including radios and washing machines, rose sharply, then dropped. Sales of mechanical refrigerators, by contrast, were a minor source of strength, increasing from fewer than 5,000 in 1920 to 778,000 in 1929. But the great source of strength in consumer durables, not only accounting for most of the rise in the early years of the decade but moderating the decline later on, was the passenger automobile, that quintessentially American device for augmenting the ego of the individual and freeing it from many of the restrictions of time and distance. Sales of cars rose from 1,900,000 units worth $1.8 billion in 1920 to 3,900,000 units (a 100 per cent rise) worth $2.7 billion in 1926 to 4,800,000 units worth $3 billion in 1929 (all prices wholesale).

Note, however, that the *growth* in auto sales, especially in dollars, *did* taper off. Why? For one thing, dollar value per unit dropped as the industry saturated the class market and shifted to a mass market. For another, it is obviously impossible for any new product to maintain its early growth *rate*—a fundamental fact on which Joseph Schumpeter erected much of his wave theory of depressions.

Again, the mass-production industries did not have the mass markets they have today. Finally, auto manufacturers, for all their high-pressure salesmanship, did not measure their markets as accurately or tap them as effectively as they do today. Henry Ford was a good if somewhat extreme example. Because he believed in giving the people any model they wanted so long as it was the Model T and any color they wanted so long as it was black, he put out his Model A two or three years later than he should have, and so restricted the market.

Too Many "Homes"

What accounted for the spectacular decline of residential construction in the late 1920's was that both house and apartment construction had outpaced their market. Partly because mass immigration had ended, the U.S. population growth rate turned down sharply. Population had increased 14 million between 1910 and 1920, another 9,400,000 between 1920 and 1925—but only 7,200,000 in the next five years. Yet the building industry, rushing in to make up for the deficits of World War I, which concentrated so many people in the cities, erected 937,000 housing units in 1925 (only 22 per cent less than in 1954 when the urban population was some 40 per cent greater). And the overbuilding was usually accompanied by a bank-loan-fed inflation in real-estate prices, which like stock-market prices often outran real values and discounted future values egregiously.

A Lopsided Market

A part of the faltering in both the housing and durable markets is explained by the fact that the middle-class market was much smaller than it is today, both because average income per capita was lower and because the national income was not so evenly distributed as it is today. As *Fortune* showed in "The Changing American Market" (August, 1953), 15,600,000 or 43 per cent of all family units in 1929 received less than $2,000 cash (in 1953 dollars) whereas 11,700,000 or 23 per cent of all family units do so today. The 43 per cent obviously was not in the market for much except bare necessities.

The concentration of income in the upper groups actually increased, especially in the latter half of the Twenties:

The share of the disposable national income claimed by the top 1 per cent of incomes, between 1920 and 1929, increased by half, from 12 per cent to 18 per cent. And the share claimed by the top 5 per cent increased from 24 per cent to 33.5 per cent.

Between 1920 and 1929 profits, interest, and rent, which went largely to upper-income groups, increased 45 per cent, whereas total wages and salaries, which comprised the bulk of the income of the lower and middle-income groups, rose only 13 per cent. At the same time consumer prices, after rising between 1922 and 1926, declined only 3 per cent between 1926 and 1929.

Between 1920 and 1929, while factory productivity or output per man hour was increasing 55 per cent, hourly wage rates in manufacturing rose only 2 per cent. One reason for labor's surprising inability to get more benefit from its rising productivity was that the labor movement, after the bitter strikes of 1919, was persuaded into uncritical "cooperation" with management. This was the great era of company unions, open shops, and shrewd paternalism. It was also an era of weak labor leadership. "If he (Judge Gary) sent less than ten hay wagons of roses to (Gompers') funeral (in 1924)," wrote H. L. Mencken, "then he is a niggard indeed. For Sam got upon the back of the American labor movement when it was beginning to be dangerous, and rode it so magnificently that at the end of his life it was tame as a tabby cat."

There was also a growing imbalance in the distribution of corporate profits. Corporations with profits of more than $1 million accounted for 65 per cent of all corporate profits in 1925, 71 per cent in 1927, and 80 per cent in 1929. Economists argued that monopoly pricing and excessive market power accounted for a great part of the trend toward profit concentration. Actually, big companies tended to dominate profit figures partly because they had the resources to become more efficient. Their ability to "administer" prices cannot be overlooked, however, in accounting for the fact that consumer prices did not fall as rapidly as productive efficiency rose.

The Heady Philter

Let us recapitulate. Undeveloped marketing methods, declining population growth, declining foreign investment, low farm prices, sticky

consumer prices, the real-estate inflation, and the substantial and growing concentration of profits in large corporations and of individual incomes
in the upper-income groups even as the luxury markets were becoming
saturated—all these caused the growth of consumer durables practically
to stop in the mid-Twenties, and caused residential construction to turn
down sharply. Thus it was inevitable that business' capital outlays would
stop growing, and might even decline. The combination clearly made for
a cyclical adjustment.

But before a genuine adjustment to correct the imbalances could occur,
the stock-market boom began. This boom, by mounting and accelerating a
false recovery early in 1928, postponed a real adjustment, and put the economy on an increasingly precarious footing.

It enabled hundreds of thousands of speculators to spend more on luxuries than they otherwise would have spent, and thus super-imposed
a consumption boomlet on the stock-market inflation. Above all, the
stock-market inflation helped maintain business' capital outlays at a level
unjustified by business conditions. Those outlays rose from $6.8 billion
in 1920 to $9.3 billion in 1926. Instead of falling when consumer durables
and residential construction turned down in the mid-Twenties, capital outlays continued around the $9.4 billion level until 1929, when they actually
jumped by $1.3 billion. The stock-market boom, by driving down yields,
made new-issue flotation cheap and easy, and encouraged business to buy
more capital goods than it needed.

The stock boom stimulated over-building of commercial and office structures; physical volume of commercial building in 1929 was larger than
it ever has been since. And the boom also resulted in speculative excesses,
such as mortgage bonds issued for amounts greater than costs. Some $8
billion worth of mortgage bonds were sold between 1920 and 1929.

The stock-market boom, in other words, not merely concealed the defects of the economy, it seemed to cure those defects. The patient's blood
count was dropping, but the heady philter of speculation deluded him
into believing he never felt better.

Boom Unrestricted

And what started the stock-market boom? For one thing, dividends
began to catch up with profits in the middle Twenties, and the advantages
of investing in stocks consequently became evident to more and more
people who had more and more money to invest—a condition not too
different from the mid-Fifties. The concentration of profits in the blue
chips also made them inordinately preferable to other stocks.

There were no restrictions on margin such as there are today. The
amount of cash a man needed to buy a share was decided by brokers and
their banking connections, and in the mid-Twenties, 10 per cent was
usually sufficient. And there were virtually none of today's restrictions on

pool operators, who could drive up the price of stocks by selling them to
one another.

In this unhealthy state of affairs, the Federal Reserve, in August, 1927,
actually made speculative credit still more plentiful—by reducing the rediscount rate from 4 to 3.5 per cent and by purchasing government securities
in the open market. The Fed did this partly to encourage business at home,
which was then slipping a bit (the "adjustment" of 1927), but principally
to help Britain stay on, and France get on, the gold standard. The widespread agreement that the Fed's action bears considerable responsibility
for the stock-market inflation is more than shared by Herbert Hoover.
"But the policies assumed by that System," he writes, "must assume the
greater responsibility. . . . There are crimes far worse than murder for
which men should be reviled and punished."

Before passing on, let us note the dilemma that faced the Federal Reserve. If it was expected to use monetary policy to avoid deflation and
depression, how could it stop the stock-market inflation? The Fed, after
all, was a relatively new institution that had been denounced for causing
the 1920–21 crash by its stringent credit policies. And the Fed lacked the
power it now has to set margins, and it lacked the backing of an SEC
with the power to police the issuing and buying and selling of securities.

"Wicked Manipulations"

Starting about 1928, the market ceased to be a reasonably sober reflection
of economic conditions and became a morbid demonstration of mass avarice.
Before mid-1928, broadly speaking, a man paid a certain price for a share
of stock because he was pretty sure it would return him more, over the
long run, than a bond or other investment, and he was inclined to bid
up the price only when he felt his judgment of the company's earning
power was correct. After mid-1928 people bought stocks on about the same
basis they had bought Florida real estate only a few years before.

It has been estimated that enough Florida lots were sold to provide one
for every family in th U.S.; and in his book *The Legendary Mizners*, the
late Alva Johnston wrote that some Miami lots could justify their 1925
price only if 200-story skyscrapers were erected on them. Many of the shares
in the 1929 stock market could have justified their prices only by the year
2000.

But the "market" in those days represented not merely the spontaneous
reactions of hundreds of thousands of speculators. It also represented the
contrived pressure of operators who sold dubious foreign bonds, who promoted domestic issues many corporate layers removed from any productive
property, who peddled the ubiquitous tips, and who worked the many
variations of the pool racket.

The boom "set the stage for wicked manipulations and promotions,"
Herbert Hoover remarks accurately. "It also furnished ammunition to
radicals for their attacks on the whole American system. The exhibition

of waste, fraud, and greed . . . appears in their literature as a typical phenomenon of our free civilization, whereas it was the exception."

When two or three million little speculators entered the market, the pickings were all the better. It is true that the common people were given plenty of warning; Roger Babson was only one of many doom criers. But as every decline promptly turned into recovery and a still greater ascension, people who had nervously considered selling when they had a 30 per cent profit grew ever bolder; if their shares had now doubled in value there was no reason why they shouldn't triple. Many outward signs, moreover, were good, at least until early 1929.

The Great Credit Inflation

What gave the boom such uncontrollable momentum was that a great part of the stock buying was done on credit—how much nobody knows, but certainly much more than was done recently, when more than 40 per cent of all *individual*—i.e., non-professional and non-institutional—transactions were made on margin.

Brokers' loans, which had amounted to $1.5 billion in 1923, increased from $4.5 billion early in 1928 to more than $7 billion by June, 1929, and to $8.5 billion by fall. By then the average yield was less than a third of the interest that speculators had to pay to carry the shares.

About three-quarters of the money came not from the banks, but from individuals and corporations that saw a chance to make 10 per cent or more, with no risk to speak of, on their spare cash, and let the banks handle it. Many companies, indeed, floated new issues not for capital investment but for the sole purpose of investing the cash in the call-money market. And it was this tremendous rise in speculative credit that tightened credit for ordinary business operation—which was one reason why the Federal Reserve was reluctant to restrict credit still more.

So Anaconda rose from 54½ early in 1928 to 162 in September, 1929; G.E. from 128¾ to 396; Montgomery Ward from 132¾ to 466½; Radio from 94½ to 505 (without paying a dividend); Westinghouse E. & M. from 92 to 313. And thus it was that the total value of stocks on the New York Stock Exchange rose from $49 billion in December, 1927, to $87 billion on October 1, 1929.

"So Foul a Sky . . ."

Such "appreciation," occurring when margin requirements were only 10 per cent (though they rose to as much as 50 per cent in the summer of 1929), meant that a man with $10,000 in cash in January, 1928, could have put it in blue chips and theoretically run it up to more than $1,500,-000 by August, 1929. For $10,000 would have given him about $100,000 worth of "buying power," and within two or three months a 10 per cent rise in stock values would have given him another $100,000 or so in buying power, and he could, in this fashion, have doubled his "equity" every three months or less.

By early 1929 hundreds of knowledgeable people, among them the governors of the Federal Reserve, were wringing their hands, and dozens of magazines and papers, including the New York *Times* and the *Commercial and Financial Chronicle,* were calling the folly what it was. But almost nothing could be done.

The Federal Reserve issued its famous warning of February 2, 1929, stating that a member bank "is not within its reasonable claims for rediscount facilities when it borrows either for the purpose of making speculative loans or for the purpose of maintaining speculative loans. . . ." Although call-money rates went up to 20 per cent in February, and for a while it seemed as if a monumental "correction" would occur, the market receded only temporarily. Whether Charles Mitchell's audacious follow-up statement that his National City Bank, to avoid a panic, was prepared to lend $25 million in call money at rates beginning at 15 per cent started the market upward again is debatable. But upward the market went. The Federal Reserve's last attempt to stay the tide by raising the rediscount rate to 6 per cent in August, 1929, however, may have had some effect on the market. The Dow-Jones index had risen from 315 in June to 380 in August, and rose only one point higher in September.

As the madness of 1929 approached its climax, the stock market not only failed to anticipate the general state of the economy—which it usually does by six months or so—but it lagged behind by several months. The market rose despite the fact that inventories had begun to mount in midsummer, that wholesale prices had turned down in July, that industrial production had declined in August, and that capital-goods orders had tapered off as early as March.

In a more narrow or "technical" sense, the crash had actually been signaled by a turndown in low-priced securities late in 1928, and by sporadic temporary declines in the summer and early autumn of 1929. (The market, then as now, was selective.) Some of the bears were obviously selling short. The warning signs grew with successive waves of selling in September and early October, 1929, which reduced prices 15 per cent below their peak. And the grand October liquidation culminated not merely in the famous Black Thursday of October 24, when nearly 13 million shares changed hands and thousands of margins were exhausted, but also in a still blacker Monday and Tuesday the next week. By the end of October the Dow-Jones index had fallen to 230—from a high of 381 in September.

The Market's Revenge

Of all the man-made forces behind the break and the ensuing panic, few were more powerful than the short interests, which began to mount in mid-summer. "The short interests," says Sidney Weinberg, "were substantially responsible for the severity of the stock-market crash." Today a short sale cannot be made except at a price higher than the last reported sale. In those days short sales could be made at prices below the market level, and thus could be used to drive down and demoralize the market. One of the most spectacular short-sellers was Albert H. Wiggin, chairman of the Chase Bank, who made $4 million selling short between October and December 11, 1929. What gave Mr. Wiggin's achievement a great deal of adverse publicity later on was the disclosure that he not only sold short before and during the crash, even while he was a leading member of the famous bankers' consortium to stabilize the market, and that he had not only made the $4 million selling his own bank stock short, but that he had sold some of the stock to his own bank, and borrowed from his bank to buy the stock to cover his short sales.

An even more important factor in the panic than short selling, perhaps, was the fact that marginal speculators, when forced to cover their debts, had to sell the stock or turn it over to the brokers. The more stock they put up for sale or turned in, the more prices fell—and of course the more stock that had to be sold. Worse, panicky outside lenders called in their loans, which forced the sale of stock to repay the loans. The volume of brokers' loans declined $2.5 billion in three weeks. To avoid losing their shirts, brokers tried to sell in an orderly fashion the stocks they took over. But every time the market rallied, the new rush to sell precipitated a new decline. Neither speculators nor brokers were any longer free agents, expressing their faith in the future of the nation's business (which has turned out to be a pretty well-founded faith), or betting that a given stock was worth so much. They were flotsam in the torrent, and the fact that they were sensitive and even intelligent flotsam that did not believe in being rushed away by torrents did not help them at all.

This peculiar ability of a chaotically falling market to take its revenge not only on speculators but on the whole economy that let it occur cannot be overemphasized. It was overlooked for a good time after the crash. Some called the crash a Prosperity Panic, in which, as Professor Irving Fisher put it, the lunatic fringe was being shaken out. "The depression in Wall Street," said the New York *Sun*, "will affect general prosperity only to the extent that the individual buying power of some stock speculators is impaired. No Iowa farmer will tear up his mail-order blank because Sears, Roebuck stock slumped."

The Grand Liquidation

Alas the forces the crash set in motion penetrated to every corner of the economy, where powerful deflationary influences—declining construction, declining consumer durables, declining farm prices—were already at work. The crash further deflated all values and almost destroyed the U.S. banking system.

When the 1920's ended, shattering as the end was, few Americans as yet understood what they were in for. One of the few who did was the hitherto dogmatically optimistic Andrew Mellon. Mr. Mellon now had only one "hope" for the nation: "Liquidate labor, liquidate stocks, liquidate the farmers, liquidate real estate." If Mr. Mellon's formula had included business, it would have come close to being a good description of what eventually happened.

[11]

Business Cycles in the
Interwar Period:
The "Quantitative–Historical"
Approach*

ROBERT A. GORDON†

Editors' Note

How much do we really know about business cycles? It may be distressing, but not surprising, to learn that there are still many unanswered questions about business cycles that happened decades ago, despite the great efforts already made. Even today, there is no wide agreement as to the causes of the cycles in the interwar period, much less consensus on more recent events. The beginning of wisdom is to know what questions to ask. In this regard, Gordon's article makes a major contribution. But will its ambitious agenda be accomplished? Certainly, the statistical approach is fundamental, but it should not be the only method of attack. The historical approach also must be employed since it will presumably explain behavior

* From *The American Economic Review*, Vol. XXXIX, No. 2 (May, 1949), pp. 47-63. Reprinted by permission of *The American Economic Review* and the author.

† Professor and chairman of the Department of Economics, University of California, R. A. Gordon (1908–   ) enjoys a growing reputation among his confreres on the contemporary scene. Educated at Johns Hopkins and Harvard, he served with the faculty at Harvard before joining the University of California. Extracurricular activities include appointments with the Brookings Institution, 1940–41; U.S. delegate to International Rubber Conference, 1944; and the Committee for Economic Development, 1954–58. Gordon is a frequent contributor to professional journals—attested by his several appearances in this volume—and additionally has to his credit *Business Leadership in Large Corporations* (1945); *Higher Education and Preparation for Business* (1959); and *Business Fluctuations* (1961).

in particular cycles rather than generalize about all of them. Clearly, much more work will have to be done on interwar business fluctuations before the postwar movements can be understood. This article states the problem in an empirical context, notes the major studies already written and the leading methodologies, and highlights some of the broad tendencies evident in the statistics.

❦ A review of the literature speedily convinces one that we still know distressingly little about the causes of economic fluctuations in the United States in the period between the two Great Wars. In this paper, I shall indicate what, in my opinion, are some of the most important unanswered questions about this period and how we may best go about trying to answer them. In a sense, this paper is a first report on a larger project dealing with American business cycles during the interwar years which is now in progress.[1]

1. *Questions We Need to Answer*

The need for more detailed study of this period is easily documented. Even the best of the existing studies of business cycles during the interwar years have not brought about general agreement among economists as to the nature and causes of the major cyclical fluctuations between 1919 and 1939.[2] To be more specific, consider the following questions, to which, so far as I know, satisfactorily detailed answers do not now exist.

1. What were the most important secular forces operating upon the American economy during the interwar period, and how were these secular forces related to both the boom of the twenties and the depression

[1] This project is being financed by the Rockefeller Foundation and by the Bureau of Business and Economic Research of the University of California. The generous assistance of both organizations is gratefully acknowledged.

[2] The best studies of interwar cycles in the United States are probably: S. H. Slichter, "The Period 1919–1936 in the United States: Its Significance for Business Cycle Theory," *Review of Economic Statistics*, Vol. 19 (Feb., 1937), pp. 1-19; J. A. Schumpeter, *Business Cycles* (New York, 1939), Vol. II, Chs. 14-15, and "The Decade of the Twenties," *American Economic Review*, May, 1946, pp. 1-10; J. Tinbergen, *Statistical Testing of Business-Cycle Theories, II, Business Cycles in the United States of America, 1919–1932* (Geneva, 1939); Thomas Wilson, *Fluctuations in Income and Employment* (London, 1942), Part II; N. J. Silberling, *The Dynamics of Business* (New York, 1943), esp. Chs. 12-15; L. R. Klein, *Economic Fluctuations in the United States, 1921–41* (in press, to be published by the Cowles Commission for Research in Economics); *ibid.*, "The Use of Econometric Models as a Guide to Economic Policy," *Econometrica*, April, 1947, pp. 111-151. See also Slichter's article on the 1937 downturn, *Review of Economic Statistics*, August, 1938, pp. 97-110, and Kenneth Roose, "The Recession of 1937–38," *Journal of Political Economy*, June, 1948, pp. 239-248.

of the thirties? It is now generally accepted that secular and cyclical movements are interrelated and that an understanding of the causes of short-run instability requires a detailed knowledge of the long-run forces operating on the economy.[3]

2. The role of World War I in influencing cyclical and secular developments needs further study, particularly for the United States—where war-created dislocations were less obvious than in Europe. In this connection, we need to compare secular movements before 1914 with the changes which occurred after the war. To what extent, and in what sense, did World War I create a "break in trend" in important sectors of the economy?

3. Partly because of our uncertainty regarding the answers to these questions, there is no consensus on how to interpret the total pattern of change during the interwar years. For example, should the entire period 1921–33 be considered a "major" cycle, on which were superimposed several minor cycles? How shall we draw the secular movements during 1919–39? Should we recognize both "primary" and "secondary" trends? And so on.

4. We need more study of the timing and extent of the apparent "drying-up" of investment opportunities at the end of the twenties. For each major industry, what was the nature of the market situation and the prospects for further investment in 1928–29, and how did the changes which occurred during the twenties affect developments from 1929 on? To what extent were the deflationary forces at work merely cyclical, and to what extent also secular?

5. We have few detailed studies of significant cyclical turning points during the interwar period.[4] In particular, there is no adequately detailed study of the 1929 turning point, which should include a detailed analysis of the behavior of significant industries in the neighborhood of the downturn in total activity. Studies of turning points should be integrated with an analysis of the preceding cumulative phase and should aim at throwing light on three questions: where and why deflationary or expansionary

---

[3] Writers with such different approaches to business cycle analysis as Schumpeter, on the one hand, and A. F. Burns and the National Bureau of Economic Research, on the other, seem to agree on this point. Schumpeter's views are well known. Note the emphasis given in the National Bureau's research program to the studies of secular changes in income, production, employment, and productivity since 1900 or earlier in various sectors of the economy. In addition to these individual studies, see the interpretive summary of findings by George Stigler, *Trends in Output and Employment* (New York, 1947).

[4] There is some consideration of timing relationships at the turning points in 1927, 1929, and 1932–33 in W. C. Mitchell and A. F. Burns, "Production during the American Business Cycle of 1927–1933," *National Bureau of Economic Research Bulletin 61* (November, 1936). See also the turning point analysis in Slichter's two articles on the interwar period. Slichter's articles, excellent as they are in some respects, have two main defects. They are not sufficiently systematic and detailed in their study of timing relationships at the turning points, and, more important, his study of turning points is not integrated with an analysis of underlying cyclical and secular developments. The latter criticism applies also to Roose's study of the turning points in 1937 and 1938. (See his article previously cited and his doctoral dissertation on which the article is based.)

stimuli originate, through what channels they are transmitted, and approximately what weights should be attached to the various originating forces. While discouragingly little can be done with this third question, some rough quantitative statements should be possible.[5]

6. The facts regarding the relations between income and consumption, in the aggregate and for significant segments of the economy, need to be more fully explored, both for the twenties as a whole and for the 1929 downturn. The main job here is putting together the numerous partial, and partly contradictory, pieces of evidence. Reliance on a few aggregative series, without examination of other relevant evidence, is not enough.

7. It is generally agreed that, over and above the causes that initiated the downswing of 1929–33, a combination of additional factors contributed to the peculiar severity of the decline. But we are unable to give precise answers to such questions as the following:

a) What, specifically, was the role of the various causes which have been cited as contributing to the length and severity of the Great Depression?

b) What happened after 1929 to each of the main sources of investment in the twenties? In what industries was investment particularly deficient, and what can we say about the causes of these deficiences (in terms of both the demand and supply of investment funds)?

c) How was the world-wide collapse in international trade related to developments in the United States? How were cyclical forces transmitted internationally, both on the downswing and during the stirrings of revival in 1932–33?

d) If we do make a distinction between the forces that initiated the depression and those that accentuated its severity, how did the interrelationships between these two sets of forces change as time went on? In this connection, more attention needs to be paid to the abortive recoveries in 1930 and 1931. The reasons for these slight revivals and the causes of their quick termination should throw valuable light on the deflationary forces operating during 1929–32.

8. The attention of business cycle students has usually centered on upper turning points, to the neglect of the factors responsible for initiating revivals. We need a careful study of the lower turning point in 1932–33. What industries led in the brief 1932 upturn? Which most strongly resisted further deflationary pressures? What, generally, were the favorable and unfavorable factors in the business situation in 1932? Similar questions can be asked concerning developments in March, 1933, and again at the end of 1933 after the brief "NRA boom" had collapsed.

9. The considerable literature on the cycle of 1933–38 does not give clear-cut answers to either of the two key questions: (1) What were the

---

[5] Eventually, the techniques and models of the sort being developed by Leontief may permit us to make significant statements about the quantitative importance of various initiating forces uncovered by an integrated study of a particular turning point and the preceding cumulative phase.

immediate causes of the turning points in 1937 and in 1938? (2) What factors were responsible for the unsatisfactory nature of the recovery during 1933–37? The first question requires a detailed turning-point analysis of the sort that we referred to in discussing the 1929 peak. To secure a more satisfactory answer to the second question, we need to complete the study of secular forces mentioned earlier and to compare in detail the factors affecting production and investment in 1935–39 with those prevailing in the late twenties.

10. Thus far we have emphasized the gaps in our knowledge concerning the "major cycle" of 1921–33 and the cycle of 1933–38. While our information about the cycle of 1919–21 is fairly good, we need to know much more concerning the "minor cycles" between 1921 and 1929. Time does not permit a detailed listing of the more important questions that remain unanswered here.[6]

11. *The Statistical Approach to Empirical Business Cycle Research*

The questions we have raised obviously imply an application of the so-called "historical" approach to empirical business cycle research, in contrast to what may be termed the purely statistical approach. A few comments on the usefulness of both methods in "explaining" past cyclical fluctuations may be in order.

The various versions of the "statistical" approach have this in common. For periods covering several business cycles, they look for patterns of systematic behavior in significant statistical series which can form the basis of generalizations about the nature and causes of business fluctuations. Either whole cycles or the successive data for individual months or years are taken as "observations" on "underlying" patterns of behavior, and statistical techniques are then applied to these observations in order to uncover the typical patterns and interrelationships which may exist.

Two versions of the statistical approach are currently attracting attention: the econometric work of Tinbergen and the Cowles Commission group[7] and the business cycle studies of the National Bureau of Economic

---

[6] The reader will undoubtedly want to supplement this list of questions with others which he thinks are equally or more significant. In particular, he may miss any reference to such debated issues as the effects of monetary policy on developments before and after 1929, the role of capital gains in stimulating spending, the effect of the stock market crash, and so on. Such questions would automatically come up for consideration in dealing with the issues raised in the text. The form in which I have put the latter suggests the directions in which I think empirical work can be most profitably pursued. The result should throw light on many questions besides the ones specifically raised in the text.

[7] See J. Tinbergen, *op. cit.*, also his *Statistical Testing of Business-Cycle Theories: I, A Method and Its Application to Investment Activity* (Geneva, 1939), and his paper on "Econometric Business Cycle Research," reprinted in *Readings in Business Cycle Theory* (Philadelphia, 1944); L. R. Klein, "The Use of Econometric Models as a Guide to Economic Policy," *op. cit.*; *ibid.*, "A Post-mortem on Transition Predictions of National Product," *Journal of Political Economy*, August, 1946, pp. 289-308; also the monograph by Klein previously cited. See also T. Haavelmo, "Statistical Testing of Business-Cycle Theories," *Review of Economic Statistics*, February, 1943, pp. 13-18, and the essay on

Research.[8] It may seem odd to classify together two groups which differ so radically on fundamental problems of methodology,[9] but there is a basic similarity between the two which should not be neglected. Both are interested primarily in typical, statistical relationships and behavior. In contrast to the historical approach, emphasis is not placed upon detailed, over-all studies of individual cycles or turning points. Particular cycles or cyclical phases are "explained" chiefly through generalized explanations which apply to all cycles in the period under study. In addition these and other versions of the statistical approach find it difficult to handle information which cannot be quantified and expressed in the form of averages or functional relationships.[10]

The heart of the econometric approach is the search for "structural behavior equations" which will explain the movement over time of significant economic variables in terms of other variables which are included in the model. Basically, it represents a sophisticated and elaborated application of least-squares analysis applied to time series.[11] Equations are first set up to reflect the investigator's judgment of the significant relationships which govern changes in economic activity, and statistical techniques are then applied to the data to secure the parameters for these equations. The equations thus secured are taken to describe the dynamic behavior of the economy and to "explain" why the endogenous variables change as they do over the business cycle.

Current econometric research in business cycles has a number of serious weaknesses. As tools of empirical research, econometric models are too simple and too rigidly bound by the set of hypotheses chosen. To permit of statistical estimation, these models must contain relatively few equations (even twenty or thirty are few in this context), and the total number of

---

"Econometrics," by Wassily Leontief in H. S. Ellis, editor, A *Survey of Contemporary Economics* (Philadelphia, 1948), especially pp. 403-407.

[8] See, in particular, A. F. Burns and W. C. Mitchell, *Measuring Business Cycles* (New York, 1946), and the mimeographed chapters of W. C. Mitchell's *What Happens during Business Cycles.*

[9] See, for example, T. C. Koopmans' highly critical review of *Measuring Business Cycles* in *Review of Economic Statistics*, August, 1947, pp. 161-172, and the forthcoming exchange between Koopmans and Rutledge Vining to be published in the same journal.

[10] These comments require some qualification with respect to the National Bureau's methods. The qualifications would apply more to the potentialities of the Bureau's approach than to the results thus far published. While averages and cycle "patterns" bulk large in what the Bureau has thus far done, the data for individual cycles are available for analysis, and the statistical records for individual cycles or specific series can be analyzed in conjunction with nonquantitative information.

[11] The advance of modern econometric business cycle research over earlier correlation studies has been chiefly along two lines: (1) the construction of complete equation systems or models to portray the behavior over time of all aggregative variables thought to be significant in explaining and predicting the level of business activity and (2) the adoption of probability reasoning in applying these models to reality and the consequent use of recent contributions to the theory of statistical inference in estimating the parameters of the equations used.

variables must be correspondingly limited. As a result, the variables studied tend to be broad aggregrates and broad index numbers. Further, the functional relationships are taken to be of a simple form and, more important, are assumed not to change in the period being covered. This is a dangerous assumption to make when not all of the possibly significant variables are included in the model.

Reliance on broad aggregates and on unchanging, simple functional relations is particularly questionable in a field where observation tells us that the behavior of components is of strategic importance and that the role of these components varies from cycle to cycle and even within the same cycle. In addition, econometric studies of the cycle suffer from the same technical weaknesses that have always plagued multiple-correlation studies of time series—intercorrelation among the "explanatory variables" (nearly all of which move roughly in the same cyclical pattern) and a reduction in "degrees of freedom" as the number of variables is increased.[12]

Econometric studies leave untapped all information which cannot be put into the chosen system of equations. "Exogenous variables" are included as given data—which means that the attempt is made to measure the effects of such variables on the other parts of the model, but no effort is made to explain the behavior of these "exogenous" events. But numerous factors are not taken into account at all—because precise data are not available, because these factors are not measurable, because they may be judged to be nonsignificant on a priori grounds, and so on.

The econometric approach excludes two types of study of considerable importance in business cycle research. It does not attempt to trace channels of transmission of initiating forces, partly because this involves dealing with an unwieldy mass of variables, partly because the econometric technique precludes *ad hoc* judgments by the investigator regarding cause and effect sequences. Secondly, the method deals with a given time period in isolation. No attempt is made to relate observed behavior during this period to what has gone on before, or to separate secular and cyclical forces (which can be done only if the period of investigation is related to preceding decades).[13]

---

[12] Econometric studies of economic behavior over time have thus far been further hampered by the almost exclusive use of annual data, which are too crude for business cycle analysis. Resort to quarterly or monthly data raises another problem, that of high correlation between successive pairs of observations of the same variables. See, however, Koopmans' comment that "statistical theory is sufficiently flexible to face" situations in which there is high serial correlation, as in quarterly and monthly data, though the "mathematical and computational difficulties inherent in such a situation pose technical problems which need to be overcome." *Op. cit.*, p. 170.

[13] As a matter of fact, current econometric business cycle research does not even require the assumption that business cycles exist. The method is applicable to static models of the Keynesian type or to "dynamic" models which introduce lags and rates of change. Even the dynamic models do not recognize the cycle as a unit of experience requiring separate analysis; the models "explain," through the invariant functions included, why the endogenous variables are what they are in any particular unit of time, regardless of the particular cycle or cyclical phase into which that unit of time falls.

For these reasons, among others, econometric techniques give us high correlations but fail to yield convincing explanations of the causes of cyclical fluctuations. They may tell us that a given set of observed facts is not inconsistent with the hypotheses embodied in the model chosen. But if the facts are equally consistent with a quite different but equally plausible set of hypotheses, we are not much better off than when we began. And there may be still other hypotheses, not yet tested, which fit the facts equally well.[14]

The techniques thus far employed by the National Bureau also do not take us very far in answering the questions raised regarding cyclical behavior in the interwar period. The National Bureau has sought to uncover the average or typical behavior of economic series over a large number of cycles. Thus far, the emphasis in the Bureau's specific work on business cycles has been on typical patterns of behavior displayed by individual series during "specific" and "reference" cycles—on "specific" and "reference" cycle *patterns.*

The delineation of such patterns serves a useful purpose, for it increases our ability to generalize about the characteristics which business cycles tend to have in common. But, if causal relationships vary from cycle to cycle as much as observation leads us to expect, this form of the statistical approach is not a substitute for detailed historical studies of individual cycles.[15] Also, the Bureau's business cycle research thus far has been concerned primarily with setting forth the facts, in the form of measures of average cyclical behavior of specific series. The task of explanation and interpretation still lies ahead.

In this connection, the Bureau's choice of cycle units probably lessens somewhat the usefulness of the work thus far done. Mechanical criteria are set up for marking off cycles in aggregate activity and in specific series, and these criteria preclude the recognition of possible "major cycles" underlying the business cycles which are recognized. Thus, for our period, the Bureau mechanically marks off "business cycles" according to the familiar turning points (which are listed in footnote 22). No measures

---

[14] Hence I view with skepticism Schumpeter's statement that "the highest ambition an economist can entertain who believes in the scientific character of economics would be fulfilled as soon as he had succeeded in constructing a simple model displaying all the essential features of the economic process by means of a reasonably small number of equations connecting a reasonably small number of variables." ("The Decade of the Twenties," *op. cit.,* p. 3.) Will it ever be possible to display "all the essential features" of economic behavior in this fashion? If the number of variables is "reasonably small" and therefore composed of broad aggregates, can we get the amount of detail we need to speak with confidence of specific causes? And as pointed out, models that seem to "fit the facts" do no more than tell us that one set of hypotheses is not inconsistent with these facts. Other sets of hypotheses may be equally consistent. In this respect, the writer shares the skepticism voiced by Keynes in his review of one of Tinbergen's studies, though Keynes did not always stand on firm ground in his detailed technical criticism. Cf. *Economic Journal,* September, 1939, pp. 558-568.

[15] Nor, I gather, would Mitchell or Burns suggest that it was. In this connection, see the comments on the potentialities of the National Bureau's methods in footnote 10.

are computed for the underlying swing of 1921–33; the decline of the thirties is related only to the truncated expansion of 1927–29. Each of the shorter cycles becomes a unit in the averages which are computed.[16]

Since so much of the evidence points to the need of treating the period 1921–33 as a cyclical unit, we are enjoined from using many of the results of the National Bureau's analysis of the cycles during this period. At the same time, however, we shall place heavy reliance upon what are perhaps the Bureau's two main contributions to empirical business cycle research thus far: their invaluable compilation of original data, corrected for seasonal variation,[17] and their many excellent monographs on the behavior of income, production, prices, and other variables in different sectors of the economy.

III. *The Historical Approach*

The essential characteristics of the historical approach to empirical cycle research are these. The emphasis is on explaining behavior during particular cycles, rather than on obtaining general conclusions that apply to all cycles within a given period. Full use is made of qualitative as well as quantitative information. The approach does not require precise measurement of functional relations or the preliminary setting up of complete theoretical models. Causal inference depends upon personal interpretations and judgment after detailed examination of the available evidence. A variety of statistical techniques—including econometric studies—may be employed. In addition, the approach should entail placing the cycle or period being studied in the context of the dynamic forces operating over a considerable period in the past.

The historical, no less than the statistical, approach entails initial theorizing—setting up working hypotheses. But the role of theory in both approaches can vary over a wide range. At the one extreme, complete theoretical models may first be constructed, in terms of which an attempt is made to "explain" historical events. This, for example, is the method used by Schumpeter, and also in the econometric model-building of the Cowles Commission group. More often, the historical approach utilizes theory chiefly as a guide to suggest significant types of relationships to examine in attempting to explain particular fluctuations.[18] This particular relation between theory and empirical research can be extended into the formal "testing" of alternative theories.[19] The econometric approach can

---

[16] See Mitchell's and Burns's brief comments on the relative advantages of treating the cycle of 1921–33 as a single unit of experience and of breaking the period up into segments corresponding to the shorter cycles. "Production during the American Business Cycle of 1927–1933," *op. cit.*, p. 2.

[17] The attitude of unstinting co-operation by Professor Burns and his fellow workers at the National Bureau in making this material available calls for special acknowledgment.

[18] This is essentially what is done in Slichter's study of turning points during 1919–36.

[19] This is Wilson's aim in the empirical section of his *Fluctuations in Income and Employment*. Even when formal testing of alternative theories is not the primary aim of a

also do this by trying different models, each being tested against the data in turn.

The three most important historical studies of business cycles in the interwar period are probably those of Schumpeter, Slichter, and Wilson.[20] Each contributes significantly to our knowledge, but, in varying degrees, each falls short of providing satisfactory answers to most of the questions asked in the preceding pages.

Time does not permit a full critical evaluation of these studies here, but some of their limitations may be mentioned briefly. Of the three authors, only Schumpeter attempts to place the interwar period in the setting of secular movements originating before 1914, and his analysis is seriously hampered by his adherence to an unchanging theoretical and statistical model. None of the studies attempts to assess the *quantitative* significance of secular and cyclical developments in strategic sectors, and none provides an analysis of the major turning points in the detail and along the lines which we have described as necessary. All three studies generally fail to present the available evidence in sufficiently detailed and systematic form.

We may conclude that the possibilities of applying the historical approach to a study of business cycles in the interwar period have been far from exhausted. It also seems reasonable to say that, in further applications of the historical approach to this period, the following lines of inquiry need particularly to be emphasized:

1. Consideration of the fluctuations during 1919–39 against the background of secular and cyclical change during the several preceding decades.

2. Heavy emphasis upon the behavior of *segments* of the economy— particularly the components of total investment and also output and employment in particular industries.

3. Detailed study of the "anatomy" of turning points, with attention being paid to particular industries and particular types of spending as well as to significant aggregative variables.

4. Rough assessment of the quantitative importance of various segments of the economy affecting total employment and investment at turning points and during cumulative phases.

5. Finally, such a study should emphasize systematic coverage and presentation of data so that the reader can check the author's judgments and interpretation as the analysis progresses. In the past, historical studies have too frequently been marred by the use of statistics merely for illustrative purposes.

For lack of a better term, we may refer to this method of analysis

---

historical study, the analysis almost always permits some conclusions regarding the extent to which particular explanations are consistent with observed relationships during the period examined. Thus Slichter's article on the period 1919–36, which disavows the primary aim of checking theories against observed behavior, has a final section of "Tentative Conclusions," a good many of which are concerned with the extent to which the evidence examined supports or refutes particular theories. (*Op. cit.*, pp. 17-19.)

[20] The full references are given in footnote 2.

as the "quantitative-historical" approach. Our emphasis, as in purely statistical studies, is on quantitative measurement; but we deal with individual cycles and turning points and utilize qualitative evidence and personal judgment as they seem to be required.

While our approach is quantitative as well as historical, we recognize that frequently it is impossible to arrive at convincing judgments regarding the actual magnitude of various forces which we may be able to isolate as probable causes of particular fluctuations. As Schumpeter has noted,[21] organic processes do not lend themselves to quantitative evaluation of causes, but certainly more is possible here than has thus far been attempted in historical studies.

IV. *Cyclical Patterns in the Interwar Period*

So much for how, in my opinion, the job should be done. In the little time remaining, I should like to comment briefly on the cyclical contours of the interwar period.

We can accept immediately the turning-point dates which the National Bureau has tentatively established for the cycles between 1919 and 1939.[22] From this and other evidence, we secure the five business cycles that are usually recognized for the interwar period: 1919–21, 1921–24, 1924–27, 1927–33, and 1933–38.[23] The evidence is overwhelming, however, that not all of these cycles stand on the same footing. Whatever our opinion as to the occurrence of "major" cycles before 1914, it is clear that we should group together the three "business cycles" from 1921 to 1933, particularly if we are to attempt to explain the causes of the Great Depression following 1929.

We can therefore describe the cyclical pattern of the interwar period as consisting of (a) the postwar cycle of 1919–21, (b) the "major cycle" of 1921–33, on which were superimposed the short and relatively mild cycles of 1921–24[24] and 1924–27 and which culminated first in the spurt of

---

[21] "The Decade of the Twenties," *op. cit.*, p. 8.

[22] These are:

Troughs: April, 1919, September, 1921, July, 1924, December, 1927, March, 1933, May, 1938.

Peaks: January, 1920, May, 1923, October, 1926, June, 1929, May, 1937.

See Burns and Mitchell, *op. cit.*, p. 78.

[23] What the writer means by "business cycles" is indicated by the following definition. Business cycles consist of recurring alternations of expansion and contraction in aggregate economic activity, the alternating movements in each direction being self-reinforcing and pervading virtually all parts of the economy. Further, but merely as a working rule which may on occasion be broken, we specify that business cycles usually last from about two to about twelve years. We may measure "aggregate economic activity" for this purpose by taking total output or total employment. Except for its criterion of "aggregate economic activity," this definition is similar to that of the National Bureau but has the virtue of being briefer. Cf. Burns and Mitchell, *op. cit.*, p. 3.

[24] As we shall emphasize later, the upswing of the minor cycle of 1921–24 was anything but mild. The 1921–23 upswing must be studied as part of the underlying expansion of 1921–29 as well as of the 1921–24 cycle.

1928–29 and then in the prolonged and severe downswing of 1929–33, and (c) the "New Deal" cycle of 1933–38, with its unusually long but halting expansion,[25] which terminated with the sharp recession of 1937–38.

The cycle of 1919–21 consists of two asymmetrical phases. The decline in output and prices was much greater, in both amplitude and duration, than the upswing. The general contours of this cycle and the fact that important indicators had been reflecting an underlying expansion since 1914 suggest that 1919–21 was part of a longer cyclical swing—a major cycle—which began about 1914 and may have reached its peak (so far as physical volumes are concerned) in 1917 or 1918.[26] The three-year moving averages in Chart I delineate this major swing quite well.

The downswing of 1920–21 is usually compared to the depressions of the 1870's, 1880's, 1890's, and 1930's, as well as to that of 1907.[27] Actually, despite the sharpness of the drop in many business indicators, the depression of 1921 does not belong in the same class with most of these other depressions for a number of reasons.[28] The downswing was relatively short.[29] While the depression involved drastic liquidation of prices, inventories, and short-term debts, it led to only the most temporary impairment of the business community's "propensity to invest." According to Kuznets' estimates, most of the decline in gross capital formation between 1920 and 1921 was accounted for by the difference in inventory accumulation. When adjusted for price changes, private business construction in 1921 was about as high as in 1920, and residential construction was larger. The flow of producers' durables declined by about a third, but this loss was more than regained by 1923. The moderate decline in consumers' expenditures between 1920 and 1921 apparently reflected merely the drop in prices. Kuznets' estimate of total consumers' outlay in constant prices is higher for 1921 than for 1920.

Add to these facts the character of the recovery between 1921 and 1923. The annual production series in Chart I, as well as other physical-volume series which are not plotted, suggest that the 1921–23 rise was

---

[25] The longest earlier expansions recorded by the National Bureau (going back to 1854) were associated with the Civil War (46 months) and World War I (44 months). (See Burns and Mitchell, *op. cit.*, p. 78.) Since 1938, a new record has been established by the expansion which began in that year and ended in the latter part of World War II.

[26] The peak in prices and in total spending, of course, did not come until 1920.

[27] Cf., for example, A. R. Eckler, "A Measure of the Severity of Depressions, 1873–1932," *Review of Economic Statistics*, May, 1933, pp. 75-81; and J. B. Hubbard, "Business Declines and Recoveries," *ibid.*, February, 1936, pp. 16-23. Hubbard puts the 1920–21 decline in the same class (as to severity) with the downswings of 1882–85 and 1907–08 but rates it as being considerably less severe than the depressions of the '70s, '90s, and 1930's. Eckler rates it as of the same order of severity as the declines of 1873–78 and 1892–94 and as being more severe than those of 1882–85 and 1907–08. Burns and Mitchell include 1920–21 in their list of the five most severe depressions since the Civil War. (*Op. cit.*, pp. 455, 462.) Their table on p. 403 suggests that it was more severe than the contractions of 1882–85, 1893–94, or 1907–08.

[28] Though it did mark the end of what we call a major cycle.

[29] Cf. the durations of other contractions listed in Burns and Mitchell, *op. cit.*, p. 78.

CHART I

ANNUAL MEASURES OF PHYSICAL VOLUMES, WITH THREE-YEAR MOVING AVERAGES

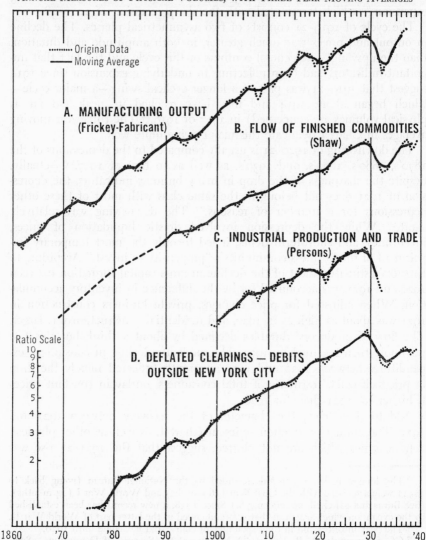

The nature and sources of the data are as follows:

A. Frickey's index of manufacturing production, 1860–1899, and Fabricant's index, 1899–1937, both on the base of 1899. See Edwin Frickey, *Production in the United States, 1860–1914*, p. 54, and Solomon Fabricant, *The Output of Manufacturing Industries, 1899–1937*, p. 44.

B. Flow of finished commodities plus construction materials, in 1913 prices, from W. H. Shaw, *Value of Commodity Output since 1869*, pp. 76-77.

C. Index on 1923–25 as a base, from W. M. Persons and LeB. R. Foster, "A New Index of Production and Trade," *Review of Economic Statistics*, August, 1933, p. 155, col. 3.

D. Outside bank clearings to 1919 and outside debits thereafter, deflated by Snyder's "Index of the General Price Level." Originally taken from F. R. Macaulay, *The Movements of Interest Rates, Bond Yields and Stock Prices in the United States since 1856*, Table 30, and continued by the National Bureau of Economic Research. This series has been transcribed directly from the National Bureau's files.

the most vigorous cyclical expansion since the turn of the century and perhaps since the Civil War.[30] Nearly all the serious depressions of the past have been followed by one or more "submerged" cycles, in which industrial output failed to reach as high a level, relative to the underlying trend, as did the preceding peak. Such "submerged" cycles seem to have occurred after the crises of 1837, 1857, 1882, 1893, and even 1907, as well as after the 1929–33 downswing.[31]

This does not seem to have happened after 1921. The ensuing expansion put the 1923 peak in most production series significantly above that in 1920. (See Charts I and II.) Of course, we are not sure how much allowance to make for trend, and it is possible to draw the underlying trend so sharply upward that the "trend adjusted" figure for 1923 is no higher than for 1920. There is strong reason to believe, however, that the trend in total output and in industrial production was not so steeply inclined.

Let us now look at the period 1921–29. Taking first the cycle of 1921–24, we note immediately the asymmetry between the expansion of 1921–23 and the contraction of 1923–24. Monthly indices of industrial production are unanimous in indicating that the downswing was, in absolute terms, less than half the preceding rise. Indeed some annual measures show little or no decline in 1924.

The recovery after mid-1924 was very rapid until the early months of 1925. Then ensued a period of remarkable stability, but with continued expansion, until the beginning of 1928. Expansion during 1925–26 was generally at a much slower rate than during 1921–23. The recession of 1927 was so mild as to show up in many series merely as a decline in the rate of advance.

Then followed the boom of 1928–29. Industrial production advanced at the most rapid rate since 1923, and the rise in GNP between 1928 and 1929 was the largest of any year since 1923.[32] I should like to emphasize

---

[30] A table in Burns and Mitchell, *op. cit.*, p. 403, confirms this conclusion, although it must be noted that these authors dealt only with trend-adjusted series. The total rise after the decline of the seventies was probably greater (making no allowance for trend), but it was not as rapid. In addition to the series in Chart II, the writer has examined the monthly indices of the American Telephone and Telegraph Company (since 1899) and Babson (since 1871) and the annual indices of Barron's (since 1899) and Silberling (which goes back to 1700). The series for monthly deflated outside bank clearings (continued by bank debits after 1918) does not suggest that the 1921–23 expansion was as vigorous as some of the cyclical upswings before 1914. (See Burns and Mitchell, *op. cit.*, chart facing p. 372.) Given the well-known weaknesses of deflated clearings and debits as measures of the physical volume of business activity, I am inclined to place more confidence in the direct measures of physical volume.

[31] As in the 1930's, the long decline following 1873 prevented the emergence of a short cycle before the next major expansion began. The ensuing long upswing was part of a major cycle, superimposed on a marked upward trend, which led to a peak in the early eighties substantially above that of 1873. But even with the help of the underlying secular rate of growth, industrial production did not exceed the 1873 peak until about 1878. Compare Chart I and Edwin Frickey, *Economic Fluctuations in the United States* (Cambridge, Mass., 1942), chart facing p. 180.

[32] However, the annual estimates of Kuznets (for the GNP), by Shaw (for total commodity flow) and by Fabricant (for manufacturing output) all agree that, taking two

CHART II

GROSS NATIONAL PRODUCT, CAPITAL FORMATION AND CONSUMERS' OUTLAY, 1929 PRICES
1869–1943

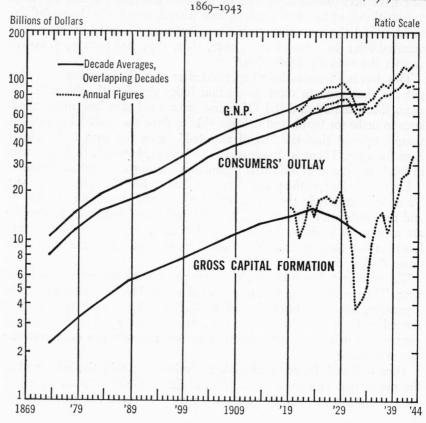

Source: Simon Kuznets, *National Product since 1869*, pp. 52, 119.

several points about this final spurt in output: the rapidity of the rise, the fact that the expansion started from a relatively high level, and the composition of the increase in output and GNP. Regarding this last point, we should note the sharp rise in inventory accumulation, the marked increase in the flow of producers' durables, and the fact that manufacturing suddenly became again the chief generator of expanding incomes and employment. (During 1923–28, finance, service, and government each accounted for a larger increase in national income than did manufacturing, and employment in manufacturing actually declined during these years.[33]) As a result of the increase in inventory accumulation and in producers' du-

---

year intervals, the total rise from 1927 to 1929 was somewhat less than during 1924–26 and, of course, considerably less than during 1921–23.

[33] Cf. Simon Kuznets, *National Income and Its Composition, 1919–1938* (New York, 1941), Vol. I, pp. 310, 314.

rables, gross capital formation rose sharply in 1929, despite a decline in construction. And here we may point to another significant contrast, which is brought out in Chart II. Whereas the rise in GNP from 1923 to 1928 took the form primarily of an expansion in consumption, capital formation changing relatively little, gross investment rose relatively much more than consumption in 1929 and even matched the absolute increase in the latter.

We thus get a picture of an underlying expansion continuing from 1921 to 1929, but with much the larger part of the rise occurring in the first two years of sharp recovery and in the last year's final spurt. During the five intervening years, from 1923 to 1928, we find the underlying expansion taking the form of a continued rise in consumption but with little expansion in investment. We should now look at the components of consumers' outlay and capital formation in more detail, but the pressure of time makes that impossible here.

The 1929–33 decline was the longest since the contraction of the seventies. In amplitude, it was almost certainly the most severe since the Civil War, and perhaps in our entire history.[34] This long downswing is clearly not symmetrical with the rise during 1928–29. If we are to find a meaningful cyclical unit in which to include this decline, clearly we must take the entire period 1921–33. We do not need a rigid model such as Schumpeter's to insist that the major swing of 1921–33 is a more significant unit to study than the cycle of 1927–33.

Further evidence of the cyclical unity of the period 1921–23 is provided in Chart I. Here three-year moving averages have been drawn through several annual series measuring changes in the physical volume of production and trade. (Between 1885 and 1914 and again during the 1920's minor cyclical fluctuations regularly ranged between three and four years in duration.[35]) In all of the series shown, the moving average traces out a major cycle from 1921 to 1932 or 1933 which is striking in its amplitude and regularity of movement. The chart also suggests that there has been no other major cycle of comparable amplitude since the 1870's. While the expansion of 1921–29 was perhaps not unprecedented, the decline after 1929 clearly was.

Chart I deserves careful study. It lends support to the hypothesis that a distinction should be made between major and minor cycles, but it also suggests that the major swings have not followed any regular pattern and sometimes scarcely seem to show up at all. So far as the observed behavior of output is concerned, the chart lends no support to rigid—as opposed to flexible—versions of the major-minor cycle hypothesis. Major cycles,

---

[34] Cf. Eckler, *op. cit.*; Hubbard, *op. cit.*; and Burns and Mitchell, *op. cit.*, pp. 403, 455. See also such measures of economic activity going back to the Civil War or earlier as those of Silberling (*The Dynamics of Business*, pp. 39, 50-51), Ayres (Cleveland Trust Index), and Babson (going back to 1871).

[35] Cf. Burns and Mitchell, *op. cit.*, p. 78.

granted they exist, do not seem always to include some given number of minor cycles. They may include none at all.

Charts I and II together also deserve study for the light they may throw on the secular forces operating on the twenties and thirties. There seems to be some evidence in these charts that the rate of growth in output was subject to some degree of retardation before 1929 and perhaps before 1914. This is a point on which there is disagreement, and I shall not push the issue here.[36] Our ability to generalize regarding the degree of secular retardation, if any, is further complicated by the fact that there have been long-term oscillations in the rate of growth—what A. F. Burns has called trend-cycles.[37] To this writer, Charts I and II suggest that the underlying rate of growth in the twenties—particularly in capital formation— was less than it was between the nineties and 1914, and significantly less than it was in the seventies and eighties. However, we need to disentangle the "primary" from "intermediate" (or "trend-cycle") movements, and even then we may not be able to reach clear-cut conclusions as to the relative roles of cyclical and secular forces in the twenties and thirties.[38]

A final word about the thirties. The interwar years after 1933 cover only one complete cycle—with a rise from March, 1933, to May, 1937, and a subsequent decline to about May, 1938. Here again there is a marked lack of symmetry between the expansion and contraction phases. The upswing was the longest in the National Bureau's records; and, since it began from a low level, the total rise was very large, even though output and employment at the peak were little if any higher than in 1929. The contraction was very short. Though the decline was precipitous, it ended quickly enough to leave the trough far above the levels of 1932–33. The recovery after the 1938 low point was rapid, so that by the end of 1939 the 1937 level had been reattained. Hence, so far as statistical behavior is concerned, the downswing of 1937–38 does not belong high on our list of "severe" depressions. It apparently belongs in the same category as the downswings of 1920–21 and 1907–08.[39]

---

[36] Stigler believes that there was no retardation between 1899 and 1929 (*Trends in Output and Employment*, p. 10). More cautious statements that the evidence is inconclusive will be found in A. F. Burns, *Production Trends in the United States since 1870* (New York, 1934), pp. 271-279, and Frickey, *op. cit.*, pp. 199-201. Kuznets, on the other hand, finds clear indications of retardation in the rate of growth of the national income. See *National Income: A Summary of Findings* (New York, 1946), pp. 34-39. The fact of retardation in total output is also accepted by A. G. Hart in *Money, Debt and Economic Activity* (New York, 1948), p. 265.

[37] Cf. Burns, *Production Trends*, Ch. 5; Kuznets, *National Income: A Summary of Findings*, pp. 60-71. These "trend-cycles" or intermediate swings in rates of growth are not to be confused with the "long waves" associated with the name of Kondratieff.

[38] This subject is pursued further in the larger study referred to in this paper.

[39] The decline in production was roughly of the same order of magnitude in all three downswings, although the monthly rate of decline was considerably greater in 1937–38 than in the other two cases. In all three cases, about the same period elapsed before the level of the preceding peak was again reached. These comparisons are based upon a study of Babson's and the American Telephone and Telegraph indices, both unadjusted for trend.

v. *Conclusion*

I must apologize for the briefness and generality of my remarks about the cyclical contours of the interwar period. Because of the time limitation, they violate in part some of the criteria set up earlier in this paper for historical research in business cycles. Even a description of broad cyclical patterns, if it is to be useful in later analysis, requires more historical perspective, a more detailed breakdown of aggregates, and greater recognition of non-quantitative information than I have been able to present here. These criteria will be more strictly adhered to in the larger project to which I have referred.

12

The 1957–58 Business Contraction: New Model or Old?*

GEOFFREY H. MOORE†

Editors' Note

The National Bureau of Economic Research has developed leading, coincident, and lagging indicators, statistical series which measure cycle developments even as they occur. For example, if on past experience certain data such as manufacturers' durable goods orders consistently change direction before the whole economy does, then such orders become a leading indicator. Other data, such as the gross national product itself, move directly in line with the general business cycle and thus become coincident indicators. Still others, for example unemployment, may lag behind, change direction after the whole economy, and thus fall in the category of lagging indicators. The indicator approach argues that all three types—leading, coincident, and lagging—should provide the temperature readings of the business cycle.

At any moment of time, the leading, coincident, and lagging indicators proceed, in terms both of timing and of amplitude, to a point comparable with earlier recorded cycles. Such a comparison provides the basis for classifying current movements as more or less severe than earlier ones and for determining how much longer the current cycle will run if history repeats itself. The approach assumes the usefulness of averaging earlier

* From *The American Economic Review*, Vol. XLIX, No. 2 (May, 1959), pp. 292-308. Reprinted by permission of *The American Economic Review* and the author.

† Dr. Geoffrey H. Moore, Associate Director of Research for the National Bureau of Economic Research, is a distinguished scholar in the field and third in the line which started with the late Wesley C. Mitchell, the father of the National Bureau, and continued with Professor Arthur F. Burns, who is represented earlier in this book. A Harvard Ph.D. (1947) and university professor, he has written: *A Significance Test for Time Series* (1941); *Production of Industrial Materials in World War I and II* (1944); *Statistical Indicators of Cyclical Revivals and Recessions* (1950).

cycles, or classifying previous cycles into several groups, more or less severe. Contemporary judgments are then expressed in the context of these averages. Since most of the recorded cycles took place in the prewar period, such a procedure has the disadvantage of diminishing the importance of government intervention so widely prevalent in the postwar period. Accordingly, in recent years, the National Bureau has also placed greater emphasis on diffusion indexes as measures of the inner workings of the economy from the cycle viewpoint.

Moore's article is a representative piece of National Bureau literature. The 1957–58 contraction, the most severe thus far recorded in post–World War II history, is particularly noteworthy since it did not develop into a major depression.

1. *Towards an Appraisal*[1]

❧ The business cycle is not dead. The 1957–58 contraction and the recent recovery demonstrated that it is still to be reckoned with. It is not the same identical cycle we have known in the past. The business cycle is like an automobile. Every new model is different, with bigger fins (they even call them stabilizers), automatic transmission, safety belts, and a smoother ride. But a car is still a car. What we know about the basic characteristics of business cycles should be taken into account in any calculations of the short-run future of the economy. Where these characteristics have changed, we should take the changes into account, too. What did the 1957–58 experience contribute to this knowledge?

This paper atempts to make a start on this appraisal by examining, first, the substantial similarities between the 1957–58 contraction and preceding contractions; then the substantial differences. This is not an easy classification to make. Really it serves only an expository purpose. There are all shades of difference, just as with the new automobiles. Moreover, where the difference represents the latest extension of a trend in cyclical behavior, both the similarity and the difference deserve emphasis. Thus a comparison of this sort is complicated. Couple this with the fact that there are a great many aspects of cyclical behavior to examine, and a lot of history, the justice of my claim that this appraisal is only a beginning is apparent.

[1] I am indebted to Arthur F. Burns for comments on an earlier draft of this paper, and to Sophie Sakowity, Dorothy O'Brien, Sandra Renaud, and Irving Forman for the statistical computations and charts.

II. *Features of the 1957–58 Contraction Substantially Similar to Earlier Contractions*

Duration. At first sight it might seem that in respect of duration the 1957–58 contraction is more different from than similar to its predecessors. In terms of the National Bureau's business cycle chronology, the contraction lasted nine months—from the peak in July, 1957, to the trough in April, 1958. Only three of the preceding twenty-four contractions, going back to 1854, were shorter than this. The median is twice as long, eighteen months.

However, a considerable number of contractions, especially since World War I, have not been much longer. The 1923–24 contraction was fourteen months; 1926–27, thirteen months; 1937–38, thirteen months; 1948–49, eleven months; 1953–54, thirteen months. The contractions that immediately followed World Wars I and II, in 1918–19 and 1945, also were short—seven and eight months, respectively. Only the 1920–21 and 1929–33 contractions were substantially longer—eighteen and forty-three months. There is some indication, therefore, that business cycle contractions in the United States have typically become somewhat shorter than they were before World War I, and the 1957–58 contraction adds one more bit of evidence on this score (Chart I).[2] Since the length of a business cycle contraction cannot be determined with absolute precision (because the peak and trough dates themselves are uncertain), close comparisons are not warranted.

There is another aspect, also, to this matter of duration. From some points of view, the duration that is of most consequence is that of the period when economic activity is, in some sense, "depressed." The contraction is only the initial part of this period, and although undoubtedly it is the part that is of greatest concern, the recovery period may also be a time of economic distress and uncertainty, particularly if it is prolonged.

In a recent study, two ways of measuring this period of depressed activity were proposed.[3] One used a single monthly index of production— the Federal Reserve index of mining and manufacturing production—and measured the interval from the business cycle peak to the month when the index regained the level it had at the peak. The other was based on a collection of ten indicators of aggregate economic activity and measured the interval from the business cycle peak to the month when half the indicators had regained their respective levels at the peak date. Other measures might readily be conceived, but these seemed adequate for the purpose, provided no implication was drawn that the attainment of preceding peak levels indicated a satisfactory, less than satisfactory, or better than satisfactory state of affairs.

---

[2] The monthly business cycle chronology, 1854–1957, is given in *Measuring Recessions*, by Geoffrey H. Moore, Occasional Paper 61 (NBER, 1958), p. 260.

[3] *Ibid.*, pp. 280–281.

The durations of periods of "depressed activity" have ranged from a year and a half to two years in mild or moderate recessions like those of 1949 or 1954, two and a half to three years in severe recessions like those of 1921 and 1938, and seven years or more in the Great Depression. These periods seem to bear a rough relationship to the severity of the decline during the contraction, mainly because the recovery periods (from the trough to the preceding peak level) have usually been substantially longer following severe declines than following mild ones.

It is too early to tell how closely the current period of depressed activity will resemble those in other cycles. Since the 1957–58 decline was intermediate in severity (see below), the period of depressed activity, to be in line with historical experience, should be within a range of a year and a half to two and a half years.[4] In terms of the industrial production index, the actual period may fall within this range, since by November, 1958, sixteen months after the July, 1957, business cycle peak, the index had recovered about three-fourths of its decline from peak to trough.

In terms of the other measure mentioned above, the recovery date may have been reached by November, 1958. Five of the ten aggregate indicators had exceeded their July, 1957, levels by that date. These were gross national product, personal income, retail sales, bank debits outside New York, and wholesale prices. These are all dollar value or price series. The five that had not yet recovered their pre-recession levels are industrial production, carloadings, nonagricultural employment, the unemployment rate, and corporate profits. All of these except profits are physical volume series. It appears, then, that the period of depressed activity will be longer when activity is measured in physical terms. Subsequent revisions of the figures may, of course, alter these results.

Severity. In terms of severity, or magnitude of decline from peak to trough, the 1957–58 contraction closely resembled many of its predecessors. Despite its brevity, the decline was somewhat larger, according to most measures of business activity, than in each of the four milder contractions since 1920, but much smaller than in the three severe contractions of 1920–21, 1937–38, and 1929–33.[5] The intermediate position of the 1957–58

---

[4] This range can be narrowed if account is taken of the length of the contraction period. Since the period of depressed activity consists of two phases—contraction and recovery—when the contraction period is known, only the recovery period need be estimated, and presumably this should lead to a more precise estimate of the full period. The eighteen-to-thirty month range for the full period was defined on the basis of a consideration of the apparent intermediate severity of the contraction before its actual severity or length was known (see *ibid.*, pp. 265, 289-291). Since the actual duration of the contraction was nine months and its severity was in the intermediate range, an appropriate estimate for the recovery period in the light of these facts and the historical record might be put at nine to fifteen months. This would yield an estimate of eighteen to twenty-four months for the period of depressed activity.

[5] For the percentage changes in seven measures of business activity during these contractions, see *ibid.*, p. 261. The corresponding percentage declines for the July, 1957–April, 1958 contraction are: nonagricultural employment, 4.4; gross national product, 3.7; retail sales, 3.4; bank debits outside N.Y.C., 5.9; industrial production, 12.2; and

CHART I

LENGTH AND MAGNITUDE OF BUSINESS CONTRACTIONS IN THE UNITED STATES, 1857–1958

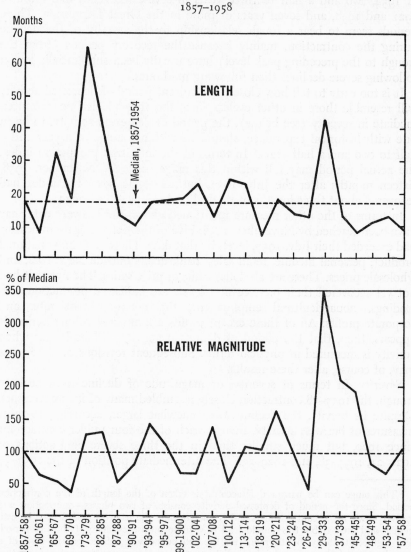

Duration is measured from monthly business cycle peak to trough. Relative magnitude is based on the average decline from specific cycle peak to trough in three indexes of business activity, each adjusted for long-term growth (A.T.&T., Persons-Barrons, and Cleveland Trust Company). The average decline in each cycle is taken as a percentage of the median decline for the twenty-four contractions, 1857–1954.

SOURCE: National Bureau of Economic Research, October, 1958.

contraction is shown also by a much longer record (Chart I). The average decline during 1957–58 in three indexes of business activity was very close to the median of all the cyclical declines in those indexes since 1854. In other words, about half the declines were larger than the latest one and half were smaller.

The 1957–58 contraction resembled its predecessors, also, in respect of the time when its relative severity became apparent.[6] Historical studies have shown that rates of decline during the few months in most measures of aggregate economic activity do not furnish a reliable gauge of the ultimate severity of a contraction. After six months or so have elapsed, however, the comparative declines in different contractions array themselves fairly well in relation to the ultimate extent of the declines. If the declines in certain "leading" indicators are analyzed in this way, the changes during the first four months or so of the contraction yield fairly reliable indications of severity. This much seems clear from an analysis of the seven business recessions between 1920 and 1954.

Developments during the 1957–58 contraction, on the whole, supported these results. After the first four months of the contraction had elapsed, comparisons of the declines in a group of ten leading indicators with the corresponding four-month declines in earlier recessions, suggested a contraction of intermediate severity. Subsequent comparisons compiled month by month for the same series continued to indicate this. On the other hand, the comparative picture shown by ten indicators of aggregate activity became reasonably clear, and like that shown by the leading series, only after about seven months of the contraction had elapsed. This type of analysis, it should be understood, did not pinpoint the magnitude of the 1957–58 decline but rather defined a broad range within which it might fall.

Scope. The contraction that began in 1957 quickly embraced a large proportion of the nation's economic activities. Until July or August, declines had occurred more or less sporadically in various sectors or types of economic processes. In September these declines became general. By the end of the year, among the ten aggregative indicators mentioned previously the only one that was at a higher level than it had been in July was the wholesale price index. Employment was lower in manufacturing, mining, construction, transportation, communication, and wholesale and retail trade.

It was the scope of these declines, as much as any other single thing, that identified what was going on as a business recession. Or, to put it differently, the characteristic of generality was one of the features of the 1957–58 contraction that puts it in a class with all the other business contractions of history. Burns and Mitchell, it may be recalled, included this characteristic as part of their definition of a business cycle: ". . . a cycle con-

personal income, o.9. The average unemployment rate for 1958 was 6.8 per cent. The 1957–58 contraction ranks fifth in severity (mildest first) among the eight contractions since 1920 according to the first four measures cited and the unemployment rate; it ranks fourth according to the other two measures.

[6] See *ibid.*, pp. 265, 282-286.

sists of expansions occurring at about the same time in many economic activities, followed by similarly general recessions, contractions, and revivals which merge into the expansion phase of the next cycle. . . ."[7] Chart II shows how this characteristic, measured by means of a diffusion index, has been identified with busines cycles in recent years.

The chart displays another prominent characteristic of business cycle expansions and contractions; namely, that they become less widely diffused before they end. The 1957–58 contraction was no exception to the rule. Indeed, one of the earliest signs that the contraction might be drawing to a close, though it was by no means conclusive at the time, was the diminution of the scope of the contraction that began to be observable last winter. More industries, more areas, and probably more business enterprises were experiencing declines in production, employment, orders, and profits in October or November last year than at any time since, with the exception in some instances of February, 1958. The comprehensive diffusion index in Chart II reached its lowest ebb in November, when only 12 per cent of the 280-odd series covered by the index were rising and 88 per cent were falling. In December the percentage rising increased to 21 per cent and in January, 1958, to 31 per cent. It remained at about that level until May, when it jumped to 57 per cent.[8] Since then it has stayed in the neighborhood of 70 to 75 per cent.

Shift in Composition of Output. One of the typical features of brief business cycle contractions is that a large proportion of the decline in output is attributable to a decline in investment in inventories. At the business cycle peak, usually a portion of output is being devoted to the accumulation of inventories, so that the current rate of output exceeds the volume of sales. Two or three quarters after the peak, inventory liquidation is usually under way, so that output is less than sales. As a result, the decline in output exceeds the decline in sales, often by a wide margin. This was the case in 1957–58 and also in 1953–54 and 1948–49. In each of these brief contractions, the decline in inventory investment exceeded the decline in total final purchases and hence was a dominant factor contributing to the decline in gross national product. Information on this point for earlier contractions is less adequate, but as far as it goes it supports the generalization.[9]

Wider relative swings in the output of durable goods than in nondurable goods during business cycles have long been observed. Between July,

---

[7] *Measuring Business Cycles* (NBER, 1946), p. 3.

[8] The dates cited accord with the plotting of the chart, which since 1948 is based on directions of change in the component series over three-month spans. E.g., the percentage rising from August to November is plotted in November, the percentage rising from September to December is plotted in December, etc. It should be understood that the figures cited were not available in the months designated, but usually about one month later. For a full description of this index see the paper by Julius Shiskin, "An Experiment with New Measures of Recession and Recovery," presented at the meeting of the American Statistical Association, December, 1958.

[9] See Moses Abramovitz, *Inventories and Business Cycles* (NBER, 1950), Chap. 21.

CHART II

A COMPREHENSIVE DIFFUSION INDEX AND AN INDEX OF
BUSINESS ACTIVITY, 1921–58

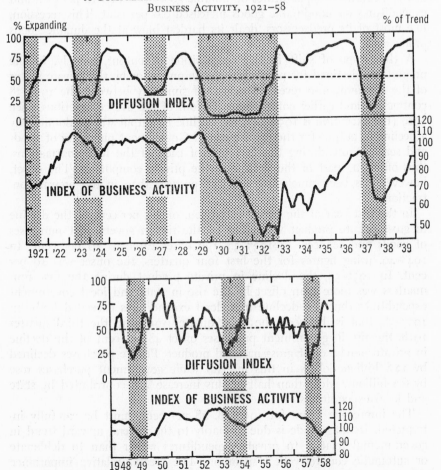

Shaded areas represent contractions of business cycles and white areas expansions, according to NBER chronology.

Diffusion index plotted on arithmetic scale; index of business activity plotted on ratio scale.

SOURCE: Diffusion index, 1885–1939, based on 404 economic series, is from G. H. Moore, *Statistical Indicators of Cyclical Revivals and Recessions* (NBER, 1950), pages 14-17. Diffusion index, 1948–58, based on 213-279 economic series, is from Julius Shiskin, "An Experiment with New Measures of Recession and Recovery" (Bureau of the Census, mimeographed, November, 1958), pages 37-39. The 1885–1939 index is not only based on a different sample of series than the later index, but is constructed in such a way that more of the minor fluctuations are ironed out. Index of business activity is published by the Cleveland Trust Company and is adjusted for long-run trend.

1957, and April, 1958, the Federal Reserve index of durable manufactures declined 19 per cent and the index of nondurable manufactures declined 4½ per cent. Between the third quarter of 1957 and the second quarter of 1958, consumer expenditures on durable goods declined 12 per cent and expenditures on nondurable goods increased 0.6 per cent. This recession, like most of its predecessors, dealt its hardest blow at the durable goods producers.

A third type of shift in the composition of output, namely, in the proportions destined for purchase by government or by the private sector of the economy, also reveals a degree of similarity between the 1957–58 contraction and earlier contractions. In four of the five contractions since 1929 (the exception is 1953–54), the decline in output was predominantly a decline in output for the private sector. Government purchases of goods and services rose during the first year of each of the four contractions, thus offsetting part of the decline in the private component. The offset, however, has been much larger in the postwar than in the prewar contractions.

In the first year of the 1929 contraction, only 5 per cent of the decline in gross private product was offset by the rise in government purchases of goods and services. In 1937–38, the offset came to 16 per cent. In 1948–49, using figures for the first four quarters, the offset was 19 per cent. In 1953–54, the decline in private product during the first four quarters was more than offset by the rise in state and local government expenditures, but the decline in federal expenditures exceeded both. In 1957–58, that is, between the third quarter 1957 and the third quarter 1958, the rise in government purchases offset 48 per cent of the decline in private purchases of gross national product. Private purchases declined by 12.8 billion dollars in this interval while government purchases rose by 6.2 billions. More than half of this increase was contributed by state and local expenditures.

The impressive figure for 1957–58, 48 per cent, must be carefully interpreted. Its magnitude is due primarily to the general upward trend in governmental relative to private expenditures rather than to deliberate or automatic countercyclical spending. The greater relative importance of state and local than of federal expenditures as an offset suggests this, among other things. Furthermore, the offsets to the initial declines in private product, i.e., *before* the first year had elapsed, were not nearly so large as those just mentioned. Thus the offset provided by total government purchases in the recent contraction was only 14 per cent in the first quarter after the peak, 11 per cent in the first two quarters, and 19 per cent in the first three quarters. It reached 48 per cent only after four quarters, by which time the reduction in the private component had already become very much smaller.

Early Decline in Profit Prospects and Investment Commitments. The circumstances attending the onset of the 1957–58 contraction resembled, in certain important respects, those frequently described by writers on business cycles. Mitchell, for example, described the later stages of a business boom as follows:

> The very conditions which make business profitable gradually evolve
> conditions which threaten a reduction of profits. . . . The decline in sup-
> plementary costs per unit ceases; equipment of less than standard efficiency
> is brought back into use; the price of labor rises while the efficiency of
> labor falls; the cost of materials, supplies, and wares for resale advances
> faster than selling prices; discount rates go up at an especially rapid pace,
> and all the little wastes incidental to the conduct of business enterprises
> grow steadily larger. . . . In many industries the increase in industrial
> equipment has been so rapid that the full output can scarcely be marketed
> at the high prices which must be asked. In the trades engaged in con-
> struction work the volume of new contracts declines when the rise in
> long-term interest discourages borrowing, and when the cost of construc-
> tion becomes excessive in the eyes of investors. The decline in bank re-
> serves ultimately makes the banks disinclined to expand loans further—
> a development which diminishes the ability of many enterprises to buy
> as freely as they had planned. . . .
> Since these various stresses become more severe the longer prosperity
> lasts and the more intense it becomes, and since a set-back suffered by any
> industry necessarily aggravates the stress among others by reducing the
> market for their products, a reduction in the rate of profits must infallibly
> occur. But . . . this reduction comes much later in some branches of busi-
> ness than in others, and varies widely in its severity. Even in the same
> industry different enterprises have exceedingly dissimilar fortunes. . . .
> Indeed, what quantitative information we possess indicates that in the
> very last year preceding a crisis a large number, perhaps a majority, of en-
> terprises are still making profits as high as or higher than in any preceding
> year. But . . . the critical point is reached . . . as soon as a decline of
> present or prospective profits has occurred in a few leading branches of
> business and *before that decline has become general.*[10]

This was written in 1913; yet with minor changes it might be a description of the course of events in 1955 and 1956. Higher overhead, materials,
labor, and construction costs; higher interest rates and tight money; plant
and equipment expanding amid evidences of excess capacity; a decline
in new appropriations and contracts for industrial construction; declining
profit margins in an increasing number of industries and declining profits
in an increasing number of business enterprises—all were present and
most can be accounted for, statistically.

A picture of part of this process is drawn in Chart III. At the beginning of 1955, profit margins per dollar of sales were rising in nearly all
manufacturing industries and aggregate profits were rising in a substantial
majority of the larger corporations (only firms that publicly report quarterly

[10] Wesley C. Mitchell, *Business Cycles*, Part III, pp. 494-495, 502-503 (University of
California Press, 1913).

CHART III

DIFFUSION IDEXES OF PROFITS AND CAPITAL INVESTMENT

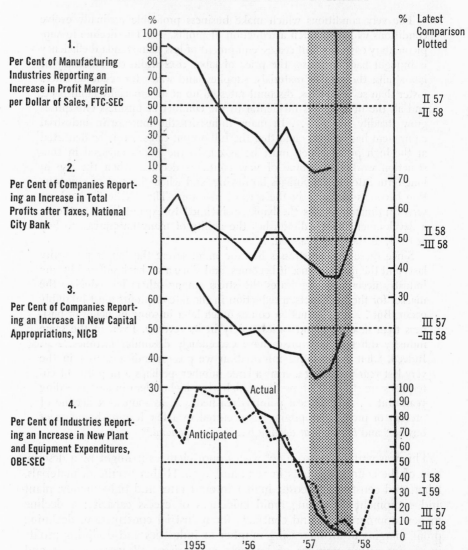

1.

Per Cent of Manufacturing
Industries Reporting an
Increase in Profit Margin
per Dollar of Sales, FTC-SEC

2.

Per Cent of Companies Report-
ing an Increase in Total
Profits after Taxes, National
City Bank

3.

Per Cent of Companies Reporting an Increase in New Capital
Appropriations, NICB

4.

Per Cent of Industries Reporting an Increase in New Plant
and Equipment Expenditures,
OBE-SEC

Latest
Comparison
Plotted

II 57
-II 58

II 58
-III 58

III 57
-III 58

I 58
-I 59

III 57
-III 58

Series 1, 3, and 4 are based on changes over four-quarter intervals, centered in the middle of the interval. Series 2 is based on quarter-to-quarter changes (adjusted for seasonal variation) and is centered in the first month of the second quarter. Shaded area represents business cycle contraction (July, 1957–April, 1958); unshaded areas are expansions.

profits are included in the sample). By 1956 these majorities had become minorities. In 1955 a majority of the larger corporations were increasing their budget appropriations for new capital, and virtually all major industries were increasing their actual and anticipated expenditures on new plant and equipment. By 1956 a reduction in new capital appropriations had become the more typical corporate policy, though it was not until 1957 that reductions in anticipated or actual expenditures on plant and equipment became widespread.[11]

Other Timing Sequences. Many other timing sequences that have persisted in business cycle downturns of the past reappeared at the 1957 downturn. Chart IV records the timing sequences exhibited by twenty-one economic indicators that were selected in 1950 and classified into leading, roughly coincident, and lagging groups on the basis of their cyclical behavior prior to 1938. The correspondence between the leads and lags of these indicators at the July, 1957, peak and their average (median) timing at preceding business cycle peaks is not close, but it is unmistakable. Six of the eight leading series reached peaks prior to July, 1957, and none later than July, whereas four of the five lagging series reached peaks later than July and none earlier. The lead of corporate profits was exceptionally long. That of freight carloadings was long (fifteen months) but not exceptional in view of the declining trend of rail traffic in recent years (carloadings led by twenty-one months at the 1948 peak, and by thirty-one months at the 1953 peak). The long lead of the average work week in manufacturing industries was unprecedented but needs to be interpreted in light of the fact that manufacturing activity as a whole was the first major sector of the economy to exhibit recessionary tendencies. The peak in manufacturing production was reached in December, 1956, or February, 1957, and in manufacturing employment in December, 1956—seven months before the July, 1957, business cycle peak from which all the leads are measured. The long leads in some of the other indicators that predominantly reflect manufacturing activity also should be interpreted in the light of this fact.

At the upturn in the spring and summer of 1958 the turns in this set of indicators were far more concentrated than at the downturn. The longest lead was five months (stock prices and basic prices) and the longest lag was about the same, making a span of ten or eleven months altogether. The sequences also were less clear. One of the leading indicators (contracts for commercial and industrial construction) lagged at the April, 1958, turn and two were coincident; the rest began to rise two to five months before the turn. Three of the lagging series lagged as usual, but

---

[11] For analyses of the historical record of the cyclical diffusion of profits and the timing of investment commitments and outlays see Arthur F. Burns, "New Facts on Business Cycles," in *Frontiers of Economic Knowledge*, pp. 107-134; Thor Hultgren, *Cyclical Diversities in the Fortunes of Industrial Corporations*, Occasional Paper 32; Wesley C. Mitchell, *What Happens during Business Cycles*, pp. 158-170; Geoffrey H. Moore, "The Diffusion of Business Cycles," in *Economics and the Public Interest*, pp. 35-64.

CHART IV

LEADS AND LAGS AT BUSINESS CYCLE PEAKS AND TROUGHS,
TWENTY-ONE INDICATORS

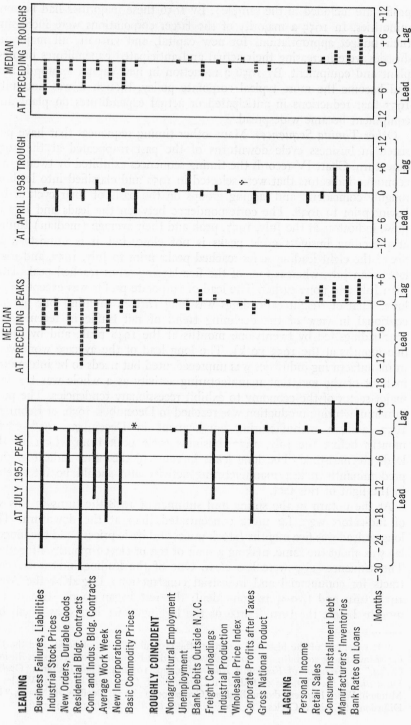

LEADING

Business Failures, Liabilities
Industrial Stock Prices
New Orders, Durable Goods
Residential Bldg. Contracts
Com. and Indus. Bldg. Contracts
Average Work Week
New Incorporations
Basic Commodity Prices

ROUGHLY COINCIDENT

Nonagricultural Employment
Unemployment
Bank Debits Outside N.Y.C.
Freight Carloadings
Industrial Production
Wholesale Price Index
Corporate Profits after Taxes
Gross National Product

LAGGING

Personal Income
Retail Sales
Consumer Installment Debt
Manufacturers' Inventories
Bank Rates on Loans

AT JULY 1957 PEAK

MEDIAN
AT PRECEDING PEAKS

AT APRIL 1958 TROUGH

MEDIAN
AT PRECEDING TROUGHS

* No cyclical peak corresponding to July, 1957.
† No cyclical trough corresponding to April, 1958.

retail store sales led by one month and personal income by two. The lead of personal income was not particularly unusual; leads occurred at six of the eight preceding troughs.

Although the upturns in different aspects of economic activity were more concentrated than at the previous business cycle trough in 1954, the degree of concentration was not unprecedented. A similar situation prevailed, for example, at the trough in 1938. Moreover, it would be unrealistic to expect that the sequence among the individual series at any given business cycle turn would closely resemble the average sequence. The sequence at each turn generally varies considerably from the average sequence.

III. *Unusual Features of the 1957–58 Contraction*

Some features of the 1957–58 contraction are unusual in the sense of seldom if ever having been observed before, while other unusual features have antecedents in earlier contractions and merely represent a further secular change in cyclical behavior. Indeed, we have already encountered one example of the latter: the increasing potency of governmental expenditures in offsetting cyclical declines in the private sector. The distinction is important, for secular shifts in cyclical behavior may continue and knowledge of them may help us to analyze subsequent contractions. In what follows we shall try to draw this distinction whenever we can.

Financial Distress. Many of the business cycle contractions of the more remote past were accompanied by severe financial distress, credit liquidation, wholesale cancellation of orders, hoarding, and other manifestations of loss of confidence or even panic. These conditions were either absent in 1957–58 or present on only a moderate scale.

The difference can perhaps be put most plainly by referring again to Mitchell's 1913 account of the cycle. The chapter following the above-cited description of the later stages of prosperity is entitled "Crises." By this term Mitchell meant an acute stage of credit liquidation—a period when banks and other creditors demand repayment of a part of their outstanding loans and are reluctant to grant new ones. Sometimes the crisis was accompanied by a panic, bankruptcy of some conspicuous enterprise, or a run on the banks. At other times the crisis was simply a period of severe financial strain which eased gradually into a depression.

Despite the fact that, as pointed out earlier, developments immediately before the 1957–58 contraction were similar in many respects to those that Mitchell described as culminating in a crisis, the consequences were different. The improvements in our financial structure that provide some insurance against disasters of this sort are well known. Some of the insurance is provided by institutional changes outside the financial area.

There is, of course, no guarantee in these safeguards that a credit crisis will never occur again. If, through speculation or relaxation of credit standards, a serious deterioration in the quality of credit should develop, as happened in the twenties, a drastic credit liquidation might ensue. Most of the new countercyclical weapons are either not designed to or are not so likely to be employed to prevent the excesses in the granting of credits that can develop during a boom. Nevertheless, the 1957–58 contraction provided the severest test in the postwar period of the effectiveness of our safeguards against financial collapse, and the results were encouraging.

Stability of Personal Income. A second and not unrelated feature of the 1957–58 contraction was the impressive stability of total personal income in face of the sharp drop in production, employment, and profits. Relative to these declines, the stability in income was unprecedented, but it was nevertheless the manifestation of a trend. Income declined about 1 per cent during the nine-month business cycle contraction of July, 1957–April, 1958. This small decline was only about a fourth as large as the declines in gross national product or in nonagricultural employment, less than a tenth as large as the decline in industrial production, and only 3 per cent as large as the decline in corporate profits. In the first nine months of the contraction that began in 1929, the percentage decline in personal income exceeded those in GNP and employment, was half as large as the decline in industrial production, and nearly one-sixth as large as the reduction in corporate profits. In each successive contraction between 1929 and 1957, the drop in personal income during the first nine months became progressively smaller relative to those in production, employment, and profits. The factors that appear to be primarily responsible for this are: the declining relative importance of farm income and its insulation from recession in recent years, the growing importance of government payrolls and their insulation from recession, and the rising relative magnitude and countercyclical behavior of transfer payments, mainly unemployment compensation payments.[12]

The personal income figures we have been discussing are before taxes. On an after tax basis, that is, in terms of disposable income, the trend towards greater stability during business cycle contractions has been even

---

[12] These effects can be demonstrated by a hypothetical calculation of what the decline in total personal income would have come to in any given contraction if the percentage changes in each component were unaltered but the relative size of each component shifted as it has in the course of time. For example, in the 1937–38 contraction, personal income declined 7.7 per cent, on an annual basis. If the composition of income had been as it was in 1953, when farm income was a smaller fraction of the total and government payrolls and transfer payments much larger fractions, the decline would have been 5.6 per cent. By 1957, the decline would have been 5.3 per cent. Thus in effect the shift in the sources of personal income that has taken place in the past twenty years would have moderated the decline in the total by nearly a third, other things remaining the same. A similar calculation based on the 1948–49 experience shows that the 1 per cent decline in personal income (annual figures) in that contraction would have been a 1 per cent increase if the composition had been what it was in 1957. Both calculations take into account shifts in other components of income besides farm income, government payrolls, and transfer payments. For further details see my introduction to Daniel Creamer's *Personal Income during Business Cycles* (NBER, 1956), pp. xxviii-xxxi.

more marked. One would expect, then, that this stability would have a substantial effect on the behavior of consumer expenditures, as well as a less readily measurable effect on the business cycle itself. Consumer spending does appear to have become decidedly more stable relative to declines in output and employment, and it seems likely that income stability has been a factor in this. Further study of the components of expenditure and their relation to declines in income and to changes in the use of credit is necessary before one could be confident about this, however.

Prices; Wages; Monetary Policy; Foreign Trade. At the end of the contraction the consumers' price index was about 2½ per cent above its level when the contraction began. Aside from the brief business contractions of 1919 and 1945, when consumer prices also rose substantially, this was the first recession since World War I to witness such an increase. The increases were concentrated among foods and services; prices of apparel and household goods held steady or declined slightly. The total index itself began to level off at about the time the business contraction ended, i.e., in March or April, 1958, especially if allowance is made for some slight seasonal movements. Wholesale commodity prices, again with the exception of foodstuffs, responded more perceptibly and promptly to the recession, but the total index excluding farm products and foods did not drop more than a fraction of 1 per cent below its level when the recession began. A similar stability prevailed in the 1953–54 recession, but in most earlier recessions reductions in wholesale prices were larger and more widespread. Allowance should, of course, be made for the brevity and moderate severity of the 1957–58 contraction, as well as for the changing composition of most of the available price indexes and the ways in which actual prices may differ from reported prices. The subject warrants further study, but a trend towards increasing stability or stickiness of prices during recession both at retail and at wholesale seems to be developing. In this respect the farm price support program bears a share of responsibility.

The 1957–58 recession caused virtually no slackening in the rate of advance in hourly rates of pay. The rate of increase in average hourly earnings in manufacturing as a whole did diminish somewhat, but this is largely accounted for by reductions in the amount of time paid for at overtime rates and in employment in the more highly paid durable goods industries. During the thirty-five month period of business expansion from August, 1954, to July, 1957, straight-time hourly earnings rose twenty-nine cents in durable goods manufacturing industries and twenty-three cents in nondurable industries. During the next nine months of business contraction, a period about one-fourth as long, the increases were almost precisely one-fourth as great: seven cents and six cents per hour, respectively. Increases in hourly wages during brief and moderate recessions are somewhat less unusual, historically, than increases in consumer prices. Yet here, too, there is evidence of a larger degree of insulation from the pressures that accompany a contraction in business activity, in part because of the greater prevalence of long-term union contracts with built-in wage improvement factors and escalator clauses.

If the prices of commodities, services, and labor are becoming more immune to recession, that does not appear to be true of the price of money. The reversal in monetary policy in the autumn of 1957 helped to bring interest rates down farther in the same period of time than in any recession since the Federal Reserve System was established. The free reserves of member banks rose in the first nine months of recession by larger dollar amounts than in any of the five preceding recessions for which figures are available. The money supply decreased sharply at first but by April, 1958, was increasing at a faster rate than at the corresponding point (ninth month after the peak) in any of the contractions since 1920.

The behavior of foreign trade also was unusual. Imports declined irregularly, but the decline was smaller than in the corresponding periods of most of the preceding seven contractions. Exports, on the other hand, dropped more sharply than in most of the preceding recessions. As a result, the drop in exports greatly exceeded the decline in imports. This had happened in none of the preceding seven contractions. It caused a drop of three billion dollars (annual rate) in net exports in the GNP accounts between the third quarter of 1957 and the second quarter of 1958—again an unprecedented decline for the first nine months of a business cycle contraction.

IV. *Historical Perspective and Its Pitfalls*

Though the differences are important, the similarities between the 1957–58 contraction and its predecessors are sufficient to demonstrate that business cycle phenomena continue to exert a profound influence upon our economy. Accordingly, what has been learned in the past about such phenomena can usefully be applied to the present and the future. There is need, however, to guard against oversimplification in the use of historical perspective. Comparisons of this recession with the other two postwar recessions became so popular during the past year that a few warnings would seem to be in order. With suitable changes in wording, they apply to recoveries as well as recessions.

First, do not confine comparisons to the immediately preceding recession or even the last two. There is too much variability in these phenomena for a sample of one or of two observations to be very helpful—though one or two is better than none. For many years after the Great Depression, that catastrophe became the prototype with which all recessions were compared. More recently, the 1953–54 contraction became a sort of standard of comparison. These two are at opposite poles as far as duration, severity, and most other respects are concerned. There is no particular reason for subsequent contractions to be like either one.

Second, do not confine comparisons to an average of preceding cycles. Surely an average is better than a single observation. But again there are wide variations about averages of cyclical behavior. When these variations reflect progressive changes, as we noted in some instances above, it is essential to take them into account. Even when they do not, they are instructive.

Third, be aware that current developments can fall outside the range of previous experience, but use that range as a guide to help avoid the biases we are all heir to. Many of the forecasts of the 1954-55 recovery, for example, fell far below the range of previous experience. A similarly conservative tendency appears to characterize many of the forecasts that have been made about the current recovery. Conservatism is a fine thing, and so is optimism. Both should be tempered by experience.

FOR FURTHER READING

The historical analysis of business cycles is still a neglected field. However, one valuable study of an important episode is that of Kenneth D. Roose, *The Economics of Recession and Revival—An Interpretation of 1937–38* (New Haven: Yale University Press, 1954), which takes a close look at the 1937–38 downturn, one of the sharpest on record. For the reader who has only experienced the mild downturns of the postwar period, an awareness of what can happen to production and incomes in a few short months will be revealing. Another book which almost everyone interested in economics should read is that by John K. Galbraith, *The Great Crash*, 1929 (Boston: Houghton Mifflin, 1955). This entertaining account of the 1929 debacle, while a best seller, nevertheless deserves the attention of those for whom that historic period is only a subject of conversation among their elders. Since the National Bureau techniques for assessing business cycle developments are now so widely accepted, it is mandatory to read the basic work on the subject, Arthur F. Burns and Wesley C. Mitchell, *Measuring Business Cycles* (New York: National Bureau of Economic Research, 1946). The National Bureau has performed a valuable service in publishing a two-volume study, edited by Geoffrey H. Moore, on *Business Indicators* (Princeton: Princeton University Press, 1961). This summarizes all the work done at the Bureau on the leading indicator approach; presents the latest version of what indicators are considered as leading, coincident, or lagging; contains the statistics used for the indicator method; and makes a number of new empirical contributions to the broad subject of business cycles. In a word, it is essential reading for anyone seriously interested in the subject. A perspective somewhat different from that of the National Bureau is presented in an important book by Bert G. Hickman, *Growth and Stability of the Postwar Economy* (Washington, D.C.: Brookings Institution, 1960), a major contribution toward understanding what has happened to the business cycle in recent years. Since many of the empirical advances in tracing economic fluctuations have taken the form of a wide variety of anticipations or intentions surveys covering many aspects of the economy, the student should read *The Quality and Economic Significance of Anticipations Data* (Princeton: Princeton University Press, 1960), which contains references to all the leading surveys, what they have shown, and how they can or cannot be used to determine the future of business spending for plant and equipment, consumer spending for durable goods, investments by life insurance companies, and so forth. The advent of high-speed data processing has introduced a new dimension into empirical business cycle research. For this purpose, the study by Julius Shiskin, *Electronic Computers and Business Indicators* (New York: National Bureau of Economic Research, 1957) is important. Shiskin, incidentally, has been the prime mover behind the publication of a new official release which contains a sizable number of leading, lagging, and coincident indicators, all seasonally adjusted (*Business Cycle Developments*, a monthly report by the U.S. Department of Commerce). Finally, the reader should follow for himself the contemporary tracing of the business cycle as it unfolds month by month, and quarter by quarter. Many publications are available for this purpose, but among these, two of the leading bank letters are worthy of mention, particularly since they are available gratis on a continuing basis: the *Monthly Letter—Business and Economic Conditions* of the First National City Bank of New York and *Business in Brief* of the Chase Manhattan Bank of New York.

PART III

Business Cycle Theory

INTRODUCTION

The articles of Parts I and II recounted the many types of fluctuations to which economic activity is subject and explored the problems involved in describing and measuring one kind of fluctuation, namely, the business cycle. Nevertheless, our knowledge of business oscillations is not wholly empirical. Theory plays a vital role in motivating research and in providing useful insights for the interpretation of data.

The perennial question of whether economics is an art or science may never be settled, depending as it does on the definitions accepted by the debaters. It need not concern us here. It is important to emphasize, however, that the modern economist advances his professional knowledge by employing the *scientific method*. This demands extensive fact-gathering on the phenomenon under scrutiny, the careful formulation of a hypothesis to explain the relationship among the relevant variables, testing of the hypothesis by further resort to experience, and, finally, the acceptance or rejection of the hypothesis. Upon verification of the hypothesis, a new principle, which may in turn spark further research or offer a valuable tool to decision-makers in business or government, becomes incorporated into the body of economic thought.

In order to understand any complex phenomenon—for example, the business cycle—one must make certain simplifying assumptions (that is, formulate a hypothesis) and proceed from there. Mere accumulation of data will not furnish a ready explanation of the behavior reflected in the data. In systematizing and rationalizing the empirical evidence, the analyst supposes a set of general relationships to exist among the observed events. Herein lies the function of economic theory: to discover the underlying forces which condition productive activity and to describe cause-and-effect associations which may serve as a basis for prediction. Thus our economist, as well as his confreres in the physical sciences, looks to theory for unifying principles to link the component parts of an intricate reality and to create a mental unity out of a vast array of tabulated data.

Economists of the eighteenth and nineteenth centuries, possessing only the most rudimentary data on the contemporary economic scene, evolved the original postulates or "laws" of economic thought deductively from the nature of man and his institutions. The hallowed "Law of Diminishing Marginal Utility," still a standard feature of principles textbooks, illustrates the point. Although deductive reasoning formed the basis of much classical economic literature, as an exclusive methodological approach it obviously possesses many drawbacks from the nature of the subject under investigation. Moreover, the enlightened management of an industrial society would soon require great quantities of statistics on movements in the general economy, its individual sectors and particular industries. Therefore, with the proliferation of economic and demographic data and improvement in the techniques of induction, these original postulates guided research but, in turn, became subject to verification. Today, economic thought matures by a balanced methodology of deductive and inductive reasoning.

Nowhere do we see this process of hypothesizing and verification more clearly than in cycle theory. The preceding articles have tended perhaps to overstress one side of the process, namely, induction. The following selections will somewhat redress the balance and provide an introduction to each of the major lines of inquiry elaborated in the succeeding sections. To begin, we have selected an excerpt from Professor Haberler's *Prosperity and Depression,* for it expounds most lucidly the logical nature of cycle theory. The selection from Professor Heimann's *History of Economic Doctrines* discusses in broad fashion the important advances in the field with special emphasis on the neoclassical and modern periods.

One aspect of modern cycle theory merits independent comment: that is, econometric business cycle models. The attempt to mathematize economic problems goes far back into the history of economic thought, certainly to Hermann Gossen (1810–1858) who believed that mathematics would end the dissonance of conflicting theoretics, and perhaps to Sir William Petty (1623–1687), the author of *Political Arithmetick* (1672). The econometricians of today, however, have shouldered a broader and more complex task than the mathematical economists of tradition in striving to blend economic theory, statistics, and mathematical economics in their constructions. The successes and difficulties, the limitations and the potential which have beset this attempt are sympathetically evaluated in the excerpt from R. A. Gordon's *Business Fluctuations.*

The reader should note that no one theory or explanation of the business cycle receives the general approbation of the majority of professional economists, although at certain stages of economic history particular theories have been especially influential. In general, diversity of opinion continues to characterize the field, and the tendency persists for each economist to construct his own theory, introducing various points of emphasis which suit his unique experience. This naturally makes for a healthy spirit of controversy, typical of all vital intellectual disciplines. Better still, in recent decades it has yielded exceptional advances and provided public authorities with the knowledge of how at least to moderate cyclical oscillations. For the reader, sadly, there seems no alternative but to canvass each concept, compare it with other ideas on the same subject, and arrive at his own conclusions. Nonetheless, the reward should match the effort, for in doing so the diligent scholar will become familiar with many valuable concepts and insights which bring a measure of reason to our complex world.

13

The Explanation of the Business Cycle*

GOTTFRIED HABERLER†

~~~~~~

Editors' Note

The jacket description of Professor Haberler's *Prosperity and Depression* ("As a classic of business cycle literature . . . since gone through three editions [and now a fourth] and has been translated into Japanese, Swedish, Spanish and German") ranks as fact, not the "puffing" of salesmanship. A comprehensive and authoritative analysis of cycle theories, it must stand side by side with Mitchell's *Business Cycles: The Problem and Its Setting*. Both are milestones in cycle literature, and the reader desirous of starting a home library on the topic must surely begin with them.

In a general way, the business cycle finds its ultimate causation in either the nature of man (human motivations, psychological factors, and so forth), the nature of his society (institutional arrangements as private property or the structure of the banking system), or the geophysical environment (sunspots, crop variations, or the discovery of new resources). These factors may in turn be regrouped to distinguish between external, noneconomic, or exogenous factors (not inherent in the operation of a capitalist economy) and internal, economic, or endogenous factors (*sui*

---

* Reprinted by permission of the publishers from Gottfried Haberler, *Prosperity and Depression*, pp. 5-12; Cambridge, Mass.: Harvard University Press, Copyright, 1958, by The President and Fellows of Harvard College.

† Born in Purkersdorf, Austria, on July 20, 1900, Professor Haberler has had a unique career in European and American academic, governmental, and business circles. At various times he has held professorships in economics and statistics at the University of Vienna and Harvard University. From 1934 to 1936, he served with the Financial Section, League of Nations, and in 1943 became associated with the Board of Governors, Federal Reserve System. Always active in the affairs of professional associations, he was nominated Chairman of the Board, National Bureau of Economic Research in 1956. He is today Professor of Economics and Galen L. Stone Professor of International Trade at Harvard University.

generis to the private enterprise system). Schemata of this sort, though useful in classifying cycle theories, may not, Professor Haberler points out, be altogether enlightening. The exogenous factor of one set of assumptions may in a different set of circumstances work endogenously (witness Schumpeter's innovation theory). Pointing a way out of this methodological dilemma, Haberler asks us to study primarily the structure of the system and to treat the so-called exogenous factors as modifying influences for good or ill. "The Explanation of the Business Cycle," in *Prosperity and Depression*, is preliminary to the theory discussions. It will serve the same purpose in our book of readings.

❧ Before we begin the exposition of the various theories of the business cycle, some remarks may be advisable on the general logical nature of any explanation of the cycle, and on the mutual relation between various possible explanations (theories). The implications of these observations will be fully realised only in the light of subsequent pages where these formal principles are, so to speak, put to work. Nevertheless, it seems useful to touch upon these things at the beginning in order to avoid misunderstandings. The study of the various theories will be more fruitful if the following general remarks are kept in mind.

Plurality of Causes

Such a complex phenomenon as the business cycle, which embraces almost all parts of the economic system, does not easily lend itself to explanation by any one factor. Even if we assume from the beginning that the same explanation of the business cycle holds good in the highly industrialized countries of Western Europe and America as well as in industrially less developed countries such as New Zealand or Roumania, and in the twentieth century as well as at the beginning of the nineteenth —neither of which assumptions is by any means self-evident—it is not easy to speak of *the* cause of the business cycle. Few writers have ventured to proclaim just one single factor as *the* cause of the business cycle or of depression in particular. In fact, explanations which run in terms of one single cause have been more and more discredited and should be regarded with suspicion. The majority of modern writers on the subject are careful to point out that a whole set of factors, and perhaps not always the same combination of factors, contribute towards producing an alternation of prosperity and depression. Frequently, the difference between various theorists is rather a difference in the emphasis laid upon the different factors than a difference in the enumeration of contributing causes and conditions.

Even those writers whose theory centers round one single factor which they make responsible for the business cycle—e.g., crop variations, or inventions, or the acceleration of derived demand, or changes in demand, or waves of optimism and pessimism—are forced to admit that what they call *the* cause of the business cycle can produce its effect only in a certain economic institutional environment. They assume, explicitly or implicitly, a certain structure of the exchange economy, a certain rigidity of wages and contracts, a certain behaviour of investors, the presence or absence of a certain amount of knowledge and foresight amongst entrepreneurs, a certain monetary organisation, etc. The business cycle might well not appear (*a*) if those "active" forces (crop changes, inventions, changes in demand, etc.) were absent, or (*b*) if one or several of the significant features in the economic institutional framework were changed; if, for example, wages and contracts were perfectly plastic, if entrepreneurs behaved in a different way, if they possessed perfect foresight or if the monetary organisation were different and monetary authorities took steps to prevent repercussions: in a word, if they were to behave differently from what they actually do.

It might therefore just as well be maintained that the rigidity of our economic system, or its financial or monetary organisation, or particular features of the latter, are the causes of the cycle as that inventions or crop changes or changes in demand are responsible.

Theories Differ Mainly as to Emphasis

Normally, a complex phenomenon such as the business cycle is caused and conditioned by a large number of factors and circumstances. Even if the same theory holds good for all cycles, there is still room for a multitude of "different" explanations which need not all be logically exclusive and contradictory. Each of them stresses one or other of the relevant factors and conditions and calls it the "dominant" or "causally relevant" one. The other factors are neglected, or it is assumed that they do not change or cannot be changed, or that it is for some reason not desirable to change or eliminate them (*e.g.*, inventions) or that their changes cannot be further explained (at least not by the economist) and that they must therefore be taken for granted. In particular, monetary and nonmonetary explanations of the business cycle seem to be frequently reconcilable. The non-monetary theorist (who stresses, *e.g.*, the impact of inventions, or changes in demand with intensified changes in derived demand) often tacitly assumes—or ought logically to assume—the willingness and ability of the banking system to expand credit on existing terms, whereas the monetary theorist takes such disturbing events as inventions or changes in demand for granted and blames the monetary authorities for not adjusting the terms of credit.

Classification of Causal Factors

These considerations suggest that it is useful to distinguish certain types of causal factors. One may draw a distinction, for instance, between active and passive factors or, in other words, between causes and conditions or between conditions *per quam* and conditions *sine qua non*. Inventions, crop changes, changes in demand are active factors, while institutional circumstances such as are mentioned above should be classified as passive conditions. Sometimes this distinction may be useful; but frequently it is difficult or impossible to draw a sharp line between the two types of factors. How is it possible to decide whether any given action on the part of the banks, such as lowering the discount rate when reserves are running high or failure to raise the rate when the demand for credit rises (*i.e.*, when the "natural rate" has risen), is an "active" or a "passive" factor? This is obviously a terminological question and it is fruitless to press for an answer in every single case.

The real distinction—in some cases—is between *controllable* and *uncontrollable* factors.[1] The weather, *e.g.*, is uncontrollable, while institutional factors are at least in theory controllable. Among factors, furthermore, which can in principle be controlled, there are those which one does not find it desirable, for one reason or another, to control or to eliminate altogether—*e.g.*, inventions, or the liberty of the recipient of income to spend his income or to save it, or to exercise freedom of choice in regard to his consumption or occupation. Needless to say, opinion as to what it is possible and desirable to control or influence varies from time to time and from person to person.

A more usual if less pragmatic classification is that of causes which originate within and causes which originate outside the economic system. Wars, inventions, crop changes (so far as they depend on the weather and are not economic adjustments to changes in demand, prices or cost), spontaneous changes in demand (so far as they are due to changes in taste and are not simply a reaction to changed supply conditions) are examples of outside causes. Changes in production due to changed demand conditions, price changes due to rise in cost, intensified demand for producers' goods due to changes in demand for consumers' goods are examples of economic causes. But what is to be called an *economic* and what a *non-economic* factor or circumstance is frequently rather a matter of convention than of argument.

Exogenous and Endogenous Theories

Closely connected with the distinction between economic and non-economic factors and causes is the distinction between "*exogenous*" and

---

[1] *Cf.* J. M. Clark, *Strategic Factors in Business Cycles*, New York, 1935, pages 4-5 and *passim*.

"*endogenous*" theories of the business cycle. Exogenous theories are those which assume external disturbances—*e.g.*, crop changes or inventions—in order to explain the business cycle. Endogenous theories rely exclusively on movements which can be explained economically. This distinction, too, is not always definite. Is the monetary theory, which explains the business cycle in the light of certain actions or a certain policy on the part of the banking authorities, to be regarded as exogenous or endogenous? If the banks lower the rate of interest, thereby inducing a credit inflation, their action will presumably be regarded as an exogenous factor: but suppose they do not raise the rate sufficiently in face of a rising demand for credit (due, *e.g.*, to inventions) with the same result in the shape of a credit inflation—is that the operation of an exogenous factor?

It has been attempted to give more precision to the distinction between exogenous and endogenous theories by saying that the former assume movements in the data, while the latter suppose the data to remain constant.[2] This distinction is precise enough once the general theoretical system on which a writer builds his theory of the business cycle has been determined and accepted; but it is not possible to lay down beforehand once and for all what phenomena are to be regarded as accepted data and what are magnitudes to be explained and determined in the light of those data. What the theory of yesterday accepted as data, we try to explain to-day; and the independent variables (data) on which we build to-day may become dependent variables to-morrow. All attempts to make a definite distinction between data and results lead back to the earlier conception which regards forces or movements of a "non-economic" nature or "external" to the economic system as the "data" of economic theory. But this distinction between "economic" and "non-economic" phenomena is a purely conventional one. There is no reason why forces or movements not to be classified as economic should not become "dependent" or "explained" variables of a general—as distinct from an economic—theory.

With very few exceptions, all serious explanations are neither purely exogenous nor purely endogenous. In almost all theories, both the "originating factors" and the "responses of the business system" (to use the expression of J. M. CLARK[3]) play a rôle. On the one hand, a purely exogenous theory is impossible. Even if one assumes a weather cycle, the peculiar response of the business system, which converts harvest variations into a general alternation of prosperity and depression, has still to be explained. On the other hand, a purely endogenous theory is hardly satisfactory. It is not likely that, without outside shocks, a cyclical movement would go on for ever: and, even if it did go on, its course would certainly be profoundly influenced by outside shocks—that is, by changes in the data (however these may be defined and delimited by economically explained variables).

---

[2] See especially Tinbergen: "Suggestions on Quantitative Business Cycle Theory" in *Econometrica*. Vol. III, No. 3, July 1935, page 241.

[3] See his book: *Strategic Factors in the Business Cycle, passim.*

The interaction of exogenous and endogenous forces is intricate, and the logical possibilities of their mutual impacts are numerous. We shall not, however, discuss these problems in the abstract here at the beginning. They will find their solution as we proceed in our theoretical enquiry, especially in Part II of the present report.

Inherent Instability in the Economic System

One methodological rule of thumb may be suggested at this point, however, although it will find its full justification only later. For various reasons, it seems desirable, in the explanation of the business cycle, to attach as little importance as possible to the influence of external disturbances. In the first place, large swings in the direction of prosperity and depression as we find them in real life are difficult to explain solely by exogenous forces; and this difficulty becomes an impossibility when the alleged "disturbances" do not themselves show a wave-like movement. Even if a periodic character is assumed (*e.g.,* in the case of crops or inventions), the hypothesis is full of difficulty. The responses of the business system seem *prima facie* more important in shaping the business cycle than external shocks. Secondly, historical experience seems to demonstrate that the cyclical movement has a strong tendency to persist, even where there are no outstanding extraneous influences at work which can plausibly be held responsible.[4] This suggests that there is an inherent instability in our economic system, a tendency to move in one direction or the other. If it is possible (as we believe) to demonstrate that such a tendency exists and to indicate the conditions under which it works, it will be comparatively easy to fit all kinds of external perturbations, including all State interventions, into the scheme. Exogenous forces will then figure as the originators or disturbers of endogenous processes, with power to accelerate, retard, interrupt or reverse the endogenous movement of the economic system.[5]

Mechanical Analogy

A frequently used analogy may be adduced, not to prove anything, but to make the meaning of what has been said clearer. We can compare the economic system with a pendulum or with a rocking-chair. A rocking-chair may be made to perform fairly regular swings by quite irregular impulses (shocks) from the outside. (Besides it may conceivably have a mechanism installed which makes it swing without outside forces operating on it.) In the explanation of the movement of the chair we must now distinguish two factors: the structure of the chair and the impulses from the outside—

---

[4] What is to be regarded as "outstanding" and "plausible" is, of course, a matter of dispute. As there is always something happening somewhere, it is always possible to find some external events which can be made the basis of a tentative explanation.

[5] For this reason, anything like perfect regularity in respect of the amplitude, length, intensity and concomitant symptoms of the cyclical movement is *a priori* improbable.

endogenous and exogenous factors. The structure of the chair is responsible for the fact that irregular shocks are transformed into fairly regular swings. An ordinary chair would ordinarily respond quite differently, although some particular kinds of impulses are thinkable (regular pushes and pulls) which would make it move in regular swings.

Naturally, the structure of the rocking-chair—and hence the nature of the swings produced by external shocks—may be very different in detail. The system might be so constructed that incessant regular swings are produced if, after having been pushed, the system is left to itself. Or else the swings may gradually disappear—that would be the case with an ordinary rocking-chair; we speak in that case of "damped oscillations" and may distinguish various degrees of dampening. The opposite may be true, the swings may become more and more violent; the fluctuations are then said to be "explosive" or "antidamped," or the system is in an unstable equilibrium.

The methodological suggestion made above then comes to this. We tentatively assume that, for the explanation of the fairly regular swings of the economic system (just as for those of the rocking-chair), it is more important to study the peculiar structure of the system and hence its responses to outside shocks than to look for regularities in the occurrence of these shocks. This hypothesis is, of course, subject to subsequent confirmation or rejection.

If, therefore, in many of the following sections, not much is said about such external influences (and in particular about the various forms of intervention in the economic process by the State or other public bodies, which figure so prominently in the daily comments of economists, politicians and economic journals on contemporary events), this must not be taken to imply that, in our opinion, or in the opinion of the writers whose theories are reviewed, these factors do not influence the economic situation. Our object is in the first instance to isolate the responses of the economic system, in order to stage the scene and to describe the environment in which the external influences have play.

14

Business Cycles *and* The Emergence of the System of Economic Fluctuations[*]

EDUARD HEIMANN[†]

Editors' Note

It is no small task to undertake a history of economic thought. This vast subject presumes acquaintance with the major works of the great economists, the nuances injected by their apostles, and the philosophic, sociological, and historical factors influencing economic literature. Along the way, many perennial issues will surely demand fresh comment, for example, the methodology and logic of economic thought, the mutability of economic "laws," and the "scientific" nature of the inquiry. Little wonder that these histories are generally rather verbose, carefully documented, and buttressed by extensive quotations.

All the more remarkable therefore is Professor Heimann's *History of Economic Doctrines*, from which our selection is taken. He characterizes his brief work as "a critical survey of, and introduction to, the entire field of economic theory." However, it must rank above the survey level, for only one with a sure command of the literature could write so concisely of its evolutionary development yet so authoritatively and with such comprehension. A book of "ideas rather than authors," Heimann's his-

[*] From *History of Economic Doctrines: An Introduction to Economic Theory*, by Eduard Heimann. Copyright 1945 by Oxford University Press, Inc. Reprinted by permission.

[†] Professor Heimann, born in Berlin July 11, 1889, received his Ph.D. from the University of Heidelberg. From 1925 to 1933 he taught at Hamburg and in 1933 joined the faculty of the New School for Social Research (New York), serving as Dean of the Graduate School in 1946–47. He has written numerous articles and books on such contemporary problems as freedom and order, Christianity and the social crisis, the conflict of communism, fascism, and democracy.

tory had by 1959 gone through eight printings and earned a solid reputation with university students and faculty, and those members of the public with an interest in economics.

Heimann treats cycle theory not as something grown in a vacuum; rather, he relates it fully to those factors guiding the maturation of economic thinking. Accordingly, the excerpts quoted below, surveying the development of cycle theory, provide that kind of background "briefing" so useful to more detailed examination.

Business Cycles

❦ The crucial problem of neo-classicism is the economic crisis: how can a general disturbance arise in a system regulated by price? Say had flatly denied the possibility of such a disturbance. Only the socialists had made the theory of the crisis an integral part of their system of thought, which is dynamic and points beyond capitalism. And before them the two great theorists of the classical school, Ricardo and Malthus, had, in different ways, recognized the possibility of a disturbance. They had come to this conclusion by taking a circular-flow approach to the problem and had found that certain qualitative aggregates have peculiarities which deflect the regular circular flow of economic activities. But their school had repudiated these results. Now it was the neo-classicists who were faced with the problem of the crisis.

In this respect, the neo-classical theorists were under an even greater handicap than were their classical predecessors. The neo-classical objection to classicism is that it did not adhere to the logic of its own argument; for according to classical price theory, the system is self-regulatory by virtue of the price mechanism. The neo-classicists contend that, if the pricing process wipes out qualitative differences everywhere in the economic system, then there is no obstacle to the flow of economic activity. The more neo-classicism progressed in the formal logic of this argument, the further it was removed from economic reality, which is not as smooth as the theory would have it. The theory of the crisis must follow from the general concepts of the system of theory, just as the crisis in reality results from the system of free enterprise; one must reflect the other. The problem is that of deriving a theory of a general disturbance from presuppositions according to which such a disturbance is rendered impossible by the regulatory mechanism of the economic system. This is almost like squaring the circle.

Of the first generation of neo-classical theorists, the founders and their closest disciples, Jevons was the only one to consider the problem; but his approach did not lead him to the crucial issue. For Gossen, Walras, Menger, and Clark the problem does not exist; and Pareto's contribution is of forbidding abstruseness and certainly outside his system of thought. Wieser, who so much surpassed his fellow theorists by his far-sighted critical attitude, explicitly followed Say in denying the possibility of a general disturbance. Boehm-Bawerk, in a passing remark, made it clear that he regarded the theory of the business cycle as the capstone which would complete the structure of economic theory; but he himself never undertook to construct it. And Marshall was so preoccupied with a theoretical analysis of the innumerable small changes in the economic system, in all directions and at every moment, that he treated the massive changes of the cycle, as it were, as a datum and inquired into the reactions of the business world to the business cycle instead of taking the business cycle itself as the problem to be solved.

Various methods of solving it were available. In the first place, the business cycle could be traced to a disturbance coming from outside the system and forcing it to a gradual adaptation to, or absorption of, the disturbing element. No general-equilibrium theory need or can deny the possibility of such an extraneous disturbance; every change is a disturbance in this sense, and the economic system is characterized not by the absence of such outside influences, but by its own resilience, its ability to establish a new equilibrium. Accordingly, Jevons attributed the business cycle to the periodically recurrent disturbances caused by sun spots, which produce fluctuations in agricultural crops; an increase in these, in turn, stimulates the demand for industrial goods and hence increases employment. The same theory had already been suggested by Juglar, whose name must head every list of business-cycle analysts, and a variant was later employed by the mathematical economist Henry Ludwell Moore of Columbia University. Even if the assumption is abandoned that there is a periodicity in the fluctuation of agricultural crops, it is still possible that a chance expansion of agricultural production may result in an expansion of business. This more restricted theory has been elaborated by Pigou, who has most fully investigated the impact of rising crops on business and credit. But whatever the merits of Pigou's theory, it can never be, and was not intended as, more than a partial explanation of the business cycle; the theory presupposes that productive resources are not fully utilized, since otherwise production could not be expanded in response to improved agricultural conditions.

A second way out of the impasse must be credited to Pigou, who had the wisdom to realize that there is no logical reason why the recurrent disturbances of the economic system should have but one cause; no logic can preclude the possibility that different causes take turns in the history of the phenomenon or combine in the same cycle. Pigou has stressed a possibility that had already been recognized by his predecessors, namely that booms and depressions are caused by miscalculations on the part of businessmen with regard to future market conditions. It is a fact that "business confidence" or lack of it feeds on itself, since the holding back of sales in the expectation of higher prices or the rushing of sales in the expectation of lower prices cannot fail to bring about at least a short-lived boom or depression. However, it is questionable whether this explanation really gets to the bottom of the matter; such fluctuations in business sentiment may be only one phase in a cycle and may be traceable to more fundamental causes in the economic system. Although the logic in the argument which attributes the periodic breakdown of the self-regulatory mechanism of the economic system to cumulative errors on the part of those in charge of the system is unassailable, the argument itself is certainly not impressive.

The contribution of Irving Fisher can perhaps be characterized as parallel to Pigou's. Fisher describes an important phase of the cycle, which reinforces it, once it begins for other reasons. As prices rise, money depreciates in value, and the real value of the nominal rate of interest diminishes. From the nominal rate one has to deduct the expected rate of depreciation of money, that is, of the loan when it will become due. In other words, for the real rate to remain unchanged, the nominal rate would have to increase by the depreciation rate of money. This argument presupposes the price rise of the boom; the contrary holds as prices fall in the depression. Fisher's theory thus explains a strong incentive to further expansion on the basis of credits in the boom and to contraction in the depression.

The third way out of the impasse is to ignore the general structure of the system of economic theory and to concentrate on the analysis of the cycle as an isolated problem. This way suggested itself to those who were opposed to economic theory on principle. It was only natural that the serious analysis of the business cycle should be inaugurated by economists who rejected the theoretical system according to which a crisis is impossible. The lone and long-ignored pioneer in this analysis is Juglar, who, as early as 1860, took the decisive step from the idea of the crisis as a periodic breakdown of an otherwise smoothly working system to a statistical investigation of the business cycle. According to Juglar, "the sole reason for the crisis is the boom"; the capitalist system develops, not along a straight line broken by periodic depressions, but with wide fluctuations of employment, income, and output, in which every phase follows from the preceding one, and there is no equilibrium. In this way, the problem was for the first time fully understood: what is the reason, not of the crisis, but of boom and crisis, that is, of the cycle? It is on this basis that the great achievements of Spiethoff and Mitchell stand. These we have already discussed. For all their merits, however, their explanations of the business cycle proved incomplete because unrelated to a general system of economic theory which could explain the movements that were supposed to lead to the fluctuations. Cassel's theory is open to the same criticism; although, unlike Spiethoff and Mitchell, he is a neo-classical economist, he in no way relates his theory of the business cycle to his general-equilibrium theory and does not explain the contradiction between them. This point too has already been discussed.

Thus, Mises and Schumpeter must be credited with having made really significant progress because, instead of being content with highly original theories of the business cycle, they integrated their own original theories into the general system of economic thought. The question then is: to what extent was the problem solved?

Mises reversed the socialist argument. The socialists had pointed to the crisis as the sign that capitalism is unstable and decaying. Mises, who more than any other economist regards laissez-faire as the system of equilibrium, blames the crisis on arbitrary tampering with that delicate mechanism. Whereas Cassel's theory of the crisis cannot be fitted into a system of thought built around the price theory, Mises's theory, and that of his disciple Hayek, is an integral part of the system because it describes an illegitimate but regularly recurrent interference with the natural flow of economic activities. This disturbing element is the inflationary proclivities of both governments and banks, which lead to over-expansion of credit. It would be quite possible to keep these tendencies towards inflation under control, just as, according to Smith, it is possible to control the tendency towards monopoly; but in reality the harmful forces assert themselves.

Businessmen always cry for "cheap money"; governments, in their eagerness for popularity, are prone to yield to this pressure; and banks gladly lower the rate of interest by creating additional loans and thus increasing their business. Accordingly, everything conspires to deflect the rate of interest from its proper position as analyzed by Boehm-Bawerk and thereby to make so long a period of production—so large an output of producers' goods—appear profitable that the available subsistence fund is not sufficient to sustain producers for so long a period. When this situation becomes apparent, consumption goods rise in price and producers' goods fall, bringing losses to their producers. Thus the structure of production is disrupted. The difference between the prices of producers' goods and those of consumers' goods is the profit which accrues from the use of the former for the production of the latter; Boehm-Bawerk and his pupils contend that under conditions of equilibrium the interest rate is equal to this profit. Hence, Mises argues that the rise in the price of consumers' goods in relation to the price of producers' goods restores the correct rate of interest by disrupting the distorted structure of production resulting from the distorted rate of interest.

This theory has been further elaborated by the Austrian-born London theorist Friedrich A. von Hayek and has become one of the major business-cycle theories of our day. According to Hayek, the rise of prices resulting from the creation of new, illegitimate bank credit forces the recipients of fixed incomes, or of incomes which do not rise in proportion to the rise in prices, to forego the services of factors of production which they formerly used. The same thing happens when people voluntarily save their money. But the "forced saving" imposed by credit expansion on those who cannot afford to buy at the higher price is not likely to be continued when the credit inflation stops; the former level of consumption will be immediately restored, whereas voluntary savings are likely to be continued. The restoration of the former level of demand then draws factors of production into the consumers' goods industries and may leave the far-reaching projects of expansion unfinished and the capital invested in them lost. Lionel Robbins of the London School of Economics has undertaken to verify this thesis by using the statistical material provided by the great depression of 1929. The main objection to Hayek's theory, raised by Neisser, is that the restoration of the consumption level does not have harmful effects if the expansion stimulated by credit inflation has already resulted in enlarged output; the total level is then higher than it was. Apart from its political implications, however, the Mises-Hayek thesis certainly gives an accurate picture of what happens in the last phase of the boom, when labor is fully employed and a continuous stream of credit raises wages and destroys profit.

The explanatory value of theories like those of Mises and Hayek is, of course, limited because of the fact that the disturbing element to which they trace the cycle is regarded as illegitimate, i.e. outside the activities necessary for the carrying on of the economic process. Hence, the importance of these theories in the development of economic thinking is considerably surpassed by Joseph A. Schumpeter's achievement in at last providing a theoretical understanding of the cycle as a phenomenon quite legitimate and even indispensable in capitalism. Each cycle leaves a net gain in income, output, and employment, as evidenced by the hundred years of progress between the Napoleonic Wars and the First World War. This led Sombart, the historian, and Schumpeter, an Austrian-born Harvard theorist, to interpret the business cycle optimistically as the special form in which capitalist industry grows, an encouragement to all sorts of experiments in the boom and a severe test of soundness in the depression.

Schumpeter solves the problem of the business cycle by introducing into the system of static equilibrium a dynamic factor which upsets the equilibrium, namely the entrepreneur, in the new and specific sense of the person who does not simply produce things desired by the consumers in the traditional way, but conceives of new products, new methods of production, and new industries. In the system of static equilibrium, all the factors of production and all purchasing power are needed for normal circulation; thus, in order to be able to bend factors to his own purposes, the entrepreneur must be given command over them. It is the banker who provides him with newly created purchasing power, after considering the many projects submitted for financing; the banker limits the total volume of his loans, in order to remain liquid, by charging an interest that is intended to exclude the weaker applicants or those who are less reliable. The entrepreneur then uses the credit to purchase factors of production; he can offer higher wages, and thus divert the factors of production from the channels of the static economy, because he expects higher profits to result from the application of his new ideas. In this way, additional purchasing power circulates, wages and prices rise, and the boom begins. Once the new production has come to an end, the output becomes larger and cheaper, the credits are repaid from the proceeds of the new sales, and the volume of purchasing power shrinks. For these reasons the return to static equilibrium comes as an unpleasant surprise but also indicates that the whole process is self-regulating.

What Schumpeter describes is essentially the rise from one state of equilibrium through a disequilibrium to a new state of equilibrium on a higher plane. In other words, the crisis is not inevitable; what happens is only that static equilibrium is restored after the rush to a higher plane, and the crisis could be avoided if people were not thrown into panic by the interruption of the boom. Graphically represented, the cycle would appear not as a wave fluctuating around a rising average but only as the upper half of such a wave. Thus it can be seen that Adam Smith's idea of harmonious growth guided by price still exercises an important influence upon the theory of this most advanced neo-classical economist and places a limitation even on his epoch-making achievement. In Schumpeter's most recent presentation of his doctrine the crisis is again absent from the primary development of his principle and introduced only in a second step.

Schumpeter's achievement is not confined merely to the development of a new theory of the business cycle; he opened up an entirely new vista. What he provides is a theory of economic dynamics, different from the equilibrium which is the subject matter of the static theory. According to Schumpeter, the crisis is not produced by extraneous disturbances, miscalculations, or illegitimate influences on credit policy; what happens is that there is movement and growth, which in due time has to give way to the readjustment of the economic system by the tendency towards equilibrium. The only predecessor of Schumpeter to hold such a dynamic conception, although he approached it from a different standpoint, is Marx; Schumpeter, however, makes full use of the refined neo-classical instruments of thought, the beginnings of which Marx had spurned.

Credit, profit, and interest, according to Schumpeter, are phenomena only of the expanding phase of the business cycle and vanish with it. Prosperity is, in fact, always accompanied by increasing credits and profits, and it has become an accepted doctrine that in a state of equilibrium, in which aggregate price covers aggregate cost, including interest, there is no room for profit beyond this. Thus, the classical theory, which identified profit with interest, is justified anew: it always is a theory of equilibrium, which in Schumpeter's system is reduced to the second phase of the cycle. However, the moot point in Schumpeter's theory is the exclusion of interest itself from the static equilibrium. According to Schumpeter, once equilibrium is reached, round-about production becomes synchronized with consumption; that is, both processes are simultaneous and continuous, consumption need not wait for production to be completed, and no limitation need be placed on the period of production. This argument had been employed by J. B. Clark against Boehm-Bawerk; Schumpeter uses it to deny the possibility and necessity of interest in a state of static equilibrium.

Moreover, he cannot, from his starting point, provide an analysis of the peculiarities of the structure of fixed capital.

The Emergence of the System of Economic Fluctuations

The economic and social turmoil after the First World War, first in Germany and then in the other occidental countries, naturally stimulated the quest for a new principle of economic theory—different from the principle of equilibrium—which would logically lead to a theory of fluctuations as the normal condition of capitalist industry. In other words, the shackles of classical and neo-classical price theory had to be broken by the unqualified acceptance of the circular-flow principle in order that the theory of the business cycle, and more generally the theory of economic fluctuations, could be adequately formulated.

The discussion was opened by a group of German theorists who later came to the United States. Adolph Lowe acted as the herald of the new doctrine in the struggles of the 'twenties, demanding the reconstruction of economic theory in terms of the circular-flow principle. He sees in technical progress, as did Marx and Schumpeter, the dominant dynamic force of this age, and sketched a system of thought which would renew, with modern means and in the light of modern developments, Marx's attempt to describe periodic fluctuations around a general course of economic transformation. Emil Lederer, like Schumpeter, laid greater emphasis on the credit phenomena accompanying technical progress. He made an exhaustive study of the many different cases in which technical progress may or may not lead to unemployment, depending on whether or not the immediate dismissal of workers is offset by the effects of general expansion. A new industry, financed by new credits and producing new goods, enlarges both the total supply and the total demand; it is in this way that capitalism has continually grown. But, according to Lederer, Lowe, and Neisser, the mechanization of existing industries may lead to a shrinkage in the economic system. This argument is disputed by the "compensation theory" of the classical school, according to which the dismissal of workers resulting from the introduction of labor-saving devices is compensated by the setting free of their wages for reinvestment, which cannot fail to reabsorb the workers. However, the re-employment of the workers requires additional capital for the equipment of new jobs as well as the old wage fund—where is this capital to come from, unless it is provided by chance? Moreover, those who receive the money saved by the dismissal of the workers—consumers if the product sells at a lower price, producers if the price remains the same—must use this money to buy the things produced for the dismissed workers; otherwise these products would remain unsold and the crisis would begin. But then that money cannot be used for reinvestment, and the dismissed workers remain excluded from employment and consumption. This reasoning, based on the principle of the circular flow of goods, is sound. But, though it demonstrates the possibility of permanent technological unemployment, the theory does not provide an explanation of the business cycle, which, whatever its ultimate source, is directly caused by a fluctuation in purchasing power.

This point is taken into consideration in Lederer's theory of the business cycle, which, though taking its start from Schumpeter's theory, is free from the classical prejudice of economic harmony. The additional credit which is granted to entrepreneurs introducing new projects necessarily results in a profit margin over aggregate cost, since the covering of costs would have required only unchanged purchasing power. Profits are preponderantly invested in further expansion, while the lagging-behind of wages undermines the demand for the new larger output and brings about the crisis; in the downward movement again, profits fall first and wages lag behind, thus bolstering up demand and eventually stopping the downward movement. Hans Neisser, starting from Say's law of markets, has provided what is up to the present day the most comprehensive catalogue of such changes in both production and consumption as may lead to a withdrawal of purchasing power from the market and thus to a crisis. Following a suggestion of Schumpeter, Neisser also shows how the international division of labor makes the study of the cycle in only one country inadequate, since the successive phases of the same cycle may occur in different countries.

The main approach to the rebuilding of the system of economics was, logically, from the side of purchasing power, i.e., of monetary theory. Wicksell, Schumpeter, and Hahn were the pioneers, who also influenced the economists of Lederer's group. Keynes is the undisputed head of this school.

Wicksell was the first, after 150 years, to establish a connection between the theory of money and that of interest. No one since David Hume had done so; everybody was awed by the insistence of the classical economists that a policy of "easy money," which businessmen invariably demand and the confused mercantilists recommended, could not lead to anything but inflation. Starting from the classical conception of capital and credit, Wicksell called "normal" or "natural" that rate of interest at which the available supply of capital was absorbed by those seeking funds for profitable investment; in other words, the rate of interest at which saving is equal to investment. This rate is thus equal to marginal profit. Now if the chances of making a profit are improved by technical progress or other causes, the unchanged interest rate of the banks proves to be too low to meet the increased demand for credit. The demand must be satisfied by creating new money, which, in this age of bank accounts and checks, is not technically distinguishable from the already existing money. Entrepreneurs use the loans to pay higher incomes to workers and landowners, and the demand for goods increases. Hence the price level rises as long as interest, although rising, has not caught up with profits; the price level falls as long as interest is too high, even though it too is falling. In other words, the boom and the depression result from the lagging of interest rates behind profits. What is implied in this theory, although not explicitly formulated at that early date (1898), is Keynes's thesis that there is an upward movement if investment exceeds savings and a downward movement if investment falls short of savings.

Schumpeter's much more radical theory of credit and interest is an integral part of his dynamic theory, which we have discussed above. Though original, it was anticipated in one important respect by the Scottish banker Henry Dunning McLeod, whose voluminous writings in the second half of the last century had been contemptuously rejected by his contemporaries. According to McLeod, credit is not a transfer of purchasing power from a saver through a bank to a debtor-investor, but purchasing power is created by the bank—in the form of bank accounts—for the express use of the debtor. McLeod had then traced the business cycle to fluctuations in the volume of bank credit, which varies incomparably more than the volume of money saved. Schumpeter likewise takes bank credit as capital—the means of building up new enterprises—but he deviates from McLeod in limiting the possibility of bank credit to a dynamic development, that is, such applications for credit as are designed to transform production. Only such credit as serves to direct resources into new productive channels and thus anticipates future additional goods is capital and can earn an interest, since interest must be paid out of entrepreneurial profits. Accordingly, in a state of static equilibrium, there is no credit and no interest. The bank must charge an interest on its credits because the circulation of its credits diminishes its liquidity; the interest so charged places a limit on the number of applications for credit and on the ensuing loss of liquidity. Thus, Schumpeter is the founder of the new theory of interest, which was called the theory of liquidity preference, first by Hahn and then by Keynes. According to Schumpeter and Hahn, interest does not make saving equal to investment, as the classical theory holds; interest makes investment equal to bank credit. Savings, says Schumpeter, are too insignificant to support the dynamic development of production, and the interest that they receive is only reflected from the interest on the investable funds created by the banks. This point had already been made by Hermann, as early as 1832.

McLeod's theory was made respectable and refined considerably by R. G. Hawtrey of the British Treasury, according to whom the business cycle is a "purely monetary phenomenon" governed by variations in the interest rate. These variations, although too small to influence industrial investments directly, are of decisive importance for the carrying of merchants' stocks and consequently for the orders from merchants to manufacturers. Hawtrey holds that the gold standard is responsible for the downward trend, which is the result of the rise in interest rates needed to protect the gold reserve, and he recommends to the authorities a policy of credit control in order to stabilize the flow of purchasing power, which consists almost exclusively of bank money. The specific role assigned to interest and the association of the business cycle with the gold standard makes this a somewhat frail theory.

The contribution of Albert Hahn, a former German banker, is remarkable despite the fact that it was ignored by the English-speaking theorists.

In his credit theory he follows McLeod rather than Schumpeter; his emphasis is on the technical mechanism of credit and its operation. His theory of interest is that of Schumpeter. But Hahn suggests new approaches to the problem of the relation between saving and investment. He revived the thesis of Malthus, later much emphasized by Keynes, that saving, far from automatically bringing investment with it, is in itself a reduction of effective demand. Moreover, Hahn added what Keynes later called the doctrine of the rising propensity to save or falling propensity to consume, in the normal progress to greater wealth. Hahn infers from this doctrine and from the theory of Malthus that, if a crisis is to be avoided, rising investment must offset rising saving. This thesis is also at the center of Keynes's system. Whereas Wicksell, who held a similar theory, had presupposed full employment, Hahn associates the fluctuations of investment with those of employment and output.

All these motives were richly elaborated by John Maynard Keynes, now Lord Keynes, a Cambridge man, and used as material in the building of a new structure of thought. Keynes goes far beyond Wicksell and Hahn in developing the theory of saving and investment, proving that saving and investment, for all their dynamic relationship, are always equal for the economy as a whole. Total income is equal to total output and spending is equal to consumption; hence, income that is not spent but saved, and production that is not consumed but invested are equal. But the intentions of savers on the one hand and investors on the other are not connected and may diverge. There may be more intended investment than saving, the momentary result being that stocks of consumption goods fall short of demand and are depleted. In other words, this rush for goods brings about an unintended disinvestment, which reduces aggregate investment to an amount equal to savings. In the longer run the depletion of consumers' goods leads to more orders, more investment, higher incomes, and a rising saving quota, until saving equals intended investment. If saving exceeds investment, the demand for goods falls short of the supply, and the expected disinvestment does not take place; this unintended investment raises total investment to an amount equal to saving in the short run, and reduces orders, investment, and income in the longer run, until the saving quota out of a lower income is only equal to intended investment. This is the mechanism which, within the fundamental condition of equality between saving and investment, makes for fluctuations of income and employment.

Like Hahn, Keynes holds that the rising propensity to save is the gravest and ever-present danger to the stability of the system. This theory must be classified with the underconsumption theories, like that of Malthus, because they all trace the downward movement of the economic process to the inability of the community to consume its growing income. And this tendency is not easily reversible. Alvin H. Hansen of Harvard, the leading representative of the theory in the United States, has demonstrated how vast is the amount of more or less irrevocable, institutionalized saving, e.g.

in private and social insurance. The use of boom profits for hastily writing off new plants, while considered sound financial practice from the point of view of an isolated enterprise, does much to break the boom. Investment, on the other hand, fluctuates with the prospects of net profit, which is the difference between expected gross profit and interest. Gross profit depends on the application of new ideas, which raise the "marginal efficiency of capital." Interest, however, is regarded as independent of such considerations and determined solely by the liquidity preference of the public.

This theory of interest assumes a new dimension in comparison with those of Schumpeter and Hahn, which connect interest only with the liquidity preference of the credit-issuing banks. Keynes's extension of the theory of interest is an application of Marshall's theory of money, which has been handed down by an almost purely oral tradition, and of the coincident, independently conceived theory of Mises. Marshall and Mises replace, in the quantity theory of money, the inconvenient and unsystematic concept of the circulation velocity by its reciprocal, the demand for money, in the sense of people's desire to hold it in order to be liquid. This desire will normally be for the equivalent of a certain quantity of goods in order to cover the period between expected income payments or expected business proceeds, and to meet possible emergencies. The demand for money in this sense will thus rise as prices rise and fall with falling prices, but will be lower in the expectation of rising prices (since people try to purchase goods before their prices rise and thus add to the inflation by adding to the demand) and will be higher when a fall in prices is expected, with the opposite effect. The desire to hold money in the expectation of falling prices is the third motive for liquidity added by Keynes; the speculative motive for holding money. When prices—e.g. bond prices, which rise as the general rate of interest falls—have sufficiently risen to make some owners apprehensive of the future price, these owners liquidate their assets and hold cash. Only if prices fall and interest rises again will they part with their money, and the rate at which they do so is the measure of their liquidity preference. Hence, interest is determined by forces independent of investment and may be, and actually is for long periods of time, too high for that volume of investment which would provide full employment.

The relation between interest and saving is here the opposite of that posited by classical theory, according to which a rise in the rate of interest not only checks investment but stimulates saving, and a fall in the rate of interest has the opposite effect; in this way, a unique equilibrium is reached between saving and investment, which are not naturally equal. According to Hahn's and Keynes's doctrine, the volume of saving is not only dependent on the rate of interest but on the size of the income out of which the saving is to be done: the saving rises with the income and more than the income. Hence, a rise in the rate of interest, by checking investment, diminishes income and both the absolute and the relative amounts of saving out of that income; conversely, a lower rate of interest stimulates investment—if there is a given expectation of profit—and increases income and the absolute and relative amounts of saving. What interest equates is neither saving and intended investment nor bank credit and intended investment, but the supply of money issued by the banking system and the amount which the public wants to hold; this amount is determined by the schedule of liquidity preference and by the size of the income, which in turn is determined by the volume of investment at the given rate of interest.

Two special theories fit into this system of thought and help to explain the modes and sizes of the fluctuations in the economic process. The first is the "multiplier" theory: any increment to the circulating purchasing power, such as is invariably connected with the rising phase of the business cycle, causes an addition to total income larger than the amount of the increment. The reason is that the first recipient, into whose income the additional money enters, buys additional goods and, in payment therefor, passes the money on to his supplier, for whom in turn it is again additional income. Thus, the original increment is "multiplied" in any one income period, according to the circulation velocity of incomes, until theoretically one circuit is completed and the money arrives at its starting point again. This ideas was closely analyzed by Pigou, who gave the credit for it to Walter Bagehot, famous British financial expert and writer of the last century. Later, in the great depression, R. F. Kahn of Cambridge investigated the effects of relief payments on total income and added to the theory the important observation that even if payments continued indefinitely the effect would not be multiplied to infinity, because leakages diminish the amount passed on at every step in the circulation, as debts are repaid to grocers and bakers and by these to wholesalers and banks; furthermore, the amounts paid for imported materials leave the circulation of the country. Kahn shows that, given a stable percentage of leakage at every step, the effect of the original payment is multiplied over an indefinite period of time by the reciprocal of the leakage, e.g. three times if the leakage is one third. Further discussion, climaxed by the work of John Maurice Clark, showed the impossibility of assuming that the percentage of leakage is constant, since debt repayments reach their end, new savings may or may not follow, etc. The main result of the discussion was the realization that the tangible effects of an increase in income are limited to a relatively short period of time. Keynes generalized the multiplier theory: any addition to purchasing power, whether inaugurated by public policy or private investment, produces a multiplied effect, and the downward spiral must be explained conversely.

The other special theory is of incomparably greater importance. It is called variously the "theory of the accelerator" or the "principle of derived demand" or the "principle of the relation," and was first developed by the French theorist Albert Aftalion; Spiethoff too suggested it. The chief authority on this subject too is Clark, and Harrod has integrated the theory into the Keynesian system of thought. According to this theory, the fluctuations in the demand for durable goods—both producers' and consumers'—are far more violent than the fluctuations in the demand for transient goods, because, once durable goods have been produced, the demand for them has been satisfied for several years to come, and normal production is reduced to the annual replacement quota. Suppose the latter is 10 per cent, and the demand increases by 10 per cent of its former volume, the output for one year must then be raised to twice the former amount (which was only the replacement quota) and then reduced to whatever the new replacement quota may be. Conversely, a decrease of the demand by 10 per cent would temporarily halt production, since one of the ten replacement quotas would no longer have to be filled. Any change in the mere rate of increase or decrease of the demand thus produces a cyclical movement in production because of the key position of the replacement quota in the durable-goods market. The Norwegian Ragnar Frisch and Clark have greatly refined this theory and have again shown that crude arithmetical reasoning must be avoided. But the unsettling consequences of the operation of this principle can be appreciated when it is realized that demand shifts more and more to highly durable goods. And the even more significant conclusion follows that, with heavy industry geared to the demand of a rapidly expanding and mechanizing industrial world, any diminution in the rate of expansion is likely to bring disaster. In an appraisal of the future of an uregulated system, the decreasing population rate, which diminishes the demand for houses, and the cessation of capital export as young countries provide for their own industrialization, must be accounted unfavorable tendencies, while the spread of further technological improvements makes for a more favorable prospect; the deciding factor may be the post-war reconstruction demand and assistance to backward countries in raising their productivity.

Keynes's system of economic theory is far from complete. It is a dynamic theory of employment and makes reference to the factors which bring about the business cycle, but it is not yet a real theory of the cycle. The way out of our difficulties through the creation of additional demand, either by public investment or public consumption, is not controversial in principle, although its political implications are. But some implications of the theory are dubious. As popularly understood, Keynes's theory traces the discouragement of investment to an interest rate that is too high. But this interpretation is not quite consistent with the doctrine that the cycle is traceable to violent fluctuations in the expectation of profit while liquidity preference is much more stable. The rate of interest cannot be lower than zero, yet even a zero rate would be "too high" for a period in which losses are expected from investment.

More generally, Keynes's system, first conceived in the great depression, may seem to later historians as a reflection of special troubles rather than as a balanced presentation of the economic world as a whole. His theory may be said to over-emphasize Quesnay and Marx as against Adam Smith. For the equilibrating forces of the price mechanism, although too weak to prevent the depression, were still too strong to permit the system to be completely disrupted; a minimum of spontaneous order survived even in the crisis. And the problems of equilibrium, overshadowed by the depression, would be raised again if specific conditions of stability in the financial and in selected industrial sections of the economc system were realized. More specifically, modern theory has swept aside rather than refuted or considered older theories. In a reorganized and stabilized world the length of the period of production as studied by Boehm-Bawerk would be of paramount importance again, and neither profit expectations nor liquidity preferences would fluctuate as violently as in the past once freedom from fear removed the main reasons for such fluctuations.

Keynes's system is predicated on a very definite assumption with regard to wages, namely that the present institutional organization of society makes it impossible for workers to increase employment by lowering their real wages, even if they wanted to do so, because a cut in money wages may bring down prices and thereby raise real wages. This doctrine is tantamount to the assumption that wages are more or less stable—an assumption which inevitably leads to a number of consequences at variance with orthodox reasoning. Here then is the point on which the attack on Keynes's system seems to concentrate: the system is supposed to be valid only if wages are kept from fluctuating with prices, a condition which in itself, whether or not it can be altered, is contrary to the classical theory of a price-regulated economy. Pigou, the main target of Keynes's criticism, has rejoined by pointing out this implication. If this criticism is well founded, the "general theory" of Keynes would be revealed as a special theory distinguished by realism and closeness to the facts of history, but not necessarily in conflict with the more abstract classical doctrine. Much bewilderment and confusion, which inevitably attends the advance into new territory, would thus be relieved.

[15]

Econometric Model Building*

ROBERT A. GORDON†

Editors' Note

It will ever be the wish of economists to give their science the precision of quantification. From the small beginnings of Sir William Petty and Hermann Gossen, today's student rummages about in the subspecialties of mathematical economics, statistical economics, and econometrics—all of which resort in varying degree to mathematical symbolism. The mathematical economist expresses the principles and postulates of economic theory in mathematical form and draws from the stated assumptions theoretical conclusions. Although results may not differ significantly from those arrived at by verbal argumentation, the precision of mathematical deduction is imparted to the whole. Since, however, the method assumes all theoretical relationships to be instantaneously fulfilled, few attempts are made to fit the equations with behavior data.

Statistical economics, on the other hand, eschews theory and concentrates on the simple presentation or comparison of data. In a sense, it "lets the figures speak for themselves." Yet the matter is not that simple. Figures do not always provide an unequivocal testimony. Economic theory is needed to illuminate significant relationships, and in any case a great deal of theory is necessarily involved in collecting and processing data.

Econometricians strive for a greater realism. They attempt to overcome the limitations of statistical economics by relating economic theory to the interpretation of statistics and to improve on purely mathematical economics by giving due weight to the characteristics of the data in model construction.

Is the economist's search for certitude in a field where human decisions are crucial a mere chimera?

* From *Business Fluctuations*, by Robert A. Gordon, 2nd ed. (New York: Harper & Brothers, 1962), pp. 388–398. Reprinted by permission of Harper & Brothers.
† See p. 206.

The growth of contemporary physics and chemistry has made physical scientists increasingly aware that there is no perfect "fit" between mathematics and nature when problems of even moderate complexity are brought under consideration. The life sciences, for the most part, have remained still more refractory to quantization techniques. . . . Moving into the social sciences, this limitation becomes more acute because of the great complexity and contingency inherent in such subject matters. While recent research has shown that much can be done by applying scientific method to the study of human problems, it also introduces a note of caution against too naive employment in the social sciences. . . . These limitations, of course, are clearly recognized by mathematicians who are engaged in business and economic analysis. Von Neuman and Morgenstern make no extravagant claims for their theory of games as applied to economic behavior. [William A. Wallace, O.P., "The Role of Mathematics in Liberal and Professional Education," in John J. Clark and Blaise J. Opulente (ed.), *Thought Patterns: Business and the Liberal Arts*, (New York: St. John's University Press, 1962, pp. 25-26).]

Professor Gordon's article deserves the care and attention of all students of business forecasting or cycle theory.

❧ An increasing number of economists have presented their theories explicitly in the form of business-cycle models. A few economic variables are chosen as being of primary importance, and it is then shown how fluctuations are generated by the relationships that are assumed to hold among the variables. These models can be expressed in mathematical or literary form. Rigorous demonstration that cyclical variations result from the assumed relationships virtually requires that the latter be stated in mathematical terms.

During the last 25 years or so, important work has been done in the construction of *econometric* models. Econometrics is a special type of economic analysis in which economic theory (formulated in mathematical terms) is combined with statistical measurement of economic phenomena.[1] Econometric business-cycle research consists of the following steps: A system of equations (i.e., a model) is set up to represent a particular theory of how certain variables interact with each other to determine the behavior of the economic system through successive periods of time. By

---

[1] Cf. W. Leontief, "Econometrics," in H. S. Ellis, ed., *A Survey of Contemporary Economics*, 1948, p. 388 n. Leontief's paper provides a useful brief survey of developments in this field of economic analysis. For a more extended but still elementary exposition of econometric methods, see J. Tinbergen, *Econometrics*, 1951. At a more technical level, see L. R. Klein, *A Textbook of Econometrics*, 1953.

statistical methods these equations are then "fitted" to the actual statistical data to determine the numerical values of the constants in the equations chosen. The model is then tested to see if the results adequately explain what has actually happened. If the equations fit the data well, and the sampling errors involved are small, the investigator concludes that the theoretical relationships embodied in his equations are consistent with the actual behavior of the economy, at least for the period studied. This does not mean that this particular theory has been "proved" to be correct. For there may be other theories and other sets of equations that will fit the data equally well.[2]

The final test of an econometric model lies in its ability to predict. These models are dynamic in the sense that some of the equations connect variables referring to different moments of time. If a model is to hold for the future as well as for the past, we should be able to substitute into the equations past and present values for some of the variables, and the model should then predict for us what the values of some of the other variables will be next month or next year. So far, no econometric model has met this forecasting test with any marked degree of success.

The following are the main features of econometric business-cycle models.[3]

1. The variables involved are broad aggregates, such as total consumption, total investment, total profits, and so on.

2. The models are considered to be complete, but only in a formal, logical or mathematical, sense; that is, there are as many equations as there are unknowns (i.e., variables whose behavior is to be explained).

3. The models are dynamic in that some of the equations connect variables referring to different time periods. Some of the variables may also be expressed as rates of change.

4. Four kinds of equations may be used: (a) *identities* or definitional equations, which are true by definition (thus: price times quantity equals value, saving equals investment [*ex post*], and so on); (b) *institutional rules,* such as equations that describe the reserve requirements of the banking system or the relation between corporate income taxes and corporate incomes; (c) *technological transformation functions,* such as the way output varies with employment; (d) *behavior equations,* representing the way groups of firms or individuals react to given stimuli (for example,

---

[2] For more detailed discussion of the nature of the econometric approach to business-cycle analysis, see T. C. Koopmans, "The Econometric Approach to Business Fluctuations," *American Economic Review,* vol. 39, May, 1949, suppt., pp. 64-72; Jan Tinbergen, "Econometric Business Cycle Research," reprinted in *Readings in Business Cycle Theory,* pp. 61-86; L. R. Klein, *Economic Fluctuations in the United States, 1921–1941,* 1950; and, by the same author, "Statistical Testing of Business Cycle Theory: the Econometric Method," in Erik Lundberg, ed., *The Business Cycle in the Post-War World,* pp. 222-245.

[3] This summary is based on that of T. C. Koopmans, *op. cit.,* p. 64. Cf. also C. F. Christ, "Aggregate Economic Models," *American Economic Review,* vol. 46, June, 1956, pp. 385-388.

the consumption function, showing how consumers respond to changes in income, and demand equations, which relate the quantity bought of a commodity to its price, to the prices of other commodities, to income, and to perhaps other variables).

All econometric models contain both endogenous and exogenous variables. The former are the ones whose behavior is to be explained by the equations chosen. The exogenous variables are taken as given. They represent forces at work which the model does not try to explain. One measure of the usefulness of a model lies in its treatment of exogenous variables. If important economic magnitudes whose behavior we want to explain are treated as exogenous, the model is of limited usefulness. Thus a model that treats investment as exogenous says in effect: Consumption, employment, and the other endogenous variables will change in certain ways as investment varies (in accordance with the equations used), but we cannot say why or when investment changes. To solve for the endogenous variables, we must wait to find out what investment will be.[4]

Some variables must, by the nature of the case, be considered exogenous—in particular, those that are determined by government policy; for example, the supply of money and government spending. Population or the labor force is another type of exogenous variable that, for obvious reasons, we cannot explain entirely in terms of the behavior of a few other economic magnitudes.

A simple example may help to make these concepts clearer. A simplified version of a model that has actually been fitted to American data for the interwar period runs as follows:[5]

$$(1) \quad C = a_0 + a_1 W + a_2 P + u_1$$
$$(2) \quad I = b_0 + b_1 P + b_2 P_{-1} + b_3 K_{-1} + u_2$$
$$(3) \quad W = c_0 + c_1 Y + c_2 Y_{-1} + c_3 t + u_3$$
$$(4) \quad C + I + G = Y$$
$$(5) \quad P + W = Y$$
$$(6) \quad \Delta K = I$$

The a's, b's, and c's in these equations are the constants for which we have to determine numerical values. The capital letters represent the variables, which are tied together in the way described by the equations. All the variables are expressed in "real" terms; i.e., they are corrected for price changes. Let us now look at the six equations one by one.

(1) The variables in the first equation are total consumers' expendi-

---

[4] At least one recent model of the United States economy displays some interesting, though limited, possibilities, despite the fact that all noninventory investment is taken to be exogenous. See the reference to the model by Duesenberry, Eckstein, and Fromm, p. 277 below.

[5] This model is taken with permission from L. R. Klein, *Economic Fluctuations in the United States, 1921–1941*, Cowles Commission for Research in Economics Monograph No. 11, p. 62, with no change other than the substitution of Latin for Greek letters.

tures (C), total payrolls (W), and total nonwage income, which for short we can refer to as profits (P). The equation states that consumption varies with changes in total wages and profits; in other words, this is the consumption function. The coefficient a_1 tells us how much consumption will change for every change of a dollar in payrolls, and similarly for a_2. Since we do not expect this equation to hold perfectly for every year, we add the variable u_1 to represent the "disturbance"—that is, the amount by which unmeasured influences cause C to deviate from the calculated value.

(2) The second equation is the investment function. Investment (I) is made to depend on current profits (P), last year's profits (P_{-1}), and the stock of capital at the end of last year (K_{-1}). In all cases, the subscripts give the date for which the variable in question is to be taken. Again we insert a residual variable (u_2) to express the fact that this equation does not hold perfectly.

(3) This equation expresses the demand for labor. The total wage bill (in constant dollars) is made to depend on current output (Y) and last year's output (Y_{-1}). It is also assumed to vary in accordance with a trend factor c_3t; that is, independently of Y and Y_{-1}, we expect W to change by a constant amount each year in response to the growing bargaining strength and productivity of labor. The variable t represents time (in years) measured from some base period. Here also we add the residual variable u_3.

The remaining equations are identities to complete the system.

(4) We are already familiar with this equation, which states that consumption plus investment plus government spending is equal to total output (Y). Since, by definition, this equation must hold perfectly, we do not have to add another u variable to cover other influences at work.

(5) This is the other side of the income equation and is also true by definition. Total income or output (Y) goes to either wages or profits (which are defined to include all nonwage incomes).

(6) This is also a definition. The amount of net investment in any year (I) is equal to the net change in the stock of capital during the year (ΔK).

All of the variables are defined in "real" terms; that is, they are corrected for price changes. Thus Y is a measure of the real national income, which is equivalent to total output. We are dealing with the net national income, after the deduction of depreciation and business taxes.

Of our six equations, the first three are behavior equations and the last three are identities. In all we have six equations to explain six endogenous variables (C, I, W, P, K, and Y). In addition we have the exogenous variables t and G. We do not attempt to calculate G; we look up the actual data to find out what value for G to use in any particular year.

Having these equations, the econometrician would next apply the appropriate statistical methods in order to ascertain the numerical values of the a's, b's, and c's—that is, the constants in the equations. Since this is not a textbook in statistics or econometrics, this is a good point at which to leave him.[6]

It is clear that this is much too simple a model for useful results. The aggregates are too broad, and obviously important variables are omitted. In particular, we need to break down investment and set up separate equations for inventories, business equipment, industrial and commercial construction, and residential construction. There is no consideration of government taxes; there are no variables for the money supply, holdings of liquid assets, or interest rates. In addition, consumption is related to national income rather than to disposable income; hence, the influence of changes in business savings and personal taxes is concealed.[7]

The author of this model, Lawrence Klein, has also developed much more elaborate models which he has applied to American data. His most recent published model, for the years 1929–1952, contains twenty equations, an equal number of endogenous variables, and an additional number of exogenous variables.[8] Among the 20 endogenous variables for which equations are given are, for example, consumption, gross investment, corporate saving, corporate profits, total compensation separately for private and for public employees, gross national product, the wage level, farm income, personal and business liquid assets, and short- and long-term interest rates. Although this may seem to be a very complicated model, it still is too aggregative, particularly in its failure to break down total investment into its significant components.

Sometimes an econometric model may give us useful partial insights even though it treats as exogenous (i.e., does not try to explain the behavior of) some variables that we know to be important sources of cyclical instablility. For example, a recent model of the American economy treats total noninventory investment, as well as government spending, as exogenous.[9] Since the behavior of fixed investment is not explained, this cannot be considered a complete business-cycle model. But it serves a useful purpose in describing how the economy responds to possible changes in either private investment or government spending. This is done in this model by a set of equations which relate, respectively, consumers' expenditures to disposable income, disposable income to personal income,

[6] For a technical discussion of estimating methods, see the textbook by Klein previously cited. For two excellent nontechnical discussions, see Christ, *op. cit.*, pp. 397-401, and K. A. Fox, "Econometric Models of the United States," *Journal of Political Economy*, vol. 64, April, 1956, pp. 128-142.

[7] In applying this model to the United States, Klein elaborated it to the extent of dividing W into two variables, W_1 (wages paid by private enterprise) and W_2 (wages paid by government), and adding business taxes as an additional variable. *Economic Fluctuations in the United States, 1921–1941*, pp. 64-66.

[8] L. R. Klein and A. S. Goldberger, *An Econometric Model of the United States, 1929–1952*, 1955. For valuable reviews of this study, see the articles by Christ and Fox previously cited.

[9] James Duesenberry, Otto Eckstein, and Gary Fromm, "A Simulation of the United States Economy in Recession," *Econometrica*, vol. 28, October, 1960, pp. 749-809. The model is intended to apply only to postwar recessions.

and personal income to GNP.[10] An equation for inventory investment is also included. In effect, this is a model to test the stability of the economy's responses to an assumed change in either private (noninventory) investment or government expenditures. What is measured in particular is the strength of the automatic stabilizers, given the relation of consumers' expenditures to disposable income and given the way inventory investment typically responds to changes in conditions during the business cycle. This particular model suggests that, in the absence of a collapse of private long-term investment, the American economy today is quite stable and that the multiplier effects of a moderate deflationary decline in government expenditures or fixed investment are relatively small.[11]

Econometric models are less than 30 years old. The possibilities of constructing and using them to explain the business cycle were first pointed out by Ragnar Frisch, a Norwegian mathematical economist, in 1933.[12] While a number of economists and statisticians have worked with such models since then, econometric business-cycle research in recent years has been associated particularly with the names of Jan Tinbergen of the Netherlands and Lawrence Klein of the United States. After a good deal of earlier pioneering work, Tinbergen published in 1939, under the auspices of the League of Nations, two volumes which have become classics in the field of econometric business-cycle research.[13] The second of these volumes represented an econometric study of business fluctuations in the United States during the period 1919–1932.

Although the logic underlying econometric model-building remains largely as Tinbergen expressed it, a great deal of work has been done since in improving the statistical methods that are used to estimate the coefficients in the equations comprising a business-cycle model. Considerable progress has been made in working out methods for determining simultaneously the coefficients of all the equations in a model and in relating the estimating problems that arise to recent developments in the theory

---

[10] A considerable number of equations have to be combined to relate personal income to GNP—for example, equations that attempt to account for the behavior of depreciation, indirect taxes, corporate taxes and retained earnings, and various kinds of transfer payments. As we saw in Chapter 3, these are the items that have to be subtracted or added in the national income accounts as we move from GNP to personal income payments. It should also be noted that the authors intend this to be a model appropriate for recessions only, since some of the equations were fitted only for recession periods.

[11] It is interesting to note, incidentally, that the Klein-Goldberger model, described on p. 277, also turns out to be very stable, even with the treatment of private investment as an endogenous variable. That is, the sort of economic system described by this model would not go on generating cyclical fluctuations without recurring disturbances or shocks. Irma and Frank L. Adelman, "The Dynamic Properties of the Klein-Goldberger Model," *Econometrica*, vol. 27, October, 1959, pp. 596-625.

[12] "Propagation Problems and Impulse Problems in Dynamic Economics," in *Economic Essays in Honour of Gustav Cassel*, 1933, pp. 171-205. Pioneering work in this area had already been done by Tinbergen.

[13] *Statistical Testing of Business-Cycle Theories: I. A Method and Its Application to Investment Activity* and *II. Business Cycles in the United States of America, 1919–1932*. See also his *Business Cycles in the United Kingdom, 1870–1914*, 2nd ed., 1956.

of statistical inference.[14] At the same time, various economists have experimented with actual models applied to specific periods of business-cycle history, not only in the United States but also in some other countries.

Econometric business-cycle models have not, so far, materially increased our ability to explain or predict business fluctuations. This is not surprising, because the difficulties that have to be overcome are well-nigh insuperable, even after the statistical and computing problems are solved.

The basic difficulty is this: An econometric model purports to explain how the economy behaves during a particular period. The equations used, which are selected on the basis of initial theorizing by the investigator, represent a set of hypotheses as to how the economy functions. After the coefficients are computed for these equations, we may find that the model yields accurate estimates for all the important endogenous variables during the period covered. But we still do not know whether we have explained anything. The endogenous variables may also depend on other factors which are not covered in the model, but these additional influences may not have been at work during this period. We have here the same problem that always arises when we apply the methods of multiple correlation analysis to economic time series. The high correlation coefficients that may be obtained do not prove that the independent variables explain or "cause" the behavior of the dependent variable. They may both depend on some other variable which has not been included. Or the correlation may hold only because certain conditions, the nature of which has not been investigated, are true; and these conditions may not continue to hold in the future.

This last point raises the problem of extrapolation and prediction. At best, a model can "explain" only some past period. To apply it to a later period we must assume that the "economic universe" has not changed, that the variables in the model will be related to each other in the future in precisely the same way as in the past. This is always a dangerous assumption to make, and it almost always turns out to be a false one. The danger is the greater, the fewer the variables in our model. The more limited the model, the more likely is it that we have left out something that, though not important in the past, may become important in the future. Even if we have not omitted any important variables, the significant relationships are almost certain to change unpredictably in one way or another. All sorts of institutional changes may alter the basic relationships that the equations in our model attempt to describe. Consumption may seem to depend only on disposable income during the period covered, and

[14] The pioneering work here was done by the Cowles Commission (now Foundation) for Research in Economics. See especially T. C. Koopmans, ed., *Statistical Inference in Dynamic Economic Models*, 1950; and W. C. Hood and T. C. Koopmans, eds., *Studies in Econometric Method*, 1953. For a good introductory discussion, see E. G. Bennion, "The Cowles Commission's 'Simultaneous Equation Approach'," *Review of Economics and Statistics*, vol. 34, February, 1952, pp. 49-56.

we may find that later it also responds to changes in liquid-asset holdings. During one period, private long-term investment may seem to be highly sensitive to current changes in profits and relatively insensitive to the prices of capital goods or to increases in the stock of capital; at a later period, these additional variables may take on a new importance. These issues are particularly significant if we project our model very far past the period originally covered, or if major structural changes suddenly occur—say, because of a war. Even very short-period projections may give inaccurate predictions. The constants in our equations represent, in a sense, average behavior over the period studied. These averages conceal a good deal of short-period variability.[15] Thus we come back to the point made before. It is humanly impossible to put into a system of equations every single influence that has affected or may affect the variables we want to study. Some influences, indeed, cannot even be expressed in quantitative form.[16]

Despite such difficulties, work in this field is likely to continue unabated. Anything approaching complete success (in the sense of ability to predict) is highly improbable, but the rewards of even partial success make the attempt well worth while. After all, it is only in this direction that economists can aspire to put their field on the same "scientific" plane as that of the natural sciences. Econometric model-building represents a striving for the goal Schumpeter described when he said that "the highest ambition an economist can entertain who believes in the scientific character of economics would be fulfilled as soon as he succeeded in constructing a simple model displaying all the essential features of the economic process by means of a reasonably small number of equations connecting a reasonably small number of variables."[17] Although this goal is almost certainly an impossible one, continued striving for it will teach economists a good deal that will help them in using the blunter tools with which most of their work will have to be done.

As econometric models are improved and more detail added, they might also become useful tools of government policy, and indeed they have already been used for this purpose in some countries. Models, either for particular sectors or for the whole economy, can be constructed to point up the influence of variables under the control of the government, and the equations in the model can help government officials to estimate the effects

---

[15] Current econometric models generally assume that all relationships are linear and that they remain unchanged over the period studied. Both assumptions are obviously risky ones to make. The functions included in a model may change not only in what seems to be a haphazard way but also in some systematic manner over the course of the cycle or from one cycle to the next.

[16] The reader will recall our summary in Chapter 11 of the nature and causes of cyclical fluctuations. Note the variety of possibilities that may occur and the fact that no two cycles reflect exactly the same set of forces. See also the comments by Milton Friedman in Universities—National Bureau Committee for Economic Research, *Conference on Business Cycles*, 1951, pp. 107-114.

[17] "The Decade of the Twenties," *American Economic Review*, vol. 36, May, 1946, p. 3.

on various sectors of the economy of deliberate changes in the variables that the government can control—for example, through a reduction in taxes or a change in unemployment benefits.[18]

So far we have been considering econometric models that attempt to deal with the economy as a whole by exploring the mutual interrelations among a workably small number of aggregative variables. We may refer to these as comprehensive models. In addition, as earlier chapters have suggested, there has been a good deal of useful econometric business-cycle research that has dealt only with particular sectors of the economy. There have been, for example, many econometric studies of the consumption function. There have also been a number of econometric studies either of total investment or of particular kinds of investment—for example, inventory investment, residential construction, and investment in public utilities and in manufacturing.[19] And one will find, scattered through the literature, econometric studies of other variables that enter into business-cycle analysis, of which interest rates, various kinds of prices, the demand for consumers' durable goods, foreign trade, and corporate saving might be cited as examples.

---

[18] Cf. Jan Tinbergen, *On the Theory of Economic Policy*, 1952, and *Economic Policy: Principles and Design*, 1956. Econometric models useful for government-policy purposes do not necessarily have to be dynamic; that is, they may not involve any lagged relationships. Even though static, they can help the policy-maker to estimate the effect of an assumed change in one or more variables on certain other variables in a particular year, although the model will provide no information as to what will happen in subsequent years as a result of the internal working of the system. A study of static relationships can provide some guide to policy in a dynamic world, even if it cannot provide an explanation of why the world continues to change.

[19] A few recent examples are J. R. Meyer and Edwin Kuh, *The Investment Decision*, 1957 (on investment in manufacturing); Avram Kisselgoff and Franco Modigliani, "Private Investment in the Electric Power Industry and the Acceleration Principle," *Review of Economics and Statistics*, vol. 39, November, 1957, pp. 363-379; P. G. Darling, "Manufacturers' Inventory Investment, 1947–1958," *American Economic Review*, vol. 49, December, 1959, pp. 950–962; and Robert Eisner, "A Distributed Lag Investment Function," *Econometrica*, vol. 28, January, 1960, pp. 1-29 (for long non-financial corporations).

FOR FURTHER READING

Inasmuch as business cycle theory represents a specialization within the general body of economic thought, it can endure only if causally related to a synoptic view of the entire process of production and distribution. Accordingly, the reader desirous of probing deeper into the evolution of business cycle theory will greatly profit by completing Professor Heimann's brief but perceptive *History of Economic Doctrines*. For the ambitious, we suggest Professor Lewis H. Haney's more detailed and philosophic *History of Economic Thought* (New York: Macmillan Company, 1949), or M. Blaug's *Economic Theory in Retrospect* (Homewood, Ill.: Richard D. Irwin, 1962). Fortified with a broad conception of the scope and method of economic theory, he may further pursue his studies in Professor Haberler's *Prosperity and Depression*; Chapters 2, 3, and 4 of Wesley C. Mitchell's *Business Cycles: The Problem and Its Setting* (New York: National Bureau of Economic Research, 1927); and Mitchell's *Business Cycles and Their Causes* (Berkeley: University of California Press, 1941). These latter will prove an excellent basis for understanding and evaluating post–World War II theoretical advances. In this respect, we also recommend Chapters 26, 27, and 29 of John M. Clark's *Social Control of Business* (New York: McGraw-Hill, 1939). The publications of the National Bureau of Economic Research, professional journals, and the bulletins of research foundations will provide examples of current theoretical work.

In the special field of econometrics, we suggest as a useful introductory text Michael J. Brennan, Jr.'s *Preface to Econometrics* (New York: South-Western Publishing Company, 1960). Part XI of Philip C. Newman,

Arthur D. Gayer, and Milton H. Spencer's *Source Readings in Economic Thought* (New York: W. W. Norton, 1954) is an excellent presentation of the mathematical strain in economic thought. For particular readings in econometric cycle theory, we can do no better than refer the reader to the citations in Professor Gordon's article.

SECTION A

Underconsumption Theories

✗ ❀ ✗

INTRODUCTION

Underconsumption theories comprise perhaps the oldest "explanations" of the business cycle. That the problem of underconsumption should have occupied economists for so long is understandable, since want of purchasing power typifies all business contractions and if, in some fashion, society could sustain the demand for goods then manifestly prosperity would endure *ad infinitum*. Easily recognizable symptoms, however, do not invariably offer accurate clues to the nature or root cause of the disease. Thus underconsumption theories, especially the earlier expositions, are more speculations on economic crisis than analytic inquiries into the causes of those rhythmic expansions and contractions of economic activity termed "business cycles."*

The annals of economic thought reveal that economists subscribing to the underconsumption view attribute the deficiency in purchasing power to sundry causes. The more naive among them pictured a crisis developing out of the tendency of production to outdistance the capacity to consume as capital accumulated or technological innovations were introduced. Robert Owen (1771–1858), in the *Report to the Committee for the Relief of the Manufacturing Poor* (1817), gave eloquent testimony to this position. Others feared that purchasing power would in some way be hoarded and fail to materialize in a demand for goods. François Quesnay (1694–1774), for example, warned against the pernicious effects of sterile savings withdrawn from circulation.

Actually, the underconsumptionists have brooded excessively over the role of savings. A downward turn of production could conceivably result if the accumulated savings of society were not invested or if, through savings, the demand for consumer goods were forced below a level of profitable production. By the same token, if all savings were automatically invested in new plant and equipment, trouble could still arise if the eventual supply of new consumer goods rolling into the market precipitated price declines.

In short, the underconsumptionists or "oversavers" make the demand for consumer goods the central fact of economic life. Only as long as the demand for consumer goods is sustained—so they maintain—will employment in the capital goods industries be assured. Should any disturbing

---

* Some economists demur at the use of the term "business cycle." They properly contend that the phrase implies a uniformity in duration and amplitude of fluctuation not typical of the movements under study. The reader will recall from Part I that although "business cycles" have many common characteristics, nevertheless, each cycle differs in many significant ways from every other cycle. Not only have economists not achieved a consensus on a single, dominant cause of recession and revival, but the discernible initiating forces need follow no special time sequence and may differ greatly in magnitude. Moreover, the disappearance of the gold standard has altered the periodic quality of business fluctuations. Variations in the supply of bank credit may still produce corresponding oscillations in business activity but today's central bank is no longer *required* to expand and contract credit in response to an inflow or outflow of gold reserves. See Irving Fisher, "Our Unstable Dollar and the So-called Business Cycle," *Journal of American Statistical Association* (June, 1925); Ruth Mack, "Notes on Subcycles in Theory and Practice," *American Economic Review* (May, 1957); Adolph G. Abramson and Russell H. Mack, *Business Forecasting in Practice: Principles and Cases* (New York: John Wiley & Sons, 1956), pp. 202-205; Maurice W. Lee, *Economic Fluctuations: Growth and Stability* (Homewood, Ill.: Richard D. Irwin, 1959), pp. 22-29; and Robert Aaron Gordon, *Business Fluctuations* (New York: Harper & Brothers, 1961), pp. 352-358.

Conversely, it appears well nigh impossible to avoid the expression "business cycle," for it bears a popular connotation, associated in the public and professional mind with short-term, cumulative fluctuations (two to eleven years from peak to peak and trough to trough) in the general economy and indigenous to the institutional arrangements of a private enterprise system. In this sense, we shall employ the phrase "business cycle" and hope thereby to sidestep the semantics of the argument.

element—such as an increase in the rate of saving—upset the market for consumer goods, the entire economy must suffer the repercussions.

If the early classical economists did not commonly accept the underconsumption thesis, the school, notwithstanding, had some notable adherents. Thomas R. Malthus (1766–1834), famed for his controversial *Essay on Population*, certainly envisioned the possibility of a "general glut" caused by an insufficiency of demand. Simonde de Sismondi (1773–1842) and Karl Rodbertus (1805–1875), the latter one of the most influential of socialist writers, both foresaw in capitalistic production a tendency toward "crisis" because of the low incomes paid to the laboring masses. None of these authors, however, attempted to explain the disruption of production as a *periodic* phenomenon: that is, a recurring cycle.

Succeeding authors have put the underconsumption story on a firmer intellectual foundation. John A. Hobson (1858–1940), whose views are reproduced below, may be numbered among these later apostles. We will not anticipate his remarks except to note that both he and Karl Marx (1818–1883) accounted for the irregular nature of business activity as part of a continuing inclination to disequilibrium associated with capitalism and its institutional arrangements. In the Marxian analysis, a violent liquidation was prerequisite to the restoration of equilibrium.*

Up to now, we have talked of essentially nonmonetary interpretations. Two contemporary economists, R. G. Hawtrey† and R. F. Harrod,‡ have written extensively on a monetary underinvestment explanation of underconsumption. They contend that as income increases in a period of expansion, the rate of consumption falls behind and savings grow. Unless investment is sufficient to absorb the increased saving at the peak of prosperity the economy must relapse into recession. The best-known exponent of this version, and one of the "influentials" of our age, was, of course, J. M. Keynes (1883–1946). Chapter 3 of Professor Dillard's *The Economics of John Maynard Keynes*, included in this book (pp. 296–316), ably recapitulates the general theory of Keynes. Kenneth E. Boulding's "The Consumption Concept in Economic Theory" (*The American Review*,

---

* Interestingly enough, where communist governments have come to power they have consistently favored the heavy, capital goods industries at the expense of consumer goods output. In doing so, they have reversed the economic history of the Western countries. In the Western world the process of industrialization extended over many generations, and only in the final phase of development did the production of the so-called capital goods industries exceed that of the consumer goods industries. These Marxian countries, especially the U.S.S.R., are achieving a high rate of heavy industrial progress at the cost of a very low standard of living for the overwhelming majority of the population—in short, by saving!

† See p. 424 for a review of Hawtrey's career and principal writings.

‡ Harrod's chief work, the *Trade Cycle*, was published in 1936. His other books: *A Page of British Policy*, 1946; *Are These Hardships Necessary?* 1947; *Toward a Dynamic Economics*, 1948; *Policy Against Inflation*, 1958. He has also published widely in professional journals, the more recent contributions including: "Notes on the Trade Cycle," *Economic Journal* (June, 1951), and "Measures to Prevent a Slump," *Foreign Affairs* (July, 1949).

Vol. XXV, No. 2, May 1955, pp. 1–14) illustrates certain relationships between production and consumption, summarizes the main contributions of Keynesian thought, and examines the serious dilemma facing "mature capitalism"—to increase consumption or to decrease production through depression and unemployment.

In rounding out an all-too-brief preface, we must take cognizance of one further variation of the underconsumption theme, the works of Emil Lederer and Hans Neisser. Both emphasize monetary factors, but, unlike the underinvestment theorists of the preceding paragraph, Lederer stresses the disproportionality of price movements which cause income to lag behind output in expansion and to exceed output in contraction. Neisser gives a greater proportionate influence to international conditions.

[16]

The Failure of Consumption*

JOHN A. HOBSON

Editors' Note

John A. Hobson (1858–1940)—economist, educator, and social reformer—while a student at Oxford University was influenced by the social philosophies of Arnold Toynbee, John Ruskin, and other liberal thinkers. His own social philosophy manifestly colored his thinking on educational and economic problems. In the area of education, Hobson labored to encourage the organization of university extension teaching programs for the education of the working class. So oriented philosophically, his underconsumption diagnosis of the economic ills afflicting society need occasion no great surprise. This was early expressed in the *Physiology of Industry* (1889), *The Evolution of Modern Capitalism: A Study of Machine Production* (1894), and *The Economics of Unemployment* (1931). Chapter 2 of the last-named volume, frequently cited in anthologies on economic thought, outlines Hobson's explanation of the cyclical crisis affecting capitalist production. In it, he argues forcibly that underconsumption is the inevitable concomitant of inequalities in the distribution of income.

A critic of the established order, Hobson still did not accept the Marxian interpretation. He looked to the reform of society, not revolutionary change. He stressed the need to consider the human costs of production as well as the monetary costs and took the orthodox economists to task for failing to consider this aspect of economic life.

A social reformer must popularize his views. Hobson's writings are therefore somewhat less "intellectual" than the professional economist would desire, accounting in part for his lack of influence with the "chiefs." However, for those who are at times appalled by the arid exchanges in pro-

* From *The Economics of Unemployment* by John A. Hobson (London: George Allen & Unwin, 1931), Chap. 2, pp. 29-41. Reprinted by permission of George Allen & Unwin, Ltd.

fessional journals, Hobson may prove a welcome relief. He at least set forth his ideas in lucid, unobfuscated prose.

~~~~~~

❧ During the war, and for some time after, trade was prosperous and employment full, because there was an assured effective demand for all that could be produced. In other words, consumption kept pace with production, taking off without delay all that was produced. The full pace of this artificially stimulated production could not, indeed, have been maintained indefinitely. But, if this war-economy could have been converted into a peace economy operating at, say, four-fifths the full war pace, the fighters absorbed into the working classes on a shorter working day, producing the housing, railway developments and other work of capital repair and extension, while public expenditure was maintained on a high-tax basis without further borrowing or inflation, there seems no economic reason (apart from political and social considerations) why effective demand for British products should have failed and depression supervened. The high level of wages and full employment for our workers would have enabled the size of the effective demand to compensate for the slack demand of foreign customers, as during the war itself. This policy could not, indeed, have continued indefinitely for this or any other highly peopled country. For a considerable export trade is indispensable for a people who must buy half of their food and much of their materials abroad. But this signifies that a world-depression, or any other world-problem, cannot finally be solved for any single country on its separate national policy. Cyclical depressions are the gravest of international diseases, and demand an agreed diagnosis and a common line of treatment—industrial, commercial and financial.

The general shrinkage of effective demand which constitutes a cyclical depression implies a failure of consumption to keep pace with production in the industrial world taken as a whole. There may be areas, whole countries, where production is active, as during the present depression. But their very activity is aggravating the depression elsewhere.

A period of depression is marked by under-consumption and under-production. But it is not a matter of indifference through which of these two gates of explanation we enter. The business world, employers and workers alike, are, as we have seen, strongly and variously committed to the belief that at any given time there is a limited market, in the sense of an effective demand insufficient to take all the goods they can produce, on terms enabling production to continue. In other words, the limited market signifies a normal tendency for consumption to fall below production. Every one knows that in ordinary times it is easier to buy than to sell, and that more and more economic activity is given to pushing wares and the arts of salesmanship, while an ever-increasing proportion of the retail prices paid for most goods is swallowed up in costs of distribution.

But in focussing our attention upon under-consumption, or the chronic failure of consumption to keep pace with production, it is necessary to define our meaning of consumption. The term is applied in the business world not only to the withdrawal of final commodities for purposes of personal consumption, but to the use of raw materials, fuel and other capital goods which are said to be consumed when they are worked up into other products. Although in periods of general depression both sorts of consumption are reduced, the latter sort is not properly regarded as part of the problem of under-consumption. In this analysis we shall confine the terms consumption and under-consumption to the effective demand of final consumers for finished commodities.

For only thus can we challenge sharply and clearly the accepted economic dogma, which renders it impossible to get a comprehension of the real social economic significance of unemployment. The orthodox economist regards all the opinions and practices, to which we have appealed in support of a belief in a limited market, as based on fallacious thinking. He is convinced that general over-production is impossible, though it stares him in the face at the outbreak of each cyclical depression. Under consumption is for him equally absurd. For does not everything that is produced belong to its producers, who must either want to consume it, or to consume something else against which they can exchange it, or to use it for producing more things which they will consume later on? The wants of man being expansible without limit, how is it possible that too much can be produced? If he is confronted with the progress of a trade cycle, the full activity in boom years evoking an output which presently becomes so large that it can only be marketed at lower prices—this fall of prices proceeding until a level is reached at which costs of production are no longer covered and surplus stocks of goods are accumulated, which, if thrown upon the market, could only be sold by driving down prices to a still lower level—this economist refuses to recognise this condition as over-production, and confines his attention to the resulting stoppage of industry which he rightly diagnoses as under-production. Now a trade depression manifestly is a state of under-production, but this state is the product of an excessive activity preceding it. Over-production, congestion, stoppage, is the visible order of events. Theoretically, no doubt, it ought not to be possible. Every increase of output ought to find its outlet in consumption without reducing prices below the level at which it pays to produce.

But since it does not work this way, it is well to inquire why it does not. Why does consumption fail to keep pace with increased powers of production? Or, conversely, why do the powers of production increase faster than the rate of consumption?

The answer is found in two related phenomena: first, the conservative character of the arts of consumption, or standards of living, as compared with the modern arts of production; second, the ways in which the current distribution of income confirms this conservatism of consumption.

In primitive societies the standards or methods of work are almost as conservative as those of consumption. Of civilised societies, and especially of modern industrial nations, this is no longer true. Invention and business initiative, enlisted in the cause of quick profiteering, transform with great rapidity the arts of industry, raising this productivity by leaps and bounds. Though modern man, in his capacity of consumer, is far more progressive than his ancestors, his power of taking on new economic needs and of raising rapidly the quantity, variety and quality of his consumption, is limited by a narrowness of imagination and a servitude to habit which are far less dominant in production. There is in modern business a strong stimulus to progress in the great gain which comes to the man of inventive and initiative power, while, on the other hand, there is a strong stimulus to the early imitation and adoption of new superior methods by the whole body of members of a trade, who are otherwise outcompeted and ruined by their conservatism. Now a large part of consumption is carried on in the privacy of separate homes, under the bonds of custom, and withdrawn from any strong continual stimulus to imitation and competition; and though changes are quicker and more numerous in those factors of consumption, such as dress, travel and recreation, which are subject to publicity and imitation and carry personal prestige, the capacity of assimilating easily and quickly large new personal expenditure is comparatively rare. Indeed, it is needless to set out in detail the evidence for the comparative conservatism of consumption. For, if everyone was driven by a natural impulse to raise his consumption immediately, so as to absorb the whole of any enlargement in the output of industry which came to him as income, there could be no increase in the provision of capital, and all further progress in the arts of production, so far as they demanded capital, would be inhibited.

Indeed, it must be admitted that upon this natural conservatism of present consumption, strengthened and directed by reasonable regard for future consumption, the economic progress of mankind depends. It is this conservatism that is expressed in saving. The real economic function of saving must be clearly kept in mind. It does not consist in not spending, i.e. in putting money income in a bank, or even in making an investment. It consists in paying producers to make more non-consumable goods for use as capital, instead of paying them to make more consumable goods and consuming them. This is the vital distinction between spending and saving, so often obscured by dwelling upon the merely monetary aspect.

Now, if we hold, as seems to be the case, that a depression is due to, or testifies to, the existence of an excess of producing power and a corresponding deficiency of consuming power, we can only mean that somehow or other there has been over-saving or under-spending on the part of industrial society, in the sense that more non-consumable, i.e. capital, goods have been created than have been capable of being properly utilised for the supply of future consumption. This is not a theory or an explanation, but rather a description of the actual facts. At a time of depression large bodies of capital stand idle, together with the labour and business ability that could operate them. They simply represent a surplus or excess of former savings, which cannot get used without delay and waste for the productive end for which they were designed.

I am aware that long before this many readers will be bursting with impatience, because they think I am ignoring what seems to them other and truer explanations of depression, resting upon the play of psychological-financial forces. Now, without denying the important part taken by these forces in exaggerating the fluctuations of concrete industry and commerce, I propose to show that they are secondary and not primary causes, and have no initiatory and independent influence. Having this intention, I must first complete the chain of reasoning by which I trace the under-production and under-consumption, which are the chief factors of a depression, to the normal tendency to save a larger proportion of income than can effectively and continuously function as capital.

I have referred to a natural conservatism in the arts of consumption in part explanation of the failure of consumption to keep full pace with the more progressive arts of production. But this natural tendency is strongly reinforced by inequalities in the distribution of income, which place a larger proportion of the aggregate incomes in the possession of comparatively small classes, who, after satisfying all their economic desires, have large surpluses for automatic saving and investment. The great bulk of the saving, normally applied to capital purposes in this and other industrially developed countries, belongs to this almost automatic accumulation of the surplus incomes of the well-to-do. I speak of it as 'almost automatic,' meaning that its provision involves no appreciable sacrifice in current satisfaction from consumption on the part of its possessors, and very little thought, excepting as regards its application for investment.

That the large incomes resulting from the inequality of wealth distribution enlarge the volume of savings, available for the increase and improvement of the capital structure of industry, is the accepted view of most economists.[1]

An interesting, though necessarily speculative, estimate of savings in relation to incomes was presented by Mr. Ireson in 1910,[2] to the following effect:

---

[1] Cf. Pigou, *Wealth and Welfare*, p. 354; Stamp, *The Principles of Taxation*, p. 164; Keynes, *The Economic Consequences of the Peace*, p. 19.

[2] *The People's Progress*, p. 146. Mallock, *Capital, War and Wages*, pp. 34-35, estimates that "at present some three-fourths of these savings—the total being about £15 per head of the occupied population—come from the richer classes, the savings of those per head being about £170, and those of the poorer majority being not so much as £4."

Families with	Average Income per Family	Average Spending per Family
	£	£
Over £5,000	12,100	7,600
From £700 to £5,000	1,054	690
From £160 to £700	357	329
From £52 to £160	142	138
Under £52	40	40

There is nothing unreasonable in the conclusion, suggested by this table and supported by *a priori* considerations, that any approximation towards equality of incomes would reduce the proportion of income saved to income spent. At a time like the present, when the aggregate amount of saving is greatly reduced, it is natural that qualms should be felt as to the effect of any movements making for a greater equalisation of incomes, and a consequent reduction of the automatic savings from high incomes. Under such circumstances my thesis, that under-consumption due to oversaving arising from maldistribution of income, is the normal cause of cyclical depression, is liable to grave misunderstanding.

I hasten, therefore, to explain that the over-saving of which I speak refers solely to the proportion of saving to spending, and does not imply any fixed limit to the amount that can be serviceably saved. This thesis may be presented in the following form:

Just as waste of productive power admittedly occurs by misapplication of capital, skill, and labour, as between one trade and another, or one area of investment and another (too much applied here, too little there), so income as a whole may be wastefully applied as between purchase of commodities and purchase of new capital goods.

For just as it is clear that waste ensues unless some accurate proportion is kept between the amounts of capital, skill, and labour placed in the several productive processes required for converting raw materials into finished goods, so there is waste if these finished goods are not effectively demanded and consumed as fast as the productive processes enable them to pass into the form of finished goods. In other words, consumption is simply the final link in a chain of economic processes, each of which should be kept in accurate proportion to the preceding ones, unless stoppage and waste are to occur. This is quite evident if the series of processes comprising the production, sale and consumption of any single commodity such as bread, or boots, is taken under survey. Having regard to the current condition of the arts of industry, there will be a just balance both between the productive power applied at the respective stages of production on the one hand, and between the quantity of purchasing power applied to buy the bread or boots, and the quantity applied to maintain and improve the productive processes as a whole, upon the other hand. And what applies to any kind of commodity applies to commodities in general. In the use of the current income there must exist, at any time, an economically right proportion between expenditure in withdrawing commodities from the retail shops for consumption, and expenditure in maintaining and enlarging the plant and materials functioning in each stage of production. Or, putting it otherwise, saving and investment for enlargement of production are only economically valid on condition that the enlarged production is accompanied or soon followed by a proportionately enlarged consumption. In the last resort the rate of saving (in this sense) must bear an accurate proportion to rate of spending. This proportion of saving may be exceeded by any person or group, or even (within limits), any nation, but it must be kept by industrial society as a whole. Any attempt on the part of the whole society to live beyond its income is soon frustrated, for it is impossible to continue taking out more consumables than are passed through the productive processes. A nation may let down its productive plant, and stocks of materials or semi-manufactured articles, in order to over-consume for a brief spurt, as we did in the emergency of war; but even this national over-consumption was only rendered possible by the belligerent nations drawing upon the surplus accumulations of the neutral world. The world as a whole would be pulled up very soon in any collective refusal of its inhabitants to make the necessary provision for future production.

There might, indeed, be under-saving, in the sense of a refusal to save enough to realise the enlargements and improvements of the machinery of production that are required to furnish a larger output of commodities for a higher standard or a growing population.

Such a society might be said to over-spend and under-save, though it would not strictly speaking live beyond its income. Such under-saving on the part of society would mean a retardation or even a paralysis of economic progress.

This, indeed, presumably is what our economists consider would be the natural result of a process of equalisation of incomes. As under this condition the proportion of savings to consumption would be reduced, the growth of capital, and therefore the progress of production would be checked. And this seems true on one assumption, viz. that the total income to be spent or saved is not directly affected in its dimensions by the process of 'equalisation.' Suppose, however, that this equalisation, with its increased pressure of demand for consumables, kept the machinery of production more fully and more quickly working to supply the increased outflow of consumables, this would constitute an actual increase of real income, by reason of the higher productivity of the capital and labour continuously under full employment. Under such circumstances, although a smaller proportion of the larger income might be saved, and a larger proportion consumed, the actual amount of saving might be as large as or even larger than before, and, being more fully utilised as capital, might maintain as high a rate of economic progress as before.

This is the thesis which I here maintain.

The waste of production actually experienced in our normal operation of industry, by slowing down and stoppages, represents an attempt to save and employ as capital a larger proportion of income than *can* function in supplying the reduced consumption. This is to be attributed to a maldistribution of income, which upsets the true balance between present and future consumption that would obtain in a well-constituted society.

A self-sustaining individual (were such possible) would balance as exactly as he could present labour against future enjoyment. So would any group whose earnings were strictly proportionate to efforts. Such group-economy would apply a certain proportion of its present toil to making more or better tools, so as to lighten future toil and make it more productive of consumables. But there would be no tendency to sacrifice so large a proportion of possible present enjoyment as to provide more tools than were wanted, and more than could possibly be put continuously to full use in the production of future goods. But if in any society you get considerable groups of men whose incomes come to them by others' toil instead of their own, and if these incomes are so large as to afford little or no additional satisfaction by any considerable increase of their expenditure, this natural balancing of present against future enjoyment is upset. It becomes too easy for a rich man, living on unearned income, to cause an excessive proportion of the labour which he commands, but does not himself perform, to be directed to the production of future goods which he, or someone else, may or may not consume. In other words, the 'surplus' nature of much of the income which results from inequality of distribution disturbs the true balance of productive activities, and disturbs it normally in the direction of the postponed consumption of articles which, if consumed now by those into whose hand they would fall, would satisfy no felt want but would spell repletion.

A Preliminary Summary
of the General
Theory of Employment*

DUDLEY DILLARD†

***

Editors' Note

We must concur with Professor Dillard when he ranks Lord Keynes as "one of the great economists of all time and as the most influential economic thinker the twentieth century has so far produced." Keynes shifted the attention of economists from their orthodox preoccupation with the study of individual behavior (microeconomics) to the study of aggregates (macroeconomics). By denying that capitalism was self-adjusting and by demonstrating an innate tendency of mature capitalism to reach an equilibrium at less than full employment, he not only preached economic heresy but forced a reorientation of the discussion toward the factors which govern the level of employment.

Keynes' exposition struck at the doctrinal roots of private enterprise. In vain were the protests of the Keynesians that the master was at heart a conservative, a man of considerable financial means, and in true light a "doctor of capitalism." The patient simply had no stomach for this kind of salvation. Time, however, inexorably cooled the heat of debate; and the government's role in maintaining employment, which generated so much

***

* Dudley Dillard, *The Economics of John Maynard Keynes* (chap. 3, pp. 28-55), © 1948. Prentice-Hall, Inc., Englewood Cliffs, N.J. Reprinted by permission.

† Dudley Dillard, (1913–   ), Professor and Chairman of the Department of Economics, University of Maryland, enjoys a solid reputation among the ranks of American scholars and teachers. In addition to service with the Federal Government from 1942–44, Professor Dillard has held teaching positions at the University of Colorado and the University of Delaware. His principal interests lie in economic theory, economic development, and the history of economic doctrines.

discord in the 1930's and '40's, became a commonplace in the '50's and '60's. In no small measure, the transition reflected the influence of *Treatise on Money* (1930) and *The General Theory of Employment, Interest, and Money* (1936). The latter, for good or ill, swayed the fiscal and monetary policies of many Western nations, including the United States. Although history may subsequently revise the ultimate standing of Keynes, no one can claim to understand the extant politico-economic environment without an acquaintance with his teachings.

The purpose of Professor Dillard's summary is to "give the reader a bird's eye view" of Keynes' whole theory before essaying a detailed examination of its individual parts. Because this article is readable and accurate in its presentation, it is frequently used to introduce students to the complexities of Lord Keynes' thought.

❧ This analysis supplies us with an explanation of the paradox of poverty in the midst of plenty. For the mere existence of an insufficiency of effective demand may, and often will, bring the increase of employment to a standstill *before* a level of full employment has been reached . . . Moreover the richer the community, the wider will tend to be the gap between its actual and its potential production; and therefore the more obvious and outrageous the defects of the economic system.

J. M. Keynes, *The General Theory of Employment, Interest and Money*.[1]

The Principle of Effective Demand

The logical starting point of Keynes' theory of employment is the principle of effective demand.[2] Total employment depends on total demand, and unemployment results from a deficiency of total demand. Effective demand manifests itself in the spending of income. As employment increases, income increases. A fundamental principle is that as the real income of a community increases, consumption will also increase but by

---

[1] Reprinted by permission of Harcourt, Brace & World, Inc.; The Trustees of the Estate of the late Lord Keynes; and Macmillan & Co., Ltd.

[2] As explained below, the adjective "effective" is used to designate the point on the aggregate demand curve where it is intersected by the aggregate supply curve. There are other points on the aggregate demand curve but these are not effective in determining the actual volume of employment. "Effective" is also helpful in emphasizing the distinction between mere desire to buy and desire plus ability to buy. Only the latter has economic significance.

less than income. Therefore, in order to have sufficient demand to sustain an increase in employment there must be an increase in real investment equal to the gap between income and the consumption demand out of that income. In other words, employment cannot increase unless investment increases. This is the core of the principle of effective demand. Since it is fundamental to the general theory of employment, it will be restated on an expanded basis in the following paragraphs.

AGGREGATE DEMAND AND AGGREGATE SUPPLY

The term "demand" as used by Keynes refers to aggregate demand of the whole economic system. Aggregate demand must be clearly distinguished from the demand for the products of individual firms and individual industries which is the usual type represented in supply and demand diagrams. The demand for a firm or industry means a schedule of various amounts of a commodity which will be purchased at a series of prices. Price means the amount of money received from the sale of a given physical quantity of output, such as a bushel of wheat or a ton of steel. Since the output of the entire economic system cannot be measured in any simple physical unit like a bushel or ton, Keynes uses the amount of labor employed as the measure of output as a whole. The aggregate demand "price" for the output of any given amount of employment is the total sum of money, or proceeds, which is expected from the sale of the output produced when that amount of labor is employed. The aggregate demand curve, or "aggregate demand function" as Keynes calls it (represented by DD in Figure 1), is a schedule of the proceeds expected from the sale of the output resulting from varying amounts of employment. As more labor is employed, more output is produced, and the total proceeds are greater. In other words, aggregate demand price increases as the amount of employment increases, and decreases as the amount of employment decreases.

In Figure 1 the aggregate demand price or proceeds is represented along the vertical axis, and the quantity of employment (N) along the horizontal axis. The aggregate demand schedule slants up toward the right, indicating that demand increases with employment. This contrasts with an industry demand curve which slants down toward the right, indicating that the quantity sold will increase as the price falls.

In a business-enterprise economy in which production is motivated by profit, each business man will employ that number of workers which will yield him the greatest profit. The total number of men employed in the whole economy is the total or aggregate of those employed by all entrepreneurs. A certain minimum amount of proceeds will be necessary to induce employers as a whole to offer any given aggregate amount of employment. This minimum price or proceeds which will just induce employment on a given scale is called the aggregate supply price of that amount of employment. The aggregate supply function is a schedule of the minimum amounts of proceeds required to induce varying quantities of employment.

As the amount of proceeds increases, a greater amount of employment will be offered to workers by employers. Therefore, the aggregate supply schedule (ZZ in Figure 1), like the aggregate demand schedule, slants up toward the right as the amount of employment (N) increases. It will not, however, follow the same course. There will be some amounts of employment for which the proceeds expected will exceed the proceeds necessary to induce a given volume of employment and there will be some amounts of employment for which the proceeds expected will not be suf-

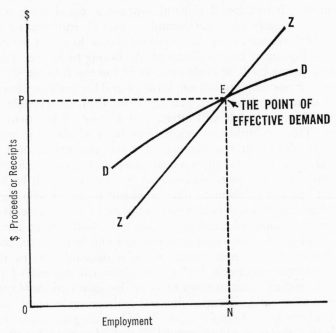

DD—The Aggregate Demand Schedule: The proceeds or receipts (P) *expected* to be forthcoming for output produced by vary-ing amounts of employment (N).

ZZ —The Aggregate Supply Schedule: The proceeds or receipts (P) which will *just induce* given amounts of employment (N).

FIGURE 1. AGGREGATE DEMAND AND AGGREGATE SUPPLY.

ficient to induce that amount of employment. In between there will be some amount of employment for which the expected proceeds will just equal the necessary proceeds to make the employment profitable to en-trepreneurs. At this point the aggregate demand function intersects the aggregate supply function, and the point of intersection determines the actual amount of employment at any time. This is the crux of Keynes' theory of employment. The aggregate demand schedule (DD) and the aggregate supply schedule (ZZ), as represented in Figure 1, intersect at the point E, corresponding to the amount of employment N. E at the point of intersection represents *the effective demand*. At this point, entrepreneurs maximize their expected profits. If either more or less employment were offered, profits would be less. Thus at any one time, there is, according to Keynes' theory, a uniquely determined amount of employment which will be most profitable for entrepreneurs to offer to workers. There is no reason to assume this point will correspond to full employment. The labor market is not, as a rule, a seller's market. Aggregate demand and aggregate supply might be equal at full employment, but this will occur only if investment demand happens to equal the gap between the aggregate supply price corresponding to full employment and the amount which consumers in the aggregate choose to spend for consumption out of income at full employment. According to Keynes, the typical investment demand will be inadequate to fill the gap between the amount of income corresponding to full employment and the consumption demand out of that income. Therefore, the aggregate demand schedule and the aggregrate supply schedule will intersect at a point of less than full employment. This establishes an equilibrium from which there will be no tendency to depart in the absence of some external change. In the absence of a large volume of expected proceeds from the sale of investment goods, the total proceeds expected by employers will be less than is necessary to induce them to offer employment to all who are willing to work. Full employment is important only as a limiting case. It may be defined as an amount of employment beyond which further increases in effective demand do not increase output and employment (p. 26).*

The maxim that "supply creates its own demand" means that *any* increase in employment will lead to an additional amount of proceeds sufficient to induce entrepreneurs to offer the increased employment. If this maxim were valid, aggregate demand and aggregate supply would be equal for all amounts of employment (N). On a diagram similar to Figure 1, the classical theory would represent DD and ZZ as equal for all amounts of employment (N). Since the expected proceeds would always be adequate to induce more employment, competition among entrepreneurs for workers and among workers for jobs would lead to an expansion of employment as long as anyone is involuntarily unemployed. The classical theory breaks down in attempting to apply Say's law to the demand for investment. For while it is true that more employment will create more income of which some will be spent for consumers goods, all of it will not be spent in this way and there is no reason to assume that the difference will be devoted to investment expenditure. If investment does not increase when employment increases, the sum of consumption demand and investment demand will be less than the aggregate supply price for the higher level of employment. Entrepreneurs will reduce employment to a

---

* Editor's note. Page references within the excerpt apply to Keynes' work, *The General Theory of Employment, Interest, and Money,* unless otherwise indicated.

level at which the aggregate supply price exceeds the consumption demand by the actual amount of investment.

FURTHER STATEMENT OF THE PRINCIPLE OF EFFECTIVE DEMAND

Since there is little that is novel about the aggregate supply function, the essence of Keynes' theory is found in his analysis of the aggregate demand function. Since employment depends on demand and total demand is equal to total income, the general theory of employment is also a theory of aggregate demand or of aggregate income. Since the value of total output is equal to total income, Keynes' theory may also be called a theory of aggregate output. Employment results in the production of output on the one hand and in the creation of income on the other. Total output will have a value equal to total income. Total output consists of the production of consumers goods and the production of investment goods.[3] Total income is earned from the production of consumers goods and the production of investment. If we start from less than full employment, any *increase* in employment must be divided between consumption output and investment output in a manner which corresponds to the way in which income receivers choose to divide their *increase* in income between consumption expenditure and saving.

Assuming as Keynes does the aggregate supply function to be given, the thesis of his *General Theory* is that employment is determined by aggregate demand, which in turn depends on the propensity to consume and the amount of investment at a given time.

Since employment is assumed to be uniquely correlated with income, we may show income along the horizontal axis in place of employment, which was represented there in Figure 1. The value of total output is shown along the vertical axis. Since total income is equal to the value of total output, the equilibrium adjustment must lie along the 45° line indicated in Figure 2.[4] The point of effective demand (E) will be on the

---

[3] Any number of divisions of total output could be made. For some purposes it is convenient to make a three-fold division of total national product by setting the contribution of government apart in a separate category. For other problems a four-fold division into consumption, private investment, government investment, and foreign investment (net exports) is used. In *The General Theory* Keynes uses only the two-fold division into consumption and investment. At this point in our discussion it would complicate the analysis and add little to the essential meaning of Keynes' theory to depart from his simple classification of output as consumption and investment. This two-fold division is not arbitrary. It is based on the empirical premise that the behavior that determines consumption and that which determines investment are different in a way which has great practical significance. One is stable in relation to income and the other is highly unstable and largely autonomous.

[4] The 45° line in Figure 2 is not the same as the aggregate supply schedule in Figure 1. The 45° line is merely a line along which income equals output for any value of output. Keynes did not use a diagram to explain his theory of effective demand, but geometrical drawings have been widely used for this purpose. Figure 2 differs from

45° line at the point at which the volume of investment is equal to the distance between this line and the consumption schedule, CC.

The consumption schedule (propensity to consume) will be discussed in detail later. This schedule represents the stable relationship which Keynes assumes to exist between the size of the national income and the

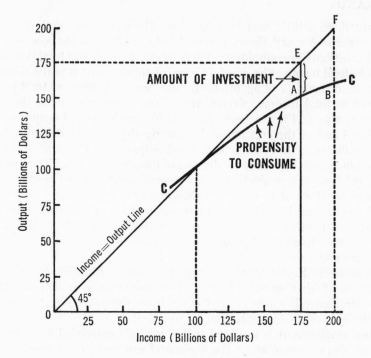

FIGURE 2. INCOME DETERMINED BY THE PROPENSITY TO CONSUME AND THE AMOUNT OF INVESTMENT.

amount which will be spent by the public for consumption. In Figure 2 the consumption schedule is drawn to represent the following assumed relations between income and consumption, in billions of dollars:

Income	100	125	150	175	200
Consumption	100	120	137.5	150	160

most of the diagrams of this type in that it shows "output" along the vertical axis. It would perhaps be more appropriate to call this the "demand for output." If Figure 2 were to be broken down into more detail, it would show income, which is along the horizontal axis, divided into two parts, consumption expenditure and saving; and output, which is along the vertical axis, divided into consumption output (or consumption demand) and investment demand. This presentation has pedagogical advantages over diagrams which show consumption, investment and saving along the vertical axis. The proportionality of the two parts of these two lines is an essential condition of an equilibrium position. It also can be used to show the meaning of the equality of saving to investment.

This schedule follows the fundamental maxim that when income rises, consumption also rises, but less than income. The difference between income and consumption increases from zero at $100 billion of income, to $5 billion at $125 billion, to $12.5 billion at $150 billion, to $25 billion at $175 billion, and finally to $40 billion at the assumed full employment income of $200 billion.

If AE ($25 billion) is the amount of investment at a given time, the total output most profitable for entrepreneurs to produce will be $175 billion. This total output will consist of two parts, $150 billion worth of consumption output in addition to $25 billion worth of investment output. Total income, which is equal to total output, will also be $175 billion. If the amount of investment becomes less than AE, income must fall below $175 billion. When investment is zero, income will be $100 billion, and all output will be consumption output. The distance FB ($40 billion) represents the amount of investment that would be necessary to raise income to the full employment level of $200 billion.

Since consumption expenditure increases by less than income when income increases, there can be no increase in employment unless there is an increase in investment. This means that investment must increase to fill the gap between income and consumption. Less than 100 per cent of any increase in aggregate income will be spent for consumption goods and consequently less than 100 per cent of output must be in the form of consumption goods. Otherwise what is produced will not correspond to what is demanded out of the higher income. In the absence of an increase in the demand for investment, business men who employ additional workers to produce more output will be unable in the aggregate to sell what they produce except at losses. If newly employed workers are set to producing all consumers goods, there will be an insufficient demand to buy these goods at prices profitable to entrepreneurs because only a part of the newly created income will be spent to buy consumers goods. In the circumstances illustrated in Figure 2, let us suppose entrepreneurs were to hire the unemployed workers to produce an additional $25 billion worth of consumers goods. This would make a total output of $175 billion of consumption output and $25 billion of investment output, and a total income of $200 billion. Since out of this income only $160 billion will be spent for consumption, there will be $15 billion worth of unsold consumption output. Losses will result because all the additional workers have been employed to produce consumers goods and only part of the additional demand will be for consumers goods. But if newly employed workers are set to producing less than 100 per cent of consumers goods, there will be no market for the non-consumer (investment) goods in the absence of an increase in the demand for investment. Losses will result in either case because the proceeds received by entrepreneurs will be less than sufficient to cover the total costs (aggregate supply price) of the higher level of employment. Consequently output and employment will reach an equilibrium only at the point where income exceeds consumption by the actual amount of investment. This illustrates again the principle that employment cannot increase unless investment increases. This principle rests on the assumption that the propensity to consume (consumption function) remains unchanged.

The Propensity to Consume

Consumption demand depends on the size of income and the share that is spent for consumers goods. We have already observed that for any level of national income there is a fairly stable proportion which will be spent for consumption by the public. If the American public chooses to spend $160 billion for consumption when the national income is $200 billion, the average propensity to consume at this point is 80 per cent. Some income recipients will spend more than 80 per cent and others will spend less than 80 per cent of their incomes for consumption, but the average (arithmetic mean) will be 80 per cent. At different levels of national income the amount of consumption will change, and the proportion which total consumption is of total income will also change. The absolute amount of consumption will increase as income increases, and will decrease as income decreases. A schedule showing the various amounts of consumption which correspond to different levels of income is the "schedule of the propensity to consume," which for the sake of brevity is referred to simply as "the propensity to consume." It is a functional relationship indicating how consumption varies when income varies. Such a relationship may be shown for an individual or family consumption unit, but in Keynes' theory it is the relationship between aggregate community consumption and aggregate community income that is important.

Keynes' assumption that the propensity to consume is relatively stable in the short run is a generalization about actual experience and is an essential part of the structure of his theory. If this assumption is valid, the amount of community consumption varies in a regular manner with aggregate income. What the actual schedule of the propensity to consume will be at any time depends on the established customs of the community, the distribution of income, the tax system, and other factors. A high propensity to consume is favorable to employment because it leaves relatively small gaps between income and the consumption out of income corresponding to different levels of employment. If the schedule of the propensity to consume is relatively low, the gaps between income and consumption will be greater and, in order to maintain high levels of employment, the amount of investment must be relatively great. If the average propensity to consume were 100 per cent for all levels of income, full employment would be assured because no investment would be required. As income was received, it would all be spent for consumers goods. Supply would create its own demand. However, it is a characteristic of the actual world that the average propensity to consume is less than 100 per cent for all high levels of employment. Only if employment falls low enough, will a point be reached where consumption is equal to income. This is a lower limit below which employment will not fall, except perhaps temporarily. In wealthy industrial societies this level of employment is so low that it would provoke revolutionary action if long maintained. Investment is required to maintain employment above a relatively low and socially intolerable level.

The Inducement to Invest

Effective demand for investment is more complex and more unstable than effective demand for consumption. As previously indicated, investment means producing more than is currently consumed, and takes the form of adding to the accumulated wealth of society. Although investment sometimes takes the form of additions to the stocks of finished goods in the hands of retailers and wholesalers, its most important form is in expenditures by business men for factories, machinery, and other forms of producers goods. The inducement to business men to build factories and to invest in other ways arises from the expectation that such investment will prove profitable. Since these expectations are often based on precarious estimates of the future, the volume of investment is subject to wide fluctuations. Business men will borrow to invest up to the point at which the expected return from new investment is equal to the cost of borrowing funds with which to carry out the investment. The inducement to invest is determined in Keynes' analysis by the business men's estimates of the profitability of investment in relation to the rate of interest on money for investment. The expected profitability of new investment is called the marginal efficiency of capital.

THE MARGINAL EFFICIENCY OF CAPITAL

The marginal efficiency of a capital asset is the highest *rate* of return over cost expected from producing one more unit (a marginal unit) of a particular type of capital asset. In the language of the man in the street, it may be thought of as the expected rate of percentage profit per year on real investments of the most efficient type. Assume that in a growing community a store building that can be built for $20,000 will yield $1200 per year in rental and has depreciation and maintenance of $200 per year, giving a net return of $1000 per year. If the rate of interest is 4 per cent, this building is worth $25,000 ($1000 divided by .04). A building of this type already constructed should be worth $25,000. However, it will be preferable to borrow $20,000 at 4 per cent to build a new building, and receive a net return of $1000 or 5 per cent. The efficiency of this type of capital asset is 5 per cent, which is higher than the rate of interest of 4 per cent. If 5 per cent is the highest rate of return which can be secured from any type of real investment, the marginal efficiency of capital *in general* is 5 per cent. Investment continues as long as the expected rate of return exceeds the rate of interest. If the cost of construction of a new asset is less than the purchase price of the old asset of the same type, it will be profitable to build a new one rather than to buy the old one. This explains what is meant by the expected rate of profit being in excess of the rate of interest.

Keynes uses the term marginal efficiency of capital rather than expected rate of profit or some other conventional term like the marginal productivity of capital because he wishes to emphasize the dynamic setting in which the present and future are linked by the expectations of investors. In the example of the store building referred to above, the fact that the current yield from such assets is $1000 per year does not justify the assumption that the yield will continue at this level in the future. It may rise above $1000 in some years, fall below $1000 in other years, or behave in almost any other way depending on the future course of events, some of which may be foreseen clearly but not with certainty, others which may be only dimly anticipated, and still others which are completely unforeseen at the time the investment is made. In this dynamic setting, the investor is extremely cautious about investments that will realize their value, if at all, only over many years to come. The longer the period involved, the greater the chance that unforeseen events will intervene to disappoint today's investors. The role of capital assets as a link by which wealth-holders bridge the gap between the present and the future is one of the fundamental ideas underlying Keynes' entire analysis.

The marginal efficiency of capital is characterized by short-term instability and a tendency toward long-term decline. Fluctuations in the marginal efficiency of capital are the fundamental cause of the business cycle. Feverish building activity in the capital goods industries that marks the later phase of the expansion stage of the cycle results from the optimistic expectations of investors. For some time the increased activity brings larger profits and adds fuel to prevailing optimism. Meanwhile, however, great additions to the existing supply of capital goods force down the expected rate of return below the rate of interest. The cessation in capital accumulation (investment) which follows leads inevitably to collapse and depression. This transition from expansion to contraction is frequently highlighted by the gyration of the stock exchange, whose violent fluctuations are an objectification of the instability of the marginal efficiency of capital. The speculation and financial manipulation that characterize stock market activities are among the chief manifestations of the instability of capitalist economies.

Since every new investment competes with every old investment, there is a tendency in the secular long run for the growing abundance of capital assets to cause a decline in the rate of return. This tendency may be offset by unusual circumstances like those which characterized the western world during the nineteenth century when rapid growth in population, the existence of great undeveloped geographical frontiers, and great technological innovations like the railroad provided unprecedented demands for new capital, and forestalled the fall in the rate of return to capital. Geographical expansion has come to a close with the end of the frontiers in America and elsewhere, population growth has slowed down, and inventions are more of the labor-saving than of the capital-absorbing type. These under-lying structural changes of recent decades provide a plausible explanation for the mass unemployment which struck capitalist economies in the 1930's. However, the unemployment trends set up by a falling marginal efficiency of capital can be offset, at least temporarily, by a corresponding fall in the rate of interest.

THE RATE OF INTEREST

The rate of interest, the other factor which determines the volume of investment, depends upon two things: (a) the state of liquidity preference and (b) the quantity of money. The former is the demand aspect and the latter the supply aspect of the price of money, that is, the rate of interest. Liquidity preference refers to the desire of people to hold some of their assets in the form of money. The quantity of money refers to the amount of funds in the form of coins, paper currency, and bank deposits outstanding in the hands of the public.

There are several reasons why people may wish to hold wealth in the form of money. Classified according to motive, these include the transactions motive, the precautionary motive, and the speculative motive. The demand for money for the transactions motive refers to the use of money as a medium of exchange for ordinary transactions such as buying raw materials, paying rent, paying wages, paying dividends, et cetera. For any given level of employment, output, and prices, there is a relatively definite and stable quantity of money needed for this purpose. As the level of employment and output rises, the number of transactions will, of course, increase and thus increase the demand for money for transactions. Likewise, a general rise in prices or wages will increase the amount of money needed for transactions. The precautionary motive for holding money arises from the need for meeting unforeseen emergencies which will involve outlays greater than those involved in the usual anticipated transactions. Here again the amount of money needed to satisfy this demand is relatively stable and predictable.

The type of liquidity preference which is important in relation to the rate of interest is that arising in connection with the speculative motive. Keynes defines the speculative motive as "the object of securing profit from knowing better than the market what the future will bring forth" (p. 170). Quite apart from needs for money as a medium of exchange, people hold money as a store of wealth. They hold their assets in this form because they prefer it to any other means of storing wealth. This is a type of speculation because in holding their wealth in the barren money form, people are speculating on the chances that conditions will change so they will be able to convert their money into earning assets on better terms at a later date, and on terms which will be enough better to offset any earnings that might be made by parting with liquidity now. Chiefly responsible for this type of preference for money is uncertainty concerning the future rate of interest. If it is thought that the interest rate may rise in the future, there will be an incentive to hold money and avoid buying income-yielding securities such as bonds. A future rise in the rate of interest may wipe out an amount of the capitalized value of purchased assets to an extent that will more than offset any temporary returns in the form of interest or dividends. The lower the interest rate goes, the stronger becomes the incentive to hold wealth in the form of money. There is an increasing danger of capital loss arising from a slight rise in the interest rate. The long-term rate of interest will be especially sensitive to liquidity preference because over a long period the uncertainty of events increases in a sort of geometric proportion.

In the light of these circumstances, the demand for money to satisfy the speculative motive is subject to erratic fluctuations, in contrast with the relatively stable demand for the transactions and precautionary motives. When liquidity preference for the speculative motive weakens, the interest rate will fall, and when liquidity preference for the speculative motive strengthens, the rate of interest will rise. Liquidity preference rises and falls according to the changing attitudes of the public toward the economic and political future. Thus the level of the interest rate depends upon factors which are highly psychological in nature. The so-called psychological factors are themselves conditioned by more objective events in the economic and political arena.

A rise in the interest rate resulting from increased liquidity preference indicates that the desire to store wealth in the form of money is not an absolute desire, but one which is relative to the desire for rewards offered by other alternatives. If the reward for surrendering liquidity is high enough—that is, if the interest rate is high enough—illiquidity will be risked. The interest rate is a price which fluctuates according to the supply and demand for money. The supply is fixed by the banking system and the demand is determined by the preference for holding cash. As long as the supply remains fixed, the price, or rate, varies with the demand. The rate of interest is the price which "equilibrates the desire to hold wealth in the form of cash with the available quantity of cash" (p. 167). If the rate of interest were lower at any particular time the public would want to hold more cash than is available, and if the rate of interest were higher at any time, the public would not wish to hold all the cash that is available.[5] Interest is the reward paid for the use of money, and the reward, like any price, must be neither too high nor too low in relation to the supply.

Although the public does not control the quantity of money, the banking system does. All the public can do when it wants to hold more money and there is no more money is to bid up the price, the rate of interest. But the banking authorities are in a position to answer the demand for

---

[5] The word "cash" as used here is equivalent to "money" including demand deposits.

more money by increasing the supply, and thus preventing the rate of interest from rising. Consequently, the position of the banking and monetary authorities is strategic in relation to the rate of interest. By pursuing a policy of a flexible money supply, the banking system can, within limits, control the rate of interest. If the banking authorities cannot control the psychological ups and downs of the public in its attitude toward liquidity preference, they can at least offset the effects of these changes on the interest rate by letting a public which desires to hold more cash actually hold more cash. It is crucial to Keynes' position that the monetary authorities should be strong and during depressions should pursue an easy money policy which will lower interest rates and permit them to remain low.

In the transition from depression to recovery, the demand for money for transactions will be increasing. If this increased demand must be met by drawing upon money used to satisfy the speculative motive, the rate of interest will rise, and recovery will be impeded. Therefore, unless the banks are ready to lend more cash, or unless the liquidity preference of the public for the speculative motive decreases considerably, the volume of investment will fall off and recovery may be nipped before it has really begun. This shortage of money would retard investment and recovery no matter how much the desire of the public to save might increase.

The Relation of Investment to Consumption

There exists a definite relation between the amount of consumption output and the amount of investment output which it will be profitable for entrepreneurs to produce. Given the propensity to consume, the amount of consumption demand depends on the size of national income. National income is created partly from the output of consumption and partly from the output of investment. The volume of investment depends on the inducement to invest as determined by the principles discussed in the preceding section. Hence, the amount of consumption goods that it will be profitable for entrepreneurs to produce depends partly on the amount of investment output that is being produced. If the inducement to invest is such that entrepreneurs in the United States are producing $40 billion worth of investment goods, and if the propensity to consume is four-fifths, it will pay to produce $160 billion worth of consumption output in addition to the $40 billion worth of investment output. The output is divided four-fifths to consumption and one-fifth to investment because demand is in the ratio of four to one. If output is to be sold without losses, it must be proportioned between consumption goods and investment goods in the ratio which corresponds to the ratio in which income receivers choose to divide their incomes between consumption expenditure and saving. The *amount* of total output it will pay to produce in this ratio depends on the amount of investment demand.

In the arithmetical example cited in the preceding paragraph, the $160 billion of effective demand for consumption comes from the income, some of which is earned in investment activity. For example, men working on the construction of a factory (investment goods) spend part of their incomes for groceries and clothes (consumption goods) just as do men who work in factories turning out consumers goods. Thus if the number employed in building factories decreases, so will the demand for consumption goods decrease. Using the above figures, suppose investment falls from $40 to $39 billion. If the ratio of consumption to investment remains 4 to 1, there will have to be a fall in consumption to a level of 4 times $39 billion or $156 billion. From a fall of $1 billion in investment there results a fall of $4 billion in consumption, making a total fall of $5 billion. National income decreases from $200 to $195 billion ($156 plus $39 equals $195). While the ratio may not remain exactly 4 to 1, it will not change very much as long as total income remains in the neighborhood of $200 billion.

What would happen if entrepreneurs did not reduce their output of consumption goods by $4 billion when investment falls from $40 billion to $39 billion? Suppose they continued to produce the same amount of consumers goods as before, $160 billion worth. They would be unable to sell all the consumers goods produced, because the workers who lost their jobs in investment activity and other income recipients whose incomes had been lowered as a result of the falling off of investment would not spend as much for consumers goods as before. When incomes are less, consumption expenditure will be less, given the propensity to consume. The original impact of the $1 billion fall in investment is to lower income from $200 billion to $199 billion. But this is not the end of the process. Retailers and others whose sales are reduced will suffer reduced income, wholesalers who sell to retailers will also suffer reduced income, and the manufacturers who sell to wholesalers will suffer likewise. This process of cumulative income reduction will go on until the total fall in income resulting from a decline in consumption demand is 4 times the fall in investment demand. The over-all ratio of 4 to 1 between consumption and investment will be reestablished at 156 to 39, or at a total income of $195 billion.

What would be the result of applying the classical theory to the above situation? Under conditions of full employment assumed by the classical theory, income and total effective demand remain constant in the short period. Effective demand will always be sufficient to lead to full employment. Starting with an income of $200 billion, divided $160 billion to consumption and $40 billion to investment, a fall in investment of $1 billion would have to result in an *increase* in consumption from $160 billion to $161 billion. This would change the ratio of consumption to investment in a way inconsistent with Keynes' principle of effective demand. It would also seem to violate common sense because it assumes consumption will increase at the very time when men are losing jobs and spending less for consumers goods than before. Although the classical analysis may seem to violate common sense, it is not without an answer as to why decreases in investment lead to increases in consumption. The answer relates to the classical theory of the rate of interest, which brings the volume of investment to equality with the volume of saving.

Summary of the General Theory of Employment

From the foregoing discussion and from Figure 3 it may be seen that there are several alternative ways of expressing the essence of the general theory of employment. An over-all summary may be stated in the form of the following propositions:

1. Total income depends on the volume of total employment.
2. According to the propensity to consume, the amount of expenditure for consumption depends on the level of income, and therefore on total employment (from No. 1 above).
3. Total employment depends on total effective demand (D), which is made up of two parts: (a) consumption expenditure (D_1) and (b) investment expenditure (D_2).
   $(D=D_1+D_2)$
4. In equilibrium, the aggregate demand (D) is equal to the aggregate supply (Z). Therefore, aggregate supply exceeds the effective demand for consumption by the amount of the effective demand for investment. $(D=D_1+D_2,$ or $D_2=D-D_1.$ Since $D=Z,$ therefore $D_2=Z-D_1.)$
5. In equilibrium, aggregate supply is equal to aggregate demand, and aggregate demand is determined by the propensity to consume and the volume of investment. Therefore, the volume of employment depends on (a) the aggregate supply function, (b) the propensity to consume, and (c) the volume of investment.
6. Both the aggregate supply function, which depends mainly on physical conditions of supply, and the propensity to consume are relatively stable, and therefore fluctuations in employment depend mainly on the volume of investment.
7. The volume of investment depends on (a) the marginal efficiency of capital and (b) the rate of interest.
8. The marginal efficiency of capital depends on (a) the expectations of profit yields and (b) the replacement cost of capital assets.
9. The rate of interest depends on (a) the quantity of money and (b) the state of liquidity preference.

These propositions contain the essentials of the general theory of employment. Our further discussion will involve a more detailed analysis of the factors influencing effective demand. Concerning the aggregate supply function, Keynes has nothing of importance to add to traditional treatments of the subject matter, although his form of expression is somewhat novel.

We may now carry our provisional survey one step further and indicate some of the interrelations among these main elements of the theory. Employment depends on effective demand, which is determined by the propensity to consume and the inducement to invest. If the propensity to

A Theory of Employment (N), Income (Y), and Effective Demand (D)				*Characteristics*
Consumption (C)	Propensity to Consume	Average Propensity to Consume $\left(\dfrac{C}{Y}\right)$		"Basic" national income where $\dfrac{C}{Y}=1$, that is, where $C = Y$. As income increases consumption increases, but by less than income.
		Marginal Propensity to Consume $\left(\dfrac{\Delta C}{\Delta Y}\right)$	Derive Investment Multiplier (k) $k = \dfrac{1}{1 - \dfrac{\Delta C}{\Delta Y}}$	$\dfrac{\Delta C}{\Delta Y}$ always less than 1. k always more than 1.
	Size of Income			An increase in investment causes a multiple increase in income.
Investment (I)	Rate of Interest (r_i)	Liquidity Preference (L)	Transactions Motive (satisfied by M_1)	Involves money as a medium of exchange.
			Precautionary Motive (satisfied by M_1)	
			Speculative Motive (satisfied by M_2)	Involves money as a store of value.
		Quantity of Money (M) ($M = M_1 + M_2$)		Can be controlled by monetary authority.
	Marginal Efficiency of Capital (r_m)	Expectations of Profit Yields		Unstable. Influenced by stock market, business confidence, etc.
		Replacement Cost, or Supply Price of Capital Assets		Cycle: fluctuates Long run: declines

1. Employment (and income) depend on effective demand.
2. Effective demand is determined by the propensity to consume and the volume of investment.
3. The propensity to consume is relatively stable.
4. Employment depends on the volume of investment if the propensity to consume is unchanged.
5. Investment depends on the rate of interest and the marginal efficiency of capital.
6. The rate of interest depends on the quantity of money and liquidity preference.
7. The marginal efficiency of capital depends on the expectations of profit yields and the replacement cost of capital assets.

FIGURE 3. AN OUTLINE OF THE GENERAL THEORY OF EMPLOYMENT

consume remains unchanged, employment will vary in the same direction as the volume of investment. Investment tends to increase either with a fall in the rate of interest or a rise in the marginal efficiency of capital, or both. But the tendency for investment to increase through a fall in the rate of interest may be offset by a simultaneous fall in the marginal efficiency of capital. An increase in the general level of economic activity will increase the demand for money as a medium of exchange and, by draining the fund of money available as a store of value, will increase the rate of interest unless the monetary authority and banking system act to increase the total supply of money. And even though the quantity of money may be increasing, the rate of interest may nevertheless rise as a result of an unfavorable shift in the attitude of wealth-holders toward liquidity. Expectations of rising future yields from capital assets will tend to raise the marginal efficiency of capital and thus raise investment and employment. This favorable effect may be offset by a simultaneous rise in the current supply price (cost of production) of capital assets.

Although rising investment will usually be accompanied by rising employment, this need not happen if the propensity to consume is falling. On the other hand, employment can rise without a rise in investment if the propensity to consume is rising. As a rule, however, the propensity to consume, or consumption function, is stable in the short run.

Finally, increases in investment bring about increases in income, and out of larger income there arises a greater demand for consumption which leads to still further increases in income. Taken in reverse, this process means that a fall in investment will decrease income and out of the decreased income there will be less demand for consumption, which leads to still further decreases in income. Once set in motion, movements of income and employment tend to be cumulative. These cumulative movements account for the fluctuating nature of employment. Limits to amplitude of fluctuation are set in the downward direction at the level at which income falls to equality with consumption, and in the upward direction at full employment. Actual fluctuations will not, as a rule, range all the way from one extreme to the other. An upward movement will characteristically stop short of full employment and a downward movement will usually stop short of the point at which income has fallen to equality with consumption. What the actual range will be depends upon the strength or weakness of the propensity to consume and the inducement to invest under the prevailing circumstances.

Practical Meaning of the Main Concepts

Among all the terms and concepts used by Keynes in *The General Theory of Employment, Interest and Money*, the three which stand out above all the rest as the strategic, independent variables are the propensity to consume (consumption schedule), the marginal efficiency of capital (investment-demand schedule), and the rate of interest (liquidity-preference schedule). The choice of these three independent variables or strategic factors arises from the nature of Keynes' interest in practical policy. The ultimate purpose of his theory is to explain what determines the volume of employment, or in terms of the practical problems involved, what causes unemployment. To explain the cause means, in a significant sense, to point to those factors or to a course of action which, if changed or followed, will remedy the malady. Thus when we say a common cold is caused by sitting in a draft, we usually mean that by not sitting in a draft a cold will not occur or is less likely to occur. To explain unemployment means to indicate those aspects of the economic system which need to be changed or subjected to social control in order to assure a high level of employment. Keynes says: "Our final task might be to select those variables which can be deliberately controlled or managed by central authority in the kind of system in which we actually live."[6]

Realistic theory is necessarily conditioned by the theorist's sense of values and by his ideas as to what is practicable policy. The realistic nature of Keynes' theory may be attributed largely to his vital concern with a specific type of economic program. This does not mean that Keynes' theoretical concepts are worthless in relation to policies other than those advocated by him, nor does it mean that his policies or any other policies necessarily follow from his abstract, theoretical concepts. However, a recognition of the social values and practical aims of a pioneering theorist like Keynes gives a richer insight into the meaning of his abstract theoretical concepts and propositions. A concept like the propensity to consume, or consumption function, is a formal, mathematical relationship between amounts of consumption corresponding to amounts of income for the community as a whole. But this is only the bare bones. The full meaning of this formal concept as used by Keynes emerges in terms of the use to which he puts it. He uses it to show the necessity of a high rate of consumer expenditure, which, perhaps, can be obtained by a more equal distribution of income and wealth. He uses it to indicate the desirability of steeply progressive taxation and large government outlays for social services. The propensity to consume is further refined in the form of the marginal propensity to consume, which is used to derive the concept of the investment multiplier. The common-sense meaning of the investment multiplier is that in times of depression when private investment lags, government investment in public works will increase the national income not only by the amount of the public outlay but by some multiple of it.

In these terms Keynes makes a case for public works and becomes an advocate of public spending. His theory is referred to as a "spending" theory. To call a theory a spending theory has no meaning except in relation to some fairly specific steps or policies that may be followed to increase aggregate demand above what it would be in the absence of such

---

[6] Keynes, *The General Theory of Employment, Interest and Money.* New York: Harcourt, Brace and Co., Inc., 1936, page 247.

policies. When we trace the concepts to their practical consequences, the lifeless forms of abstraction begin to take on definite shape and meaning. We see them emerging as plans of action, altered behavior, policies. The theory is put into practice. Only when theory is put into practice—that is, only when we trace the theory to its practical consequences—can we hope to test its validity by an appeal to facts and thus arrive at an evaluation of its probable workability in the actual world.

The operational or practical meaning of Keynes' theory will be referred to often in this book in the belief that this method will facilitate the understanding of what is likely to appear to be an intrinsically difficult body of doctrine. At this juncture we allude briefly to the operational significance of Keynes' theories of the rate of interest and the marginal efficiency of capital, the two independent variables which, along with the propensity to consume referred to in the preceding paragraph, determine the level of employment. The uniqueness of Keynes' theory of the rate of interest runs in terms of the importance of controlling the quantity of money. The novel concept is liquidity preference for the speculative motive. Wealth-holders have a preference for keeping their assets in a liquid form, the form of money, and it is this desire to hoard which determines the level of interest rates. An easy money policy under a strong monetary authority can keep down the interest rates and thus stimulate investment and employment. However, Keynes' practical sense is too strong to lead him to attach sole importance to interest rates and so we find a parallel stress on the marginal efficiency of capital. The chief characteristic of the marginal efficiency of capital is its great instability. It may fall so low in depression that no reduction in interest rates will induce private investment. To alleviate the consequences of instability in the marginal efficiency of private capital, Keynes advocates government direction of total investment, including public investment, to compensate for the inevitable fluctuations in private investment. A low rate of interest and a high marginal efficiency of capital are the conditions favorable to investment and employment. Since the natural tendency is for the rate of interest to stay up and the marginal efficiency of capital to come down, laissez-faire policies will leave the volume of investment short of what is necessary for full employment. Both of these determinates of investment involve psychological attitudes toward the future which cause investment to be much less stable than the volume of consumption. The instability of these factors determining investment leads Keynes to say that employment is determined by investment.

The Paradox of Poverty and Potential Plenty

Keynes' principle of effective demand furnishes an explanation of the paradox of poverty in the midst of potential plenty, one of the grave contradictions of modern capitalism. A poor community will have little difficulty employing all its resources because it will tend to spend on consumption a large proportion of its total income. Only a small gap needs to be filled by investment, and since the stock of accumulated capital assets will be slight in the poor community, the demand for investment will be brisk. A wealthy community, on the contrary, will have great difficulty maintaining full employment because the gap between income and consumption will be large. Its investment outlets must be great if there are to be enough jobs for all. Failing to find these outlets, the potentially wealthy community will be forced to reduce its actual output until it becomes so poor that the excess of output over consumption will be reduced to the actual amount of investment. To make matters worse, the very fact that a community is rich in accumulated capital assets weakens the inducement to invest because every new investment must compete with an already large supply of old investments. The inadequacy of demand for investment reacts in a cumulative fashion on the demand for consumption. The factories that are already built cannot be used because more factories are not being built. Unemployment on a mass scale exists in the midst of potential plenty. Thus as Keynes says, "the richer the community . . . the more obvious and outrageous the defects of the economic system." Keynes finds no reason to assume that the growing gap between income and consumption at high levels of employment will be filled automatically, that is, without conscious social action, except under special historical circumstances like those existing in the nineteenth century or in time of war. War has a distinct if ironical advantage over peaceful industry in that it calls for the production of things which are to be exploded and shot away and do not remain to compete with more production of the same type at a later date. If war and threat of war are banished from the world, the capitalist countries will once more be confronted with the tasks of finding sufficient outlets for new investment to provide employment for all of its millions of workers who cannot be employed in consumption industries.

FOR FURTHER READING

The literature of underconsumption is prolific. On a historical tack, the reader may profitably refer to Book II, chap. 2 of Malthus' *Political Economy* (1820) or Sismondi's *New Principles of Political Economy* (1819). Karl Rodbertus' *Our Economic Condition* (1842) and Karl Marx's *Capital, A Critique of Political Economy* (1867), are erudite interpretations of the socialist position on underconsumption. For more recent interpretations, a complete reading of John A. Hobson's *The Economics of Unemployment* (London: George Allen & Unwin, 1931), Clifford H. Douglas' *Social Credit* (New York: W. W. Norton, 1933), and Henry Smith's "Marx and the Trade Cycle," *Review of Economic Studies*, IV (June, 1937), is clearly advisable. Naturally, the cited works of Hawtrey and Harrod and J. M. Keynes' *The General Theory of Employment* (New York: Harcourt, Brace, 1936) must be studied for comprehension in depth of the topic. The significance of Keynes' work is critically evaluated in L. R. Klein's *The Keynesian Revolution* (London: Macmillan, 1947); A. C. Pigou's *Keynes's "General Theory"* (London: Macmillan, 1951); and H. G. Moulton's *Controlling Factors in Economic Development* (Washington, D.C.: Brookings Institution, 1949).

But summaries of underconsumptionist literature are available. See John W. McConnell, *The Basic Teachings of the Great Economists* (New York: New Home Library, 1943), pp. 260-270 (rather dated for modern theory but, nevertheless, a useful, nontechnical introduction to economic thought for the laymen); Carl A. Dauten, *Business Fluctuations and Forecasting*

(New York: South-Western Publishing Company, 1954), pp. 297-302; Robert Aaron Gordon, *Business Fluctuations* (New York: Harper & Brothers, 1961), pp. 380-385; Maurice W. Lee, *Economic Fluctuations: Growth and Stability* (Homewood, Ill.: Richard D. Irwin, 1959), chaps. 10, 11 and 12.

SECTION B

Cumulative Expansion
and Contraction:
The Multiplier and Accelerator

INTRODUCTION

At the close of the previous section, we noted the importance of consumption in maintaining employment and stable economic growth. The matter does not end there, however, for changes in consumption will affect the level of investment which in turn will lead to changes in income and consumption. These interactive effects between consumption and investment are dealt with in the present chapter on the accelerator and multiplier principles.[1]

[1] Before embarking on a study of articles treating of the accelerator and multiplier principles, our budding economist will profit from a second perusal of R. A. Gordon's excellent summary of econometrics, its assumptions, mathematical techniques, and limita-

Partly because of the ease with which they relate to the study of growth factors, accelerator–multiplier models have enjoyed considerable attention in the post–World War II era. Highly abstract and mathematical, these models follow the Keynesian tradition in making investment determine aggregate income and output. By the same token the quantity of investment will hang upon total income and output rather than on the availability of savings per se or the level of interest rates. Period analysis and the use of lag relationships also characterize the accelerator–multiplier models.

Broadly speaking, we may identify two categories of business cycle models: First, those models which see the prime mover behind cyclical fluctuations in the relationship of the accelerator principle to induced investment. The accelerator models of J. R. Hicks,* R. F. Harrod,† Paul Samuelson,‡ and perhaps Richard Goodwin§ are probably to be reckoned among this group. In the Hicksian prototype, by way of illustra-

---

tions. Gordon's comments are equally apposite to the discussion of the essentially mathematical models, albeit simple ones, selected for presentation here.

The student should also have the definitions of important terms clear in his mind as he reads the articles that follow. Erwin Nemmers and Cornelius C. Janzen, *Dictionary of Economics and Business* (New Jersey: Littlefield, Adams, 1958), define the investment multiplier (p. 160):

The reciprocal of the *marginal propensity to save* (q.v.). The ratio of the change in national income consequent upon a change in investment to that change in investment. When there is an increment of aggregate investment, other things unchanged, national income will change by an amount which is K times the increment of investment. K is the investment multiplier. Hence, the greater the marginal propensity to consume, the greater the investment multiplier.

They define the acceleration principle thus (p. 4):

In business cycle theory, the principle that changes in demand for finished goods and services (consumption) tend to give rise to much greater changes in the demand for those producers' goods (investment) which are used to make the consumer goods. The acceleration coefficient is the ratio of change in investment to the accompanying change in consumption.

Although economists will put different emphases on the relative importance of each of these two concepts, or introduce time lags into their operation, or quibble with this or that phrase within either description, the definitions above have a certain general acceptance and the reader should keep firm hold upon them for an intelligent appreciation of our authors' remarks.

* A *Contribution to the Theory of the Trade Cycle* (Oxford: Clarendon Press, 1950). See also S. S. Alexander, "Issues of Business Cycle Theory Raised by Mr. Hicks," *American Economic Review* (December, 1951); James Duesenberry, "Hicks on the Trade Cycle," *Quarterly Journal of Economics* (August, 1950) included in this section; Arthur F. Burns, *The Frontiers of Economic Knowledge* (Princeton: Princeton University Press, 1954), pp. 236-267.

† *The Trade Cycle* (Oxford: Clarendon Press, 1936); *Towards a Dynamic Economics* (London: Macmillan, 1948).

‡ "Interactions Between the Multiplier Analysis and the Principle of Acceleration," *Review of Economic Statistics* (May, 1939) reproduced here.

§ "A Model of Cyclical Growth," in Erik Lundberg, (ed.), *The Business Cycle in the Post-War World* (New York: St. Martin's Press, 1955).

tion, the size of the accelerator and the propensity to consume measure the amplitude of fluctuation. When expansion grinds to a halt because of shortage of resources, the acceleration principle, thrown into reverse, sets off a decline in investment. During the ensuing contraction, induced investment falls to zero and the accelerator ceases to function. However, with autonomous investment continuing at the secular rate, the time must come when excess capacity will be absorbed and cyclical expansion renewed. Thus, although monetary elements may accentuate the difficulties of retrenchment, real factors, according to Hicks, dominate and eventually limit the upswing.

A second category of models represent a reaction against those which place investment in exact relationship to the acceleration principle. James Duesenberry, for example, eschews an explanation solely in terms of endogenous factors and stresses other causal possibilities: monetary disturbances, speculative activity, or variations in autonomous investment. Robert Solow* points out that technological conditions make it possible to combine labor and capital in varying proportions; the level of output, accordingly, depends upon the varying combinations of labor and capital employed. Nicholas Kaldor,† on the other hand, believes that the rate of profit and the share of profits in total income set the level of investment. *In praesenti*, these latter models provide a more flexible theory of investment in which factors other than changes in income and consumption receive due weight in motivating investment decisions.

In evaluating the efforts of Mr. Hicks and his successors to incorporate within a set of equations the constituent causes of income and output variations, we cannot resist the temptation to quote Hamlet, himself a "model builder" of less elegant accomplishment:

> There are more things in Heaven and earth, Horatio,
> Than are dreamt of in your philosophy.

So it is with the multiplier–accelerator theories of the business cycle. Though complex of construction and employing advanced mathematical techniques, they are, nevertheless, too simple in that they deal with but a few variables (aggregates) and perforce ignore the myriad significant changes which take place in particular parts of the economy. Even apart from the practical difficulties of distinguishing between induced and autonomous investment, such vitally important cyclical events as innovations, fiscal and monetary changes, price–cost relationships, and the role of expectations receive scant attention from the model builders.

Jan Tinbergen—probably influenced by Santayana's dictum, "It is a great advantage for a system of philosophy to be substantially true"‡—in 1942§

---

* "A Contribution to the Theory of Economic Growth," *Quarterly Journal of Economics* (February, 1956).

† "A Model of Economic Growth," *Economic Journal* (December, 1957).

‡ *The Unknowables.*

§ "Critical Remarks on Some Business Cycle Theories," *Econometrica* (April, 1942).

put to statistical test some of the theories based upon the accelerator principle. He found no consistent lag between fluctuations in the production of investment and consumption goods. Other empirical studies also have failed to develop support for the premises or conclusions of the accelerator–multiplier models.*

Well, if all this be true, why bother to take up the topic of accelerators and multipliers? We think the answer was best expressed in these remarks from a review of L. R. Klein and others, "An Econometric Model of the United Kingdom," *The Economist* (June 3, 1961):

> The book is, in fact, likely to command more respect than understanding. Most people will be impressed rather than informed when they read the computation procedure involved maximizing likelihood functions, each "formed from the joint distribution of the stochastic terms in the reduced forms for the endogenous variables entering into the equation." This may suggest that the book is required reading only for the longest-haired eggheads (if there be such creatures) and that is probably right. Nevertheless, it is a good idea for at least the short-haired eggheads to know what the whole thing is about. Is it a waste of scarce and highly skilled manpower or could it actually be useful? . . .
>
> All this may suggest that the book is a waste of effort. Such a conclusion is, however, quite unwarranted. In economics knowledge grows and rarely leaps. Just as the first flying machines were not useless, even though they barely left the ground, so this model is not useless. It is a stimulus and a challenge to further research.

---

* Simon Kuznets, "Relation Between Capital Goods and Finished Products in the Business Cycle," *Economic Essays in Honor of Wesley Clair Mitchell* (New York: Columbia University Press, 1935); Jan Tinbergen, "Reformulation of Current Business Cycle Theories as Refutable Hypothesis," *Conference on Business Cycles* (New York: National Bureau of Economic Research, 1951).

[18]

Interactions Between the Multiplier Analysis and the Principle of Acceleration*

PAUL A. SAMUELSON

Editors' Note

If the collegians of this generation are familiar with any name in economics, it is most likely that of Paul A. Samuelson (1915–   ), for his principles textbook has become a sort of McGuffey's reader to introduce freshmen to the "mysterious reasonings" of economists. The first recipient of the John Bates Clark medal awarded by the American Economic Association to the most distinguished economist under the age of forty, and the youngest president of the Association, Samuelson is perhaps the leading economist of the younger school; that is, he received his graduate training in the 1930's and the main body of his work has appeared in the past two decades. In addition to a professorship on the faculty of the Massachusetts Institute of Technology, Samuelson has had a long career as consultant to various government agencies: National Resources Planning Board (1941–43), War Production Board (1945), and U.S. Treasury (1945–52). His books include: *Foundations of Economic Analysis* (1947); *Economics, An Introductory Analysis* (1948); *Readings in Economics* (1955).

We have noted previously that the articles chosen for this sub-Part—with one possible exception—have the purpose of encouraging the intelligent reader to further study of a rather complex area of investigation. It would serve no purpose therefore to initiate his studies with current litera-

* Reprinted by permission of the publishers from *Review of Economics and Statistics*, Vol. XXI, No. 2 (May, 1939), pp. 75-78; Cambridge, Mass.: Harvard University Press, Copyright, 1939, by The President and Fellows of Harvard College.

ture, if the fundamentals of the argument were lost to him. Samuelson's 1939 article in which, unlike his predecessors, he varied the values of the multiplier and the accelerator, stands as a pioneer effort on the interaction of these two principles.

The relationship of accelerator and multiplier has much significance for cycle theories. An increase in the demand for consumer goods, through the operation of the accelerator, results in a magnified demand for capital goods. These higher capital expenditures in turn, through the operation of the multiplier, increase the income stream by an amount greater than the increment of investment. Higher incomes lead to further increases in consumer demand, and a cumulative process ensues. Depending on the values assigned to the multiplier and the accelerator, one may theoretically describe cycles of different amplitudes and duration. These are the considerations in Samuelson's article.

❦ Few economists would deny that the "multiplier" analysis of the effects of governmental deficit spending has thrown some light upon this important problem. Nevertheless, there would seem to be some ground for the fear that this extremely simplified mechanism is in danger of hardening into a dogma, hindering progress and obscuring important subsidiary relations and processes. It is highly desirable, therefore, that model sequences, which operate under more general assumptions, be investigated, possibly including the conventional analysis as a special case.[1]

In particular, the "multiplier," using this term in its usual sense, does *not* pretend to give the relation between total national income induced by governmental spending and the original amount of money spent. This is clearly seen by a simple example. In an economy (not necessarily our own) where any dollar of governmental deficit spending would result in a hundred dollars less of private investment than would otherwise have been undertaken, the ratio of total induced national income to the initial expenditure is overwhelmingly negative, yet the "multiplier" in the strict sense must be positive. The answer to the puzzle is simple. What the multiplier does give is the ratio of the total increase in the national income to the total amount of investment, governmental and private. In other words, it does *not* tell us how much is to be multiplied. The effects upon private investment are often regarded as tertiary influences and receive little systematic attention.

---

[1] The writer, who has made this study in connection with his research as a member of the Society of Fellows at Harvard University, wishes to express his indebtedness to Professor Alvin H. Hansen of Harvard University at whose suggestion the investigation was undertaken.

TABLE 1.—THE DEVELOPMENT OF NATIONAL INCOME AS A RESULT OF A CONTINUOUS LEVEL OF GOVERNMENTAL EXPENDITURE WHEN THE MARGINAL PROPENSITY TO CONSUME EQUALS ONE-HALF AND THE RELATION EQUALS UNITY
(Unit: one dollar)

Period	Current governmental expenditure	Current consumption induced by previous expenditure	Current private investment proportional to time increase in consumption	Total national income
1	1.00	0.00	0.00	1.00
2	1.00	0.50	0.50	2.00
3	1.00	1.00	0.50	2.50
4	1.00	1.25	0.25	2.50
5	1.00	1.25	0.00	2.25
6	1.00	1.125	−0.125*	2.00
7	1.00	1.00	−0.125	1.875
8	1.00	0.9375	−0.0625	1.875
9	1.00	0.9375	0.00	1.9375
10	1.00	0.96875	0.03125	2.00
11	1.00	1.00	0.03125	2.03125
12	1.00	1.015625	0.015625	2.03125
13	1.00	1.015625	0.00	2.015625
14	1.00	1.0078125	−0.0078125	2.00

* Negative induced private investment is interpreted to mean that for the system as a whole there is *less* investment in this period than there otherwise would have been. Since this is a marginal analysis, superimposed implicitly upon a going state of affairs, this concept causes no difficulty.

In order to remedy the situation in some measure, Professor Hansen has developed a new model sequence which ingeniously combines the multiplier analysis with that of the *acceleration* principle or *relation*. This is done by making additions to the national income consist of three components: (1) governmental deficit spending, (2) private consumption expenditure induced by previous public expenditure, and (3) induced private investment, assumed according to the familiar acceleration principle to be proportional to the time increase of consumption. The introduction of the last component accounts for the novelty of the conclusions reached and also the increased complexity of the analysis.

A numerical example may be cited to illuminate the assumptions made. We assume governmental deficit spending of one dollar per unit period, beginning at some initial time and continuing thereafter. The marginal propensity to consume, α, is taken to be one-half. This is taken to mean that the consumption of any period is equal to one-half the national income of the previous period. Our last assumption is that induced private investment is proportional to the increase in consumption between the previous and the current period. This factor of proportionality or *relation*, β, is provisionally taken to be equal to unity; i.e., a time increase in consumption of one dollar will result in one dollar's worth of induced private investment.

In the initial period when the government spends a dollar for the first time, there will be no consumption induced from previous periods, and hence the addition to the national income will equal the one dollar spent. This will yield fifty cents of consumption expenditure in the second period, an increase of fifty cents over the consumption of the first period, and so according to the *relation* we will have fifty cents worth of induced private investment. Finally, we must add the new dollar of expenditure by the government. The national income of the second period must therefore total two dollars. Similarly, in the third period the national income would

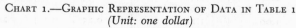

CHART 1.—GRAPHIC REPRESENTATION OF DATA IN TABLE 1
(*Unit: one dollar*)

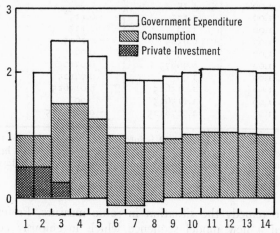

be the sum of one dollar of consumption, fifty cents induced private investment, and one dollar current governmental expenditure. It is clear that given the values of the marginal propensity to consume, α, and the *relation*, β, all succeeding national income levels can be easily computed in succession. This is done in detail in Table 1 and illustrated in Chart 1. It will be noted that the introduction of the acceleration principle causes our series to reach a peak at the 3rd year, a trough at the 7th, a peak at the 11th, etc. Such oscillatory behavior could not occur in the conventional model sequences, as will soon become evident.

For other chosen values of α and β similar model sequences can be developed. In Table 2 national income totals are given for various selected values of these coefficients. In the first column, for example, the marginal propensity to consume is assumed to be one-half, and the *relation* to be equal to zero. This is of special interest because it shows the conventional multiplier sequences to be special cases of the more general Hansen analysis. For this case no oscillations are possible. In the second column the oscillations in the national income are undamped and regular. In column three things are still worse; the oscillations are explosive, becoming larger and larger but always fluctuating around an "average value." In the fourth column the behavior is no longer oscillatory but is explosive upward approaching a compound interest rate of growth.

By this time the investigator is inclined to feel somewhat disorganized. A variety of qualitatively different results emerge in a seemingly capricious manner from minor changes in hypotheses. Worse than this, how can we be sure that for still different selected values of our coefficients new and stronger types of behavior will not emerge? Is it not even possible that if Table 2 were extended to cover more periods, new types of behavior might result for these selected coefficients?

Fortunately, these questions can be given a definite negative answer. Arithmetical methods cannot do so since we cannot try all possible values of the coefficients nor compute the endless terms of each sequence. Nevertheless, comparatively simple algebraic analysis can be applied which will yield all possible qualitative types of behavior and enable us to unify our results.

The national income at time t, Y_t, can be written as the sum of three components: (1) governmental expenditure, g_t, (2) consumption expenditure, C_t, and (3) induced private investment, I_t.

$$Y_t = g_t + C_t + I_t.$$

But according to the Hansen assumptions

$$C_t = \alpha Y_{t-1}$$
$$I_t = \beta[C_t - C_{t-1}] = \alpha\beta Y_{t-1} - \alpha\beta Y_{t-2}$$

and

$$g_t = 1.$$

Therefore, our national income can be rewritten

$$Y_t = 1 + \alpha[1 + \beta]Y_{t-1} - \alpha\beta Y_{t-2}.$$

In words, if we know the national income for two periods, the national income for the following period can be simply derived by taking a weighted sum. The weights depend, of course, upon the values chosen for the marginal propensity to consume and for the *relation*.

This is one of the simplest types of difference equations, having constant coefficients and being of the second order. The mathematical details of its solution need not be entered upon here. Suffice it to say that its solution depends upon the roots—which in turn depend upon the coefficients α and β—of a certain equation.[2] It can be easily shown that the whole field

---

[2] Actually, the solution can be written in the form

$$Y_t = \frac{1}{1-a} + a_1[x_1]^t + a_2[x_2]^t$$

of possible values of α and β can be divided into four regions, each of which gives qualitatively different types of behavior. In Chart 2 these regions are plotted. Each point in this diagram represents a selection of values for the marginal propensity to consume and the *relation*. Corresponding to each point there will be a model sequence of national income

TABLE 2.—MODEL SEQUENCES OF NATIONAL INCOME FOR SELECTED VALUES OF MARGINAL PROPENSITY TO CONSUME AND RELATION
(*Unit: one dollar*)

Period	$\alpha = .5$ $\beta = 0$	$\alpha = .5$ $\beta = 2$	$\alpha = .6$ $\beta = 2$	$\alpha = .8$ $\beta = 4$
1	1.00	1.00	1.00	1.00
2	1.50	2.50	2.80	5.00
3	1.75	3.75	4.84	17.80
4	1.875	4.125	6.352	56.20
5	1.9375	3.4375	6.6256	169.84
6	1.9688*	2.0313	5.3037	500.52
7	1.9844	.9141	2.5959	1,459.592
8	1.9922	− .1172	− .6918	4,227.704
9	1.9961	.2148	−3.3603	12,241.1216

* Table is correct to four decimal places.

through time. The qualitative properties of this sequence depend upon whether the point is in Region A, B, C, or D.[3] The properties of each region can be briefly summarized.

REGION A (RELATIVELY SMALL VALUES OF THE RELATION)

If there is a constant level of governmental expenditure through time, the national income will approach asymptotically a value $\dfrac{1}{1-\alpha}$ times the constant level of governmental expenditure. A single impulse of expenditure, or any amount of expenditure followed by a complete cessation, will result in a gradual approach to the original zero level of national income. (It will be noted that the asymptote approached is identically that given by the Keynes-Kahn-Clark formula. Their analysis applies to points along the α axis and is subsumed under the more general Hansen analysis.) Perfectly periodic net governmental expenditure will result eventually in perfectly periodic fluctuations in national income.

---

where x_1 and x_2 are roots of the quadratic equation

$$x^2 - \alpha[1 + \beta]x + \alpha\beta = 0,$$

and d_1 and d_2 are constants dependent upon the α's and β's chosen.

[3] Mathematically, the regions are demarcated by the conditions that the roots of the equation referred to in the previous footnote be real or complex, greater or less than unity in absolute value.

REGION B

A constant continuing level of governmental expenditure will result in damped oscillatory movements of national income, gradually approaching the asymptote $\frac{1}{1-\alpha}$ times the constant level of government expenditure. (Cf. Table 1.) Governmental expenditure in a single or finite number of periods will result eventually in damped oscillations around the level of income zero. Perfectly regular periodic fluctuations in government expenditure will result eventually in fluctuations of income of the same period.

REGION C

A constant level of governmental expenditure will result in *explosive,* ever increasing oscillations around an asymptote computed as above. (Cf. column 3 of Table 2.) A single impulse of expenditure or a finite number of expenditure impulses will result eventually in explosive oscillations around the level zero.

CHART 2.—DIAGRAM SHOWING BOUNDARIES OF REGIONS YIELDING DIFFERENT QUALITATIVE BEHAVIOR OF NATIONAL INCOME

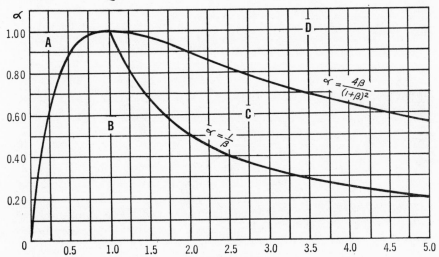

REGION D (LARGE VALUES OF THE MARGINAL PROPENSITY TO CONSUME AND THE RELATION)

A constant level of governmental expenditure will result in an ever increasing national income, eventually approaching a compound interest rate of growth. (Cf. column 4 of Table 2.) A single impulse of net investment will likewise send the system up to infinity at a compound interest rate of growth. On the other hand, a single infinitestimal unit of disinvestment will send the system ever downward at an increasing rate. This is a highly unstable situation, but corresponds most closely to the pure case of pump-priming, where the total increase in national income bears no finite ratio to the original stimulus.

The limitations inherent in so simplified a picture as that presented here should not be overlooked.[4] In particular, it assumes that the marginal propensity to consume and the *relation* are constants; actually these will change with the level of income, so that this representation is strictly a *marginal* analysis to be applied to the study of small oscillations. Nevertheless, it is more general than the usual analysis. Contrary to the impression commonly held, mathematical methods properly employed, far from making economic theory more abstract, actually serve as a powerful liberating device enabling the entertainment and analysis of ever more realistic and complicated hypotheses.

---

[4] It may be mentioned in passing that the formal structure of our problem is identical with the model sequences of Lundberg, and the dynamic theories of Tinbergen. The present problem is so simple that it provides a useful introduction to the mathematical theory of the latter's work.

[19]

Hicks on the Trade Cycle*

JAMES S. DUESENBERRY†

Editors' Note

Model building is necessarily a somewhat rigid analytical device, for it must rest upon contrived assumptions relating to the nature of the economy, individual behavior, and the values of the multiplier and accelerator. Duesenberry has attempted a more flexible approach to the construction of cycle models. His researches, for example, stress the existence of not one consumption function, but many.‡ In *Income, Saving and the Theory of Consumer Behavior,* he urged the necessity of recognizing the social character of consumption patterns. The model developed in *Business Cycles and Economic Growth* allows exogenous factors to disturb the growth trend of the model and induce cyclical expansions or contractions. From this frame of reference, Duesenberry undertakes the study of J. R. Hicks, *A Contribution to the Theory of the Trade Cycle* (Oxford: Clarendon Press, 1950).

The commentary "Hicks on the Trade Cycle," which critically evaluates the Hicksian cycle model, is one of acknowledged excellence. After deftly summarizing Hicks's position, Duesenberry examines with great penetration the assumptions and methodology employed. In so doing he illumi-

* Reprinted by permission of the publishers from *The Quarterly Journal of Economics,* Vol. LXIV, No. 3 (August, 1950), pp. 464-476; Cambridge, Mass.: Harvard University Press, Copyright, 1950, by The President and Fellows of Harvard College.

† James S. Duesenberry (1918–   ) has taught at the University of Michigan and Harvard and during 1954–55 worked under a Fulbright Research Professorship at Cambridge University, England. He is a contemporary economist of growing reputation, and his studies on consumption, cycles, and growth have secured for him an attentive audience. In addition to contributions to professional journals, he has written *Income, Saving and the Theory of Consumer Behavior* (1949) and *Business Cycles and Economic Growth* (1958).

‡ "Income-Consumption Relations and Their Implications," *Income, Employment and Public Policy, Essays in Honor of Alvin Hansen* (New York: W. W. Norton, 1948), p. 54.

nates some of the differences among the model builders, alluded to in our introductory remarks.

❧ Mr. Hicks's contribution to trade cycle theory[1] is, as we have learned to expect, ingeniously contrived and urbanely expressed. In this very concise volume we are offered a theory of the trade cycle in the full sense of the word. This is neither a catalogue of factors affecting income nor a commentary on business cycle history. Instead it is a fully worked out theory in which it is shown that a few simple hypotheses are sufficient to produce cycles of the type which have been observed. In this respect it is much more like the theories of Wicksell, Hawtrey, Schumpeter, and Hayek than the more eclectic theories which have appeared in recent years. The content of the hypotheses is different, but the character of the argument is the same.

Hicks begins by taking a strong position on the question of the periodic character of the cycle. It seems to him that "the economic history of the last 150 years organizes itself so easily into a series of 7 to 10 year cycles with certain interruptions traceable to major wars that the reality of the cycle seems . . . unmistakable." He makes a bow to the works of Slutzky[2] and Yule,[3] but is unimpressed by the possibility that observed cycles should have been produced by the summation of random shocks. It is the approximate but not precise regularity of cyclical fluctuation which he sets out to explain. This is done by introducing a set of assumptions which will make cycles of the kind described inevitable. For this purpose the assumptions must be such that the cycle to which they lead is regular enough but not *too* regular. In addition the cycles must appear even though some parameters in the assumed relations vary over fairly wide ranges.

Hicks requires just five assumptions to produce the desired result. They are as follows: (1) Real consumption expenditure is a function of real income in the recent past. His results can be obtained with any of a wide variety of lag structures and with changing parameters in the consumption function. (2) Autonomous investment, i.e., investment which is independent of output, rises through time at a more or less constant percentage

---

[1] J. R. Hicks, A *Contribution to the Theory of the Trade Cycle* (Oxford: Clarendon Press, 1950).

[2] Eugen Slutzky, "The Summation of Random Causes as the Source of Cyclic Processes," *Econometrica*, April 1937.

[3] G. V. Yule, "Why Do We Sometimes Get Nonsense Correlations? A Study of Sampling and the Nature of Time Series," *Journal of the Royal Statistical Society*, January 1926.

rate. Again fluctuations and occasional shifts in the rate of growth are permitted. (3) A substantial amount of investment is induced by changes in output. The accelerator must have a rather high value; i.e., in interacting with the multiplier it must tend to produce explosive cycles. (4) At any point in time there is a ceiling beyond which output cannot be increased. (5) The value of the accelerator is much smaller on the downswing than on the upswing. This is due to technical limitations on the possibility of disinvestment.

Given these assumptions the argument is fairly simple. It is first shown that if autonomous investment rises at a constant percentage rate there will be an equilibrium growth pattern for income. Money income will grow at the same rate as autonomous investment and the ratio of income to autonomous investment will depend on the values of the multiplier and accelerator. This is, of course, the familiar Domar-Harrod[4] proposition. Next follows an explanation of the interaction of multiplier and accelerator. The exposition here is excellent and every student will find the mathematical appendix useful. It is shown that, when autonomous investment rises trendwise, cyclical fluctuations about the trend will arise which are perfectly analogous to the fluctuations about the static equilibrium when autonomous investment is constant.

So far the argument is familiar but at this point something new is added. It has sometimes been maintained that the values of the multiplier and accelerator must be such as not to produce antidamped cycles or exponential growth rates of income, because we do not observe any economic explosions. The cycle has to be kept going by erratic shocks. Hicks feels that the erratic shock-damped cycle mechanism would not produce cycles having as much regularity as actual cycles seem to have. A regular cycle could be produced if the accelerator were always just equal to one, but that seems too improbable. Consequently, he assumes that the accelerator is usually large enough to produce antidamped cycles or explosions. The assumption of a ceiling for output is then invoked to explain why actual explosions do not take place.[5]

Suppose the system to be in equilibrium. Autonomous investment and income are rising at constant rates. If there is a bulge in autonomous investment, the interaction of multiplier and accelerator will carry income away from its equilibrium path. If there were no ceiling, income might rise indefinitely; but, when the ceiling on output is reached, the accelerator cannot work any longer. As soon as output ceases to grow the accelerator drops to zero. Income must then fall because autonomous investment alone cannot support an income above the equilibrium. But as soon as income falls, the accelerator begins to work on the downside and

---

[4] Domar, Evsey, "Capital Expansion, Rate of Growth and Employment," *Econometrica*, April 1946; Roy Harrod, *Toward a Dynamic Economics* (London: Macmillan, 1948).

[5] Cf. Alvin Hansen, *Monetary Theory and Fiscal Policy* (McGraw-Hill Book Company, 1949), pp. 148-150.

therefore the fall in income overshoots the equilibrium. Its fall is checked because negative investment cannot be greater than depreciation. Income then levels out (or rather reaches a new path of steady growth). Autonomous investment is still rising, however, so that as soon as the capital stock has been sufficiently reduced by passage of time, income again begins to rise toward the equilibrium position. But because of the instability resulting from the multiplier-accelerator interaction it again overshoots the mark and hits the ceiling. The whole cycle is then repeated. The ceiling and floor are on a rising trend because they depend on the size of the capital stock. Thus one bulge in autonomous investment is sufficient to produce an undamped cycle about a rising trend.

Since the repetitiveness of the cycle requires only that the accelerator be greater than one, it is possible for its value to shift over fairly wide ranges. The only effect of these shifts will be to cause variations in the length of the cycle. Similarly there can be as many erratic fluctuations in autonomous investment as one likes without destroying the basic regularity of the cycle. These are the characteristics which make the theory attractive. One can keep the original assumptions and still introduce enough variation in the parameters and shocks to produce the great variety of cyclical patterns which economic history reveals.

Hicks's theory is an elegant one, but if we look at it closely its validity seems doubtful. There are a number of weak points in the theoretical structure. In addition there is considerable doubt about the empirical validity of some of the fundamental assumptions.

First of all, Hicks's idea of the relation of the equilibrium growth rate to autonomous investment seems to be wrong. He feels that he has improved Harrod's analysis of equilibrium growth by assuming that autonomous investment increases at a steady rate. Hicks supposes that the equilibrium rate of growth depends on the rate of increase of autonomous investment. But as Domar[6] pointed out some time ago the equilibrium rate of growth depends only on the size of the multiplier and the productivity of new investment. The equilibrium rate of growth must be such that each year's income exceeds that of the previous year by just enough to permit absorption of the product of the additional capacity installed in the previous year. That means that investment must rise each year by an amount which depends on the multiplier (which determines the amount of income generated by investment) and by the inverse of the accelerator (which determines how much income is required to absorb the output added by last year's investment). The required rate of growth is simply the product of the marginal propensity to consume and the inverse of the accelerator. It is quite independent of the distribution of investment as between autonomous and induced investment.

In calculating the equilibrium rate of growth Hicks is wrong in applying the accelerator to increases in output rather than to the difference be-

---

[6] *Op. cit.*

tween the increase in demand and the increase in capacity. In other words, he assumes that the autonomous investments have no productivity. If we use Hicks's method of calculation but assume that autonomous investment adds to output as much as induced investment, we arrive at Harrod's equilibrium growth rate formula.

A second weakness arises out of his neglect of the discontinuity in his difference equations when he calculates the amplitude of the cycles they generate. He assumes that the accelerator is usually great enough to produce either exponential growth in income or antidamped cycles.

Exponential movements, when there are distributed lags in both consumption and investment, occur only when the accelerator is quite high. It must be around three for reasonable values of the marginal propensity to consume. There is no empirical evidence at all for believing that the accelerator is ever as high as three. The argument then depends on the occurrence of antidamped cycles. If Hicks had neglected the irreversibility of the accelerator on the downswing he could have got antidamped cycles by simply assuming a high value for the accelerator. But he (correctly) argues that disinvestment is limited by the size of depreciation allowances. This implies that after a downswing we do not follow the course of the cycle which produced the previous upswing. Instead we start a new cycle on the basis of new initial conditions. In the trough of the depression the accelerator is not working because there is excess capacity. Income movements therefore do not follow the course indicated by the multiplier-accelerator mechanism. That mechanism comes into play only when excess capacity has been eliminated. We have to regard each cycle as starting at the date of elimination of excess capacity. It is a new cycle having nothing to do with the previous upswing. Accordingly, its amplitude will depend on the initial conditions, that is, on the income in the period in which excess capacity is eliminated and in the following period or periods (depending on the distribution of the lags). Consequently there is no reason for the second cycle to have a greater amplitude than the first even if the multiplier-accelerator coefficients imply antidamped cycles. As a matter of fact, if we accept the rest of Hicks's assumptions, the amplitude of each cycle as a percentage of the equilibrium income should be about the same. This is so because the initial conditions for each cycle depend on the amount of disinvestment taking place in the trough of the previous depression. That in turn depends on the stock of capital, which ought to rise at roughly the same rate as the equilibrium income. We may conclude that a more or less steady cycle can be maintained without a ceiling even if the multiplier and accelerator coefficients imply antidamped cycles.

Once we have reached that conclusion we may call in question the existence of the ceiling. Hicks appears to have introduced the ceiling because the observed phenomena could not be explained without it. His reasoning, if I take him rightly, is as follows. First, we have observed a cycle with a fairly regular period for a long time. It is very improbable that this should have resulted from the continued existence of an accelerator just large enough to keep the cycle going without damping or antidamping tendencies. He rejects the idea that the basic cyclical mechanism is of the damped type but is kept going by random shocks. The only remaining possibility is that the fundamental multiplier-accelerator mechanism leads to explosive or antidamped movements. Since we do not observe such movements there must be a limit on output which prevents the accelerator from working. *Ergo*, the cyclical cat can only be killed by choking it with cream.

But if we are correct in maintaining that the irreversible accelerator prevents antidamped cycles from expanding in amplitude, the ceiling ceases to be a logical necessity. It may exist, but we can only tell whether it does or not by looking at the facts.

There can be no question but that there is always some limit to the possible output of a community. The question is whether we are likely to reach that limit. We can try to answer that question in two ways. Proceeding directly we can ask how many booms have ended because of shortages in investment goods. There do not seem to be many cases of that sort. In particular it seems very hard to argue that the boom of the 1920's ended in the way Hicks suggests. There are cases, however, which at first glance seem to fit Hicks's model. The boom of 1868–73 in England was, according to Rostow,[7] ended by a coal shortage. But the collapse was not brought on in the Hicksian fashion. The coal shortage resulted in rising coal prices. The high profits of the industry led to the sinking of new pits, but their output was not immediately available. Meanwhile investors reduced orders on the expectation of a fall in prices. The reduction in orders produced a temporary fall in income and a great drop in coal prices. Recovery of output came quickly but in the meantime the new pits were in production and coal prices did not rise again. No doubt similar cases could be found, though I suspect there would be more of them in the United States than in England. But such cases do not fit Hicks's model: here the boom is brought to an end by the rise in prices and the accompanying speculative forces—not by the inability of investors to make physical investments. Hicks recognizes that the pressure on productive facilities might lead to inflation but argues that bottlenecks will check investments before prices rise. Moreover, as soon as prices fall the investors who withdraw from the market because of high prices come back in again. This indicates, if nothing else does, that there is more to the cycle than the mechanical operation of the multiplier and accelerator. It may be noted that the events of 1921 bear out the view that temporary declines in income do not destroy a boom when the basic investment situation is favorable.

Hicks has given no evidence for the view that booms are checked by bottlenecks and so far as I am aware there is none. On that basis alone

---

[7] Walt W. Rostow, *British Economy of the 19th Century* (Oxford: Clarendon Press, 1948).

his argument might be rejected. But the concept has been in use for a long time. It appears in Hayek's theory and in many others. Most recently Mr. Domar[8] has used it in arguing that the equilibrium rate of growth is higher than our resources will permit us to attain. In view of the importance of the idea it may be worth while asking what are its logical foundations and whether there are any hidden flaws in those foundations.

A limit to output in the capital goods industries can be reached either because of a shortage of labor or because of a shortage of equipment in those industries. If we conceive of an ordinary peacetime boom the latter is not likely to be a very serious possibility. The cyclical mechanism is supposed to be one in which output increases because of increases in the rate of investment while investment is induced by increases in output. The induced investment occurs not only in the industries producing consumption goods, but in those producing investment goods as well. Consequently when those industries near capacity levels of operation, they may be supposed to expand as well as the others. If investment in those industries proceeds on the accelerator basis there is no reason offhand why they should not expand fast enough to meet the demands on them. However, it may be argued that these industries have special characteristics. Some, like steel, have long construction periods so that the capacity coming into use in one year was induced by the increase of demand two years before. If output were increasing at an increasing rate, output might catch up with capacity. The practical importance of that consideration is largely vitiated by the existence of stand-by capacity. Because of technical improvements it becomes profitable to build new equipment to replace old equipment even when the latter is perfectly usable. In many industries that equipment is not scrapped but is kept available for just such periods of very high output as are under consideration here.

In other cases, such as in the metal fabricating industries, plants producing investment goods can subcontract work to plants using machine tools for production of consumption goods. The latter can be produced when necessary by less capital-using methods, e.g., by stamping or molding. The result is that there is a good deal of flexibility in production methods when there is real pressure on equipment resources. The problem here is one of overcoming a lag, not of overcoming an absolute shortage. Lags aside, as much equipment can be built as labor supplies will permit.

Of course, as we have already indicated, bottlenecks do sometimes occur. But there is no reason to suppose that serious bottlenecks, as opposed to general labor shortages, are a regular feature of booms. With that qualification it seems reasonable in the absence of evidence to the contrary to suppose that the problem of equipment shortage boils down to one of labor shortages.

Let us then examine the probability that labor shortages will occur and check the boom. Here the case for shortages looks better. We know that

[8] *Op. cit.*

most booms are accompanied by "full employment" in the sense that relatively few people are seeking work. If we often find that there is no excess supply of labor during most of a boom, is it not plausible to suppose that the boom is brought to an end by a shortage of labor?

It is remarkable that during the 1920's unemployment in the United States appeared to be very low while the economy continued to expand. That seems to imply that the total demand expanded just fast enough to absorb the increase in labor force resulting from population increase plus the labor released by increases in labor productivity. Had that occurred, it would have been a remarkable coincidence. What actually happened, of course, was that large numbers of workers moved from farms (particularly marginal farms) to take employment in urban industry. Their marginal productivity on the farms was very low so that no serious repercussions were felt in that sector. In other words, from being underemployed (but not unemployed in any of the usual definitions) they became fully employed. The country was in effect equipped with a "reserve army" of labor willing to take employment in urban industry when such employment became available.

The existence of such a reserve army is of course in contradiction to classical wage theory. In that theory when differences in marginal productivities (and wages) exist between workers who can be substituted for one another those differences should be eliminated by competition. The low-paid workers should try to obtain employment in the high-wage industry by offering to work for less than the going rate. Similarly the high-wage employers should try to force down the wage rate by recruiting additional supplies of labor from the low-wage industry. The result should be an equalization of wages at a rate between the two old ones with a concomitant expansion in the high-wage industry and contraction in the low-wage one. All this is, of course, qualified by considerations of immobility and nonpecuniary advantages.

In fact, however, differences in wages persist not merely because of immobility (in the sense that workers are unwilling to move) or of nonpecuniary advantages, but also because of the passivity of both workers and employers. Workers who would like to work in a high-wage industry (even at a rate considerably less than the going one) do not try to gain employment there by offering to work for less than the going rate. Instead they merely wait until a job opportunity occurs. Similarly employers do not typically try to force down wage rates by bringing in new workers. They are satisfied if they can keep them from rising. It is this passivity on the part of both parties (all this seems to have been nearly as true before trade unions became very strong, as it is now) to the "competitive wage struggle" which makes the existence of the reserve army possible. In the nineteenth century the reserve was even larger because of migration from Europe which varied with the United States trade cycle. But even in the 1920's some millions of workers moved from farms to urban industry. Of course there must be some rate of increase of output so great that workers cannot be brought in fast enough to meet the demand. But it does not follow that it is often reached. In any case, the fact that the economy reaches "full employment" in a boom is no evidence that a labor shortage is impending. (It may be said that there will be skill shortages even if there is no shortage of labor in general. The example of the war seems to show, however, that the possibilities of upgrading semi-skilled workers are very great so that skill shortages are not really so very probable. There may, of course, be specific shortages in some places, but it is pushing things a bit far to attribute a major depression to a shortage of key men.)

Labor shortages have at times resulted in inflations (although most of the peacetime inflations in this country are more closely connected to speculative movements than to labor shortages). But what should be emphasized is the fact that, in the United States at least, there is never an effective ceiling on the *level* of output. The ceiling, if any, is on the rate of increase of output. In general there can be a much greater expansion of output in a boom than one would expect if one supposes that "full employment" sets an upper limit on output. It is also important to note that the process of industrialization has consisted to a large extent of drawing in the "reserve army" of low productivity labor into higher uses. This has been accomplished by booms in which output pushed through the "full employment ceiling."

What has been said applies chiefly to the United States. In European countries and particularly in England the situation is different. There the farm population has been a small proportion of the population for a long time. But population increase was very large and Great Britain has sent out emigrants in large numbers for many years. It is hard to see how one can argue that a country with large migration outwards suffered very seriously from labor shortages.

If the above arguments are correct then we must conclude that (1) the ceiling concept is unnecessary for an explanation of the cycle, and (2) its existence is extremely doubtful. Hicks's theory is then much simplified. It boils down to the proposition that there is a multiplier-accelerator process which tends to produce antidamped cycles which are kept in check by technical limitations on the accelerator on the downswing. The cycle is on an upward trend because of a rising trend in autonomous investment. (The latter idea does not seem too plausible. It can easily be replaced by introducing an irreversible consumption function which keeps the income in a depression from falling back to the level of the previous depression.)[9] The resulting theory is not obviously inconsistent with observation, but it is perhaps a little too simple.

Hicks's argument and many similar ones are based on a division of investment into three classes: autonomous investment, induced invest-

---

[9] Cf. James S. Duesenberry, *Income, Saving and the Theory of Consumer Behavior* (Cambridge: Harvard University Press, 1949), pp. 114-115.

ment, and replacement investment. Like many other concepts in business cycle theory the above classification is somewhat poorly related to the underlying micro-theory of investment.

From the way in which the terms are used by Hicks and others it appears that replacement investment is made necessary by the physical deterioration of equipment. Similarly, induced investment is necessitated by rising costs owing to high intensity of operation of equpment. Autonomous investment is brought about by technical developments of various kinds.

In fact, we cannot make a clear distinction between these three types of investment except in certain rather special cases. Putting aside investment for production of new products or by new firms, we can say that investment takes place when in view of output expectations it will cost a firm less to produce all or part of its output with new equipment than with its existing equipment. The cost comparison is one between the operating costs with existing equipment and operating costs plus capital costs for new equipment. The comparison will be favorable to the purchase of new equipment when (1) the new equipment is technically superior to the old, (2) the old equipment has high maintenance or operation costs because of its age, or (3) output is so high that the existing equipment must be operated at high intensity, which raises operating costs. Any one of these three situations will lead to the purchase of new equipment but they all influence the decision jointly and their combined influence may lead to equipment purchases when no one of them separately would do so. In general all three considerations will be present and the distinction between types of investment loses most of its usefulness.

Investment in new products may still appear to be autonomous. Actually, the amount of such investment will certainly depend on the level of aggregate demand to some extent. Similar considerations apply to investment by new firms.

If we argue that we cannot separate out a special category of induced investment, what happens to the accelerator? It does not disappear but it operates in a somewhat more complicated way than one might suppose from reading the accelerator theorists. Let us consider what happens at the bottom of a depression. In Hicks's model a depression once started continues until excess capacity is eliminated by the passage of time. When that is accomplished replacement begins to take place, income rises and the multiplier-accelerator process begins again.

If we look at investment from the point of view described above we get a somewhat different picture. Once a depression sets in, income falls to a level set by (1) the character of the consumption function, and (2) the amount of investment which firms find it profitable to make even at very low levels of aggregate output. The latter will depend primarily on the amount of technical development. Some new products may be developed which can make their way even when aggregate demand is low. Shifts in demand may keep some industries operating at high levels or even make them expand, so that it pays them to buy new equipment even in the bottom of the depression. Some technical developments may be so cost-saving that firms will buy equipment even though output is low (so that they are using only their most efficient equipment). The amount of this investment will be small in the early stages. As time passes, however, technical developments accumulate and more firms will be induced to undertake investment. This causes a rise in output. The rise in output will have a two-fold effect. First, the firm that found it profitable to invest at the old level of output will find it profitable to do so again. At the old output they found that the difference in operating cost between new equipment and the least efficient equipment in use was great enough to justify replacing that equipment with new equipment. The equipment thus replaced would ordinarily be kept for reserve. When output expands they are back in the old situation. They will have to use that reserve equipment and it will again pay to replace it with new equipment.

Secondly, there were firms which did not find it profitable to invest at the old level of output. When output rises, some of them will find that they have to use less efficient equipment to produce additional output. It may turn out that this equipment is sufficiently inferior to new equipment to justify investment in the latter. Thus the rise in ouput will probably produce a rise in investment and thereby a further rise in output. The same argument holds in the new situations. All firms which invested before will invest again, and some additional ones will invest. The "accelerator" applied to the second rise in income will be greater than that applied to the first. As the process continues the accelerator will continue to rise, approaching an upper limit set by the condition that all firms are participating in the investment process. If that point is reached the ordinary multiplier-accelerator analysis is appropriate.

The model just given is rather similar to that obtained when it is assumed that different industries have different degrees of excess capacity when the upturn starts. The differences are (1) that the somewhat inconvenient capacity concept can be scrapped without losing the essential concept of the accelerator; and (2) that the volitional element in investment decisions and the importance of technical change are emphasized.

The volitional element is important because no one has to invest. Buying new equipment reduces operating costs, but that is worthwhile only if the equipment is more or less fully used for some years. A rise in output only affects expectations as to what future output will be. The response to such a rise can vary widely according to the circumstances surrounding the rise in output. All that is well known, but it certainly needs to be emphasized.

The amount and distribution of technical change during the depression will be of equal importance in governing the course of the recovery. If the first upturn is generated by technical developments in a few industries while others have had no such developments, the recovery will be weak. The investment of the first group of firms will raise output and they will invest again. But if no developments have taken place since the boom in the other industries the latter will not invest because of the rise in output. The accelerator will not grow and the recovery will soon collapse. The accelerator may increase to the upper limit or, depending on the technical situation, it may stop growing at any point. If it stops before it is sufficiently large to produce a strong upward movement the boom will end. The economy will then be in a worse state than before, since it will have "used up" all the technological development accumulated since the last boom. Thus the course of a recovery will be much influenced by the amount and character of technical development, and a strong recovery from a depression is by no means inevitable.

In addition to these complications others connected with the relation of profits to investment decisions, and the connections of monopoly and freedom of entry with technical development become important when we use the accelerator concept in a less mechanical way. These considerations will make each cycle a unique one in a fundamental sense.

The basic concept of multiplier-accelerator interaction is an important one but we cannot really expect to explain observed cycles by a mechanical application of that concept. Furthermore, whatever cycle possibilities might exist if there were no technical development, it seems clear that none of the cycles which have been observed can be explained without reference to changes in technique.

Hicks's theory has come in for some rather severe criticism in these pages. Nevertheless, it is an ingenious piece of work and will repay the efforts of the student of business cycles. The treatment of difference equations both in the text and in the mathematical appendix is, from an economist's point of view, a very illuminating one.

In one sense this is the first coherent theory of the cycle to appear for some years. Fluctuations in income and employment appear to have occurred for many years and we have not yet succeeded in giving a satisfactory explanation of them. Models such as those of Tinbergen and Klein produce cycles only with the aid of frequent outside shocks. That may well be the explanation of the cycle, but if one is impressed with its regularity, then something more basic is required. Hicks has tried to give us a more fundamental explanation. While the explanation is not completely satisfactory, his contribution will stand as a challenge to every business cycle theorist to see if he can do better.

[20]

Diffusion, Acceleration, and Business Cycles*

BERT G. HICKMAN†

Editors' Note

If the acceleration concept is a valued tool of cyclical analysis, it is none-theless a limited one. Many assumptions circumscribe the practical appli-cation of the principle. Is there, for example, in each industry a constant ratio between consumer outputs and the quantity of capital equipment? Are entrepreneurs aware of these ratios and do they consciously strive to maintain them? Will the acceleration principle operate where idle man-power and equipment exist? Many economists, including J. R. Hicks, think not. What are the effects of tax legislation and technological change on depreciation policies and hence on the capital replacement ratio?‡ Is not the option to invest, that most volatile of all economic choices, vastly oversimplified by the acceleration hypothesis? These considerations

---

* Copyright 1959 by the American Economic Association. Reprinted, with the per-mission of the author and the Association, from the *American Economic Review*, Vol. XLIX, No. 4 (September, 1959). The article was prepared as part of a broad study of the growth and stability of the postwar economy undertaken for the Brookings Institu-tion. The interpretations and conclusions are those of the author and do not necessarily reflect the views of other members of the Brookings staff or of the administrative officers of the Institution.

† Bert G. Hickman of the Brookings Institution, Washington, D.C., is another con-temporary economist devoting his energies to the challenge of business fluctuations and economic stabilization. He is the author of *Growth and Stability of the Postwar Economy* (1960). Fortunately for those with an interest in the topic, the Brookings Institution has made available a series of reprints of Hickman's investigations, many of which have appeared in scholarly or professional journals: "Federal Spending and the Stability of the Postwar Economy" (1958 reprint); "The Contraction of 1953–54" (1958 reprint); and "Postwar Cyclical Experience and Economic Stability" (1958 re-print).

‡ See Delmar D. Ray, *Accounting and Business Fluctuation*, Gainesville, Fla.: Florida Press, 1960, Chapters IV and V.

prompted us to choose Hickman's "Diffusion, Acceleration, and Business Cycles" to round off the sequence on accelerators and multipliers. By relating rates of change in the output of specific industries to aggregate investment, Hickman casts doubt on the realism of many accelerator models. He purports to show that investment is "more nearly a function of the level of output than its rate of change. . . ." More than that, the article offers a useful illustration of how economic knowledge grows through a process of hypothesizing and verification, deduction and induction, and the vital importance of isolating those key assumptions on which any theory must rest.

▂▂▂▼

❦ The acceleration principle is a key element in many modern aggregative models of the business cycle.[1] Coupled with the multiplier, it can be made to yield a series of self-generating cycles, provided that the phenomenon of excess capacity is ignored, as in Paul Samuelson's classic model [12]. Even when discarded as the usual cause of the upturn, as it was by J. R. Hicks [6], the accelerator remains the crucial factor on the downturn, because it is used to explain an endogenous lead of investment over national output. The principle derives its peculiar power and its attraction, in other words, from the proposition that a mere retardation in the rate of increase of real national income during a cyclical expansion may cause an absolute decline of investment and hence of production.

I propose to show that it is unnecessary to invoke the accelerator to explain how a downturn of aggregate investment may occur when aggregate output retards (decelerates), that it is substantially incorrect to do so, and that more than token weight must be given to other determinants of investment decisions which acceleration theorists themselves recognize are of some, though not "fundamental" importance. The negative aspect of my argument consists principally of the demonstration that fixed investment in the bulk of manufacturing industries is more nearly a function of the level of output than its rate of change, together with tentative evidence that accelerator-induced inventory investment may play a minor role in business downturns. The positive contribution is to emphasize the fact that a business expansion becomes less widely diffused over the economy as aggregate activity retards, and to show how the individual production *declines* which regularly accompany aggregative *retardation* may induce a downturn of aggregate investment by affecting the capital

---

[1] The author is a member of the senior research staff of the Brookings Institution. His thanks are due to Moses Abramovitz and W. H. White for valuable comments and suggestions.

outlays of the declining industries and by weakening investment incentives generally.

According to the acceleration principle, net investment for purposes of capacity expansion is a function of the rate of change of output. This follows from the assumption of a technologically determined, fixed ratio of capital to output in the individual firm. If output is constant at an economically efficient level of capacity utilization, no increase of capacity is called for. If output rises and the increase is thought to be permanent, it will pay to augment capacity in proportion to the *change* in output, so that net investment will rise by an amount determined by the output change. If output subsequently rises more slowly, net investment will decline, since the required increment to capacity will have diminished.

Now, no one contends that investment in new capacity invariably behaves in the foregoing manner. For one thing, the principle does not come into play until output has increased enough from a cyclical trough to eliminate the excess capacity which had developed during the preceding contraction—which means that it cannot be used to explain the upturn itself.[2] Acceleration theorists recognize, moreover, that a current rise of output may not always be regarded as permanent, that not all of the deficiency of capacity need (or can) be made up quickly, and that the cost and availability of capital funds may enter the investment decision. (Indeed, these factors are often represented explicitly in modified accelerator models.) Nonetheless, they are inclined to treat such considerations as secondary qualifications to the "fundamental" technological relationship expressed in the acceleration hypothesis. But are the qualifications sufficiently secondary so that the predictions of the original formulation remain valid?

Few economists have denied that expansions and contractions of output will induce corresponding fluctuations of investment—including replacement expenditure and "autonomous" investment as well as expenditure for capacity expansion—since current profits rise and fall with production and affect both expected returns from investment and the internal supply of capital funds. Moreover, if production presses on capacity and the condition is expected to continue, capacity expansion is indicated—unless near-term expectations suggest that a postponement would be profitable. In much the same way, when production and profits are falling, the appearance of surplus capacity is an additional, and powerful, incentive to defer investment. These capacity effects are only part of the story, however, and certainly need not be controlling, nor do they require investment to fluctuate in proportion to the rate of change of production.

---

[2] This statement would have to be modified in the extreme case where gross investment dropped to zero and output remained at a floor long enough to permit the gradual elimination of excess capacity and a subsequent rise of replacement demand. This is not regarded as a realistic situation even by acceleration theorists, however. Hicks, for example, assumes that the recovery is started by an uptrend of autonomous investment [6, pp. 101-5].

These considerations suggest the testable hypothesis that for individual industries and periods as short as business cycles, fixed investment is more nearly a function of level of output than its rate of change.[3] But if this is correct, investment will usually lag production or synchronize with it, and this means that the acceleration hypothesis will be either inapplicable or invalid in most instances. That is, either output will not have retarded before falling, or if it did, the retardation will not have caused investment to lead output—and it matters little which, if either situation occurs commonly enough. Cases where investment led production would be consistent with the acceleration hypothesis, provided output retarded prior to the investment decline. Such cases could also result from other factors, however, and additional evidence would be necessary to select among the alternatives in such instances.

But all this has to do with the individual industry. Paradoxically enough, it is conceivable that a mere retardation of aggregate output could result in a decline of aggregate investment even though investment was a function of the level instead of the rate of change of output in every single industry.[4] This is because there is a strong correlation between the industrial coverage of a business expansion, as measured by a "diffusion index" which shows the ratio of expanding industries to all industries, and the rate of change of aggregate production.[5] When aggregative retardation occurs, it is not exclusively or even primarily because all individual outputs are increasing more slowly—the image which is probably at the back of the mind when the accelerator is applied to aggregate output—rather, it is principally because fewer industries are expanding at all and more have begun to decline.[6] But individual production declines will induce individual investment declines, and under certain conditions to be examined later, the individual declines could cause aggregate investment to lead aggregate output. Persons with a taste for "as if" theorizing and high levels of aggregation, could describe this situation by a model in which aggregate investment was a function of the rate of change of aggregate output. It would be incorrect, however, to justify the assumed relationship by appeal to a technologically determined capital-output ratio, or to argue that it reflected accelerator-induced investment reductions in individual firms. To do so would be to mistake what was basically a diffusion phenomenon for another sort of behavior with a different rationale.

---

[3] This is not to deny that the assumption of a comparatively fixed ratio between real capital and output is useful in the longer-run analysis of investment in individual industries. See below, fn. 23.

[4] This case is a logical extreme, involving unnecessarily strong assumptions. My general thesis that the relation between diffusion and aggregate activity is a key element in business cycles does not hinge on this one possibility.

[5] A. F. Burns [1] and G. H. Moore [10], working along lines pioneered by Wesley Mitchell, developed diffusion indexes and demonstrated their major cyclical properties in 1950.

[6] See Hickman [4], especially Chart 48, which shows that variations in the rate of change of aggregate manufacturing employment are due more to variations in the proportion of expanding industries than to changes in the average rate of expansion per industry, although both influences are involved.

There are three main divisions to the paper. We begin with an empirical examination of industrial (manufacturing and mining) investment in plant and equipment since the second world war. The purpose is twofold: to test whether fixed investment does or does not lead production in the separate industries and the aggregate, and to investigate the conditions under which aggregate investment would lead aggregate output even if investment in each industry were a coincident or lagged function of its own output and of nothing else. The second section is concerned with the relationship of sales diffusion on the retail level to production diffusion in manufacturing, and more generally, with the relative importance of diffusion and acceleration as causes of turning points in inventory investment and business cycles. The paper closes with a qualitative analysis of the relation between diffusion and aggregate activity and of its implications for investment and cycle theory.

1. *Industrial Production and Investment, 1947–1958*

Quarterly indexes of total industrial production and real gross expenditure for industrial plant and equipment are graphed for the period 1947–1958 in the upper panel of Chart 1.[7] The fact that capital formation is measured gross is no handicap in the present connection. Although the acceleration principle deals with *one* variety only of *net* investment—that needed to increase the capacity to produce existing products—it would cease to be interesting if it consistently failed to explain observed downturns of gross investment merely because other categories continued to increase.

The vertical lines on the chart show the dates of the quarterly peaks and troughs of industrial production associated with the business cycles of the period. It will be seen that there is a one-to-one correspondence between the cycles in production and investment, but that the turns do not in general coincide. Investment regularly lags production on the upturns. With regard to the peaks, investment leads by two quarters in 1948 and one in 1953, but turns simultaneously with output in 1957.[8]

---

[7] The investment figures were derived from the SEC-OBE estimates of capital expenditure by adjusting the raw data for price changes and seasonal variations. Details are given in the notes to Table 1. Deflation procedures are necessarily crude and may affect the timing comparisons between production and investment. The deflated indexes used here are less favorable to my hypothesis than the current dollar estimates, since rising prices will, if anything, make a deflated series turn down earlier than its undeflated counterpart. With regard to the downturn of 1957, for example, timing comparisons based on the undeflated investment figures would reduce the number of individual investment leads from 3 to 0, and would increase the length of the investment lags in 3 other industries. Deflation did not alter any turning points during the Korean period, however, nor did it affect the general consensus of investment leads during 1947–48.

[8] These timing comparisons are based on small differences at two of the downturns. Production was nearly as high in the fourth quarter of 1948 as in the third, so that its peak might be considered to lag investment by 3 quarters instead of 2. Similarly, in 1957 the level of investment declined only fractionally from the first to the second quarter, so that it could be considered to lag production by one quarter.

CHART 1.—INDUSTRIAL PRODUCTION AND INDUSTRIAL FIXED INVESTMENT, TOTALS, QUARTERLY CHANGES, AND DIFFUSION INDEXES, SEASONALLY ADJUSTED, QUARTERLY, 1947–1958

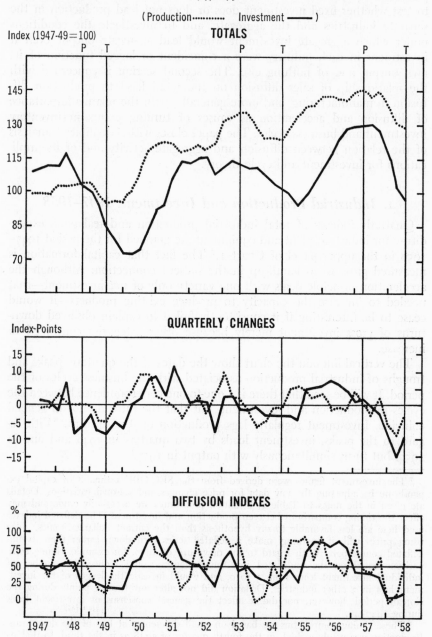

Vertical lines indicate peaks and troughs of industrial production. For sources and notes see Table 1.

The investment lags on the upturn need cause no concern, for every-one agrees that output must usually rise before improved profits and in-creased rates of utilization become positive spurs to fixed investment over the broad range of commodity-producing industries. The downturns are another matter. The prima-facie case for the acceleration hypothesis is strongest in 1948, when the lead of investment was both long in duration and substantial in amplitude. Production, moreover, did retard one quar-ter before the peak of investment (see the absolute quarterly changes of production shown in the middle panel of the chart).

One must remember, however, that the early postwar years were abnor-mal and turbulent. The investment data for 1946 are unavailable, but they would show a swift rise as manufacturers reconverted to peacetime produc-tion and undertook programs of modernization and expansion to meet postwar levels of demand. Put a bit differently, the first postwar expansion began from a position of *deficient* capacity. From the engineering stand-point, a decline of investment was indicated once satisfactory postwar levels of capacity had been attained, even if production had continued to rise as rapidly as before. It appears likely that this stage of satisfactory capacity had been attained in most manufacturing lines by the end of 1947, after two years of intense investment activity and partly because, it is true, output rose more slowly in 1947 than in 1946. When to this sup-position is added the continuing uncertainty as to whether the postwar inflation could be liquidated without a severe depression, it is easy to ac-count for the decline of investment during 1948.

All this is quite consistent with modified versions of the acceleration principle, of course, for these are usually flexible enough to handle situa-tions of initial disequilibrium and inelastic expectations. It does seem plausible, however, that these last determinants of investment were at least as important as the rate of change of production during this first postwar expansion.

The lead of investment was notably briefer and milder in 1953 than in 1948. It may be objected that the peak of investment should be dated in the second quarter of 1952 instead of the first quarter of 1953, but in that case we not only have investment leading production, but leading it dur-ing a period of accelerated production increase. Actually, neither aggregate production nor its rate of change was closely linked to total investment during this period, because the expansion was dominated by the Korean war and mobilization from mid-1950 to mid-1952, but was capped there-after by a boom in civilian goods. The corresponding shifts of output com-position and their consequences for investment will be discussed presently.

Finally, no lead of investment whatever appears in 1957, despite the fact that aggregate production was retarded after 1955 and actually decreased during the first three quarters of 1956, before rising in a last spurt to its ultimate peak.

None of the foregoing is conclusive. Because of its technological ra-tionale, the acceleration principle must hold for individual industries, if it holds at all, so that final judgment on it must await examination of the industry detail. Before we take that step, however, it will be convenient to view the behavior of industrial production and investment in the light of the correlation between aggregative acceleration and industrial diffusion. Attention is therefore directed to the bottom panel of Chart 1, which contains diffusion indexes of investment and production corresponding to the aggregates already studied. Industrial production, for example, was broken down into 16 component industries, and the percentage of them experiencing increases of production in each quarter was then computed. The diffusion index of investment expenditures was similarly prepared for the same set of industries.

A comparison of the diffusion index of production with aggregate production will quickly demonstrate that the former leads the latter. Each decline of aggregate production is preceded by a period during which the proportion of expanding industries declines, until finally the aggregate turns down, usually when production is falling in more than half the industries. Not only that—and here is visual proof of the point stressed earlier—but variations in the rate of change of aggregate production are closely correlated with variations in the percentage of expanding industries, as may be seen from the middle and lower panels. Exactly the same observations may be made with regard to the relationships among the three investment curves.

Of greater interest at the moment, however, is the relationship between production diffusion and investment diffusion. Investment diffusion usually lags the peaks and troughs of production diffusion by one or two quarters. If investment in each industry were a lagged function of output in that industry and of nothing else, we would observe just such a correlation between the diffusion indexes. As aggregate output retarded, and production declined in more industries, so too, with a lag, would investment in more industries.

Assume furthermore that each industry was the same size, as measured by value added, and that the individual production cycles were identical except for the time-phasing.[9] This would assure a perfect correlation between the percentage of expanding industries and the rate of change of aggregate production. Suppose also that investment per unit of output and the time-lag of investment were identical for each industry.[10] This would assure a perfect correlation between investment diffusion and the rate of change of aggregate investment. Taken altogether, these assumptions would mean that each of the investment curves in the three panels of the chart should be a lagged replica of the corresponding production curve.

Since the actual correlations approach but do not equal the hypothetical

---

[9] Or, more realistically, that the average size and amplitude of the industries included in the expanding and contracting groups remained constant even as the size and composition of the groups varied over time.

[10] Or that the average investment-output relationships were the same for the expanding and contracting groups.

ones—and in particular, since total investment sometimes leads total production—we are led to ask what factors might account for the departures. First, investment in each industry may not be simply a lagged function of its output. This important question aside for the moment, there may be imbalances among the industries with regard to size or amplitude of production. Such imbalances do exist even on the average,[11] but they are comparatively minor, and in any event are unimportant for our problem. Production imbalances would merely make aggregate production turn down before (or after) the proportion of declining industries exceeded one-half.[12] Aggregate investment would then also decline before (or after) investment was falling in half the industries, but it would still lag aggregate production.

Finally, it might be the case that one or more industries had a larger (or smaller) influence on investment than on output, either because the capital-intensities or the time-lags differed markedly from the industrial averages. In particular, if the early decliners invested heavily per unit of output, and with short or average lags, aggregate investment could lead aggregate output even though this was not true of any single industry. Since aggregate production seldom declines until half the industries are contracting, such an instance of disproportionate influence on investment would usually be reflected in a downturn of total investment before investment was falling in half the industries. This is not the explanation of the investment lead on the downturn of 1953, however, for the proportion of industries in which investment was declining fell below 50 per cent in the same quarter that aggregate investment dropped. (What actually happened was that investment led output in several industries.) And, as far as 1957 is concerned, investment inequalities *delayed* the downturn of aggregate investment, since the proportion of industries experiencing investment declines fell below 50 per cent two quarters before the rate of change of investment became negative. We will return to these general considerations after an examination of the cycles of production and investment in the component industries.

Chart 2 reveals substantial variation from industry to industry with regard to production, investment, and the relationship of the two: so much as to disabuse one of the notion that investment is a simple, stable function of either output or its change. Despite these differences, however, a common cyclical pattern may be detected among the production indexes. The variety of investment behavior is more pronounced and no attempt will be made to account for it fully. It will be possible, nevertheless, to

---

[11] The average size of the industries in the expanding and contracting groups remains fairly constant as industries shift from one group to the other, but there is a positive correlation between the number of rising (falling) industries and the average amplitude per rising (falling) industry [4]. This was demonstrated for employment in the paper cited, but it is also true of production.

[12] Suppose the early declines occurred among larger-than-average industries or were of more-than-average amplitude. Total production would then fall while the contracting industries were still a minority.

reach some firm conclusions on the issue of whether as a rule investment does or does not lead production in the several industries.

The timing of the peaks and troughs of production and investment in each industry is compared with those of aggregate industrial production in Table 1. The average lead or lag at each turning point is recorded at the bottom of each column. With regard to the general peak of 1948, for example, it will be seen that the individual investment series led total production by an average of 3.5 quarters, whereas the several production indexes showed an average lead of .5 quarter. More relevant for us is the comparison between the peaks of production and investment in each industry, which shows that investment lagged in only 2 of 16 industries in 1947–48. The abnormal character of that expansion and its implications for investment behavior were discussed earlier. For the same reason, there is no need to dwell on the timing relationships at the troughs.

Several peculiarities of the Korean expansion must be kept in mind for a correct reading of that period. The recovery which began in 1949 was accelerated by the outbreak of hostilities in June 1950, and from then until early 1951 most industries participated in a phase of intensive, heavily speculative, expansion. This phase gave way to a lull in civilian goods production which lasted until about mid-1952, whereas defense production rose all the while. During this interval also, fixed investment was subject to a variety of selective controls and incentives. Controls were relaxed thereafter and civilian production boomed during the last four or five months of 1952 and the first half of 1953.

Most of the individual industries had two humps in production corresponding to the first and last phases just described. These humps also appear in the total production index (Chart 1). I have not included the first of them in the timing comparisons of Table 1, but if that were done, investment would lag output in the overwhelming majority of industries which participated in the lull (Chart 2). With regard to the peak that actually terminated the expansion in 1953, we find investment lagging production in 6 industries and turning simultaneously in 3 more. It led, however, in the 7 remaining cases. As we know, aggregate investment also led aggregate production by one quarter. Why was this so, when slightly less than half the industries were investment leaders?

The wide fluctuations and early declines of investment in iron and steel, nonferrous metals and transportation equipment reflect the fact that these industries were strongly influenced by the Defense Facilities Expansion Program of the Korean war.[13] Investment was clearly not a function either of current output or its change in these industries; rather, its course was determined by the timetable of the mobilization. If these 3 are excluded

---

[13] Projects completed under Certificates of Necessity from 1951 through September 30, 1954 [13] accounted for half or more of the investment by these three industries during those years. The proportion was also substantial—about 45 per cent—in paper and chemicals, but was 25 per cent or less in the other groupings included in our breakdown.

TABLE 1—QUARTERLY LEADS (−) OR LAGS (+) OF PRODUCTION AND FIXED INVESTMENT IN INDIVIDUAL INDUSTRIES RELATIVE TO PEAKS AND TROUGHS OF AGGREGATE INDUSTRIAL PRODUCTION

Industry	Peak (III 48)		Trough (II 49)		Peak (II 53)		Trough (III 54)		Peak (I 57)	
	Prod.	Invest.	Prod.	Invest.	Prod.	Invest.	Prod.	Invest.	Prod.	Invest.
Primary iron and steel	+2	0	+2	+2	0	−4	0	+1	−4	+2
Primary nonferrous metals	0	−5	0	+5	0	−3	−2	+3	−5	+2
Electrical machinery	−3	−5	0	+3	+1	+2	−1	+3	−1	−2
Nonelectrical machinery	−1	−6[a]	+2	+2	0[c]	0	+1	+2	−1	+3
Motor vehicles and equip.	none	−6[a]	none	+3	0[c]	+4	0	−3	−5	+1
Other transportation equip.	+2	−1	+3	+3	+2	−5[d]	+1	0	+1	−2
Stone, clay & glass prod.	0	−4	0	+1	+1	−7[d]	−2	−1	−3	−2
Other durable goods	0	−5	0	+2	+1	−8	0	+2	−5	−3
Textile mill products	−1	0	0	+2	0[c]	0[c]	−2	0	−4	−1
Rubber products	−6[b]	−6[a]	+1	+2	+1[c]	+3	0	+2	−5	−1
Paper and allied prod.	0	−6[a]	0	+2	+1	+2[c]	−2	+3	+2	+2
Chemicals & allied prod.	+1	−6[a]	0	+2	+1	0[c]	0	+2	0	0
Petroleum & coal prod.	+1	−2	+2	+4	+1	+4[c]	0	+4	none	−2
Food and beverages	none	0	none	+3	+1	+2[c]	0	+2	+1	−2
Other nondurable goods	−2	−5	+2	+4	0	+2	0	+2	0	0
Mining	0	+1	+1	+5	0	+2	0	+2	0	0
Average	−0.5	−3.5	+0.9	+2.8	+0.6	−0.7	−0.6	+1.6	−2.0	−0.5

a Lead at least this long, although no investment data available for 1946 to check for earlier leads.

b Although data prior to 1947 are not included in Chart 2, inspection of the 1946 figures shows that the first quarter of 1947 was the peak in rubber production.

c During the Korean expansion, two peaks are often found for production and/or investment in a given industry. Unless the later of the two is markedly lower than the first, it is chosen for comparison with the general peak of II Q 1953.

d "Local" peak lags industrial production by one quarter—see Chart 2.

Source: Indexes of production from Federal Reserve Board. Expenditures on new plant and equipment in current dollars from U. S. Department of Commerce, Office of Business Economics, and Securities and Exchange Commission, adjusted for seasonal variation and corrected for price change by the author. The price deflator was a weighted average of an index of wholesale prices of producer goods for manufacturing industries (Bureau of Labor Statistics, weight 62 per cent) and an index of construction costs of commercial and factory buildings (E. H. Boeckh and Associates, weight 38 per cent). The weights reflect the relative importance of structures and equipment in manufacturing establishments in 1947, as given in Survey of Current Business, Nov. 1956, p. 9, Table 1. The index of industrial investment shown in Chart 1 is the sum of the individual series as separately adjusted and deflated.

CHART 2.—PRODUCTION AND FIXED INVESTMENT IN SIXTEEN INDUSTRIES, SEASONALLY ADJUSTED, QUARTERLY, 1947–1958

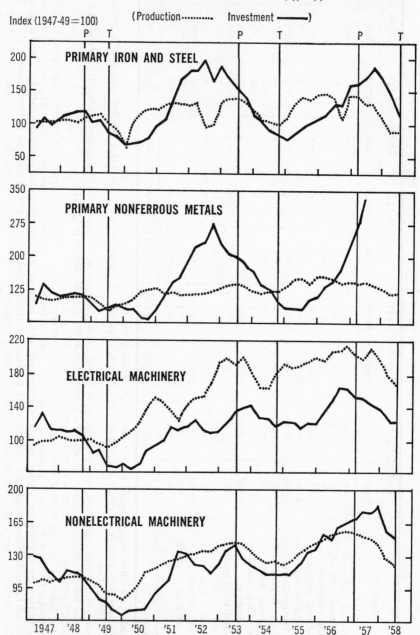

Index (1947-49=100)   (Production·········   Investment ——)

PRIMARY IRON AND STEEL

PRIMARY NONFERROUS METALS

ELECTRICAL MACHINERY

NONELECTRICAL MACHINERY

Vertical lines indicate peaks and troughs of industrial production.
For sources and notes see Table 1.

CHART 2 (*Continued*)

Index (1947-49=100)

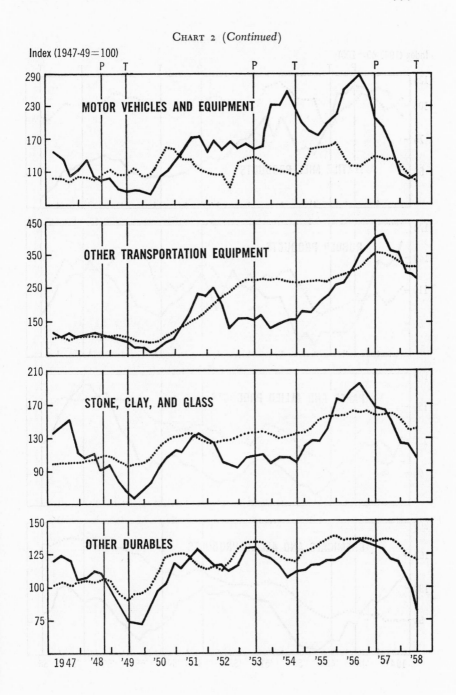

CHART 2 (*Continued*)

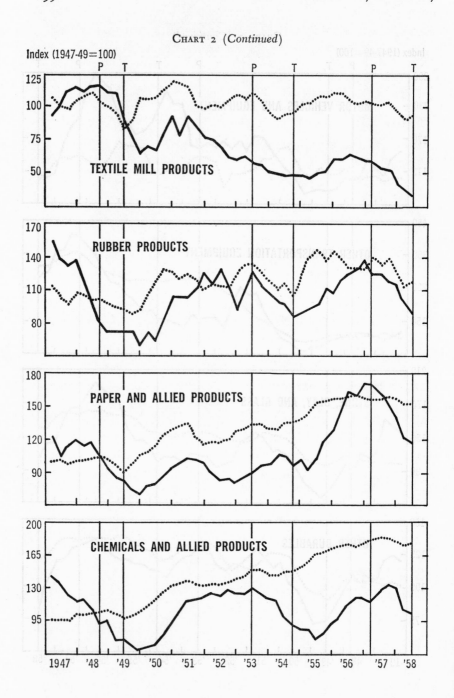

Index (1947-49=100)

TEXTILE MILL PRODUCTS

RUBBER PRODUCTS

PAPER AND ALLIED PRODUCTS

CHEMICALS AND ALLIED PRODUCTS

1947 '48 '49 '50 '51 '52 '53 '54 '55 '56 '57 '58

CHART 2 (*Continued*)

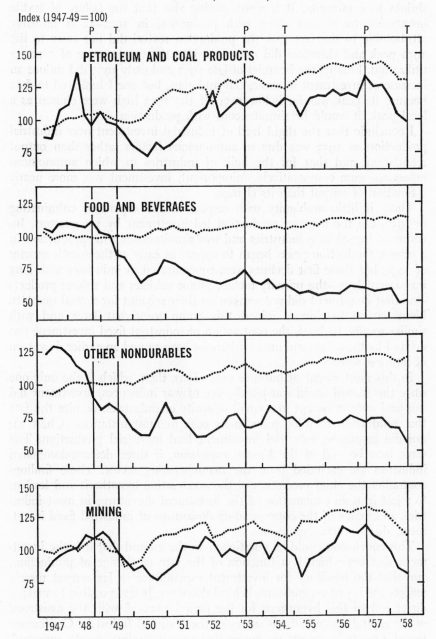

Index (1947-49=100)

from the total, the aggregate investment of the remaining 13 industries lags their aggregate production, and the proportion of investment leaders shrinks to a minority. It is worth noting also that the failure of textile investment to recover along with production in 1952–53 is probably attributable to the fact that the production revival did not carry to the 1950 peak and therefore did not move into the upper range of capacity utilization. Finally, the boomlet of late 1952 and early 1953 did induce an increase of investment in stone, clay and glass, but one I hesitated to date because its peak was far below 1951. If the 1953 high were chosen as a local peak, it would be simultaneous with production.

I conclude that the slight lead of industrial investment over industrial production in 1953 was due to autonomous factors rather than output retardation, and that for the bulk of industries in which autonomous influences were comparatively unimportant, investment was more nearly a function of output than its change.

There is little ambiguity with respect to the expansion culminating in 1957. On the average, production led investment by 1.5 quarters. Investment lagged in 9 industries and was simultaneous with production in 4 others. Production peaks began to appear as early as the fourth quarter of 1955, but these first declines were concentrated in industries with long investment lags—the primary metals, motor vehicles and rubber products —so that investment did not weaken on their account for several quarters. Nonelectrical machinery joined this group somewhat later and with similar results. In brief, the contraction of industrial fixed investment was delayed by these lags and might otherwise have caused an earlier downturn of business activity.

In this most recent of business expansions, then, which is the only one since the second world war largely free of war influences, investment did not lead output, except in a small minority of industries, despite the fact that production retarded prior to its peak in most instances (Chart 2); nor did aggregate industrial investment lead industrial production. The same may be said of the Korean expansion, if three defense-dominated industries are excluded from the manufacturing sector. These findings contradict the chief prediction of the acceleration hypothesis and lead us to reject it as an explanation of the investment downturns in most industries, and hence of the corresponding downturns of industrial fixed investment, during these expansions.

This conclusion could be questioned on the ground that it is the investment *decision* which is a function of the rate of change of production, and that the tendency for investment expenditure to lag output merely reflects the lag of expenditures behind decisions. It was possible to make a direct test of this hypothesis for the period 1955–58 with the assistance of the capital appropriations survey of the National Industrial Conference Board. Quarterly reports on appropriations outstanding, newly approved, committed or spent, and canceled, are available for 500 large manufacturing corporations and by major industries [3]. Since appropriations provide the budgetary authority to go ahead with investment projects, they are an ideal index of investment decisions for the present purpose. They measure decisions at a point where they are comparatively firm, just one stage before contracts are let or orders placed.

The turning points of new appropriations and of appropriation backlogs for these large corporations were compared with the corresponding Federal Reserve indexes of production. For all 500 companies, new approvals reached a peak in the second quarter of 1956, to be followed by appropriation backlogs (end of quarter) in the first quarter of 1957 and by capital expenditures in the third.[14] Thus new approvals led the index of manufacturing production, whereas appropriation backlogs synchronized with it. Evidently it is important to decide which concept of appropriations is the best measure of planned investment. Reflection indicates that the logical choice is the backlog of unexpired appropriations. This is because it is the relation of new approvals to expiring appropriations, rather than the trend of new approvals, which counts for future expenditures. In the early months of an investment boom, new approvals run far ahead of current commitments or expenditures, and the backlog mounts. Later, when new approvals begin to decline, it is not necessarily because firms wish to reduce capital outlays: they may merely be curbing the rate of increase of projected expenditures. As long as new approvals (net of cancellations) exceed current commitments or expenditures, the backlog of uncommitted or unspent appropriations will continue to rise, and this means that the amount of planned (currently budgeted) investment is still increasing. As a corollary, the pattern of new expenditures resembles that of backlogs instead of new approvals.

Comparable data on production and appropriations are available for 10 of the industries we have examined.[15] New appropriations led production by from one to 4 quarters in 4 industries, were coincident in 3, and lagged one or 2 quarters in the 3 remaining cases. Appropriations backlogs led in only two industries (by one and 2 quarters), were coincident in 4, and lagged in 4, by intervals of two to 4 quarters. Thus investment decisions as well as expenditures tend to lag or synchronize with output.

II. *Role of Inventory Investment in Business Downturns*

The technological rationale of the acceleration principle is weaker for inventory than for plant investment, but perhaps the economic compulsion to maintain a fairly rigid ratio of capital to output is stronger in the

---

[14] When measured in current dollars, the peak in the SEC-OBE estimate of new plant and equipment expenditure by manufacturers also occurs in the third quarter of 1957.

[15] Primary iron and steel; primary nonferrous metals; electrical machinery; nonelectrical machinery; stone, clay and glass; petroleum and coal products; textile mill products; rubber products; paper and allied products; and chemicals and allied products. I adjusted the appropriations data for seasonal variation. However, comparison of unadjusted production and appropriations yields the same timing results.

case of stocks; and in any event, a constant marginal relationship between sales changes and inventory investment is sufficient to cause inventory cycles [9] [11]. Inventory investment (net change in inventories), moreover, is intrinsically short-run and quickly adaptable to changing conditions of production and sale. It is quite possible, therefore, that accelerator-induced swings of inventory investment may cause business downturns.

Thus far we have studied retardation and diffusion only on the level of industrial production. Now it is conceivable that production diffusion is due to acceleration effects stemming from retardations or accelerations of final demand. Suppose it were true, for example, that when retail sales retarded, this was not because sales of some goods were falling, but because sales of all types were rising more slowly than before. Assume also that retailers reduced orders for goods for stock when sales decelerated, producing first a retardation and eventually a downturn of total orders for stock and for sale even though sales were still rising. To cap it all, assume that the same thing occurred at each level of distribution and production—that because of accelerator-induced inventory effects, the orders by wholesalers from manufacturers first retarded and then led their own sales downward; and that orders placed by manufacturers of finished consumer goods for manufactured materials or components first retarded and then led their own production, etc., etc. We would then observe a sequence of production declines, and over time an increasing proportion of contracting industries, as a result of a sustained general retardation of retail sales unaccompanied by specific declines.[16]

Whereas the foregoing sequence is possible, the weight of empirical evidence goes against it. Ruth P. Mack's thorough-going case study of demand propagation showed that the cycles in production of hides, leather and shoes tended to be synchronous with retail shoe sales, and gave no sign of progressively earlier timing at the "earlier" stages of processing [7]. Other evidence, admittedly incomplete because of the paucity of matched data for the various stages of production and sale of specific final products, suggests that manufacturers' buying does not lead orders received by them for their own goods [8]. Since orders may be transmitted rapidly through the vertical market structure, the likely result will be approximately synchronous production cycles on the earlier levels, but cycles which might or might not lead retail sales, depending on whether and by how long retailers' orders lead retail sales.[17] However, because

---

[16] It is necessary to assume that there is a period of retardation not only of sales, but also of purchase orders at each stage. This is because the orders of one stage are the sales, often with a lag, of the next. Suppose retail sales retarded, and as a result, retailers' orders retarded for, say, 4 months and then fell. This would mean that wholesale trade would be retarded for 4 months, and the orders of wholesalers to manufacturers could then retard for, say, 3 months before falling, etc. If retail retardation caused an immediate decline of purchase orders, in contrast, wholesalers' and manufacturers' orders would drop concomitantly and there would be no opportunity for prior turns at the earlier stages of production and sale.

[17] New orders by department stores sometimes lead their sales by several months, although they usually are synchronous [8, pp. 24-26].

lags of manufacturing production behind incoming orders will tend to cancel leads of purchase orders by retailers over retail sales should the latter occur, factory sales and production may well synchronize rather closely with retail sales [8, pp. 47-48].

It appears improbable, therefore, that an increasing proportion of manufacturing industries would experience production declines unless there were also an increasing percentage of final products experiencing sales reductions. This judgment is supported broadly, though not conclusively, by the data contained in Chart 3. Indexes of total retail sales and of manufacturing sales and production are included in the top half of the chart. Below them appear corresponding diffusion indexes and rates of change, smoothed by moving averages to suppress random variations. The data are defective in two respects for our purposes. Most serious is the fact that the breakdown of industries underlying the diffusion indexes of manufacturing sales and production differs considerably from the breakdown of retail sales by type of store.[18] Second, retail sales measure only one category of final demand which impinges on manufacturing industry.

Despite these deficiencies, the data tell a coherent story. First, comparison of retail sales with their diffusion index reveals the expected correlation between rate of change and extent of diffusion. This is enough to show that even when it comes to final demand, aggregative retardation manifests itself in individual declines as well as retardations. Particular products or lines will usually retard before reversing, but the leads are apt to be short, and it may be just as well to neglect them when it comes to generalizing about the relationships among sales retardation, inventory adjustments, and purchase orders by retailers in the aggregate—although this is more in the nature of hypothesis than conclusion. The close correlation between retardation and diffusion of retail sales shows that production diffusion is not a consequence merely of individual decelerations in retail markets, but it does not exclude the possibility that acceleration effects are present as well, causing brief leads of purchase orders over sales of individual items or lines.

Second, it is readily apparent that manufacturing sales and production move in tandem, although sales are more subject than output to random variations. Especially notable is the fact that the turning points are virtually synchronous, with sales either leading by one month or coincident with production on four of the five cyclical turns. Approximate synchro-

---

[18] The components for the diffusion index of retail sales include motor vehicle dealers; tire, battery and accessory dealers; furniture and home-furnishings stores; household-appliance and radio stores; lumber and building-materials dealers; hardware stores; apparel stores; drug and proprietary stores; eating and drinking places; grocery stores; general merchandise stores; and liquor stores. The industries included in the diffusion indexes of manufacturing sales and production are primary metals; fabricated metals; machinery; transportation equipment; lumber and furniture; stone, clay and glass; food and beverages; tobacco; textiles; paper; chemicals; petroleum and coal products; and rubber. I have not included the heterogenous groupings of "other" durables and nondurables in the computations.

CHART 3.—RETAIL AND MANUFACTURERS' SALES AND MANUFACTURERS' PRODUCTION, TOTALS, MONTHLY CHANGES, AND DIFFUSION INDEXES, SEASONALLY ADJUSTED, MONTHLY, 1949–1958

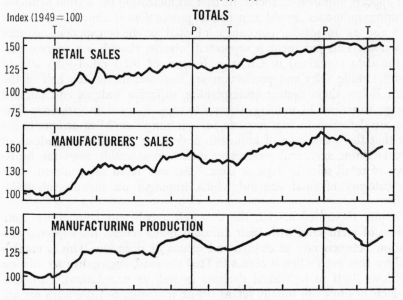

Index (1949=100)

TOTALS

RETAIL SALES

MANUFACTURERS' SALES

MANUFACTURING PRODUCTION

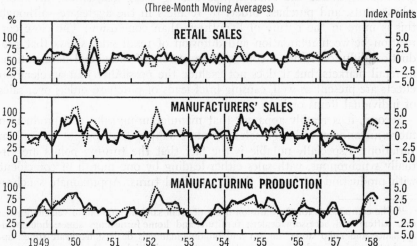

DIFFUSION INDEXES (——) and MONTHLY CHANGES (·······)
(Three-Month Moving Averages)

%   Index Points

RETAIL SALES

MANUFACTURERS' SALES

MANUFACTURING PRODUCTION

1949   '50   '51   '52   '53   '54   '55   '56   '57   '58

Vertical lines indicate peaks and troughs of manufacturing production.
Sources: Department of Commerce and Federal Reserve Bank.

nization is also the rule for individual industries, to judge from the diffusion indexes. These curves bear the expected relationships to the rates of change of their respective aggregates.[19] More to the point, they are also correlated with one another, just as one would predict if production were a positive, nearly synchronous function of sales in each industry.[20] Because of the nature of the data, each "industry" may embrace separate stages of production and sale, but for reasons already cited, the several stages probably are closely synchronized.

It is a matter of some importance that sales and production are approximately synchronous for the individual industries. Lloyd Metzler [9] and Ragnar Nurkse [11] have shown that efforts by businessmen to adjust inventories in proportion to recent changes in sales may cause aggregate production to decline simultaneously with aggregate sales and realized inventory investment. But the coincident downturn of sales and production in these models results from the (immediate acting) feedback of production income on effective demand. When production and sales decline simultaneously in a particular industry, however, it can scarcely be argued that its own production cutback induced its own sales decline. This would make no difference if all industries declined together, but as has been emphasized throughout this paper, the downturn of aggregate output is preceded by a fairly prolonged period of retardation during which there is a growing accumulation of individual production declines. Since production tends to turn with or behind sales in these instances of early decline and while aggregate income is still rising, it would appear that for individual manufacturing industries the simplest explanation is the correct one: namely, that causation runs from sales decline to production downturn.[21]

Manufacturers' inventory investment could, nevertheless, contribute to a downturn of business activity through its feedback effects on national income, without necessarily causing manufacturing output to decline prior to manufacturing sales in any industry or in the aggregate. First, realized inventory investment may lead production even if the latter is synchronous with sales. Provided the early decrease of inventory investment in a given industry were caused by sales retardation, this would be the accelerator at work. If the industry bulked large in total inventory

---

[19] The correlation of sales movements is even closer when the measures of monthly change and diffusion are based on deflated sales.

[20] Inspection of the data for the separate industries confirms that production turns with or shortly after deflated sales in the overwhelming majority of instances.

[21] In many manufacturing industries the advance warning provided by new and unfilled orders will minimize the tendency for production to lag sales. Metzler's assumption that current production decisions are based on past levels and rates of changes of sales is perhaps more applicable to retailers than manufacturers, since retailers do not usually possess advance information about their own sales. The explanation offered by Mack and Zarnowitz [8] of the lead of retailers' orders over retail sales on some downturns, incorporates a corrective-order accelerator similar to Metzler's, along with allowance for the influence of short-term market prospects on purchase decisions.

investment, or if investment leads occurred in a sufficient number of industries, manufacturers' inventory investment could decline while manufacturers' sales and production were still on the upgrade. Secondly, the same aggregative result could arise even if realized inventory investment were synchronous with sales in each industry, provided the early decliners were above-average investors (relative to sales). This is analogous to the case of unequal weighting discussed above in connection with fixed investment, and does not involve acceleration effects. Third, manufacturers' realized inventory investment might be coincident with sales in each industry and the aggregate (the case of equal weighting), but factory sales and production might lead national product.

It would be interesting to compare the timing of real inventory investment with sales and production in each industry, but this would be a research project in itself. As for inventory investment in manufacturing as a whole, quarterly changes in the estimated book value of manufacturers' stocks as published by the Department of Commerce, show moderate leads or coincident turns with manufacturing production during the postwar cycles, and it is doubtful that correction for price movements would alter this relationship appreciably. This in turn implies that manufacturers' inventory investment will sometimes lead the business cycle by half a year or more, especially when, as in 1956–57, inventory investment leads manufacturing production and the latter also declines considerably earlier than total business. The important point, however, is that this route takes us right back to demand diffusion, for if aggregate income is retarded by a downslide of inventory investment, the retardation will manifest itself partly in specific declines affecting particular products or industries.

All the same, if the income retardation is due to a reduction of manufacturers' inventory investment, is this not the accelerator in action, at least in situations where realized inventory investment leads sales and production in individual industries? Yes it is, but its role is more limited than usually implied. This sort of inventory effect may contribute indirectly to a general downturn by retarding aggregate income, but it will not in itself cause a decline of aggregate output. If inventory investment falls while production is still rising in an industry, it obviously has not acted directly to decrease production, and its indirect effect is to slow the increase of personal production income and consumer demand, rather than to reduce them.[22] This differs considerably from a situation in which a decision to reduce inventory investment is in itself a decision to decrease production in advance of sales.

Finally, we compare sales of manufacturers with those of retailers. Here are both similarities and differences, as must be expected since manu-

---

[22] This is the case when the reduction of inventory investment is offset by diminished business saving within the manufacturing sector. If the reduction should cause an early decline of demand for raw materials, however, it might decrease production and income in the extractive industries. As far as minerals production is concerned, however, it usually turns with or after manufacturing production.

facturers also sell producer goods and supply government demands. The two series do display similar contours through most of the period, however, amplitudes aside. The major discrepancies are during the Korean war and in 1957. At other times, interestingly enough, retail sales led or were virtually synchronous with those of manufacturers. These tendencies toward parallelism appear also in the indexes of sales diffusion, with retail diffusion synchronous or leading on the turns in 1949, 1953, 1954, and 1958. The reader is reminded that these last indexes differ in composition. Nevertheless, the correlation is consistent with the hypotheses and evidence already considered, and it is difficult to believe that it is an accidental one.

The principal discrepancy occurring during a "normal" period came in 1957, when manufacturing sales and production led retail sales by half a year. This experience should not be taken as verification of the acceleration principle as applied to retail inventory investment, however, if for no other reason than the fact that retail sales *accelerated* to their final peak. What happened was this. As we already know, sales of producer goods began falling early in 1957, primarily because of, and augmenting the spread of, production declines among manufacturing industries many of which dated back a year or more. When retail sales accelerated during the spring and early summer, and retail diffusion therefore increased, correlative increases appeared in manufacturing. These increases among consumer goods were too small to offset fully the declines in other demands, however—partly because retailers did *not* increase their orders enough to maintain stock-sales ratios—so that manufacturing production did move upward, but insufficiently to regain the peak. The closing spurt of retail sales, incidentally, indicates that the main channel by which the early decline of manufacturers' inventory investment could help induce a downturn—that is, by retardation of personal income and consumption—was blocked temporarily by other factors, including increases in government expenditure and net foreign investment during the first half of the year and a rise in the ratio of consumption to disposable income in the third quarter.

Despite the gaps in the evidence presented—the lack of data on diffusion of government demands, the imprecise information on the timing of manufacturers' inventory investment and retailers' orders, and the slender sample of observed cases of vertical synchronization of production and sales for specific products or lines—the tentative conclusion appears warranted that acceleration-induced inventory investment may be a comparatively unimportant initiating (as contrasted with amplifying) factor in business contraction. Its main effect may well be to retard income growth and thereby to augment the spread of specific declines, rather than to cause a direct reduction of aggregate demand. It is certainly consistent with the known facts to assume that the adverse effects of aggregative retardation are due principally to individual declines instead of individual retardations, that sales and production on all market levels tend to be synchronous with sales of the final products from which their demands are derived, and that such departures from synchronous timing as may result from inventory change are small enough to be neglected.

III. *Diffusion, Investment, and Cycles*

Let us now inquire further into the phenomenon of diffusion and its relationship to the level and rate of change of aggregate activity. There are three intriguing questions: Why the positive correlation between diffusion and the rate of change of aggregate activity? What are the implications of that correlation for the theory of investment? For the theory of business fluctuations?

The answer to the first question becomes apparent when one asks whether all individual outputs should be expected to rise or fall in a fixed proportion to real national income. This is obviously absurd, since the structure of demand and supply, and with it the composition of prices and output, is constantly being altered by the differential impact of dynamic factors like technological change, population growth, and shifting tastes. When aggregate money income may rise freely and individual supplies are elastic, most demands and outputs will rise, although some more slowly than others. Once a restriction is placed on the advance of either real or money income, however, it becomes virtually certain that expansion will continue in some directions at the expense of contraction in others.

Suppose a full-employment ceiling is encountered, for example, so that the advance of real national income is limited to the rate made possible by growth of the labor force and man-hour productivity. Firms and industries favored by bright profit prospects because of process or product innovations are unlikely to remain content with such a slow rate of progress, and will doubtless bid vigorously for resources. And, of course, on the side of final demand, households, businesses and governments are apt to diminish some demands in order to augment others within the budget constraint imposed by real income. The result will be that some industries will be squeezed between upward shifting cost curves and more slowly rising or falling demand schedules, and will be forced to curtail production.

Should a monetary ceiling be approached instead of or in addition to one on real income, differential impacts are again to be expected. General credit restraints do not retard all demands evenly, and some will decline as others increase, with corresponding effects on supplying industries owing to specialization in production and the resulting resource immobilities.

Finally, the scope and rate of expansion will be positively correlated even when the latter is unchecked by external constraints. There are two main possibilities: First, individual demands may diminish for reasons unrelated to the level of national income, such as prior errors of business judgment about investment or production, autonomous changes of taste, market saturation after a period of vigorous growth, or special circumstances due perhaps to replacement waves or peculiarities of market structure, as in cobweb situations or the building cycle. If resources are imperfectly mobile, these specific reductions may not be offset immediately by increases elsewhere, with the result that aggregate income will increase more slowly or decline.

Secondly, aggregative retardation may occur independently of external ceilings or individual maladjustments, but with adverse consequences for particular demands all the same. The marginal propensity to consume may decline, for example, retarding aggregate demand relative to income and inducing declines in specific industries. A similar result may follow with a fixed marginal propensity to consume if personal income retards because of a drop of inventory investment. Another possibility which may generate endogenous "free cycle" downturns analogous to those of accelerator-multiplier models, will be discussed presently.

The empirical correlation between industrial diffusion and the rate of change of aggregate activity, then, has a solid rationale in the theory of resource allocation under conditions of disturbance and disequilibrium, of shifting functions and ceaseless change. What are the consequences for investment theory? The most obvious consequence is that the composition of investment matters, in the sense that it affects the behavior of aggregate capital formation. I would like to sketch a conceptual scheme which provides, I believe, a useful framework for the analysis of the interaction between components and aggregate.[23]

The first element of the framework is that "law of industrial growth" which says that individual industries pass through a life cycle of several stages: introduction of the product and a period of vigorous expansion as it wins general acceptance, then slower growth as it nears market saturation, and eventual decline. These phases would occur, I assume, even if national income were stationary, and would have obvious consequences for the composition of demand and production. Since national income itself has a rising trend, however, each industry growth curve will be tilted upward to reflect the increase which would occur even with constant output composition. Now, since the life span of an industry is usually long—at least if it is not defined too narrowly in terms of product —a given segment of its growth curve during a period of say, 5 or 10 years, may be approximated by a straight line of constant percentage increase. The line may tilt up or down depending on the growth stage, and represents the prevailing tendency of output due to the combination of specific growth factors affecting the industry and the secular uptrend of national income.

Next, make gross investment a positive function of level of output. This means that industries with strongly rising production tendencies during our 5 to 10 year period, will have correspondingly rapid investment

---

[23] In doing this, I will merely be restating propositions made familiar by a long line of students of the cycle, including Schumpeter, Mitchell, Robertson, Burns, Hansen, Haberler, Fellner, and Gordon.

uptrends. It may be objected that rapid capacity growth could be achieved with a constant, though large, annual flow of net investment. If we measure our production growth tendencies at constant percentage rates, however, this implies that steady growth would require an increasing amount of net investment per year: increasing, in fact, at the same percentage rate as production if capacity were always adjusted optimally to output.[24] Additionally, replacement demand will increase over time in growing industries, although not in constant proportion to output if growth occurred at different rates in previous decades. Remember, these are not rigid relationships we are assuming, but merely positive correlations between average growth rates of production and investment.

Actual growth will not, of course, occur steadily. National income will fluctuate, and with it production in each industry, according to its price and income elasticities. And, as noted earlier, there will be factors which foster independent fluctuations specific to certain industries. Nor will investment proceed steadily, for it varies with output during the short run as well as over the decade. Notice that our formulation simultaneously embraces those autonomous investment determinants which underlie industry growth curves, and the tendency for movements of national income to induce fluctuations of investment by influencing individual outputs. What is left out, because imperfectly reflected in output if at all, is autonomous investment of the sporadic variety—the defense investment of the Korean war is a pertinent example—and the influence of cost and availability of external funds.

Now we are in a better position to understand the implications for investment of the correlation between retardation and diffusion. When national output rises more slowly, it is primarily because more industries are contracting than before, and these decreases spell trouble for the affected firms—they are members of "sick" industries or of industries in late stages of growth, or they are experiencing temporary difficulties due to special factors. In any event, this is more serious than if all industries were retarded evenly and none declined. In that case, profits would continue to rise everywhere, unless margins narrowed sufficiently to offset rising outputs, whereas when individual declines occur profits are virtually certain to fall in the distressed sectors. But a situation where production and profits are falling is more detrimental to investment than one in which output is merely retarded. On the financial side of the investment decision, retained profits are an important source of investment funds. Expected returns from investment are doubtless sensitive to current profits,

---

[24] The postulated relation between production and investment "trends" amounts to a loose application of the acceleration principle to the case of long-term adjustment of capacity to ouput, but without the implication that investment fluctuates with the rate of change of output in the short run. Notice that under the assumed trend conditions, net investment would always be in fixed proportion to both the level of output and its absolute change. The factor of proportionality in the latter case would be the accelerator coefficient, and in the former, the product of the accelerator coefficient and the growth rate of output.

moreover, especially when the latter are declining during a period of general business expansion and are therefore symptomatic of weakness within the industry.

As far as the declining industries are concerned, then, investment is likely to fall, whereas it would probably continue to rise if output were merely retarded. But will not investment be enough higher in the expanding industries by virtue of the fact that their outputs and perhaps their profits can now increase more than otherwise, to compensate the decreased investment of the distressed sectors? This sort of offsetting certainly does occur, particularly when the specific declines are not an independent cause of the retardation of aggregate income but are themselves induced by expansions in other industries within a given over-all constraint. As we shall see, however, there are several reasons why the offsetting is unlikely to persist indefinitely. This brings us to the last question: How does our conception of the typical investment-output relationship in individual industries fit into the theory of business fluctuations? First, as regards the upper turning point, how can general contraction set in if investment usually synchronizes with production or lags it in each industry? There are several possibilities.

For one, investment may lead output in some industries and on some occasions even if it does not do so typically. Financial constraints may prompt investment leads, for instance, as may autonomous political or military events. And, of course, some categories of final demand, not ordinarily classified as investment, are partly independent of real income and may decline autonomously. Government expenditures and consumer demands for durables are the principal examples. Now, in all these cases, the specific "investment" declines may readily be absorbed if other demands are rising sufficiently, but if they occur at a time when the offsetting movements of investment in the expanding and contracting sectors of the economy are approximately balanced, it may require only one individual lead to cause a general downturn.

It must be emphasized in connection with the role of income-autonomous demands in the downturn, that my empirical analysis of fixed investment was confined to manufacturing and mining industries: that is, it dealt with industries producing goods instead of services. This is important because services cannot be stockpiled by buyers and must be produced as consumed, with the result that production of marketed services often continues to increase (at a retarded rate) during mild contractions of national income. Yet fixed investment in these industries —public utilities, housing, trade and the like—often fluctuates with the business cycle. Evidently in such cases, investment is linked only loosely to sales or production in the short run, and it is certainly conceivable that investment declines in these industries are caused by production retardations via the accelerator mechanism. Notice, however, that even if such accelerator-induced declines do occur, they will not initiate a general downturn unless they come during the expansion phase of the business cycle. Residential construction did lead on the downturns in 1948 and 1956–57, but these declines were clearly caused by financial constraints rather than an excess supply of housing. Investment by public utilities, moreover, has either failed to fall or has lagged on the three postwar downturns. Of course, three instances do not make a timeless generalization, and it is necessary to remember that when excess capacity does develop in the housing market, the condition may persist for many years, and that business contractions are apt to be especially severe during the long downswings in building. But this is an example of a maladjustment which may develop in a particular industry independently of the level or rate of change of national income, and has little bearing on the processes by which business expansions are regularly reversed, or on the accelerator as a general theory of short-term investment demand.

Closely related to the foregoing point is our second observation, that a downturn may be delayed as well as precipitated by specific income-autonomous demands. This occurred in 1957, for example, when industrial investment lagged industrial production and yet led the business cycle,[25] because offset temporarily by autonomous increases in other sectors, which then ceased to rise or fell before they could feed back to the industrial sector.

Third, investment inequalities among industries may cause a downturn of aggregate investment before aggregate production even when there are no individual investment leads. Actually, it is more likely that inequalities will delay the investment decline, as in manufacturing industry during 1956–57. This is because unequal lags can act only in the direction of greater or lesser delay, whereas there is no systematic reason why capital-intensive industries should be the first to decline.

Fourth, the composition of the aggregate may matter in the sense that individual investment demands are partly a function of the extent of diffusion. This hypothesis was advanced by Burns. "The rise in construction and financing costs during an expansion impinges broadly on the investing class and would check the investment boom sooner or later even if prosperity diffused itself uniformly over the economic community. But this does not happen, and the uneven spread of expansion is our second vital fact" [2, p. 22]. As the proportion of firms experiencing rising profits begins to shrink, firms become more hesitant about investing *now*: "The firms whose fortunes are waning are likely to be among the first to reduce investment expenditure, and their curtailments spread doubt among others whose profits are still rising, but many of which have come to feel that investment costs will be reduced before long from the abnormal level to which they have been pushed by prosperity" [2, p. 22].

Here, diffusion becomes an expectational variable affecting the timing of investment expenditure and capable of causing an endogenous down-

---

[25] The peak of industrial production came in the first quarter, that of industrial investment in the first or second (see fn. 7), and the business peak in the third.

turn. It could do this even in the absence of resource immobilities and external constraints on aggregate activity. If investment in each industry is a function of general diffusion as well as its own output; if the individual production tendencies imply that some will be forced into declines because others expand more rapidly than aggregate income; and if the average propensity to consume is constant at less than one, aggregate income will turn down endogenously, provided the individual investment sum to less than the average propensity to save when diffusion falls below some critical value. Burns refers to profits diffusion, but the correlation with output diffusion is so close that one may stand for the other. The major difference that could arise would be a price-cost squeeze which narrowed margins sufficiently to offset stable or rising outputs and caused profits to lead production.

Abramovitz has directed my attention to a fifth way in which the spread of individual declines may act to depress aggregate investment. When the proportion of firms enjoying increasing profits diminishes, this reacts adversely on the prices of the stocks of unfortunate firms on the market and sympathetically on all share prices. The uncertainty and pessimism caused by the accumulating declines, may depress the market while total profits are still rising. Hence it becomes more difficult to market new issues on favorable terms, and investment plans may be postponed even by firms which are still prospering.

I have concentrated my attention on the downturn, since this is where the relationship between diffusion and the rate of change of aggregate activity is most critical for cycle theory. The apparatus I have sketched is also useful for the study of contraction and recovery, however, and of the relation between growth and stability. Just as the accelerator has pre-empted attention in cycle theory in recent years, so also has it, or its cousin the capacity principle, in growth theory. Earlier writers, such as Schumpeter, Robertson and Hansen not only got closer to those mainsprings of growth—innovation and population—which are usually autonomous in the modern models, but they also merged more intimately the determinants of growth and fluctuation. For them, business cycles were the necessary consequence of industrial progress, and the dispersion which occurred among industries during a cycle was critical to its development. Whether contractions are long or short, deep or shallow, depends partly on the influence of population, technology and other income-autonomous factors as they are expressed in the prevailing production and investment tendencies of the industries within the economy, and partly on the response of spending units to changes of income, capacity utilization, financial conditions, and prices. The autonomous factors deserve more attention than they have received of late, and industrial disaggregation is one of the most promising lines of attack.[26]

---

[26] On this subject, see [5] and the works cited there. The topic is treated more extensively in my forthcoming Brookings study of the growth and stability of the postwar economy.

References

1. A. F. BURNS, "New Facts on Business Cycles," *30th Annual Report of the National Bureau of Economic Research*, 1950, reprinted in his *The Frontiers of Economic Knowledge*, New York 1954, pp. 107-34.
2. ——, "Hicks and the Real Cycle," *Jour. Pol. Econ.*, Feb. 1952, 60, 1-24. Reprinted in *The Frontiers of Economic Knowledge*, New York 1954, pp. 236-67.
3. M. COHEN and M. R. GAINSBRUGH, "Capital Appropriations: A Leveling Out?" *Conference Board Bus. Record*, Sept. 1958, 15, 345-58.
4. B. G. HICKMAN, "An Experiment With Weighted Indexes of Cyclical Diffusion," *Jour. Am. Stat. Assoc.*, Mar. 1958, 53, 39-53.
5. ——, "Postwar Cyclical Experience and Economic Stability," *Am. Econ. Rev.*, Papers and Proceedings, May 1958, 48, 117-34.
6. J. R. HICKS, *A Contribution to the Theory of the Trade Cycle*. London 1950.
7. R. P. MACK, *Consumption and Business Fluctuations*. New York 1956.
8. —— and V. ZARNOWITZ, "Cause and Consequence of Changes in Retailers' Buying," *Am. Econ. Rev.*, Mar. 1958, 48, 18-49.
9. L. A. METZLER, "The Nature and Stability of Inventory Cycles," *Rev. Econ. Stat.*, Aug. 1941, 23, 113-29.
10. G. H. MOORE, *Statistical Indicators of Cyclical Revivals and Recessions*, Nat. Bur. of Econ. Research Occas. Paper 31. New York 1950.
11. R. NURKSE, "The Cyclical Pattern of Inventory Investment," *Quart. Jour. Econ.*, Aug. 1952, 66, 385-408.
12. P. A. SAMUELSON, "Interactions Between the Multiplier Analysis and the Principle of Acceleration," *Rev. Econ. Stat.*, May 1939, 21, 75-78; reprinted in *Readings in Business Cycle Theory*, Philadelphia 1944, pp. 261-69.
13. Office of Defense Mobilization, *Expansion Progress, Projects Under Certificates of Necessity*, Washington, Apr. 1955.

❧ ❀ ❧

FOR FURTHER READING

The reader who has grasped the fundamental concepts developed by our authors can do no better than to undertake a complete reading of R. F. Harrod, *The Trade Cycle* (Oxford: Clarendon Press, 1936) and *Towards a Dynamic Economics* (London: Macmillan, 1948); J. R. Hicks, A *Contribution to the Theory of the Trade Cycle* (Oxford: Clarendon Press, 1950); and J. S. Duesenberry, *Business Cycles and Economic Growth* (New York: McGraw-Hill, 1958). These will require patient study and, on occasion, purposeful rereading. The sequence, however, affords an excellent picture of the development in accelerator-multiplier models since the middle 1930's.

Numerous articles reflect the growing interest, mostly post–World War II, in this line of investigation. A few citations will suffice: R. F. Kahn, "The Relation of Home Investment to Unemployment," *Economic Journal*, Vol. XLI, No. 162 (June, 1931); Simon Kuznets, "Relations Between Capital Goods and Finished Products in the Business Cycle," *Economic Essays in Honour of Wesley Clair Mitchell* (New York: Columbia University Press, 1935); A. F. Burns, "Hicks and the Real Cycle," *Journal of Political Economy*, Vol. LX, No. 1 (February, 1952); Moses Abramovitz, "Influence of Inventory Investment in Business Cycles," *Conference on Business Cycles* (New York: National Bureau of Economic Research, 1951); Lloyd A. Metzler, "Business Cycles and the Modern Theory of Employment," *American Economic Review*, Vol. XXXVI, No. 3 (June, 1946); Joan Robinson, "Mr. Harrod's Dynamics," *Economic Journal*, Vol. LIX, No. 233 (March, 1949); Ruth Mack, "The Direction of Change in Income and the Consumption Function," *Review of Economics and Statistics*, Vol. XXX, No. 4 (November, 1948); S. C. Tsiang, "Accelerator,

Theory of The Firm, and the Business Cycle," *Quarterly Journal of Economics*, Vol. LXV, No. 3 (August, 1951); A. D. Knox, "The Acceleration Principle and the Theory of Investment," *American Economic Review* (June, 1953); Gardner Ackley, "The Multiplier Time Period," *American Economic Review*, Vol. XLI, No. 3 (June, 1951).

For less technical summaries of the accelerator–multiplier principles and interactions, see: G. Haberler, *Prosperity and Depression* (Geneva: League of Nations, 1937), pp. 85-105; Maurice W. Lee, *Economic Fluctuations— Growth and Stability* (Homewood, Ill.: Richard D. Irwin, 1959), pp. 350-394; R. A. Gordon, *Business Fluctuations* (New York: Harper & Brothers, 1952), chaps. 5, 6, 12, and 13; Carl A. Dauten, *Business Fluctuations and Forecasting* (New York: South-Western Publishing Company, 1954), pp. 285-290, 310-327.

SECTION C

Investment
Theories

INTRODUCTION

It seems safe to say that among all the forces making for cyclical behavior, investment is the most important. The critical investment sector generates cycles, particularly the more severe ones. For example, the sharpest recession since the end of World War II is generally agreed to have occurred in 1957–58. Over that two-year period, real gross national product declined by about 1½ per cent, but outlays for plant and equipment fell roughly 16 per cent, as did total private investment outlays. Investment includes such activities as the construction of homes, office buildings, shopping centers, machinery and equipment, factory building, and inventories— quite a list.

Why, then, is investment so important for business fluctuations? Simply put, investment is lumpy—it comes in large chunks like a factory building, an electric generator, or an assembly line. Investment decisions have a long-time horizon, and once begun, are changed with great difficulty and at considerable expense. The production period of investment goods is a long one, measured in terms of months, or even years. While this investment is going on, incomes are raised without concomitant increases in finished goods. When the investment is completed, new goods and services pour onto the market, but the incomes generated by the act of investment itself stop. It is clear that this set of circumstances can result in cycles.

Yet of all the theoretical explanations of the business cycle, those relating to investment have been the most inadequate. One reason for this is the inability, thus far, of the econometrician and statistician to develop quantitative relationships which explain past performance and predict future behavior, even though a number of attempts have been made. At present, business predictions utilize surveys of business spending plans. For example, the econometric model developed at the University of Michigan contains a number of equations for various aspects of the economy, but in making forecasts for the next year, the model builders invariably rely upon McGraw-Hill's annual survey of capital budgets. Although this survey and others—in particular the Department of Commerce and Securities and Exchange Commission reports on planned business outlays for plant and equipment—have proved helpful in forecasting investment expenditures, the surveys are themselves occasionally subject to cyclical influences. To illustrate: in a period of rising business activity, a survey of next year's spending taken in the fall of the previous year will be exceeded by one taken in the winter, and this, in turn, will be exceeded by one taken in the spring of the year in question. Putting it another way, the surveys mirror the optimism or pessimism generated by the swings of the cycle. Nevertheless, if properly interpreted, they do improve the estimates of key variables in econometric forecasting and contribute to our understanding of the investment process.

The search for a better theoretical explanation of investment cycles will continue. Most encouraging in recent years has been the realization that investment can be treated formally as a variant of the broad problem of stocks and flows. The notion of capital stock, the relationship of capital stock to output, and the disaggregation of capital stock for purposes of analysis—all offer promise. In the context of renewed emphasis on theories of growth (Part IV), the concept of capital stock has a primary role. Here lies the promise of a more satisfactory theory of investment in business cycles. An analytical device of this sort would offer a framework for statistical and econometric relationships, which would also be extremely desirable in longer-range projections, say for the next decade, where it helps little to ask others what they intend to do. Only an analysis of investment in terms of capital stock will make that possible.

The Role of Investment[*]

ALVIN H. HANSEN[†]

Editors' Note

Alvin H. Hansen (1887–   ), one of America's leading economists, has long been interested in business cycles and his name is indelibly linked in the history books with the secular stagnation controversy of the 1930's. As the leading American disciple of John Maynard Keynes, he has had an extensive influence on both the academic community and public policy makers. Through his leading student, Paul Samuelson (an early and continuing adviser to President Kennedy), through the members of the Kennedy Council of Economic Advisers, and through his students in all parts of the executive branch of the federal government, Hansen's ideas are now being put into practice.

The role of investment has always been prominent in Hansen's thinking. That is why he pays particular attention to the work of Tugan-Baranowsky, who held that fluctuations in the rate of investment dominate and control the cycle, whereas saving and income are passive factors. But what is unexplained is the reasons for these fluctuations. The "pull" of the economy on investment is the main contribution of Spiethoff. He highlights the investment vacuum at the start of the business recovery and the investment opportunities which are the key to the investment boom. Fulfilling the investment needs provided by new territories and new opportunities in fixed investment results in a "stormy demand." The process of saturation follows and the cycle repeats itself, with new opportunities reappearing at a later date. Schumpeter's innovator, also, helps to explain

* Reprinted from *Business Cycles and National Income* by Alvin H. Hansen. By permission of W. W. Norton & Company, Inc. Copyright 1951 by W. W. Norton & Company, Inc.

† After completing graduate work at the University of Wisconsin (A.M. 1915, Ph.D. 1918), Hansen taught at the Universities of Wisconsin, Brown, and Minnesota before joining the Harvard faculty in 1937. He served as economist with the U.S. Department of State (1934–35) and was a special economic adviser to the Federal Reserve Board in 1940–45. In 1938, he was elected to the presidency of the American Economic Association.

the fluctuations in investment. The innovator changes permanently the production function and this requires a lot of fixed investment. Innovations cluster and produce cycles thereby, because the few new ideas attract a great following. These "herdlike" movements result in cumulative investment booms. The recession, in Schumpeter's view, is the period of absorption of all the previously introduced innovations.

Although these authors by themselves have not made the definitive analysis of investment, they all focus on its exogenous or autonomous character. This also explains why to date there have been no satisfactory statistical explanations of spending on capital goods and why so much reliance is currently placed on surveys of business plans for prospective plant and equipment outlays.

Michel Tugan-Baranowsky (1865–1919)[1]

🌿 We begin first with Tugan-Baranowsky's interesting analysis of the different theories of crises up to the end of the nineteenth century. This will serve not only as an introduction to Tugan-Baranowsky's own theory, but also as a supplement to the preceding three chapters, in which we have surveyed the early conceptions and also the development of business-cycle theory in England from Lauderdale to Marshall. Tugan-Baranowsky's summary is particularly to be welcomed since, except for his treatment of Jevons, his discussion relates to the early continental theories, and not to the early English theories which we have considered in the preceding chapters.

Tugan-Baranowsky classified all theories into three groups: (1) the theories of production (Jevons); (2) the theories of exchange, credit, and monetary circulation (de Laveleye, Juglar); and (3) the theories of distribution of income (Sismondi, Rodbertus). All these are efforts to explain that enigmatic phenomenon—the cyclical character of industrial life, the successive phases of upswing and depression. But so far, says Tugan-Baranowsky, economic science has not been able to offer a solution for this difficult problem.

JEVONS AND THE ROLE OF HARVESTS[2]

Many economists have sought to show that the periodic industrial crises spring from periodic fluctuations of crops. In fact, however, the industrial

[1] In this entire section on Tugan-Baranowsky, I have endeavored to give a precise and carefully paraphrased summary of his *Les Crises industrielles en Angleterre* (1913), especially Part II, Chapters II and III.

[2] W. S. Jevons, *Investigations in Currency and Finance*, Macmillan & Co., Ltd., London, 1884.

cycle is regulated, says Tugan-Baranowsky, by its own laws, which are quite independent of harvest movements.

The ingenious theory of Jevons—relating the periodicity of crises to the periodicity of sun spots—is not supported, in Tugan-Baranowsky's view, by the facts. In order to get his neat periodicity figures, Jevons is obliged to resort to forced interpretations. He omits certain crises altogether, and includes doubtful ones. In general, the industrial cycle has, Tugan-Baranowsky believes, no exact periodicity. It varies from seven to eleven years. The industrial cycle is not based on astronomical phenomena subject to a rigorous mathematical periodicity. Instead, industrial fluctuations are tied to characteristics inherent in the nature of the economy itself.

EXCHANGE, CREDIT, AND MONETARY CIRCULATION: DE LAVELEYE, JUGLAR

De Laveleye[3] argues that crises are invariably preceded by an export of gold. Other circumstances vary: this one is invariable. Accordingly he concludes that the loss of gold is the true cause of crises. Immediately the reserves of the Bank of England diminish, credit is restricted, alarm spreads through the country, and commodity prices fall.

But, says Tugan-Baranowsky, the change in the balance of payments is a secondary phenomenon which itself needs to be explained. These movements are symptoms of industrial cycles. Moreover, the loss of gold, while preceding violent crises, did not precede the long periods of stagnation which, toward the end of the nineteenth century, characterized English industry.

Juglar,[4] says Tugan-Baranowsky, has the distinction of being the first to demonstrate the high periodicity of industrial fluctuations in England, France, and the United States. After studying the accounts of the Bank of England, the Bank of France, and the leading American banks, Juglar came to the following conclusion: Without interposing any theory or hypothesis, observation of the facts suffices to disclose the law of crises and their periodicity. Epochs of activity, prosperity, and high prices always end in crises, and these are followed by some years of depressed activity and low prices.

Wars, droughts, abuse of credit, excessive issues of bank notes—all these are not able to provoke an industrial crisis if the general economic situation does not warrant it. They may hasten the arrival of a crisis, but only when the economic situation is such that a crisis is inevitable. The industrial crisis does not come abruptly; it is always preceded by a high animation of industry and commerce whose symptoms are so characteristic that it is possible to forecast the approach of a crisis.

Whence comes this regular succession of periods of activity and depres-

---

[3] E. de Laveleye, *Le Marché monetaire et ses crises depuis cinquante ans*, 1865.
[4] Clément Juglar, *Des Crises commerciales*, 1st ed., 1860; 2nd ed., 1889.

sion? Juglar, says Tugan, can find only one primary cause: the periodic fluctuation in commodity prices. The period of prosperity which precedes the crisis is always characterized by high prices. As prices rise, exports become difficult, the balance of payments becomes less favorable, gold flows out. The crisis approaches when the price movement slows down. In a word, the unique cause of the crisis is the cessation of the price rise.

But Juglar's theory does not resolve, says Tugan-Baranowsky, the problem of crises. If one compares it with de Laveleye's one sees that Juglar has indeed moved a step forward. He has shown that the monetary difficulties which signal the approach of the crisis are only secondary phenomena associated with the price movements. But there is no really satisfactory explanation for the factor which Juglar regarded as at the bottom of the problem of crises: the fluctuation of prices.

Tugan's discussion no doubt underrates the contribution made by Juglar. The vast assemblage of data in Juglar's "great book of facts" laid bare successive phases in a recurring movement. Thus Juglar was one of the first to see that the problem is not one of *crises* but one of *cycles*. Moreover, he regarded depression as the inevitable result of the maladjustments of the boom phase of the cycle. In this sense prosperity could be regarded as the unique cause of the depression.[5]

DISTRIBUTION OF INCOME: SISMONDI, RODBERTUS

The third group of theories finds the explanation of crises in the domain of income distribution. Sismondi's[6] theory of markets is at the same time a theory of crises. The cause of the crisis phenomenon is inadequate consumption, due to the poverty of the masses. The market for industrial products is too restricted, compared with the productive capacity of modern industry.

But, says Tugan-Baranowsky, the history of crises contradicts this doctrine. If one accepted this theory, the prosperity which follows each depression would be absolutely incomprehensible. The crisis, and the stagnation which follows, certainly does not enrich the people; it impoverishes them. How, then, after some years of depression, is a revival of prosperity possible? If this theory were correct, the poverty of the people would prevent any expansion of industry. Industrial stagnation would become chronic. Now in fact one observes something quite different—namely, a rapid growth of production, notwithstanding the interruptions caused by periods of depression.

This simple observation, says Tugan-Baranowsky, shows that the theory which finds the cause of industrial crises in the insufficient consumption of the people must be erroneous. According to this principle we should expect to find chronic stagnation, not a periodic recurrence of the cycle.

---

[5] See J. A. Schumpeter, *Business Cycles*, McGraw-Hill Book Company, 1939, p. 139; also *Quarterly Journal of Economics*, February, 1950, p. 149.
[6] Sismondi, *Nouveaux Principes d'Economie Politique*, 2nd edition, 1827.

Put in modern terms, a low propensity to consume might explain continuous underemployment equilibrium, but not cyclical oscillations. Sismondi, as was also true of Lauderdale and Malthus, was trying to explain unemployment and depression, but he offered no explanation of the *cycle*.

To the same group belongs the theory of Rodbertus with his iron law of wages. According to this law, wages are always at the minimum of subsistence, while productivity increases with industrial progress. New techniques augment the output of workers, but the worker continues to receive the same low wage. Thus the *relative share* of the worker falls with the progress of technique.

Logically the theory of Rodbertus,[7] says Tugan-Baranowsky, is well constructed. Unlike Sismondi's it does not consider the *absolute* poverty of the workers as causing the crisis, but rather the fact that the workers' *share* diminishes with technical progress. Thus Rodbertus finds the cause of the crisis, not in an excess of production, but rather in a lack of proportionality in the distribution of the product.

The defect in this theory, according to Tugan-Baranowsky, is that it does not accord with the facts. The iron law of wages does not conform to the cyclical movement of wages, since in fact wages rise in the period of prosperity. Moreover, it is those branches of industry which produce capital goods that suffer the most from crises and depressions, not those which produce consumers' goods for the working classes.

Thus Tugan-Baranowsky concludes that none of the theories examined can explain the cycle; it still remains enigmatic and incomprehensible.

A TURNING POINT IN BUSINESS-CYCLE THEORY

We come now to Tugan's own analysis, which represents a violent break with the past. In one sense there is "nothing new under the sun," at least not in economics. It has been said that there is not a new idea in Adam Smith; yet this book turned economic thinking upside down. In some measure, the same can be said about Tugan-Baranowsky with respect to business-cycle theory. He cut his way through the jungle to a new outlook. He began a new way of thinking about the problem.

The history of crises in England, he begins, reveals a recurrent ebb and flow of economic life. The cycle is long or short according to the concrete economic conditions of each historical period. The cycle is not a phenomenon regulated by a mathematical law. Crises have recurred at intervals of seven to eleven years. The movement is periodic in the sense that there occur successive phases of prosperity and depression which rise and fall like a cycle. The industrial cycle may be conceived of as a law inherent in the very nature of the capitalist economy.

The problem of crises can only be resolved, says Tugan, by leaning on a good theory of markets. Now most representatives of contemporary eco-

---

[7] Tugan-Baranowsky's reference to Rodbertus' principal exposition of his theory is to his "Letters" addressed to Kirchmann.

nomic science, he points out, hold at bottom a warped theory of markets, namely, Say's Law. It is therefore no wonder, he thinks, that economists have found no solution of the business cycle.

There follows then a discussion which runs very much along the same lines as that developed by Malthus. As with Malthus, the analysis suffers from the absence of the concept of the consumption function.

Thanks to the money and credit economy, says Tugan-Baranowsky, all the oscillations of the economy acquire a much greater amplitude. But monetary factors only aggravate the cycle. Money is not the primary cause. The industrial cycle has its roots deep in the very nature of the capitalist economy. The inherent characteristics of the modern economy render the cycle inevitable.

That, however, does not explain why the phases of prosperity and depression succeed each other with such amazing regularity. The history of the industrial cycle, however, gives the answer.

THE ROLE OF IRON AND INSTRUMENTS OF PRODUCTION

The most characteristic feature of these industrial fluctuations, according to Tugan, is the coincidence of the movements of the *price of iron* with the phases of the cycle. The price of iron is invariably high in prosperity and low in depression. The prices of other products oscillate with much less regularity. This indicates a close relation between the *fluctuation in the demand for iron* and the phases of the cycle. The demand for iron rises in the period of prosperity and falls in the period of depression. Now iron is the material used in making the *instruments* of production. One can estimate the demand for the means of production in general by the demand for iron.[8] The expanding phase of the cycle is then characterized by the augmentation of the demand for the means of production, the descending phase by the decline in this demand.

Now the means of production (iron, coal, timber, etc.) are strongly in demand when large additions are made to the fixed capital of the country—railroads, factories, buildings, houses. The phase of prosperity is the period of very active construction, the creation of new industrial enterprises.

A characteristic of many crises is the speculation in real estate. These are the outgrowth of the expansion of fixed capital, but they are symptoms, not causes, of the industrial cycle.

FLUCTUATIONS IN THE OUTPUT OF FIXED CAPITAL

The branches of production which disclose the most violent fluctuations are those which produce fixed capital goods. These fluctuations are reflected in a general rise and fall in economic activity throughout industry. The reason for this is the interdependence of the various branches of industry in the whole economy.

The production of fixed capital creates a demand for other goods. In

---

[8] Cassel's indebtedness to Tugan-Baranowsky is evident here.

order to create new enterprises, it is necessary to procure the primary materials of production, namely consumption goods for the workers. Expansion of output in one branch increases the demand for the products of other industries. Thus in the period of rapid growth in fixed capital accumulation one observes a general augmentation in the demand for goods.

Here, in a general way, is a description of the multiplier process. But lacking the concept of the marginal propensity to consume, Tugan-Baranowsky was not able to make a precise formulation of the problem.

THE SAVING-INVESTMENT ANALYSIS

But why does not the growth of fixed capital proceed steadily, bit by bit, instead of by violent leaps and bounds? The explanation, says Tugan-Baranowsky, must be found in the conditions underlying the accumulation of capital in the modern economic order.

The discussion which follows is highly significant for the development of the saving-investment analysis, but there are nonetheless some important gaps which had to be filled by others. Tugan-Baranowsky, however, started a stream of thinking among Continental economists which, fed from another source (namely, Wicksell), finally emerged in the modern theory perfected by Keynes.

FREE CAPITAL AND PRODUCTIVE REAL CAPITAL

In all rich capitalist countries, says Tugan-Baranowsky, free capital, which is not yet embodied as fixed capital in any branch of industry, rapidly accumulates under the prevailing economic conditions. This capital makes its appearance in the market in the form of disposable capital or loanable funds. It is free capital. The banks are reservoirs into which this disposable capital flows and from which it is distributed as loanable funds. Now one must be careful, he says, not to confuse the accumulation of loanable funds with the growth of productive real capital. The growth of loanable funds (free capital) does not per se imply any accumulation of real capital or any increase in fixed-capital formation. The difference between productive capital and loan capital is clearly seen in the case of government loans. Let us assume, he suggests, that the state places loans for unproductive purposes. The creditors of the state are the capitalists who advance the loanable funds, and they remain as creditors after the funds are spent. The increase of government debt does not augment the real productive capital of the country. Nevertheless, government securities are regarded as capital no less than the securities issued by industrial enterprises which represent real capital.

Thus the accumulation of loanable capital is something entirely different from the growth of real productive capital. The loanable funds can accumulate not only when there goes on an expansion of production but even when production declines. In fact, loanable funds do accumulate, says Tugan-Baranowsky, in such conditions.

In the capitalist society, there are several kinds of incomes which depend very little, or not at all, upon the general movement of the national income. The most fluctuating incomes are the profits of enterpreneurs; next are the earnings of workers. These two fluctuate with the cycle. But some incomes are derived from fixed yields that are quite independent of the various phases of the cycle. Thus, for example, the intrest payments on bonds and mortgages do not vary with prosperity and depression. Income from real estate is often fixed over long periods. All told, the sum total of incomes which do not fluctuate, or flutuate very little with the cycle, constitutes a considerable fraction of the national income. And the fixed-income groups, who gain in purchasing power when prices fall, are often able to augment their current savings. Without doubt, the accumulation of loanable cash funds proceeds with more regularity than the formation of fixed capital. Loanable funds accumulate steadily, but their conversion into productive capital proceeds by leaps.

Many times, in the course of his descriptive analysis of each crisis in English history, Tugan-Baranowsky had occasion to call attention to the considerable accumulation of bank reserves immediately after the end of each crisis. At the same moment the savings deposits of individuals in the banks are increased. This indicates the accumulation of disposable cash funds seeking investment outlets. The low rate of discount which follows a crisis and which persists for some years bears testimony to the superabundance of uninvested funds. In general, the prosperity phase is characterized by a considerable investment of capital (via the transformation of free capital into fixed capital); the depression phase is characterized by an accumulation of loanable, free, mobile capital.[9]

This is so evident, says Tugan-Baranowsky, that a number of economists, especially J. S. Mill, have concluded that the immediate cause of the revival is the low rate of interest; this provokes the speculation in the money market which leads to the ensuing collapse. Mill is perfectly right, says Tugan-Baranowsky, in calling attention to the rapid accumulation of loanable capital after the crisis which causes a low rate of interest and favors the development of speculation. But he completely ignores the more profound factors inherent in an economy using capital goods.

The accumulation of loanable cash funds continues, as we have seen, in all phases of the cycle; but the embodiment of this free capital into the form of productive capital, the investment of the loanable funds in industry, encounters an obstacle. The presence of this obstacle is indubitable. During the stagnation years, the market overflows with loanable funds. In order to transform this capital into productive capital, a certain proportionality in the allotment of disposable capital among the different branches of production is needed. Now in arriving at this proportional distribution, one encounters, in view of the anarchy of the individualistic competitive economy, a great difficulty. The following situation develops: The disposable, loanable cash funds accumulate steadily; they energetically seek investment outlets, but none can be found. Uninvested capital earns no

---

[9] Compare this terminology with Cassel's "disposable capital."

interest. But the larger the accumulation of inactive capital, the greater the pressure to find an outlet into productive investment. On the one side industry is saturated with capital, and on the other the new free capital, daily accumulating, endeavors to force itself into industry. A moment finally arrives when the resistance of industry is vanquished; the loanable funds find outlets here and there and begin to be transformed into productive capital. A new period of prosperity begins.

In the transformation of loanable capital into productive capital, the first step alone is difficult. By reason of the mutual interdependence of all industry, expansion in one direction tends to spread over the whole economy. The loanable funds or disposable capital may take the form of idle deposits in banks, thus representing latent purchasing power. This purchasing power, which accumulates in bad years, exercises no influence on the market for goods, since the loanable capital is not invested. But when for one reason or another an investment outlet is found, then latent purchasing power transforms itself into effective purchasing power. A new productive capital is created which increases the demand both for means of production and for objects of consumption. Industry finds a new market, created by the expansion of production itself, by reason of the expenditure of enormous loanable funds which before had remained inactive in the banks. It matters not, so far as industry is concerned, what is the origin of the unexpected growth of demand. What is important is that the demand grows and grows until it absorbs all the accumulated loanable funds. Prices rise and production expands all along the line. The upswing phase is kept up by the continued creation of productive capital goods.

Some years pass by. The accumulated loanable funds are bit by bit exhausted. Without doubt the expansion of production creates a considerable quantity of new free saving. But the market rapidly absorbs it all, since the entrepreneurs are eager to take advantage of the favorable situation. Each one seeks to get all the capital he can for his enterprise. All capital reserves are used. The extraordinary expansion of credit, so characteristic of this phase of the industrial cycle, is indicative of the intensive investment of capital. The high rate of interest which one observes toward the end of this phase of the cycle is a certain proof of the exhaustion of loanable funds.

Let us pause here and take stock. According to Tugan-Baranowsky, prosperity is ushered in via an expansion of investment. This leads (if we apply modern concepts to Tugan's analysis) to the multiplier process via an induced rise in consumption. But it is the increase in investment which generates prosperity.

Now this analysis turns the tables upside down. Tugan's theory is the opposite of Sismondi's, for example. *Investment* is the prime mover. And when it moves forward, it pulls up with it all other branches of the economy, including the consumption goods industries. Income, in Keynesian language, rises by a multiple of the net increment of investment. This is the doctrine expounded by Tugan-Baranowsky.

And the expansion is financed from three sources: (1) idle balances,

(2) the growth in current savings generated out of the enlarged income, and (3) expansion of bank credit.

The creation of new productive capital comes to an end when the loanable capital is exhausted. Thus the industrial crisis follows the financial crisis. Depression arrives after the creation of productive capital has suffered a decline.

Tugan-Baranowsky refers to the remarkable article by John Mills on credit cycles. But he finds it unsatisfactory. Mills tells only one side of the story—the psychological phenomena which accompany the industrial cycle. He neglects completely the objective causes of the cycle. In the end it is cold objective facts that control, not simply psychological moods of optimism and pessimism. The hour of reckoning comes sooner or later.

THE BOOM AND THE UPPER TURNING POINT

The period of prosperity is generated, according to Tugan-Baranowsky, out of the expenditure of the accumulated loanable funds. Necessarily this backlog of latent purchasing power is eventually used up. During the period of prosperity new fixed capital is created. Production is directed toward the output of iron, machines, tools, construction materials. Finally the new capital is completed—new factories, new houses, new ships, new railroad lines. The demand for all the materials used in the production of fixed capital suffers a decline. Few new industries are started. But the producers of machines, tools, iron, tile, and lumber are not able to withdraw their capital from their enterprises, and with heavy capital investments in plant and equipment, they are under pressure to continue production. There follows a saturation, an overproduction, of the means of production —capital goods of all kinds. This partial overproduction of the instruments of production, by reason of the interdependence of the different branches of industry, results in a general overproduction. Prices fall. A period of general economic decay ensues.

LACK OF PROPORTIONALITY

It is, moreover, evident, he says, that the general decline in the number of new enterprises necessarily causes a derangement in the proportional distribution of the productive forces. The equilibrium of aggregate demand and aggregate supply is shattered. Since the new enterprises create an enlarged demand not only for producers' goods but also for consumers' goods (the multiplier effect) it follows that, once new enterprises fall off, the branches of industry which furnish consumers' goods also suffer a decline in demand no less than those which furnish the means of production. The "overproduction" becomes general.

In Tugan-Baranowsky's somewhat equivocal language, the explanation of the "overproduction" is to be found in the lack of proportionality between the different branches of production.[10] The productive capacity of

[10] Compare with Schumpeter's period of readjustment following a period of rapid innovations. See discussion later in this chapter.

society has outrun the power of consumption. In other words, it is a saving-investment problem. Difficulties arising in the domain of money and credit, says Tugan-Baranowsky, are merely secondary phenomena, which result from the fundamental lack of proportionality in the area of saving and investment. This is clearly what Tugan-Baranowsky is driving at when he speaks of the productive forces outrunning the power of consumption.

Quite apart from the repercussions following a decline in new industries, there is another factor which leads to disproportionality in production. In the prosperity phase, some branches enjoy a greater expansion than others. They offer a rich field for speculation. At the end of the ascending phase of the cycle the proportionality of production is accordingly disturbed, and a new balance can only be restored through a destruction of a part of the capital of those branches of industry which have had an excessive expansion.

Thus a general stagnation follows the upswing, and the cycle passes from the phase of prosperity to the phase of depression. During the depressed phase, disposable or free capital (loanable funds) accumulates; then comes a new period of prosperity during which this "free capital" is spent on fixed capital—and the latent purchasing power becomes activated. Eventually comes the crisis, and we start all over again.

THE ANALOGY OF THE STEAM ENGINE

The working of this mechanism Tugan-Baranowsky compares to the operation of a steam engine. It is the accumulation of loanable capital which plays the role of the steam in the cylinder; when the pressure of the steam against the piston attains a certain force, the piston is set in motion, and is pushed to the end of the cylinder; here the steam escapes and the piston returns to its former position. The accumulated loanable funds operate in the same manner in industry when they reach a certain volume. The funds are set in motion—i.e., expended on fixed capital goods. Once the loanable funds are exhausted, industry returns to its former position. In this manner crises recur periodically.

CONSUMPTION AND INVESTMENT

The capitalist economy is subject to laws inherent in its own inner nature. Common sense is a poor guide toward an understanding of these laws. The capitalist system is highly complex. Each individual member of society is guided by his personal interests. But the collective end result of all these individual volitions, each independent of the other, is something qualitatively different. Here we encounter the logician's "fallacy of composition." What is true for the individual is not necessarily true for the group. The laws of movement of the complex whole are not determined by the volition of individuals, but on the contrary each individual is subject to the laws of the whole. With regard to the cycle, this antinomy arises conspicuously. On the one hand, investment is the only means of satisfying the propensity to save; but on the other hand investment can have no meaning except as the means of supplying the needs of consumers. On a commonsense basis, investment is for the purpose of supplying consumption needs. Yet in reality, in the capitalist economy, the relation between investment and consumption is reversed. In the prosperity phase, it is not an increase in consumption which commands an increase in investment; it is investment which regulates consumption. The phases of the industrial cycle are determined not by the laws of consumption but by the laws of investment.

Thus it is the fluctuations in the rate of investment that dominate and control the cycle; and consumption rises and falls in response to these movements. This is the theory, highly original[11] and essentially novel at the time he was writing, advanced by Tugan-Baranowsky.

A FLUCTUATING RATE OF INVESTMENT VS. A STEADY RATE OF SAVING

Combined with a fairly steady rate of saving from income, Tugan-Baranowsky sees a rather violent fluctuation in the rate of investment. In the prosperity phase, investment outruns current saving, and the difference between the two is filled by (a) the activation of idle balances (dishoarding) and (b) the expansion of bank credit. In the depression phase, investment falls below current saving, and the difference between them "runs to waste" in idle balances (hoarding) and repayment of debt to banks.[12] This is the nature of the cycle as Tugan-Baranowsky sees it. But his theory of investment demand is inadequate, and his explanation of the turning points is unsatisfactory. What is it, specifically, that starts investment on the upswing, and why does it turn down?

With Tugan-Baranowsky, investment is *pushed* up by the action of lenders eagerly seeking financial investment outlets. But this entirely leaves out of account the "pull" which comes from new technological developments and from *growth* in the economy. This is the most serious defect in Tugan-Baranowsky's analysis, and Spiethoff, as we shall soon find, was quick to see it. With respect to the downturn, Tugan's main explanation

---

[11] Keynes, in the *Treatise* (Vol. II, p. 100) says he finds himself in strong sympathy with that school of writers of which Tugan-Baranowsky was "the first and the most original," and especially with the form which the theory takes in the works of Tugan-Baranowsky himself.

Keynes then offers two criticisms (p. 101). The first, which follows Pigou, is, I think, not justified. Contrary to the Pigouvian interpretation, Tugan-Baranowsky's accumulations are purely monetary—idle balances. The second quite rightly touches on a weak link in Tugan-Baranowsky's chain—the role of unequal income distribution in promoting an unsteady rate of expansion.

Not wholly satisfied with Tugan-Baranowsky's treatment, Keynes then points to Schumpeter's important contribution to the theory of fluctuation.

[12] Tugan-Baranowsky's "saving" must be interpreted to mean the same thing as Robertson's saving out of "disposable" (i.e., yesterday's) income. Tugan's theory was the first of those cycle theories (of which Keynes' *Treatise on Money* was a variant) which stress the divergence of investment and saving.

is the exhaustion of idle balances, which, together with the limits to bank credit expansion, forces a curtailment of investment. But there is also the suggestion, inadequately stated, of the temporary exhaustion of investment opportunities, the fall in the marginal efficiency of capital.

Arthur Spiethoff (1873–   )

The great influence of Tugan-Baranowsky's book on the whole course of business-cycle thinking after the turn of the century is revealed in the literature which rapidly appeared, especially the influential writings of Arthur Spiethoff and Gustav Cassel. Spiethoff's early articles carry on almost every page the imprint of Tugan-Baranowsky's analysis. In the case of Cassel, one can go further, and say that the ideas, and often even the forms of expression, come almost *en masse* from Tugan-Baranowsky. It is often said that Cassel's business-cycle theory was derived largely from Spiethoff, and this is indeed more or less true. There is, however, strong internal evidence that however much he may have drawn from Spiethoff, very much of it flowed directly from Tugan-Baranowsky. It is, of course, true that, in the process of reworking the whole subject matter, both Spiethoff and Cassel left the strong imprint of their own forceful and original thinking in the important contributions which they made. In the meantime, however, the fountainhead of this whole stream of thinking— Tugan-Baranowsky—has unfortunately been somewhat neglected.

Spiethoff himself, however, has warm praise for his predecessor. In his "Die Krisentheorien von M. v. Tugan-Baranowsky und L. Pohle"[13] he refers to Tugan-Baranowsky's work as the first scientific monograph on crises. On December 17, 1901, shortly after Tugan-Baranowsky's *Studien zur Theorie und Geschichte der Handelskrisen in England* had appeared in Germany,[14] Spiethoff delivered an address at a meeting of the Political Science Association in Berlin entitled "Vorbemerkungen zu einer Theorie der Überproduktion."[15] This address shows unmistakably how forcefully this new way of thinking about crises and the industrial cycle had captured the imagination of the young man who rapidly became the leading German specialist on business cycles.[16]

FACTORS CAUSING THE UPSWING

As we have already noted, the weakest part of Tugan-Baranowsky's exposition was his analysis of the causes underlying the fluctuations in investment. Why, asks Spiethoff, is there first a period in which large masses of loan capital are piled up without being invested, followed by a period of

---

[13] *Jahrbuch für Gesetzgebung, Verwaltung und Volkswirtschaft*, 1903.

[14] Jena, 1901.

[15] Published in *Jahrbuch für Gesetzgebung, Verwaltung und Volkswirtschaft*, 1902.

[16] Tugan-Baranowsky, in his French edition (p. 277, note), refers to his earlier work as the point of departure for the studies of Spiethoff, Pohle, and others, who, he says, adopted it in whole or in part.

"stormy investment"?[17] And it is with respect to this point that Spiethoff made his most significant contribution.

Spiethoff accepted unreservedly Tugan-Baranowsky's view that the essential character of the industrial cycle is the fluctuation in the rate of investment, and also the conception (so radically different from that of the prevailing underconsumptionists) that investment is the dynamic factor, with consumption passively responding as income rises and falls.

With Spiethoff, prosperity begins in especially hopeful branches in which capital expects unusual profits, and from these there is developed a general impetus. First, existing production plants are brought into full use. There follows the second stage, in which new plants are built. These new plants swallow up a large volume of investment capital and constructional raw materials of different kinds. But while this construction is going on there is no counterbalancing output of finished goods. In the third stage of the cycle the new plants begin to turn out finished products. Finally, the "last period is the reverse of the second; a feverishly increased production throws its products on the market without being met by a like consumption."[18]

The upswing is initiated, not in the consumers' goods industries, but in the great industries which furnish the materials required for construction and the manufacture of equipment—iron, steel, lumber, cement, bricks, etc. Great tasks confront these industries, as the expansion gets under way, and when these are completed the "stormy demand" which dominates the boom phase comes to an end. Each upswing springs from exceptional investment opportunities, which provide a powerful impulse toward expansion. The impulse may come from investment in new machinery and equipment by reason of new technological developments and inventions. Or it may come from the opening up of new opportunities in relatively undeveloped countries—new markets which require loans and investments from the advanced industrial countries. Whatever the impulse, the important fact is that, at the beginning of each great upswing, industry stands before a "vacuum"—namely, unsatisfied investment opportunities at home and abroad.

INVESTMENT SATURATION

Eventually, these new requirements are met; industry becomes equipped with new capital facilities and new techniques; both the newly opened territories and the older industrial areas find themselves, to a degree, "saturated" with equipment.[19] But it is not merely a matter of new undertakings: there is also the replacement of old equipment with improved machinery. All this vast demand for new developments and improvements is, after some years of high investment activity, for the most part satisfied; and

---

[17] *Jahrbuch für Gesetzgebung, Verwaltung und Volkswirtschaft*, 1903, p. 696.

[18] Spiethoff, "Vorbemerkungen zu einer Theorie der Überproduktion," *Jahrbuch für Gesetzgebung, Verwaltung und Volkswirtschaft*, 1902, p. 730.

[19] *Ibid.*

then a kind of saturation process (*Sättigungsprozess*) sets in. The then prevailing level of technique sets a fairly definite limit to the amount of capital goods—mines, iron and steel works, railroads, transportation equipment, locomotives, factories, machines, electrical apparatus—which can be usefully employed in production. While there is a vast latent demand for consumers' goods as a whole—a demand which is in general highly elastic with respect to both price and income—the demand for capital goods and for the materials needed for the construction of durable goods is highly inelastic and is eventually satisfied. It is then no longer a matter of "filling an empty vessel," but rather of "keeping it full." After the new plant, machinery, and equipment have been erected and installed, one does not build them all over again; there remains only the task of maintenance and replacement.[20] If one misjudges the "filling of the vacuum" and mistakenly considers it a case of "continuing demand," one will overshoot the mark, in view of the inelastic demand for capital goods.[21]

SPIETHOFF VS. TUGAN-BARANOWSKY

We now see clearly the important new contribution made by Spiethoff. The expansion phase of the cycle—prosperity and boom—does not and cannot come merely from the pressure exerted by loanable funds seeking investment outlets in real capital formation. The period of high investment activity is mainly the result of a "pull," not a "push from behind." Technological developments and the opening up of new territory create a vacuum whose vast "suction power" pulls the economy forward in leaps and bounds. Discoveries and technological advances enlarge the "bucket of capital formation," and there is a crying need to get it filled. This is the period of prosperity; it is ushered in by autonomous investment.

But the need or usefulness of additional capital is rigorously limited. Once the bucket (whose size is fixed by the requirements of technological progress) is full, any additional capital formation rapidly becomes useless; the marginal efficiency of capital falls rapidly toward zero. Thus investment ceases; the period of prosperity comes to a dead stop.

Spiethoff stresses again and again the "saturation process." He who today buys a machine, or builds a factory or a house, has no need, like the man who buys a loaf of bread, to repeat the performance tomorrow or the next day; he must wait until perhaps ten or more years hence.

---

[20] "The demand for productive equipment and for durable consumers' goods is not continuous; and when an economy has been fully supplied with such goods, the plant and machines which produced them are thrown out of work. Once the iron industry of a country has produced the necessary railways, mere repair and upkeep are insufficient to keep the industry operating at capacity." Arthur Spiethoff, *Encyclopædia of the Social Sciences*, Vol. XI, pp. 513-517.

[21] Spiethoff, "Vorbemerkungen," p. 731. While Spiethoff's concepts are not sharply defined, it is quite clear from the context that his "inelastic demand for capital" means that once the "bucket is filled," the marginal efficiency of capital would fall rapidly toward zero with every further net addition to the stock of capital goods.

All this is very different from the explanation offered by Tugan-Bara-nowsky. Nevertheless, Spiethoff is prepared to support Tugan-Baranowsky's explanations of the boom and of the upper turning point as well as his own. He regards them as complementary, not contradictory. There can be a "push" as well as a "pull" in the upswing period, and at the upper turn-ing point a sharp *check* to further expansion, no less than a *petering out* of the forces of expansion. Spiethoff accordingly declared that the period of expansion may be halted not merely by the inelasticity of the demand for capital—the decline in the marginal efficiency of capital—but also by the limited supply of funds seeking investment (disposable capital). Thus there are, he believed, two rather rigorously fixed limits to the process of expansion: (1) from the side of the demand for real capital, and (2) from the side of the supply of disposable capital seeking investment outlets.

On both these grounds, he argued,[22] it is quite impossible that the ex-pansionist movement could go on indefinitely on a balanced or propor-tional basis. The boom and the collapse may, of course, be artificially intensified by overspeculation and violent price movements. But quite apart from these more superficial factors, the basic fundamental causes are the two factors mentioned above—the inelastic demand for real capital and the limited supply of disposable capital.

SAVING AND INVESTMENT

The production of equipment is conditioned, Spiethoff explains, by an investment of free or disposable capital. At the beginning of a period of prosperity a very large mass of loanable capital, gathered during the depres-sion, is available for investment. This mass is being added to continually, but is nevertheless constantly being absorbed. Eventually the time is reached when production can no longer lean back on the gatherings of depression but must look to the current flow of saving.[23]

At the upper turning point, then, as Spiethoff sees it, the production of fixed capital has grown beyond the prevailing needs and also beyond the available investment-seeking capital. Through these causes the production of fixed capital is undermined.

The influence spreads from the industries affected to other industries; and so general overproduction develops. In the ensuing depression new undertakings are looked upon with suspicion, and the possessors of free capital will rather let their stores lie idle or be satisfied with small interest than take steps toward investment in fixed capital.[24]

With the curtailment of the production of fixed capital there follows an unavoidable pressure on consumers' incomes, for both the profits of the employer and the rewards of labor will decline. With the resulting worsen-

---

[22] Spiethoff, "Vorbemerkungen," p. 732.

[23] *Ibid.*, pp. 730-733; see also "Krisen," *Handwörterbuch der Staatswissenschaften* (1925), VI, p. 74.

[24] Spiethoff, "Vorbemerkungen," pp. 737-738.

ing of incomes, consumption is injured. Underconsumption follows from the fact that certain parts of the productive processes stand still.

THE IMPACT OF FLUCTUATIONS OF INVESTMENT ON CONSUMPTION

The fall in the rate of profit and the low reward of labor reduce consumption, the decreasing consumption lowers prices, the fall in prices reduces production still further, the curtailment in production diminishes again the reward of labor and the rate of profit. There arises a formal vicious circle, and the interdependent effect of the different lines of industry on one another nourishes and increases the tendency to depression.[25]

During depression the chief problem confronting the industrialist is that of reducing costs through increased productivity and labor-saving machinery. But these improvements intensify depression. Many plants lose their value because of the new technique. The labor-saving machinery may either displace workers or press many skilled workers into the ranks of the unskilled.[26]

During prosperity the income distribution does not affect the general expenditure, for even though a part of the income flows into the hands of the people who will not immediately consume it but instead will invest it in fixed capital, still these funds are not abstracted from the income flow. In depression, however, the unequal division of incomes does affect the general expenditure. This is true because that part of the income which is saved *is* likely in such periods to be abstracted from expenditure, since it fails to find investment outlets, and is gathered instead into great idle masses of loan capital.[27]

Every limitation of production weakens afresh the buying and consuming power and is therefore a cause of the spread of the "overproduction" into other parts of the economy. It is therefore of the greatest importance that production be kept up as far as possible and not reduced except for the most pressing causes. It may be more profitable for the entrepreneur to sell a smaller quantity for higher prices rather than a greater quantity for lower prices, but depression and unemployment will be increased thereby. This is a case where the individual entrepreneur's interest in special branches is opposed to the general interest and where the cartel contributes to the injury of industry in general.[28]

THE ROLE OF TECHNOLOGY AND NEW TERRITORIES

With Spiethoff, then, the "real difference between prosperity and depression consists in the increasing or decreasing production of fixed capital

---

[25] *Ibid.*, p. 741.

[26] *Ibid.*, pp. 741-742.

[27] *Ibid.*, p. 743; see also "Krisen," *Handwörterbuch der Staatswissenschaften* (1925), VI, p. 80.

[28] Spiethoff, "Vorbemerkungen," p. 745.

and in the decreasing or increasing store of investment-seeking capital."[29]

According to Spiethoff, prosperity is initiated when new territories or new inventions open up new opportunities for investment in fixed capital. The accumulation of idle loan capital during the depression produces after a while a corrective, but that alone is not sufficient. Through the pressure of the mobile loan capital, the rate of interest falls continually lower, and when this tendency coincides with the recovery of the rate of profit in industry a certain condition of equilibrium may be reached. But the entrepreneurs have need for *special* inducements for great investments, and without these a large production of fixed capital will not occur. If unusual opportunities for gain appear, an excessive production of fixed capital will probably ensue. If, on the other hand, great losses have recently been sustained, an exaggerated fear of the risks of investment will prevail. The production of fixed capital is therefore never uniformly progressive, but always proceeds by fits and starts and is followed by reaction and depression. Every false estimate of the future needs, every great technical change, must disturb the equilibrium of prices and the harmony of consumption and production.[30]

If we stand at the beginning of a new period of outstanding inventions, says Spiethoff, then the end of crises is not in sight. Moreover, the territories which are to be added to the European industrial *Kultur* carry similar obstacles and dangers, for every addition of new territory carries with it the tendency to excesses and overproduction. If industry is on the forward march in its extension to peoples who have not yet been made its subjects, then the outlook is not good for the prevention of periodic crises. But we may expect that by the progress of social reform, by a continued adaptation of the capitalistic method of production, the industrial catastrophes will take on a more and more civilized form and finally lose themselves in a milder crossing from prosperity to depression. This development is not a necessary one, but it is worthy, Spiethoff believes, of our earnest labor and effort, and it is also a possible one.[31]

According to Spiethoff, there is no reason to doubt that people will gradually be able to adjust themselves to the capitalistic process of production. The history of crises teaches that its character has largely changed, that we have overcome many "children's diseases" of the capitalistic manner of production.[32]

With respect to these longer-run developments, Spiethoff's analysis was overly optimistic. As outlets for investment declined, once the whole world was equipped with the modern technique, he believed that spurts of investment would subside and so the cycle would tend to die down. But he failed to ask the question whether consumption could *automatically* be expected to rise sufficiently, in relation to income, to fill the gap left by the receding

---

[29] *Ibid.*, p. 753.
[30] *Ibid.*, pp. 748-749, 754-755.
[31] *Ibid.*, pp. 758-759.
[32] *Ibid.*, pp. 756-758.

tide of investment. No adequate analysis of this problem was made until the appearance of Keynes' *General Theory* in 1936.

RÉSUMÉ OF TUGAN-BARANOWSKY AND SPIETHOFF

In Tugan-Baranowsky's view, the rate of accumulation of free capital or loanable funds goes on steadily. But the accumulations of free capital are "pushed out" into real capital by a jerky process. Once a forward movement is started, expansion proceeds cumulatively because of the interdependence of industries. Any forward thrust spreads throughout the economy. It would keep on expanding more and more were it not for the "reining-in" effect due to the eventual exhaustion of "free capital." Similarly, the cumulative downward movement is sooner or later checked by the increasing pressure of loanable funds seeking real investment outlets. This stops the decline in investment and eventually starts it up again. The higher the propensity to save the greater the amplitude of the fluctuations.

Spiethoff asked why the flow of loanable funds might not move smoothly into investment *at a steady rate*. He offered the explanation that the boom is caused by a suction apparatus, so to speak—the investment vacuum created by technological inventions and the opening of new territories. But why the *fluctuations?* Why not a *steady* suction, and so a steady rate of investment?

Here it becomes necessary to draft into service *initiating* factors on the one side and a *cumulatively responsive mechanism* on the other side. If inventions and discoveries come unevenly like a throw of dice, these *intermittent* shocks may operate upon an economic structure capable of making *cyclical* adjustments. For this case, the Spiethoff analysis is adequate. But suppose these external shocks are distributed *evenly* over time. Suppose there is a steady rate of progress in inventions and discoveries. What then? The answer given by various theorists is that even so the response of the economic structure to these exogenous factors may still produce a cyclical movement. In this case, however, something more is needed than the analyses thus far made. And so we turn to Joseph A. Schumpeter.

Joseph A. Schumpeter (1883–1950)

THE INNOVATION PROCESS

Schumpeter enters into the argument with his concept of "innovation." *Invention* may indeed proceed at a uniform rate, but *innovation* (given the herdlike characteristic of entrepreneurs) cannot do so in the very nature of the case. Innovation necessarily wells up in a great tidal wave, and then recedes. That is the inherent nature of the process of innovation.[33] Thus the business cycle consists in essence in the ebb and flow

---

[33] Schumpeter's theory runs in terms of a process inherent in the inner nature of a dynamic economy in which the impelling factor is the innovating entrepreneur. See

of innovation, together with the repercussions resulting therefrom. An economy which experiences innovation, and which is directed by innovators and operated by entrepreneurs having the instincts of the herd, necessarily displays wavelike movements. Innovation involves capital investment, "which accordingly is not distributed evenly in time but appears *en masse* at intervals."

Innovation is an historic and irreversible change in the way of doing things. If instead of varying the quantities of the factors, we vary the form of the production function, we have an innovation. "We will simply define innovation as the setting up of a new production function."[34] This covers not only new techniques, but also the introduction of new commodities, new forms of organization, and the opening up of new markets. Innovation combines factors in a new way. Innovation represents a jump from an old production function to a new production function. The old marginal cost curve is destroyed and a new one put in its place each time there is an innovation. An innovation means a *shift* in the marginal productivity curve.

Major innovations entail the construction of new plant and equipment, but not every new plant embodies an innovation. "Add as many mail coaches as you please, you will never get a railroad by so doing."[35] To do something new is very much more difficult than to do something that belongs to the ordinary run of economic routine. The two tasks differ qualitatively. Whenever "the trade beholds the new thing done and its major problems solved, it becomes much easier for other people to do the same thing, and even to improve upon it." Thus innovations do not remain isolated events, and are not evenly distributed over time. They tend to "cluster," to come in "bunches," simply because "first some, and then most, firms follow in the wake of successful innovation."[36]

We must distinguish, says Schumpeter, between innovation *possibilities* and the *practical realization* of these possibilities. Prosperity does not arise merely as a result of inventions or discoveries. It waits upon the actual development of *innovations*, which is the driving power of the period of prosperity. Only a few leaders have the intelligence and energy to found new undertakings, to develop new possibilities. While only a few can *lead*, many can *follow*. Once someone has gone ahead, it is not difficult to imitate him. Few are capable of securing financial backing for a new venture of which bankers and investors are skeptical; but once one such new estab-

Joseph A. Schumpeter, "Über das Wesen der Wirtschaftskrisen," *Zeitschrift für Volkswirtschaft*, 1910, pp. 271-325; *Theorie der wirtschaftlichen Entwicklung*, Duncker & Humblot, Leipzig, 1912; "Die Wellenbewegung des Wirtschaftslebens," *Archiv für Sozialwissenschaft und Sozialpolitik*, 1914, pp. 1-32; *The Theory of Economic Development*, Harvard University Press, Cambridge, 1934; *Business Cycles*, McGraw-Hill Book Company, New York, 1939, Vols. I and II.

[34] Schumpeter, *Business Cycles*, pp. 87-88.

[35] J. A. Schumpeter, *Readings in Business Cycle Theory*, The Blakiston Company, Philadelphia, 1944, p. 7. See also his "The Explanation of the Business Cycle," *Economica*, December, 1927.

[36] Schumpeter, *Business Cycles*, p. 100.

lishment is a going concern, others can easily secure credit and capital for similar undertakings. If a new process is put into successful operation, others can simply copy. If the first one has found the right location, others can simply locate near him. Experiments with workers and customers benefit other entrepreneurs who learn from these experiments.

The problems confronting those who imitate innovations are more difficult than those of the ordinary routine business. But they are not nearly so great as those faced by the leaders who blaze the trail. And whenever a few successful innovators appear, immediately a host of others follow. The appearance of one or a few entrepreneurs facilitates the appearance of others, and these, the appearance of more, in ever-increasing numbers. This is the basis of the "wave movement" of industrial activity.[37]

THE HERDLIKE MOVEMENT

Thus the process of expansion is not simply a process of cumulation—the favorable "secondary waves" which flow to interrelated industries from the initial impulse. The expansion proceeds by "rushes" because a forward push by innovators impels a "herdlike" movement of followers who see the tempting profit possibilities opened up. The boom is a phenomenon caused by the herdlike action of entrepreneurs who *en masse* rush into the new openings. Even though inventions were uniformly distributed over time, fluctuations in the rate of investment would still occur, owing to the discontinuity of innovational activity. "Breaking through" the established routine is not something that occurs at a uniform and smooth pace. Innovation is discontinuous. The new combinations are not evenly distributed over time. They appear "discontinuously in groups or swarms."[38]

The "swarm-like appearance of new enterprises" is *intensified* by the cumulative process—the secondary waves which spread all over the business sphere. "Many things float on this 'secondary wave,' without any new or direct impulse from the real driving force."[39] Moreover, errors of optimism may intensify the boom. These are supporting and accentuating circumstances, but not a primary cause of cyclical movements. The central driving force is the appearance of an innovation which sets going the herdlike movement of entrepreneurs.

THE END OF THE BOOM

Schumpeter differs from Spiethoff not only in his explanation of the origin of the boom but also in his analysis of the termination of the boom.[40]

[37] J. A. Schumpeter, "Die Wellenbewegung des Wirtschaftslebens," *Archiv für Sozialwissenschaft*, 1914, pp. 28-32; also *Theory of Economic Development*, Harvard University Press, 1934, p. 228.

[38] Schumpeter, *Theory of Economic Development*, p. 223.

[39] *Ibid.*, p. 226.

[40] Schumpeter does say that as a "description of the actual facts" he can accept Spiethoff's explanation as far as it goes (*Theory of Economic Development*, p. 215). But he does not stop here.

He accepts Juglar's statement that the "only cause of the depression is prosperity," and this he interprets to mean that "depression is nothing more than the economic system's reaction to the boom, or the adaptation to the situation into which the boom brings the system."[41] The disturbances arising from innovation cannot be currently and smoothly absorbed. These disturbances are "big"; they disrupt the existing system and enforce a distinct process of adaptation.

A railroad through a new country upsets all conditions relating to the location of industry, all cost calculations, all production functions in the area. Hardly any "ways of doing things" remain as before. In the wake of big industrial changes, the various elements of the system do not move in step. Some industries move on, others stay behind. Discrepancies arise. The depression is a process of adaptation to the changed conditions ushered in by the boom.

THE RECESSION: A PERIOD OF READJUSTMENT

The process of introducing innovations into the productive system is the essence of the boom. Progress not only proceeds by jerks, but also by one-sided rushes with disruptive consequences. The development is "lopsided, discontinuous, disharmonious." The history of capitalism is "studded with violent bursts and catastrophes." Evolution is a disturbance of existing structures, more like a series of explosions than a gentle transformation.[42] But these new methods cannot become incorporated into the circular flow, cannot become integrated into a new equilibrium system, without an intervening period of readjustment. This process of absorption and liquidation, of incorporating the new things and of adapting the economic system to them is, according to Schumpeter, the essence of the recession.

In the recession period, the economic system is struggling toward a new equilibrium position following the disturbances caused by the boom. The economic nature of depression lies in the diffusion of the achievements of the boom over the whole economic system through the mechanism of the struggle for equilibrium.[43]

Any innovation—be it a new method of production, new goods, the opening up of a new market, any new combination of productive forces—will alter the buying power of consumers, the prices of raw materials, the quantity of sales, etc. These are the basic facts upon which industrial plans are formed. The old plans, formerly correct, no longer fit the facts of the industrial situation. A process of accommodation to the new facts, a fitting of the innovation into the general industrial system, becomes necessary. If the innovations appear simultaneously and in large numbers, then the data change so rapidly that adjustment becomes extremely difficult. Little by little the adjustment is made and a new equilibrium is reached.

---

[41] Schumpeter, *Theory of Economic Development*, p. 224.
[42] Schumpeter, *Business Cycles*, pp. 101-102.
[43] Schumpeter, *Theory of Economic Development*, p. 251.

We may define the period of depression as one in which there is being completed an accommodation to the new industrial situation created in the preceding period by the appearance of many relatively sudden innovations. A reorganization of the price system, of incomes, of production to fit the new demand situation, is inevitable. This process is the content of the period of depression, and it takes place with losses, resistance, and disillusionment. Thus we come to the conclusion that it is the multiplicity of innovations in the period of prosperity which disturbs the equilibrium and changes the basic industrial data so that a period of readjustment of prices, values, and production necessarily appears.[44]

NEIGHBORHOODS OF EQUILIBRIUM

Cyclical movements are movements away from neighborhoods of equilibrium, and back again. It is the process of innovation which drives the system away from equilibrium into a boom of capital investment. This is the phase of "prosperity," and it is followed by "recession"—the struggle back to equilibrium. But as the depressive forces gather momentum, the system usually outruns also this neighborhood of equilibrium and thus plunges beyond—down into the "depression excursion." From here the recuperative forces of adjustment bit by bit promote "revival" and gradually pull the economy back again toward equilibrium. From here a new swarm of innovations starts the economy on a new cycle. Starting from the neighborhood of equilibrium, the innovational surge drives the economy on into the next phase of "prosperity." Innovators supply the propelling force which generates a new cycle.[45]

BANK CREDIT AND INNOVATIONS

Schumpeter stresses not only innovations and economic progress but also the role played by bank credit in economic development. Indeed, bank credit expansion is intimately connected, he believes, with the process of innovation.

"Neutral money"[46] might indeed very probably prove to be the appropriate monetary arrangement in a static equilibrium in which a continuous production process was constantly being maintained—Schumpeter's *"Kreislauf"* or "circular flow." But in a dynamic society in which "development" is going on, a more flexible money system is necessary. "Development," in Schumpeter's sense, is something quite distinct from and foreign

[44] Schumpeter, "Die Wellenbewegung des Wirtschaftslebens," *Archiv für Sozialwissenschaft*, 1914, pp. 17-20, 23-24.

[45] Schumpeter, *Readings in Business Cycle Theory*, pp. 8-11. For a detailed discussion of the four phases in relation to the neighborhoods of equilibrium see pp. 7-9 of this book.

[46] By "neutral money" is meant, in effect, a constant money supply, the idea in the minds of the advocates of such a monetary policy being that money would then be "neutral" in its effect upon the production process. While, as indicated, this might be true under conditions of static equilibrium, the situation in a dynamic economy is quite different.

to the circular flow. It is spontaneous and discontinuous change in the channels of the circular flow. These changes appear on the side of production, not on the side of consumption. They are technical innovations in the production process. Development means the carrying out of new combinations. And for the carrying out of these combinations, credit is primarily necessary. The detachment of productive means, already employed elsewhere, from the circular flow, and the allotment of them to new combinations—this is the function of credit. These necessary funds are obtained through the creation of purchasing power by the banks. With the help of these credit means of payment, innovators who carry out new combinations are able to gain access to the existing factors of production. The banker, therefore, is "essentially a phenomenon of development." It is through the issue of credit that the carrying out of new combinations is made possible. Swarms of innovations have periodically in past history been floated into their places in the new structure of production on the tide of an expanding volume of bank credit.[47]

The essence of economic development, Schumpeter explains, consists in a *different* employment of *existing* productive resources. New combinations require the withdrawal of primary factors from their previous employments, and this "cannot be achieved otherwise than by a disturbance in the relative purchasing power of individuals."[48] It is this function that credit performs. The purchasing power which the entrepreneur—the innovator —needs "does not flow towards him automatically as to the producer in the circular flow, by the sale of what he produced in preceding periods."[49] In the circular flow, there is no need of credit; only for development does it play a fundamental role. The quantity of credit operates as an order on the economic system to accommodate itself to the purpose of the entrepreneur. Credit bridges the gap between products and means of production in the carrying out of new combinations.

EXOGENOUS AND ENDOGENOUS FACTORS

Under the impulse of entrepreneurial activity (i.e., innovation) the economic system draws away from the neighborhood of equilibrium. But the farther it moves away from equilibrium, the stronger is the pull back to equilibrium. In the downward readjustment (recession) the economy is likely to "overshoot" and pass through the neighborhood of equilibrium into the depression phase. Again the economy is pulled back toward equilibrium. Once there, it does not come to rest, because it is just in the neighborhood of equilibrium that the economic climate is favorable for innovations.[50] Thus, in a very fundamental sense Schumpeter's theory runs

---

[47] Schumpeter, *Theory of Economic Development*, Chapters II and III.

[48] *Ibid.*, p. 96.

[49] *Ibid.*, p. 102.

[50] In his *Economics of Welfare* (1920), Pigou pointed out that inventions become important only when they are applied, and their *time of application* is determined by states of confidence.

in terms of an endogenous, self-perpetuating process—a process inherent in the inner nature of a dynamic economy in which the impelling force, which cycle after cycle renews the wavelike movement, is the innovating entrepreneur.

Yet economic development (and the wave movement in economic life) is not merely a product of the innovational process. It is also a product of far-reaching structural changes in technique, within which pattern of change the innovational process occurs. A case in point was the shift to a new technological plateau ushered in by the railroad. In this respect exogenous factors, notably revolutionary inventions, play a highly significant role, especially with respect to secular trends (the Kondratieff long waves) against which background the regular business cycles (Juglar's) unfold.

Economic fluctuations are concerned with "economic changes inherent in the working of the organism itself."[51] Yet we are faced with an economic process which is continually being disturbed by external factors. These external factors "induce a process of adaptation in the system" which will produce wavelike oscillations.[52] The influence of external factors is never absent, and they are often of such a nature that we cannot dispose of them simply according to the "schema of, say, a pendulum continually exposed to numerous small and independent shocks."[53] External factors are always important and sometimes dominant.[54]

---

[51] Schumpeter, *Business Cycles*, Vol. I, p. 7.
[52] *Ibid.*, p. 11.
[53] *Ibid.*, p. 12.
[54] *Ibid.*, p. 72.

[22]

Investment Behavior
and Business Cycles*

ROBERT A. GORDON†

Editors' Note

This article is a contemporary statement, couched in theoretical terms, of the role of investment. Without significant fluctuations in investment, the business cycle would be moderate and of short duration. There would be narrow fluctuations in consumption expenditures and wide movements in inventories. Historically, at least, there have been major fluctuations in investment, and the investment boom of 1955–57 and the subsequent sharp decline in 1957–58 suggest that this process has not been entirely eliminated from the American economy. Here Gordon stresses the need for analysis in terms of the capital stock, and thus joins forces with those who believe that the stock-flow approach to investment will result in better predictions of future trends in capital outlays.

The appropriate level and the composition of the capital stock are the key, not in terms of a static concept, but in terms of forward planning. "Appropriate" is defined in terms of what would be appropriate if the attempt were made to achieve that particular capital stock. This stock is always changing and this involves long-term anticipations of the future. Exogenous and endogenous factors are considered, as are interactions between secular and cyclical changes. Altogether, the article represents one of the best restatements of investment theory as it relates to business cycles.

* Reprinted by permission of the publishers from *Review of Economics and Statistics*, Vol. XXXVII, No. 1, (February, 1955), pp. 23-34; Cambridge, Mass.: Harvard University Press, Copyright, 1955, by The President and Fellows of Harvard College.
† See p. 206.

Still to be accomplished, however, is the empirical amplification of such a theory.

❧ Most economists agree that the primary source of cyclical instability is to be found in the determinants of investment behavior.[1] Current cycle theory largely takes the following simple form. Today's value of output is equal to today's aggregate demand, which is the sum of consumption and investment (plus government expenditures). Consumption is assumed to be more or less inflexibly tied to current or past income. Hence the essence of the problem is to find the determinants of current investment. These determinants, so far as they are considered endogenous, are usually taken to be either the rate of change in total output (the acceleration principle) or the *level* of total output and the size of the total capital stock.

The business-cycle models which result from this approach are open to a number of objections. They are unable to account for the important differences among past cycles; they abstract from most of the complexities of economic growth; they ignore some features of the cumulative process which observation suggests may be important in shaping the course of the cycle; and they yield explanations of investment behavior which, as often as not, do not seem to fit the facts.

The purpose of the present paper is to suggest a different approach to the study of economic fluctuations—one which links cyclical change more closely to the underlying forces making for growth and structural change than is usually the case today.[2] First, we shall examine whether cyclical fluctuations are likely to take place in the absence of significant variations in (long-term) investment. Following this, we shall attempt to lay the groundwork for a theory of investment behavior in terms of the opening up of investment opportunities and the varying inducements to exploit these opportunities. The analytical framework resulting from these two sections is then used to elaborate and refine the usual distinction between major and minor cycles. In a concluding section, we shall try briefly to evaluate this way of looking at the causes of cyclical instability.

---

[1] This is a revision of the major part of a paper presented at the Conference on Policies to Combat Depression, held by the Universities-National Bureau Committee for Economic Research at Princeton on October 30-31, 1953. I am indebted to the Bureau of Business and Economic Research of the University of California for assistance in the preparation of this paper and to a number of my colleagues at Berkeley for their helpful comments.

[2] In this respect, this paper owes an obvious debt to Schumpeter, Hansen, and Robertson. See also the reference to Thomas Wilson in footnote 12 below.

1

History tells us that, even without significant fluctuations in long-term investment, we can get cyclical movements in income and employment, albeit of moderate amplitude. Something of this sort is what economists have in mind when they refer to "minor cycles" or "inventory recessions." Such minor cycles not only involve moderate fluctuations in income and employment (and relatively wide fluctuations in inventory investment); they also are associated with typical cyclical patterns in different sorts of commodity prices, in interest rates and security prices, in the money supply, and in other variables—about which current cycle theory has relatively little to say.[3]

Our first task, then, is to sketch the outlines of a dynamic response mechanism which can generate fluctuations in income, employment, prices, etc., even in the absence of fluctuations in long-term investment (i.e., expenditures on producers' durables and construction). This analysis serves two purposes. It helps to explain why minor cycles occur. And it describes the cyclical response mechanism which interacts with the determinants of long-term investment to create wider fluctuations.

We may indicate the outlines of our model, perhaps too elliptically, as follows. Today's volume of output is the result of yesterday's short-period production plans. The latter depend on how businessmen react to the current level of and recent changes in a number of variables—their sales (which in turn depend on the components of final demand, including investment in inventories), the prices of what they buy and sell, the important monetary variables, and the current state of their inventories. It is not important for our purpose to try to spell out the precise nature of these variables or the exact way in which they are related to the volume of planned output.

Today's aggregate (money) demand is the sum of today's consumption and investment (including production withheld for stock); and this aggregate demand (equal to income) determines, with today's volume of output resulting from yesterday's production plans, today's prices.[4] Today's

---

[3] The best known current theory of inventory cycles is, of course, that of Lloyd Metzler. See his papers in the *American Economic Review*, XXXVI, (June 1946), 278-91, and *The Review of Economic Statistics*, XXIII (August 1941), 113-29, and XXIX (February 1947), 1-15. Metzler has nothing to say about the cyclical behavior of any variables other than output, consumption, and inventories; and he takes all non-inventory investment to be autonomously determined. Schumpeter is the only writer I know to develop a single theoretical explanation which yields simultaneous cycles of different durations and amplitudes, including the Kitchin or minor cycle. Eventually, however, he came to believe that a special theory such as Metzler's might be necessary to explain the minor cycle. See his paper in Universities-National Bureau Committee, *Conference on Business Cycles* (1951), p. 154. For Alvin Hansen's views on the causes of minor cycles, see *Business Cycles and National Income* (New York, 1951), ch. 2.

[4] It is most useful, in this connection, to assume that prices react only slowly and partially to changes in the relation between output and aggregate money demand, so that unplanned changes in inventories also occur.

consumption is related to yesterday's and today's income but also to other variables.[5] Today's long-term investment depends on a complex of factors that we shall examine in section II.

We can add to these rudiments of a cyclical mechanism two additional relationships, although they are not essential. The supply of money is elastic but not perfectly so, so that after some point further expansions in output bring about some increase in interest rates and in the degree of credit rationing. Secondly, we assume that, as employment (output) rises, beyond some point money wages also rise.

Now these imperfectly specified relations can be assumed to take particular forms and can be combined into a formal dynamic model. However, we shall not make that attempt here. All that we want to do here is to indicate, without any attempt at precision, that the sort of model adumbrated in the preceding paragraphs is likely to generate fluctuations, entirely apart from induced or autonomous changes in long-term investment. Since production plans are made in advance of sales and in response to factors partly different from those which determine the (subsequent) demand for the planned output, businessmen will experience price changes or unplanned changes in inventories. As a result, production plans are subject to continuous revision; and, depending on the nature of the assumed relationships, cumulative movements in output, prices, and employment can (and in practice do) result. Production plans will be continuously revised not only because of unanticipated discrepancies between planned output and demand but also because of induced changes in cost-price relationships and in the important monetary variables. With an imperfectly elastic money supply, for example, the tightening of credit brought on by continued expansion of output is likely to lead to a widespread change in attitudes toward liquidity (defined as a preference for cash or highly liquid assets *rather than goods*), so that production plans are changed in order to convert inventories (and also accounts receivable) into cash and to reduce current liabilities. Expectations of changing prices also affect liquidity attitudes.[6]

Thus, even without significant fluctuations in long-term investment, we can get cyclical movements in income and employment. Such fluctuations

---

[5] A few words about the sort of consumption function that is relevant here. We assume some variability in the relation between consumption and disposable income and also between the latter and gross national product. The former relation is affected by such factors as the stock and distribution of liquid assets, the behavior of consumers' debt, consumers' stocks of durable and semi-durable goods, changes in the distribution of income, and consumers' expectations regarding prices and their future incomes. The relation between disposable income and GNP is influenced particularly by business savings and the behavior of taxes. The result is that as gross output changes cyclically, the over-all marginal propensity to consume that output may vary both erratically and in systematic fashion.

[6] A firm's desire for liquidity increases if it considers that the probability of realizing capital losses on its real assets (particularly inventories) has increased, or if it feels greater uncertainty as to its ability to meet its obligations as they come due. And conversely for a lessened desire for liquidity.

will tend to be of moderate amplitude and short duration and, in terms of the components of final demand, will be reflected in fairly narrow fluctuations in consumption but in wide movements in inventory investment.

Depending upon the circumstances, revision of short-period production plans can affect long-term investment plans. Whether this occurs depends upon the strength of the minor-cycle forces at work and on the prevailing state of investment opportunities. Hence we must now turn to a consideration of what is probably the most troublesome problem in business-cycle analysis—the determinants of (long-term) investment behavior.

II

We may begin our study of investment behavior with what seems to me a useful distinction between "underlying investment opportunities," on the one hand, and inducements to exploit these opportunities, on the other. This is not an easy distinction to handle, and I have not been able to make either concept as precise as I should like. Nonetheless, I think the distinction can serve a number of useful purposes, and it seems to me to throw light on some of the destabilizing forces operating on private investment which most of current cycle theory does not take adequately into account.

The *stock* of underlying investment opportunities at any moment may be defined as the difference between the existing capital stock and that which businessmen would find it most profitable to have if they were well informed regarding all current cost and demand relationships and also the forces making for long-run growth in the economy. Thus we may speak of an "appropriate" level *and composition* of the capital stock, and we may look on all investment (which is not based on mistaken expectations) as an attempt to modify the existing capital stock in the direction of that which is "appropriate," not only to the current situation but also to that which is expected in the future.

Borrowing a term from Harrod, we may also describe the appropriate capital stock as that which would be "warranted" (or justified), as to both its total size and its composition, given the underlying determinants of economic growth. It is the capital stock which would justify itself if the business community as a whole sought to achieve it. Thus, the appropriate capital stock is to be considered with respect not to the present level of income but to that level which would result from attempts to achieve the appropriate capital stock, given knowledge of the underlying determinants of growth, including the factors making for changes in the composition of output.[7]

---

[7] What stock of capital is appropriate depends on the level and rate of growth of output which would result from the attempt to achieve it, and this in turn depends, among other things, on the rate of investment, i.e., on the rate per time period at which the existing stock of capital rises toward the appropriate stock. Here an adaptation of Lerner's distinction between the marginal productivity of the capital stock and the

The appropriate capital stock is always changing, thereby creating new investment opportunities. It reflects (correct) anticipations regarding that segment of the future which is within the businessman's horizon; and, as time passes, more of the future becomes relevant. What capital stock is appropriate also depends on what capital stock now exists, as well as on relative factor prices (including interest rates), the nature of consumers' preference maps, existing and foreseeable technological possibilities, and the nature of competitive relationships.

Obviously there is a resemblance between this notion of an appropriate capital stock and Richard Goodwin's concept of a desired stock of capital that underlies his flexible accelerator.[8] But there are several important differences. Goodwin, like most current cycle theorists, is concerned only with the total stock of capital, not with its composition. Secondly, Goodwin's desired stock of capital is not affected by changes in interest rates or relative prices (particularly capital-goods prices). And, thirdly, he relates the desired stock of capital, through the accelerator, to the *current* level of output, whereas we relate the appropriate stock of capital to whatever (secularly) changing level and composition of output businessmen would consider in their long-term planning on the basis of correct long-term expectations. This involves taking into account some segment of the future. It also involves some notion of "normal."

This last point needs further elaboration. If, in the context of expected future growth, there should be a cyclical decline in output, we would say that the appropriate stock of capital had not declined for that reason alone and that therefore the decline in output *per se* did not reduce the stock of investment opportunities. What had happened in this case was an impairment in the inducement to exploit a given stock of investment opportunities. This is a distinction of some importance for policy and also conforms with common-sense notions regarding the meaning of "underlying" investment opportunities. If only the inducement to invest is impaired, then measures aimed at raising the general level of income will have the desired leverage effect on private investment. If, however, there is a deficiency in investment opportunities, then merely raising the level of

---

marginal efficiency of investment is helpful. [See *The Economics of Control* (New York, 1944), pp. 334-42.] Given technology and all the relevant cost and demand relations, then the interaction of interest rates, cost functions and capacity ceilings in the capital-goods industries, and various sorts of lags will determine the "equilibrium" amount of net investment per time period. The income corresponding to this rate of investment helps to determine what stock of capital is appropriate. (I am indebted to Robert Dorfman for this suggestion.) While this is the "equilibrium" rate of investment, the actual behavior of investment will be strongly influenced by the cyclical inducements discussed later in the text.

[8] See his "A Model of Cyclical Growth," presented at the Round Table on Business Cycle Problems of the International Economic Association, September 1952. Also his papers in A. H. Hansen, *Business Cycles and National Income* (New York, 1951) and in *Income, Employment and Public Policy: Essays in Honor of Alvin H. Hansen* (New York, 1948).

income—say, by fiscal measures—may not be enough to restore private investment to a satisfactory level.

Changes in investment opportunities come about for reasons which are both exogenous and endogenous with respect to the cyclical model that we are building. Technological change is in large part exogenous for our purpose. It affects investment opportunities by changing the appropriate composition of output (e.g., through new products) and therefore the appropriate capital stock, or by changing the size and composition of the capital stock which is appropriate for a given output. Technological change is the principal (but not the only) source of one of the types of investment discussed later, namely, that which does not depend on the behavior of aggregate output in the economy as a whole. We do not exclude the possibility that some technological change is endogenous, being related to some aspect of the cyclical response mechanism.

Thus we start with the notion of a set of investment opportunities which responds to various influences which are wholly or partly non-cyclical in origin—technological change, population growth, government intervention, changes in tastes, etc. The opportunities are partly in new industries, partly in new ways of doing things in old industries, partly in expanding some old industries to take advantage of changed tastes or changed price relationships, partly in expanding old industries generally as population and per capita income reflect the underlying forces making for growth, partly in meeting past and current replacement needs. Another source of investment opportunities, in house-building, reflects the interaction of divergent rates of growth in population, in per capita income, and in the stock of housing, as well as the influences determining building costs and the availability of mortgage credit. To all of these must be added governmental action, particularly changes in government spending. Government decisions to spend may themselves be considered new investment opportunities, and in addition they create opportunities for private investment. Investment opportunities are further widened or narrowed by purely cyclical changes—e.g., through innovations induced by rising profits and changing cost-price relationships, through changes in interest rates and the prices of capital goods, and, most important, by the rate at which existing opportunities are exploited through current investment.

We now have to ask what determines the rate at which given investment opportunities are exploited. If investment opportunities were perfectly known, there would be, for any appropriate capital stock, an equilibrium rate of investment per unit of time determined, in effect, by certain lags and the elasticity of supply both of loanable funds and of capital-goods output.[9] In fact, of course, investment opportunities are not known with certainty. The appraisal of investment opportunities is strongly influenced by current expectations as to future profits and sales and by current attitudes toward liquidity, and these expectations and attitudes vary as a re-

---

[9] See footnote 7, above, and pp. 411-412 below.

sult of the cyclical response mechanism outlined in the preceding section. Thus we may speak of cyclically changing inducements to exploit a given (or also changing) stock of investment opportunities. In the early stages of cyclical revival (or during many cyclical downswings), the stock of investment opportunities may be large enough to support a full-employment level of investment, but the cyclical inducements to invest may be so weak as to result in a much lower level of investment.

Now the higher the level of investment opportunities as previously defined, all other things being equal, the more favorable will be business expectations. But expectations may change for other reasons—for example, because of cyclical changes in demand resulting from the operation of the cumulative process, because of the imbalances resulting from past mistakes, or because of other factors operating to affect business confidence.

We can relate our findings thus far to the usual way of expressing an investment function as follows. The volume of current investment is a function of the (changing) state of investment opportunities, of other variables which also influence profit and sales expectations, and of the variables influencing liquidity attitudes. We cannot conveniently list or quantify all of the forces determining the state of investment opportunities. Hence, if we try to express investment only as a function of the other variables, we face the certainty that the nature of the function will change over the cycle in unpredictable ways.

It is useful to differentiate among the more important types of investment on the basis of the different ways in which investment opportunities are created. Thus we may divide total gross domestic investment into the following categories: replacement expenditures, expansion in capacity required by an increase in total output, net investment intended to exploit new investment opportunities which come about for reasons other than an increase in total output, residential building, and inventory investment. For our present purpose, we can ignore inventory investment, which was briefly considered in section I.

Consider first replacement. Investment opportunities are created by wear and tear and obsolescence and are reduced by actual expenditures for replacement. In depression, replacement expenditures tend to be reduced though there may be little decline in investment opportunities (in our sense).[10] Postponing replacement means that the stock of investment opportunities available for future exploitation is increasing. Eventually, improved profit expectations and liquidity attitudes lead to a surge of deferred replacement demand, which aims at restoring the stock of capital to its previous level and in the improved form made possible by recent

---

[10] This result arises because we define investment opportunities independently of the effect on investment incentives arising from a temporary decline in demand. If existing investment opportunities of all sorts would be, if exploited, sufficient to maintain the former high level of output, then the opportunity for replacement also would exist. What has happened is an impairment in the inducement to exploit replacement opportunities.

technical change.[11] Afterward, replacement may fall to a lower level governed by current retirements, reflecting a decline in the stock of investment opportunities on account of replacement, even though other types of investment are still expanding.

Let us now consider investment aimed at expanding a particular type of capacity beyond its previous level. Such expansion may reflect a like expansion in total output, but nothing more than this. This would be the case of old industries, in which production tends to be a constant or slowly changing fraction of total output in the economy as a whole, and in which also no important technological changes are occurring. This is the sort of case really implied in attempts to use the acceleration principle to explain the behavior of total investment. Here investment opportunities are created through growth in aggregate income; they are exploited in response to changing profit expectations and liquidity attitudes as part of an interdependent cyclical response mechanism.

The kind of investment opportunities mentioned in the preceding paragraph depends only on growth in aggregate income, given an unchanging composition of output and a technologically determined capital-output ratio. (This does not mean, however, that *in the short run* these opportunities are necessarily exploited in precisely the way the acceleration principle implies.) But many of the investment opportunities existing in any period have a different origin. They arise because a new composition of output may have become appropriate, or because changes in technology or relative factor prices call for a different composition of the capital stock. Investment booms to a considerable extent represent the exploitation of this kind of investment opportunity. And the "using-up" of such opportunities is one reason why aggregate investment eventually declines. Thomas Wilson has recently given the name "structural effect" to the influences which lead to this type of capital formation.[12]

Investment opportunities created in this way may persist through several

---

[11] The reader may have noted that we are implicitly making a distinction between replacement and net investment that is different from that implied in most recent business-cycle models. Assume that during a depression, the capital stock declines because gross investment is less than depreciation and that, eventually, when conditions improve, firms begin to expand capacity again. Most economists would say that *all* of such expansion in capacity represented net investment, to be explained by whatever investment function was being used. We would say, on the contrary, that all expenditures aimed at bringing capacity back to its former level represented (deferred) replacement, and that this type of expenditure is to be explained in a different way from those investment outlays undertaken in order to expand the capital stock above its previous level. This is reminiscent of the "Duesenberry-Modigliani" effect in recent discussions of the consumption function.

[12] See his "Cyclical and Autonomous Inducements to Invest," *Oxford Economic Papers*, New Series, V (March 1953), 65-89, esp. 81-85. Indeed, there is a close kinship between Wilson's entire paper and the analysis of investment behavior presented here. W. W. Rostow is another writer who has emphasized the importance of changes in the composition of investment as a factor in cyclical and secular change. See "Some Notes on Mr. Hicks and History," *American Economic Review*, XLI (June 1951), 316-24. Obviously, this sort of analysis owes a great deal to Schumpeter.

business cycles, as did the opportunities created by the railroad, the auto·mobile, or electric power. These opportunities may expand suddenly, and also gradually. But there is no reason why new opportunities of this sort should be created precisely at the rate at which old ones are exploited. The larger the stock of such opportunities at any time, the stronger the inducement to invest; but the rate at which such investment actually takes place depends upon how the cyclical inducements to invest operate in the industries affected, so that such "autonomous" or "structural" investment is also induced by the "endogenous" variables in our system.

We need not at this point say much about investment in housing. Here again our concept of investment opportunities has an obvious application. Because of the very high capital-output ratio, new opportunities in this field (which come chiefly from population growth and migration) call for an increase in the capital stock which is quite large in terms of the usual rate of aggregate investment in the economy as a whole—and lags and supply inelasticities spread this increment in the capital stock over a considerable period, usually over more than one business cycle. As has been pointed out by numerous observers, a serious decline in the exploitable stock of investment opportunities in residential and commercial building is an important factor explaining the unusual severity of some business depressions.

Two elements must now be added to our explanation of the cyclical behavior of investment. First, investment opportunities, once created, are not completely and instantaneously exploited, no matter how favorable may be profit and sales expectations and liquidity attitudes. There are two reasons for this. In the first place, we must take account of a variety of lags: delays in perceiving the available opportunities, the time required to arrange financing, to place orders, and to produce the necessary capital goods, and so on. In the second place, imperfectly elastic supply curves for loanable funds and capital goods—and ultimately capacity ceilings in the capital-goods industries—place an upper limit on the amount of investment which can take place in the short run.[13]

Now let us add the second element. We assume that, in a relatively mature and industrialized economy, the ability to produce (or import) capital goods and to finance their installation is sufficiently great so that during periods of boom there can be a gradual using up of the stock of

---

[13] Cf. footnote 7 above. It is possible to make either of two assumptions here. First, we can assume a marginal efficiency of investment function which declines in part because of supply inelasticities in the capital-goods industries, the upper limit on current investment being imposed by the eventual equality of the marginal efficiency of investment and the rate of interest. Or we can assume, given sufficient inflexibility of prices, that an upper limit on investment is imposed by capacity ceilings in the capital-goods industries. This latter assumption is an essential feature of Richard Goodwin's approach, and it has also been used by Mrs. Robinson. In this connection, see also the explicit statements regarding the role of the capacity ceiling in the capital-goods industries in Kaldor's recent article, "The Relation of Economic Growth and Cyclical Fluctuations," *Economic Journal*, LXIV (March 1954), 53-71.

investment opportunities.[14] The demand for capital goods per time period may or may not exceed the capacity of the capital goods industries. In peak boom periods, capacity in these industries may be a limiting factor. Even when it is, however, the rate of investment which is possible can, if sustained, eventually reduce investment opportunities enough to cause a fall in total investment. Whether it does or not depends on the rate at which new opportunities are being opened up.

III

Let us now merge the arguments of the two preceding sections and see what sorts of fluctuation are likely to result. In terms of the forces which are likely to end a boom and bring on a cyclical downswing, we can distinguish at least four possibilities.

First, we have the case described in section I. Here the cyclical response mechanism operates without affecting long-term investment. The downturn comes because of a downward revision in short-period production plans; but the stock of investment opportunities remains large enough to maintain investment, and there is no significant deterioration in the inducements to exploit these opportunities. *Long-term* profit and sales expectations remain favorable, and any increase in the desire for liquidity can be satisfied by temporarily curtailing production in order to reduce inventories. When a downswing occurs in this way, it is likely to be mild and brief. We can call this type of fluctuation a "pure" minor cycle. It becomes less pure as changes in production plans lead also to changes in the inducements to undertake long-term investment. This brings us to our next case.

It is possible, once a downswing begins, for business confidence to become so impaired that long-run possibilities are not correctly appraised for some considerable time, even though investment opportunities remain large enough to maintain long-term investment at its previous peak rate. The deterioration of short-period expectations may affect longer-term

---

[14] This assumption is implied when writers, such as Kaldor or Kalecki, make the current rate of investment a decreasing function of the stock of capital. (Cf. Kaldor's recent article cited in the preceding footnote, especially p. 63.) Lawrence Klein has used the same assumption in his econometric work. A similar assumption is made in Richard Goodwin's models, also by Mrs. Robinson in *The Rate of Interest and Other Essays* (London, 1952), pp. 131-35. This assumption is an essential part of all those cycle theories which emphasize the role of innovations—notably in Schumpeter's explanation and also in those of Alvin Hansen and D. H. Robertson.

The pure acceleration-multiplier models, including the nonlinear version made popular by Hicks, operate a bit differently in this respect. Leaving aside autonomous investment, about which such models have very little to say, investment opportunities are being continuously created by increases in output and then completely and promptly exhausted, either simultaneously or with a predetermined constant lag. In our terminology, investment rises or falls whenever acceleration or retardation in the growth of total output causes a change in the rate at which new investment opportunities are being created.

expectations, and the increased desire for liquidity may become too great to be satisfied merely by reducing inventories.[15] When this happens, long-term investment declines along with total output, and the resulting decline in activity may be quite pronounced. Each successive decline in income may serve to weaken further the cyclical inducements to invest, even though the stock of investment opportunities remains large.

What is important about this case (and this is true also of the next case to be discussed) is that the revival of long-term investment is brought about endogenously through the operation of the cyclical response mechanism: as soon as excess inventories are liquidated, prices stop falling, etc. Thus, while contractions which arise in this way may be quite sharp, they are not likely to last long. They represent one of two types of "intermediate" or "hybrid" downswings (intermediate between a "pure minor" and a "pure major").

Our third category results in the other type of hybrid contraction. During the boom, as investment and output rise, interest rates and the prices of capital goods increase. This by itself does not necessarily bring on a decline in investment. We have already allowed for the effect of supply inelasticities in our definition of the appropriate capital stock and of investment opportunities. During expansion, the marginal efficiency schedule of investment shifts upward and then may stabilize at a high level so that, even with upward sloping supply functions for loanable funds and capital goods, a full-employment rate of investment is attained. However, in a particularly vigorous and speculative boom, with or without intervention by the monetary authorities, interest rates and/or capital goods prices may rise beyond the levels that would permit continuance of a full-employment level of investment. The capital shortage reduces the stock of investment opportunities, possibly to the point where it can no longer support the current level of investment. Even if the stock of investment opportunities remains large enough under these conditions, current investment may still fall for any one of several reasons. (1) The marginal efficiency schedule for current investment is not likely to be completely interest inelastic, so that rising interest rates can have some effect on current investment once the schedule stops shifting upward. (2) A continued rise in capital-goods prices can shift the marginal efficiency schedule downward. (3) The schedule may shift downward because of growing expectations that interest rates and capital-goods prices will be

---

[15] The size of the stock of investment opportunities at the time of the downturn should make a considerable difference in this case. The more plentiful are investment opportunities, the less likely is a reversal of short-term expectations to bring about a decline in the cyclical inducements to undertake long-term investment. It is possible also that the *kind* of opportunities makes a difference. The more important are the opportunities for so-called autonomous investment, and the less investment is geared to anticipated changes in total output, the more resistant will long-term expectations be to a given downward revision in short-period expectations. I would emphasize, however, that even the most "autonomous" kind of investment is not completely insensitive to cyclical changes in profit expectations and liquidity attitudes.

more favorable later on. (4) Capital rationing may force investment below its former level. Whatever the precise mechanism, a monetary or real capital shortage *may* choke off the boom, but this is only one of several ways in which the boom can end.

For our present purpose, what is important about a decline that begins in this way is that the automatic corrective forces inherent in the downswing are sufficient in themselves to bring about eventually a revival of investment. The elimination of the capital shortage is enough to raise the stock of investment opportunities back toward its former level. Current investment becomes more attractive. And, of course, the stock of investment opportunities may increase for other (exogenous) reasons, also. The downswing may force the level of investment quite low, because of the induced and cumulative deterioration in expectations. But, as in our other two cases, the seeds of revival are in the downswing. Like the preceding hybrid case, contractions arising in this way may be quite sharp, since long-term investment also falls, but they are not likely to be of long duration.

Finally, we have our fourth type, when a high level of investment has been maintained for a long enough time so that long-term investment opportunities become seriously impaired, even without the advent of a capital shortage. The boom may actually go on for some time after investment opportunities have declined to the point where, if they were correctly appraised, less than the current level of investment would be undertaken. If this happens, potential overcapacity in some lines is being created, and the eventual decline will be worse than it otherwise would be. The decline, when it finally comes, may be ushered in by the same sequence of events that we associate with minor recessions; but, as the contraction gathers momentum, the impairment of investment opportunities is increasingly recognized; the decline in long-term investment accelerates; and output drops to very low levels.

This is the case of a "pure" major depression. Two essential points about it need to be noted. (1) The decline in investment is associated with a reduction in investment opportunities, brought about not by a fall in the appropriate capital stock but because the existing capital stock was approaching that which was appropriate. (2) The forces making for revival that gradually emerge from a cyclical contraction are not enough in themselves to restore the stock of investment opportunities. Eventual improvement of short-term expectations and liquidity attitudes will also bring about improvement in the inducements to exploit existing investment opportunities, but the ensuing expansion will be weak and will not carry to a high level of employment if the stock of investment opportunities remains deficient.

To avoid any misunderstanding, let me emphasize that this description of a major depression in terms of reduced investment opportunities is not intended to mean what has been widely debated under the heading of secular stagnation. We assume that the deficiency of investment opportunities is only temporary, but that it does continue long enough to create serious difficulties. It may be primarily associated with over-building in one or more important expanding industries (as occasionally happened with the railroads in the nineteenth century), or the approach to maturity of a group of industries, or the making up of deficiencies in the stock of housing, or the end of a boom associated with major structural changes in the economy (as the rapid growth in the trade and service industries in the 1920's). During the depression we can assume that the stock of investment opportunities will begin to accumulate until it is again able to support a high level of employment—because of deferred replacement, continued growth in population, continuing technological change, new opportunities opened up by changed cost-price relations, and so on. In general, the stronger the underlying forces making for growth, for rapid technological change, and for changes in the composition of output, and the less the degree of over-building during the preceding boom, the more rapidly will the stock of investment opportunities accumulate as a major depression wears on.

IV

The four possibilities just described can be used as the basis for a three-fold classification of cycles, which represents an elaboration of the usual distinction between major and minor cycles. First, we can have a pure minor cycle, with no significant fluctuations in long-term investment, the contraction phase of which is marked chiefly by a sharp decline in inventory investment and some fall in income and consumption. Such were the American contractions of 1923–24, 1927, and 1949. The very mild reconversion recession at the end of World War II does not, however, fit this description.[16]

The minor cycle shades into our second type, which culminates in what we may call a hybrid contraction. This sort of decline can result from either the second or third possibilities described above. In this case the contraction can be quite severe, and long-term investment can fall very sharply, but the decline will not last long. I suggest that it is more useful

---

[16] According to Barger's figures, the sum of producers' durables and private construction declined by ten per cent or less in the 1924 and 1927 recessions. H. Barger, *Outlay and Income in the United States, 1921–1938* (New York, 1942), p. 114. The decline in gross private domestic investment exclusive of inventories was also mild in the 1949 recession. I would not class the mild and brief reconversion dip at the end of World War II as a minor recession in my sense. I think it is more informative to characterize this episode as a case of the overlapping of two major cycles. The decline in government spending at the end of the war was so quickly offset by the upsurge in private investment opportunities (and the upward shift in the consumption function) that there was little opportunity for a downward cumulative spiral to carry very far. The usual sort of minor-cycle readjustment in inventories did not occur. In a recent article, C. A. Blyth has argued that there *was* a substantial reduction in private expenditures on plant and equipment in the 1949 recession. See "The 1948–49 American Recession," *Economic Journal*, LXIV (September 1954), 486-510.

to think of the depressions of 1907 and 1937–38 and (with some qualifi-cations) 1921 in these terms, as hybrid contractions, than as major depres-sions resulting essentially from the same sorts of causes as the prolonged depressions of the 1870's or 1930's.

Finally, we have the case of the major cycle proper, which ends in a prolonged (and usually severe) depression associated with a significant impairment of investment opportunities. To this category apparently be-long the depressions of the 1870's, 1890's, and 1930's, and probably also the depression of 1882–85.[17]

In the way that major cycles are usually marked off by observers, they may end in either a true major or a hybrid depression, to use our termi-nology. Ordinarily, a major cycle is said to end when there is a sharp decline in long-term investment.[18]

In practice, one set of investment stimuli may follow upon another with-out the intervention of either a major depression or a hybrid contraction. For this reason I have sometimes found it useful to speak of "incomplete" and of "overlapping" major cycles, when two major expansions, each as-sociated with a particular set of investment opportunities, follow each other with no intervening contraction or at worst a very short one.[19]

In this connection, it is worth noting that there has been no complete major cycle in the United States since 1933. A major upswing did begin in that year, but it did not end in 1937. The decline of 1937–38 was a hybrid contraction, superimposed on a long but weak major upswing. There was no significant change in the state of investment opportunities in 1937–38. Then in 1940 a new set of investment opportunities took over and sparked the accelerated expansion of 1940–45, which was geared to war expenditures. Thus the recorded upswing of 1938–45 is not homogeneous with respect to the underlying investment opportunities which kept it going.

We have already commented on the mild reconversion recession at the end of the war.[20] Since 1945 we have had a prolonged boom, interrupted

---

[17] The 1882–85 decline had some of the earmarks of a hybrid contraction, but there does seem also to have been a decline in investment opportunities in railroads. Cf. Rendigs Fels, "The American Business Cycle of 1879–85," *Journal of Political Economy*, LX (February 1952), 60-75.

[18] Cf. Hansen's chronology of major depressions in *Business Cycles and National Income*, ch. 2.

[19] "An incomplete major cycle would consist of an underlying expansion phase which did not continue long enough to generate a major depression before a new set of invest-ment stimuli took hold and created a new major upswing. . . . The concept of over-lapping major cycles differs only in degree. In this case, a major expansion does continue long enough to generate a decline of some severity. But during this cycle new invest-ment stimuli may be accumulating and gain strength, and they may take hold quickly enough to cut short the decline and lead to a prompt and vigorous recovery. Thus a new major cycle may overlap the old." R. A. Gordon, *Business Fluctuations* (New York, 1952), pp. 268-69. While I find these concepts useful, the terms "incomplete" and "overlapping" may be unfortunate. However, I have not been able to think of better ones.

[20] Cf. p. 415, note 16, above.

by the clearly minor recession in 1948–49 and by the contraction that be-gan in 1953. Here again, however, the underlying major expansion has not been homogeneous in terms of underlying investment opportunities. Korea added a new set of stimuli to those which were already maintaining the level of aggregate demand.

In the last 20 years, then, we have had four successive sets of stimuli operating to expand aggregate demand (during 1933–39, 1940–45, 1945–50, and since 1950). It is not surprising, therefore, that during this period there has been no complete major cycle ending in a significant impairment of investment opportunities and a major depression. What is perhaps surprising is that we have been able to avoid a hybrid contraction for so long.[21]

All this suggests a conclusion which, while perhaps obvious, has not, I think, been sufficiently recognized in the literature on business cycles. While it is useful to mark off cyclical turning points and to examine the whole cycles that we thus obtain, such combinations of expansion and contraction are not necessarily the most significant units for the analysis of economic change. We may have to combine some of the recorded cycles in order to study the effect of a given set of investment opportunities work-ing itself out through a major boom and decline (1921–33, for example), or we may have to subdivide what is statistically a single phase of the cycle to explain how changes in investment stimuli brought about the statistical results that we are trying to explain (the long upswing of 1938–45 or the unusually long period of high-level activity after World War II). Perhaps this is to say nothing more than that a simplified picture of a more or less invariant cyclical process is not enough, by itself, to explain how the fluc-tuations we call business cycles emerge out of the underlying forces making for growth and structural change.

V

The approach outlined in the preceding sections has a number of advantages over the growth and business-cycle models to which we have become accustomed in recent years. First of all, it takes account of the fact that growth is a complicated process, involving not only a secular increase in total output but also both gradual and discontinuous changes in the composition of output and in the composition of the capital stock. Secondly, it offers a picture of the cyclical self-generation process that takes account of more elements of reality than do most recent cycle models; and it recalls to our attention important dynamic forces that much of the neo-Keynesian literature has tended to neglect: expectations, price changes, cyclical changes in liquidity attitudes, etc. Thirdly, I think, it throws ad-ditional light on the ways in which secular and cyclical change interact.

---

[21] The considerations suggested in footnote 15 are relevant here. There also seem to have been important changes in the cyclical response mechanism since the 1930's.

And, finally, it offers a set of hypotheses for explaining the important differences among the business cycles of experience.[22]

The approach to investment behavior outlined in the preceding pages offers a general framework into which can be fitted most of the recent literature dealing with the cyclical behavior of investment. The acceleration principle becomes a special kind of special case. Investment opportunities arise in only one way, through changes in total output; and they are exploited in a certain way, in response to the same changes in output. The Kalecki-Kaldor type of investment function is another kind of special case, to which we have already referred, and so also is Goodwin's application of the notion of a flexible accelerator. Our approach fits even better all of the innovation theories.

Our approach also helps to evaluate the usual distinction between autonomous and induced investment. All investment depends in the first instance on the creation of investment opportunities. These opportunities may arise through the growth of total income, or because some product comes to claim a larger share of total income, or because, given the level and composition of output, new techniques call for a different composition of the total stock of capital. Once investment opportunities exist for any of these reasons, then the operation of the cyclical mechanism, particularly as it affects profit and sales expectations and liquidity attitudes, determines the actual time path of investment. In this sense, there is no private investment that is completely autonomous with respect to the important cyclical variables.[23]

The approach outlined here, even in the very general form in which it has been put, provides a useful set of hypotheses, and a list of possible forces operating on investment, which can be a guide in the study of particular cyclical episodes. It can also be useful in current appraisal and prediction. Granted that we can never know precisely the size and composition of the appropriate capital stock at any time and hence cannot get a reliable measure of the current stock of investment opportunities. Nonetheless, detailed studies can tell us a good deal about the state of investment opportunities in particular sectors and whether, over some given time in the future, investment is likely to rise, fall, or maintain its current level. Such studies of investment opportunities would be a useful

---

[22] See also Thomas Wilson's comments on the most useful way of studying the causes of cyclical fluctuations in his paper previously cited, especially pp. 87-89. There are also interesting similarities between the present paper and Kaldor's elaboration of his model to allow for "dynamic" elements in "The Relation of Economic Growth and Cyclical Fluctuations," cited in footnote 13 above, although I should have to disagree with some of his conclusions regarding the relations between growth and business cycles.

[23] Cf. this with Sidney Alexander's concept of "timing-induced autonomous" expenditures, in "Issues of Business Cycle Theory Raised by Mr. Hicks," *American Economic Review*, XLI (December 1951), 861-78. See also Thomas Wilson's discussion of "Cyclical and Autonomous Inducements to Invest," *op. cit.*, and Rendigs Fels's attempt to merge Schumpeter's and Hicks's models in "A Theory of Business Cycles," *Quarterly Journal of Economics*, LXVI (February 1952), 25-42.

supplement to the important surveys of planned investment expenditures that are now published.

Our study of investment behavior and the resulting classification of cycles has an obvious implication for public policy. In the case of minor and both types of hybrid contractions, government measures aimed at priming the pump are likely to have the desired leverage effects. Government measures which raise private incomes, improve liquidity positions, and bring about more favorable business expectations are likely to induce a cumulative rise of private investment back to its previous boom level. But in the case of a true major depression, measures aimed merely at maintaining or increasing disposable income and consumption will not be enough in themselves to restore private investment to the level needed for full employment. This is the case in which pump-priming will have only limited success, and the leverage effects of expansionary measures will be disappointingly small.[24] It is the hybrid depression which offers the fullest scope for the conventional instruments of stabilization policy, and it is this type of depression which economists usually seem to have in mind when they deal with problems of business-cycle policy.

---

[24] This does not mean that nothing can be done, but only that private investment will not necessarily respond vigorously to a rise in national income. In this case three lines of action are available to the government: to shift the consumption function upward, to substitute government expenditures for the lacking private investment, or to set about expanding private investment opportunities—for example, through tax incentives, pushing down interest rates and prices of capital goods, special aid to particular industries, various measures to stimulate residential building, etc.

FOR FURTHER READING

The writers who have been cited in this section are those who have emphasized nonmonetary investment factors which bring about fluctuations in business activity. Most modern investment theories stress monetary factors. Yet among the older writers, Gustav Cassel's *The Theory of Social Economy* (London: Ernest Benn, 1932) pays particular attention to the role of real investment (see particularly Chap. 19). Spiethoff's famous article on *"Krisen"* is now available in English as "Business Cycles" in *International Economic Papers*, No. 3, pp. 75-171. See also Arthur Schweitzer, "Spiethoff's Theory of the Business Cycle," *University of Wyoming Publications*, VIII, (April, 1941), 1-30, and Gottfried Haberler, *Prosperity and Depression* (Geneva: League of Nations, 1940), pp. 72-84. An interesting American exposition of this point of view is contained in George Hull's *Industrial Depressions* (New York: F. A. Stokes, 1911). The nonmonetary investment approach is also discussed in Wesley Mitchell's *Business Cycles: The Problem and Its Setting* (New York: National Bureau of Economic Research, 1927), pp. 23-29. Finally, Joseph Schumpeter's *The Theory of Economic Development* (Cambridge: Harvard University Press, 1934) should be carefully read not only for his contribution to the specific problem at hand, but also for a major contribution toward understanding the dynamics of modern capitalism.

SECTION D

Monetary Theories

❋❋❋

INTRODUCTION

Although we attempt to classify cycle theories in such categories as under-consumption, overproduction, and under- or overinvestment, monetary factors are almost always present in the analysis. The divergence of the monetary and nonmonetary theories, in many instances a matter of emphasis, lies principally in the fact that money and credit are paramount in the former and merely passive agents in the latter. Thus we have counted Hawtrey and Keynes in Section A as representing one facet of underconsumption, i.e., underinvestment theories of underconsumption. The studies of both men, however, leaned heavily to the monetary side and might therefore with equal justification have appeared in this section. Accordingly, it seemed propitious to incorporate below an excerpt from R.

G. Hawtrey's *Trade and Credit*. The problem of classifying the monetary theorists well illustrates the larger predicament of all anthologies which must pigeonhole the ideas of men who probe deeply into a given subject.

Monetary theorists argue that cyclical turning points occur as a result of changes in the average amount of money in circulation: that is, variations in the supply of money induce changes in total spending and affect thereby the level of business activity. In a modern credit economy, bank deposits compose the major form of money, and hence the proponents of the monetary approach tend to assume that it is the action of commercial banks in expanding and contracting the money supply which is the primary factor accounting for the volatility of business.

Since the turn of the century, monetary theory has pursued two distinct, but in a measure related, lines of investigation. A few economists in the United States and Great Britain (R. G. Hawtrey, for example) sought to establish a nexus between the quantity of money and the level of demand. If the quantity of money declined, demand would slacken, production fall off, and a pervasive contraction ensue. Opposite effects, of course, result from accretion in the circulating media. Some of Hawtrey's insights mirror the influence of the American economists Irving Fisher and Alvin Hansen.

More recently, in this tradition, may be listed Clark Warburton* and Milton Friedman.† Warburton reasons that economic stability depends upon the money supply growing at the same rate as the trend in total output. Monetary policy may inhibit a proper expansion in the supply of money with unfortunate consequences. Milton Friedman pitches his argument on the supply of money as related to the expected level of income over a number of years (permanent income). The latter determines the demand for money. If the supply of money rises faster than this demand, the excess cash balances will drive up money expenditures and income. Consequently, permanent income rises, and, *pari passu*, the demand for cash balances. Therefore, the money supply conditions the level of both income and production.

The Austrian School of economists, on the other hand, harkening back to Knut Wicksell's distinction between a natural and market rate of interest, stress abuse of credit as the main cause. Banks with excess reserves reduce interest rates below the "natural" level. These low rates foster a basic maladjustment in the structure of industry through encouraging

---

* See "The Misplaced Emphasis in Contemporary Business-Fluctuation Theory," *Journal of Business of the University of Chicago* (October, 1946); "Volume of Savings, Quantity of Money, and Business Instability," *Journal of Political Economy* (June, 1947); "The Theory of Turning Points in Business Fluctuations," *Quarterly Journal of Economics* (November, 1950); "How Much Variation in the Quantity of Money Is Needed?" *Southern Economic Journal* (April, 1952); "Money and Business Fluctuations in the Schumpeterian System," *Journal of Political Economy* (December, 1953).

† See *A Program for Monetary Stability* (New York: Fordham University Press, 1959); "The Demand for Money: Some Theoretical and Empirical Results," *Journal of Political Economy* (August, 1959).

the production of capital goods beyond the point justified by the demand for consumer outputs. Thus, although the overinvestment theory of the Austrians focuses on savings and investment, the relationship of the two is conditioned by the credit policies of the banking system—that is, by monetary factors.

In judging the worth of the monetary doctrines, the reader should bear in mind the following criticisms leveled at the school. All agree that fluctuations in aggregate demand are also fluctuations in money spending. Nevertheless, purchasing power *per se* does not create an effective demand; the desire for goods or the will to spend must also exist. If desire be wanting, no amount of monetary juggling or indiscriminate price cutting will convert a period of contraction into one of renewed expansion.

Monetary theories, by nature, overstate the influence of the interest rate in fixing the level of production and employment. One can easily demonstrate that variations in the national product more often than not are caused by nonmonetary factors: innovations, novel methods of doing business, evolving patterns of consumption, and changes in real or money costs. (In fact, does not the emphasis, in Hayek's article, on entrepreneurial anticipations, consumption habits, and the industrial structure represent a striving toward a more comprehensive explanation of the cycle?)

We must not go too far, however, in minimizing the monetary elements in business fluctuations. No matter how favorable the nonmonetary stimuli, expansion will not long endure without the sanction of monetary support. The monetists have served well in alerting us to the cumulative expansions and contractions which monetary factors, if not carefully managed, can set in motion.

The Trade Cycle*

RALPH G. HAWTREY

~~~~~~

Editors' Note

R. G. Hawtrey (1879–   ), educated at Eton and Trinity College, Cambridge, served in various capacities with the British Treasury in 1904–45. During this period, he earned an international reputation on currency, credit, and banking problems. In 1946, he was chosen president of the Royal Economic Society. Within his field of specialization Hawtrey has been a prolific author: *Good and Bad Trade: An Inquiry into the Causes of Trade Fluctuations* (1913); *The Exchequer and Control of Expenditure* (1921); *Currency and Credit* (1923); *The Economic Problem* (1926); *The Gold Standard in Theory and Practice* (1927); *Trade and Credit* (1928); *Trade Depression and the Way Out* (1931); *The Art of Central Banking* (1932); *Capital and Employment* (1937); *A Century of Bank Rate* (1938); *The Balance of Payments and the Standard of Living* (1950).

Hawtrey's article "The Trade Cycle," and the succeeding one by Hayek, typify the two lines of inquiry which have characterized the development of monetary theory in the present century. Defining demand as "money" and employing a circular-flow analysis, Hawtrey believes that changes in the supply of bank credit generate cyclical changes in spending. Movements in interest rates are effective primarily on the accumulation of inventories, low rates favoring inventory rebuilding and expansion. However, expansion can proceed only as long as bank reserves allow for additional credit advances. A rise of currency in circulation or the export of gold may deplete bank reserves, impair the flow of credit, and initiate recession.

A careful scrutiny of Hawtrey's and Hayek's articles, with special atten-

---

* From *Trade and Credit* by Ralph G. Hawtrey (London: Longmans, Green, 1928), chap. v, pp. 330-349. Reprinted by permission of Longmans, Green & Co., Ltd.

tion to points of similarity and difference, will afford good practice for further sallies into monetary theory.

❧ The output of literature on the subject of the trade cycle has increased beyond precedent since the war, but the numerous writers who have contributed to it have not always noticed that for the time being there *is* no trade cycle. The essential characteristic of the trade cycle is its periodicity. That of course is the meaning of the term, *cycle*. What struck the pre-war economists was that the alternation between good and bad trade was regularly spread over a period of from seven to eleven years, and that it was world-wide. Otherwise there would have been nothing to explain. That the state of trade should vary is what every one would expect. Were it always the same, like the temperature of the human body, that would have been at least as much in need of explanation as the trade cycle itself.

Since the war there have been ups and downs in trade, but they have not synchronised, or have only very partially synchronised, in different countries, and there has been no trace of regular periodicity. This change is significant, and ought to throw light on the explanation of the trade cycle. I shall return to it later on.

Clearly, in investigating the trade cycle, the first thing to consider is, what *are* the phenomena that vary periodically. The alternation is of good with bad trade, or of prosperity with depression. But these are vague terms. Students of the trade cycle are aware that the alternation is apparent at many different points. There is scarcely any field of economic activity which does not exhibit it.

But among the multifarious symptoms of the trade cycle, two tendencies stand out conspicuously and may well be treated as fundamental, a fluctuation in productive activity and a fluctuation in the price level. A fluctuation in productive *activity* is not to be confused with a fluctuation in *production*. The one is measured by the amount of effort put into production, the other by the amount of output resulting. Output depends partly on effort and partly on other factors, such as technical processes and natural conditions.

Output may furnish a good measure of productive activity, when disturbing factors are absent or, if present, are allowed for. But employment is a better test. When the percentage of available workmen unemployed increases, productive activity is diminishing, and *vice versa.*

The trade cycle is composed of periods of good trade, characterized by rising prices and low unemployment percentages, alternating with periods of bad trade, characterized by falling prices and high unemployment percentages.

Since productive activity and the price level increase and decrease together, it necessarily follows that there is a corresponding fluctuation in the total *demand* for all products expressed in terms of money.

The money of which demand consists is provided directly or indirectly from people's incomes. The total of the incomes which people in any community have to spend I call the *consumers' income*; the total which they do spend I call the *consumers' outlay*. Consumers' income and consumers' outlay tend to be equal. The means of payment (comprising money and bank credit), which people have in hand, I call the *unspent margin*. Consumers' income and consumers' outlay can only differ in amount when the unspent margin changes.

The term "consumer" as here used must not be interpreted too narrowly. People spend their incomes not only on consumable products, but on investment. "Consumer" must be regarded as including "investor," and the consumers' outlay as including investment. For money invested is *spent*. It is spent on capital goods.

On the other hand, the consumers' outlay does not include the expenditure of traders on buying or producing goods to sell again. Such expenditure is not incurred out of a trader's income, but out of his turnover, the gross receipts of his business. All that comes out of his income is such additional capital as he puts into his business out of his own savings. This is expenditure from income on investment, whether the money be spent on an extension or improvement of fixed capital, or on a net addition to goods held in stock.

So understood, the consumers' outlay is the whole effective demand for everything that is produced, whether commodities or services. The trader who buys to sell again is merely an intermediary passing on a portion of this demand to one of his neighbours. The cyclical alternations in effective demand must therefore be alternations in the consumers' outlay.

Demand however is *relative*, and some economists have sought to explain the depression which marks the adverse phase of the trade cycle as due, not to an actual decrease in the consumers' outlay, but to an excess in the output of products.

The classical economists argued that general over-production was impossible, because no one produced except with a view to consuming, and therefore demand was necessarily equal to supply. Moreover, production was at its greatest during the active phase of the trade cycle, and fell off during the phase of depression, at the very time when the symptoms of over-production appeared. These difficulties could be met if the over-production were supposed to take the form of accumulation of excessive stocks of commodities. If production outstrips demand, it was said, a part of the products remains unsold, and traders, encumbered with unsold goods, become reluctant to produce more. Restricted production means restricted employment. Those conditions will continue so long as unsold stocks remain above normal. The redundant goods have to be sold off at a sacrifice of price. When that process is completed, traders' stocks will have been brought into relation with a reduced scale of production and consumption. The pressure on markets being then relieved, there is found to be a margin of unemployed capital and labour, anxious to start producing. When production revives, the existing stocks of commodities are found to be insufficient for the needs of markets, and the process of replenishing stocks makes for active production. Production in fact exceeds consumption, and will continue to do so till excessive stocks have again been accumulated, and the cycle is then started afresh.

This is a version of the over-production theory of the trade cycle. The theory by itself was incomplete, because it offered no explanation of why the accumulation and liquidation of stocks synchronized in different industries and different countries, or why the process should have a period of from seven to eleven years, or even why it should ever begin at all.

Accordingly the theory was further elaborated. To explain the length of the period, it was pointed out that, when output has to be increased in order to replenish stocks, the capacity of the industries concerned might have to be extended by the construction of new plant and fixed capital. That would take a considerable time. Not only does the construction of a piece of capital equipment often take months or even years, but the capacity of the constructional trades themselves is limited, and when they are congested with orders they cannot undertake prompt completion.

At the end, therefore, of a time of depression, the period of recovery would be prolonged during the process of extending the equipment of industry. The climax would come when the fresh capital came into use, and the swollen output of consumable commodities would increase stocks up to normal and thereafter would exceed demand.

To explain why the movements synchronised in different industries, recourse was had to two arguments. In the first place, it was said, prosperity in one industry created demand for the products of others, and they in turn became prosperous and created further demand for one another's products. Secondly, the activity of an industry depended on psychological causes. Producers become enterprising when they *expect* good markets; they become cautious when they *expect* markets to flag. Such expectations, it is said, are contagious; they are subject to the laws of crowd psychology. Optimism in one industry spreads to others; optimism in one country breeds optimism in all. In the same way pessimism when once it gets started tends to become universal.

The over-production theory thus elaborated represents, I think, fairly the explanation of the trade cycle prevalent among what I may call the classical school of economists. In many respects it fits the facts well. Experience shows that at a time of good trade the constructional trades are more active than the others, and when the tide turns they are more depressed. Stocks of commodities are redundant when trade is bad, and short when trade is good.

One thing, however, I have omitted. I have said nothing about monetary changes, or about the regulation of credit, upon which monetary changes usually depend. Economists of the classical school do not leave the monetary factor out altogether. But they regard it as subsidiary, and as merely modifying and perhaps intensifying tendencies otherwise accounted for.

But in the over-production theory, as I have just stated it, there are *presupposed* certain assumptions as regards money and credit.

The theory finds the explanation of trade activity in the replenishment of stocks depleted during the preceding depression, and of the depression in the liquidation of stocks accumulated during the preceding activity. The replenishment of stocks consists in an excess of traders' purchases over their sales. It is an addition to their physical capital, and must be paid for. The necessary funds can be provided either by savings out of income or by means of bank credit.

If they are provided by savings out of income, that means that a part of the consumers' outlay is diverted to the accumulation of stocks. If the consumers' outlay itself remains unchanged, what is left to provide the effective demand for commodities for consumption is correspondingly diminished. On that assumption there is nothing in the replenishment of stocks to make trade active.

If on the other hand traders increase their stocks with money borrowed from the banks, this is no longer so. The banks can *create* the necessary funds. The trader becomes indebted to the banker for the amount of his loan, and the banker becomes indebted to the trader for an equal amount on current account.

The trader can use the banker's obligation as a means of payment; he can assign it by cheque to those from whom he buys. He can thus add to his stocks of commodities without diminishing the amount of the consumers' outlay in other directions.

If the consumers' income and the consumers' outlay be supposed to balance at £1,000,000 a day, or £30,000,000 a month, and if traders set out to add £5,000,000 worth of commodities to their stocks in the course of three months, providing the necessary funds from their own savings, then the traders' demand for their own consumption will be diminished by that amount and the consumers' outlay as a whole for three months will be reduced from £90,000,000 to £85,000,000. If on the other hand the traders borrow the £5,000,000 from their bankers, the consumers' outlay will remain at £90,000,000, and the total demand experienced by producers will be increased to £95,000,000.

Here we have a definite addition to the consumers' outlay, a demand springing out of nothing. That does not however tell the whole story. It is important to trace as clearly as possible the ulterior effects of the creation of additional bank credit, and we shall return to the subject presently. Meanwhile it is enough to note that *without* the creation of additional bank credit, or some process equivalent to it, the desire of traders to add to their stocks will not on balance occasion any activity in trade at all.

Exactly the same line of argument applies to the creation of additional fixed capital. If the fixed capital is paid for from savings out of income, the amount of income available for other purposes is diminished by an equal amount. Professor Aftalion has maintained that the characteristic of the active phase of the trade cycle is a scarcity of consumable commodities relative to demand. In order to increase the supply, he contends, it is necessary in the first instance to extend the capital equipment of industry. That takes time, and while it is in progress the prices of consumable commodities are abnormally high, while the prices of capital goods, the products of the constructional and engineering trades and their materials, are also high, because they reflect the anticipations of ultimate profit from the sale of increased supplies of consumable goods. It would not be easy to establish the assumption here implicitly made, that at the end of the depression the capital equipment is not sufficient to give full employment to the population. But apart from that Professor Aftalion's argument really presupposes that the consumers' outlay provides an undiminished demand for consumable goods, while the additional supply of capital goods is paid for from some other source. In other words, whether by the creation of bank credit or some other means, the consumers' outlay is assumed to have been increased.

The same criticism is applicable once again to the supposed spread of prosperity from one industry to another. If the consumers' outlay is unchanged, then any increase in the amount spent on the products of one industry can only be at the cost of diminishing the amount spent on the products of others. So long as the consumers' outlay is supposed fixed, there is only one way in which it can be reconciled with an increase in economic activity, and that is by a general fall in prices. But this is the exact reverse of what experience of the trade cycle records; the active phase is invariably accompanied by rising prices, whereas falling prices are an outstanding characteristic of the phase of depression.

There remains the argument from the psychology of traders. Cannot trade become active because traders *expect* a good demand, even though their expectation is erroneous? And may not depression likewise be due to an expectation of a poor demand? An optimistic trader who gives orders for an additional supply of commodities need not pay for them till they are delivered. Meanwhile the producers will be the more fully employed on account of the additional orders. But the burden of financing the orders is not escaped. The producers must meet their outlay upon wages and other current costs from some source or other. Either they must borrow from their bankers, or they must meet these costs out of their own incomes. In the one case bank credits are created; in the other the consumers' outlay is encroached upon.

A speculative movement may lead to lucrative orders being given to producers for the delivery of goods at future dates. The prospective profit on such orders is part of a producer's income. If he refrains from anticipating the profit, and only borrows so much as is essential to pay current costs, he may be regarded as applying that part of his income to holding the goods in course of manufacture and in the interval before delivery. Here we have an increase in the consumers' income which does not depend on the creation of bank credits. But the addition so made to income is tied up with the goods in course of manufacture, and cannot come into the market for any other purpose till the order is completed and the goods are delivered. The purchaser must then pay for them, and he can only find the necessary means either from income or by borrowing.

If the speculator's expectation of a favourable market is mistaken, he will make a loss, or at any rate a smaller profit than he anticipated. This loss must be set against the producer's gain, and the consumers' income as a whole will not have been increased. Complicated as the effect of speculation may be, the amount of the consumers' income and the consumers' outlay remains the governing factor.

And at this point we may return to the question of their relation to the creation of bank credits. We saw that, if traders set out to increase their stocks of goods, and borrow the means of paying for them, there is an increase in the total effective demand. The traders' demand for additional stocks of goods, while it lasts, is *added* to the consumers' outlay, which comprised the pre-existing demand for goods for consumption.

The usual method of proceeding would be for a merchant or dealer in commodities to give orders to producers for fresh supplies, and it would be the producers in the first instance who would borrow. They might draw bills on the merchant and get them discounted by the banks, or they might obtain advances from the banks.

The sums credited to the producers are applied by them to pay the costs of production. But the costs of production are composed of the *incomes* of those who contribute to production, whether by their services or by the use of their property. The cost of materials used in production is similarly composed of the incomes of other producers. Thus the whole amount of the funds created by the banks is received as income, whether profits, wages, salaries, rent, or interest, by those engaged in producing the commodities.

The effect is to distribute the money advanced among them, and to increase their balances of cash by the amount distributed. There has in fact been an increase in the unspent margin, the total quantity of money and bank deposits. According to the quantity theory of money, that should tend, other things being unchanged, to raise prices.

We cannot assume without further consideration that other things will be unchanged. If the recipients of this extra money, both profit-makers and wage-earners, added it to their cash balances and kept it unspent, there would be no increase in the consumers' outlay, and no tendency for prices to rise. But this is extremely unlikely. Some of the recipients would be wage-earners newly brought into employment, who would spend their money on necessary consumption. Others would certainly spend some of their additional earnings on consumable goods. Others again would save part of the money, but saving would ordinarily take the form, not of hoarding money or of leaving it on current account at a bank, but of investing it. And money invested is spent on fixed capital.

A little of the money would remain behind in balances, for a man whose earnings are increased would hold on an average somewhat larger amounts of cash in hand than before; but probably much the greater part of the additional income is immediately in one way or another spent. It is spent on buying things from traders, who find their stocks of goods diminished, and are put in a position to pay off part of their indebtedness to their bankers with the cash received.

But we started by supposing that dealers in commodities desired to *increase* their stocks of commodities, and found it worth while to borrow from their bankers in order to hold additional stocks. Now we find that by doing so they bring into being a new consumers' demand, which tends to deplete their stocks almost as fast as they are replenished. What the traders have accomplished is limited to the excess of their purchases for stock over their sales to consumers, and the net increase in their indebtedness to the banks is so much as is required to finance this excess. The net increase in the unspent margin, the quantity of the means of payment, is equal to the same excess; seen from another point of view it is that part of their increased receipts which people leave in balances rather than spend or invest.

The traders' desire for increased stocks remains unsatisfied, and they continue giving increased orders to the producers. It may be pointed out that the consumers' outlay is increased as soon as the producers begin to borrow. The producers and their employees have more to spend while the orders are still uncompleted. The dealers find that the goods they have immediately in hand are actually diminished, though against the shortage they have command of a greater future supply. By the time an order is completed, the whole of its value will have become available to the producers as income. The net effect in increasing stocks will be limited to so much of this income as is kept in hand by the recipients in balances.[1]

In order to complete their programme of increasing stocks, the dealers in commodities must go on giving fresh orders, till the amount so kept in hand in cash balances is great enough to equal the additional stocks desired. But meanwhile the producers will be becoming more and more active, and there is a limit to their activity. As more and more producers become employed up to capacity,[2] they will tend to raise prices. And as

---

[1] The recipients may spend this income not on commodities but on personal services. But those who are paid for rendering these services will in turn either spend the money or retain it in balances.

[2] The limit of capacity may be imposed by the available labour supply before all the available plant is active. This may occur in one locality or industry, or in industry as a whole.

the dealers experience more and more difficulty in placing orders and in securing early delivery of those placed, they will tend to defend their stocks against depletion by raising prices against the consumer. Here we have that rise of prices which the quantity theory of money tells us ought to occur. It comes about because people spend the money they receive, but only in so far as their expenditure cannot be met by increased production. If we go back for a moment to the over-production theory, we can now see not merely that it presupposes an increase of bank credits as a pre-requisite condition of increased trade activity, but that the increase of bank credits gives rise to a complicated succession of reactions tending to intensify the activity far beyond its immediate effect.

It is equally true that when traders seek to diminish their stocks of commodities, there will be no flagging in the activity of trade unless they take steps to diminish their indebtedness to the banks. A dealer who reduces his stock, by restricting purchases or hastening sales, finds himself with more cash in hand. But if he spends the cash (whether on consumable commodities or on investments), it is paid away directly or indirectly to producers, and the adverse effect on markets is counteracted. The more normal course of events is that the dealers give less orders to the producers, the producers borrow less from the banks, they and their employees have less to spend, and the dealers consequently find that they sell less.

Here, as in the contrary case of the increase of orders, a *vicious circle* is set up. The dealers want to diminish their stocks of goods, but, when they restrict the orders they give to the producers, the consumers' outlay falls off, and their sales are so reduced that their stocks are little diminished.

The foregoing analysis of the effects of an acceleration or retardation of the creation of bank credit has been simplified by the omission of any reference to the investment market and the supply of fixed capital. The capital equipment of industry and transport for the most part differs essentially from those consumable goods which can be accumulated by merchants in stock. The effective demand for capital goods emanates from savings. These savings are a part of the consumers' outlay.

Nevertheless here also bank credit is a factor. It enters into the matter in at least three ways. A contractor who produces capital equipment may borrow from his banker for the interval before he receives payment. When the requisite funds have been raised in the investment market to pay for the capital equipment, a part of the shares or securities issued may be temporarily carried by underwriters or by dealers in the investment market with borrowed money. And finally an industrialist may avoid application to the investment market altogether, and may pay for an extension of his fixed capital by means of an advance from his banker, which he will hope to pay off out of profits in a short period of years. An increase or decrease of the bank credits created for these purposes has substantially just the same effect as an increase or decrease of those created to carry stocks of consumable commodities. The fundamental principle applicable to all cases is that no one borrows from a bank to hold the proceeds idle;

he pays them away immediately, and they pass into circulation and swell the consumers' income and the consumers' outlay.

We have now shown that the variations of effective demand, which are the real substance of the trade cycle, must be traced to movements in bank credit. But we have still to explain why and how such movements in bank credit will occur.

Under pre-war conditions the creation of bank credit was governed by the supply of gold. If the lending operations of the banks were accelerated, and the consumers' outlay increased, we have seen that there would be an increase in people's cash balances. The balances of the well-to-do may be held in the form of bank credit, but those of the wage-earning classes must be in actual money, whether coin or paper. When the earnings of the working classes are increased, they begin to absorb cash, and the cash reserves of the banks are thereby weakened. Even in countries where paper money was used, the law did not allow of its indefinite increase without a prescribed backing of gold. Sooner or later therefore the restrictions on the supply of money would compel the banks to limit their lending.

That the transition from activity to depression was marked by a restriction of credit occasioned by a shortage of cash reserves in the banks is a fact proved by experience. But we still have to explain why the process by which the banks were led first to expand and then to contract credit was spread over a long period of years.

To a bank lending is the source of profit, and it will seek to lend as much as it can. But if any bank lends more freely than its neighbors, it will begin to lose cash at the clearing. This is a more immediate check upon it than the withdrawal of cash into circulation, and tends to make all the banks in a country keep pace with one another. It does not of itself prevent the whole community of banks from accelerating their lending operations together, but it prevents any sudden spurt except in concert. Such a simultaneous spurt may occasionally occur, when for example there is a reduction of bank rate, but in general the expansion of credit would be gradual.

And if the expansion of credit in one country with a gold standard outstrips the expansion of credit in the others, it will have to meet an adverse balance of payments. As we saw, an expansion of credit increases the consumers' outlay; it therefore makes the country a more favorable market to sell in. It attracts imports and diverts goods from export to the home market. The adverse trade balance thus occasioned has to be paid for in gold, and it can only be corrected, and the drain of gold stopped, by a contraction of credit.[3]

Therefore just as one bank has to keep pace in lending with other banks in the same country, so one country must keep pace with the others. The desire for profit always points toward expansion, but, each bank and each

[3] When the balance of payments of any country is disturbed by any independent cause (e.g. external borrowing or lending, or good or bad crops) its credit position will diverge for the time being from that of its neighbours. [See my *Currency and Credit*, pp. 110-16 and 163-74 (3rd edition).]

country being imbued with caution lest it go too fast, the progress of the credit expansion is necessarily very gradual and slow. It is not merely like a procession keeping pace in response to a central command, which would no doubt move somewhat more slowly than a free individual. It is rather like a crowd moving without organisation towards an objective, under the condition that any individual who goes faster than the rest is immediately pulled back.

There is another factor which materially affects the rate of progress of the credit cycle. What ultimately limits the expansion of credit is the absorption of money into circulation, and we saw that it is absorbed mainly by the wage-earning classes, who receive and pay small sums, and have no banking accounts (excepting savings bank accounts which are really a form of investment). This absorption lags behind the credit expansion.

When employment improves and wages rise, the working classes spend the greater part of what they receive on consumable goods. The residue builds up their cash balances very slowly. The rise of wages lags some way behind the rise of prices and profits. In the course of revival after a depression, when the stage is reached at which industry is working approximately up to capacity, and prices are perhaps not far from normal, wages are still below normal. After an interval, when wages have reached normal, the cash holdings of the working classes have still not been brought up to their normal proportion to wages. There ensues a period when these cash holdings continue to increase. By the time they have increased not merely up to normal, but so far beyond it as to make a shortage in the cash reserves of the banks, considerable further progress will have been made with the credit expansion, and wages themselves will be well above normal. At that stage the banks will begin to restrict credit. By that time prices and profits will be swollen, and the consumers' outlay will be much above its normal amount. Producers will be working up to capacity under the pressure of an accumulation of forward orders. The restriction of credit will not be fully effective till these orders have been worked through; for so long as producers are engaged upon them they must borrow on any terms. There will therefore be an uncomfortable interval while producers remain busy, but the shadow of credit contraction is already upon trade. During that interval the workpeople will still be fully employed, wages cannot be reduced, and they will be absorbing cash. When at last the credit restriction becomes fully effective, and unemployment develops, the absorption of money into circulation will have reached a maximum.

The process of getting money back from circulation into the reserves of the banks is a slow and painful one. The pressure of unemployment and inadequate wages has to drive the working classes to draw upon their supplies of cash, or at any rate to prevent them increasing those supplies, while the new gold from the mines flows into the banks.

It would not be possible to calculate *a priori* what period the completion of a cycle of these processes would occupy. But at any rate it is not surprising that the period should extend over a considerable number of years.

The regulation of credit in an international system by reference to gold reserves supplies an adequate explanation of the rate of progress of the cycle and its periodic character, *once it is started*. But why does it start at all?

The answer to this question is that credit is *inherently unstable*. We have already referred to the "vicious circle" of expansion and contraction. Activity causes credit expansion, credit expansion increases demand, demand evokes greater activity. Depression damps down borrowing, diminished borrowing brings with it curtailed demand, curtailed demand means more depression.

It follows that a small or casual credit movement, whether expansion or contraction, tends to exaggerate itself. Once started, it grows, and will continue growing till the banks take active steps to stop it. Under the conditions we have assumed, they do not take these steps till the reserve position is affected, and by the time that occurs the movement will have gathered considerable momentum. The process of checking and reversing this momentum will be a fairly protracted one.

Therefore even if a state of perfect credit equilibrium could be established, it would give way at the first small disturbance, and a cyclical movement would develop. No other originating cause is called for than the endless fortuitous variations in the credit position and in traders' expectations, which are always occurring.

We have now travelled a long way from the over-production theory with which we started. In fact we have shown that trade depressions cannot be due to over-production; the disparity that arises between supply and demand cannot be due to an excess of supply, but must be due to a deficiency of demand. Demand, that is to say, the consumers' outlay, is curtailed owing to a restriction of credit. If the restriction of credit did not occur, the active phase of the trade cycle could be indefinitely prolonged, at the cost, no doubt, of an indefinite rise of prices and an abandonment of the gold standard. There is no over-production. Throughout the active phase production is at a high level, but that is because it can barely keep pace with consumption. Stocks of commodities are then below normal, and are still below normal when the restriction of credit brings the turning-point.

The standard of sufficiency in stocks is itself *relative*, and is dependent among other things upon the state of credit. It is usual for merchants to carry a part of their stocks with borrowed money, and any increase or decrease in stocks probably means an increase or decrease in their indebtedness. Interest on temporary advances is a small item to a manufacturer, whose main preoccupation is to keep his plant fully employed. But it is of considerable account to a merchant who makes a profit, often a very small percentage, on buying and selling large consignments of goods. To a merchant the inconvenience of letting his stocks fall a little below the usual amount is probably very slight. When the rate of interest rises, his idea of what is a reasonable amount to hold in stock is immediately modified; he begins to hasten his sales and restrict his orders.

The serious glut of goods which is so characteristic of a trade depression occurs at a later stage, when the contraction in the consumers' outlay has made itself felt in a decline of sales. Stocks then become actually greater than normal.

An expansion of credit is similarly started through the sensitiveness of merchants to the rate of interest. Merchants are tempted by cheap money to hasten their purchases.

It is obvious that much depends upon the psychology of the merchants and other traders, and particularly on their expectations as to the course of markets. One who expects demand to grow will hasten to buy. He anticipates the advantages of prompt sales or high prices or both. When prices are rising, the holding of goods in stock is itself profitable; when prices are falling, the holding of goods in stock is a source of loss. When prices are rising, a very high rate of interest may fail to deter merchants from borrowing; when they are falling, an apparently low rate of interest may fail to tempt them.

Here we find a new point of contact with the classical school of economists. They lay great stress on the state of business confidence and find one explanation of the trade cycle primarily in a rhythmical recurrence of errors of optimism and errors of pessimism.

It is taken for granted that the optimism and the pessimism are *mistaken*. But in reality this is not so. Optimism means the expectation that prices will rise or demand at a given price will expand. Pessimism means the expectation that prices will fall or demand at a given price will shrink. At a time of good trade, optimism is not mistaken at all, but is a perfectly correct view, and the same is true of pessimism at a time of bad trade. Each state of expectation tends to bring about its own fulfilment. The optimists borrow freely, and the spending power thus created brings about the rise of prices they hope for; the pessimists refrain from borrowing and the shortage of spending power brings about the fall of prices they fear. It is only at the turning-points, when the banks check borrowing, or succeed in reviving it, that the optimists and pessimists are respectively mistaken. And they may not be mistaken even there; they may have sufficient insight into the credit situation to anticipate the action of the banks. If this wisdom were general, the change from one phase of the cycle to the other would then be inaugurated without any initiative from the banks, by a spontaneous decrease or increase, as the case may be, in the borrowing operations of the traders. In practice, no doubt, there are invariably found some mistaken optimists when the decline starts, and some mistaken pessimists when the revival starts. But their existence is not essential to the credit theory of the trade cycle.

Traders' expectations, whether erroneous or correct, form one element in the problem of the regulation of credit. But under prewar conditions the regulation of credit was guided by the state of gold reserves. If traders' expectations were of a kind to support and assist the action of the bankers in encouraging or discouraging borrowers, that facilitated their task. But if traders' expectations tended in the contrary direction, the bankers could not surrender their policy. They were bound to take whatever measures were necessary to make it prevail.

In fact *three* distinct influences have to be taken into account, and the state of trade depends upon their resultant. First, there is the rate of interest on the merchants' borrowings. Secondly, there is their expectation as to the course of prices. Thirdly, there is the actual extent of their sales. The first is within the control of the bankers. The second is psychological, but can be *influenced* by extraneous circumstances. The third depends on the net effect of the first two upon the consumers' outlay.

The inherent instability of credit, which becomes apparent in the vicious circle of expansion and the vicious circle of contraction, is due to the mutual relations of these three factors. Optimism encourages borrowing, borrowing accelerates sales, and sales accentuate optimism. Pessimism discourages borrowing, and the consequent decline in sales intensifies pessimism.

If merchants refused to be influenced in any way by expectations as to the future state of markets, the psychological factor would drop out, but the credit cycle would still persist. Borrowing would respond to the rate of interest, and the volume of sales would respond to the volume of borrowing. Therefore business psychology, though in practice a very important factor in the trade cycle, is not essential to it.

In general, traders' expectations conformed under pre-war conditions almost too easily to the state of credit. Difficulties in enforcing the control of credit occurred at the climax of trade activity, but that was chiefly on account of the heavy commitments which involved traders in further borrowing on any terms. A conflict between business sentiment and credit policy was more likely to occur in the depths of trade depression. After an overdose of credit contraction it was sometimes difficult to induce traders to embark on fresh enterprises, when everything seemed likely to end in a loss owing to falling prices.

A complication is introduced into the control of credit in that the psychology of the trader influences the velocity of circulation of money. When prices are expected to rise, people hasten to spend money, and hold smaller balances relatively to the extent of their transactions; when prices are expected to fall, they lose little by letting balances accumulate. The result is that a contraction of credit may have very little visible effect upon the amount of bank deposits. Borrowing is checked, but because balances are less quickly spent, existing indebtedness is not paid off.

In 1920 when bank rate in London was raised to 7 per cent, and the most intense deflation was set on foot, the total amount of bank deposits in England actually increased.

I started by saying that since the war there has been no trade cycle. This is in itself a valuable confirmation of the monetary explanation. For if the cause of the trade cycle is to be found in the gradual progress of a credit expansion in an international gold standard system, we should expect that when there is no such system there would be no cycle. In the United States there has been a gold standard since June, 1919, but the momentum of an international system has not been at work. In the interval of six and a half years trade in that country has risen to three successive maxima, in May, 1920, in March, 1923, and in February, 1925, with severe depressions in 1921 and in the early part of 1924.

Other countries have experienced similar short-period fluctuations, having little connection with those of the United States. Some in the throes of monetary collapse have become painfully familiar with the "catastrophe boom," the exaggerated activity associated with a rapid depreciation of the currency. Others, under the shadow of deflation, have suffered from chronic depression and unemployment. Thus the evils of fluctuations have not been avoided. This experience, however, has given us valuable assistance towards finding a remedy for the trade cycle. The Federal Reserve Banks have been confronted with the problem of how to avoid an undue expansion of credit and rise of prices, when exceptional gold imports have so swollen their reserves as to make the statutory proportions completely inoperative. They have been compelled to seek some other guide than the reserve proportions, and substantially they have adopted the policy of stabilizing prices. The too ready acceptance of reserve proportions as the guide to credit policy was the real cause of the trade cycle before the war. Reserve proportions gave too tardy a warning of a credit expansion, and the credit expansion was allowed to gather impetus for years before the banks took effective steps to stop it. The trade depression was the accompaniment of the prolonged credit contraction which was thereafter necessary to restore the cash position of the banks. If the expansion is stopped before it goes too far, the need for anything more than a slight and transitory depression is avoided. American experience shows convincingly that for a single country this can de done. There is no reason in principle why the same remedy should not be applied to an international system, provided the authorities responsible for controlling credit are willing to co-operate. For Europe international co-operation with a view to preventing undue fluctuations in the purchasing power of gold was agreed on in principle at the Genoa Conference in 1922. Since then progress has been made towards that ideal not only in Europe but in America too, and we may hope that the trade cycle, the sinister cause of so much distress before the war, and particularly of periodical unemployment epidemics, will become a thing of purely historical interest.

[24]

Price Expectations, Monetary Disturbances and Maladjustments[*]

FRIEDRICH A. HAYEK

Editors' Note

A mere listing of F. A. Hayek's (1899–) academic and governmental assignments is sufficient to indicate the supranational scope of his professional activities and reputation: Austrian civil service, 1921-26; Director, Austrian Institute for Economic Research, 1927-31; Tooke Professor of Economic Science and Statistics, University of London, 1931-50; Professor of Social and Moral Science, University of Chicago, 1950– . His principal publications, apart from numerous articles, include: *Prices and Production* (1931); *Monetary Theory and the Trade Cycle* (1937); *Monetary Nationalism and International Stability* (1937); *Profits, Interest and Investment* (1939); *The Pure Theory of Capital* (1941); *The Road to Serfdom* (1944); *Individualism and Economic Order* (1948).

The editors feel Hayek's elaborate theorizing constitutes the best expression of the monetary, overinvestment hypothesis. Unlike Hawtrey and Keynes, he does not see in the structure of capitalism a tendency toward unemployment. Rather Hayek assumes a full employment equilibrium at which interest will approximate the difference between the value of present goods and future goods and argues that lowering interest rates below this equilibrium level initiates the sequence of events comprising the business cycle. The conservative nature of Hayek's diagnosis, as compared to that of Keynes and Hawtrey, lies in Hayek's treatment of savings.

---

[*] From *Profits, Interest, and Investment* by Friedrich A. Hayek (London: Routledge, 1939), pp. 135-136 and 351-365. Reprinted by permission of Routledge & Kegan Paul Ltd.

According to him, it is a *shortage* of saving that turns expansion into contraction, i.e., when investment exceeds the voluntary savings of consumers. The virtue of individual thrift, without which the folklore of capitalism would scarcely survive, endures Hayek's analysis if not the Keynesian treatment.

~~~~~~

I

❧ The most characteristic feature of the work of our generation of economists is probably the general endeavour to apply the methods and results of the pure theory of equilibrium to the elucidation of more complicated "dynamic" phenomena.[1] Perhaps one might have expected all generations of economists to have striven to approach nearer to reality by gradually relaxing the degree of abstraction of pure theory. Yet advance in this direction was not great during the fifty years preceding say 1920. The development of economics has not proceeded along the systematic lines of the textbook which advances step by step from the general to the particular. The answers to the pressing questions of real life could not wait till the slow progress of pure theory provided a scheme which would allow of immediate application in the more practical work.

It seems that as regards the attitude towards the applications of pure theory to the most complicated phenomena of economic dynamics, crises and industrial fluctuations, we can distinguish three main types. In many instances the men who most strongly felt the urgency of the problems existing in this field and attempted to solve them had little knowledge of the state of economic theory. This group includes, in addition to numberless cranks, several clear thinkers of rich experience to whom we are greatly indebted. A second group of men which is hardly less important consisted of scholars who, although well versed in current theoretical speculation, regarded it as of little use for the task in which they were mainly interested. Both groups have considerable achievements to their credit and I shall later have occasion to mention some important contributions from about 1850 onwards which we owe to them. It is by no means clear that this debt is smaller than that which we owe in this field to the third group, namely to those scholars who attempted—as it may appear to us, prematurely—to apply an over-simplified and defective theory to these complicated phenomena. Although their endeavour to justify in this way

---

[1] This essay reproduces the main argument of a lecture delivered on December 7th, 1933, in the *Sozialökonomisk Samfund* in Copenhagen and was first published (in German) in the *Nationalökonomisk Tidskrift*, Vol. 73, No. 3, 1935, and later (in French) in the *Revue de Science Economique*, Liège, October, 1935.

their concentration on pure theory and to demonstrate its usefulness was undoubtedly right, and although their instinct that only this path would ultimately lead to a really satisfactory explanation was right, the result of these early attempts, from the celebrated *Théorie des Débouchés* onwards, was frequently to press the problems into the strait-jacket of a scheme which did not really help to solve them.

II

It was only the modern development of equilibrium analysis together with the increasing awareness of the conditions and limitations of the applicability of the equilibrium concept which has taught us to recognize the nature of the problems existing in this field and which has indicated the paths towards their solution. And even if the different students of these problems proceed along different routes, it is probably true to-day to say that in all countries with a great theoretical tradition the efforts of the younger men in our subject is directed towards bridging the gulf between "statics" and "dynamics." To some the differences which exist here between different "schools" may appear very large. Yet whether the different individuals, in their zeal to advance, stress the deficiencies of the existing "static" theory more or less strongly appears to me to be based much more on differences of temperament than on differences in the aims or in the methods used. I believe that the great majority of the younger economists share the belief that the continuity of the development can be preserved and that only this will help us to reach our goal.

What we all seek is therefore not a jump into something entirely new and different but a development of our fundamental theoretical apparatus which will enable us to explain dynamic phenomena. Not very long ago I myself still believed that the best way to express this was to say that the theory of the trade cycle at which we were aiming ought to be organically superimposed upon the existing theory of equilibrium. I am now more inclined to say that general theory itself ought to be developed so as to enable us to use it directly in the explanation of particular industrial fluctuations. As has recently been shown very convincingly by Dr. Lutz,[2] our task is not to construct a separate theory of the trade cycle, that is of a construction of a detailed scheme which will fit all actual trade cycles, but rather a development of those sections of general theory which we need in the analysis of particular cycles—which often differ from one another very considerably.

A great part of this work will certainly consist in the elaboration of particular chapters of general theory, especially of the theory of capital and the theory of money, in the direction of a more careful analysis of the processes resulting from any change in the data. It is, however, the common peculiarity of all such attempts to make the theory more realistic

---

[2] F. Lutz, *Das Konjunkturproblem in der Nationalökonomie.* Jena, 1932.

that they soon bring us back to the fundamental problem of all economic theory, that is to the question of the significance of the concept of equilibrium and its relevance to the explanation of a process which takes place in time. There can be no doubt that here some of the formulations of the theory of equilibrium prove to be of little use and that not only their particular content but also the idea of equilibrium as such which they use will require a certain amount of revision.

That this concept of equilibrium has in the past not always had the same meaning and that this meaning has often not been very clear can hardly be denied. This is at least true of the application of the concept of equilibrium to the phenomena of a competitive society, while if applied to the economic activities of an isolated person or of a centrally directed communist system it probably has a definite meaning. While in this latter case we can legitimately speak of a necessary equilibrium between the decisions which a person will make at a given moment, it is much less clear in what sense we can apply the same concept to the actions of a great number of persons, whose successive responses to the actions of their fellow-beings necessarily take place in time, and which can be represented as a timeless equilibrium relationship only by means of unrealistic special constructions.

Equilibrium analysis certainly needs, if we want to apply it to a changing competitive system, much more exact definitions of its basic assumptions than are commonly given. The realistic significance of the tendencies towards a state of equilibrium, traditionally described by pure theory, can be shown only when we know what the conditions are under which it is at least conceivable that a position of equilibrium will actually be reached.

The main difficulty of the traditional approach is its complete abstraction from time. A concept of equilibrium which essentially was applicable only to an economic system conceived as timeless could not be of great value. Fortunately in recent times there have been considerable changes on this very point. It has become clear that, instead of completely disregarding the time element, we must make very definite assumptions about the attitude of persons towards the future. The assumptions of this kind which are implied in the concept of equilibrium are essentially that everybody foresees the future correctly and that this foresight includes not only the changes in the objective data but also the behavior of all the other people with whom he expects to perform economic transactions.[3]

It is not my intention to enter here more fully into these recent developments of equilibrium analysis and I hope what I have said will suffice to explain certain conclusions which I want to draw from them as to the study of dynamic phenomena. It appears to me that from this new angle it should at last become possible to give somewhat more definite

---

[3] Since the above was written I have further elaborated and partly revised this discussion of the relationship between equilibrium and foresight in a paper on "Economics and Knowledge," published in *Economica* for February, 1937.

meaning to certain concepts which most of us have been using somewhat loosely. I am thinking in particular of the statement frequently made that a whole economic system (or a particular price, as e.g., the rate of interest) either is or is not in equilibrium.

It is evident that the various expectations on which different individuals base their decisions at a particular moment either will or will not be mutually compatible; and that if these expectations are not compatible those of some people at least must be disappointed. It is probably clear also that expectations existing at a particular moment will to a large extent be based on prices existing at that moment and that we can conceive of constellations of such prices which will create expectations inevitably doomed to disappointment, and of other constellations which do not bear the germ of such disappointments and which create expectations which —at least if there are no unforeseen changes in external circumstances —may be in harmony with the actual course of events. This consideration appears to me to provide a useful starting point for further developments of the theory of industrial fluctuations.

III

Every explanation of economic crises must include the assumption that entrepreneurs have committed errors. But the mere fact that entrepreneurs do make errors can hardly be regarded as a sufficient explanation of crises. Erroneous dispositions which lead to losses all round will appear probable only if we can show why entrepreneurs should all simultaneously make mistakes in the same direction. The explanation that this is just due to a kind of psychological infection or that for any other reason most entrepreneurs should commit the same avoidable errors of judgment does not carry much conviction. It seems, however, more likely that they may all be equally misled by following guides or symptoms which as a rule prove reliable. Or, speaking more concretely, it may be that the prices existing when they made their decisions and on which they had to base their views about the future have created expectations which must necessarily be disappointed. In this case we might have to distinguish between what we may call justified errors, caused by the price system, and sheer errors about the course of external events. Although I have no time to discuss this further, I may mention that there is probably a close connection between this distinction and the traditional distinction between "endogenous" and "exogenous" theories of the trade cycle.

The most interesting case, for our present purpose, of such decisions of entrepreneurs where the outcome depends entirely on the correctness of the views *generally* held about future developments, is, of course, the case of investments in so far as these are affected by the situation of the capital market in general and not by the special position of particular industries. Here the same cause may bring about malinvestments not only in one or a few but in all industries at the same time. The success of almost any investment made for a considerable period of time will depend on the future development of the capital market and of the rate of interest. If at any moment people begin to add to the productive equipment this will as a rule represent only a part of a new process which will be completed only by further investments spread over a period of time; and the first investment will therefore prove to have been successful only if the supply of capital makes the expected further developments at later dates possible. In general it is probably true to say that most investments are made in the expectation that the supply of capital will for some time continue at the present level. Or, in other words, entrepreneurs regard the present supply of capital and the present rate of interest as a symptom that approximately the same situation will continue to exist for some time. And it is only some such assumption that will justify the use of any additional capital to begin new round-about methods of production which, if they are to be completed, will require continued investment over a further period of time. (These further investments which are necessary if the present investments are going to be successful may be either investments by the same entrepreneurs who made the first investment, or—much more frequently—investments in the products produced by the first group by a second group of entrepreneurs.) If these expectations are to be realised it is necessary not that the supply of capital during the relevant period remains absolutely unchanged, but, as I have tried to show on another occasion,[4] that during no interval of time should it fall by more than has before been utilised to start new processes (as distinguished from continuing uncompleted ones).

Very large and unforseen fluctuations of saving would therefore be sufficient to cause extensive losses on investments made during the period preceding them and therefore to create the characteristic situation of an economic crisis. The cause of such a crisis would be that entrepreneurs had mistakenly regarded a temporary increase in the supply of capital as permanent and acted in this expectation. The only reason why we cannot regard this as a sufficient explanation of economic crises as we know them is that experience provides no ground for assuming that such violent fluctuations in the rate of saving will occur otherwise than in consequence of crises. If it were not for the crises, which therefore we shall have to explain in a different way, the assumption of the entrepreneurs that the supply of saving will continue at about the present level for some time would probably prove to be justified. The decisions of the entrepreneurs as to the dates and quantities of consumers' goods for which they provide by their present investments would coincide with the intention of the consumers as to the parts of their incomes which they want to consume at the various dates.

---

[4] Cf. the article on "Capital and Industrial Fluctuations," *Econometrica*, Vol. 2, No. 2, April, 1934 (now reprinted as appendix to the second edition of *Prices and Production*) where I have also somewhat more fully explained the distinction between complete and incomplete processes of production alluded to in the text.

IV

It is, of course, a well-known fact that the current supply of money-capital is not necessarily identical with the amount of current savings. All sorts of monetary disturbances, shortly described as changes in the quantity of money and changes in the velocity of circulation of money but in fact much more variegated in nature than these terms at first suggest, may change the supply of money capital independently of the supply of savings. This means, however, that entrepreneurs will often base their decisions about their investment plans on a symptom which in no way indicates even the current willingness of the consumers to save, and therefore provides no guide whatever for a forecast of how they will distribute their income in the future between consuming and saving. Entrepreneurs will make their decisions about the volume of their investments, i.e., about the quantities of consumers' goods they will produce at various dates, as if the present distribution of monetary demand between consumers' goods and investments corresponded to the way in which the consumers divide their income between consuming and saving. The result of this must be that the proportion in which entrepreneurs will divide their resources between production for the near future and production for the distant future will be different from the proportion in which consumers in general want to divide their current income between current consumption and provision for consumption at a later date.

In such a situation there exists evidently a conflict between the intentions of the consumers and the intentions of entrepreneurs which earlier or later must manifest itself and frustrate the expectations of at least one of these two groups. The situation is certainly not one of equilibrium in the sense defined before. A condition of equilibrium would require that the intentions of the two groups are at least compatible. It precludes a situation in which current prices, and particularly current rates of interest, create expectations concerning the future behaviour of some members of the society which are entirely unfounded. An equilibruim rate of interest would then be one which assured correspondence between the intentions of the consumers and the intentions of the entrepreneurs. And with a constant rate of saving this would be the rate of interest arrived at on a market where the supply of money capital was of exactly the same amount as current savings.

If the supply of money capital is increased, by monetary changes, beyond this amount, the result will be that the rate of interest will be lowered below the equilibrium rate and entrepreneurs will be induced to devote a larger part of the existing resources to production for the more distant future than corresponds to the way in which consumers divide their income between saving and current consumption. At the time when the entrepreneurs make this decision the consumers have no possibility of expressing their wishes with sufficient emphasis since their money incomes are as yet unchanged while the expansion of credit has increased the fund available for investment. The investment of these funds, however, must in the course of time increase total income by nearly the full amount of these funds, either because wages are raised in order to attract people away from producing consumers' goods towards producing capital goods, or because the funds are used to employ formerly unemployed workers. This will certainly tend to increase the intensity of the demand for consumers' goods—how far will depend on how consumers distribute their additional money income between consuming and saving.

The first point which we must keep in mind here is that this increase in aggregate money incomes cannot mean an increase of real incomes and is much more likely to mean a decrease of real incomes to many individual consumers. However great the amount of money at the disposal of the consumers, they can never consume more than the current supply of consumers' goods—and if the new investments have led to a diversion of already employed factors into longer processes of production, this must lead, to that extent, to an actual decrease of the current output of consumers' goods. The increase in the returns from the existing permanent resources in consequence of the new investments will not come until much later. But even when the first results of the new investments begin to come on the market, this increase in the output will amount to only a fraction of the additional incomes and, as will appear in a moment, it is this relation between the increase in incomes and the increase in the output of consumers' goods which is relevant to our problem.

There is little reason to assume that, in the circumstances we are considering, the share of the increased money incomes spent on current consumption will be diminished. The willingness to save on the part of the consumers will have been little affected by these changes; and their capacity to save will, if anything, have decreased. Only in so far as redistributions of income have taken place during the whole process, favouring those more inclined to save at the expense of those less inclined to save, a certain increase in the proportion of the income actually saved may be expected. But whether the consumers divide their additional money income in the old proportion between current consumption and saving, or whether the proportion is slightly more favourable to saving, the increase in money incomes will in any case lead to an increase in the monetary demand for consumers' goods and therefore to an increase in the prices of consumers' goods.

This increased intensity of the demand for consumers' goods need have no unfavorable effect on investment activity so long as the funds available for investment purposes are sufficiently increased by further credit expansion to claim, in the face of the increasing competition from the consumers' goods industries, such increasing shares of the total available resources as are required to complete the new processes already under way. That this requires a continued expansion of credit proceeding at a progressive rate and that this, even apart from all legal or traditional obstacles, cannot be continued indefinitely, even if it were only because it would inevitably lead to a cumulative rise in prices which earlier or later would exceed any limit, is not difficult to see.[5] What is mainly of interest for our present purpose is, however, what will happen when the inevitable moment comes when the demand for consumers' goods begins to rise not only absolutely but also relatively to the funds available for investment.

V

We have now reached the point where the conflict between the intentions of the consumers and the intentions of the investors begins to manifest itself—the conflict caused by the distortion of the capital market by credit expansion. The entrepreneurs who have begun to increase their productive equipment in the expectation that the low rate of interest and the ample supply of money capital would enable them to continue and to utilise these investments under the same favourable conditions, find these expectations disappointed. The increase of the prices of all those factors of production that can be used also in the late stages of production will raise the costs of, and at the same time the rise in the rate of interest will decrease the demand for, the capital goods which they produce. And a considerable part of the newly created equipment designed to produce other capital goods will stand idle because the expected further investment in these other capital goods does not materialise.

This phenomenon of a scarcity of capital making it impossible to use the existing capital equipment appears to me the central point of the true explanation of crises; and at the same time it is no doubt the one that rouses most objections and appears most improbable to the lay mind. That a scarcity of capital should lead to the existing capital goods remaining partly unused, that the abundance of capital goods should be a symptom of a shortage of capital, and that the cause of this should be not an insufficient but an excessive demand for consumers' goods, is apparently more than a theoretically untrained mind is readily persuaded to accept. Yet the truth of these apparent paradoxes appears to me to be established beyond doubt. Before I proceed to explain them further it is perhaps not inappropriate to show that some of the most experienced observers of the crises of the mid-nineteenth century had been constrained to accept them.

Their explanations of these crises were usually expressed in terms of an excessive conversion of circulating capital into fixed capital, induced by the creation of "fictitious capital,"[6] and leading in the end to a scarcity of "disposable" or "floating" capital which made a completion of many of the newly started ventures impossible. The author who mainly devel-

---

[5] See in this connection my article in *Econometrica*, already quoted, particularly pp. 161 ff.

[6] On the origin of this term see now J. Viner, *Studies in the Theory of International Trade*, 1937, p. 196 note.

oped and popularised this doctrine in connection with the great railway booms and the following crises in the middle of the nineteenth century was the first editor of the *Economist*, James Wilson. It was later taken up by a group of Manchester economists and finally introduced into academic economics by Bonnamy Price in England and Courcelle-Seneuil and V. Bonnet in France. And Yves Guyot even summed up the fundamental idea in the following characteristic sentence (I quote from the English translation of his *La Science Economique*): "Commercial and Financial Crises are produced, not by over-production, but by over-consumption."[7]

Perhaps it may be claimed that a doctrine which gained such wide acceptance right at the beginning of the systematic study of industrial fluctuations cannot be as much opposed to sound common sense as it seems to appear to many to-day after a century of propaganda in favour of underconsumptionist explanations. That these early attempts did not have a more lasting success was probably due to the vague meaning of the various capital concepts which they had taken from the City jargon of the time. It is not difficult to see that with this very imperfect conceptual apparatus the adherents of this theory must have found it difficult to explain convincingly what they had rightly seen and to defend their accounts against criticisms. Even to-day we have not yet quite outgrown the stage in which the ambiguity—or rather lack—of meaning of the various concepts of capital which we still employ is a constant obstacle to real understanding. This is not least true of the term of "scarcity of capital" itself, and of the closely related concept of "free capital" to which it refers. Even if we connect fairly clear ideas with the term "scarcity of free capital," and even if the term is often used with advantage, nevertheless it is in a sense misleading and will easily lead one to ask meaningless questions. The difficulty is that the term appears to refer to some single, measurable entity, some amount of money or "subsistence fund" which represents the "free capital" and which in real life simply does not exist. What we actually mean when we speak of scarcity or abundance of free capital is simply that the distribution of demand between consumers' goods and capital goods compared with the supply of these two kinds of goods in either relatively favourable or relatively unfavourable to the former.

VI

More important, however, is another difficulty connected with the traditional concepts of capital. It is this difficulty which seems to me to necessitate a restatement of the Wicksell-Mises theory of industrial fluctuations in the form which I have tried to sketch in this lecture. Prevailing ideas about how capital would normally be kept quantitatively intact in changing circumstances suggested the notion that a period of intense in-

---

[7] Yves Guyot, *Principles of Social Economy*, London, 1884, p. 249. For a slightly fuller account of these theories of the middle of the nineteenth century see the appendix to the third chapter of the second edition of *Prices and Production*, 1934.

vestment activity followed by a period when the value of much of the capital so created was destroyed might be treated as periods of alternating accumulation and decumulation of capital. For most practical purposes this may indeed represent a fairly adequate description of the real facts. Theoretically this way of approach appeared particularly attractive because it seemed to make it possible to describe the conditions of a stable equilibrium in the way which at the present moment is very fashionable; in terms of the correspondence between (net) saving and (net) investment. Yet the first serious attempts exactly to define these two magnitudes, which are supposed to correspond in some quantitative sense, proved that these concepts had by no means a very clear meaning. Both concepts depend, as can be easily shown, on a vague idea that capital is "normally" kept or preserved constant in some quantitative sense: savings being that part of income which is not consumed we have to know first what income is, that is, we have to determine what part of total (gross) receipts has to be deducted for the amortisation of capital; and similarly we can determine the magnitude of new investments only if we first decide what amount of investment activity is required in order merely to maintain old capital. Whether we are able to decide what savings and what investment are depends therefore on whether we can give the idea of maintaining capital intact a clear and realistic meaning.

That this can be easily done is usually taken for granted; in fact it seems to be regarded as so obvious, that a more careful study of the question has mostly been regarded as unnecessary and has hardly ever been attempted. As soon, however, as one makes any serious attempt to answer this question, one finds not only that the concept of the maintenance of capital has no definite meaning, but also that there is no reason to assume that even the most rational and intelligent entrepreneur will ever in dynamic conditions be either willing or able to keep his capital constant in any quantitative sense, that is with respect to any of the measurable properties of capital itself. How entrepreneurs will behave in particular circumstances and whether the value of the capital under their control will experience unexpected increases or decreases in value will, of course, depend on the wisdom and foresight of the entrepreneurs. But, as I hope to show more fully on another occasion,[8] even if we could assume that entrepreneurs possessed full knowledge of all the relevant future events there would be no reason to expect that they would act in such a manner as to keep the value of their capital (or any other measurable dimension of this capital itself—as distinguished from the income derived from it) at any particular figure.

If the "Wicksellian" theory of crises were really as dependent on the traditional concepts of saving and investment as would seem to appear from the extensive use of these terms in the current expositions of it, the

---

[8] Cf. now the article on "The Maintenance of Capital," *Economica*, August 1935, pp. 247 ff.

considerations just advanced would constitute a grave objection to it. Fortunately, however, there is no such necessary connection between that theory and these concepts. In the form in which it has, tentatively and very sketchily, been restated in the earlier part of this lecture, it appears to me to be quite independent of any idea of absolute changes in the quantity of capital and therefore of the concepts of saving and investment in their traditional sense. The starting point for a fully developed theory of this kind would be (*a*) the intentions of all the consumers with respect to the way in which they wish to distribute at all the relevant dates all their resources (not merely their "income") between current consumption and provision for future consumption, and (*b*) the separate and independent decisions of the entrepreneurs with respect to the amounts of consumers' goods which they plan to provide at these various dates. Correspondence between these two groups of decisions would be characteristic of the kind of equilibrium which we now usually describe as a state where savings are equal to investments and with which the idea of an equilibrium rate of interest is connected. A rate of interest below that equilibrium rate would then induce entrepreneurs to devote a smaller share of the available resources to production for current consumption than the share of the income earned by these resources actually spent on consumption. This may mean that entrepreneurs lengthen the investment period by more than is justified by the voluntary "saving" of the entrepreneurs in the usual (net) sense of the term, or that they do not shorten the existing processes of production sufficiently to take full account of the "impatience" of the consumers (that is, in the usual terminology, of their desire to consume capital). It need not therefore be capital consumption in the absolute sense of the term, which is the essential characteristic of a crisis (as I have myself suggested on earlier occasions) but merely that the consumers demand a more rapid supply of consumers' goods than is possible in view of the decisions of the entrepreneurs as to the form and volume of their investments. Practically this correction probably makes little difference, but theoretically the statement of the theory can be made unobjectionable only if we free it from any reference to the absolute quantity of capital.

VII

It is scarcely possible to give in a short lecture more than a mere sketch of the developments taking place at the moment in trade cycle theory. And I need hardly add that in my view this development is still very far from complete and that what we can say to-day must necessarily be tentative and will probably undergo much further revision as time goes on. But even when at last we are able to state this particular argument in a more unobjectionable and convincing form than we can to-day, this will not mean an end but only a beginning. Even when we have answered the question how entrepreneurs will react to the expectations of particular price changes there will remain the much more difficult and important question of what determines the expectations of entrepreneurs and particularly of how such expectations will be affected by any given change of present prices. All these questions are still a more or less unworked field in which the first pioneer work has been done by one or two Scandinavian economists. And while I cannot quite agree with Professor Myrdal when he alleges that in my theory there is no room for the role played by expectations[9]—to show how important a place they do play was in fact one of the purposes of this lecture—I am on the other hand in complete agreement with him when he stresses the great importance of this element in the further development of the theory of industrial fluctuations. I have no doubt that in this field the whole complex of the theory of uncertainty and risk, to which Scandinavian economists have recently given so much attention, will become increasingly important.[10]

---

[9] Cf. G. Myrdal, Der Gleichgewichtsbegriff als Instrument der geldtheoretischen Analyse, *Beiträge zur Geldtheorie*, Ed. by F. A. Hayek, Vienna, 1933, p. 385.

[10] See in this connection J. R. Hicks, "Gleichgewicht und Konjunktur," *Zeitschrift für Nationalökonomie*, Vol. IV, No. 4, 1933, and "A Suggestion for Simplifying the Theory of Money," *Economica*, February, 1935.

❌ ❈ ❌

FOR FURTHER READING

The articles of this section have discussed from a theoretical viewpoint the impact of money and credit policies on economic well-being. Although we do not wish to anticipate the objectives of Part IV, the reader may desire to explore some of the complexities of implementing theory and fixing guidelines for monetary and fiscal management. We recommend, in this respect, Arthur I. Bloomfield, *Monetary Policy Under the International Gold Standard, 1880–1914* (New York: Federal Reserve Bank of New York, 1959); The American Assembly, *United States Monetary Policy* (New York: Columbia University Press, 1958); William McChesney Martin, "The Battle Against Recession," *Federal Reserve Bulletin* Vol. 44, No. 5 (May, 1958); John Kenneth Galbraith, "Does Monetary Policy Really Work?" *Congressional Record*, April 1, 1958; Milton Friedman, "Federal Reserve Policy and 100 Percent Money," *Monetary Policy and the Management of the Public Debt*, Hearings before the Subcommittee on General Credit Control and Debt Management of the Joint Committee on the Economic Report, 82d Congress, 2d Session (Washington, D.C.: U.S. Government Printing Office, 1952); Harold G. Moulton, *Can Inflation Be Controlled?* (Washington, D.C.: Anderson Karmer Associates, 1958).

Since it is impossible to pursue the study of monetary policy without reference to the allied tool, fiscal management, we suggest the reader supplement the above by dipping into *The Treasury and the Money Market* (New York: Federal Reserve Bank of New York, 1954); Robert V. Roosa, *Federal Reserve Operations in the Money and Government Securities Markets* (New York: Federal Reserve Bank of New York, 1956); Committee for Economic Development, *Managing the Federal Debt* (New York: Committee for Economic Development, 1954); Joint Committee on the Economic Report, *Monetary, Credit, and Fiscal Policies* (Washington, D.C.: U.S. Government Printing Office, 1950); Committee for Economic Development, *The Budget, The Economy, and Tax Reduction in 1956* (New York: Committee for Economic Development, 1956); W. Randolph Burgess, "The National Debt," Statement submitted to the Committee on Finance, United States Senate (85th Congress, 1st Session, July 29, 1957); Joint Committee on the Economic Report, *Monetary Policy and the Management of the Public Debt*, Parts I and II (Washington, D.C.: U.S. Government Printing Office, 1952).

Henry C. Murphy skillfully treats the special case of war finance and its impact on the economy in his *National Debt in War and Transition* (New York: McGraw-Hill, 1950). It is an essential reading in applied economics.

SECTION E

Psychological Factors

✘ ❋ ✘

INTRODUCTION

In reviewing monetary interpretations of the business cycle, we observed the general difficulties involved in classifying particular theories. Most speculations on the origins of the cycle recognize a monetary factor. Similar considerations apply here. Economists invariably allude to "motivations," "expectations," "intentions," optimistic or pessimistic evaluations of the future; their hypotheses ineluctably subsume, implicitly or explicitly, premises about the behavior of consumers, businessmen, or other segments of the economy. Classification therefore becomes again a question of emphasis. We shall canvass in this chapter only those writers who see economic oscillations as originating in psychological factors.

One version of psychoeconomics—perhaps the best publicized—sees the reactions of businessmen to the uncertainties and complexities of modern business as causative. Thus W. H. Beveridge,* an early advocate, believed that the excessive reactions of entrepreneurs to a changing business environment produce alternating periods of expansion and contraction. Better known for this position is the English economist A. C. Pigou, whose views are summarized below by Professor Mitchell. Pigou, however, espoused a broader view of the cyclical process which after allowing for psychologically induced errors of pessimism and optimism becomes in effect an overinvestment theory.†

Contemporary business cycle theory, however, assigns a more specific, less generalized, role to psychological factors than did Pigou. The latter in the final analysis discerned a cyclical pattern in business psychology which became manifest in a general economic cycle. Recent work, on the other hand, brings the psychological element into play only at critical points in the response mechanism. To illustrate: Keynes held the marginal efficiency of capital would decline as expansion progressed. This fall in the *expected rate of future return* on investment reflects real changes in the business situation; that is, an increasing cost of new capital goods and falling rate of profit which make additional investment less attractive. Forced to reassess their position, businessmen would curtail their "expectations," adversely affecting the level of investment and putting the brakes on expansion. Therefore, the state of business psychology determines the marginal efficiency of capital. It only remains to add, according to Keynes, that during a period of expansion businessmen would have a tendency to overestimate future returns on current investment.‡

Emphasis on "expectations" and "intentions" has in a practical way influenced the art of economic forecasting. Since statistical data do not precisely forecast turning points of business conditions, the forecaster will likely supplement his data by attempting to gauge the attitudes of the participants. A number of ready-made surveys are there to assist him: "What Businessmen Expect" in *Dun's Review and Modern Industry*; "Business Outlook" in *Fortune*; "Business Situation" in *Survey of Current Business*; *The Annual Survey of Business Anticipations of Plant and Equipment Expenditures* by the Securities Exchange Commission and the Department of Commerce; *Business Plans for New Plants and Equipment*, a McGraw-Hill survey; *Quarterly Survey of Capital Appropriations of the 1,000 Largest Manufacturing Firms*, National Industrial Conference Board. Whether these forecasts are self-defeating by inducing corrective action or self-substantiating by a kind of hypnosis is part of the larger

---

* *Unemployment, A Problem of Industry* (London: Longmans, Green, 1910).

† *Economics of Welfare* (London: Macmillan, 1920); *Industrial Fluctuations* (London: Macmillan, 1927).

‡ J. M. Keynes, *The General Theory of Employment, Interest and Money* (New York: Harcourt, Brace, 1936). See chap. 3, "A Preliminary Summary of the General Theory of Employment," of Dudley Dillard's *The Economics of John Maynard Keynes* (New York: Prentice-Hall, 1948), reproduced on pp. 296-316 of this volume.

question of how psychological factors should be considered in a complete explanation of the cycle.

Economic decisions are made by human beings and not by events. The economist therefore cannot avoid the psychological factor in his theorizing. He must ask, however: How much do psychological factors shape economic events? Do they simply intensify pre-existing economic movements or are they sufficiently powerful in themselves to mold the trend of things? Is it possible through scientific manipulation of public opinion to mitigate cyclical fluctuations? No one has the final answers to these speculations.

[25]

The Emotional Factors in Business Decisions[*]

WESLEY C. MITCHELL

~~~~~~

Editors' Note

Wesley C. Mitchell (1874–1948) at the time of his death was perhaps the world's leading authority on the business cycle. The subject became for him a lifetime study, to be pursued not by the elaborate deductions of the equilibrium economists but rather by the methods of a truly empirical science.

Nowadays we can begin laying the foundation for a type of economics that will have a demonstrable relation to the actual conditions with which men have to deal because it can be based upon an analytic study of actual behavior. This empirical science, whose birth pangs we are witnessing, will be as definitely a by-product of a later phase of money economy as mercantilism and the speculations of Ricardo were by-products of earlier phases.[†]

More fortunate than many prophets, Mitchell lived to see his vision achieve reality with the founding of the National Bureau of Economic Research and the truly impressive flow of empirical investigations emanating from universities and foundations.

Yet Wesley Mitchell was no narrow specialist prosecuting his line without regard to larger considerations. For him, "business cycles encompassed the entire field of economics, and a theory of business cycles was to be a

---

[*] From *Business Cycles: The Problem and Its Setting* (New York: National Bureau of Economic Research, 1927), pp. 17-20. Reprinted by permission of the National Bureau of Economic Research, Inc.

[†] "The Role of Money in Economic History," *Journal of Economic History*, Supplement IV (December, 1944), p. 66.

theory of capitalism itself."* Business fluctuations were inherent in a private enterprise economy, a money economy based upon production for profit and a responsive price structure. Even a minimal comprehension of the business cycle phenomenon therefore demands a quantitative and qualitative description, historically oriented, of the institutional arrangements of capitalistic society.

These views were given scholarly expression in *Business Cycles* (1913); *Business Cycles: The Problem and Its Setting* (1927); *The Backward Art of Spending Money* (1937); *Measuring Business Cycles* (co-author with A. F. Burns, 1946); *Lecture Notes on Types of Economic Theory* (1949); and posthumously, *What Happens During Business Cycles* (1951).

The following excerpt on "The Emotional Factor in Business Decisions" is taken from *Business Cycles: The Problem and Its Setting*. This is fitting, for no one was better aware than Mitchell "that business is affected by numberless factors, physical, psychological, political, economic or social in origin. . . ." Principally, he condenses the views of A. C. Pigou, the major proponent of a psychological explanation of business fluctuations.

❧ Everyone recognizes the uncertainties with which business men must contend in planning their operations; but most writers on business cycles hold that uncertainty merely provides opportunity for the working of other factors to which they attach greater significance. One of these factors is the "psychological," or more accurately, the emotional influences which warp business judgment. The best exposition along this line is that given by Professor A. C. Pigou of Cambridge University. In his opinion "the movement of business confidence" is "the dominant cause of the rhythmic fluctuations that are experienced in industry": "optimistic error and pessimistic error, when discovered, give birth to one another in an endless chain."

After stating the conditions which make it difficult to avoid errors in planning production, Professor Pigou attacks the problem why the majority of these errors run in the same direction, instead of cancelling each other. It is at this point that his explanation diverges from the path that contents Dr. Hardy. While the latter relies upon the similarity of the price and order data used by producers and by speculators to account for the similarity of their errors, Professor Pigou has recourse to waves of elation and discouragement which sweep over the business community.

---

* A. F. Burns, "Mitchell and the National Bureau," in *Frontiers of Economic Knowledge*, (published for the National Bureau of Economic Research by Princeton University Press, Princeton, 1954), p. 91.

Let us suppose the business world to be in a neutral position, not suffering from either type of error. On this situation there supervenes some real cause for increase in the demand for business activity.

Then, because business men cannot foresee the results which will be produced by their own and other men's response to the stimulus, errors of the optimistic type will begin to be made. But why should these errors multiply so rapidly and grow so huge?

When an error of optimism has been generated, (Professor Pigou answers) it tends to spread and grow, as a result of reactions between different parts of the business community. This comes about through two principal influences. First, experience suggests that, apart altogether from the financial ties by which different business men are bound together, there exists among them a certain measure of psychological interdependence. A change of tone in one part of the business world diffuses itself, in a quite unreasoning manner, over other and wholly disconnected parts. . . . Secondly . . . an error of optimism on the part of one group of business men itself creates a justification for some improved expectation on the part of other groups.

Thus the optimistic error once born grows in scope and magnitude.

But since the prosperity has been built largely upon error, a day of reckoning must come. This day does not dawn until after a time long enough to construct new industrial equipment on a large scale, to bring the products of the new equipment to market, and to find that they cannot be disposed of promptly at profitable prices. Then the past miscalculation becomes patent—patent to creditors as well as to debtors, and the creditors apply pressure for repayment. Thus prosperity ends in a crisis. The error of optimism dies in the crisis, but in dying it

gives birth to an error of pessimism. This new error is born, not an infant, but a giant; for an industrial boom has necessarily been a period of strong emotional excitement, and an excited man passes from one form of excitement to another more rapidly than he passes to quiescence.

Under the influence of the new error, business is unduly depressed. For a time there is relatively slow extension of facilities for production. In consequence,

a general shortage of a number of important commodities gradually makes itself apparent, and those persons who have them to sell are seen to be earning a good real return. Thereupon, certain of the bolder spirits in industry see an opportunity and seize it.

Business begins to pick up slowly and gradually.

The first year or two, say, is taken up with a wholly justified expansion. But, after the first year or two, further expansion represents, not a correction of the past error, but the creation of a new one.

And the new error grows until it has betrayed business men into courses which end in a fresh crisis.[1]

Professor Pigou represents waves of elation and depression as arising from changes in the business situation, changes which are magnified into business cycles by the emotions they excite. Dr. Maurice Beck Hexter, Director of the Federated Jewish Charities of Boston, has thrown out the suggestion that these waves of feeling have an origin independent of the business world.

By an elaborate statistical analysis of vital and economic data, Dr. Hexter has reached the conclusion that

> . . . fluctuations in conceptions *precede* fluctuations in wholesale prices by about eight months; fluctuations in the birthrate *precede* fluctuations in unemployment by about seventeen months . . . fluctuations in the death-rate *precede* fluctuations in wholesale prices about seventeen months; and . . . fluctuations in the death-rate *precede* fluctuations in unemployment by about ten months.

A causal explanation of these relations is suggested by the powerful emotional reactions excited in men by the death of friends and the prospect of having children. Dr. Hexter argues thus:

> Business enterprise is the application of mental effort to the transforma-
> tion of our physical environment. Anything which affects the emotions of
> men must necessarily affect their ability to make decisions, anticipate de-
> cisions, or postpone decisions. If these times of postponed decisions or
> accelerated judgments or stimulated efforts are not isolated, but, on the
> contrary, run in wave-like movements, we think that there may be some-
> thing to (*sic*) the suggestion that varying birth-rates and fluctuating
> death-rates can and do affect business cycles. The errors of optimism
> and the errors of pessimism may be closely connected with these varia-
> tions in human emotions. It may very well be that these waves of emotion
> which run through society from time to time are very closely related to
> these variations in births and deaths.[2]

It will be noticed that Dr. Hexter's hypothesis is related to Professor Huntington's quite as closely as to Professor Pigou's. But Hexter differs from Huntington in that he does not seek to connect fluctuations in vital statistics with fluctuations in the weather.

---

[1] A. C. Pigou, *The Economics of Welfare*, 1st ed., London, 1920, Part vi, chapter vi. The quotations are from pp. 833, 839, 840, 843 and 844. In companion chapters, Professor Pigou shows how the results of the "dominant cause" are modified by other factors, such as harvest fluctuations, and the workings of the monetary system. Professor Pigou has dropped this discussion from his second edition, hoping to incorporate it "in the next year or two" in "a study of industrial fluctuations." See preface of the 2d ed., 1924.

[2] Maurice B. Hexter, *Social Consequences of Business Cycles*. Boston and New York, 1925, Part ii. The quotations are from pp. 169, 174 and 175.

✕ ❋ ✕

FOR FURTHER READING

~~~~~~

Psychological factors weave in and out of almost every cycle theory, making it somewhat difficult to assemble a bibliography on the topic without overlapping citations presented elsewhere. Pigou, however, stressed the psychological more than others, and we suggest therefore a complete reading of *Industrial Fluctuations* (London: Macmillan, 1927) and *The Theory of Unemployment* (London: Macmillan, 1933). See also, in this connection, Albert Aftalion, "The Theory of Economic Cycles Based on the Capitalistic Technique of Production," *Review of Economic Statistics* (Vol. 9, October, 1927). Earlier literature mainly attracts the interest of the historian seeking out the origins of this view.

We have noted that in recent years economists have given more attention to the role of expectations in economic decisions. See J. M. Keynes, *The General Theory of Employment, Interest and Money* (New York: Harcourt, Brace, 1936), chap. 22. Unfortunately the disciples of Keynes have not rushed to follow the master's lead. Nonetheless, other economists, especially those concerned with forecasting for business or government, have picked up the thread. The result is a growing body of literature, at present not altogether assimilated into the body of economic theory. See George Katona, *Psychological Analysis of Economic Behavior* (New York: McGraw-Hill, 1951) and "Federal Reserve Board Committee Reports on Consumer Expectations and Savings Statistics," *Review of Economics and Statistics* (February, 1957); Margaret E. Thomas, "The Predictive Value of Consumer Expenditure Data as a Method of Forecasting Economic Fluctuations," presented at the 1954 meeting of American Statistical Association; Elmer C. Bratt, *Business Forecasting* (New York: McGraw-Hill, 1958), pp. 146-150, 168-171.

PART IV

Economic Stabilization, Growth, and Inflation

INTRODUCTION

This final Part is concerned with the problems of public policy and the economist's contribution to solving them. The experience of the Great Depression, during which profound institutional realignments altered the very fabric of our society, made the succeeding generation very conscious of the problem of economic stabilization. In earlier times, few thought that anyone could do anything about economic change and development. Now the controversy is between those who want to do a little and those who want to do a great deal.

The great debates on policy have veered between the Scylla of stagnation and the Charybdis of inflation. There is wide agreement that economic growth is essential for meeting the aspirations of the American people. There is less agreement as to what if anything should be done with the fruits of growth. On the one hand, there are those who argue that raising the standard of living of the country's population is the main purpose of economic growth, and that this will happen more or less automatically. On the other hand, there are those who argue that America's position in the world requires a faster rate of growth, not only to improve this country's level of living, but to help improve standards in the underdeveloped countries and to maintain a strong defense posture in a world divided into two armed camps. The problem of inflation, furthermore, complicates the issue. Can the economy grow at a faster rate without inducing inflation? What should public policy do about this possible conflict? Despite the great efforts already made to answer these and allied questions, the final verdict has not been rendered. It is safe to say that much of the public debate on economic policy in this decade will continue to focus on these issues.

Whatever the resolution of these debates may be, it is obvious that the huge size of the government sector and the large sums being spent on defense, space, and atomic energy programs with concomitant necessity for large tax receipts makes the question of government intervention one of form rather than substance. The role of economics in the setting of national policy has been officially recognized since the founding of the President's Council of Economic Advisers in 1946. This institution and the equally important and coordinate Joint Economic Committee of Congress have had a continuing and major influence not only on federal policy but also on the economics profession and the business community. The annual Economic Reports of the President and the reports of the Council of Economic Advisers further serve to keep public policy issues uppermost in the country's consciousness.

Unresolved is the question of whether the postwar business cycle differs materially from earlier cycles. Many argue that new institutional arrangements, an increased awareness of the problem, and the greater role of the federal government together have reduced the amplitude of the business cycle; some even suggest that it may in time be eliminated. Others argue that the relative mildness of postwar business cycles emanates from World War II and its aftermath and that we have yet to make the great postwar readjustment which may be more severe than many seem willing to admit. Only time will tell who is right.

Finally, there is still considerable controversy over the nature of government policies for stabilization and growth. What are the proper roles of fiscal policy, monetary policy, and debt management? Some economists prefer to rely more on the last two; others want to place the main emphasis on the first. Still others think there is no conflict at all; rather, that each policy has its appropriate place and all three can be coordinated. Value judgments galore enter into this discussion and the economist frequently finds himself in a position where he has to choose among policies on the basis of noneconomic considerations. Yet in the end that is not too surprising, since the subject matter—man and his progress—covers far more than economic variables. Nevertheless, economics does have an important part to play and the articles presented in Part IV were chosen to highlight some of these issues, as they relate to the present and as they can shed light on the future.

[26]

Built-in Stabilizers
of Our Economy*

PAUL A. SAMUELSON†

Editors' Note

Although his professional work is of the highest caliber, Samuelson never-theless finds time to write popular articles on economics for the foreign press, particularly in England and Japan.

This article, written for a wide nonprofessional audience, pinpoints the nature and role of the built-in stabilizers. Thus a progressive tax system, which also imposes heavy corporate income taxes, generates wider swings in tax receipts than take place in national income. As business booms, corporate tax accruals rise more than proportionately, as do the personal income tax receipts; the reverse, of course, is true in recessions. On the outlay side, the unemployment compensation system was specifically de-signed to react to business trends; farm price support programs and social security have had a comparable effect. These effects are built in, since they require no special action on anyone's part. Also, the mammoth out-lay represented by government spending is ordinarily not subject to cyclical fluctuations. Much has been written on the role of built-in stabilizers, but this article is a gem in its brevity.

❧ The new Administration is on the spot. It takes over at a time when the country is at its peak of prosperity. Almost anyone can find a job.

---

* From *The Reporter* (February 17, 1953, Copyright 1953 by The Fortnightly Pub-lishing Co., Inc.), pp. 13-15. Reprinted by permission of *The Reporter* and the author.
† See p. 323.

Output is at its postwar high. Even prices have been generally stable for the last year.

In contrast, Franklin Roosevelt took over when the economy was at its lowest point. Things could perhaps have gotten worse. But, proclaiming that America had nothing to fear but fear itself, he was singularly able to capture the imagination of the people, stem the waves of pessimism that had swamped Hoover's well-meaning economic maneuvers, and establish a reputation for miraculously pulling the country out of the Great Depression.

Is there a real danger that Eisenhower may share Herbert Hoover's uncomfortable role in history—that of taking over a prosperous-seeming economy just at a time when the clouds of depression are forming on the horizon? Less than six months after the 1929 inauguration, business activity had begun to recede from its peak, a historical parallel that may well haunt Eisenhower's advisers.

My own diagnosis makes me discount such a gloomy analogy, principally because I believe that various changes during the past quarter century have given our economy a built-in stability it never had before.

FLATTENING CYCLES

Many forecasters have been expressing fears of a business downturn during the last half of 1953. They may possibly be right. Even if a downturn does not materialize so soon, the historical record of American business cycles does not reassure us that sometime during Eisenhower's four-year term another recession will not occur. The record shows that every so often merchants and manufacturers can scarcely help getting too eager in their inventory buying. While the boom psychology is on, businessmen's frantic attempts to order more goods stimulate too rapid an expansion; inevitably there comes a day when shelves are overloaded with goods and orders are canceled; this fills the warehouses of the man up the line and he has to lay off workers, thereby accentuating the drop in purchasing power and in business generally.

Exactly this happened in 1920–1921, in 1937–1938, and quite recently in 1948–1949. Something like the usual inventory cycle took place between early 1951 and the present time: After the immediate Korean War splurge, retail trade and civilian industries—such as textiles, shoes, and durable appliances—went into a mild slump from which they did not revive until after the settlement of last summer's steel strike. Few noticed this because of the defense build-up; but the evidence is to be seen in the chart of physical production if not in the national income indexes.

It is interesting to compare the magnitude of these four successive inventory cycles. The 1920 collapse in prices was by far the sharpest. The 1937 decline in employment and activity was sharp, but by early 1938 many programs were under way to reverse the tide. After the Second World War the long-predicted recession did not materialize until the fall of 1948, and it then turned out to last less than eight months. Those of us who waited for depression bargains were disappointed: All that happened was that prices and wages stood still for a change rather than continuing to rise. As for the minor recession of 1951, any movement that only the specialists know about and that the public is generally unaware of cannot be very important.

Why this dramatic flattening of the ups and downs of business? Why is it that a new voter who has been alive some 255 months should have lived through only about thirty months of decline in general business activity? Clearly the war and the postwar emergency have had much to do with the recent buoyancy of the economy. Clearly too, the prewar improvements in business were made possible by the low level of the economy some twenty years ago, and even then were not sufficient to bring us back to anything like full employment prior to the war itself.

DEFENSIVE WEAPONS

Nonetheless there seems to have been a profound change in the inherent stability of the American economy. We read every day about the wonderful marvels of the electronic age—of the control gadgets that enable gunners to track an airplane from the deck of a tossing ship, of others that keep the temperatures of our rooms at specified levels. We have yet to realize that our economic system itself contains stabilizers that offer powerful resistance to extreme departures from existing levels in production and spending.

Today's *tax system* is closely geared to changes in national income. Even before Eisenhower confers with his Congressional leaders, any slump in spending and business activity will show itself in lower personal and corporate incomes and in lower collections of income and payroll taxes. Such reductions in tax payments by individuals and businesses automatically tend to cushion the decline. Conversely, when inflationary pressures increase, tax payments go up regardless of any change in tax rates, thereby tending to reduce purchasing power and to lessen the inflationary pressure.

Many of the *government expenditure programs*—such as unemployment compensation, social security, and farm-price supports, which both political parties uphold and are mostly here to stay—tend automatically to move against the current of business activity. When general demand expands employment, then unemployment compensation drops off; when unemployment develops, payments to the out-of-work increase without anyone's having to survey the situation or dream up politically acceptable programs.

The general scope of *government use of resources* is much bigger than it used to be. This huge inert element in the total tends to reduce the oscillations of the system. If the farmer and manufacturer at the same time become pessimistic and begin to contract their purchases, they react upon each other in a self-aggravating way. And you can blame neither one, for when one's income is cut and his purse is thin, he must spend less.

But government expenditure does not behave in this cyclically reinforcing way, in the United States or anywhere else. Regardless of the expected pattern of prices and markets, government continues to need battleships and bombers, judges and policemen, county agricultural agents and civil servants.

In theory, when business declines, the government could try to do what any business firm does. It could balance its budget, letting unemployment grow as it would. It could raise its tax rates and cut its expenditure activities down to its shrinking level of tax receipts. In practice, no national government in a democracy can ever do this. And none of Eisenhower's advisers want this to happen.

OFFENSIVE WEAPONS

By themselves, the built-in stabilizers can go a long way toward moderating short inventory swings in business. But alone they only undo part of the harm caused by other unstable forces. Suppose—as I believe far from inevitable—there should be a serious post-defense slump in private capital expenditures because of our tremendous accumulations of completed plant and equipment. Then the built-in stabilizers would have to be reinforced by more offensive measures.

Our Congressional and political attitudes have become such that I would regard such positive actions as being scarcely less probable than the purely automatic stabilizers. A recent survey of 373 readers of a business journal showed that ninety per cent of them expected the government to take such action if it became necessary. Among the electorate at large, there is this same general feeling. The campaign speeches of Eisenhower and the incoming Congress could not be more explicit: No one intends to sit idly by while a serious depression materializes.

Here are the principal public and private programs likely to be introduced if there is a serious continued drop in investment spending:

Tax reduction. Everyone loves Santa Claus, and both parties can be expected to vie with each other in reducing the currently high load of taxes if falling prices and employment make present tax rates unnecessary. The first to go, regardless of the business outlook, will undoubtedly be the excess-profits tax on corporations. As far as the personal income tax is concerned, the problem will not be to get Congress to make cuts but rather to persuade Congress not to disregard any threatening inflationary upsurge. Already the Washington hotels are filled with business spokesmen seeking relief from the present high excises on liquor, tobacco, furs, cosmetics, transport, and so on. So these depression-fighting tax measures will not be overlooked. Indeed, we may be more likely to get large budget deficits from this new Congress than from its predecessors.

Credit control. The Federal Reserve authorities have come out from under the thumb of the Treasury and have been quietly putting the brakes on over-all monetary expansion, making credit harder to get and more expensive. From all we know about the new Eisenhower appointees, they can be expected to intensify action along this anti-inflationary front if prices should zoom. W. Randolph Burgess, formerly of the National City Bank and now Treasury consultant on management of the public debt, has repeatedly gone on record in this regard; Gabriel Hauge, Eisenhower's brain-truster and speech writer on economic affairs, is thought to be an exponent of the use of monetary devices; Marion Folsom of Eastman Kodak, the new Under Secretary of the Treasury, was head of the Committee for Economic Development, which has repeatedly espoused a stabilizing monetary policy; Chairman William McChesney Martin, Jr., of the Federal Reserve Board has been held over because he is known to oppose the Truman-Snyder pegged-bond policy that enabled banks blithely to sell their government bonds and lend the proceeds.

These measures of monetary contraction can be put into reverse if the problem becomes one of depression rather than inflation. The more these measures actually bite in on the inflationary side, the greater will be their likely effect in offsetting any developing slump. However, most economists believe monetary policy is less potent in coaxing out investment during deep slumps than in choking it off in time of boom.

Government expenditure programs. Few realize that the nondefense programs of the government have been running at a considerably lower percentage of the national income than before the war. There are many new cars on our highways; but because of the urgency for defense we have kept road construction down.

Similarly, if one examines the budget item by item and makes prewar comparisons, he will find that the growth of ordinary government expenditure has been much less, particularly in terms of the prewar dollar, than has the growth of the rest of the economy. I think this a good thing—to the extent that it reflects greater private uses of economic resources and to the extent that our high levels of business activity have released the government from any obligation to engage in made-work projects of dubious value. But to the extent that it reflects a determination to give highest priority to defense and security needs, any future lessening of those needs can be expected to have the following consequences: The money and resources released from the defense effort we shall want to spend in part privately on clothing, housing, appliances; in part, we shall want to spend them publicly on schools, roads, parks, beaches, research laboratories, and other construction.

There is no danger that there will be too few public works to spend our money on. But if Congress acts in time and if we are to get the most for our money, advanced scheduling of stand-by programs is needed—and here we are falling behind.

DEFENSE BOONDOGGLING

There is one other possible anti-depression measure—and one of which I thoroughly disapprove. We could use the defense program as the excuse for expanding general demand whenever markets decline. There will be pressures in this direction from workers, farmers, and businessmen who would rather work on building up stockpiles than have their present activities cut back. I do not think that up until now there has been Machiavellian reliance on the defense program to keep up business activity, and I do not expect the situation to change in this respect. However, Congress will undoubtedly be under considerable political pressures, and an enlightened public opinion can help immensely.

The problem is the more difficult for the following reasons. First, no one can indicate precisely how large defense spending need be. If war is really imminent, which no man can know, we are spending far too little. If there is an over-all business contraction, it is perfectly appropriate for us to expand the defense program in those marginal areas which we have previously refused to enter for fear of adding to inflation. Extreme wisdom will be needed to distinguish between defense spending that will counteract an incipient depression and that which represents boondoggling.

Out of a long list of further unwise anti-depression programs I shall here warn against only two: the use of hasty, unplanned, and unnecessary foreign aid simply to keep up spending; and the revival of tariffs and protectionist measures to help any and every industry that is experiencing a loss of domestic markets.

PERPETUAL PROSPERITY?

Does all this suggest that America has tamed the business cycle for all time and can now usher in an era of perpetual prosperity? It would be absurd to fall back into the fatuous optimism of the pre-1929 era. We shall still have fluctuations. But it is equally absurd not to recognize the important new stabilizers in our economic system. The extreme variations can be substantially moderated.

What needs strongest emphasis, in my judgment, is not the differences in economic policy that a Republican Administration is likely to pursue as compared to a Democratic one. There are discernible differences. But just as the Russians are fooling themselves when they confidently expect the capitalist system to go into a major collapse, so many Democrats are fooling themselves when they think that the new Administration is sure to bungle the stabilization program and discredit itself by killing off prosperity.

The American people expect much of Eisenhower and the new Congress. In this sense the Administration is on the spot. But no one party has a monopoly on common sense, and the economic decisions will not be insoluble or even terribly difficult so long as the key problem is to maintain high employment rather than to control inflation.

27

Postwar Cyclical Experience
and Economic Stability*

BERT G. HICKMAN†

Editors' Note

Cycle theorists cannot agree as to whether or not there has been a permanent change in the nature of the business cycle since the end of World
War II. This article argues that there has been no basic change in the
nature and causes of business fluctuations in recent years. It concedes,
however, that postwar cycles do differ from earlier ones in their structure
and in the particular mix of autonomous factors, especially government
defense spending. Although the discussion refers only to the 1948–49 and
1953–54 downturns, the argument could be extended to include the later
1957–58 and 1960–61 experiences. It is indeed true that over the past
fifteen years which have been characterized by high level employment and
rapid growth in output there have been no severe contractions. (However, some might argue that the failure of unemployment from 1955
through 1962 to fall back to the 4 per cent rate which held in earlier
years might be viewed as a longer-run tendency worthy of concern.) Such
a happy state of affairs did exist in earlier periods. The postwar economy
differs from that of earlier times in that it has not suffered a major price
deflation, which, if past performance were a sure guide, should have resulted after the end of a major war. The legacy of the war and the continuing cold war have been major factors in the relative stability of

---

* Copyright 1958 by the American Economic Association. Reprinted, with the permission of the author and the Association, from the *American Economic Review*, Vol.
XLIX, No. 2 (May, 1958). The article was prepared as part of a broad study of the
growth and stability of the postwar economy undertaken for the Brookings Institution.
The interpretations and conclusions are those of the author and do not necessarily
reflect the views of other members of the Brookings staff or of the administrative
officers of the Institution.
† See p. 343.

investment, but this does not prove that private outlays on capital goods could not at a later date fall precipitously. Thus far, Hickman argues, postwar cycles have been mild because they have not been widely diffused. The analysis is made in terms of a study of the diffusion of production series, industry by industry, and this represents a major advance in research. All in all, the following article, a contribution by one of the leading students of business cycles of the new postwar generation, sheds important light on the nature of postwar business cycles.

❧ Twelve years unmarked by serious economic contraction have elapsed since the end of World War II.[1] The impressive postwar record of growth and resistance to depression is partly responsible for the widespread tendency to emphasize aspects of recent experience which are believed to be new or abnormal and are thought to have contributed importantly to economic stability. The structural changes of the past twenty-five years, it is asserted, have so altered the response mechanism of the economy that wide swings are a thing of the past. At the other pole is the argument that postwar prosperity has been due to war or cold war influences which are not only autonomous but abnormal in their persistence for nearly two decades. If either of these explanations is correct, it has obvious implications for future stability. So also does a third possibility; namely, that although the postwar economy differs from its predecessors in details of structure and the mixture of autonomous factors at work, there has been no essential change in the nature or causes of business fluctuations.

I am not prepared to make a categorical choice among these alternatives, although I lean toward the last. One of my purposes in this paper is to show why I find the choice to be difficult, and why certain inferences which are sometimes drawn from observable characteristics of recent fluctuations appear to me to be quite inconclusive. The other purpose is to call to mind a few of the important autonomous forces which are known to have affected business cycles in the past and to stress their influence in the postwar era.

The Postwar Cycles in Historical Perspective

An obvious first question is whether the postwar business fluctuations have differed so much from those of earlier years that one is almost forced

---

[1] This paper presents some early results from a study of the growth and stability of the postwar economy which I am undertaking for the Brookings Institution.

to conclude that abnormal external factors or decisive structural changes must be the cause of contemporary behavior.

The long-run development of production in the United States reveals striking gains, but growth has been far from steady (Chart I). Since the absence of a major contraction is a distinctive feature of the postwar era, the most comparable intervals with regard to stability and continuity of growth lie between the severe contractions of the past. Among the latter may be ranked the contractions of 1873–78, 1882–85, 1892–94, 1907–08, 1920–21, 1929–32, and 1937–38.[2] The contraction of 1944–46, while large in terms of production, was mild insofar as the development of unemployment or excess capacity is concerned.

It is apparent that the postwar period is not in a class by itself in its freedom from depression. Beginning with the segment of 1866–73, the intervals between severe contractions before World War II measured respectively 7, 4, 7, 13, 12, 8 and 5 years, while the postwar experience has spanned 12 years thus far.[3] If the comparatively mild though long-lived contraction of 1882–85 is excluded from the class of major contractions, moreover, the two short periods which are second and third on the foregoing list would be replaced by a single interval of 14 years.

The duration of the contemporary period, on the other hand, becomes 19 years if it is extended to include World War II. The vital question, however, is whether by virtue of structural changes or abnormal forces the economy has been inherently more stable in the postwar years. The influence of World War II and its aftereffects cannot be neglected in either of these connections, but the fact remains that the relevant period for study and comparison begins in 1946 rather than 1938, and to this period we now return.

It is somewhat surprising to discover that the average annual rate of increase of production has been smaller in the postwar years than in the comparison periods (Table 1). Some of the earlier periods, however, began with recoveries from deep troughs in which surplus capacity had developed on a large scale, permitting rapid advances until the slack was eliminated. Allowance should be made for this fact, since the present period did not begin from a position of underutilization.

A correction for the capacity factor can be made by selecting periods of approximately equal labor force utilization. Estimates of the percentage of the labor force which was unemployed during the various comparison periods are shown in Table 2. By this important criterion, the economy has fared well in the postwar years, and indeed better than in any period covered by the unemployment data with the exception of 1900–1907. The

---

[2] The dates are from the business cycle chronology of the National Bureau of Economic Research. They do not necessarily agree with the peaks and troughs of the corresponding contractions in the production series included in Chart I, although the disagreements are few.

[3] The first segment dates from the end of the Civil War even though no severe contraction occurred at that time.

TABLE 1—AVERAGE ANNUAL PERCENTAGE RATES OF INCREASE OF PRODUCTION,
SELECTED PERIODS, 1866–1956*

Period	Manufacturing Production (1899=100)	Gross National Product (1947 Dollars)	
		Total	Per Capita
1. 1866–73	6.0		
2. 1878–92	5.7		
a) 1878–82	13.2		
b) 1885–92	6.7		
3. 1894–1907	7.1	4.7†	2.8†
4. 1908–20	5.5	4.2	2.5
5. 1921–29	6.3	4.8	3.3
6. 1932–37	15.7	8.2	7.5
7. 1938–44	24.2	11.8	10.7
8. 1946–56	4.8	4.0	2.2

* Percentage growth rate computed from an exponential curve fitted to the annual data by the use of Glover's mean value table (J. W. Glover, *Tables of Applied Mathematics*, George Wahr, Ann Arbor, Michigan, 1923, pages 468 ff.).

† Computed for the period 1897–1907.

SOURCES: Index of manufacturing production:

    1860–99. Edwin Frickey, *Production in the United States 1860–1914* (Harvard University Press, 1947), Table 6.

    1900–1937. Solomon Fabricant, *The Output of Manufacturing Industries 1899–1937* (National Bureau of Economic Research, 1940), Table 1.

    1938–56. *Economic Report of the President* (January, 1957), Table E-27. Converted to 1899=100.

Gross national product:

    1897–1928. Raymond W. Goldsmith, *A Study of Saving in the United States*, Vol. III (Princeton University Press, 1956), Table N-2. The series was adjusted to the level of the Department of Commerce estimate for 1929 and converted to 1947 dollars.

    1929–56. The Department of Commerce estimates as given in *Economic Report of the President* (January, 1957), Table E-4.

Population:

    1897–1928. *Historical Statistics of the United States 1789–1945* (U. S. Bureau of the Census, 1949), page 26.

    1929–56. *Economic Report of the President* (January, 1957), Table E-14.

average unemployment ratio for the twenties, however, is raised by the high rates of 1921 and 1922. If those years of initial expansion are disregarded, the resulting average for 1923–29 is about equal to 1946–56.

Here, then, are two periods—1900–1907 and 1923–29—during which over-all resource utilization was comparable to present times. Computing production growth rates for these periods, we find that it is still true that growth was slower in recent years than around the turn of the century (Table 3). Contemporary growth has been more rapid than in the middle and late twenties, however, although the excess can scarcely be considered a difference in kind.

So much for the growth of physical activity during the postwar period

TABLE 2—UNEMPLOYMENT AS A PERCENTAGE OF THE CIVILIAN LABOR FORCE,
AVERAGES FOR SELECTED PERIODS, 1900–1956

Period	Average Unemployment Ratio
1. 1900–1907	2.9
2. 1908–20	5.4
3. 1921–29	5.1
4. 1932–37	20.2
5. 1938–44	9.8
6. 1946–56	3.9

SOURCES: 1900–1928. Stanley Lebergott, "Annual Estimates of Unemployment in the United States, 1900–1954," *The Measurement and Behavior of Unemployment*, A Conference of the Universities—National Bureau Committee for Economic Research (Princeton University Press, 1957), page 215. 1929–56. *Economic Report of the President* (January, 1957), Table E-17.

as a whole. Let us now take a closer look at the two post-World War II business cycles and see how they compare in amplitude and duration with their predecessors (Table 4). Both postwar expansions were considerably longer than the average of previous upswings, though they were not the longest on record. Similarly, the postwar contractions were briefer than the average, but there were several earlier downswings of approximately equal duration. With regard to amplitudes, the first postwar upswing was among a number of mild expansions on record, while the second was about average. The downswings of 1948–49 and 1953–54 had amplitudes below the average for all prior contractions but well within the range of previous minor recessions. The postwar fluctuations are clearly similar with respect to amplitude and duration to a number of their forerunners. The differences between them and earlier cycles are no greater than the differences among earlier cycles.

Thus far, three major aspects of postwar economic performance have been set against the perspective of history. The postwar record has been good on all three counts of freedom from severe contraction, maintenance of high-level employment, and rapid growth of production. It is not unique

TABLE 3—AVERAGE ANNUAL UNEMPLOYMENT PERCENTAGE AND AVERAGE ANNUAL
RATE OF GROWTH OF PRODUCTION, SELECTED PERIODS, 1900–1956*

Period	Average Unemployment Percentage	*Average Annual Percentage Increase of*		
		Manufacturing Production	Gross National Product (1947 Dollars)	
			Total	Per Capita
1. 1900–1907	2.9	6.6	4.4	2.4
2. 1923–29	3.8	4.2	3.1	1.6
3. 1946–56	3.9	4.8	4.0	2.2

* For sources and methods, see Tables 1 and 2.

TABLE 4—DURATION AND AMPLITUDE OF BUSINESS CYCLES, 1854–1954

Expansions				Contractions			
Business Cycle		Dura-tion (Months)	Ampli-tude (Per Cent)	Business Cycle		Dura-tion (Months)	Ampli-tude (Per Cent)
Trough	Peak			Peak	Trough		
Dec. 1854	June 1857	30	12.3	June 1857	Dec. 1858	18	21.0
Dec. 1858	Oct. 1860	22	16.8	Oct. 1860	June 1861	8	14.1
June 1861	Apr. 1865	46	18.1	Apr. 1865	Dec. 1867	32	11.4
Dec. 1867	June 1869	18	6.9	June 1869	Dec. 1870	18	7.9
Dec. 1870	Oct. 1873	34	18.4	Oct. 1873	Mar. 1879	65	26.9
Mar. 1879	Mar. 1882	36	27.6	Mar. 1882	May 1885	38	27.9
May 1885	Mar. 1887	22	22.7	Mar. 1887	Apr. 1888	13	11.2
Apr. 1888	July 1890	27	16.6	July 1890	May 1891	10	17.0
May 1891	Jan. 1893	20	16.3	Jan. 1893	June 1894	17	30.7
June 1894	Dec. 1895	18	25.3	Dec. 1895	June 1897	18	24.3
June 1897	June 1899	24	26.6	June 1899	Dec. 1900	18	14.4
Dec. 1900	Sept. 1902	21	14.2	Sept. 1902	Aug. 1904	23	14.4
Aug. 1904	May 1907	33	20.2	May 1907	June 1908	13	29.5
June 1908	Jan. 1910	19	25.6	Jan. 1910	Jan. 1912	24	12.0
Jan. 1912	Jan. 1913	12	13.6	Jan. 1913	Dec. 1914	23	23.2
Dec. 1914	Aug. 1918	44	29.8	Aug. 1918	Apr. 1919	8	22.0
Apr. 1919	Jan. 1920	9	17.9	Jan. 1920	July 1921	18	34.7
July 1921	May 1923	22	38.0	May 1923	July 1924	14	21.8
July 1924	Oct. 1926	27	17.8	Oct. 1926	Nov. 1927	13	9.3
Nov. 1927	June 1929	19	16.7	June 1929	Mar. 1933	45	75.1
Mar. 1933	May 1937	50	63.7	May 1937	June 1938	13	45.4
June 1938	Feb. 1945	80	72.7	Feb. 1945	Oct. 1945	8	41.0
Oct. 1945	Nov. 1948	37	14.7	Nov. 1948	Oct. 1949	11	17.5
Oct. 1949	July 1953	45	23.9	July 1953	Aug. 1954	13	14.3

SOURCE: National Bureau of Economic Research.

NOTES: The amplitudes are averages of three trend-adjusted indexes of business activity: AT&T, Persons-Barrons, and Ayres. Before 1879, the entries are for the Ayres index alone. The amplitudes for each index are based upon the specific cycles in the index. The method by which specific cycle amplitudes are computed is explained in Arthur F. Burns and Wesley C. Mitchell, *Measuring Business Cycles* (National Bureau of Economic Research, 1947), Chapter 2.

in any of these respects or in the combination of them, however. It is not until we turn to the behavior of prices that a pronounced contrast with earlier events is found, and even then it is with developments in other postwar decades rather than with the entirety of previous experience.

To judge from the historical record, the absence of postwar deflation is an outstanding characteristic of the contemporary era. It is not, however, evidence that a basic change in the nature of business cycles has necessarily occurred.

The long-term development of production has been more regular than the course of prices (Chart I). Production has risen with only minor setbacks except during major contractions. Prices have also declined during severe contractions, but for the rest, they have sometimes increased, some-

CHART I MANUFACTURING PRODUCTION, REAL GROSS NATIONAL PRODUCT, AND
WHOLESALE PRICES, 1866–1956

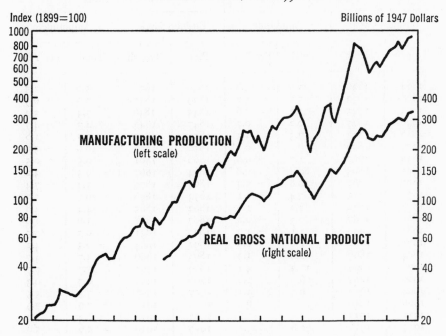

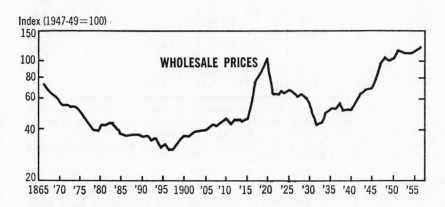

For source and notes see Tables 1 and 5.

TABLE 5—AMPLITUDE OF WHOLESALE PRICES DURING BUSINESS CYCLES, 1834–1954
(In Per Cent)*

EXPANSIONS				CONTRACTIONS			
Business Cycle		Amplitude		Business Cycle		Amplitude	
Trough	Peak	Total	Per Year	Peak	Trough	Total	Per Year
1834	1836	27.5	13.8	1836	1838	− 5.0	− 2.5
1838	1839	5.2	5.2	1839	1843	−26.0	− 6.5
1843	1845	1.2	0.6	1845	1846	3.4	3.4
1846	1847	0.2	0.2	1847	1848	− 4.7	− 4.7
1848	1853	7.5	1.5	1853	1855	3.7	1.8
1855	1856	0	0	1856	1858	−10.0	− 5.0
1858	1860	− 1.7	− 0.8	1860	1861	0.5	0.5
1861	1864	89.4	29.8	1864	1867	− 9.5	− 3.2
1867	1869	−10.8	− 5.4	1869	1870	− 7.4	− 7.4
1870	1873	− 3.4	− 1.1	1873	1878	−26.3	− 5.3
1878	1882	7.2	1.8	1882	1885	−14.4	− 4.8
1885	1887	− 0.3	− 0.2	1887	1888	1.6	1.6
1888	1890	− 2.1	− 1.0	1890	1891	− 0.5	− 0.5
1891	1892	− 6.6	− 6.6	1892	1894	− 8.3	− 4.2
1894	1895	1.9	1.9	1895	1896	− 4.7	− 4.7
1896	1899	12.3	4.1	1899	1900	7.7	7.7
1900	1903	6.0	2.0	1903	1904	0.3	0.3
1904	1907	9.3	3.1	1907	1908	− 3.5	− 3.5
1908	1910	12.0	6.0	1910	1911	− 7.9	− 7.9
1911	1913	7.6	3.8	1913	1914	− 2.4	− 2.4
1914	1918	92.6	23.2	1918	1919	5.6	5.6
1919	1920	11.3	11.3	1920	1921	−36.8	−36.8
1921	1923	3.2	1.6	1923	1924	− 2.4	− 2.4
1924	1926	1.9	1.0	1926	1927	− 4.6	− 4.6
1927	1929	− 0.2	− 0.1	1929	1932	−32.0	−10.7
1932	1937	33.3	6.7	1937	1938	− 8.9	− 8.9
1938	1944	32.3	5.4	1944	1946	16.4	8.2
1946	1948	32.7	16.4	1948	1949	− 5.0	− 5.0
1949	1953	11.0	2.8	1953	1954	0.2	0.2

* The business cycle dates are from the chronology of the National Bureau of Economic Research. The percentage changes during expansions are computed from trough to peak and those during contractions, from peak to trough.
SOURCE: Index of wholesale prices (1947–49 equals 100) is from a mimeographed release of the Bureau of Labor Statistics.

times decreased, and sometimes remained virtually unchanged during business cycles (Table 5). Since a variety of price tendencies have been compatible with production tendencies which are similar to those of the postwar years, it cannot be concluded that recent price behavior is prima facie evidence that business cycles have changed.[4]

[4] This is not to say that the characteristics of cycles are unrelated to price trends. Prices trended irregularly downward from the end of the Civil War until the late 1890's, and during that span several prolonged contractions occurred. Prices subsequently followed a rising trend through World War I, and there were no contractions during

What is the proper interpretation to place upon the finding that in a number of important performance characteristics the post-World War II business fluctuations fall within the range of their predecessors? Pronounced contrasts between recent and earlier behavior would be consistent with the hypothesis that business cycles now differ because of abnormal autonomous factors or of structural changes that altered the response mechanism, or some combination of the two. The fact that such differences do not exist does not disprove the hypothesis, however. It is entirely possible for varying combinations of autonomous factors or for different economic structures to yield the same general outcome. The multiplicity of theories of the business cycle is in itself evidence of that, as is the stubborn persistence of the phenomenon in the real world. At the same time, one cannot be as confident that a fundamental change has occurred as he would be if contemporary experience were outside the previous range; and the mere fact that business cycles have persisted during a long history of institutional development and economic growth cautions against quick inferences that lasting structural changes are responsible for recent stability and will continue to induce stability in the future.

The Diffusion of Business Cycles

Contemporary observers have not overlooked an interesting feature of recent business fluctuations; that is, the tendency for offsetting movements to occur among the various sectors of the economy. Sustained declines of business fixed investment occurred during the contractions of 1948–49 and 1953–54, but residential construction and personal consumption led on both recoveries. The outbreak of Korean hostilities stimulated private as well as public demand, and the subsequent reaction to the early speculative buying diminished the pressure on resources just as an accelerated mobilization program was getting underway. After lagging behind homebuilding and consumption on the 1954 upturn, business fixed investment rose steeply as residential construction declined, and when business investment began to taper off in 1956, federal spending commenced to rise.

It is tempting to speculate that these tendencies are a reflection of new structural developments which have inhibited the transmission of inflationary or deflationary impulses from one sector to another, and there has been a fair amount of popular discussion of "rolling readjustments" and "the breakup of the business cycle." Propositions which might be advanced in support of the hypothesis include the following. The automatic stabilizers have reduced the value of the multiplier during expansions and

---

that period which were both extended and deep. Burns and Mitchell found evidence that contractions tend to be long or short according as the trend of prices is rising or falling (*Measuring Business Cycles*, National Bureau of Economic Research, 1947, pp. 431-440). They express confidence, on the other hand, that the business cycles occurring during upswings of long waves in commodity prices do not differ substantially from the cycles during the long downswings of prices.

by moderating the fall of disposable income in contractions, have fostered favorable conditions for autonomous upward shifts of the consumption function such as occurred during 1949 and 1954.[5] Business fixed investment is less responsive than formerly to slowdowns or declines in sales, because businessmen are looking farther into the future and expect growth to continue, as evidenced by the increased use of capital budgeting techniques and long-term projections in the formation of investment programs. Financial reforms have strengthened the banking system and the capital markets, inhibiting speculative tendencies and mitigating the threat of secondary deflation.

The list could be lengthened, but to little purpose since I am not prepared at this time to assess the significance of individual structural changes. I will therefore confine myself to an indirect approach to the problem, by again asking whether the phenomenon is a new one requiring a new explanation.

The answer, of course, is that it is not, which will surprise few students of business cycles and none who has stressed the importance of disaggregation. Even on a broad aggregative level, there are similar instances of counterbalancing movements during earlier cycles. Residential construction reached a peak of the long building cycle in 1925, which means that it rose during part or all of the contractions of 1920–21 and 1923–24, but fell during the expansion of 1927–29. Professor Kuznets' estimates of annual consumption expenditures in 1929 prices show increases during the contractions of 1923–24 and 1926–27.[6]

These illustrations are drawn, of course, from the minor fluctuations of the twenties. But that is just the point. Let us accept the working hypothesis that the contractions of 1948–49 and 1953–54 were mild because they were not widely diffused. If a similar relationship between amplitude and diffusion is to be found during the mild contractions of the middle twenties, contemporary experience can hardly be cited as proof of a basic change in the response mechanism.

That a similar relationship did exist during the earlier contractions is shown, not only by the aggregative data already mentioned, but also by the diffusion index graphed in Chart II. This index measures the percentage of manufacturing and mining industries in which production

---

[5] In this context, "automatic stabilizers" consist of any leakages which regularly moderate the marginal response of disposable income to GNP, including induced changes in business saving. There is evidence, however, that the over-all response has been diminished in the postwar period because of the augmented importance of taxes and transfers. See my paper, "Federal Spending and the Stability of the Postwar Economy," *Federal Expenditure Policy for Economic Growth and Stability, Papers Submitted by Panelists Appearing Before the Subcommittee on Fiscal Policy* (Joint Economic Committee, 85th Congress, 1st Session, November 5, 1957), which contains a comparison with the twenties. It should also be noted that tax cuts helped to raise disposable income in 1954.

[6] Simon Kuznets, *National Product Since 1869* (National Bureau of Economic Research, 1946), Table I 15.

CHART II INDUSTRIAL PRODUCTION AND ITS DIFFUSION, 1919–39 AND 1947–56

Part A. 1919–1929

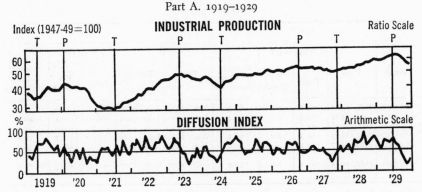

Part B. 1929–1939

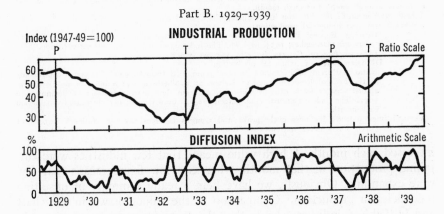

Part C. 1947–1956

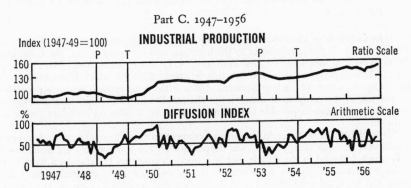

Vertical lines indicate business cycle peaks and troughs as dated by the National Bureau of Economic Research.

For sources and notes see Table 6.

TABLE 6—AMPLITUDE AND DIFFUSION OF INDUSTRIAL PRODUCTION DURING
BUSINESS CYCLES, 1919–39 AND 1947–56
(In Per Cent)

EXPANSIONS*		Amplitude†		Average Monthly Index of Diffusion‡	CONTRACTIONS*		Amplitude†		Average Monthly Index of Diffusion‡
Trough	Peak	Total	Per Month		Peak	Trough	Total	Per Month	
Mar. 1919	Feb. 1920	25.7	2.3	65.5	Feb. 1920	July 1921	−31.8	−1.9	45.3
July 1921	June 1923	63.3	2.8	67.4	June 1923	July 1924	−18.4	−1.4	42.3
July 1924	Oct. 1926	32.5	1.2	61.3	Oct. 1926	Nov. 1927	− 7.5	−0.6	44.9
Nov. 1927	Aug. 1929	24.5	1.2	66.1	Aug. 1929	July 1932	−54.1	−1.5	29.1
July 1932	May 1937	132.1	2.3	62.2	May 1937	May 1938	−33.8	−2.8	30.7
Oct. 1949	July 1953	45.7	1.0	59.9	July 1953	Oct. 1949	−10.5	−0.9	39.9
					Oct. 1949	Aug. 1954	−10.2	−0.8	42.3

* The peaks and troughs are those of the cycles in industrial production which correspond to business cycles as dated in Table. 4.

† Amplitudes of expansions are measured from trough month to peak month and of those of contractions from peak month to trough month.

‡ Arithmetic mean of the diffusion index during the cyclical phase.

SOURCES: Index of industrial production:

    1919–53. Federal Reserve Monthly Index of Industrial Production, *Federal Reserve Bulletin,* December, 1953, page 86. The index is adjusted for seasonal variation.

    1954–56. *Federal Reserve Bulletin,* various issues.

    Diffusion index of industrial production:

    National Bureau of Economic Research, computed from seasonally adjusted components of the Federal Reserve Index of Industrial Production. The number of industries included was 15 from 1919 to mid-1923, 25 from then until 1939, and 26 beginning in 1947. The index measures the percentage of industries which increased production each month.

Vertical lines indicate business cycle peaks and troughs as dated by the National Bureau of Economic Research. For sources and notes see Table 6.

increased each month. A high value means that few industries were curtailing production in that month, whereas a low figure means that few were expanding. Obviously, we have here a ready summary of offsetting tendencies in production.[7] Comparison of the values shown in the chart and in Table 6 indicates clearly that the two recent contractions are in the same class as those of the mid-twenties with regard both to amplitude and diffusion.[8]

---

[7] The emphasis of the NBER on the importance of diffusion goes back, of course, to Wesley Mitchell. Some references to the literature will be found in my "An Experiment With Weighted Indexes of Cyclical Diffusion," *J. of Amer. Statis. Asso.,* Mar., 1958, pp. 39-53. This experiment demonstrates that a simple diffusion index based only on the direction of change of each component differs little from indexes which are weighted by the size of the component industries or the amplitudes of the individual fluctuations. This finding removes a possible objection to the use of a diffusion index for the present purpose.

[8] It is of little importance in the present connection that the contraction of industrial production in 1920-21 apparently was deeper though not more widely diffused than the two which followed in the decade, but it is worth noting that the statistical bases of the indexes are weaker for the years prior to 1923, and that more comprehensive indexes show the expected correlation between diffusion and amplitude even in 1920-21. Cf. Arthur F. Burns, "New Facts on Business Cycles," *30th Annual Report of the National Bureau of Economic Research,* 1954, reprinted in the same author's *The Frontiers of Economic Knowledge* (Princeton University Press, 1954), pp. 107-134.

Autonomous Factors in the Postwar Cycles

Economists are generally agreed that severe contractions result from substantial declines of fixed investment. These may occur because the stock of investment opportunities becomes temporarily insufficient to maintain an adequate level of expenditure or because the desire to exploit the existing opportunities is impaired for a time by adverse price or sales expectations, liquidity considerations, deterioration of business confidence, monetary or real capital shortages, etc.[9]

Following Professor Gordon, we may note several ways in which fixed investment opportunities are created: replacement requirements; demand for additional capacity induced by income growth with a given composition of output and given capital-output ratios; opportunities arising because a new composition of output becomes appropriate owing to the development of new products, changing tastes, divergent income elasticities, etc.; alterations in the composition of the capital stock made attractive by changes in technology or relative factor prices; and new opportunities in the field of housing stemming chiefly from population growth and migration. The crucial point to recognize is that investment opportunities may be created by factors which are to an important degree autonomous with respect to the level or rate of change of aggregate economic activity, even though the rate at which they are exploited may be modified by current and prospective short-term movements in sales, prices, profits, etc. This line of thought suggests that the postwar contractions have been mild, not alone because of structural changes in the cyclical response mechanism, but also because autonomous factors have helped to assure an adequate stock of investment opportunities. What might some of those factors be?

High on the list must be placed war and cold war. The second World War left as part of its heritage to the forties an abundance of investment opportunities and the psychological and financial conditions favorable to their implementation. The importance of federal expenditure in the present-day economy springs largely from security needs, and to the formerly paramount destabilizing potential of private investment must now be added that of government spending. As I have emphasized elsewhere,[10] largely for autonomous reasons federal expenditure has been the most variable major component of final demand in the postwar economy and has contributed much to such short-term instability as has occurred. Each

---

[9] Cf. Robert A. Gordon, "Investment Behavior and Business Cycles," *Rev. of Econ. and Statis.*, Feb., 1955, pp. 23-34, and also his "Types of Depression and Programs to Combat Them," *Policies to Combat Depression*, A Conference of the Universities— National Bureau Committee for Economic Research (Princeton University Press, 1956), pp. 7-25. Professor Gordon acknowledges his intellectual debt to Schumpeter, Hansen, and Robertson.

[10] The statements in this and the next paragraph are based upon the evidence and analysis contained in the paper cited in footnote 5.

retrenchment of federal spending, however, has left it higher than before; and over the decade as a whole it has been a broadly expansive force.

This last need not have been the case, of course. It is sometimes asserted that the new importance of government demand for output has placed a high floor under the economy. But if big government is regarded as a structural feature of the economy, the fact that the overwhelming bulk of federal purchases of goods and services is for national security and may therefore shift up or down with changes in the international political or military situation must also be accepted. Even if it is assumed that a pronounced curtailment of government spending is not likely to recur for some time to come, it must be recognized that private fixed investment is still sizable enough to fall as far below its full employment share of GNP as it did after 1929. If government has placed a high floor under aggregate activity, it is not because of any inherent stability of federal expenditure or because it has displaced what were previously the least stable elements of effective demand. Rather, it is because of structural changes which have accompanied the growth of government—financial reforms, tax and transfer stabilizers, and the assumption of federal responsibility for full employment—and altered the response mechanism; or because the knowledge and ability have been developed to take appropriate discretionary actions to counteract fluctuations in effective demand.

The role of technology and other factors in the creation of investment opportunities in individual industries should also be stressed. If the composition of output were fixed, each industry could grow only at the rate and in the time pattern set by aggregate output, and investment opportunities would consist only of those induced by output growth. In actuality, of course, individual industries grow more or less rapidly than national output; indeed, the processes of growth make this inevitable. Cost-reducing innovations or factor substitutions alter relative prices and outputs even with a given composition of demand. New products compete with the old. Tastes change. Because income elasticities differ, unequal increases occur in the demands for individual products as national income grows. Thus, observed changes in the composition of output are partly the cause of investment opportunities and partly the effect of their exploitation. Moreover—and this is the critical point—investment demand is almost certain to be larger when changes in output composition are appropriate than when they are not. For one thing, autonomous increases may occur in some sectors even when excess capacity prevails generally. For another, as Professor Fellner has emphasized, the disinvestment which may be forced upon a displaced industry is limited per unit of time by the annual rate of depreciation and is likely to be outweighed by the net investment required in a growing industry.[11]

---

[11] William Fellner, *Monetary Policies and Full Employment* (University of California Press, 1946), Chap. 4. The replacement demand lost could exceed the net investment gained if the growing industry required considerably less real capital per unit of output or if the declining industry lost considerably more output than the other gained through the substitution.

TABLE 7—DISTRIBUTION OF PERCENTAGE CHANGES IN PRODUCTION OF 146
MANUFACTURING INDUSTRIES BETWEEN 1947 AND 1956*

Percentage Change of Production	Number of Industries
Over 600†	2
400 to 599	3
200 to 399	2
160 to 199	1
120 to 159	2
110 to 119	3
100 to 109	3
90 to 99	2
80 to 89	3
70 to 79	7
60 to 69	9
50 to 59	2
40 to 49	14
30 to 39	12
20 to 29	14
10 to 19	19
0.1 to 9	14
0 to −9	14
−10 to −19	9
−20 to −29	5
−30 to −39	3
−40 to −49	2
−50 to −59	0
−60 to −69	1

* Based upon estimates of annual production in 1947 and 1956.
† The two industries in this class experienced production increases of respectively 4000 and 4050 per cent. Note that the class intervals are uneven above 120 per cent.
SOURCE: Production data from Board of Governors of the Federal Reserve System.

Individual industries have grown at widely divergent rates in the post-war economy. Table 7 contains a frequency distribution of the percentage changes in production of 146 manufacturing industries between 1947 and 1956. They range from a positive extreme of 4,000 per cent to a maximum decline of 65 per cent, and they vary considerably even within the more normal limits of growth. Clearly, substantial shifts occurred in the composition of output over the decade.

Let us go a step further. If irregular fluctuations are ignored, we can think of particular industries as subject to individual growth forces which are modified by cyclical influences. Each industry will respond to cyclical movements of aggregate activity according to its price and income elasticities. These elasticities will depend partly upon characteristics of the product and market which are independent of the rate of growth of the industry, but they will also be influenced by the latter. Since rapidly growing industries are increasing their share of national income, they should resist contractions of aggregate demand. Similarly, stable or declining industries should be stimulated less during expansions than their more fortunate competitors. These observations lead to the hypothesis that systematic differences in the extent of participation in business cycles should exist among industries which are grouped according to their growth over an interval spanning several cycles.

The hypothesis is confirmed by the measures of diffusion presented in Chart III and Table 8. Monthly diffusion indexes were prepared for 146 manufacturing industries and for three approximately equal subgroups classified by amount of growth between 1947 and 1956. Since nongrowth factors affect cyclical sensitivity, it was necessary to control such factors in establishing the growth groupings. Details are given in the notes to Table 8.

Inspection of the chart and table reveals the following facts. The average level of diffusion over the entire decade is highest for the group of rapid growth industries and lowest for the slow group. The same relationship holds for periods of expansion marked off by the business cycle chronology of the National Bureau of Economic Research, but it fails during the contractions.

Another look at the chart shows, however, that the over-all diffusion index indicates a shift from a majority to a minority of expanding industries prior to the business cycle peaks, and vice versa at the troughs. These leads partly reflect the fact that the peaks and troughs of manufacturing production are flat, so that the shift in the preponderance of expanding or contracting industries is not associated with a sharply defined reversal of manufacturing output in the vicinity of the business cycle turning points. Other factors help to account for the leads, but the important point in the present connection is that the relevant "contraction" periods are those during which the over-all diffusion index is consistently below 50 per cent in the neighborhood of the cyclical contraction. When average levels of diffusion are computed for periods of contraction so defined, the predicted relationship among the growth groups holds precisely for the first contraction and breaks down only slightly for the second. Finally, it may be observed that the medium and slow groups tend to fall below the 50 per cent level earlier and stay below it longer than the group of rapidly growing industries.

What are the broad implications of this sensitive test, which requires that industries experiencing rapid growth resist deflationary forces with regard even to the direction in which their outputs are changing?[12] First, it supports the hypothesis that mild cyclical movements are mild because they are not widely diffused rather than its converse that they are not widely diffused because they are mild. This is because a classification based upon production changes bridging a decade reveals group differences in diffusion which persist through several cycles and are therefore partly in-

---

[12] Because of the correlation that exists between extent of diffusion and average amplitude of the component industries ("An Experiment with Weighted Indexes of Cyclical Diffusion," *op. cit.*) it is likely that the group differences in diffusion are reinforced by group differences in average amplitudes. It should be emphasized that the relationship between growth characteristics and cyclical diffusion is not a tautological result of the system of industry classification. On this point, also, see the above paper.

CHART III FEDERAL RESERVE INDEX OF MANUFACTURING PRODUCTION, AND DIFFUSION INDEXES BASED UPON SELECTED GROUPS OF MANUFACTURING INDUSTRIES, 1947–56

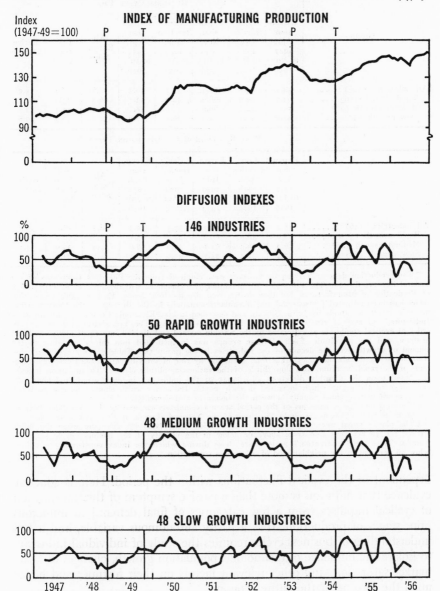

Vertical lines indicate business cycle peaks and troughs as dated by the National Bureau of Economic Research.

For sources and notes see Table 8.

TABLE 8—AVERAGE MONTHLY INDEXES OF DIFFUSION FOR SELECTED GROUPS OF
MANUFACTURING INDUSTRIES DURING SPECIFIED INTERVALS, 1947 TO 1956*
(In Per Cent)

Group	PART A. BUSINESS CYCLE PHASES†							
	Expansion Apr. 1947 to Nov. 1948	Contraction Dec. 1948 to Oct. 1949	Expansion Nov. 1949 to July 1953	Contraction Aug. 1953 to Aug. 1954	Expansion Sept. 1954 to July 1956	All Expansions	All Contractions	Entire Decade
All industries (146)	54.1	44.0	61.4	37.2	59.3	59.2	40.4	55.2
Rapid growth (50)	64.3	44.9	68.9	42.0	63.1	66.3	43.2	61.4
Medium growth (48)	54.6	41.9	60.6	33.6	58.6	58.7	37.4	54.1
Slow growth (48)	42.9	45.3	54.3	36.1	56.2	52.2	40.3	49.6

	PART B. ALL-INDUSTRY DIFFUSION INDEX PHASES‡							
	Expansion Apr. 1947 to July 1948	Contraction Aug. 1948 to June 1949	Expansion July 1949 to May 1953	Contraction June 1953 to Aug. 1954	Expansion Sept. 1954 to July 1956	All Expansions	All Contractions	Entire Decade
All industries (146)	58.4	35.6	62.2	37.5	59.3	60.7	36.7	55.2
Rapid growth (50)	68.9	38.0	69.4	42.7	63.1	67.6	40.7	61.4
Medium growth (48)	56.3	36.4	61.1	34.0	58.6	59.9	35.0	54.1
Slow growth (48)	47.4	32.4	55.7	35.6	56.2	54.3	34.3	49.6

* The production data underlying the indexes were obtained from the Board of Governors of the
Federal Reserve System. The 146 series are nonduplicative components of the Federal Reserve Index
of Production of Manufactures, but they do not comprise the total index. Each monthly production
series had been adjusted for seasonal and irregular fluctuations by the Bureau of the Census, using
methods developed largely by Julius Shiskin and described in his "Electronic Computers and Business
Indicators," *Journal of Business,* October, 1957, pages 219–267. The 146 series were arrayed in
order of cyclical amplitude as estimated by the Shiskin method and divided into equal groups of high,
medium, and low amplitude. Each of those groups was in turn split into thirds according to the
amount of growth over the decade of the industries in the group (see Table 7 for a frequency distribution of the decade increases). The final groupings by rate of growth were formed from combinations of the rapid, medium, and slow thirds of the various amplitude classes. The diffusion indexes
are based upon the monthly directions of change of the industries in each group and show the
percentage of the group which increased in each month. Industries which showed no change for a
given month were divided equally between the increases and decreases.
† The first and last expansions of the period are not completely covered by the data. The dates of
the business cycle peaks and troughs are those of the National Bureau of Economic Research.
‡ The phases based upon the over-all diffusion index were dated by observing when the index
crossed the 50 per cent line from above or below in the vicinity of the business cycle peaks or
troughs. Thus the "contraction" periods are those during which the index consistently remained
below 50 per cent in the neighborhood of a business contraction.

dependent of the cyclical fluctuations within the period. Here is concrete
evidence that diffusion is more than a passive symptom of the transmission
of cyclical impulses from a few categories of final demand to numerous
prior stages of production. It is a partly autonomous variable, and a full
understanding of business cycles requires the study of individual industries
to isolate the influence of technology, population growth, changes of taste,
market saturation, and other relevant factors on their fortunes and hence
upon the fortune of the entire economy.

It does not follow, of course, that the impulses for growth or decay
affecting particular industries operated continuously throughout the
decade, although they probably did so in many instances. Those industries

which ended the decade far above the level at which they began doubtless rose vigorously through much of the period, but this does not mean that the same forces necessarily favored the same industries in each year. Among the shifts in "tastes" affecting the composition of output were the changing requirements of national defense, for example, and these developed unevenly over time. But this is simply another way of saying that the span was not completely homogeneous with regard to the autonomous forces operating or the industries affected. It still remains true that the industries included in the first group had to expand rapidly during part or all of the decade, and that these intervals of rapid expansion overlapped enough so that a greater-than-average proportion of them were rising at any given time. The resulting offsetting movements during contractions helped to prevent a serious collapse of investment demand directly in the stimulated industries and indirectly through the support afforded aggregate income and therefore the demands for the products of other industries. Were the sample of industries extended to include the nonmanufacturing sector, similar tendencies would be found.

Conclusions

The business cycles of experience have differed according to the combination of autonomous forces and structural factors present in each historical period. A number of structural changes distinguish the postwar economy from its forerunners, and many of these changes have fostered stability by damping induced movements of effective demand. It would be premature to conclude, however, that structural developments have made major contractions a thing of the past. Forces which are partly independent of aggregate activity or its rate of change have also affected the postwar business fluctuations. These autonomous forces include war and cold war influences which have both altered the response mechanism and subjected the economy to short-term disturbances. They include also technology, population growth, and other factors which create investment opportunities in the various sectors of the economy. It must be assumed that substantial swings in government expenditure or private investment may still arise from these sources. The amplitude of induced declines has probably been diminished by structural changes, however, and should the need arise, discretionary steps can be taken to raise public or private expenditures autonomously through fiscal and monetary actions. Certainly no major contraction of the future need be as deep and prolonged as those of the seventies, eighties, or thirties.

28

Examining the New "Stagnation" Theory*

ARTHUR F. BURNS†

Editors' Note

In this highly significant article, Arthur Burns brings to bear on the major economic problem of the day his experience as the Chairman of the President's Council of Economic Advisers from 1953 to 1956, and a lifetime of research as one of the leading students of business fluctuations in this country. Burns bluntly attacks the basic thinking of President Kennedy's Council of Economic Advisers. The problem is central: Is the nation suffering from a chronic slack in production and employment which only massive government intervention can cure? He raises—and rightly so, in the opinion of the editors—the question whether this is a modern version of the secular stagnation argument so popular in earlier decades. Burns's answer is clear and pathbreaking. He views the experience since 1957 as peculiarly cyclical, not secular, and points to three important reasons why the business cycle recovery of 1958–60 was aborted. These include: (1) the violent swing in federal finances; (2) the drastic tightening of credit by the Federal Reserve authorities; and (3) the protracted steel strike in the second half of 1959. Only history will reveal the merits of his analysis.

❧ In discussing so large a topic as our current economic policies, one must make a choice. I have decided to concentrate less on the policies them-

---

* Address delivered at the University of Chicago on April 21, 1961. Reprinted from *The Morgan Guaranty Survey* of New York, May, 1961, by permission of the Morgan Guaranty Trust Company and the author.

† See p. 5.

selves than on their theoretical foundations. Policies are always based on some theory. What I shall chiefly try to do, therefore, is to examine the economic theory that underlies the major economic policies of the new Administration.

This task has been made relatively easy by the policy statement submitted by the Council of Economic Advisers to the Joint Economic Committee on March 6.

The Council's theory can perhaps be conveyed best by reading a few excerpts. According to the Council, "the American economy today is beset not only with a recession . . . but with persistent slack in production and employment, a slowdown in our rate of growth." Further, according to the Council, "economic recovery in 1961 is far more than a cyclical problem. It is also a problem of chronic slack in the economy—the growing gap between what we can produce and what we do produce . . . Especially since 1955, the gap has shown a distressing upward trend."

The essential point of this theory is that, quite apart from the recession, there is increasing slack in our economy; there is a growing disparity between actual and potential output; in short, America faces a problem of secular stagnation.

The Council informs us that "the problem of unused potential becomes continually more urgent." The gap between actual and potential output has not only been growing, but has become very large. The gap is said to have been $32 billion for 1960 as a whole. Using annual rates, the gap is estimated at $40 billion for the fourth quarter of 1960 and at $50 billion for the first quarter of 1961.

But what, it may be asked, is the large and growing gap due to? The basic reason, we are told, is that there has been a retardation of investment. The rate of increase in the stock of capital per worker has been declining. The average age of our stock of equipment has been rising. And there has not only been a retardation of investment in business plant and equipment, but public investment has also been inadequate—that is, investment in education, health, research, and development of natural resources.

It follows from the Council's analysis that if our actual output is to approximate our potential output, investment in business plant and equipment will need to be substantially increased, and so also will public investment, especially investment in human beings.

Furthermore, if we proceed to increase both private and public investment sufficiently, our economic potential itself will rise more rapidly. According to the Council, the rate of advance that our economy now achieves when it operates at full employment is 3½ per cent per year. This rate will be higher if investment is carried out on a larger scale.

The theory that I have just sketched bears some resemblance to the Keynes-Hansen theory of secular stagnation, which dominated economic thought during the 1930's and 1940's.

Just as Hansen saw secular stagnation as he looked back in time, so the

Council now sees the recent past. And just as Hansen saw secular stagnation as our fate in the future, unless appropriate remedial measures were taken in time, so the Council now sees the future.

Hansen, however, believed that private investment was bound to remain inadequate in view of the disappearance of the frontier, a declining rate of population growth, and a shift from capital-using to capital-saving innovations. Hence, he argued that it will be necessary to rely heavily on rising governmental expenditures if we are to escape a chronic condition of mass unemployment.

The Council is far less pessimistic about the prospects for private enterprise and investment. Not only does the Council argue that larger governmental spending can and will stimulate private investment, but the Council also proposes that some of our tax laws be revised in the interest of creating greater incentives for private investment. In other words, the Council seems to view the private economy as a dozing giant who, while not capable of realizing his potential through his own efforts, will come fully to life again and stay alive if the government does its part by spending more and by revising some of the tax laws.

Clearly, the Council's stagnation theory is gentler and less pessimistic than Hansen's. Indeed, it must be regarded as a gay and optimistic theory in the light of still older stagnation theories such as Friedrich Engels' or Thorstein Veblen's.

When Engels speculated about the future, he saw only the continuance of depression and the eventual breakdown of capitalism. And when Veblen turned to the future, he likewise saw chronic depression from which, to be sure, our people would be occasionally relieved but only through accidental developments.

The Council's diagnosis of the state of our economy, despite its stagnationist accent, has none of the morbid pessimism of earlier stagnation theories. A theory of secular stagnation such as the Council's therefore need not cause anxiety. Viewed coldly, it merely provides a warning. And the warning may be salutary if there is an empirical basis for the new theory. How substantial, then, is the evidence in its support? Let us turn to this question.

One piece of evidence cited by the Council is the progressive decline of business-cycle expansions in the postwar period. The expansion of 1949–53 lasted 45 months. The expansion of 1954–57 lasted 35 months. The expansion of 1958–60 lasted 25 months. In other words, successive upswings have been progressively shorter, and this is a symptom of noncyclical or secular slack.

In judging this evidence, it is necessary to recall that the expansion from 1949 to 1953 was dominated by the Korean War. This expansion might well have been shorter if the war had not lasted so long.

Historically, wartime expansions have always been exceptionally long. Indeed, the expansions of 1861–65, 1914–18, 1938–45, and 1949–53 are the longest business-cycle expansions that we have had.

Since the expansion of 1949–53 is clearly an abnormal case, it is best to put it aside. We are then left with the fact that the most recent business-cycle expansion was shorter than its immediate predecessor. There is nothing remarkable about this fact. Of itself it surely provides little reason to expect or to fear secular stagnation.

The Council cites, however, another piece of evidence—namely, unemployment was approximately 3 per cent at the peak of business in 1953, but about 4 per cent at the business-cycle peak in 1957, and about 5 per cent at the business-cycle peak in 1960. This evidence seems to suggest that successive upswings are becoming weaker.

However, as I've just noted, the peak in 1953 was a wartime peak of activity. We then had an overtime economy. It seems more sensible to regard the 3 per cent unemployment rate of 1953 as an exceptional case than to take it as a yardstick of economic performance.

This is as clear when we look back of 1953 as when we look forward, for the unemployment rate was about 4 per cent at the business-cycle peak of 1948 just as it was 4 per cent at the peak of 1957. Not only that, but the Council itself regards a 4 per cent unemployment rate as signifying a condition of practically full employment.

It is true that the unemployment rate was appreciably higher in 1960 than in 1957. This comparison is entirely valid. But one instance of higher unemployment of itself gives fragile support to the generalization that successive upswings are becoming weaker or to the theory that the gap between actual and potential output has a distressing upward trend.

The Council presents still a third piece of evidence. This takes the form of a direct measurement of the gap between actual and potential output.

Quarterly figures of the gross national product, adjusted for changes in the price level, are taken as a measure of actual output. Potential output is then measured by a curve which starts at the level of the actual output in mid-1955. This curve moves forward in time at an annual rate of increase of 3½ per cent, and it moves similarly back of 1955.

Why, it may be asked, does the curve depicting potential output start in the middle of 1955? The reason is that unemployment was then approximately 4 per cent of the labor force, and the Council regards a 4 per cent unemployment rate as a "reasonable target for full utilization of resources."

And why is this curve of potential output allowed to rise at an annual rate of 3½ per cent? Because, we are told, this rate "represents the rate of advance of gross national product (corrected for price changes) that our economy now achieves when it operates at reasonably full employment."

Once the curves of actual and potential output are drawn, the gap between them is obtained by subtraction. It is this gap which is said to show a distressing upward trend, especially since 1955.

The first and perhaps the most important question raised by this arithmetical exercise is why the curve of potential output is passed through the middle of 1955.

True, the unemployment rate was about 4 per cent in mid-1955 and actual output may therefore be taken as equal to potential output at that time. But the unemployment rate was about 4 per cent also in the second quarter of 1947, in the second quarter of 1957, and in other scattered quarters of the postwar period. Any one of these quarters or dates could have served just as well as mid-1955 for the starting point of the 3½ per cent curve of potential output.

The results, however, would have been very different. As the Council draws the 3½ per cent curve, the gap between actual and potential output in 1960 comes out $32 billion. But if the curve had been started in the second quarter of 1957, when we also had a full-employment output by the Council's criterion, the gap would have been only $20 billion.

And if the curve had been started in the second quarter of 1947, when we likewise had a full-employment output, the gap would have vanished. In fact, we would then have to say that actual output in 1960 exceeded potential output by more than $2 billion.

It is plain from these calculations that if we merely vary the starting point of the 3½ per cent curve, and do so without departing from the Council's logic, we can easily draw a more encouraging picture of the recent past than the Council has drawn.

Thus far I have followed the Council in assuming that our potential output has been growing at a 3½ per cent annual rate. I do not question the plausibility of this figure, but neither would I question the plausibility of a somewhat lower or a somewhat higher figure. We must reckon with the uncomfortable fact that small differences in the growth rate are capable of making a very large difference in projections of national output.

The Council has not described the precise derivation of its 3½ per cent growth rate. It seems clear, however, from what the Council does say that it did not use a method that is particularly appropriate on its own economic logic.

If it be assumed that a full-employment output exists when the unemployment rate is 4 per cent, then every figure of the gross national product at times when unemployment is at this level must express a full-employment output. A curve linking such figures will then automatically show the rate at which real output advances when our economy operates at reasonably full employment.

Unhappily, however, numerous pairs of such figures can be found in the postwar period, and some pairs yield a growth rate of less than 3½ per cent while others yield a higher rate.

Let me comment on one of the more decent calculations of this type. As previously noted, we had a 4 per cent unemployment rate in the second quarter of 1947 and again exactly ten years later. Between these two dates, our output grew at an average annual rate of 3.9 per cent—which is higher than the growth rate of potential output estimated by the Council.

Let us now see what happens when this 3.9 per cent curve is carried forward to 1960. At first blush, it might appear that the gap between actual and potential output would exceed the $32 billion figure computed by the Council. In fact, however, the gap turns out to be only $26 billion.

This illustrative calculation shows, once more, that it makes a good deal of difference whether the curve of potential output is started at one date or another. By starting the curve of potential output in the second quarter of 1957 instead of mid-1955, it is possible to convey, first, that the upward trend of the gap is smaller than the Council found, second, that the gap has lasted a shorter period, third, that all this is true despite the assumption of an appreciably higher growth rate of potential output than the Council estimated.

This concludes what I have to say about the Council's evidence in behalf of its theory. I hope that I have not left the impression that the new theory of secular stagnation is utterly without foundation. That would not be true. This theory *is* tied to some actual experience. But when the evidence is examined, it turns out to rest fundamentally on one fact, namely, that the business-cycle expansion of 1958–60 was exceptionally short and incomplete. When the expansion ended, our economy was still some distance from full employment.

I do not question the importance of this fact. Nor do I question its disturbing character. But I do question what inference can properly be drawn from this solitary fact.

I would urge two things. First, a theory which has such a slender foundation in experience must be viewed somewhat skeptically. Second, there is a better explanation of what happened between 1958 and 1960 than is offered by the neo-stagnation theory which of late has become quite fashionable.

Let us note, to begin with, that economic recovery proceeded very briskly until the spring of 1959. Between the first quarter of 1958 and the first quarter of 1959 the nation's physical output rose by 8 per cent. Between mid-1958 and April 1959 the rate of unemployment also fell sharply —from about 7½ to almost 5 per cent.

But soon thereafter a sharp retardation of economic growth set in. The expansion of business activity terminated in May 1960, having run its course in only two years and stopping at a time when the economy was still some distance from a full employment level.

Many factors undoubtedly contributed to the unsatisfactory character of the business-cycle expansion from 1958 to 1960, but I believe that three developments were decisive.

First of all, we had a violent shift in Federal finances. Between the first quarter of 1959 and the third quarter of 1959 the Federal cash deficit, allowing for seasonal factors, fell from an annual rate of $17 billion to $2 billion. By the second quarter of 1960, we were already operating with a surplus at an annual rate of $7 billion. Thus, in a period of little more than a year, we had a turnaround in Federal finances of about $24 billion.

This was undoubtedly one of the very sharpest shifts of Federal finance in our nation's history.

Second, the fiscal restraint on general economic expansion was accompanied—indeed preceded—by a tightening of credit conditions.

By mid-1959 commercial banks were already in debt at the Federal Reserve to the tune of $1 billion. The money supply stopped growing. Demand deposits diminished by nearly $4 billion between July 1959 and May 1960. Interest rates rose sharply, both on short-term and long-term loans. Indeed, long-term rates advanced faster than during a comparable stage of any business cycle during the past hundred years.

Still a third factor contributed significantly to the incompleteness of the expansion of 1958–60, namely, the protracted steel strike in the second half of 1959.

Anticipations of the strike first led to a sharp build-up of inventories and a boom psychology in the spring and early summer of 1959.

Once the strike came and continued to drag on, it caused both concern and confusion in the business community and led to some hesitation in placing orders for investment goods. The strike also led to some confusion in governmental circles and prevented early recognition, which otherwise might well have occurred, of the magnitude of the restraints that were being imposed by our government on economic expansion.

And when the strike finally ended, many business concerns—having in the meantime had an extraordinary stimulus and opportunity to re-examine their inventory policies—proceeded to practice new economies in managing their inventories.

In all these ways the steel strike contributed to an early end of the expansion which commenced in the spring of 1958.

If this sketch of the background of the recession is anywhere near the mark, we must attribute the incompleteness of the expansion of 1958–60 partly to the steel strike but even more to our governmental policies of restraint.

To be sure, these policies were designed to prevent further inflation and to restore confidence, both at home and abroad, in the management of our national finances. I have no doubt that these policies were sound and even essential. But, as happened in the event, they were pushed with excessive vigor and they were not checked in time.

On my reading of recent history, the neo-stagnationist theory which is now being widely used to explain the incompleteness of the expansion of 1958–60 is, therefore, quite unconvincing. To be sure, our economy faltered, so to speak, prematurely. But the early onset of recession was due to special factors, to factors of a kind that need not be repeated, rather than to some permanent or growing weakness of our economy.

I have dwelt on two very different interpretations of economic developments in recent years. These interpretations necessarily have different policy implications.

On the basis of the Council's interpretation, and to use its own language, "we face a stubborn problem of chronic slack, and the road to full recovery is a long one."

On the basis of my interpretation, there is no chronic slack of our economy. The problem of recovery that we face is not very different from that which we faced in 1949 or in 1954 or in 1958. Full employment is not a remote possibility. On the contrary, it may well be reached some fifteen or eighteen months from now.

In view of its interpretation of recent history, the Council logically concluded that "the expansionary effects of government programs will be welcome even if they occur well after the recession has been reversed."

I believe, on the other hand, that the mildness of the recent recession supports the thesis that the underlying forces of economic expansion are strong and that they have of late been only temporarily suppressed. I believe that signs of economic recovery are already here and are rapidly multiplying. In view of this fact and in view also of the substantial increases of Federal spending that were initiated in the closing months of the Eisenhower Administration and the further increases that have been set in motion by President Kennedy, I think that we would be courting inflation and a gold crisis if we now arranged new governmental spending programs so that they would mature when the economy is already advancing without them.

If we accept the Council's view that "we face a stubborn problem of chronic slack," the distinction between governmental spending to spur recovery and governmental spending to spur long-term growth becomes unimportant, and the same might be said of the distinction between governmental spending to promote social welfare and spending to promote economic growth.

On the other hand, if my diagnosis of the state of our economy is correct, these distinctions are vital. Thus, I would hold that improved medical care of the aged, however desirable it may be in the interests of human welfare, will do little or nothing to improve economic efficiency or to accelerate long-term growth, and that it is entirely misleading to favor better medical care of the aged, as is now being done, on the ground that it will also promote long-term growth.

Again, I would grant quickly that a liberalized social security program, such as President Kennedy advanced in his Economic Message to the Congress, would help to speed economic recovery. But I must go on and point out that the same can be said of any type of governmental deficit spending. Since the liberalization of the social security program is designed to be a permanent reform, rather than to serve merely as an anti-recession aid, I think that it is a mistake to advance such a program in the guise of a recovery measure. The Congress should pass this legislation only after full deliberation indicates that it is likely to promote the national welfare in the long run, and not merely in the months immediately ahead.

Once again, on the basis of the Council's analysis of the state of our economy, the problem of accelerating economic growth requires that we undertake greater public and private investment expenditures. I would readily grant this general proposition. However, the problem of accelerating long-term economic growth is excessively simplified when we suppose that it will be resolved merely by greater investment outlays.

Once aggregate spending is sufficient to maintain full employment, the rate of economic growth must depend principally on the rate at which economic efficiency increases.

Efficiency and productivity are undoubtedly promoted by some types of investment, but they can also often be promoted without any additional outlays or even with reduced outlays. We need think only of the restrictive practices that abound in construction work, in railroading, in agriculture, and in many of our manufacturing concerns.

I think that if we seriously want to accelerate economic growth, we will need to remove many of these impediments to efficiency, whether they arise from careless business management, or from the coercive power of trade unions, or from governmental legislation itself.

In the course of my remarks I have tried to indicate how a difference in interpretation of recent economic developments will lead to some differences with regard to economic policy. But I want to guard against any exaggeration of these differences.

Let me say at once that I see considerable merit in many of the proposals that the President has advanced for dealing with the recession.

I applaud his vigorous efforts to speed tax refunds, to enlarge the distribution of surplus foodstuffs to the needy, to speed early payment of dividends on veterans' life insurance, to accelerate governmental lending under existing programs, to speed procurement which has already been scheduled, and to accelerate construction work which is already under way.

I admire the President's appeal for prompt enactment of a temporary program for extending the duration of unemployment insurance benefits. The Congress has already acted favorably on this request and I hope that the Congress will go further and enact, as the President has recommended, a permanent unemployment insurance law for coping with recessions.

I also feel encouraged by the new Administration's recognition of the need to revise some of our tax laws in the interest of stimulating private enterprise and investment. I look forward hopefully to legislation along these lines.

But while I find the greater part of the President's recovery program entirely congenial, I am unable—as I have already stated—to regard liberalized social security programs, even though spending on them can get under way promptly, as sound measures for dealing with a recession.

I also doubt the wisdom of proposing a substantial increase of the minimum wage at a time of recession. I do not regard a lifting of the minimum wage as a useful anti-recession device, particularly at a time like the present when we are having a serious balance-of-payments problem.

Nor am I able to accept without some reservations the view that greater Federal investment in education, health, housing, research, and resource development is desirable in the interest of accelerating the nation's long-term economic growth. I think that some of these types of expenditure may be justified on grounds of social welfare and that others may be justified on grounds of economic efficiency, but I fail to see how all of them can accelerate the nation's long-term economic growth merely because we now call them investment.

Nor am I able to accept the view that new and larger governmental spending programs on education, health, housing, research, and resource development should be welcomed even if they materialize well after the recession has been reversed. This particular view rests precisely on the stag-nationist theorizing that I have taken some pains to scrutinize.

I have been forced by the nature of the topic on which you have invited me to speak to make some critical remarks on the economic thinking and policies of the new Administration. But I also have found much to commend.

I deem it only proper to conclude by saying that the Administration has avoided extreme economic views, that it has in no way shown hostility to business enterprise, and that the economic moves actually taken by the Administration have been more prudent than some of its economic rhetoric has at times suggested.

29

Two Views on Basic Economic Questions*

COUNCIL OF ECONOMIC
ADVISERS <u>AND</u>
ARTHUR F. BURNS

Editors' Note

The stature of Arthur Burns was such that President Kennedy's Council of Economic Advisers simply had to answer his blunt attack. The Council denied the allegation of stagnationist thinking, albeit of a "gay and optimistic" variety. Nevertheless, they continued to stress the "gap" analysis which, they argued, proved the case for further major government intervention. They argued that the major difference between themselves and Burns was as to the nature of the policies that should be pursued, not the nature of the business cycle; and in their view the policies would have to be expansionary. "If the recovery moves more rapidly than we now expect," then monetary and fiscal brakes could be applied. The actual course of events, which in the end will determine who is right in this controversy, showed that by mid-1962 the federal budget accounts, on the basis of the national income and product classifications, were still in deficit. At the same time, the economy was moving forward to record levels. Burns, in his reply to the Council, did not have the knowledge of later events which the student will have. Nevertheless he argues that policies carried out in recessions cast their shadows far into the future and that he has his regrets about the policies used in the 1957–58 downturn. In sum, this

---

* Reprinted from *The Morgan Guaranty Survey* of New York, August, 1961, by permission of the Morgan Guaranty Trust Company and the author.

controversy represents perhaps the best example in years of the role of economists in advising policy makers.

▰▰▰▰▰▰▰▰▰▰▰▰▰▰▰▰▰▰▰▰▰▰▰▰▰▰▰▰▰▰▰

The Council's View

❧ Senator Paul H. Douglas has asked the Council of Economic Advisers to analyze the position taken by Dr. Arthur F. Burns on current economic issues with special reference to the questions he has raised concerning the Council's views. The Council welcomes this opportunity to respond to Senator Douglas' request.

On April 21, 1961, Dr. Burns, first Chairman of the Council of Economic Advisers under President Eisenhower and now Professor of Economics at Columbia University and President of the National Bureau of Economic Research, appraised the views of the present Council in an address entitled "The New Stagnation Theory and Our Current Economic Policies" (later reproduced in the *Congressional Record* on April 27, and in the May issue of *The Morgan Guaranty Survey* under the title, "Examining the New Stagnation Theory"). Professor Burns' critique relates to the diagnosis of the economy which the Council presented in its testimony before the Joint Economic Committee on March 6.[1] His address served as the basis for the substance and much of the wording of the statement of Minority Views in the 1961 *Joint Economic Report* of the Joint Economic Committee, dated May 2, 1961.

Economists are fond of saying (though tired of being told) that economics is not an exact science. It is thus not surprising that Professor Burns should differ on some important points from the conclusions reached by the present Council. We believe our analysis, based on careful research, to be sound and his criticism mistaken.

But if economics is not an exact science, neither is it guesswork. And so neither is it surprising that on some important issues Professor Burns comes to conclusions which parallel or coincide with the Council's views. We welcome the establishment of a broad area of agreement and hope that controversy can be focused where there are substantial differences of analysis and opinion.

A. Major Points of Agreement

The four most important points of agreement seem to be these:

1. Professor Burns gives three mutually reinforcing explanations for

---

[1] *January 1961 Economic Report of the President and the Economic Situation and Outlook, Hearings before the Joint Economic Committee*, (Eighty-seventh Congress, First Session), pp. 290-419. See also pp. 563-614.

the short and incomplete character of the 1958–60 recovery: the shock of the "violent shift" of the Federal cash budget from deficit in 1959 to surplus in 1960; tightening of money and credit by the Federal Reserve authorities; and confusion in government and business circles and loss of momentum following upon the steel strike. With respect to governmental policies of restraint, he asserts that "they were pushed with excessive vigor and they were not checked in time." The Council has on various occasions mentioned the same points as reasons why the upswing after 1958 came to an end well short of full employment.[2] These factors are not in dispute among the majority of economists.

2. Professor Burns apparently accepts the Council's position that it is weak aggregate demand, not an unyielding core of structural unemployment, that stands between us and a 4 per cent unemployment rate. This is implicit in his assertion that the American economy may well return to full employment in 15 to 18 months (from April).[3] We do not neglect the problem of structural unemployment, but neither do we believe that the relatively high unemployment rate at the cyclical peak in May 1960 can be traced to special structural factors.

3. Professor Burns also applauds the Kennedy Administration for many of its programs for dealing with the recession and for its recognition of the need for revising the tax laws to stimulate private investment. Considerable agreement in prescription reflects considerable agreement in current diagnosis. The difference between Professor Burns and the Council in diagnosis concerns the probable speed of full cyclical recovery; the difference in prescription concerns the possibility of perverse timing of expansionary fiscal measures beyond those proposed before the date of his speech.

4. Even in his critique of the Council's analysis of the "gap" between actual and potential output, which occupies most of his attention, Professor Burns discloses large areas of agreement: he agrees that there *is* a gap, that "reasonably full employment" has been reached only fleetingly since 1956, that the peak from which the 1960–61 recession began was too low, and that the economy needs to do more than recover the ground lost in the recession. But here agreement ends, controversy begins, and labels are attached.

B. *Major Points of Disagreement*

1. "NEO-STAGNATION" THEORY

Unfortunately, Professor Burns has drawn attention away from issues and analysis by his emphasis on labels. This is doubly regrettable because

---

[2] See *Hearings*, pp. 564-565 and 572-573 (Council's answers to questions 3 and 17, respectively) for references to the steel strike and to the fiscal position. In *Life*, March 10, 1961 (p. 24), Chairman Heller enumerated in the causes of the 1960 recession "a heavy foot on the fiscal and monetary brakes."

[3] In an interview in *U. S. News and World Report*, April 24, 1961, Professor Burns referred to an unemployment rate "close to 4 per cent" as "virtually full employment."

the label he has chosen—"stagnation" or "neo-stagnation"—simply does not fit the Council's economic views. Having chosen this melancholy term to characterize the Council's position, he quickly distinguishes the Council's "stagnationism" from that of earlier economists by calling the Council's version a "gay and optimistic theory." He also concedes that the Council's theory "need not cause anxiety." What these disclaimers reveal is (a) that a label is a poor substitute for analysis; and (b) that, in this case, the label is wrong.

The distinguishing feature of the "secular stagnation" theory formulated in the 1930's was pessimism about the prospects for high private investment. Its exponents feared that full employment in a mature economy was impossible unless private consumption and government expenditure moved in to plug the hole left by severely declining investment opportunities. Rapid growth would be impossible under such circumstances. The Council has expressed no such pessimism about private investment or growth. Quite the contrary: far from suggesting that more rapid growth is beyond our reach, we have shown that our economic potential—the true measure of our capacity to satisfy needs—has been growing throughout the postwar period at faster-than-historical rates. In the light of slower growth in the last few years than in the immediate postwar period, our contention has been that the growth of our economic potential can be and should be accelerated. Our prescription for acceleration of growth has been consistent and clear: it calls for a high-investment economy, a high-research economy, a high-education economy.

2. THE GAP: FACTS AND ESTIMATES

Professor Burns criticizes the Council's "gap" analysis. The "gap" is simply the difference between the actual output of the economy and the output which could be achieved at reasonably full employment. The existence of a gap at present is not in doubt. It is attested by the unemployment rate and by excess capacity throughout American industry. The size of the gap cannot be measured with precision because the level of potential full employment output cannot be directly observed. But a reasonable estimate of potential output can be derived from careful quantitative studies of the regularities of postwar economic life. Such studies were the basis of the Council's gap figures. Without such figures, it should be noted, the Council would not have the economic benchmarks required to carry out the intent of the Employment Act of 1946.

The most detailed method used by the Council to estimate the 1960 gap is an analysis of the increase in output which would result from a reduction in the unemployment rate to 4 per cent. Although this computation—carefully anchored in the actual experience of the U. S. economy in recovering from the 1949, 1954, and 1958 recessions—is basic to the Council's analysis, Professor Burns failed to mention it in his critique of our estimate of the gap.

The Council, together with many other economic analysts, takes a 4 per cent rate of unemployment as representing substantially full employment under present conditions.[4] Given this conservative definition of full employment, the fourth-quarter 1960 unemployment rate of 6.4 per cent (seasonally adjusted) meant that excess unemployment amounted to 2.4 per cent of the labor force or 1.7 million workers. The Council's computation showed that a reduction of unemployment to the 4 per cent level would be accompanied by an increase of 8 per cent in output.

At first glance, it seems paradoxical that a reduction in the unemployment rate by 2.4 percentage points would yield a percentage expansion in output more than three times as large. The explanation is that full employment conditions have a number of favorable effects on output in addition to the basic one of putting the jobless back to work. First, new members are attracted into the labor force as job opportunities increase. Second, full employment brings an increase in average hours worked as part-time jobs are converted into full-time jobs and as overtime work increases. Third, a rapid increase in productivity per worker typically accompanies the fuller use of resources in an economic recovery; non-production workers, in particular, tend to be underutilized in recession and their productivity rises as business picks up.

Another of the ways in which the Council estimated potential output, and reached an 8 per cent gap estimate for the fourth quarter of 1960, was by passing a trend line rising at 3.5 per cent per year through the actual output series at the middle of 1955. The annual growth rate of 3.5 per cent was selected after a study of trends in labor force and labor productivity. The middle of 1955 was chosen as a base partly because it represented a period of full employment but also—and this Professor Burns fails to note—because the results thus obtained were confirmed by independent gap estimates made by the Council and others.

Professor Burns points out that if other potential growth rates and other base points are chosen, they imply results for the 1960 gap which differ, sometimes substantially, from ours. The Council's confidence in its trend projection arises from the fact that it implies gaps which bear a close and reasonable relation to observed rates of unemployment in 1960 and previous years. To be plausible, alternative trends using different growth rates and different base periods should also have this important property of consistency. We have examined Professor Burns' suggestions in this light.

a. One suggestion was to use a 3.5 per cent trend of potential GNP anchored in the second quarter of 1957, when the unemployment rate was also near 4 per cent. We have compared the percentage gaps between potential and actual GNP implied by this trend with unemployment rates observed in every quarter beginning in 1953. To accept this potential trend one must also believe (1) that actual output was above potential through-

---

[4] This figure is too high to serve as a long-run goal, but it is accepted as an interim target which could be achieved under current circumstances without serious inflationary risk. In the future, measures to improve geographic mobility, the skill structure of the labor force, and the health and education of workers, should allow the target rate to be lowered.

out the years 1955 and 1956, during which time the unemployment rate fell to 3.9 per cent in only one month; (2) that the unemployment rate corresponding, on the average, to reasonable capacity output is 4.6 per cent.

b. Another suggestion was to start the 3.5 per cent trend in the second quarter of 1947. When the gaps implied by this procedure are compared with unemployment rates in the 1953–60 period the conclusions are: (1) that real GNP was above potential throughout the period from 1953 through 1957, and indeed that the recession of 1954 was a period of above-potential output; (2) that the unemployment rate corresponding, on the average, to reasonable capacity output is 6.0 per cent!

c. A third suggestion was to fit a trend rising at 3.9 per cent per year between actual GNP in the second quarter of 1947 and actual GNP in the second quarter of 1957. Continued to 1960, this trend yields a gap of $26 billion instead of our figure of $32 billion. It also implies: (1) that output was above potential from the very beginning of 1955 to mid-1957; (2) that the unemployment rate corresponding, on the average, to reasonable capacity output is 4.6 per cent.

As this evidence strongly confirms, the Council's choice of a trend line for potential output was not capricious. We did not anchor it in 1947 or 1957, because to do so carries implausible implications about the performance of the economy in particular years and about the level of unemployment corresponding, on the average, to reasonable capacity output. And we did not use a higher growth rate than 3.5 per cent because of significant evidence that the rate of growth of potential in recent years has been lower than from 1947 to 1953.

We conclude from this review of the evidence that an 8 per cent figure for the gap in the fourth quarter of 1960 is grounded in persuasive evidence.

3. THE GAP: EXPLANATION

The Council does not hold the view that the gap is endemic to the American economy, or that it would not give way to standard fiscal and monetary measures to expand demand. On the contrary, in our statement of March 6, we assigned responsibility for the growth of unemployment and economic slack in recent years to "deficiencies in total demand," rather than to "changes in the structure of industry and manpower."[5] A Council Member said in our oral testimony of March 6: ". . . [We] would not accept the idea that we have a chronic or growing long-run problem of unemployment but, rather, that we have a problem of unemployment that we can defeat by fairly standard fiscal and monetary means provided these are applied resolutely enough."[6]

Professor Burns misread the Council's explanation of the gap when he said: "But what, it may be asked, is the large and growing gap due to? The

---

[5] *Hearings*, pp. 329-330.
[6] *Hearings*, p. 417.

basic reason, we are told, is that there has been a retardation of investment." This misinterpretation is surprising in view of the pains the Council
took to distinguish the problem of the gap from the problem of growth.

The gap problem is that demand has not been keeping up with the
estimated 3.5 per cent annual increase in potential supply. The growth
problem is that this 3.5 per cent annual increase falls short of an adequate
rate of growth in our capacity to produce. We attributed the inadequate
growth rate, not the growing gap, to "retardation of investment." It is
faster growth, not the closing of the gap, that is the primary objective of increased private investment in plant and equipment and increased public
investment in human beings. Undertaken in a time of economic slack, however, such increases have the welcome added virtue of helping to promote
recovery by swelling the demand for goods and services.

A large part of President Kennedy's program for economic recovery consists of measures to expand consumption. For example, accelerated tax
refunds and veterans' insurance dividends, temporary unemployment compensation payments, and aid to dependent children of the unemployed all
expand consumer markets. These programs operate swiftly and surely to
narrow the demand gap. Such measures as reduction of interest rates for
small business, tax credits for investment, and expenditures for research,
operate more slowly but have the virtue of simultaneously expanding demand and accelerating growth in productive potential.

4. CURRENT POLICY FOR FULL RECOVERY

The major operational difference between Professor Burns' position
and that of the Council concerns current policy—the degree and duration
of desirable fiscal stimulus.

In his April 21 speech, Professor Burns stated that "we would be courting inflation and a gold crisis if we now arranged new governmental spending programs so that they would mature when the economy is already
advancing without them."

Since April 21, in the course of the present recovery, President Kennedy
has recommended to the Congress new or expanded programs in the fields
of space, national defense, training and retraining of unemployed workers,
foreign aid, and several others. These programs, if adopted, would increase
Federal expenditures in fiscal 1962 by $724 million. The Council must
dissent from Professor Burns' implicit view that the enactment of such programs—all of them evoked by urgent national needs—will "court inflation
and a gold crisis." On the contrary, we believe that there is room for such
stimulation of the economy, and that public expenditures of high social
utility ought not to be deterred by fears that the economy will soon be up
against its capacity to produce.

Indeed, in our testimony we pointed out that the powerful Federal tax
structure would generate a considerable budget surplus at full employment,
an issue which Professor Burns ignores. We agree with other witnesses
before the Joint Economic Committee that this large "latent surplus" in

the Federal budget at present levels of expenditure makes full recovery more difficult.[7] We have not stated, nor do we believe, however, that a Federal surplus is incompatible with full employment. What we have stressed is the need for a rational allocation of the implicit surplus among increased government outlays, decreased taxes, and debt retirement to achieve higher levels of investment for growth consistent with full employment.

Professor Burns foresaw in April that "Full employment . . . may well be reached some fifteen or eighteen months from now," without any further special stimulus to the economy. According to the Council's estimates, full recovery in the third quarter of 1962 would require a 14.8 per cent increase in real GNP over the current quarter, and full recovery in the last quarter of 1962 a 15.8 per cent increase. Recovery has not proceeded at this pace in any comparable postwar period of expansion, except in 1950 under the stimulus of the Korean conflict. While it is not physically impossible for recovery to proceed that rapidly, current evidence suggests that it is highly improbable. If we were to equal the pace of recovery from the 1954 and 1958 recessions, the unemployment rate would exceed 5 per cent in the third quarter of 1962.

According to Professor Burns, "The problem of recovery that we face is not very different from that which we faced in 1949 or in 1954 or in 1958." The Council has not contended that there is any qualitative difference between the present recovery problem and earlier ones. Nor are the lessons learned from the errors of the past irrelevant to our present problem.

In every recession there is slack which must be taken up by expansion of demand; the important question is how much. According to our calculation, the percentage gap at the trough of the 1960–61 recession was greater than at the 1954 trough but about the same as at the 1958 trough. The Council has consistently stressed that the distance to full employment, not the drop from the previous peak, is the true measure of the magnitude of the recovery problem.

The 1958–59 recovery was accompanied by a much larger Federal deficit than we will experience in 1961–62. In its initial year, it was also stimulated by a strong inventory buildup in anticipation of the steel strike. As Professor Burns himself shows, a sharp reversal of the Federal fiscal position contributed to the premature end of the recovery. In retrospect, expenditure programs begun in 1958–59 and continuing or maturing in 1960 would not have been poorly timed. On the contrary, they would have given the economy a sustained stimulus just when the inevitably temporary stimulus of rapid inventory buildup was exhausted.

The Council believes that all governmental programs must meet the severe test of social priority relative to other public and private uses of the

---

[7] *Hearings*, p. 355, and in particular the testimony of Herbert Stein of the Committee for Economic Development, pp. 209-226. See also Appendix to the 1961 *Joint Economic Report* of the Joint Economic Committee, pp. 119-125.

nation's economic resources. This is true of government spending to promote long-term economic growth, and of government outlays for social
welfare. We would not support for purposes of recovery any programs
which cannot meet this test. But a time of economic slack may be an op-
portune occasion for initiating programs of high national priority which
have been waiting for room in the government budget and in the economy.
The budget must not, of course, be built up by irreversible commitments
during recessions to a level which would be regarded as undesirable at full
employment. But some programs are reversible. Moreover, the needs of
the nation, the growing "latent surplus" produced by the revenue system,
and the general growth of the economy indicate that there is economic
room for the increases in Federal expenditure recommended by the President since April.

The Council is not in any sense proposing that the monetary and fiscal
brakes be removed from our economic machine. If the recovery moves
more rapidly than we now expect, these brakes can be applied to avert
inflationary hazards. But the very existence of brakes permits the machine
to go faster with safety. In a year of urgent needs and great opportunities
there is little reason to lose precious time, production, and employment.

A SECOND LOOK AT THE COUNCIL'S ECONOMIC THEORY (BURNS)

In my Chicago address of April 21, which was largely devoted to a report
by the Council of Economic Advisers released on March 6, I expressed concern about the economic theory that underlies the major policies of the new
Administration. The Council has now issued a reply to my critique. It is a
serious and closely reasoned reply, as was to be expected. But while it
clarifies some issues, it beclouds others, and it has left my concern undiminished.

The Chicago Address

It will contribute to clarity, I think, if I summarize at the outset the
main points of the Chicago address:

1. The economic policies espoused by the Council are based on the
theory that there is "chronic slack" in our economy, that there is a "growing gap between what we can produce and what we do produce," and that
this gap has shown "especially since 1955 . . . a distressing upward trend."
Hence, in the Council's judgment, "economic recovery in 1961 is far more
than a cyclical problem"; that is, our nation has to cope not only with
a recession and its aftermath, but also with a problem of secular stagnation.

2. Before accepting this theory, it is desirable to examine the evidence
cited by the Council in its support—namely, the duration of successive

upswings of the business cycle, the level of unemployment at successive cyclical peaks, and the magnitude of the gap between what we can and what we do produce. When this evidence is analyzed, it turns out that the Council's theory rests fundamentally on the fact that the business-cycle expansion of 1958–60 was exceptionally short and incomplete. Although this is a disturbing fact, it provides a slender basis for a theory of secular stagnation.

3. Not only that, but there is a better explanation of what happened between 1958 and 1960 than is offered by the neo-stagnation theory. Although many factors contributed to the unsatisfactory character of this expansion, three developments were decisive: first, a violent shift in Federal finances after the first quarter of 1959, second, a sharp tightening of credit conditions, third, the protracted steel strike.

4. We have, then, two very different interpretations of recent economic developments. According to the theory just sketched, the early onset of recession was due to special factors that need not be repeated. According to the Council, on the other hand, the early onset of the recession provides one more symptom of the chronic weakness of our economy.

5. The two theories have different policy implications. On the basis of the Council's theory, "we face a stubborn problem of chronic slack, and the road to full recovery is a long one." On the basis of my interpretation, the current problem of recovery is not very different from the problem we had to face in 1949, in 1954, and again in 1958.

The rest of the Chicago address dealt with policy issues explicitly. Before returning to this subject, it is desirable to stop and see whether, or in what degree, the basic issues of fact and interpretation have been resolved by the exchange of views.

The Council's Reply

One way of reading the Council's Reply is as follows: Since the Council agrees with the interpretation of the incomplete expansion of 1958–60 which I had presented as an alternative to its theory of a growing gap between what our nation can produce and what it does produce; since the Council no longer speaks of a distressing upward trend in the gap, nor of chronic slack in the economy; since the Council's defense of the evidence originally presented to support its theory is confined to the statistical procedures of estimating the gap; since even this defense emphasizes the size of the gap in the fourth quarter of 1960, when the existence of a gap of some size is not in dispute; since the Council no longer claims that the problem of recovery in 1961 is far more than a cyclical problem; since the Council also agrees that the problem of speeding recovery is not very different from that faced in earlier recessions of the postwar period, but merely urges that we try to benefit from past mistakes; since the desirability of achieving a higher rate of economic growth or of meeting urgent national requirements, such as a stronger defense, is not at issue; in view of all this, it would be possible to conclude that the Council and I have now reached substantial accord in our diagnosis of the state and needs of the American economy.

Regrettably, this is not the only way of reading the record. All things considered, it is better to take the Council at its word on what is chiefly at issue than to speculate on the precise meaning of its pronouncements or reticences on subsidiary issues. The Council states plainly, and without any qualification, that it considers its earlier analysis to be "sound" and my criticism "mistaken." Not only that, but the Council defends stoutly its gap estimates and even refers, in the course of discussing a technical point, to "the growing gap." Since it is clear that the Council believes its own gap estimates, it must still believe that, quite apart from the recession, there is chronic slack in our economy. It must still believe that the gap between what we can produce and do produce has been growing, that economic recovery is therefore far more than a cyclical problem—in short, that unless the nation attends to the Council's warning, our economy faces a problem of secular stagnation. The Council's theory has not lost its true character—nor its capacity for good or evil—by appearing in a more technical dress.

Interpretation of the Postwar Period

In the Chicago address I attempted to test the soundness of the Council's theory by examining the individual blocks out of which the theory is built. I doubt whether much enlightenment can be gained by discussing in detail the individual points of the Council's Reply. It will be more useful, I think, to take another look at the general architecture of the Council's theory, and to test it by examining its implications for events about which we have some definite knowledge. If the Council's theory is sound, it should provide a reasonable interpretation of the American economy in the postwar period. Let us see whether it does this well enough to serve as a guide to current policy.

According to the Council, the potential output of our economy has grown at an annual rate of 3.5 per cent since the first quarter of 1953. The Council's Report of March 6 shows these estimates in graphic form, quarter by quarter, through 1961. In earlier years, that is, between 1947 and 1953, the growth of potential output is said to have been more rapid, proceeding at an annual rate of 4.3 per cent. Although the Council has not presented estimates of potential output for the earlier period, this can easily be done by splicing the 4.3 per cent growth curve to the 3.5 per cent growth curve in the first quarter of 1953.[1] With these records at hand,

---

[1] The Council reports that, between the first quarter of 1947 and the fourth quarter of 1953, real output grew at an annual rate of "nearly 4.5 per cent" and that "this is a reasonable approximation to the rate of growth of potential during the early postwar years." Since the Council's Appendix shows that "nearly 4.5 per cent" means 4.3 per cent, I have used the latter figure. I have spliced the 4.3 per cent curve to the

we can see how the actual output of our economy differed from what the Council tells us was its potential output, quarter by quarter, since 1947.

This comparison leads to the following results: From the beginning of 1947 through the first quarter of 1951, actual output was below the potential output. From the fourth quarter of 1953 through the second quarter of 1955, a gap again emerged. Finally, starting with the first quarter of 1956, a gap appears in every quarter up to the present time. The Council has summarized the record since 1953 by reporting that, "especially since 1955, the gap has shown a distressing upward trend." The Council has not commented on the gaps of the earlier period. But it is clear that, if the Council is right, the gap has persisted even longer than it has reported. Indeed, it appears that our nation has suffered from insufficient spending—let us keep in mind that the Council attributes the gap to a deficiency in total demand—throughout the postwar period, except for the interlude of the Korean War and a few months in 1955. Or to put this conclusion in another way: with one very minor exception, the American economy of our generation has succeeded in escaping from its chronic, persistent slack only during wartime.

This picture of the American economy as being characterized by chronic slack, caused by a chronic deficiency of demand, strikes me as a caricature. I may, of course, be mistaken. But I simply do not know how to reconcile this picture with the growth of our gross national expenditure, which more than doubled between 1947 and 1960; or with the increase of indebtedness, counting both the private and public sectors, from about $400 billion at the start to almost $900 billion at the end of this period; or with the rise of the consumer price level by nearly 40 per cent, of which only about a third occurred during the Korean War; or with the growth of real output of about 60 per cent; or with the growth of employment of nearly 10 million; or even with an average unemployment rate of 4.96 per cent—an average which omits the protracted Korean episode, but includes all the recessions of the postwar period, and is based throughout on the current definition of unemployment, rather than the more restrictive definition which ruled until the end of 1956.

These doubts are not relieved when I contemplate the remedy, required by the Council's theory, for the allegedly chronic deficiency of demand. This remedy takes no account of the specific causes of the deficiency. It calls merely for the application of "standard fiscal and monetary measures" —in other words, lower interest rates, a more rapid increase of the money supply, larger Federal expenditures, possibly also lower tax rates, in one combination or another. Surely, expansionary fiscal and monetary measures were not neglected during the postwar period. But if the Council's theory is right, they were applied on an insufficient scale or less steadily than the proposed governor of policy—that is, the gap in demand—required. Even

---

3.5 per cent curve in the first instead of the last quarter of 1953, because the Council's explicit estimates of potential output are already based on the 3.5 per cent curve back to the first quarter.

in years of boom, such as 1947 or 1956, it appears that the government would have needed to augment the nation's aggregate demand.

But if such policies had been followed, would not the pace of inflation have been faster, perhaps very much faster? I have no doubt that, in these circumstances, the rate of unemployment would now and then have been materially reduced. Yet I find it difficult to believe that the average rate of unemployment over the entire period would have been any lower, or that the average rate of economic growth would have been any higher, or that the distribution of our national income would have been more conducive to general welfare, or that the deficit in our balance of payments would have been any smaller, or that the dollar—which has come to serve as an international reserve currency—would still command much respect.

The test of experience to which I have subjected the Council's theory is not very reassuring. If it be thought that the test is severe, I can only say that a theory designed to guide the nation's economic destiny deserves nothing less. However, the implications that I have drawn from the Council's theory must not be confused with the Council's own thoughts about this or that year or years. I should expect that, when faced with an actual situation, the Council would neither take its computations as literally as I have, nor carry out the logic of its theory as remorselessly. However that may be, it appears from my test that the Council's method of diagnosing the state of the economy and its prescription for filling arithmetically contrived gaps in demand can lead to serious errors of policy.

Policies for Economic Recovery

Equipped with a theory of chronic slack in the economy, lacking faith in the capacity of private enterprise to generate full employment, anticipating a slow recovery, the Council has—quite logically—been urging a rapid expansion of Federal spending. My differences with the Council on the budgetary issue run deeper than the Council has indicated.

Let us note what is happening to Federal expenditures. Each official estimate of recent months has been a notch above the preceding one. The latest increase came on July 25, when the President announced that an additional appropriation of $3.5 billion would be requested of the Congress. Before this announcement, Federal cash payments to the public during the fiscal year 1962 were expected to be $7.8 billion higher than in fiscal 1961, when they in turn were $5 billion higher than in fiscal 1960. Again, just before July 25, the Federal cash deficit was expected to reach $4.8 billion this fiscal year. Allowing for upward revision of revenues, the deficit may now be estimated at $6.5 billion.

It may well be that the deficit will turn out to be still larger. Reversals of expenditure policy frequently result in overshooting the mark set by fiscal authorities. The present Congress seems reluctant to grant all the additional revenue the Administration has requested. More serious still, as the international situation leads to new and perhaps much larger spending on national defense, it is by no means clear that governmental outlays on objects of lesser utility will be curbed. The Council has stated that "all governmental programs must meet the severe test of social priority relative to other public and private uses of the nation's economic resources." It does not appear that this test is proving very severe. Just one day after the President made his momentous address on July 25, the House Labor Committee voted for a Youth Conservation Corps along the lines of the Civilian Conservation Corps of the depressed 1930's. The climate for larger governmental spending is now good, and the Council has helped to provide a theoretical justification for it.

Whether or not my speculations turn out to be valid, it is clear that Federal finances—as was to be expected on account of the recession—have recently deteriorated. Allowing for seasonal factors, the Federal cash budget registered a surplus at an annual rate of about $5 billion in the third quarter of 1960. From January through May of this year, however, a deficit at an annual rate of nearly $7 billion has emerged. A sharp turn-around in Federal finances has therefore already occurred. And the deficit is not only growing, but for some months must continue to grow.

Meanwhile, the economy at large has been experiencing a revival since February. The recovery is widespread and is proceeding at a rather brisk rate. Total production already exceeds the prerecession peak, and total employment is not far behind. It appears, therefore, that the bulk of the new spending commitments by the Federal government will come to fruition, not in a time of recession for which many of them were intended, but when recovery is well advanced and the economy is expanding of its own momentum—perhaps when it is already booming. New or additional governmental programs characteristically require only a modest expenditure at the start, then grow rapidly as the organization of the new activity is worked out. The full fiscal consequences of the new spending ventures lie, therefore, very much in the future.

But if governmental spending programs have a typical life history, so also has the business cycle. One of the normal features of business cycles is that the general price level tends to rise during expansions. Perhaps the present upswing will prove an exception, but as yet I know of no evidence to support this supposition. With the private economy recovering, with Federal spending already rising swiftly, with expectations of inflation beginning to spread once again, I see a greater likelihood of an upward spurt in the price level during the coming year or two than does the Council. Under ordinary conditions, having become accustomed to creeping inflation, we might not worry about another limited rise of the price level. But the state of our international balance of payments has complicated matters. In view of its precarious condition, even a modest renewal of inflation could now prove very troublesome. If our export surplus should decline appreciably, while the government continued a policy of steadily filling calculated gaps in demand, insistent pressures may arise for fact-finding boards to review planned increases of wages and prices—which would, of course, be a step toward reshaping our economy along lines of authoritarian control. Few people want such a change, certainly not the President or his Council of Economic Advisers, but economic and political forces released by our fiscal policies could move our nation in this direction.

It is true, as the Council has pointed out, that the Federal deficit in sight for fiscal 1962 is considerably smaller than it was in fiscal 1959. But what concerns me is that, in spite of the deterioration of our international financial position since 1958, the governmental approach to recession in 1960–61 has been so similar to the mistaken approach of 1957–58. Now as before, a quick reduction of taxes was talked about but never made. Now as before, the main emphasis of governmental policy has been on raising expenditures. Now as before, the spending stimulated by recession will outlast it. Now as before, programs to accelerate expenditures have proliferated—with more not only for defense, but also for public works, housing, education, research, unemployment compensation, and so on. Now as before, decisions to increase spending have not been taken all at once. Now as before, they have come in a long series, spread out over months, with few items of impressive magnitude taken by themselves. But when all the scheduled expenditures were finally added up in late 1958, they came to a much larger total than had been planned or advocated by our fiscal authorities. There is still hope that this will not happen when the accounts are struck late this year; but I cannot overlook the unexpected spurt of expenditures toward the end of fiscal 1961, or the fact that official estimates for fiscal 1962 have already had to be revised upward several times.

I have recalled the recession of 1957–58 because governmental policies for dealing with it have had consequences from which, in my judgment, our nation is still suffering. In late 1958 the European financial community, discovering that our money supply was rising sharply and the Federal deficit piling up at a time when our export surplus was dwindling and gold flowing out, first began to whisper serious doubts about the future of the dollar. The need to quiet this concern and prevent a possible gold crisis was largely responsible for the highly restrictive fiscal and monetary policies put into effect in 1959. These policies inevitably involved a risk of slowing down our economic expansion to a point that could lead to recession. As events turned out, they, together with the steel strike, did in fact lead to a mild and brief recession. The Council and I agree on this point. However, the Council also believes, if I have understood its thinking correctly, that the expansion could have continued to roll on during 1960 if only the government had undertaken larger spending in 1959, instead of curbing outlays.

But would not such a policy have hastened the economic and political disaster that the government sought to avert and in fact did avert? The heart of the problem of economic policy in early 1959 was that in the eyes of investors, particularly foreigners who do not need to continue holding billions of dollars here, our government was already spending too much. It was the very fact that governmental spending kept climbing long after the recession had ended, with the cash deficit soaring to an annual rate of over $15 billion in the first quarter of 1959, which caused fears of inflation and of possible devaluation of the dollar to spread, thereby forcing an abrupt shift of policy. I fail to see how the government could responsibly have followed any other course in 1959, although I do think that the shift need not have been so abrupt. It was not in 1959 that the fundamental mistake was made, but rather in 1958 when new governmental programs were piled up with little regard to their cost or future consequences.

The lessons of this recent episode should not be lost on us. It is precisely because the ways in which we fight recession have longer-run consequences that we must not permit even compassion for the unemployed to lead us into actions which, while immediately beneficial, may seriously injure the entire population a little later. At a time such as this, when the possibility of a devaluation of the dollar is widely discussed in business and financial circles, I do not think it is prudent to continue enlarging Federal spending programs. Since defense outlays must go up, other programs should be cut. Since our economy is recovering and employment is again rising, we can with good conscience subdue our impatience for economic improvement. Past experience is a very imperfect guide to the future, but I think that it can serve us better than the Council's bleak forecast based on its projections of potential output. If the current expansion follows anything like the rule of postwar recoveries, and this assumption seems no less reasonable today than it did three months ago, our economy should come close to having full employment toward the end of next year.

Problem of Economic Growth

The time has come to stop fighting the recession, to say nothing of fighting it on the theory that it is superimposed on a chronic deficiency of demand. Let us concentrate economic thought instead on a real problem, that of increasing the average rate of our economic growth. The Council has rightly been devoting a good deal of attention to this longer-range problem. Its call for a "high-investment economy, a high-research economy, a high-education economy" makes good sense to me, although I am not entirely happy with the apparent implication that the only path to greater future efficiency is to spend more public or private money currently.

The prosperity of a nation depends basically on the energy and skill with which people apply themselves to production—in other words, on the amount of work that is done and the efficiency with which it is done. The government can sometimes influence the outcome favorably by doing more and spending more, but it can sometimes also do so by spending less. The success of governmental policies to spur our economic growth will depend primarily on how effective they are in increasing confidence in the economic future, thereby stimulating people to use their brains, energy, money, and credit in building today for a better tomorrow.

To achieve a higher rate of economic growth, we need to give no less attention to the reduction of governmental obstacles to growth than we give to the devising of new governmental stimuli to growth. Whatever the defects of our public expenditure programs may be, whether on the quantitative or qualitative side, the Executive and the Congress at least go through the process of re-examining most of them every year. As far as the tax structure goes, there is much greater reluctance to rock the boat. Except for occasional and marginal adjustments, we have continued year after year a tax structure that practically every student knows is seriously defective. It is high time to carry out a thoroughgoing tax reform—a reform that, among other things, will serve to improve the economic climate for enterprise and investment at large, instead of on a curiously selective basis, as in the Administration's recent proposal.

Of the many reforms that are needed, I think two are especially important. First, the tax rules governing depreciation need to be amended, so that they will take realistic account both of our technological revolution and of inflation. Second, the tax rates on personal income, which for some brackets of income are nearly confiscatory, need to be generally and gradually reduced, so that personal incentives to great effort will be strengthened and the energy now expended on tax avoidance schemes may be turned back into productive channels. It should be possible to carry out such reforms without impairing tax revenues beyond the initial year. But if this cannot be done, a low but broadly based excise tax will produce substantial revenue without blunting the incentive to enterprise.

I agree with the Council that we need to enlarge the national effort devoted to scientific research and basic education, but I feel that we need also to become far more efficient than we have been in conducting our educational enterprises. We need to hasten adaptation to changing technology by undertaking extensive training programs for unskilled workers in our individual communities, as well as retraining programs for industrial workers whose skills have become obsolete. It also would be constructive to stimulate the smaller firms, which are counted in the millions, to practice greater efficiency. With proper organization, our colleges of business administration should be able to render much the same kind of assistance to small businesses that our agricultural colleges have over many years rendered to farmers.

We need to become less tolerant of the wasteful practices that we have allowed to develop all around us. I am referring not only to restraints on efficiency imposed by trade unions in railroading, construction work, and other industries, but also to the featherbedding not infrequently practiced by business executives, and to the roadblocks to efficiency that have been put up by our government, of which the farm program is only the most notorious example.

Since economic growth is bound to proceed unevenly, we must try to stiffen the resistance of our economy to occasional setbacks. In 1958 and again this year the Congress extended the duration of unemployment benefits, although it did so through tardy improvisations. Before the next recession strikes, as in time it probably will, our country should at last be armed with an unemployment insurance system that covers practically all wage-earners and automatically provides for extended benefits during periods of abnormally large unemployment. The President has wisely recommended legislation that would move our nation in this direction.

Under present conditions of world competition, a reasonably stable price level would also help to promote the long-term growth of our economy. It would therefore be desirable to amend the Employment Act by specifying that it is the continuing policy of the Federal government to promote reasonable stability of the consumer price level as well as maximum production and employment. Such a declaration of moral purpose would help to assure everyone, both in our country and abroad, that our government has a proper concern for the future as well as the present.

These are some of the things that need to be done to enlarge and sustain prosperity. But as we work for a better future, let us not exaggerate the shortcomings of our economy or belittle the achievements of the past. In the postwar period our economy has extended, if not improved on, its historic rate of growth. It has demonstrated its great resilience by speedily filling the gap left by declining Federal expenditures when World War II ended and, a few years later, when the Korean hostilities came to a close. Perhaps the greatest economic triumph of our generation, although we too often show little appreciation of it, is the reduction of the swings of the business cycle and the blunting of their impact on the lives and fortunes of individuals. We should strive to do still better in the future, and I am hopeful that our efforts will be rewarded by success. But if it turns out that we fail to achieve all the improvement we seek during the 1960's, yet do no worse than in the 1950's, our accomplishment will still be very substantial and require neither remorse nor apology.

Appendix

I am appending the following notes for readers whose interest may center on technical points. They deal primarily with the gap estimates and with alternative methods of estimating when full employment may be reached. I have also added a few remarks on the theory of secular stagnation and recovery policies.

THE GAP ESTIMATES

The Council's gap estimates, starting in the first quarter of 1953, were derived by equating potential output to the actual output in mid-1955, then allowing the curve of potential output to ascend at an annual rate of 3.5 per cent, and handling the period back of mid-1955 in similar fashion. The gap is simply the difference between actual and potential output.

In the Appendix to its Report of March 6, the Council spoke of its estimates of potential output, including the historical estimates, as being based on calculations that "are at best hazardous and uncertain." The text of the Council's Report, however, did not heed the warning of the Appendix, thus making my and other criticism inevitable. Now the Council makes a larger claim for its estimates of potential output—namely, that they are "reasonable," that they are "derived from careful quantitative studies," and that it therefore has "confidence in its trend projection."

On what quantitative studies, it is pertinent to inquire, did the Council base its estimate of an annual rate of growth of 3.5 per cent in potential output? The Council gave a sketchy answer to this question in its original Report and no information has been added by its Reply. What, then, is the visible basis for the confidence which the Council now expresses in its historical estimates of potential output? The answer to this question consists of two parts.

First, the Council reports that these estimates imply "gaps which bear a close and reasonable relation to observed rates of unemployment in 1960 and previous years." This claim is excessive. According to the Council, an unemployment rate of 4 per cent marks a period as having full employment. In mid-1955, when the unemployment rate was about 4 per cent, the Council's estimate of potential output shows virtual equality with actual output, as it should. But when we move on, we find that the estimates of potential output soar above the figures of actual output throughout 1956 and throughout the first half of 1957, despite the fact that the seasonally adjusted unemployment rate in eleven of these eighteen months was as low as or lower than in mid-1955 (when it was 4.1 per cent). These oddities suggest that 3.5 per cent overstates the annual growth of potential output, or that an exponential curve is a poor representative of potential output, or else that the concept of potential output itself requires modification. Even the Council's own equation, relating the unemployment rate to the gap, suggests that something is wrong. According to this equation, the gap vanishes at an unemployment rate of 3.7 per cent, not—as it should by the Council's logic—at 4 per cent.

The Council's report that its estimates imply "gaps which bear a close and reasonable relation to observed rates of unemployment" evidently means merely that the configuration of its gap estimates through time bears a *general* resemblance to the configuration of unemployment rates. But if this is what the Council means, no uniqueness attaches to its estimates; that is to say, several or many sets of historical estimates will meet this loose criterion equally well. For example, a curve of potential output ascending at an annual rate of only 3 per cent, similarly pivoted in mid-1955, will certainly do so. I might add, for whatever it may be worth, that this 3 per cent growth curve implies a gap of 5.3 per cent in the fourth quarter of 1960, in contrast to the Council's reported gap of 8 per cent.

Let us turn to the second part of the Council's visible evidence in support of its historical estimates of the gap. This consists of the finding that the several illustrative trends, which had figured in my criticism, yield gaps that do not bear a close and reasonable relation to rates of unemployment. The Council concludes that "this evidence strongly confirms" that its "choice of a trend line for potential output was not capricious." However, quite apart from the fact that none of my illustrative trends was suggested as a proper measure of potential output, a finding—whether well grounded or not—that these trends are faulty can tell us nothing at all about the statistical virtue of the Council's trend line for potential output.

The Council's own judgment in the Appendix of its Report of March 6 appears to be correct—namely, that its estimates of potential output "are at best hazardous and uncertain." It is difficult to see how estimates of this type could be anything but hazardous. Potential output, according to the Council, is "the output which could be achieved at reasonably full employment." Taken literally, this must mean that the potential output of a given period is the sum of (a) the actual output, (b) the additional output that could be achieved if the unemployment rate were 4 per cent instead of, say, 6 per cent, and (c) the further addition to output that could be achieved through greater efficiency of both labor and capital—apart from that which might be induced by (b). In this full sense, potential output is indefinitely larger than the sum of (a) and (b), this sum being what the Council has in mind by potential output. But even the latter quantity raises formidable difficulties. As far as (a) is concerned, we presumably know what it is. But how can we tell the magnitude of (b)? Not only is no answer given in official statistical publications, but no single true answer to this question is possible.

After all, the structure of a nation's output keeps changing. This is a particularly important feature of a free economy where people's demand may shift from automobiles to clothing to travel or whatnot. If the extra demand, which is implied by assuming that the unemployment rate comes down to 4 per cent, were supplied by high-productivity industries, (b) would be one quantity. If the extra demand were concentrated on services supplied by low-productivity industries, (b) would be another and perhaps much smaller quantity. Nor is this the only theoretical difficulty. The magnitude of (a) in any specific period must depend, among other things, on the relations among the prices of both final products and productive services during this and earlier periods. But once we assume that (b) emerges, the price relations that played their part in determining (a) will no longer be what they were. Hence, (a) itself cannot be treated as a datum. In short, unless we specify the precise assumptions concerning the economic processes involved in making total output something other than what it was or is, the magnitude of potential output is strictly indeterminate. And once we set out the assumptions of a working economic order, although a unique result becomes possible, it would still be necessary to assess the significance and relevance of the assumptions.

I have no illusions about the difficulties surrounding a theoretically valid approach to the problem of estimating potential output—even in the Council's restricted sense. I recognize that if the task of measurement is actually undertaken, some vigorous short cuts such as the Council used are unavoidable. I do not rule out the possibility of getting dependable results by this approach. However, I have reason to believe that even an improvement on the Council's method—that is, a multiple correlation of output, time, and the unemployment rate—will yield gap estimates that have an uncomfortably large dispersion. This is certainly the case with the Council's method, as Chart 5 of its Report of March 6 indicates. If all this is true of descriptions of the past, it should be still more true of projections for the future. At any rate, the enormous differences in the estimates of potential output obtained by students who have concerned themselves with this problem shout warnings about the pitfalls that surround this field of measurement. I do not believe that the art of estimating potential output has reached a point that justifies the rewriting of the economic history of the postwar period, to say nothing of using such estimates as a basis for current policy making.

As a matter of fact, in studying changes in economic conditions, it is necessary for experts to keep in mind the margins of error that attach even to measures of actual output—that is, the familiar statistics on the gross national product. Economists, no less than laymen, have gotten into the habit of assuming that there is only a single set of official estimates of the gross national product. In fact there are two estimates for every quarter, one arrived at from the expenditure side, the other from the income side. Since our statistics are imperfect, the two figures nearly always differ, sometimes by a disturbing margin. As far as expert knowledge exists on this subject, the figures derived from income data are neither better nor worse than the figures derived from expenditure data. Earlier publication and sheer convention, not science, have accorded the latter figures their practically exclusive sway. The Council's Reply calls attention to the fact that its estimate of an 8 per cent gap in the fourth quarter of 1960 was reached by more than one method. But no elaborate calculations are needed to show that this estimate may well be too high. For, even if the council's figure of potential output for that quarter is taken as it comes, the mere substitution of the less familiar gross national product figure for the conventional one (as these annual rates are given in the June 1961 issue of *Economic Indicators*) would suffice to lower the estimate of the gap by $4.1 billion, or from 7.7 to 6.9 per cent.

WHEN FULL EMPLOYMENT MAY BE REACHED

The Council observes that "the distance to full employment . . . is the true measure of the magnitude of the recovery problem" and that "the percentage gap at the trough of the 1960–61 recession was greater than at the 1954 trough but about the same as at the 1958 trough." However, "the distance to full employment" is indicated better by the unemployment figures than by the gap estimates—which are, at best, cloudy images of the unemployment figures. The highest quarterly figure of unemployment associated with the recession of 1960–61 was 6.9 per cent, with the previous recession 7.4 per cent, with the one before that 5.9 per cent, and with the 1948–49 recession, which the Council ignores, 7.1 per cent.

The Council states that "current evidence suggests that it is highly improbable" that full employment will be reached by the last quarter of 1962. Apparently, the Council reached this judgment by projecting its curve of potential output to the last quarter of 1962, then comparing the estimate so made with an estimate of actual output in the second quarter of this year. The result obtained can be no better than the Council's 3.5 per cent growth curve of potential output. A projection of this curve yields a gross national product of $580.9 billion (annual rate, 1960 prices) for the last quarter of 1962. A projection of a similarly pivoted 3 per cent curve, which meets every reasonable test as well as—if not better than—the 3.5 per cent curve, yields a figure that is $20.4 billion lower.

I believe that earlier business-cycle expansions provide a better basis than conjectures concerning potential output for judging when, if the current recovery continues to flourish, unemployment may reach a 4 per cent rate. The trough in the gross national product during the 1948–49 recession was reached in the second quarter of 1949. In the third quarter of 1949, the seasonally adjusted unemployment rate averaged 6.6 per cent. A year later, that is, in the third quarter of 1950, it was lower by 1.9 points. The drop in the unemployment rate over a corresponding interval of the business expansions starting in 1954 and 1958 was 1.8 points and 2.2 points, respectively. If, therefore, the current recovery follows approximately the course of the three preceding recoveries, the unemployment rate should be about 4.9 per cent in the second quarter of 1962. Beyond this date, the three earlier expansions no longer give a useful clue. The first fails because of the outbreak of the Korean War, the second because full employment was already virtually reached, the third because of the outbreak of the steel strike. However, common sense suggests, as does the behavior of unemployment rates during prewar expansions, that if the recovery continues with any vigor beyond the second quarter of 1962, unemployment may well reach or come close to 4 per cent towards the end of 1962.

I have now set out the reasoning on which I based the statement concerning the prospects for full employment in the Chicago address. I should, however, add a word about structural unemployment. I have been inclined to agree with the Council's position that, as aggregate demand increases, what may now appear to be "an unyielding core of structural unemployment" will largely disappear. I still believe this to be true. Yet, some tabulations I have recently seen on the concentration of unskilled and semi-skilled workers in the long-term unemployed group have made me wonder whether the Council and I may not be underestimating the difficulties posed by structural unemployment. I for one have not studied this question sufficiently.

THEORY OF SECULAR STAGNATION

The Council observes (a) that its economic views cannot be justly described as a secular stagnation theory; (b) that it has attributed the gap to deficiencies in total demand rather than to the deficiencies I had noted;

(c) that it does not hold the view that the gap is "endemic" to the American economy; and (d) that one of its members had in fact informed the Joint Economic Committee that the Council "would not accept the idea that we have a chronic or growing long-run problem of unemployment but, rather, that we have a problem of unemployment that we can defeat."

As for (a), it may suffice to point out that theories of secular stagnation are distinguished by the fact that they characteristically posit a *chronic* failure of the economy (in contrast to a merely sporadic or cyclical failure) to produce all that it is capable of producing. That is precisely the way in which the Council repeatedly described our economy in its Report of March 6.

As for (b), there is no sensible difference between my description of the Council's views (namely, that the basic reason for the alleged "growing gap" is the insufficiency, first, of investment in business plant and equipment, second, of public "investment"—that is, spending on education, health, research, and development of natural resources) and its own formulation, unless the Council believes that a deficiency of consumer spending is the basic reason for the gap.

There is no need to comment on (c), since the question whether the gap is "endemic" to the American economy is not involved in the present discussion.

I take it that the statement quoted in (d) refers to the future rather than to the past or present; for on any other interpretation the Council would be contradicting its own position (see the section on "The Chicago Address" in the text). I need hardly add that what is in question is the validity of the Council's theory that our economy has been suffering for years from a persistent, chronic, increasing slack—not whether such a condition, if it exists, can be corrected.

POLICIES FOR ECONOMIC RECOVERY

(a) The Council dissents from the view, which it attributes to me, that a particular increase of $724 million in Federal expenditures, recommended for fiscal 1962, would court inflation and a gold crisis. This view has nothing to do with what I have said or implied. What has concerned me is the extension of definite commitments for substantially larger expenditures, taken in the aggregate, not this or that recommendation, appropriation, or outlay.

(b) The Council notes that I have ignored the "latent surplus"—which, I take it, means the surplus that would emerge under conditions of full employment if both tax rates and expenditures remained unchanged. The truth is that, in view of the upsurge of Federal spending, I have taken it for granted that the "latent" or "implicit" surplus will rapidly dwindle, if not vanish. That seems to be the way in which things are working out. If present expenditure trends continue, whether or not my expectation that full employment will be approximated by the end of 1962 is borne out, it will prove very difficult to balance the budget in fiscal 1963.

(c) The Council appears to argue that, in the event it becomes clear that further stimulation of the economy would lead to inflation, monetary and fiscal brakes can be applied to prevent this from happening. I wish economic policies could be timed and executed with such nice precision. If experience is any guide, Federal expenditures are rarely reversible; they are apt to move sluggishly when they do happen to be reversed; and there is often a substantial lag between the time when monetary brakes are applied and the time they take hold. In the meantime, the economy may be damaged by inflation.

30

The Choice and Combination
of Policy Instruments*

COMMISSION ON MONEY
AND CREDIT

~~~~~~

Editors' Note

The Commission on Money and Credit was a privately financed group of leading economists, businessmen, and labor officials, established by the Committee for Economic Development to appraise the United States monetary and financial system. Their report, *Money and Credit*, is the first full-scale study since the founding of the Federal Reserve System. This article, chapter 9 of the report, considers the broad area of government action in influencing demand through monetary, debt, and fiscal policies; it obviously has great relevance for business fluctuations. It is a lucid description of what is, by and large, the current consensus on these policies —when they should be used and in what combinations. The timing effects of public policy are discussed in terms of measures which do and those which do not require legislative action. For example, the Commission argued for the granting of discretionary powers to the executive to change personal income tax rates, and this has been taken up by the Kennedy administration. A major contribution of this article is the explicit consideration of the lag between policy and its effects. In addition, volume effects are reviewed, as are the problems of the long-run policy mix. This major contribution to the literature of public policy is a primer for policy makers, setting forth what to do and in what combination in recession and recovery. Due consideration is given to margins of error. In a word, this

* The Commission on Money and Credit, *Money and Credit: Their Influence on Jobs, Prices and Growth*, chap. 9, pp. 242-258. © 1961. Prentice-Hall, Inc., Englewood Cliffs, N. J. Reprinted by permission.

article is a "must" for all those engaged in setting policy, in appraising the policy of others, and in studying the nature of the problem.

‍▃▃▃▃▃▃▃▃▃▃▃▃▃▃▃▃▃▃▃▃▃▃▃▃▃▃▃▃▃▃

❧ In this chapter the kind of "mix" of monetary, debt management, fiscal, and credit policies appropriate to differing situations is outlined in a very general way in relation to the achievement of our goals of economic growth, low-level unemployment, and reasonable price-level stability. For each kind of policy instrument has a role to play in the achievement of those goals, but each has its limitations. Sole reliance cannot be placed on any one of them.

For economic prescription to be precise, economic diagnosis must be correct. Such diagnosis is likely to be laggard, imperfect, and sometimes wrong. In actual practice we shall usually be uncertain as to the character of our economic difficulties. This necessarily limits the effectiveness of the use of any single central instrument and of a combination of them. The improvement of diagnosis is vital to the full use of the refinements suggested in this chapter; nevertheless our policy measures can be combined more effectively than in the past even with the present state of the art of appraising current business conditions.[1]

[It was previously argued] that the goals of low-level unemployment, reasonable price stability, and an adequate rate of growth cannot be achieved by policies directed only at controlling the level of demand. In this chapter attention is confined to the use of policy measures which influence the level of demand; it is assumed that appropriate measures other than those directed to altering demand will also be used.

It is inevitable that the operations of the federal government will exert a pervasive influence on the economy. The mere size of our defense program and the taxes necessary to finance it will influence every sector of the economy. Similarly, the large federal debt affects all kinds of financial transactions. A number of federal credit programs will continue in operation for the foreseeable future, and the conduct of those programs influences a wide variety of economic activities. Finally, the Federal Reserve's control of the money supply puts it inescapably in a position to influence economic activity.

The federal government must have a set of policies with respect to the level and composition of its expenditures, the structure of tax rates and composition of the debt, and terms on which it grants, insures, or guarantees loans, and the size of the money supply. And clearly it makes a difference what those policies are.

---

[1] THEODORE O. YNTEMA—This chapter suggests refinements in economic prescription that will often be impossible because of imperfect diagnosis.

Because they influence our economy in so many important ways, it is essential that federal policies on expenditures, taxation, debt management, and credit terms should be explicitly chosen in such a way as to foster the achievement of sustained high employment, reasonable price stability, and an adequate rate of growth. Those goals cannot be achieved by the private enterprise system alone or by the federal government alone, but we are not likely to achieve them unless monetary, fiscal, debt management, and credit policies are chosen with reference to their effect on the achievement of those goals. It is not appropriate to blame the government for every defect in the performance of our economy. But when the economy's performance is not entirely satisfactory, it *is* appropriate to ask whether changes in government policies can be made to improve its performance.

The magnitude of the effect of the changes of all policy measures used and the varying weights to be assigned to different policy measures differ at different phases of the business cycle and with changing underlying forces affecting the behavior of the economy. Short-run and long-run stabilization policies necessarily overlap and interact, and ideally they should not be separated arbitrarily. If all policy measures could be varied quickly and easily without administrative problems and without disrupting private planning, and if they all produced their effects quickly, there would be no need to separate the problems of cyclical stabilization from those of the longer run. Yet such is not the case, and the problems are sufficiently different to justify separate treatment.

The discussion is in three parts. Because each policy measure has different characteristics, the criteria for determining how they should be combined are considered first. The implications of the constraints imposed by the balance of payments on the choice of policy measures needed to accomplish domestic objectives are also discussed in this section.

Second, the factors to be taken into account in choosing the longer-run levels or trends in taxes, government expenditures, interest rates, credit policy, and direct controls are discussed.

Finally, policy measures for economic stabilization are considered. These encompass short-run variations of tax, expenditure, monetary, debt management, and government credit policies which are directed to preventing or recovering from recessions due to deficient demand or from inflations stemming from excessive demand.

Characteristics of Policy Measures

The objective of stabilization policy is to keep the level of demand close to the output of the economy when it is using its physical and human resources at a high level, has reasonably stable prices, and is rising at an adequate rate. The most useful kind of stabilization measure is one which can be put into action quickly, which takes effect quickly, and whose effects can be quickly stopped or reversed. For it is desirable to be able to influence expenditures of businesses, households, and governments fairly quickly in either the upward or downward direction. Unfortunately, those policy measures which are judged most effective in terms of one of these criteria are not always best in terms of the others.

TIMING EFFECTS

The measures which can be put into action most quickly are those not requiring legislative action. They include changes in monetary policy and changes in both tax rates and government expenditures which can be made by executive decision.

Changes in tax rates or expenditures requiring legislation generally take longer to be adopted than changes in administratively controlled measures. The time required to activate them could be reduced somewhat, if the type of tax or expenditure change to be made in dealing with a recession or a boom could be planned in advance.

The lag between the adoption of a policy measure and the time when it begins to have much of an economic effect is probably shortest for a change in the first-bracket rate of the personal income tax. Because of the withholding procedure, some effects of such a tax cut would take place very quickly. A substantial effect would occur within three months of the effective date of the tax reduction, and a maximum effect in about six months. A similar timing pattern would occur in response to a tax rate increase.

The effect on expenditures of changes in general monetary policy seems to have a longer lag. Since the war, six to nine months have elapsed between the date of a definite shift toward an easy money policy and the first date at which a noticeable effect on housing starts occurred. An additional six months or so has elapsed before the maximum effect on residential construction expenditures. However, commitments on new mortgages may change earlier, thereby increasing new orders for housing and stimulating activity. The lags for other types of expenditures are at least as long. The same lags are observed in a shift from an easy to a restrictive monetary policy, though they may be undesirable on other grounds. [The report noted in an earlier chapter that] measures can be adopted to shorten the interval elapsing between a change in monetary policy and its effect on economic activity.

If there are direct controls over consumer and mortgage credit, terms can be changed quickly. And such changes will affect expenditures more rapidly than general monetary policy. Credit terms can also be changed with some frequency, although not as frequently as general monetary measures.

The economic effects of decisions to increase government expenditures are felt generally as soon as orders are placed and before actual expenditures are made. A decision to curtail or slow down expenditures would similarly affect advance orders before the expenditures themselves. The impact on the economy of decisions to increase expenditures will take different lengths of time, depending on the type of government expenditure in question and the amount of advance planning which has been done. With advance planning of the type recommended in Chapter Five,* an increase in government *expenditures* can be achieved within less than a year from the time a decision is made to undertake them. The impact from the *placement* of orders will be felt much sooner.

Although it is generally advantageous to have policy measures that can be quickly activated and reversed, there may be occasions when it is desirable to stimulate expenditures for a period longer than a year without becoming committed to changes in the basic tax structure or to new permanent government expenditures. To achieve this purpose, various measures are required. Some could take effect quickly, and others could start more slowly but have more sustained effects. These measures might consist of temporary tax changes and changes in monetary policy or government expenditures.

VOLUME EFFECTS

The magnitudes of the effects of expenditure changes induced by changes in policy measures are also important. Because over $30 billion of the revenue from the federal personal income tax comes from the application of the first bracket rate, a large change of expenditure can be induced or curtailed by changes in this rate. The desire not to overuse so powerful a measure led the Commission to impose a limit on the tax change it recommends. There is the danger that the proceeds of a large tax reduction would be only partly spent in a recession, and the addition to consumer liquidity from the unspent portion of the proceeds would create the possibility of a durable goods boom after recovery was well under way. Allowing for the limit recommended, consumer expenditures could be raised or curtailed by as much as an annual rate of $5 billion within a few months.

Changes in monetary policy have resulted in large changes in expenditures on residential construction. The increase in the annual rate of expenditure induced by changes in monetary policy from tight to easy money ranged from $4 to $5 billion in 1953–54 and in 1957–58. However, the size of the effect has been partly due to the large backlog of housing

---

* Editors' note. The report therein recommended the following:

"1. There should be more adequate planning for postponable projects; suitable expenditure programs should be enacted for a number of years so as to permit greater executive flexibility in timing.

"2. For countercyclical expenditures, projects and programs should be initiated or expanded only if these expenditures are essential and useful and if the length of the project as well as its time patterns are appropriate. To combat a recession a high ratio of spending in the early period relative to subsequent periods would be favorable.

"3. Changes in planning and budgeting techniques would help to make expenditure policy more flexible. The possibility of advance appropriations for public work programs should be considered.

"4. Efforts should be made to provide incentives for state and local governments to modify their public expenditure programs in a countercyclical direction." *Money and Credit, op. cit.,* p. 141.

demand in the postwar period. So great an impact on housing from changes in monetary policy cannot be expected if the demand for housing should be weak.

Monetary policy has had unmeasured but undoubtedly substantial effects on other types of investment. However, the stimulating effect of an easy monetary policy on non-housing investment during a slump is generally believed to be much smaller than the restrictive effect of a tight money policy during a boom. In part this is because some of the investment projects most easily restrained by the effects of tight money are the ones which are also canceled by a decline in demand.

At present the increase or decrease in the volume of public expenditures which can usefully be achieved with the same speed as those induced by changes in monetary policy and without interference with the efficiency of longer-run programs is probably quite small—perhaps in the order of $1 billion. But with long range planning of the type recommended* the figure might be doubled.[2]

COMPOSITION OF DEMAND EFFECTS

The various policy measures also have different effects on the composition of aggregate demand. General monetary measures have their major direct impact on capital formation with smaller effects on the demand for consumer durables. Among the major components of capital formation, residential construction has been affected most, with lesser effects observed in state and local government construction, commercial construction, and private plant and equipment expenditures.

If fiscal measures are used, the effects on the composition of final demand depend upon whether and how expenditures are changed, or transfer payments are altered, or tax rates are changed. If tax rate changes are employed, the effects will depend on changes in the distribution of the tax burden between individuals and corporations.

Changes in government expenditures have their greatest direct impact on the capital goods industries, and because part of the expenditure change consists of wage payments, there is also an immediate indirect effect on consumers goods. Changes in transfer payments will affect the demand for consumption goods primarily.

If tax rates on individuals are changed, this will affect the demand for both consumer and capital goods. The distribution of the effect between consumer and capital goods will depend on whether the tax change bears more heavily on lower or higher income groups. An altera-

---

* See Editors' note on p. 530.

[2] STANLEY H. RUTTENBERG—I do not agree that the increase or decrease in the volume of public expenditures which can be achieved with adequate forward planning of the type recommended can be no more than $2 billion. The possible doubling of $1 billion is, it seems to me, grossly underestimated. Adequate long-range planning in an economy with public expenditures of about $100 billion should make possible a much larger sum that is susceptible to speedy flexibility.

Mr. NATHAN wishes to be associated with Mr. RUTTENBERG's comment.

tion in corporate tax rates will have its major impact on the demand for capital goods.

BALANCE OF PAYMENTS CONSTRAINTS

During most of the postwar period the United States was able to adopt domestic stabilization measures with little concern about their repercussions on the balance of payments. The achievement of external currency convertibility by the major European countries at the end of 1958 was a major step in the restoration of an international money market. Since then short-term capital flows have displayed markedly increased sensitivity to interest rate differentials among countries. Because interest rate differentials result in short-term capital movements and because the United States is a large debtor on short-term account, the choice of stabilization measures to combat domestic recessions must now take into account their balance of payments effects.

If monetary policy is used to counter recessions, the Federal Reserve should pursue those measures which provide monetary ease with minimal depressing effects on short-term interest rates if the balance of payments situation requires such action. This would attack simultaneously both the recession and short-term capital outflows. For example, increasing the reserves of commercial banks by open market purchases of other than short-term securities will result in a lesser direct impact on short-term interest rates than by purchasing short-term securities.

By placing more emphasis on fiscal policy (either increasing expenditures or decreasing taxes or some of both) as an anti-recession measure, the amount of monetary ease needed to secure business recovery can be reduced. Such a combination of measures entails a somewhat larger deficit, and the increased needs of government finance would result in upward pressure on interest rates. If this deficit is financed with short-term issues, short-term international capital flows would be discouraged, and because there would be no direct upward pressure on long-term interest rates, there would be minimum interference with domestic recovery.

Long-Run Policy Mix

There is no unique, ideal combination of policy measures which is best suited to the achievement of our major economic objectives at all times. Our economy is dynamic; it is in a constant state of flux as consumer tastes change, as new products are developed, as production processes change with new technology, as the size, geographic distribution, and skill distribution of the labor force changes, and as variations occur in many other factors which affect the level and composition of output. Most of these changes require adjustments to restore new balances between demands and outputs of particular products, and these adjustments are induced by changes in prices and responses thereto. The market mechanism is most effective in adapting to such changes if aggregate demand and its broad composition are adequate to keep production at or near high-employment levels.

The long-run rate of economic growth of a high-employment economy, depends to an important degree on the level of private capital formation. While private capital formation depends significantly on the level and rate of growth of consumption expenditures, it also varies independently of consumption. When the incentives to private capital formation are strong, a high-level investment demand requires greater levels of saving to free the resources from consumer goods output for the production of capital goods. Unless the flow of saving responds voluntarily to the increased investment demand, strong inflationary pressures will develop if other measures are not taken either to reduce consumption or to reduce government expenditures or to hold in check the increased investment spending. Contrariwise if the incentives to private capital formation are weak, the level of investment spending will be less than the flow of saving at high-level employment, and total output and employment will tend to decline. Unless current saving falls and consumption expenditures expand voluntarily to offset the decreased investment, unemployment will grow, if other measures are not taken to stimulate spending.

Monetary, credit, and fiscal policies can influence significantly the composition of demand among broad classes of expenditures as well as the aggregate level of demand. The problem of the mix of policy measures is so to influence the level and composition of demand that the aggregate levels of public plus private demands will result in sustained high-level output and employment and that the share of capital formation in total output will generate an adequate rate of growth.

At any given time there exists a basic tax structure, a pattern of government expenditure programs, a set of government credit programs, a level of money supply, a structure of interest rates, and other monetary and credit conditions. All of these inevitably affect the level and composition of demand in the economy. Both the opportunity and the necessity of adapting our programs and policy measures to the underlying trends in the economy must be continually faced. The opportunity exists because the continued growth of the economy provides more resources to use for all purposes. Also because the tax structure is progressive, tax revenues will grow more rapidly than total output in the economy. The existing monetary, credit, and fiscal structure will inevitably influence the pattern of use of the added resources. Thus the opportunity and the necessity exist to affect the way the additional resources will be used because the policy measures must be adapted to the growing size and ever-changing trends in the private sector of the economy.

As aggregate output grows the three broad classes of expenditures will also grow. Personal consumption expenditures will grow steadily with the personal incomes generated from production. Private capital formation will also grow with the level of total output. And permanent government expenditure programs will grow just because of population growth and the upward trend in pay rates. The key questions, however, are whether under the influence of existing policy measures the *total* of the three broad classes of expenditures will generate and sustain a high-employment level of output at reasonably stable prices and whether the *proportions* of the three classes of output will generate an adequate and sustainable rate of growth.

Several basic decisions by the government are involved. One is an evaluation of proposals for government expenditure programs against the alternative of an equivalent amount of private consumption expenditures and private investment. These are political decisions and should be made through the democratic process. They do have an economic impact. The Commission urges that the decisions on the introduction, continuance, or elimination of government expenditure and direct lending programs should be made in terms of a high-employment budget and on the basis of judgments as to the value of these programs relative to the value of the private consumption or investment which must be sacrificed if the government expenditure is to take place without generating excess demand and inflationary pressure.

It should be noted again that some types of government expenditures contribute directly to the pace of economic growth and should be evaluated in these terms. Some forms of public capital formation result directly in increased goods and services, other forms complement private capital and are necessary for increased private investment, and still others lead to new advances in technology which in turn stimulate private investment. If the government wants to stimulate the growth rate, expenditures such as these should have high priority.

A second set of decisions relates to the basic tax structure. The Commission believes that there should be a clear separation between the basic tax structure and temporary tax adjustments for stabilization reasons. However, because taxes affect the level and composition of personal consumption and saving, of private investment expenditures, of business saving, and work and investment incentives, the basic tax structure should be related to the strength and stability of the underlying trends in the economy. It should be designed to influence the levels of private investment and consumption and take into account the desired stimulus to private investment so that these, together with government expenditures, will generate high-level employment.

A third decision relates to changes in the money supply. The Commission urged that the money supply be increased over the long run at a rate commensurate with the high-employment potential of the economy. The public chooses to hold portions of its current saving in the form of money and highly liquid earning assets, such as savings and time deposits, savings and loan shares, savings bonds, short-term government securities, and other readily marketable short-term debt instruments. The demand for money as a liquid asset is not a constant proportion of total output in the economy. The preferences of the public for liquid assets shift between money and other liquid assets with changes in their relative yields and their relative availabilities. The monetary authority must allow for these changing preferences in providing the proper amount of money to match the proportion of saving that the public wishes to hold in this particular form.

The supply of another important type of liquid asset is under the control of the Treasury. By its debt management activities the Treasury can vary the proportion of its debt which is in the form of short-term bills and savings bonds. As the economy grows there will be an increased demand for liquid assets such as these, and the Treasury needs to take this demand into account in its long-range debt management policies. The Treasury and the monetary authority should work in harmony in the provision of money and short-term securities because to a degree at least one form is substitutable for the other.

A fourth set of decisions relates to the choice among general monetary measures, broad fiscal policy measures, particular kinds of taxes, and selective controls in regard to their influence on private investment.

There has been considerable discussion in recent years of what the level of interest rates should be to maintain a healthy growing economy. The Commission believes that Federal Reserve actions can and do affect the level of interest rates, but that there is no uniquely right interest rate level independent of the state of private investment demand and saving habits, and if the level of aggregate demand is satisfactory, if the policy for controlling the money supply outlined above is followed, and if there is no change in the private investment and saving situation, then a recommendation that interest rates should be higher or lower than they actually are requires a simultaneous recommendation for a change in fiscal policy. Under these same conditions a reduction in interest rates can only be achieved by reducing the share of government expenditures in total output or by tax measures which reduce the share of consumption, or by tax measures which reduce business investment, or by direct controls on credit which affect selected expenditures. The opposite moves would be required if an increase in interest rates were desired.[3]

With given economic conditions, there is more than one set of taxes, expenditure patterns, debt management policies, monetary conditions, and selective controls which is consistent with a given level of total demand, of private investment, and rates of growth. The choice among the alternative combinations should be made on the basis of their impact on such things as the level and composition of investment, private consumption expenditures, the level and types of saving, international capital

---

[3] CHARLES B. SHUMAN—This paragraph places too much emphasis on efforts to influence interest rates. While Federal Reserve policies inevitably affect interest rates, the criteria for policy decisions should be the economy's needs for money and credit rather than the interest rates that will result. The purposeful use of governmental powers to determine interest rates is a form of price control and, therefore, an undesirable interference with the operation of a market economy.

flows, the distribution of income, and the degree of reliance on the price system for allocation decisions.

Monetary policy and fiscal policy are to a degree substitutes for each other in their effect on private investment. Changes in mortgage credit terms and variations in business taxes (corporate tax rates, depreciation formulas, or investment allowances) are also partial substitutes for changes in interest rates. However, these measures differ in their direct effects on the composition of investment, for example, as between housing and industrial investment, and in their side effects.

For example, if it is desired to encourage business investment as well as residential construction, lower interest rates will help. If it is desired to encourage business capital formation but not residential construction, an appropriate procedure would be to get more favorable tax treatment for business investment, either through accelerated depreciation or an investment credit. If it is desired to encourage residential construction but not business investment, easing of mortgage credit terms may be appropriate. Thus different combinations of policies affect the over-all level and mix of capital formation differently.[4]

Many more alternative combinations of measures could be set forth for a variety of circumstances. The choice of a combination at a particular time involves a balancing of effects on many diverse economic and noneconomic elements in the economy; this is necessarily a broad political choice and no firm guides are available. It is important to emphasize strongly, however, that the various measures are coordinate and to some extent substitutes for each other. The decisions on the use of one type of control measure need to be made with knowledge of its ramifications and harmonized with decisions on the use of other measures. This calls for effective coordination among all government agencies involved in monetary, credit, and fiscal policies.

Stabilization Policy Mix

The general objectives of stabilization policy are to maintain levels of demand which will lead to low levels of unemployment without inflation. Not only is it necessary to have a demand target, but allowance must be made for the margin of error between the actual and the predicted course of events. How large an allowance for uncertainty must be made in the choice of policy measures depends on the flexibility of available policy measures and the speed with which they can be modified or reversed to correct errors once a mistake is recognized. It will also depend on the cost of making an error, i.e., how much of a price increase

---

[4] CHARLES B. SHUMAN—The investment credit approach is an undesirable effort to influence decisions that should be determined by the interaction of economic forces in the market place. In my opinion, it would be far better to reduce tax rates, or give taxpayers more leeway in the determination of depreciation rates, than to authorize a selective form of tax relief on the basis of the way in which earnings are utilized.

will result if demand exceeds the desired level for a given length of time or how much unemployment will result if demand is inadequate.

The stabilization problems are discussed in two parts. First, recessions are examined. This is followed by a discussion of periods of recovery, prosperity, and inflationary booms. In each case emphasis is placed on the necessity of conducting policy in such a way that efforts to solve the immediate problems do not create a new set at a later point.

RECESSION

Recessions and depressions do not have uniform patterns. Each is in a sense unique. As a result, policy guides for dealing with them are expressed only in general terms.

The objectives of anti-recession policy may be outlined as follows: when income is growing at an inadequate rate and unemployment is high and rising, measures are needed to insure that a recession does not develop; when income actually declines, action is necessary to insure that the initial decline in income does not lead to a cumulative downward spiral. In both cases action is desired to stimulate a recovery to a high level of employment.

When income fails to increase in line with our growth potential for any length of time, actions aimed at increasing demand are normally required. When unemployment and excess capacity are still modest but rising, only those policy measures should be used which can be reversed quickly and which can be applied in small increments. Monetary policy can be gradually eased and the debt structure can be shortened to provide downward pressure on interest rates; credit terms for federally insured and guaranteed mortgage loans can be eased. Placing of government orders can be expedited and government expenditures on existing programs can be increased to expand demand.

If action is confined to these policy measures, which can be moved gradually and quickly reversed, the chance that a recession will develop is reduced, while the risk of creating excessive demand is minimized.

If demand resumes its upward course, we can—according to the rapidity of its growth—refrain from further expansive action or reverse the action already taken. If demand fails to increase sufficiently, stronger policy measures to encourage demand can be undertaken gradually.

Ordinarily, temporary tax reductions should not be used before an actual decline in income has occurred. But when income grows slowly for any considerable length of time, and when unemployment and excess capacity have risen to unsatisfactory high levels, the balance between tax revenues and government expenditures should be reassessed to ascertain whether our basic fiscal policy is unduly restrictive.

When income turns down for whatever reason, there is danger that the decline will lead to a cumulative downward spiral. The first object of policy, therefore, should be to ensure that such a spiral does not develop. The automatic stabilizers have already greatly reduced our vulnerability to downward cumulative processes. All the measures appropriate in a situation where income fails to grow can be used here. It should be emphasized that those measures which have the longest lag in taking effect should be introduced at an early stage.

Temporary reductions in the first-bracket rate of the personal income tax are appropriate as soon as it is certain that income is declining. This can prevent the occurrence of any substantial reduction in disposable income and consumption expenditures. The size of the tax reduction should be based on both the rate of decline in output and the level of unemployment; it should be larger when output is declining rapidly and when unemployment is high.

STIMULATING RECOVERY

If a serious decline in consumption is avoided, a reversal of the decline is often likely within six to nine months after the onset of a recession because inventories often decline rapidly in the early stages of a recession and then level off. When inventories are declining, production is below final-product sales. When they level off, production and employment rise. The resulting increase in income should add to the strength of consumer demand and contribute to recovery.

The reversal of the movement of inventories and the stimulus to consumption provided by the tax cut and the easing of monetary and credit terms all help to stimulate private investment. Finally, those government expenditures can be undertaken which will be completed within perhaps a year from the time a decision is made to initiate them.

The policy measures just discussed are by their nature reversible so that they may be used with somewhat less caution than others. But the extent of their use and the reliance on one instrument rather than another must be varied with circumstances. If unemployment is already high or if for any reason there are strong indications that private fixed investment is declining significantly, all the policy measures under discussion should be used fully as soon as possible.

When the investment situation is less clear, and when initial unemployment is not high, it is desirable to proceed with more caution. The total effect on income of the actions taken should substantially offset the decline in private fixed investment. This should set the stage for a full recovery. The amount of action to take depends on the amount of decline in private investment to be expected and on the expected responsiveness of investment to changes in monetary and credit policy and to increasing consumer demand.

POLICY DURING THE RECOVERY

Once a recovery is under way, different policy problems arise. In the early stages of a recovery it is impossible to tell whether the measures previously taken and the underlying factors influencing private demand will increase income to a satisfactory level, generate inflationary pressures, or produce only a weak recovery.

On the one hand if restrictive action is taken too early and too strongly in a recovery, there is the risk of preventing a full recovery to a satisfactory level of unemployment. On the other hand, it is necessary to recognize that restrictive measures take effect only after a lag and that action should be taken to prevent an excessive increase in demand *before* an inflationary boom situation has actually developed. If restrictive measures are based on price movements as the principal guide to action, they will usually start too late and continue too long. Also the rate of growth of income cannot be used as the sole guide, because clearly the rate of growth of income during a recovery must be higher than the long-term growth rate if high-level employment is to be restored. These and many other indicators must be used in judging the likelihood that demand will become excessive.

In the early stages of a recovery few changes in policy measures are necessary. If, as time passes, output grows slowly and does not reach a high employment level, the measures required are those appropriate for recession policy when income fails to increase.

When an upswing is definitely under way, the temporary tax cut should be terminated and the Federal Reserve should take action to reduce bank liquidity. This latter policy should not be carried so far as to restrict bank lending; it should be designed to reduce the time required for a more restrictive policy to take effect should it later be deemed necessary. The Treasury's debt management operations can also be used to reinforce general monetary policy in reducing the liquidity of the economy and in affecting the structure of interest rates.[5]

Because monetary measures can be moved gradually in either direction, it is not necessary to make an all-out decision to take strongly restrictive action. If the economic indicators show progressively greater likelihood that excess demand will develop, Federal Reserve policy should move gradually and continually in the restrictive direction. If the first signals prove to have been false, the movement toward restriction can be reversed with little harm done.

A restrictive monetary policy will slow down the rate of increase of demand to some extent even though its direct impact may not be on the sectors in which the greatest expansion has taken place. It will take some time, however, before the expenditure effects of a restrictive monetary policy will be felt. It is important that the Federal Reserve System should take action as soon as it has a reasonable basis for judgment of the future

---

[5] STANLEY H. RUTTENBERG—I cannot concur in the recommendation that debt management be used countercyclically. I feel that the need to minimize the cost of managing the federal debt must have top priority . . . The appropriate tools for stabilization are fiscal, including tax expenditures, and monetary policies, and should not include debt management. [Comments summarized from p. 105 of *Money and Credit* and inserted here by editors.]

to compensate for the lag between decision and effect. But there will be times when the need for restrictive action cannot be foreseen in time for restrictive action to become effective when needed.

If the speed of effectiveness of monetary policy cannot be substantially increased, it may be necessary to use other measures which have a more assured and rapid influence on private expenditures. These include the regulation of credit terms on government guaranteed mortgages, and direct control of consumer credit terms.[6] The Commission has recommended that the ceiling on interest rates on government insured and guaranteed mortgages be dropped and that direct controls on the terms of such mortgages be used to influence expenditures on residential construction.[7]

Finally, government expenditures should be slowed down if this action does not interfere with vital governmental functions. If federal expenditures cannot be reduced, they should be held constant or their rate of increase held to a minimum to slow the growth of income. The same general rules apply to government credit extensions.

Despite these restrictive measures, a vigorous recovery may develop into an overinvestment boom, inventory speculation, and strong inflationary pressures. General overinvestment booms involving many sectors of the economy are most likely to arise when income is rising at a particularly rapid rate. In a period of general optimism, the real danger is that some capital formation will be carried to the point where it yields little or no return, and that some of the more speculative ventures will be carried out on a thin equity base so that a decline in profits will result in a wave of failures.

A stock market boom is also a danger. A rise in stock prices as earnings increase to new highs is of little concern. But when stock prices rise rapidly and for a considerable period, some people will buy stocks without reference to their earnings prospects but simply because prices have been rising. This kind of pyramid club can go on for some time, but history shows that it always ends. Because of losses suffered and because of the adverse effect on general expectations, a collapse of stock prices will also cause a decline in consumption and investment expenditures.

The general overinvestment boom, the growth of speculative investment, and the stock market boom reinforce each other in the boom phase, and when the downturn comes, they reinforce one another in the downward direction.

In such a situation, the objectives of policy should be to reduce the

---

[6] FRED LAZARUS, JR.—As explained previously, I am opposed to additional selective credit controls.

[7] STANLEY H. RUTTENBERG—Interest rate ceilings on FHA and VA mortgages have tended to act in a counter-cyclical fashion. They should be retained for their counter-cyclical effects as well as for their social policy effect. Standby credit controls in the field of consumer and mortgage lending are essential, but they should be a supplement to, not a substitute for, interest rate ceilings.

rate of growth of aggregate demand and, where possible, to curb investment in the particular sectors most susceptible to an overinvestment
boom. The first objective can be achieved by policy measures which restrain expenditures. These would include continuous tightening of monetary policy aided by further lengthening of the public debt. As soon as
it is certain that a vigorous recovery is developing into a boom, a temporary increase in the first-bracket tax rate should be activated.[8]

The use of whatever selective controls are available may contribute to
meeting the second objective. Increasing the margins on security loans
may restrain stock market speculation. Other selective controls can be
made more restrictive, although as was pointed out earlier, there may be
other objections to their use.[9]

A restrictive monetary and debt management policy will impinge with
special force on speculative investments which are largely financed with
borrowed funds. It is likely to restrain such investments because higher
interest rates reduce their profitability. Also when money is tight, institutional lenders generally impose tighter restraints on regular borrowers and
are reluctant to take on new customers.[10]

---

[8] See Mr. RUTTENBERG's comment on p. 539.

[9] See Mr. LAZARUS' comment on p. 540.

ROBERT R. NATHAN—Measures to affect aggregate demand are obviously essential
and important. However, instability in our economy stems in an important degree
from divergencies in various classes of expenditures. The aggregate approach may often
be less effective and more costly than selective controls. It may be much more costly
in terms of unemployment suffered in the fight against inflation, or inflation encountered in the pursuit of low unemployment, or inadequate growth resulting from
fighting inflation through aggregate demand measures. Selective controls must be pursued with care, but it is my belief that the Commission report is too cautious with
respect to the use of selective controls. [Comments from p. 76 of *Money and Credit*
inserted here by editors.]

STANLEY H. RUTTENBERG—Selective credit controls are necessary as important policy
tools to be used in an inflationary or over investment boom situation. However, it is
not sufficient just to have selective controls over consumer credit and mortgage lending.
These tools should be supplemented by selective controls over loans for inventories as
well as plant and equipment expenditures. Certainly, if one examines the business
cycle changes of the post World War II period, the most volatile sectors in the
economy have been inventories and plant and equipment. There is no justification in
my mind to try to control inventory and plant and equipment expenditures indirectly
through restricting consumer and housing credit controls. The attack should be more
directly on the specific volatile sector of the economy, namely inventory and plant
and equipment expenditures.

Mr. LUBIN wishes to be associated with Mr. RUTTENBERG's comment.

[10] STANLEY H. RUTTENBERG—I am not satisfied with the concept that monetary
restraint and higher interest rates will act as a leverage on investment by imposing
tighter restraints "on borrowers who are not regular customers." The rationing that
takes place with higher interest rates is done by the lenders and bankers when they
tighten up their requirements for loans. This could very well be discriminatory against
legitimate borrowers. Selective controls in the field of inventory and plant and equipment expenditures could be exceedingly useful as a supplement to monetary and fiscal
policy in a period of over investment booms.

Messrs. LUBIN and NATHAN wish to be associated with Mr. RUTTENBERG's comment.

A large part of business cycle history is a chronicle of speculative boom and bust. In some ways, the U.S. economy is better protected from such developments than it used to be. But it would be folly to forget the dangers of speculative booms. They are great enough to justify restrictive measures in any period in which income is rising rapidly and demand is threatening to press against capacity.

A variety of stabilization instruments are available, and in many instances a choice can be made among them. The considerations involved in the choice and combination of individual instruments are the speed with which they can be activated, take effect, and be reversed; the potency of the effect; and the sector of the economy they will influence.

The degree of freedom available in the choice of measures is limited also by other considerations. The Commission has already indicated the desirability of having the basic decisions of government expenditure, lending programs and the tax structure made in terms of a budget related to a high-employment economy. Departures therefrom for stabilization purposes would be limited to those for which temporary variations would not jeopardize the purpose of these programs. The Commission also prefers not to use direct control measures if they can be avoided. Balance of payments considerations also affect the choice of stabilization measures. All these considerations suggest that reliance cannot be placed on any single measure but that aggressive, imaginative, and integrated use of our general instruments of stabilization policy is necessary within a framework appropriate to a healthy growing economy.[11]

---

[11] GAYLORD A. FREEMAN, JR.—In general, I endorse the whole body of the recommendations of the Commisssion. I am concerned, however, that if adopted their net effect might be to increase governmental intervention in the economy. But if we accept (as I do)

  (i) the goals set forth herein,
  (ii) the fact that recurrent economic cycles interfere with the realization of such goals, and
  (iii) the conviction that such cycles can be moderated by proper use of monetary, fiscal and debt management tools,

then we are faced in each case with a decision as to whether the benefits in terms of economic stabilization more than compensate for the additional exercise of governmental influence upon the economy.

Increased governmental intervention is not desirable since

  (a) it might interfere with the performance of free markets,
  (b) it tends to concentrate greater economic power in the hands of the Executive, and
  (c) as an elected official, he is likely to err on the side of the more popular expansionary policies rather than the always unpopular restrictive policies.

Such additional power heightens the risk of a continuous bias toward inflationary pressures. On the other hand, a widely fluctuating economy not only interferes with our total productivity and distorts purchasing power, but subjects millions of our citizens to the indignity of recurrent unemployment. These conditions must be avoided and modern government has the responsibility to follow soundly conceived policies that will minimize them.

Thus with some reluctance but with no uncertainty, I accept the underlying theses of the Commission's Report. But I urge that its recommendations be enacted and administered with a scrupulous regard for the interference with long-range economic advancement that unsound or politically motivated policies might create.

Mr. SHUMAN wishes to be associated with Mr. FREEMAN's comment.

31

The Goals and Criteria
of Monetary Policy[*]

MILTON FRIEDMAN†

Editors' Note

Milton Friedman is by common consent one of the country's top economists. As a leader of the so-called University of Chicago school he is
inherently suspicious of government intervention in any form. Over the
years he has made major contributions to both theoretical and empirical
economics and his pronouncements on policy issues always receive careful
attention. Basically, he is opposed to the present reliance on government
authority for setting monetary policy. He is unhappy with the "continual
and unpredictable" shifts in this policy and its exposures to pressure groups
of all sorts. Furthermore, Friedman argues, there are no criteria for judging its performance. He objects to price stability as an immediate guide
to policy. Simply put, the Federal Reserve System—which carries out
monetary policy in this country, independently of the executive branch of
the government—should confine itself solely to the stock of money. His
policy is a simple one: namely, the Federal Reserve should increase the
monetary stock at a fixed rate no matter what the cycle does. This would

* From A *Program for Monetary Stability* by Milton Friedman (New York: Fordham
University Press, 1960), chap. 4, pp. 77-101. Copyright 1960 by Fordham University
Press, New York. Reprinted by permission of the publisher.

† Milton Friedman's career typifies the varied activities of the successful economist
in the middle twentieth century: researcher, college professor, and author. He has been
associated with the National Resources Commission; National Bureau of Economic
Research; Division of Tax Research, U.S. Treasury Department; and has been Associate
Director of Research, Division of War Research, Columbia University. He has lectured
at the University of Wisconsin, University of Minnesota, Cambridge University (Eng-
land), and presently holds the post of Professor of Economics, University of Chicago.
A prolific author, Friedman's works include: *Taxing to Prevent Inflation* (1943, with
Carl Shoup and Ruth P. Mack); *Sampling Inspection* (1948, with Harold S. Freeman,
Frederick Masteller, and W. Allen Wallis); *Essays in Positive Economics* (1953); and
A *Theory of the Consumption Function* (1957).

provide insurance against major monetary disturbances, reduce short-term monetary instability, and allow a wider scope for private initiative and enterprise. Friedman's views, always powerfully expressed, represent a minority position in current thought. As a leading exponent of the loyal opposition, his work should always be carefully considered.

❧ We are now all dressed up. Where should we go? Toward what end and in what way should we use the streamlined monetary mechanism outlined in the preceding chapters, or for that matter, our present anti-quated, creaking model?

Since at least John Maynard Keynes' tract on *Monetary Reform*,[1] it has been a commonplace that this problem has two sides, the inter-national and the internal, and that the solution adopted for the one may narrowly limit the alternatives available for the other. It so happens that these two sides come closer to being independent for the United States under present conditions than for most other countries and for most other times. Moreover, the international monetary arrangements that seem to me best leave a maximum of leeway with respect to internal policies. For these reasons, as well as the heightened interest in the problem produced by the recent declines in the U.S. gold stock, I shall consider international relations first and then turn to internal policy.

International Monetary Relations

A small country on a commodity standard that is common to much of the rest of the world—or, what is economically the same thing, that seeks to maintain fixed rates of exchange between its own currency and the currencies of most other countries without using foreign exchange controls or their equivalent—has little leeway with respect to internal monetary policy. Its stock of money must be whatever is required to main-tain external equilibrium. Internal policies and events affect internal monetary conditions primarily through their effect on the demand for and supply of foreign exchange and hence on the behavior of the stock of money that is required to maintain external equilibrium.

For most of the period prior to World War I, the United States was in this situation. Our internal price level and our internal stock of money were dominated by world-wide movements in prices and by international flows of capital that together determined the price level in the United States consistent with external equilibrium. The only important excep-tion was the period from 1862 to 1879, when the United States was

---

[1] (New York, 1924), esp. chap. iv.

on an inconvertible paper standard with flexible exchange rates and so could follow an independent internal monetary policy. Yet even the latter part of this period was dominated by the desire to resume gold payments at prewar exchange rates. In the two other periods of great instability—1837–1844 and the mid-1890's—monetary uncertainty created difficulty mostly through its effects on our international position. In both cases, doubts about the maintenance of the commodity standard led to the recurrent flights from the dollar, which is to say, to speculative capital movements, and affected other capital movements as well. The capital outflow, or reduction in capital inflow, made the internal price level consistent with maintenance of the standard lower that it would otherwise have been. The standard could be maintained, as in both cases it was albeit with some lapses, only by accepting a more severe internal deflation than would otherwise have been necessary. For the rest of the period up to World War I, it involves only mild overstatement to say that internal monetary arrangements had little or no effect on the size of the changes in the money supply that occurred. Their impact was rather on the channels through which such changes as did occur took place, and on the composition of the money supply.

Since World War I, the situation has been very different. Except for the period from March 1933 to January 1934, when, as in the greenback period, we were on an inconvertible paper standard with flexible exchange rates, we have nominally been on a gold standard, though of a different character and at a different parity after 1934 than before. Yet internal monetary behavior has been dominated by external forces on at most three occasions—in 1920–21, when the rapid approach of the Federal Reserve's gold-reserve ratio to its legal minimum triggered the sharp rise in the discount rate in January 1920 that set off or intensified the subsequent internal deflation, and when an easing of policy was postponed until the ratio had reversed its movement and seemed safely above its legal minimum; for the second time in 1931, when Britain's departure from the gold standard and the fear of an outflow of gold triggered the sharp rises in the discount rate in October 1931 that intensified the internal deflation; and, for the third time, in the period from 1934 to 1939, when the rise in the official U.S. price of gold in January 1934, combined with a capital flight from Europe in the wake of Hitler's accession to power, produced large flows of gold to the United States which were the major source of the contemporaneous growth in the stock of money. And even this last episode is somewhat dubious. If gold flows had not produced an expansion in the stock of money, it seems highly likely that a similar expansion would have been produced by other measures, since domestic policies so clearly aimed at an increase. For the rest of the period since 1914, it is hard to see any close connection between the internal behavior of the money supply and the needs of external equilibrium. External forces have manifested themselves primarily in changes in foreign holdings of dollar balances or in movements in the gold stock that have been offset by the monetary authorities—"sterilized," to use that antiseptic term which seems ironically appropriate in view of the contagiousness of the disease that resulted on two of the three occasions when gold flows were reacted to rather than offset.

There are several reasons why the United States has been able to achieve so large an apparent degree of independence in its internal monetary behavior during this period. One is that for much of the period most other countries of the world have not been on the gold standard. As far as exchange rates are concerned, it does not matter whether the dollar price of gold is free to vary and the price in foreign currency fixed, as was the case for example, in the greenback period, or whether the dollar price is fixed and the foreign price free to vary, as was the case for many countries for some years after World War I and World War II and during much of the 1930's and is now, for example, for Canada. In either case, variable exchange rates provide a means of reconciling external equilibrium with independent internal monetary policies. Another reason is the asymmetry that we, like most other countries, have displayed with respect to surpluses and deficits in our external accounts. During most of the period since World War I, it so happened that economic circumstances, our policies, and the policies of other countries produced an actual or potential surplus in our balance of payments. Prior to 1914, the resulting inflow of gold would have tended to produce increases in the money supply and this tendency would have been permitted to operate. After 1918, the monetary authorities could more readily prevent similar tendencies from being effective and were more inclined to do so. We have been willing to accept gold inflows passively and to let our gold stock grow. We have reacted very differently to gold outflows. The two clear cases in which external forces affected internal monetary behavior both involved reactions to actual or potential outflows, even though, in both cases, gold stocks were at historic highs as a result of prior gold inflows. And again in the past several years, much more concern has been expressed about gold outflows than was ever expressed about the preceding gold inflows that raised gold stocks to unprecedented levels.

Both reasons come down to one basic explanation for our large measure of independence in monetary policy despite our nominal adherence to a gold standard: the rest of the world has been largely adapting to us rather than we to them. We have become so large a part of the world that our policies have important effects on worldwide trends. Moreover, foreign payments bulk larger in the accounts of most other countries than in our own. Other countries, too, display asymmetric reactions to surpluses and deficits; our passive acceptance of gold inflows has simply thrown the necessity of adjustment on them. They too have frequently been willing to accept gold inflows—witness France in the late 1920's or Germany in recent years—but have reacted to outflows. The incompatibility of fixed exchange rates with independent monetary policies that Keynes analyzed so brilliantly has been manifested, but we have mostly been the silent partner. The measures adopted by other countries as a result of this incompatibility have varied widely, depending on internal attitudes and policies and on other problems they faced: flexible exchange rates, adopted widely after World War I and again in the later 1930's; the alteration of internal policies, attempted in Britain to some extent after 1925 and by many countries in the Great Depression; direct control of foreign exchange transactions, adopted widely after World War II; and so on.

Our domestic policies have of course not been completely independent of our foreign payments position. For example, the so-called "dollar shortage" in the postwar years doubtless made our outlays on foreign aid larger than they would otherwise have been, just as now the outflow of gold is producing some pressure to reduce foreign-aid expenditures. But the connection has been weak, and, more important for our purposes, has not taken the form, enshrined as the classical gold-standard mechanism of adjustment, of automatic adaptation of the stock of money to the needs of external equilibrium.

A full-fledged gold standard in which all money consisted of gold or warehouse receipts for gold except perhaps for a fixed fiduciary issue would have the great merits of complete automaticity and of freedom from governmental control. It would be costly in terms both of resources used to mine gold and of the price movements resulting from changes in the relative cost of producing gold and other commodities. Nonetheless, if it were feasible, the advantages might be well worth the cost. However, it seems dubious that such a monetary system is stable. It is not the system supported by most current proponents of the gold standard nor is it the system that prevailed even during the halcyon days of the gold standard in the nineteenth century, when there were large admixtures of fiduciary elements and much conscious management. It is even farther from the nominal gold standard that prevailed in the United States from World War I to 1933, let alone since 1934. During that period we have had none of the advantages of a full-fledged gold standard, and many of its disadvantages greatly exaggerated.

Only a cultural lag leads us still to think of gold as the central element in our monetary system. A more accurate description of the role of gold in U.S. policy is that it is primarily a commodity whose price is supported, like wheat or other agricultural products, rather than the key to our monetary system. Our price support program for gold differs in three important respects from our price support program for wheat: first, we pay the support price to foreign as well as domestic producers; second, we sell freely at the support price only to foreign purchasers and not to domestic; third, and this is one important relic of the monetary role of gold, the Treasury is authorized to create money to pay for gold it buys so that expenditures for the purchase of gold do not appear in the budget and the sums required need not be explicitly appropriated by Congress. This final characteristic has applied equally and for the same reason to our purchase of silver under the various price support programs that have been in effect since 1934. We have accumulated gold in the past until we now hold half the world's gold for the same reason that we have accumulated wheat—because the support price of $35 an ounce has been above the market price. In these terms, should we not welcome a situation that enables us to dispose of some part of this particular surplus?

Gold has one additional role. The Reserve System is required by law to keep a reserve in gold equal to 25% of its liabilities for Federal Reserve notes and deposits. Present reserves are well above this level and are likely to continue to be under circumstances now foreseeable. But if they should approach the 25% limit, it seems likely that the limit would be changed, as occurred when the former limits were approached in 1945, rather than the reserve position being allowed to force a monetary deflation not otherwise welcome—and this is certainly the desirable course of events. Hence, even as a monetary reserve, gold is primarily a symbol.

Since early 1958, our gold stock has declined some three billion dollars. There is no way of identifying this decline with any particular element of our balance of payments. It is simply the form in which foreigners have chosen to take part of the excess of their dollar receipts from U.S. purchases of goods and services, capital investments abroad, private gifts, and government foreign aid over their dollar expenditures on the corresponding items. So long as our present gold policy is maintained, gold is the equivalent of dollars to foreign holders. It may be preferred, either because its price is expected to rise or because it is desired for use as monetary reserves by other countries or as monetary hoards by individuals.

Because foreign aid is an independent source of dollars determined by non-market forces, there has been some tendency to link the loss of gold with foreign aid. In these terms, one might describe the loss of gold by saying that the rest of the world has decided to take a large part of the foreign aid that we have been giving them in the form of gold rather than of other goods. From our point of view, the gold in Fort Knox is serving no productive function; we use it for neither food, nor clothing, nor housing. The goods that foreign countries might take instead are contributing to our welfare. In consequence, it is very much to our interest to have foreign aid take the form of the export of gold rather than of goods. We accumulated much of the gold during and after the war because foreign countries had an urgent need for American goods in excess of the amount they could buy with dollars they earned, borrowed, or received as aid. We did not then allow the inflow of gold to influence our domestic monetary policy. It would be a mistake to allow the outflow of gold now to do so.

I see little justification for continuing our present gold policy. We are not prepared, and in my view rightly, to permit gold flows to dominate internal monetary policy. And it is hard to see why gold is a commodity whose price we should support. The chief gold producing countries are South Africa, Canada, and the U.S.S.R.; none is a country that we have felt it important to assist by economic aid; if we did want to assist them, it would be cheaper and more effective to do so by direct grants of aid; and this is certainly the case for gold mining interests in our own country.

The present gold drain offers an opportunity to reduce our stockpile of gold. It also has some value in contributing to the removal or reduction of discriminatory trade barriers or foreign exchange restrictions that have been erected by some foreign countries against goods from the United States. On the other hand, it raises the serious danger that, if the drain continues, the pressure to do something about it will lead us to take measures that are undesirable—either to raise the price of gold, thereby still further increasing the cost of the gold-support program, or to impose additional impediments to imports and stimulate exports, thereby departing still further from the free trade policy toward which we should be moving, or to tighten monetary policy more than is required for internal reasons. The way to avoid being forced into any of these measures is to cease offering to buy and sell gold at a fixed price, to eliminate the present anachronistic gold reserve requirements, and to allow the price of gold to be determined in the free markets of the world. At the same time, we should also abandon the even less justifiable commitments to purchase silver.

It is tempting to believe that the present outflow of gold means that if our price support program were eliminated the free market price of gold would rise above $35 an ounce. This might well be the case but it is by no means clear that it would be. A major reason why foreigners and others wish to hold gold is because it is convertible into dollars at a fixed price. The real demand is for dollars. If we abandoned support of the price of gold, but, let us say, retained our present stock, the demand for gold would be altered since gold would no longer have the property of conferring command over a fixed number of dollars. The result might be a decline rather than a rise in the world price of gold.

As matters now stand, the fixed gold price of $35 per ounce serves to determine exchange rates between the dollar and the currencies of other countries that also maintain a fixed price for gold. Although abandoning the fixed price for gold could be combined with rigid exchange rates through other devices, it would be far better, in my view, to allow the rates of exchange to be determined by the market. This would require that the U.S. refrain both from setting any official rates of exchange between the dollar and other currencies and from governmental speculation in exchange markets. This is essentially the arrangement that Canada adopted some years ago and that has been working well since. I have elsewhere outlined at some length the case for a system of flexible exchange rates.[2] It will suffice here, therefore, to say that such a system permits a maximum degree of international cooperation among countries, each separately following an independent internal monetary policy, without requiring exchange controls, import or export quotas, or other impediments to trade.

Internal Monetary Policy

Given that we are not and should not be prepared to permit internal monetary policy to be dominated by either gold flows or other manifestations of foreign payment arrangements, there remains the central question: what is to be our internal monetary policy?

In a celebrated article on "Rules versus Authorities in Monetary Policy,"[3] Henry Simons contrasted sharply two ways of answering this question: one, by specifying a general goal and then giving monetary authorities wide powers to use at their discretion in promoting it; the other, by assigning specific responsibilities to monetary authorities to be carried out in accordance with rules specified in advance and known to all. As Simons made clear, the contrast is not complete. The general goal alone limits somewhat the discretion of the authorities and the powers assigned to them do so to an even greater extent; and reasonable rules are hardly capable of being written that do not leave some measure of discretion. Yet the contrast is nonetheless both marked and important.

In practice, we have relied almost wholly on authorities. As was pointed out in an earlier chapter, we have done so not by intention but because the change in the role of the gold standard brought about by World War I loosened so greatly what the authors of the Federal Reserve Act had expected to be the effective "rule" limiting the discretion of the monetary authorities. In the absence of the strait-jacket of a rigid gold standard, "accommodating commerce and business," to quote the original Federal Reserve Act, imposed hardly any restrictions on the discretion of the authorities.[4]

Relying so largely on the discretion of authorities in so important an area of policy is highly objectionable on political grounds in a free society. Experience has demonstrated that it has also had unfortunate monetary consequences. It has meant continual and unpredictable shifts in the immediate guides to policy and in the content of policy as the persons and attitudes dominating the authorities have changed—from the "real

---

[2] See "The Case for Flexible Exchange Rates," in *Essays in Positive Economics* (Chicago, 1953), pp. 157-203.

[3] *Journal of Political Economy*, XLIV (1936), pp. 1-30; reprinted in Henry C. Simons, *Economic Policy for a Free Society* (Chicago, 1948), pp. 160-83.

[4] Federal Reserve Act, Section 14, paragraph 5. The Banking Act of 1933 changed the language of Section 14, paragraph 5, to specify "the maintenance of sound credit conditions, and the accommodation of commerce, industry and agriculture" as a guide to Federal Reserve action.

bills" emphasis of the early 1920's to the offsetting of inventory speculation of the mid-20's to the restraint of stock market speculation of
the late '20's to the sensitivity to external pressures and timidity in face
of internal drains of the early '30's, to the bond-support policies of the
'40's, to the sensitivity to cyclical movements and reliance on "announce-
ment effects" of the '50's. It has meant continual exposure of the authorities to political and economic pressures and to the deceptive effects of
short-lived tides of events and opinions. The role of the monetary authorities is to provide a stable monetary background, to go counter to or at
least not reinforce the ever shifting tides of current opinion and events.
This is the justification for their alleged "independence." Yet the vagueness
of their responsibilities and the wide range of their discretion has left
them no means other than "wisdom" and personal perspective of with-
standing contemporaneous pressures and has denied them the bulwark that
clearly assigned responsibilities and definite rules would have provided.

Reliance on discretion in pursuing general goals has meant also the
absence of any satisfactory criteria for judging performance. This has
made it nearly impossible to assess responsibility for success or failure
and has greatly enhanced the difficulty of learning by experience. The
Reserve System, or even monetary authorities more broadly defined,
have not been the sole agencies responsible for the general goals that
they have sought to promote, and that have become the current translation of "sound credit conditions and the accomodation of commerce,
industry, and agriculture"—such general goals as economic stability, full
employment, price stability, growth. These goals are to be approached
through the joint actions of many public and private agencies, of which
monetary authorities are only one. Success or failure in achieving them
cannot be attributed to monetary policy alone, and hence cannot be
a criterion of performance. An amusing dividend from reading *Annual
Reports* of the Federal Reserve System *seriatim* is the sharp cyclical pattern that emerges in the potency attributed to monetary forces and policy.
In years of prosperity, monetary policy is a potent instrument, the skillful
handling of which deserves credit for the favorable course of events; in
years of adversity, other forces are the important sources of economic
change, monetary policy has little leeway, and only the skillful handling
of the exceedingly limited powers available prevented conditions from
being even worse.[5]

---

[5] Even the Annual Report for 1933 comments in this vein on the Banking Holiday:
"The ability of the Federal Reserve banks to meet enormous demands for currency
during the crisis demonstrated the effectiveness of the country's currency system under
the Federal Reserve Act. . . . The crisis of February and March 1933, therefore, was
not a currency crisis but a banking crisis, and was occasioned not by a shortage of
currency but by loss of confidence in the solvency of banks and by a depreciation in
bank assets consequent upon the drop in prices of all classes of property caused by
the depression." And again, later in the same report, "It is difficult to say what the
course of the depression would have been had the Federal Reserve System not pursued
a policy of liberal open-market purchases." (Twentieth Annual Report, pp. 1, 20-21.)

The granting of wide and important responsibilities that are neither limited by clearly defined rules for guiding policy nor subject to test by external criteria of performance is a serious defect of our present monetary arrangements. It renders monetary policy a potential source of uncertainty and instability. It also gives greater power to the men in charge for good or ill, greater "flexibility" to meet problems as they arise, to use the phrase that the Reserve System likes to emphasize. If the analysis presented in the first chapter has any large measure of validity, experience suggests that eliminating the danger of instability and uncertainty of policy is far more urgent than preserving "flexibility." The major need in reforming our present control of monetary policy is, therefore, to provide more definite guides to policy and more satisfactory criteria of performance.

One way to do so that has frequently been urged is to adopt price level stability as simultaneously the specific goal for monetary policy, the immediate guide to policy, and the criterion of performance. There is much to recommend price level stability as the specific goal of monetary policy, as the way to separate the special role of monetary policy from that of other segments of economic policy in furthering our more nearly ultimate goals. The stock of money has a critical influence on the price level. No *substantial* movements in the price level within fairly short periods have occurred without movements in the same direction in the stock of money, and it seems highly dubious that they could. Over long periods, changes in the stock of money can in principle offset or reinforce other factors sufficiently to dominate trends in the price level.

I share, however, the doubts that the Reserve System has repeatedly expressed about the desirability of using price level stability as an immediate guide to policy. Entirely aside from the technical problem of the specific index number of prices that should be used, the key difficulty is that the link between price changes and monetary changes over short periods is too loose and too imperfectly known to make price level stability an objective and reasonably unambiguous guide to policy.

The Federal Reserve System does not control the price level. It controls the volume of its own earning assets and, at one remove under present circumstances or directly under the altered arrangements suggested in the preceding chapters, the stock of money. If the link between the stock of money and the price level were direct and rigid, or if indirect and variable, fully understood, this would be a distinction without a difference; the control of the one would imply control of the other; and it would be indifferent whether the guide to policy was stated in terms of the end to be achieved, stability of the price level, or the means to be used, changes in the stock of money. But the link is not direct and rigid, nor is it fully understood. While the stock of money is systematically related to the price level *on the average*, there is much variation in the relation over short periods of time and especially for the mild movements in both money and prices that characterize most of our experience and that we would like to have characterize all. Even the variability in the relation between money and prices would not be decisive if the link, though variable, were synchronous so that current changes in the stock of money had their full effect on economic conditions and on the price level instantaneously or with only a short lag. For it might then be fairly easy to substitute trial and error for a full understanding of the link between money and prices. Mistakes would not be cumulative and could be corrected quickly. In fact, however, there is much evidence that monetary changes have their effect only after a considerable lag and over a long period and that the lag is rather variable. In the National Bureau study on which I have been collaborating with Mrs. Schwartz, we have found that, on the average of 18 cycles, peaks in the rate of change in the stock of money tend to precede peaks in general business by about 16 months and troughs in the rate of change in the stock of money to precede troughs in general business by about 12 months.* The results would be roughly comparable if the comparisons were made with peaks and troughs in a price index rather than in general business. For individual cycles, the recorded lead has varied between 6 and 29 months at peaks and between 4 and 22 months at troughs. This is highly consistent behavior as such observations go and sufficient to pin down the *average* lead within a rather narrow range. But it is highly variable behavior for the individual episode with which policy must be concerned.

Under these circumstances, the price level—or for that matter any other set of economic indicators—could be an effective guide only if it were possible to predict, first, the effects of non-monetary factors on the price level for a considerable period of time in the future, second, the length of time it will take in each particular instance for monetary actions to have their effect, and third, the amount of effect of alternative monetary actions. In the present state of our knowledge, it is hard enough to conceive of an effective trial-and-error procedure for adapting to price level movements of two, three, or four years in length if monetary action taken today uniformly had its effect over a period centered, say, 14 months from now. I find it virtually impossible to conceive of an effective procedure when there is little basis for knowing whether the lag between action and effect will be 4 months or 29 months or somewhere in between. We are probably only today experiencing the effects of the rapid expansion in the money supply in the first half of 1958 in response to the 1957–58 recession. That recession itself may well have reflected in part the relatively slow rate of increase during 1956 and 1957, in its turn a reaction to the contemporaneous rise in prices. The 1956–57 price rise was itself related to the monetary expansion in 1954 and 1955 which was a reaction to the recession of 1953–54; and so on. Though oversimplified, this portrayal has enough potential validity to illustrate the problem.

---

* Editors' note. See Milton Friedman and Anna J. Schwartz, *U.S. Monetary History, 1867–1960* (Princeton: National Bureau of Economic Research, in press).

A satisfactory policy guide or rule should be connected more directly with the means available to the monetary authority than is the price level. We will, I believe, further the ultimate end of achieving a reasonably stable price level better by specifying the role of the monetary authorities in terms of magnitudes they effectively control and for whose behavior they can properly be held responsible than by instructing them solely to do the right thing at the right time when there is no clear and accepted criterion even after the event whether they have done so. In this as in so many human activities what seems the long way round may be the short way home.

The most important magnitude that the monetary authorities can effectively control and for which they have primary responsibility is the stock of money. Under present circumstances, even the stock of money is not directly controlled by the System. The System controls directly its own earning assets. As we have seen, the total of high-powered money is affected in addition by such factors as gold flows, changes in Treasury balances, and the like; and the total money stock for any given total of high-powered money is affected by the ratio of high-powered money to deposits that banks choose to hold and the ratio of currency to deposits that the public chooses to hold. These slips between control of earning assets and of the stock of money would be largely eliminated by the reforms proposed in the preceding chapters. These reforms would make changes in the earning assets of the Reserve System essentially identical with changes in the money supply and thereby give the System direct control over the money supply. But even under present circumstances, the links between Reserve action and the money supply are sufficiently close, the effects occur sufficiently rapidly, and the connections are sufficiently well understood, so that reasonably close control over the money supply is feasible, given the will. I do not mean to say that the process would not involve much trial and some error but only that the errors need not be cumulative and could be corrected fairly promptly. The process involves technical problems of considerable complexity, but they are of a kind with which the System has much experience and for which the System has trained personnel.

The stock of money therefore seems to me the relevant magnitude in terms of which to formulate monetary rules and the behavior of which should be a criterion of policy performance. The question remains, what behavior of the stock of money should we seek to achieve either by instructing the monetary authorities to do so, or by designing a system under which the desired pattern would be produced automatically?

Some years ago, I suggested as one answer to this question a largely automatic framework that would link changes in the money supply to the state of the budget.[6] Surpluses in the budget would reduce the stock of

---

[6] See "A Monetary and Fiscal Framework for Economic Stability," *American Economic Review*, XXXVIII (June 1948), 254-64; reprinted in my *Essays in Positive Economics*, pp. 133-56; also in Friedrich A. Lutz and Lloyd W. Mints, selection committee of the American Economic Association, *Readings in Monetary Theory* (1951), pp. 369-93.

money dollar for dollar and deficits would increase the stock of money dollar for dollar. The surpluses and deficits were themselves to result from the impact of changing economic conditions on a stable tax structure and a stable expenditure policy. The tax structure and expenditure policy were to be adjusted to the activities it was desired that government should undertake and not altered in reaction to cyclical movements—this is the "stabilizing budget policy" proposed at about the same time by the Committee for Economic Development.[7] This proposal would thus use the built-in flexibility of the federal budget as a means of producing countercyclical movements in the stock of money.

The research I have done since this proposal was published gives me no reason to doubt that it would work well; that it would provide a stable monetary background which would render major fluctuations well-nigh impossible, would not exacerbate minor fluctuations, and might even alleviate them. But I have become increasingly persuaded that the proposal is more sophisticated and complex than is necessary, that a much simpler rule would also produce highly satisfactory results and would have two great advantages: first, its simplicity would facilitate the public understanding and backing that is necessary if the rule is to provide an effective barrier to opportunistic "tinkering"; second, it would largely separate the monetary problem from the fiscal and hence would require less far-reaching reform over a narrower area.

The simpler rule is that the stock of money be increased at a fixed rate year-in and year-out without any variation in the rate of increase to meet cyclical needs. This rule could be adopted by the Reserve System itself. Alternatively, Congress could instruct the Reserve System to follow it. If it were adopted without any other changes in our monetary arrangements, the Reserve System would have much discretion in the precise techniques used to increase the stock of money and it could achieve the objective only with an appreciable though not large margin of error—perhaps one-half to one percentage point. If the other changes I have recommended were made, the area of discretion would be narrowed radically and so would the margin of error.

To make the rule specific, we need (1) to define the stock of money to which it refers, (2) to state what the fixed rate of increase should be or how it should be determined, (3) to state what if any allowance should be made for intra-year or seasonal movements.

(1) I have heretofore used the term "the stock of money" as if it were self-evident. Of course it is not. There is a continuum of assets possessing in various degrees the qualities we attribute to the ideal construct of "money" and hence there is no unique way to draw a line separating "money" from "near-monies"; for different purposes or at different times it may be appropriate to draw this line at different points on the continuum. In our own research we have found the most useful concept to be one that

---

[7] Committee for Economic Development, *Taxes and the Budget: A Program for Prosperity in a Free Economy* (November 1947).

includes currency held by the public plus adjusted demand deposits plus time deposits in commercial banks but excludes time deposits in mutual savings banks, shares in savings and loan associations, and the like. The Reserve System has generally used the term "money" more narrowly, to include only currency and demand deposits, and many economists have used it more broadly, to include also time deposits in mutual savings banks. I am inclined myself to favor the concept we have used because it seems to be somewhat more closely related empirically to income and other economic magnitudes than the other concepts and because it does not require classifying the deposit liabilities of individual institutions in terms of bookkeeping categories that permit much variation. But the evidence for this concept is certainly far from conclusive. More important, I do not believe it is vital which particular concept is chosen as long as first, it is at least as broad as currency plus adjusted demand deposits; second, a definite and clear-cut choice is made; and, third, the rate of increase chosen is adapted to the concept. The possible candidates for inclusion have had different secular rates of growth and are likely to continue to do so. They do not however vary radically with respect to one another over short periods and they would vary even less if some of my earlier suggestions were adopted, in particular, payment of interest on reserve balances with the Federal Reserve, and abolition of the present prohibition on the payment of interest on demand deposits and ceiling on the interest on time deposits.

(2) The rate of increase should be chosen so that on the average it could be expected to correspond with a roughly stable long-run level of final product prices. For the concept of money just recommended, namely, currency plus all commercial bank deposits, this would have required a rate of growth of slightly over 4% per year on the average of the past 90 years—something over 3% to allow for growth in output and 1% to allow for a secular decrease in velocity, which is to say for the increase in the stock of money per unit of output that the public has wished to hold as its real per capita income rose. To judge from this evidence, a rate of increase of 3 to 5% per year might be expected to correspond with a roughly stable price level for this particular concept of money. Since time deposits have grown in the past decade relative to demand deposits, and non-commercial bank time deposits relative to commercial, a somewhat lower rate of increase might be appropriate if a narrower definition were adopted, a somewhat higher rate, if a broader definition were adopted.

As with the definition, the particular rate of increase adopted seems to me less important than the adoption of a fixed rate provided only that the rate is somewhere in the range suggested and that it is adapted to the definition of money. A rate that turned out to be somewhat too high would mean a mild secular price rise, a rate that turned out to be somewhat too low, a mild secular price fall. Neither, it seems to me, would be serious. What is seriously disturbing to economic stability are rapid and sizable fluctuations in prices, not mild and steady secular movements in either direction. A fixed rate of increase in the stock of money would almost certainly rule out such rapid and sizable fluctuations, though it would not rule out mild cyclical or secular fluctuations, and it would give a firm basis for long range planning on the part of the public.

(3) I find the treatment of intra-year movements more puzzling. We now take for granted a seasonal movement in the stock of money and tend to assimilate it to other seasonal movements. Yet there is a crucial difference. The seasonal movement in the stock of money is a quasi-deliberate act of policy, not a product of climatic or similar circumstances. One initial objective of the Reserve System was to reduce seasonal fluctuations in interest rates. It has accomplished this objective by widening seasonal movements in the stock of money. I see no objection to seasonal variation in the stock of money, provided it is regular so that the public can adapt to it. On the other hand, neither do I see any objection to seasonal fluctuations in short-term interest rates. While the kind of pegging involved in eliminating seasonal fluctuations in interest rates has some special justifications, it is by no means free from the defects of other kinds of pegging. Moreover, there is no way to determine at all precisely what seasonal movement is required in the stock of money to eliminate a seasonal in interest rates. The actual seasonal that has been introduced into the stock of money has been sizable and has varied considerably from year to year. Hence, the proposal, which at first sight seems attractive, to apply a regular rate of increase to the seasonally adjusted stock of money, would involve introducing an essentially arbitrary element into the behavior of the stock of money—there is no seasonal to adjust until a decision is made what seasonal to introduce. My own tentative conclusion is that it would be preferable to dispense with seasonal adjustments and to adopt the rule that the actual stock of money should grow month by month at the predetermined rate. To avoid misunderstanding, let me note explicitly that this would be consistent with seasonal movements in currency and deposits separately, as long as they offset one another.

The proposal to increase the money stock at a fixed rate month-in and month-out is certainly simple. It is likely to strike many of you as also simple-minded. Surely, you will say, it is easy to do better. Surely, it would be better to "lean against the wind," in the expressive phrase of a Federal Reserve chairman, rather than to stand straight upright whichever way the wind is blowing. Some of my previous comments perhaps suggest that the matter is not so simple. We seldom in fact know which way the economic wind is blowing until several months after the event, yet to be effective, we need to know which way the wind is going to be blowing when the measures we take now will be effective, itself a variable date that may be a half year or a year or two years from now. Leaning today against next year's wind is hardly an easy task in the present state of meteorology.

Analogies aside, the historical record gives little basis for supposing that it is an easy task to do better than the simple rule I have suggested. Since at least the early 1920's, our monetary authorities have been trying to do just that; they have been trying to use monetary policy as an instrument for promoting stability. On the whole, the persons in charge of monetary policy have been as able, public spirited, and far-sighted a group as one could reasonably hope to have in such positions, though of course there have been some exceptions in both directions, and they have been served by a research staff that has numbered some of our leading monetary scholars and has maintained a high standard of technical excellence. Yet over this period as a whole, I doubt that many, if any, informed students of monetary affairs would disagree with the judgment that the actual behavior of the money stock has clearly been decidedly worse than the behavior that would have been produced by the simple rule—and this is true even if we leave out the war-time periods when the simple rule would almost surely have been departed from and perhaps rightly so.

The simple rule would have avoided the excessive expansion of the stock of money from 1919 to 1920 and the sharp contraction thereafter, the fairly mild but steady deflationary pressure of the later 1920's, the collapse of the stock of money from 1929 to 1933, the rather rapid rise thereafter, and the sharp decline in the course of the 1937–38 recession. In the period since World War II, the simple rule would have produced a lower rate of growth in the stock of money until the end of 1946 than was in fact realized, almost the same rate of growth during 1947, a faster rate of growth from sometime in 1947 to the end of 1949, which is to say, throughout the closing phases of the 1946–48 expansion and the whole of the 1948–49 contraction. The simple rule would have produced about the same rate of growth in the stock of money as was realized on the average from 1950 to early or mid-1953; a higher rate from then to mid-1954, or throughout most of the 1953–54 recession; about the same rate as was experienced from mid-1954 to mid-1955; a somewhat higher rate from then until the end of 1957; especially in the last half of 1957, after the 1957–58 contraction got under way; a lower rate than experienced in the first half of 1958, and about the same as the rate actually experienced from then to mid-1959.

The striking improvements in the behavior of the stock of money that would have been produced by the simple rule are for the inter-war period and for the major fluctuations of that period. It is these that make me so confident that informed students would render a nearly unanimous verdict in favor of the simple rule for the period as a whole. But, rule or no rule, changes in the monetary structure—notably federal insurance of bank deposits, the altered asset structure of banks, and the altered role of gold—and changes in the attitudes of the monetary authorities—notably their heightened sensitivity to contractions—render a repetition of major mistakes like those made during the inter-war period highly unlikely. It is nearly inconceivable that the monetary authorities would now permit the money stock to decline by one-third, as it did from 1929–33, or even by nearly 4% in 10 months, as it did in 1937. It is no doubt a merit of the rule that it provides insurance against such major mistakes but it may plausibly be argued that other factors have already provided adequate insurance—though I would be tempted to add that new mistakes are legion and insurance against major mistakes differing in kind from those in the past, in particular against unduly large increases in the money supply, is well worth while.

For the period since World War II, the contrast is not nearly so clear or sharp. The monetary authorities have followed a policy that has produced a behavior of the money supply very close to its hypothetical behavior under the rule, far closer than between the wars. In consequence, a finer criterion of performance is required to judge the desirability or undesirability of such discrepancies as there are, and this is true also for the milder discrepancies in the earlier period. My own judgment is that even for these, the rule would have produced clearly superior results, but I cannot be so sure that this judgment would be widely shared as I am for the period as a whole.

To supplement my own personal judgment, I tried to devise some objective way of grading actual performance relative to hypothetical performance under the rule. The attempt failed. The reason why it failed is, I think, most instructive. It is because the attempt to give operational meaning to "better and worse performance" revealed that such formulae as "leaning against the wind" or "countercyclical changes in the money supply," with which there might be widespread agreement, have no unambiguous specific content. I suspect that this is the only reason there is such widespread agreement. Each person can read his own content into these vague statements. If one tries to translate them into specific criteria that can be used to judge actual performance *ex post*, let alone to guide performance in the future, he finds that there are a variety of alternative translations, no one of which is fully satisfactory to any one person and on no one of which would there be anything like general agreement. In answer to the question whether it would be possible to do better than the simple rule, a majority of informed students might say "yes." Further probing would, however, reveal wide variety in the specific alternative policy regarded as "better." If each of these were made as explicit as the simple rule, I doubt that there would be anything like general assent to any one.

I can best elaborate on these remarks by describing briefly my attempts. Month-by-month, I recorded whether the growth in the seasonally adjusted actual money supply was higher or lower than the growth that would have been produced by a steady 4% rate of growth. I then tried to classify the difference as in the "right" or "wrong" direction according to an objective policy criterion.

The first criterion I tried was a simple translation of "leaning against the wind," namely, that the stock of money should grow at a slower than average rate during business expansions and at a higher than average rate during business contractions. By this criterion, for eight complete peacetime reference cycles from March 1919 to April 1958 (excluding the World War II cycle from June 1938 to October 1945), actual policy was in the "right" direction in 155 months, in the "wrong" direction in 226 months; so actual policy was "better" than the rule in 41% of the months. For the period after World War II alone, the results were only slightly more favorable to actual policy according to this criterion: policy was in the "right" direction in 71 months, in the "wrong" direction in 79 months, so actual policy was better than the rule in 47% of the months.

Even if the policy criterion could be accepted, numbers like these would not be an adequate measure of performance for three very different reasons. First, and least serious given a sufficiently long span of time, they take no account of the magnitude of the difference, only the direction. Second, and more serious, they treat each month separately, taking no account of the time sequence of deviations, and therefore neglect completely cumulative effects—a given number of deviations in the "wrong" direction could have very different consequences according as they were clustered or dispersed in time. Third, and most basic, suppose the results were less extreme and that actual policy were in the "right" direction 50% of the time. Would that mean a dead heat between the two alternative policies? Not at all. The alternative to the rule involves variability in the rate of change of the money supply; if the score is 50–50, this variability is simply a disturbance that introduces instability. Hence a 50–50 score would mean that the rule would be decidedly preferable—any alternative must be "better" much more than half the time in order to offset the harm it does through introducing random variability.[8]

The policy criterion cannot however be accepted. This is clear as soon as one goes beyond the overall results, and looks at the scoring of individual months. According to this criterion, a rate of growth higher than 4% is scored as in the wrong direction from March 1933 to May 1937. But this is absurd. Economic activity may have changed its direction of movement in March 1933 but it was still abnormally low. Surely a rule that calls for reversing policy toward "tightness" the moment a cyclical trough is reached is unsatisfactory—"ease" should be continued as long as conditions are depressed. Stating the counterpart for the peak reveals an inflationary asymmetry in reaction. There will be far less agreement that a "tight" policy should be continued beyond the peak so long as conditions are prosperous. If, however, we follow the logic both ways, we get an alternative translation of "leaning against the wind" to the effect that the money supply should grow at a slower than average rate during periods when economic conditions are "above" normal and at a faster than average rate when economic conditions are "below" normal. For simplicity, I treated the period from mid-expansion to mid-contraction as

---

[8] For a fuller analysis of this problem, see my "The Effects of a Full-Employment Policy on Economic Stability: A Formal Analysis," *Essays in Positive Economics*, pp. 117-32.

"above" normal and from mid-contraction to mid-expansion as "below" normal. By this criterion, actual policy scored much higher, being in the right direction in 56% of 377 peacetime months for the period as a whole, and in 58% of 149 months after World War II.[9]

Once again, examination of the month-by-month scoring raises serious doubts. In the Great Depression, for example, a less than normal rate of growth is scored as in the "right" direction from August 1929 all the way to the middle of 1931; and again more recently, from the cyclical peak in November 1948 through April 1949; and from the peak in July 1953 through January 1954. Some improvement might be made by adopting a less mechanical definition of "above" and "below" normal, such as the relation of income or industrial production, or some index of business conditions to its trend, or unemployment or prices to some "normal" level. But which should it be?

The two criteria so far described agree in classifying as "right" a less than normal rate of growth during the second half of expansion and a more than normal rate during the second half of contraction. This greatest common denominator of the two criteria is of course useless for future policy; it can, however, be used as at least a partial basis for judging past performance. By this third criterion, actual policy was in the "right" direction 45% of 183 peacetime months for the period as a whole, 55% of 75 months since the end of World War II.[10]

But even this common denominator is not unexceptionable. Once account is taken of the lag between monetary action and its effects, it is not at all clear that it is desirable to continue a lower-than-average rate of growth right up to the cyclical peak and a higher-than-average rate of growth up to the cyclical trough. If we could, might it not be desirable to ease monetary conditions before the peak and start tightening before the trough? Once again, reactions are likely to display an inflationary asymmetry—we readily agree at the peak, but many are likely to question the desirability of tightening before the trough is reached.

Still another range of possibilities is opened up by allowing not only for leads but also for a modified "needs of trade" argument. It has been argued that meeting a contraction arising from non-monetary forces with a larger than normal rate of increase in the money supply floods the market with liquidity, encourages investment in housing and other areas that is not viable in the longer run, and stimulates "speculation." In these ways, it creates difficulties for the future. Reverse phenomena are said to occur in the expansion. On this view, the appropriate behavior of the money supply is to move with the wind but only mildly; to grow at a

---

[9] The periods covered are from Nov.–Dec., 1918 to Nov.–Dec., 1957, excluding Nov.–Dec., 1937 to June, 1945. The numerical results are 210 months in the right direction to 167 in the wrong for the whole period; 87-62 for the period after June 1945.

[10] Actual scores were 83 out of 183 in the "right" direction for the period as a whole; 41 out of 75 for postwar period.

slower rate than normal during at least the early stages of contraction and at a faster rate than normal during at least part of the expansion.

The diversity and ambiguity concealed by the phrase "countercyclical monetary policy" itself raises something of a puzzle. How is it that there can yet be wide consensus in retrospective judgments of the major fluctuations? The answer, I conjecture, is that these involved *large* movements and that whatever the precise pattern specified, there would be general agreement that the rate of growth of the stock of money should not deviate far from some long-run average rate of growth. If this be so, then the simple rule I have proposed itself embodies an element that is common to most views about the appropriate behavior of the stock of money, is itself something of a greatest common denominator.

But whether this be the explanation or not, one thing seems clear. There is not currently any well-defined alternative to the rule I have suggested that would command wide assent, unless it be "let the Federal Reserve System do it"; and even for this alternative, there is no well-defined criterion with which there would be wide agreement for judging *ex post* whether "they" have done "it" well or poorly.

In summing up this discussion of the appropriate behavior of the money stock, I am tempted to paraphrase what Colin Clark once wrote about the case for free trade. Like other academicians, I am accustomed to being met with the refrain, "It's all right in theory but it won't work in practice." Aside from the questionable logic of the remark in general, in this instance almost the reverse of what is intended is true. There is little to be said in theory for the rule that the money supply should grow at a constant rate. The case for it is entirely that it would work in practice. There are persuasive theoretical grounds for desiring to vary the rate of growth to offset other factors. The difficulty is that, in practice, we do not know when to do so and by how much. In practice, therefore, deviations from the simple rule have been destabilizing rather than the reverse.

I should like to emphasize that I do not regard steady growth in the money stock as the be-all and end-all of monetary policy for all time. It is a rule that has much to recommend it in the present state of our knowledge. It would avoid the major mistakes that have marred our past record. It would assure long-run stability in the purchasing power of the dollar. But I should hope that as we operated under it we would accumulate more evidence and learn to understand more fully the workings of the monetary mechanism. As we did so, we could perhaps devise still better rules for controlling the stock of money that could command widespread professional support and public understanding.

Conclusion

[A summary of Professor Friedman's suggested reforms of our monetary and banking system is appended. He would expect the following benefits if they were adopted.]

The major gains would be, first, effective insurance against major monetary disturbances; second, a notable reduction in short-term monetary uncertainty and instability; third, a wider scope for private initiative and enterprise in the allocation of capital. The first would contribute to, if not effectively guarantee, the avoidance of those major economic disturbances that from time to time have threatened to tear our social fabric asunder. The second would promote a greater degree of stability in short-run movements in economic activity and thus contribute to what has become one of the major aims of national economic policy. The third would expand the area of economic freedom and promote a more efficient utilization of our resources, whether for current consumption or to increase our rate of growth.

These would be no mean accomplishments. But they would not provide a panacea for economic problems. Money is important, but only, in John Stuart Mill's words, "as a contrivance for sparing time and labour."[11] There are other sources of uncertainty and instability. No doubt they will continue to produce recurrent fluctuations in economic activity and from time to time will give rise to more serious problems of economic adjustment. Monetary policy is but one segment of total governmental policy let alone of the far wider range of private and public economic arrangements that affect the course of events. And even if we could improve governmental policy in other areas as much as our limited knowledge and understanding would permit, some uncertainty and instability would remain. After all, uncertainty and instability are unavoidable concomitants of progress and change. They are one face of a coin of which the other is freedom.

Summary of Recommendations

A. WITH RESPECT TO FEDERAL RESERVE SYSTEM:

1. Instruct the System to use its open market powers to produce a 4% per year rate of growth in the total of currency held by the public and adjusted deposits in commercial banks. The System should be instructed to keep the rate of growth as steady as it can week by week and month by month and to introduce no seasonal movement in the money stock.

2. Repeal present requirement that the Reserve System must maintain a gold reserve equal to 25% of its liabilities.

3. Require the Reserve System to pay interest to member banks on its deposit liabilities at a rate designed to be the same as the market yield on short-term government securities. Require the System to charge at cost for check-clearing or other services to member banks.

4. Repeal present control by the System over interest rates that member banks may pay on time deposits and present prohibition of interest payments by member banks on demand deposits.

---

[11] *Principles of Political Economy*, Ashley Edition (New York, 1929), p. 488.

5. Repeal present control over margin requirements on securities.
6. Repeal present power of the System to make loans to member banks, to discount paper for them, and to make loans to private individuals, corporations, or non-federal public bodies. This would eliminate any necessity for the System to establish discount rates or eligibility requirements.
7. Impose a set of fines on member banks for discrepancies between required and actual reserves.
8. Repeal present power of the System to vary reserve requirements of member banks (see also C1 and C1a below).
9. Give Reserve System power to issue its own securities, particularly if debt management functions are assigned to System.

B. WITH RESPECT TO THE TREASURY:

1. Eliminate present debt management by Treasury. Require Treasury to acquire funds it needs from Reserve System and deposit surpluses with Reserve System. This would concentrate debt management in one agency.

1a. Alternatively, if this step is not taken, modify Treasury debt management as follows:
   (1) Reduce kinds of issues offered to two—a short-term bill and a longer-term security, say an 8-year bond.
   (2) Issue both securities at regular and frequent intervals, preferably weekly, if not bi-weekly or monthly.
   (3) Announce the amount to be issued periodically as long in advance as possible and vary the amount smoothly from date to date.
   (4) Sell both issues solely at public auction and use an auction method under which all purchasers pay the same price.
   (5) As far as possible, rely on either deposits in commercial banks or in Reserve Banks for Treasury transactions, avoiding shifts between them.

2. Eliminate present commitment to buy and sell gold at a fixed price of $35 an ounce. Permit foreign exchange rates to be determined in the free market without Treasury intervention.
3. Eliminate present provisions for purchase of silver, retire silver certificates, and dispose of present silver stocks at a regular rate over the course of a decade or so.
4. Retire U.S. notes and authorize issue of Federal Reserve notes in small denominations, so that hand-to-hand currency will consist exclusively of Federal Reserve notes and coin.

C. WITH RESPECT TO COMMERCIAL BANKS:

1. Require banks accepting deposits subject to recall on demand or to transfer by check to keep reserves equal to 100% of their deposit liabilities whether demand or time in the form of either currency

in vault or interest-bearing deposits with the Reserve System. Permit completely free entry in the deposit banking business.

1a. Alternatively, if this step is not taken, revise present reserve requirements so as to make them uniform for all banks and all classes of deposits, with reserves being defined to include both vault cash and interest-bearing deposits with the Reserve System. This would mean eliminating present distinctions between central reserve, reserve city, and country banks, and between demand and time deposits.

2. Repeal present prohibition on the payment of interest on demand deposits and present limitations on interest rates that may be paid on time deposits (see A4 above for member banks).

32

Expansion and Employment[*]

EVSEY D. DOMAR[†]

Editors' Note

The Keynesian revolution turned economics upside down in the 1930's. Then, the problem was the Great Depression, and classical economic theory was found wanting for the diagnosis of actual events. However, this theoretical advance was developed under the conditions of a major and prolonged depression and as such was deemed inadequate for the problems facing the postwar world: growth and inflation. Classical economics was also concerned with growth and economic progress, but Keynesian theory focused on economic equilibrium at less than full employment. The significance of Domar's article lies in the marriage of Keynesian methodology and concept, originally conceived in a depression economy, with the classic economic problem of growth and full employment. For Domar, as for the classical economists, investment holds the key to economic expansion. However, two aspects of investment may conflict: On the one hand, it increases productive capacity; on the other, it generates income. Can you have a steady rate of economic growth involving a steady rate of investment, all under the conditions of a fully employed society? Domar's conclusion, which he expresses in simple algebraic terms, is as follows: To maintain full employment continuously, investment and income have to grow at a constant rate which must be equal to the product of the marginal propensity to save and the average

* From *The American Economic Review*, Vol. XXXVII, No. 1 (March, 1947), pp. 34-55. Reprinted by permission of *The American Economic Review* and the author.

† Evsey D. Domar (1914–   ) a native of Lodz, Poland, came to the United States in 1936. After completing his doctorate at Harvard (1947), he held teaching posts at several major American universities, among them the Carnegie Institute of Technology, University of Chicago, and Columbia University. He is the author of *Essays in the Theory of Economic Growth* (1957) and is now Professor of Economics at M.I.T.

productivity of investment. It is a conclusion still echoing through the pages of the work of other economic theorists and policy makers.

~~~~~~

> "A slow sort of a country," said the Queen. "Now *here*, you see, it takes all the running *you* can do, to keep in the same place. If you want to get somewhere else, you must run at least twice as fast as that."
> Lewis Carroll: *Through the Looking Glass*

❧ In these days of labor shortages and inflation, a paper dealing with conditions needed for full employment and with the threat of deflation may well appear out of place.[1] Its publication at this time is due partly to a two-year lag between the first draft and the final copy; also to the widely held belief that the present inflation is a temporary phenomenon, and that once it is over, the old problem of deflation and unemployment may possibly appear before us again.

<p style="text-align:center">* * * *</p>

Our comfortable belief in the efficacy of Say's Law has been badly shaken in the last fifteen years. Both events and discussions have shown that supply does not automatically create its own demand. A part of income generated by the productive process may not be returned to it; this part may be saved and hoarded. As Keynes put it, "Unemployment develops . . . because people want the moon; men cannot be employed when the object of desire (*i.e.*, money) is something which cannot be produced. . . ."[2] The core of the problem then is the public's desire to hoard. If no hoarding takes place, employment can presumably be maintained.

This sounds perfectly straight and simple; and yet it leaves something unexplained. Granted that absence of hoarding is a *necessary* condition for the maintenance of full employment, is it also a *sufficient* condition? Is the absence of hoarding *all* that is necessary for the avoidance of unemployment? This is the impression *The General Theory* gives. And yet, on a different plane, we have some notions about an increasing productive capacity which must somehow be utilized if unemployment is to be avoided. Will a mere absence of hoarding assure such a utilization? Will not a continuous increase in expenditures (and possibly in the money supply) be necessary in order to achieve this goal?

---

[1] This paper forms a sequence to my earlier article on "The 'Burden' of the Debt and the National Income," published in *The American Economic Review*, Vol. XXXIV, No. 5 (Dec., 1944), pp. 798-827. Though their titles seem different, the two papers are based on the same logical foundation and treat a common subject: the economic rôle of growth.

[2] John M. Keynes, *The General Theory of Employment, Interest and Money* (New York, 1936), p. 235.

The present paper deals with this problem. It attempts to find the conditions needed for the maintenance of full employment over a period of time, or more exactly, *the rate of growth of national income* which the maintenance of full employment requires. This rate of growth is analyzed in Section I. Section II is essentially a digression on some conceptual questions and alternative approaches. It may be omitted by the busy reader. Section III is concerned with the *dual* character of the investment process; that is, with the fact that investment not only generates income but also increases productive capacity. Therefore the effects of investment on employment are less certain and more complex than is usually supposed. In Section IV a few examples from existing literature on the subject are given, and Section V contains some concluding remarks. The most essential parts of the paper are presented in Sections I and III.

As in many papers of this kind, a number of simplifying assumptions are made. Most of them will become apparent during the discussion. Two may be noted at the outset. First, events take place simultaneously, without any lags. Second, income, investment and saving are defined in the *net* sense, *i.e.*, over and above depreciation. The latter is understood to refer to the cost of replacement of the depreciated asset by another one of *equal* productive capacity. These assumptions are not entirely essential to the argument. The discussion could be carried out with lags, and, if desired, in gross terms or with a different concept of depreciation. Some suggestions along these lines are made in Section II. But it is better to begin with as simple a statement of the problem as possible, bearing in mind of course the nature of assumptions made.

I. The Rate of Growth

It is perfectly clear that the requirement that income paid out should be returned to the productive process, or that savings be equal to investment, or other expressions of the same idea, are simply formulas for the retention of the income *status quo*. If underemployment was present yesterday, it would still remain here today. If yesterday's income was at a full employment level, that *income level* would be retained today. It may no longer, however, correspond to full employment.

Let yesterday's full employment income equal an annual rate of 150 billion dollars, and let the average propensity to save equal, say, 10 per cent. If now 15 billions are annually invested, one might expect full employment to be maintained. But during this process, capital equipment of the economy will have increased by an annual rate of 15 billions—for after all, investment *is* the formation of capital.[3] Therefore, the productive capacity of the economy has also increased.

---

[3] The identification of investment with capital formation is reasonably safe in a private economy where only a small part of resources is disposed of by the government. When this part becomes substantial, complications arise. This question will be taken up again

The effects of this increase on employment will depend on whether or not *real income* has also increased. Since money income has remained, as assumed, at the 150 billion annual level, an increase in real income can be brought about only by a corresponding fall in the general price level. This indeed has been the traditional approach to problems of this kind, an approach which we shall have to reject here for the following reasons:

1. The presence of considerable monopolistic elements (in industry and labor) in our economy makes unrealistic the assumption that a falling *general* price level could be achieved without interfering with full employment. This of course does not exclude *relative* changes among prices. As a matter of fact, if industries subject to a faster-than-average technological progress do not reduce their prices to some extent, a constant general price level cannot be maintained.

2. For an economy saddled with a large public debt and potentially faced (in peacetime) with serious employment problems, a falling price level is in itself undesirable.

3. A falling price level can bring about a larger real income only in the special case when prices of consumers' goods fall more rapidly than those of investment goods. For otherwise (with a constant propensity to save) money income will be falling as fast or faster than the price level, and real income will be falling as well. To prevent money income from falling so rapidly, the volume of real investment would have to keep rising —a conclusion which will be presently reached in the more general case.

4. Finally, the assumption of a falling general price level would obscure —and I believe quite unnecessarily—the main subject we are concerned with here.

For these reasons, a *constant general price level* is assumed throughout this paper. But, from a theoretical point of view, this is a convenience rather than a necessity. The discussion could be carried on with a falling or a rising price level as well.

To come back to the increase in capacity. If both money and real national income thus remain fixed at the 150 billion annual level, the creation of the new capital equipment will have one or more of the following effects: (1) The new capital remains unused; (2) The new capital is used at the expense of previously constructed capital, whose labor and/or markets the new capital has taken away; (3) The new capital is substituted for labor (and possibly for other factors).

The first case represents a waste of resources. That capital need not have been constructed in the first place. The second case—the substitution of new capital for existing capital (before the latter is worn out,

---

in Section II. Meanwhile, we shall disregard it and divide total national income, irrespective of source, into investment (*i.e.*, capital formation) and consumption.

The term "national income" is understood here in a broad sense, as total output minus depreciation, and does not touch on current controversies regarding the inclusion or exclusion of certain items. Perhaps "net national product" would be more appropriate for our purposes.

since investment is defined here in the net sense)—takes place all the time and, in reasonable magnitudes, is both unavoidable and desirable in a free dynamic society. It is when this substitution proceeds on a rather large scale that it can become socially wasteful; also, losses sustained or expected by capital owners will make them oppose new investment—a serious danger for an economy with considerable monopolistic elements.

Finally, capital may be substituted for labor. If this substitution results in a *voluntary* reduction in the labor force or in the length of the work week, no objections can be raised. Such a process has of course been going on for many years. But in our economy it is very likely that at least a part of this substitution—if carried on at an extensive scale—will be involuntary, so that the result will be unemployment.

The tools used in this paper do not allow us to distinguish between these three effects of capital formation, though, as will appear later, our concepts are so defined that a voluntary reduction in the number of man-hours worked is excluded. In general, it is not unreasonable to assume that in most cases all three effects will be present (though not in constant proportions), and that capital formation not accompanied by an increase in income will result in unemployed capital and labor.

The above problems do not arise in the standard Keynesian system because of its explicit assumption that employment is a function of national income, an assumption which admittedly can be justified only over short periods of time. Clearly, a full employment income of 1941 would cause considerable unemployment today. While Keynes' approach—the treatment of employment as a function of income—is a reasonable first approximation, we shall go a step further and assume instead that *the percentage of labor force employed is a function of the ratio between national income and productive capacity*. This should be an improvement, but we must admit the difficulties of determining productive capacity, both conceptually and statistically. These are obvious and need not be elaborated. We shall mean by productive capacity the total output of the economy at what is usually called full employment (with due allowance for frictional and seasonal unemployment), such factors as consumers' preferences, price and wage structures, intensity of competition, and so on being given.

The answer to the problem of unemployment lies of course in a growing income. If after capital equipment has increased by (an annual rate of) 15 billions an income of 150 billions leaves some capacity unused, then a higher magnitude of income can be found—say 155 or 160 billions —which will do the job. There is nothing novel or startling about this conclusion. The idea that a capitalist economy needs growth goes back, in one form or another, at least to Marx. The trouble really is that the idea of growth is so widely accepted that people rarely bother about it. It is always treated as an afterthought, to be added to one's speech or article if requested, but very seldom incorporated in its body. Even then it is regarded as a function of some abstract technological progress which somehow results in increasing productivity per man-hour, and which takes place quite independently of capital formation. And yet, our help in the industrialization of undeveloped countries will take the form not only of supplying technical advice and textbooks, but also of actual machinery and goods. Certainly the 80 odd billion dollars of net capital formation created in the United States in the period 1919–29 had a considerable effect on our productive capacity.[4]

A change in productive capacity of a country is a function of changes in its natural resources (discovery of new ones or depletion of others), in its labor force (more correctly, man-hours available), capital and the state of technique.[5] Since changes in natural resources and technique are very difficult concepts, we can express changes in total capacity via changes in the quantity and productivity of labor or of capital. The traditional approach builds around labor. The several studies of the magnitude of total output corresponding to full employment, made in the last few years, consisted in multiplying the expected labor force (subdivided into several classes) by its expected average productivity.[6] This procedure did not imply that the other three factors (natural resources, technology and capital) remained constant; rather that their variations were all reflected in the changes in productivity of labor.

It is also possible to put capital in the center of the stage and to estimate variations in total capacity by measuring the changes in the quantity of capital and in its productivity, the latter reflecting changes currently taking place in natural resources, technology and the labor force. From a practical point of view, the labor approach has obvious advantages, at least in some problems, because labor is a more homogeneous and easily measurable factor. But from a theoretical point of view, the capital approach is more promising and for this reason: the appearance of an extra workman or his decision to work longer hours *only* increases productive capacity without, however, generating any income to make use of this increase. But the construction of a new factory has a *dual* effect: *it increases productive capacity and it generates income*.

The emphasis on this dual character of the investment process is the essence of this paper's approach to the problem of employment. If investment increases productive capacity and also creates income, what should be the magnitude of investment, or at what rate should it grow, in order to make the increase in income equal to that of productive capacity?[7] Couldn't an equation be set up one side of which would represent the increase (or the rate of increase) of productive capacity, and the

---

[4] This figure, in 1929 prices, is taken from Simon Kuznets, *National Income and Its Composition*, Vol. I (New York, 1941), p. 268. The actual figure was 79.1 billion dollars.

[5] Taking other conditions listed on p. 37 as given.

[6] See for instance E. E. Hagen and N. B. Kirkpatrick, "The National Output at Full Employment in 1950," *Amer. Econ. Rev.*, Vol XXXIV, No. 4 (Sept., 1944), pp. 472-500.

[7] This statement of the problem presupposes that full employment has already been reached and must only be maintained. With a small extra effort we could begin with a situation where some unemployment originally existed.

other—that of income, and the solution of which would yield the required *rate of growth?*

We shall attempt to set up such an equation. It will be first expressed in symbolic form, and later (on p. 574) illustrated by a numerical example.

Let investment proceed at an annual rate of I, and let annual productive capacity (net value added) per dollar of newly created capital be equal on the average to s. Thus if it requires, say, 3 dollars of capital to produce (in terms of annual net value added) one dollar of output, s will equal one-third or 33.3 per cent per year. It is not meant that s is the same in all firms or industries. It depends of course on the nature of capital constructed and on many other factors. Its treatment here as a given magnitude is a simplification which can be readily dispensed with.

The productive capacity of I dollars invested will thus be Is dollars per year. But it is possible that the operation of new capital will take place, at least to some extent, at the expense of previously constructed plants, with which the new capital will compete both for markets and for factors of production (mainly labor). If as a result, the output of existing plants must be curtailed, it would be useless to assert that the productive capacity of the *whole economy* has increased by Is dollars per year.[8] It has actually increased by a smaller amount which will be indicated by $I\sigma$.[9] σ may be called the *potential social average productivity of investment*. Such a long name calls for an explanation.

1. As stated above, σ is concerned with the increase in productive capacity of the whole society and not with the productive capacity per dollar invested in the new plants taken by themselves, that is with s. A difference betwen s and σ indicates a certain misdirection of investment, or—more important—that investment proceeds at too rapid a rate as compared with the growth of labor and technological progress. This question will be taken up again in Section II.

2. σ should not be confused with other related concepts, such as the traditional marginal productivity of capital. These concepts are usually based on a *caeteris paribus* assumption regarding the quantity of other factors and the state of technique. It should be emphasized that the use of σ does not imply in the least that labor, natural resources and technology remain fixed. It would be more correct therefore to say that σ indicates the increase in productive capacity which *accompanies* rather than which is caused by each dollar invested.

3. For our purposes, the most important property of σ is its *potential character*. It deals not with an increase in national income but with that of the *productive potential* of the economy. A high σ indicates that the economy *is capable* of increasing its output relatively fast. But whether

---

[8] These comparisons must of course be made at a full employment level of national income. See also pp. 573-574.

[9] We are disregarding here external economies obtained by existing plants from the newly constructed ones.

this increased capacity will actually result in greater output or greater unemployment, depends on the behavior of money income.

The expression $I\sigma$ is the supply of our system; it is the increase in output which the economy *can* produce. On the demand side we have the multiplier theory, too familiar to need any elaboration, except for the emphasis on the obvious but often forgotten fact that, with any given marginal propensity to save, to be indicated, by α, an increase in national income is not a function of investment, but of the *increment* in investment. If investment today, however large, is equal to that of yesterday, national income of today will be just equal and not any larger than that of yesterday. All this is obvious, and is stressed here to underline the lack of symmetry between the effects of investment on productive capacity and on national income.

Let investment increase at an absolute annual rate of ΔI (*e.g.*, by two billion per year), and let the corresponding absolute annual increase in income be indicated by ΔY. We have then

(1) $$\Delta Y = \Delta I \frac{1}{\alpha},$$

where $\frac{1}{\alpha}$ is of course the multiplier.

Let us now assume that the economy is in a position of a full employment equilibrium, so that its national income equals its productive capacity.[10] To retain this position, income and capacity should increase at the same rate. The annual increase in potential capacity equals $I\sigma$. The annual increase in actual income is expressed by $\Delta I(1/\alpha)$. Our objective is to make them equal. This gives us the fundamental equation

(2) $$\Delta I \frac{1}{\alpha} = I\sigma.$$

To solve this equation, we multiply both sides by α and divide by I, obtaining

(3) $$\frac{\Delta I}{I} = \alpha\sigma.$$

The left side of expression (3) is the absolute annual increase (or the absolute rate of growth) in investment—ΔI—divided by the volume of investment itself; or in other words, it is the relative increase in investment, or the annual percentage rate of growth of investment. Thus the maintenance of full employment requires that investment grow at the annual percentage rate $\alpha\sigma$.

So much for investment. Since the marginal propensity to save—α—is assumed to be constant, an increase in income is a constant multiple of an

---

[10] See note 7.

increase in investment (see expression [1]). But in order to remain such a constant multiple of investment, income must also grow at the same annual percentage rate, that is at $\alpha\sigma$.

To summarize, the maintenance of a continuous state of full employment requires that *investment and income grow at a constant annual percentage (or compound interest) rate* equal to the product of the marginal propensity to save and the average (to put it briefly) productivity of investment.[11]

This result can be made clearer by a numerical example. Let $\sigma = 25$ per cent per year, $\alpha = 12$ per cent, and $Y = 150$ billions per year. If full employment is to be maintained, an amount equal to $150 \times \dfrac{12}{100}$ should be invested. This will raise productive capacity by the amount invested times σ, *i.e.*, by $150 \times \dfrac{12}{100} \times \dfrac{25}{100}$. and national income will have to rise by the same annual amount. But the relative rise in income will equal the absolute increase divided by the income itself, *i.e.*,

$$(4) \qquad \frac{150 \times \dfrac{12}{100} \times \dfrac{25}{100}}{150} = \frac{12}{100} \times \frac{25}{100} = \alpha\sigma = 3 \text{ per cent.}$$

These results were obtained on the assumption that α, the marginal propensity to save, and σ, the average productivity of investment, remain constant. The reader can see that this assumption is not necessary for the argument, and that the whole problem can be easily reworked with variable α and σ. Some remarks about a changing α are made on pp. 580–581.

The expression (3) indicates (in a very simplified manner) conditions needed for the maintenance of full employment over a period of time. It shows that it is not sufficient, in Keynesian terms, that savings of yesterday be invested today, or, as it is often expressed, that investment offset saving. Investment of today must always exceed savings of yesterday. A mere absence of hoarding will not do. An injection of new money (or dishoarding) must take place every day. Moreover, this injection must proceed, in absolute terms, at an accelerated rate. The economy must continuously expand.[12]

---

[11] The careful reader may be disturbed by the lack of clear distinction between increments and rates of growth here and elsewhere in the text. If some confusion exists, it is due to my attempt to express these concepts in non-mathematical form. Actually they all should be stated in terms of rates of growth (derivatives in respect to time). For a more serious treatment of this point, as well as for a more complete statement of the logic of the paper, see my article "Capital Expansion, Rate of Growth, and Employment," *Econometrica*, Vol. XIV (Apr., 1946), pp. 137-47.

[12] After this paper was sent to the printer, I happened to stumble on an article by R. F. Harrod, published in 1939, which contained a number of ideas similar to those presented here. See "An Essay in Dynamic Theory," *Econ. Jour.*, Vol. XLIX (Apr., 1939), pp. 14-33.

II. *The Argument Re-examined*

The busy reader is urged to skip this section and proceed directly to Section III. The present section is really a long footnote which re-examines the concepts and suggests some alternative approaches. Its purpose is, on the one hand, to indicate the essential limitations of the preceding discussion, and on the other, to offer a few suggestions which may be of interest to others working in this field.

It was established in Section I that the maintenance of full employment requires income and investment to grow at an annual compound interest rate equal to $\alpha\sigma$. The meaning of this result will naturally depend on those of α and σ. Unfortunately neither of them is devoid of ambiguity.

The marginal propensity to save—α—is a relatively simple concept in a private economy where only a small part of resources is handled by the government. National income can be divided, without too much trouble, into investment and consumption, even though it is true that the basis for this distinction is often purely formal.[13] But on the whole it sounds quite reasonable to say that if marginal propensity to save is α, then an α fraction of an increase in income is saved by the public and invested in income-producing assets.

When a substantial part of the economy's resources is disposed of by the government, two interpretations of the marginal propensity to save, or of savings and investment in general, appear possible. The first is to continue dividing the total output, whether produced by government or by private business, into consumption and investment. This method was implicitly followed in this paper. But a question arises regarding the meaning and stability of α. It makes sense to say that a person or the public save, in accordance with the size of their incomes, their habits, expectations, etc., a certain, though not necessarily constant, fraction of an increment in their *disposable* (*i.e.*, after income and social security taxes) income, but can a similar statement be made regarding total national income, a good part of which is not placed at the disposal of the public? Also it is not easy to divide government expenditures into consumption and investment.

The other method would limit α to disposable income only, and then provide for government expenditures separately. It would be necessary then to find out the effects of these expenditures on productive capacity.

Depreciation raises another problem. Since all terms are defined here in the net sense, the meaning and magnitude of α will also depend on those of depreciation, irrespective of the choice between the above two methods. Depreciation has been defined here (see page 568) as the cost of replacement of a worn out asset by another one with an equal produc-

---

[13] Thanks are due to George Jaszi for his persistent efforts to enlighten me on this subject. The division of national income into investment and consumption is really a more difficult task than my text might imply.

tive capacity. While this approach is about as bad or as good as any other, the difficulty still remains that businesses ordinarily do not use this definition, and therefore arrive at a different estimate of their net incomes, which in turn determine their propensity to save.

I do not have ready answers to these questions, though I do not consider them insurmountable. I am mentioning them here partly in order to indicate the limitations of the present argument, and also as obstacles which will have to be overcome if a more exact analysis is undertaken.

σ is even more apt to give rise to ambiguities. s, from which it springs, has been used, in one form or another, in economic literature before, particularly in connection with the acceleration principle.[14] Here it indicates the annual amount of income (net value added) which can be produced by a dollar of newly created capital. It varies of course among firms and industries, and also in space and time, though a study recently made seems to indicate that it has been quite stable, at least in the United States and Great Britain, over the last 70 years or so.[15] Whether s has or has not been relatively stable is not essential for our discussion. The real question is whether such a concept has meaning, whether it makes sense to say that a given economy or a plant has a certain capacity. Traditional economic thinking would, I fear, be against such an approach. Unfortunately, it is impossible to discuss this question here. I believe that our actual experience during the last depression and this war, as well as a number of empirical studies, show that productive capacity, both of a plant and of the whole economy is a meaningful concept, though this capacity, as well as the magnitude of s, should be treated as a *range* rather than as a single number.

In some problems s may be interpreted as the minimum annual output per dollar invested which will make the investment worth undertaking. If this output falls below s, the investor suffers a loss or at least a disappointment, and may be unwilling to replace the asset after it has depreciated.

All these doubts apply to σ even more than to s. As explained on pages 571–572, σ differs from s by indicating the annual increment in capacity of the *whole economy* per dollar invested, rather than that of the newly created capital taken by itself. The possible difference between s and σ is due to the following reasons:

1. The new plants are not operated to capacity because they are unable to find a market for their products.

2. Old plants reduce their output because their markets are captured by new plants.

---

[14] See for instance Paul A. Samuelson, "Interactions between the Multiplier Analysis and the Principle of Acceleration," *Rev. Econ. Stat.*, Vol. XXI (May, 1939), pp. 75-79; also R. F. Harrod, *The Trade Cycle* (Oxford, 1936). These authors, however, used not the ratio of income to capital, but of consumption to capital, or rather the reciprocal of this ratio.

[15] See Ernest H. Stern, "Capital Requirements in Progressive Economies," *Economica*, n.s. Vol. XII (Aug., 1945), pp. 163-71.

As productive capacity has no meaning except in relation to consumers' preferences, in both of the above cases productive capacity of the country is increased by a smaller amount than could be produced by the new plants; in the limiting case it is not increased at all, and $\sigma=0$, however high s may be. But it must be made clear that the test of whether or not σ is below s can be made only under conditions (actual or assumed) of full employment. If markets are not large enough because of insufficiency of effective demand due to unemployment, it cannot yet be concluded that σ is below s.

3. The first two cases can take place irrespective of the volume of current investment. A more important case arises when investment proceeds at such a rapid rate that a shortage of other factors relative to capital develops. New plants may be unable to get enough labor, or more likely, labor (and other factors) is transferred to new plants from previously constructed ones, whose capacity therefore declines. In its actual manifestation, case 3 can hardly be separated from cases 1 and 2, because to the individual firm affected the difference between s and σ always takes the form of a cost-price disparity. The reason why we are trying to separate the first two cases from the third lies in the bearing of this distinction on practical policy. The first two cases arise from an error of judgment on the part of investors (past or present) which is, at least to some extent, unavoidable and not undesirable. The struggle for markets and the replacement of weaker (or older) firms and industries by stronger (or newer) ones is the essence of progress in a capitalist society. The third case, on the other hand, may result from poor fiscal policy. It constitutes an attempt to invest too much, to build more capital than the economy can utilize even at full employment. Such a situation can develop if an economy with a high propensity to save tries to maintain full employment by investing all its savings into capital goods. But it should be made clear that the expressions "too much capital" or "high propensity to save" are used in a relative sense —in comparison with the growth of other factors, that is natural resources, labor and technology.

The use of σ certainly does not imply that these factors remain fixed. As a matter of fact, it would be very interesting to explore the use of a more complex function as the right side of expression (2) instead of $I\sigma$, a function in which the growth of labor, natural resources, and technology would be presented explicitly, rather than through their effects on σ.[16] I did not attempt it because I wished to express the idea of growth in the simplest possible manner. One must also remember that in the application of mathematics to economic problems, diminishing returns appear rapidly, and that the construction of complex models requires so many specific assumptions as to narrow down their applicability.

---

[16] Some work along these lines has been done by J. Tinbergen. See his "Zur Theorie der langfristigen Wirtschaftsentwicklung" in the *Weltwirtschaftliches Archiv*, Vol. LV (May, 1942), pp. 511-49.

And yet it may be interesting to depart in another direction, namely to introduce lags. In this paper both the multiplier effect and the increase in capacity are supposed to take place simultaneously and without any lag. Actually, the multiplier may take some time to work itself out, and certainly the construction of a capital asset takes time. In a secular problem these lags are not likely to be of great importance, but they may play an essential rôle over the cycle. We shall return to this question on pages 580–581.

Finally, it is possible to approach the problem of growth from a different point of view. It was established here that the rate of growth required for a full employment equilibrium to be indicated by r is equal to

$$(5) \qquad r = \alpha \sigma,$$

so that if α and σ are given, the rate of growth is determined. But the equation (5) can also be solved for α in terms of r and σ, and for σ in terms of r and α. Thus if it is believed that r should be treated as given (for instance by technological progress), and if it is also decided to keep σ at a certain level, perhaps not too far from s, then it is possible to determine $\alpha = r/\sigma$, as being that marginal propensity to save which can be maintained without causing either inflation or unemployment. This approach was actually used by Ernest Stern in his statistical study of capital requirements of the United Kingdom, the United States and the Union of South Africa.[17] I also understand from Tibor de Scitovszky that he used the same approach in a study not yet published.

It is also possible to treat r and α as given and then determine what $\sigma = r/\alpha$ would have to be. Each approach has its own advantages and the choice depends of course on the nature of the problem in hand. The essential point to be noticed is the relationship between these three variables r, α, and σ, and the fact that if any two of them are given, the value of the third needed for the maintenance of full employment is determined: and if its actual value differs from the required one, inflation in some cases and unused capacity and unemployment in others will develop.

III. The Dual Nature of the Investment Process

We shall continue the discussion of growth by returning to expression (2) on page 573.

$$\Delta I \frac{1}{\alpha} = I\sigma,$$

which is fundamental to our whole analysis. As a matter of fact, the statement of the problem in this form (2) appears to me at least as important as its actual solution expressed in (3). To repeat, the left part

---

[17] Stern, *Economica*, n.s. Vol. XII, pp. 163-71.

of the equation shows the annual increment in national income and is the demand side; while the right part represents the annual increase in productive capacity and is the supply side. Alternatively, the left part may be called the "multiplier side," and the right part the "σ side."

What is most important for our purposes is the fact that investment appears on both sides of the equation; that is, it has a *dual effect*: on the left side it generates income via the multiplier effect; and on the right side it increases productive capacity—the σ effect. The explicit recognition of this dual character of investment could undoubtedly save much argument and confusion. Unless some special assumptions are made, the discussion of the effects of investment on profits, income, employment, etc., cannot be legitimately confined to one side only. For the generation of income and the enlargement of productive capacity often have diametrically opposed effects, and the outcome in each particular case depends on the special circumstances involved.[18]

Analyzing expression (2) further, we notice that even though investment is present on both its sides, it does not take the same form: for on the σ side we have the *amount* of investment as such; but on the multiplier side we have not the amount of investment but its annual increment, or its absolute *rate of increase*.

The amount of investment (always in the net sense) may remain constant, or it may go up or down, but so long as it remains positive (and except for the rare case when $\sigma \leqq 0$) productive capacity increases. But if income is to rise as well, it is not enough that just any amount be invested: *an increase in income is not a function of the amount invested; it is the function of the increment of investment.* Thus the whole body of investment, so to speak, increases productive capacity, but only its very top—the increment—increases national income.

In this probably lies the explanation why inflations have been so rare in our economy in peacetime, and why even in relatively prosperous periods a certain degree of underemployment has usually been present. Indeed, it is difficult enough to keep investment at some reasonably high level year after year, but the requirement that it always be rising is not likely to be met for any considerable length of time.

Now, if investment and therefore income do not grow at the required rate, unused capacity develops. Capital and labor become idle. It may not be apparent why investment by increasing productive capacity creates unemployment of labor. Indeed, as was argued on page 577, this need not always be the case. Suppose national income remains constant or rises very

---

[18] The effects of labor saving machinery on employment of labor is a good case in point. Some economists, particularly those connected with the labor movement, insist that such machines displace labor and create unemployment. Their opponents are equally sure that the introduction of labor saving devices reduces costs and generates income, thus increasing employment. Both sides cite ample empirical evidence to prove their contentions, and neither side is wrong. But both of them present an incomplete picture from which no definite conclusion can be derived.

slowly while new houses are being built. It is possible that new houses will be rented out at the expense of older buildings and that no larger rents will be paid than before; or that the new houses will stand wholly or partly vacant with the same result regarding the rents.[19] But it is also possible, and indeed very probable, that the complete or partial utilization of the new buildings which are usually better than the old ones, will require the payment of larger rents, with the result that less income will be left for the purchase of, say clothing; thus causing unemployment in the clothing trades. So the substitution of capital for labor need not take the obvious form of labor-saving machinery; it may be equally effective in a more circuitous way.

The unemployment of men is considered harmful for obvious reasons. But idle buildings and machinery, though not arousing our humanitarian instincts, can be harmful because their presence inhibits new investment. Why build a new factory when existing ones are working at half capacity? It is certainly not necessary to be dogmatic and assert that no plant or house should ever be allowed to stand idle, and that as soon as unused capacity develops the economy plunges into a depression. There is no need, nor is it possible or desirable, to guarantee that every piece of capital ever constructed will be fully utilized until it is worn out. When population moves from Oklahoma to California, some buildings in Oklahoma will stand idle; or when plastics replace leather in women's handbags, the leather industry may suffer. Such changes form the very life of a free dynamic society, and should not be interfered with. The point is that there be no vacant houses while prospective tenants are present but cannot afford to live in them because they are unemployed. And they are unemployed because income and investment do not grow sufficiently fast.

The extent to which unused capacity, present or expected, inhibits new investment greatly depends on the structure of industry and the character of the economy in general. The more atomistic it is, the stronger is competition, the more susceptible it is to territorial, technological and other changes, the smaller is the effect of unused capacity on new investment. One firm may have an idle plant, while another in the same industry builds a new one; steel may be depressed while plastics are expanding. It is when an industry is more or less monopolized, or when several industries are financially connected, that unused capacity presents a particularly serious threat to new investment.

Strictly speaking, our discussion so far, including equation (2), was based on the assumption that α remained constant. If α varies within the time period concerned, the relation between investment and income becomes more involved. What the left side of the equation (2) requires is that *income* increase; and investment must grow only in so far as its growth

---

[19] It is worth noticing that in both cases the construction of the new houses represents a misdirection of resources, at least to some extent. But a complete avoidance of such misdirection is perfectly impossible and even undesirable.

is necessary for the growth of income. So if α declines sufficiently fast, a growing income can be achieved with a constant or even falling investment. But years of declining α have evidently been offset by others of rising α, because whatever information is available would indicate that over the last seventy years or so prior to this war the percentage of income saved was reasonably constant, possibly with a slight downward trend.[20] Therefore, in the absence of direct government interference, it would seem better not to count too much on a falling α, at least for the time being.

In general, a high α presents a serious danger to the maintenance of full employment, because investment may fail to grow at the required high rate, or will be physically unable to do so without creating a substantial difference between s and σ. This difference indicates that large numbers of capital assets become unprofitable and their owners suffer losses or at least disappointments (see pages 579-580). Space does not permit me to develop this idea at greater length here.[21] But it must be emphasized that what matters is not the magnitude of α taken by itself, but its relation to the growth of labor, natural resources, and technology. Thus a country with new resources, a rapidly growing population, and developing technology is able to digest, so to speak, a relatively large α, while absence or at least a very slow growth of these factors makes a high α a most serious obstacle to full employment.[22] But the problem can be attacked not only by lowering α, but also by speeding up the rate of technological progress, the latter solution being much more to my taste. It must be remembered, however, that technological progress makes it *possible* for the economy to grow, without guaranteeing that this growth will be realized.

In a private capitalist society where α cannot be readily changed, a higher level of income and employment at any given time can be achieved only through increased investment. But investment, as an employment creating instrument, is a mixed blessing because of its σ effect. The economy finds itself in a serious dilemma: if sufficient investment is not forthcoming today, unemployment will be here today. But if enough is invested today, still more will be needed tomorrow.

It is a remarkable characteristic of a capitalist economy that while, on the whole, unemployment is a function of the difference between its actual income and its productive capacity, most of the measures (*i.e.*, investment) directed towards raising national income also enlarge productive capacity. It is very likely that the increase in national income will be greater than that of capacity, but the whole problem is that the increase in income is temporary and presently peters out (the usual multiplier effect), while capacity has been increased for good. So that as far as unemployment is

---

[20] See Simon Kuznets, *National Product since 1869*, National Bureau of Economic Research (mimeo., 1945), p. II-89. I do not mean that we must always assume a constant α; rather that we lack sufficient proof to rely on a falling one.

[21] See my paper, *Econometrica*, Vol. XIV, particularly pp. 142-45.

[22] *Cf.* Alvin H. Hansen, *Fiscal Policy and the Business Cycle* (New York, 1941), particularly Part IV.

concerned, investment is at the same time a cure for the disease and the cause of even greater ills in the future.[23]

IV. An Economic Excursion

It may be worth while to browse through the works of several economists of different schools of thought to see their treatment of the σ and of the multiplier effects of investment. It is not suggested to make an exhaustive study, but just to present a few examples.

Thus in Marshall's *Principles* capital and investment are looked upon as productive instruments (the σ effect), with little being said about monetary (that is, income or price) effects of investment.[24] The same attitude prevails in Fisher's *Nature of Capital and Income*,[25] and I presume in the great majority of writings not devoted to the business cycle. It is not that these writers were unaware of monetary effects of investment (even though they did not have the multiplier concept as such), but such questions belonged to a different field, and the problem of aggregate demand was supposed to be taken care of by some variation of Say's Law.

In the business cycle literature we often find exactly an opposite situation. The whole Wicksellian tradition treated economic fluctuations as a result of monetary effects of excessive investment. It is curious that all this investment did not lead to increased output which would counteract its inflationary tendencies. Indeed, as one reads Hayek's *Prices and Production*, one gets an impression that these investment projects never bear fruit and are, moreover, abandoned after the crisis. The σ effect is entirely absent, or at least appears with such a long lag as to make it inoperative. Prosperity comes to an end because the banking system refuses to support inflation any longer.[26]

σ fares better in the hands of Aftalion.[27] His theory of the cycle is based

---

[23] That income generating effects of investment are temporary and that new and larger amounts must be spent to maintain full employment, has been mentioned in economic and popular literature a number of times. Particular use has been made of this fact by opponents of the so-called deficit financing, who treat government expenditures as a "shot in the arm" which must be administered at an ever increasing dose. What they fail to realize is that exactly the same holds true for private investment.

[24] Marshall was very careful, however, to distinguish between the substitution of a particular piece of machinery for particular labor, and the replacement of labor by capital in general. The latter he regarded impossible, because the construction of capital creates demand for labor, essentially a sort of a multiplier effect. See *Principles of Economics*, 8th ed. (London, 1936), p. 523.

[25] Irving Fisher, *The Nature of Capital and Income* (New York, 1919).

[26] Friedrich A. Hayek, *Prices and Production* (London, 1931). I don't mean to say that Professor Hayek is not aware that capital is productive; rather that he did not make use of this fact in his theory of the business cycle. See, however, his "The 'Paradox' of Saving," *Economica*, Vol. XI (May, 1931), pp. 125-69.

[27] Albert Aftalion, "The Theory of Economic Cycles Based on the Capitalistic Technique of Production," *Rev. Econ. Stat.*, Vol. IX (Oct., 1927), pp. 165-70. This short article contains a summary of his theory.

upon, what I would call, a time lag between the multiplier and the σ effects. Prosperity is started by income generated by investment in capital goods (the multiplier effect), while no increase in productive capacity has taken place as yet. As investment projects are completed, the resulting increase in productive capacity (the σ effect) pours goods on the market and brings prosperity to an end.

A similar approach is used by Michal Kalecki. The essence of his model of the business cycle consists in making profit expectations, and therefore investment, a function (with appropriate lags) of the relation between national income and the stock of capital. During the recovery, investment and income rise, while the accumulation of capital lags behind. Presently, however, due to the structure of the model, the rise of income stops while capital continues to accumulate. This precipitates the downswing.[28]

Space does not allow us to analyze the works of a number of other writers on the subject, among whom Foster and Catchings should be given due recognition for what is so clumsy and yet so keen an insight.[29] I am also omitting the whole Marxist literature, in which capital accumulation plays such an important rôle, because that would require a separate study. The few remaining pages of this section will be devoted to Hobson and Keynes.

Hobson's writings contain so many interesting ideas that it is a great pity he is not read more often.[30] Anti-Keynesians probably like him not much more than they do Keynes, while Keynesians are apt to regard the *General Theory* as the quintessence of all that was worth while in economics before 1936, and may not bother to read earlier writings. I may say that Keynes's own treatment of Hobson, in spite of his generous recognition of the latter's works, may have substantiated this impression.[31]

Even though both Keynes and Hobson were students of unemployment, they actually addressed themselves to two different problems. Keynes analyzed what happens when savings (of the preceding period) are not invested. The answer was—unemployment, but the statement of the problem in this form might easily give the erroneous impression that if savings were invested, full employment would be assured. Hobson, on

---

[28] Michal Kalecki, *Essays in the Theory of Economic Fluctuations* (New York, 1939). See particularly the last essay "A Theory of the Business Cycle," pp. 116-49. What Mr. Kalecki's model shows in a general sense is that accumulation of capital cannot proceed for any length of time in a trendless economy (*i.e.*, an economy with a secularly constant income). His other results depend upon the specific assumptions he makes.

[29] William T. Foster and Waddill Catchings, *Profits* (Boston and New York, 1925). This book is the most important of their several published works. It is interesting to note that they did come to the conclusion that ". . . as long as capital facilities are created at a sufficient rate, there need be no deficiency of consumer income. To serve that purpose, however, facilities must be increased at a constantly accelerating rate" (p. 413). This they regarded quite impossible.

[30] I am particularly referring to his *Economics of Unemployment* (London, 1922) and *Rationalization and Unemployment* (New York, 1930).

[31] See *The General Theory*, pp. 364-71.

the other hand, went a step further and stated the problem in this form: suppose savings are invested. Will the new plants be able to dispose of their products? Such a statement of the problem was not at all, as Keynes thought, a mistake.[32] It was a statement of a different, and possibly also a deeper problem.

Hobson was fully armed with the σ effect of investment, and he saw that it could be answered only by growth. His weakness lay in a poor perception of the multiplier effect and his analysis lacked rigor in general. He gave a demonstration rather than a proof. But the problem to which he addressed himself is just as alive today as it was fifty and twenty years ago.[33]

This discussion, as I suspect almost any other, would be obviously incomplete without some mention of Keynes's treatment of the σ and of the multiplier effects. Keynes's approach is very curious: as a matter of fact, he has two: the familiar short-run analysis, and another one which may be called a long-run one.[34]

Keynes's short-run system (later expressed so admiringly by Oscar Lange[35]) is based on ". . . given the existing skill and quantity of available labor, the existing quality and quantity of available equipment, the existing technique, the degree of competition, the tastes and habits of the consumer. . ."[36] Productive capacity thus being given, employment becomes a function of national income, expressed, to be sure, not in money terms but in "wage units." A wage unit, the remuneration for "an hour's employment of ordinary labor" (page 41), is of course a perfect fiction, but some such device must be used to translate real values into monetary and *vice versa*, and one is about as good or as bad as another. The important point for our purposes is the assumption that the amount of equipment (*i.e.*, capital) in existence is given.

Now, the heart of Keynesian economics is the argument that employment depends on income, which in turn is determined by the current volume of investment (and the propensity to save). But investment (in the net sense) is nothing else but the rate of change of capital. Is it legitimate then first to assume the quantity of capital as given, and then base the argument on its rate of change? If the quantity of capital changes, so does (in a typical case) productive capacity, and if the latter changes

---

[32] *Ibid.*, pp. 367-68.

[33] Contrary to popular impression, Hobson does not advocate a maximum reduction in the propensity to save. What he wants is to reduce it to a magnitude commensurable with requirements for capital arising from technological progress—an interesting and reasonable idea.

[34] This whole discussion is based on *The General Theory* and not on Keynes's earlier writings.

[35] Oscar Lange, "The Role of Interest and the Optimum Propensity to Consume," *Economica*, n.s. Vol. V (Feb., 1938), pp. 12-32. This otherwise excellent paper has a basic defect in the assumption that investment is a function of consumption rather than of the rate of change of consumption.

[36] *The General Theory*, p. 245. See also pp. 24 and 28.

it can be hardly said that employment is solely determined by the size of national income, expressed in wage units or otherwise. Or putting it in the language of this paper, is it safe and proper to analyze the relation between investment and employment without taking into account the σ effect?

The answer depends on the nature of the problem in hand. In this particular case, Keynes could present two reasons for his disregard of the σ effect. He could assume that the latter operates with at least a one period lag, the period being understood here as the whole time span covered by the discussion.[37] Or he could argue that over a typical year the net addition (*i.e.*, net investment) to the stock of capital of a society, such as England or the United States, will hardly exceed some 3 or 5 per cent; since this increment is small when compared with changes in income, it can be disregarded.[38]

Both explanations are entirely reasonable provided of course that the period under consideration is not too long. A five-year lag for the σ effect would be difficult to defend, and an increase in the capital stock of some 15 or 20 per cent can hardly be disregarded. I am not aware that Keynes did present either of these explanations; but there is just so much one can do in four hundred pages at any one time.

It would be perfectly absurd to say that Keynes was not aware of the productive qualities of capital. In the *long run* he laid great stress on it, possibly too great. All through the *General Theory* we find grave concern for the diminishing marginal efficiency of capital due, in the long run, to its increasing quantity.[39] There is so much of this kind of argument as to leave the reader puzzled in the end. We are told that marginal efficiency of capital depends on its scarcity. Well and good. But scarcity relative to what? It could become less scarce relative to other factors, such as labor, so that the marginal productivity of capital in the real sense (*i.e.*, essentially our σ) declined. But then on page 213 we read: "If capital becomes less scarce, the excess yield will diminish, without its having become less productive—at least in the physical sense."

Why then does the marginal efficiency of capital fall? Evidently because capital becomes less scarce relative to income.[40] But why cannot income grow more rapidly if labor is not the limiting factor? Could it be only a matter of poor fiscal policy which failed to achieve a faster growing income? After all we have in investment an income generating instrument; if investment grows more rapidly, so does income. This is *the*

---

[37] This again is not quite safe unless some provision for investment projects started in preceding periods and finished during the present period is made.

[38] The second assumption is specifically made by Professor Pigou in his *Employment and Equilibrium* (London, 1941), pp. 33-34.

[39] See for instance pp. 31, 105-106, 217, 219, 220-21, 324, and 375.

[40] There is a third possibility, namely that income is redistributed against the capitalists, but Keynes make no use of it.

multiplier effect of investment on which so much of the *General Theory* is built.

I don't have the answer. Is it possible that, while Keynes disregarded the σ effect in the short-run analysis, he somehow omitted the multiplier effect from the long-run?

V. Concluding Remarks

A traveller who sat in the economic councils of the United States and of the Soviet Union would be much impressed with the emphasis placed on investment and technological progress in both countries. He would happily conclude that the differences between the economic problems of a relatively undeveloped socialist economy and a highly developed capitalist economy are really not as great as they are often made to appear. Both countries want investment and technological progress. But if he continued to listen to the debates, he would presently begin to wonder. For in the Soviet Union investment and technology are wanted in order to enlarge the country's productive capacity. They are wanted essentially as labor-saving devices which would allow a given task to be performed with less labor, thus releasing men for other tasks. In short, they are wanted for their σ effects.

In the United States, on the other hand, little is said about enlarging productive capacity. Technological progress is wanted as the creator of investment opportunities, and investment is wanted because it generates income and creates employment. It is wanted for its multiplier effect.

Both views are correct and both are incomplete. The multiplier is not just another capitalist invention. It can live in a socialist state just as well and it has been responsible for the inflationary pressure which has plagued the Soviet economy all these years, since the first five-year plan. And similarly, σ is just as much at home in one country as in another, and its effect—the enlarged productive capacity brought about by accumulation of capital—has undoubtedly had much to do with our peacetime unemployment.

But what is the solution? Shall we reduce σ to zero and also abolish technological progress thus escaping from unemployment into the "nirvana" of a stationary state? This would indeed be a defeatist solution. It is largely due to technology and savings that humanity has made the remarkable advance of the last two hundred years, and now when our technological future seems so bright, there is less reason to abandon it than ever before.

It is possible that α has been or will be too high as compared with the growth of our labor force, the utilization of new resources, and the development of technology. Unfortunately, we have hardly any empirical data to prove or disprove this supposition. The fact that private investment did not absorb available savings in the past does not prove that they could not be utilized in other ways (*e.g.*, by government), or even that had private business invested them these investments would have been unprofitable; the investing process itself might have created sufficient income to justify the investments. What is needed is a study of the magnitudes of *s*, of the difference between *s* and σ which can develop without much harm and then of the value of α which the economy can digest at its full employment rate of growth.

Even if the resulting magnitude of α is found to be considerably below the existing one, a reduction of α is only one of the two solutions, the speeding up of technological progress being the other. But it must be remembered that neither technology, nor of course saving, guarantee a rise in income. What they do is to place in our hands the *power* and the ability of achieving a growing income. And just as, depending upon the use made of it, any power can become a blessing or a curse, so can saving and technological progress, depending on our economic policies, result in frustration and unemployment or in an ever expanding economy.

33

Second Essay in Dynamic Theory*

ROY HARROD†

Editors' Note

Harrod, like Domar, is associated with more recent developments of the theory of economic growth. In fact, the two are usually linked by references to the Harrod-Domar growth theory. Sir Roy is one of the great English economists, in line with Alfred Marshall, D. F. Robertson, and Lord Keynes, whose definitive biography he has written. Although acknowledging that his approach to growth theory is very similar to Domar's, Harrod argues that it is more general. He distinguishes between a warranted growth rate and a natural growth rate, a distinction which some critics have found confusing. For Harrod, the warranted growth rate occurs where the supply and demand for goods and services are in equilibrium, given the propensity to save. It is the rate of growth which the economy will maintain. (With a warranted growth rate, involuntary unemployment could occur.) If the actual rate of growth is greater than the warranted rate, then the level of investment spending which was formerly appropriate must fall short of the amount needed for the higher level of output. This stimulates the economy, which then moves further away from equilibrium. Any initiating movement that causes a discrepancy between the actual and warranted growth rates results in disequilibrium.

By contrast, the natural growth rate represents the maximum sustainable rate and implies full employment. It is a function of basic forces, such as population growth, capital accumulation, technology, and similar factors. If the natural growth rate differs from the warranted rate, economic dis-

---

* Reprinted from the *Economic Journal*, Vol. LXX, No. 278 (June, 1960), pp. 277-293, by permission of the *Economic Journal* and the author.

† A graduate of Oxford, Roy Harrod (1900-   ) served as statistical adviser to Winston Churchill (1940-42) and the Admiralty (1943-45). In addition to his continuing duties on the Oxford faculty, he was a temporary member of the International Monetary Fund (1952) and joint editor of *The Economic Journal*. He is the author of: *Are These Hardships Necessary?* (1947); *Towards a Dynamic Economics* (1948); *Life of J. M. Keynes* (1951); *Economic Essays* (1952); *The Dollar* (1953); and *Foundations of Inductive Logic* (1956).

equilibrium, with a tendency to depression or to inflation, occurs. For Harrod, public policy consists in bringing the warranted rate as close as possible to the natural rate of growth.

Harrod's first essay in dynamic theory apeared in March, 1939, while Domar's first major contribution to growth literature (see p. 566) was published in 1947. Since that time a vast body of work on economic growth has been written, amplifying and modifying these two main contributions. This article represents a further extension by one of the originators. It introduces the rate of interest as a fundamental concept in dynamic economics. Harrod's new equation is concerned with linking the interest rate to the warranted growth rate.

While the Domar and Harrod articles represent major theoretical advances, they are couched in fairly simple terms. Their significance, however, lies in the light which they shed on the present economic problem of growth, particularly since the Russian growth rate seems to be so much larger than those of the United States and Western Europe. First, the process of reaching full employment must be fully understood. Second, methods for sustaining this condition must be comprehended. Economic models like those of Harrod have proved useful in these two respects.

There is also wide agreement that such models have to be supplemented by empirical analysis which quantitatively evaluates the important factors affecting growth. Just as the Keynesian consumption function was later subjected to elaborate statistical verification, so growth theories must be subjected to empirical testing. This testing is now taking place, with regard to developed economies as well as underdeveloped ones. In the process, we are learning more about the basic forces which make for growth, such as the quality of the labor force, the size and composition of the capital stock, the role of education, institutional arrangements for channeling saving into investment, the role of government policy, the significance of technology, and the importance of basic and applied research. We are also learning about the difficulties which surround a conscious effort to accelerate economic growth.

❧ 1. I am offering this article[1] as a companion piece to one that appeared rather a long time ago and contained a form of equation, which has since become fairly well known.[2] I am now presenting a second form of equation, and submit that the two together provide the inner core of the dynamic theory of an insulated economy.[3] Demand and supply are essentially static

---

[1] I am grateful to Mr. M. F. G. Scott for certain helpful suggestions.

[2] "An Essay in Dynamic Theory," *Economic Journal*, March 1939.

[3] The dynamics of foreign trade and investment, on which Prof. H. Johnson and others have been doing notable work, must be an important part of the total theory.

concepts and not strictly applicable in dynamic analysis. But in a certain sense the equation in the previous article may be regarded as a dynamic analogue of the static law of demand; if that is allowed, the equation in this article may be regarded as an analogue of the static law of supply.

2. I do not hold that the two equations constitute what is called a "model," any more than the laws of demand and supply taken together constitute a model. Rather they should be thought of as laws expressing certain necessary relations. They are not, of course, necessary in the sense of being *a priori*, for in that case they would be empty and uninformative. They are empirical, but necessary in the sense that they flow necessarily from postulating certain very general facts in the human situation, themselves known empirically, such as the existence of a multiplicity of needs and the availability of an insufficient amount of productive resources, which can be applied to alternative uses,[4] notably to present or future satisfactions. They are prolegomena to model building. In attempting to construct a model we seek to enter more deeply into the empirical phenomena. I believe that a model can properly be distinguished from a set of fundamental laws by the presence in the former of certain adjustable parameters.

3. There has been some terminological hesitation between the use of "dynamics" and "growth theory" in relation to certain matters. I believe that a distinction can be made, and that it would be convenient to use "dynamic theory" for the relations between the rates of increase (or decrease) of certain magnitudes in a growing economy. The theory of economic growth would have a wider ambit, including dynamic theory in this narrow sense. It would comprise also such matters as the sociological effects of the impact of economic progress, the contribution of the social pattern to it, the contribution of education, both general and technological, the need for political security, the usefulness of greater or less governmental intervention in successive phases, the development of moral codes, etc. For instance, there are wise men who hold that the prevalence of graft is the greatest single obstacle to growth in some developing countries. In fine, growth economics would then constitute the "political economy" of growth, while dynamic theory would be its pure economics.

4. My original equation has been criticised for excessive rigidity, notably for not allowing for the possibility of substitution in the productive process as between capital and other factors. In my *Essay* I used the term C for the optimum amount of capital required per unit of time, given current technology, for the output of an extra unit, and C_p for the actual accretion of extra capital per unit of extra output. In my book, *Towards a Dynamic Economics*, I used C_r for the optimum amount of capital required, reserving C for the amount that actually occurred. This latter symbolism seems better, and I shall adhere to it in what follows. It is argued that the value of C_r must depend on the rate of interest, and that consequently what I

---

[4] Cf. Lionel Robbins, *Nature and Significance of Economic Science*, Chapter 1, p. 15.

have called the "natural" and "warranted" rates of growth are so dependent. Recognition of this, it is claimed, could have far-reaching effects on the analysis.

5. In self-defence I may observe that I did recognise this dependence in the *Essay*. "The value of C_r may be somewhat dependent on the rate of interest" (p. 17). If I did not develop the implication of this any further, that was mainly owing to the maxim of attempting to do only one thing at a time. I must confess, however, that I was also somewhat influenced by the view, which was prevalent in those days, that producers were but little influenced by the rate of interest in their choice of more or less capital-intensive methods of production. When entrepreneurs reported that, owing to the risks of the market or of obsolescence, a piece of equipment was normally expected to pay itself off in four or five years, how could variations in the interest rate within the range commonly experienced have any appreciable effect? This was doubtless too sceptical. Even at that time it was recognised that the rate of interest had influence on long-lasting capital installations. Since then I have been much impressed with the significance of the imperfection of the capital market. The rate of interest should be regarded as the barometric reading in that limited part of the market which is perfect (organised stock exchange, discount market, etc.). When capital disposal is short, the perfect markets record high readings; but for many the shortage impinges on them simply by would-be borrowers finding it difficult to raise money. Accordingly, a wrong impression may be gained by putting the question to producers in the form—are you influenced by the rate of interest? This implies a nice calculation, balancing a rate of interest of so and so much against an expected yield of the projected assets on their cost of production. Many of the producers who deny ever making such a calculation may none the less be influenced for or against a more capital-intensive re-deployment of their productive set-up by whether the required finance is easy or difficult to obtain. In any case, a theory which makes no allowance for the possible variation in C_r in response to the abundance or shortage of capital disposal is defective in principle. It is now sought to remedy this defect.

6. In my equation for warranted growth, which it is convenient to repeat,

$$G_w = \frac{s}{C_r}$$

s, the fraction of income saved, is taken as an independent variable. Its value is assumed to depend on the private convenience of many individuals, on the desires of many firms to finance themselves from their own ploughed-back profits, etc. This assumption of the independence of s is appropriate in its context. Indeed, the fact that the "warranted" rate of growth may not be equal to the "natural" rate depends precisely on the assumption that private motives may not yield the amount of saving that complies nicely with the needs of the society; they may generate too much or too little saving. The Keynesian origin of this idea is obvious. Natural growth (G_n) by contrast is conceived as a welfare optimum, in which resources are fully employed and the best available technology used. With natural growth so conceived, the amount to be saved becomes a "requirement," which may be greater or less than the actual s. But is not this "natural" rate itself indeterminate, unless the rate of interest is specified? There is clearly a lacuna in the theory.

7. I have to ask the reader in what follows to subject himself to a certain discipline, which may not be altogether easy. I regard the fundamental concept in dynamic economics as the rate of increase, just as the state of rest is that of statics. It is the rate of increase that obtains *at a given point of time*, given the fundamental determinants. In dynamics, or at least in Part I of dynamics—and I do not think that we can yet get beyond that—we are not, according to my view, concerned with a succession of events through time. The analogy with mechanics is, surely, precise. There we seek to determine the velocity of a particle in consequence of the forces acting upon it at a particular instant. Thereafter it may become subject to new forces. The dynamic determinants of economic progress change from time to time, and the consequence of such changes will have to be considered in due course. But, to begin with, we need to determine the rate of increase at one point. This is but applying in the realm of dynamics the procedure so well known, and, I would say, fruitful, in the theory of static equilibrium. It has always been recognised that the determinants of that equilibrium (desires of individuals, etc.) are constantly changing; none the less, it has been found serviceable to establish the equilibrium pattern required by a given set of determinants. I am convinced that we must do this in dynamics also, as an essential prelude to all else. Edgeworth once said of general value theory that "the path is short, but very slippery." If this is true of dynamics also, as is surely the case, we must proceed carefully, step by step. One consequence of this method of initial approach to dynamics is that time-lags do not appear in the equations.

8. This article is unlike the earlier *Essay* in that it will lead into the subject by reference to the welfare optimum. I believe that on a broad historic view we find that attention to the welfare optimum played a vital part in the formulation of static equilibrium theory. This may be a good precedent.

9. The second lecture in the course published as *Towards a Dynamic Economics* is called the *Supply of Saving*. This contrasts with the title of the third lecture, *Fundamental Dynamic Theorems*, and suggests, correctly, that what I had to say about saving could not be regarded as an integral part of dynamic theory. The *Supply of Saving* contains an equation (p. 42) which has been found, justifiably, somewhat obscure. The matter was rendered worse by inaccurate notation in the earlier editions. I will set it out in its most convenient form; the reader need not trouble himself, at this stage, about its justification, which will appear later. C_0 is

consumption in year o, C_r is consumption in year r, e is the elasticity of the schedule of the diminishing utility of income in its relevant range, T is "time preference" expressed in the form that, if a given unit of utility in year r is considered only half as preferable as the same unit of utility in year o, $T^r = 0.5$, and R^r is the amount of money to which 1 unit will have accumulated in r years at the current rate of interest.

$$C_r = C_0 + e\left(1 - \frac{1}{T^r R^r}\right)$$

In formulating this I was much influenced by F. P. Ramsey's famous article entitled "A Mathematical Theory of Saving."[5]

10. Ramsey's article contains a concept which he calls "Bliss," namely, "the maximum obtainable rate of enjoyment or utility." This concept is unsatisfactory for two reasons. It is unsatisfactory for dynamics, because Bliss is essentially a static concept. It is also unsatisfactory for any kind of welfare economics, because Ramsey's technique requires a comparison of the total utility achieved at "Bliss" with total and marginal utilities currently achieved, and this is manifestly altogether impracticable.

11. In my lecture on the *Supply of Saving* I gave a second equation, based on the assumption that it could be foreseen that the globe would be vaporised by a nuclear explosion n years hence. This second equation, along with n equations of the form given above, would suffice to determine the values of all the terms. Thus the Explosion would take the place of Bliss in governing the correct rate of saving. I next proceeded to some more realistic observations about a man's probable attitude to his own life and to his heirs. It was obvious that no precise theory could be based on such vague psychological speculations. Thus the matter lapsed, and my discourse on the supply of savings did not yield anything that could be included among the "fundamental dynamic theorems."

12. Although I had warned myself and others in the *Essay* that the formulation of a dynamic theory "involves something wider: a method of thinking, a way of approach to certain problems,"[6] I was still so deeply rooted in static ways of thought, when I composed the Lectures, that I did not perceive that I had under my nose what was really a dynamic equation. As Keynes observed, in relation to a different problem, namely that of his *General Theory*, it is exceedingly difficult to wrench oneself from the habits of thought in which one has been educated.

13. I now set out my "second" equation, derived from my abortive attempt, based on Ramsey, in the lecture on the Supply of Saving. Its demonstration is given in the following paragraphs. I would venture to suggest that its *simplicity* entitles it to be regarded as a fundamental equation. Let r_n be the rate of interest appropriate to a natural (welfare optimum) rate of growth, and $_{pc}G_n$ the natural rate of growth *per caput*.

---

[5] *Economic Journal*, December 1928.
[6] *Op. cit.*, p. 15.

$$r_n = \frac{p_0 G_n}{e}$$

This dispenses us both from having to have regard to "Bliss" or from having to make arbitrary assumptions about what a man may feel that he ought to do for his heirs.

14. The equation supplied in para. 9 above is based on the proposition set out in *Towards a Dynamic Economics* (p. 45) that the individual's distribution of his consumption between year 0 and year 1, in equilibrium, is given by

$$u(C_0) = RT \times u(C_1)$$

where $u(C)$ is the marginal utility of consumption. This signifies that, given the rate of interest and the time preference, consumption is so arranged that no re-distribution of it from year 0 to year 1, or conversely, would increase utility (as modified by time preference). Define, for the sake of simplicity, e as

$$e = \frac{C_1 - C_0}{C_1} \div - \frac{u(C_1) - u(C_0)}{u(C_1)} \,{}^{7}$$

Represent $\dfrac{C_1 - C_0}{C_1}$ by $G(\text{con})$

Reducing the above, it follows that, in equilibrium

$$RT - 1 = \frac{G(\text{con})}{e}$$

15. The equilibrium of static economics implies that saving is zero. A steady rate of increase implies that a constant fraction of income is saved. If the fraction of income saved is increasing or decreasing, that implies an accelerating or decelerating increase of income. Accordingly, in the equation representing the rate of increase at a point of time it should be assumed that a constant fraction of income is saved. Thus for the equation last given we may substitute:

In equilibrium, $$RT - 1 = \frac{G}{e} \qquad \ldots \ldots \ldots \ldots (1)$$

This equation defines the equilibrium behaviour for an individual, if we abstract from his employment pattern (retirement in old age, etc.), and assume a constant rate of growth of his income. If we translate this into an equation representing the situation of the community as a whole, e must be a weighted average of the e's proper to each individual in it,

---

[7] The difference between this definition and $e = \dfrac{C_1 - C_0}{C_0} \div - \dfrac{u(C_1) - u(C_0)}{u(C_0)}$ disappears when the matter is expressed in terms of differential equations.

subject to the abstractions of the last sentence. This assumes a constant income distribution. This assumption is simply carried over from the welfare optimum of static economics, where the income distribution is taken as given. Ultimately, we should be able to accommodate a steadily changing distribution of income in dynamic theory; this would (or might) entail a steadily changing rate of growth. (It is quite possible, however, the e does not differ much as between rich and poor.) With e thus re-defined, we can transform equation (1) into a community equation, in which $_{pc}G$ represents the growth of income *per caput*.

In equilibrium,
$$RT - 1 = \frac{_{pc}G}{e} \quad ^8 \qquad \dots \dots \dots \quad (2)$$

This has its own importance and should be borne in mind in what follows.

16. We may now go over to the "natural" (or welfare optimum) rate of growth. This may be regarded as, in the main (see below), exogenously determined, viz., by the growth of population and technological advance. This includes the rate of growth of skilled personnel, however obtained, *e.g.*, by governmental measures. If we are considering the welfare optimum, we should write, $T = 1$. There ought not to be a time preference! Any authority concerned with planning should, presumably, disregard it. Putting $r (= R - 1)$ for the rate of interest, we then have

$$r_n = \frac{_{pc}G_n}{e} \qquad \dots \dots \dots \quad (I)$$

In other words,

$$r_n = \frac{G_n}{e} \Big/ G_{Pop}$$

where G_{Pop} is the rate of growth of the working population.

17. As G_n is (in the main) exogenously determined, and as e certainly is, equation (I) should be regarded as stating what determines the natural rate of interest.

18. It may be objected that G_n is itself determined by the rate of interest, so that there are two dependent variables in equation (I). This must be recognised, subject to the important warnings given below, and, to accommodate the matter, we may have a second equation, showing the dependence of the natural growth rate on the rate of interest thus:

$$_{pc}G_n - f(r_n) \text{ (decreasing or increasing function)} \quad \dots \dots \quad (Ia)$$

19. There is an inclination to suppose that G_n would be greater, the lower the rate of interest. As a generalisation, this is fallacious, and due to a confusion of dimensions, which it should be the first task of a "dynamic economics" to prevent. The confusion arises from regard to two quite different propositions, as follows: (i) If the rate of interest is low, more

---

[8] In the community equation T also must be taken to represent a weighted average.

capital-intensive methods of production will be chosen by the producer, or more capital-intensive products will be preferred (because cheaper) by the consumer, than if it is high. The capital/output ratio will be higher. This means that, given the population and other factors (natural resources, trained personnel, etc.), output per person will be higher. It need hardly be said that higher production does not entail a higher growth rate. (Often the contrary!) (ii) If employment (including employment of skilled personnel) is not full, a drop in the rate of interest can increase it. While unemployed resources are coming into operation, G (actual growth rate) can exceed G_n. It need hardly be said that this does not entail a higher G_n either. It is quite an open question whether G_n will be higher or lower with a lower rate of interest. All depends on the nature of the technological innovations. If these are concentrated on substitute modes of production or substitute products where the yields on the modes and products for which they are substitutes are low, then the low-interest-rate economy will show a higher growth rate than the high-interest one. It will have the opportunity of taking advantage of a number of innovations which the high-interest economy has simply to ignore because, for it, they are outside the range of paying propositions. But if the innovations are such that the substituted processes or products were previously a long way inside the margin of substitution, the reverse may well be true. Compare two economies A and B of the same population increase, of which A uses more capital-intensive methods because its growth *per caput* and its natural interest rate are lower. A consequently has a higher income per head. Let there be an innovation available to both economies, which both will unquestionably adopt, because it is so manifestly high yielding. Thus for both it will cause the same increase in income in the sectors affected. But, because A is initially a higher-income economy, the growth entailed by this innovation will be greater in B, the high-interest country. Finally, there is the point that a *falling*, as distinct from a low, rate of interest could promote *per caput* growth. A falling *natural* rate of interest is a phenomenon of declining growth *per caput* (see para. 25). A fall in the interest rate from a supra-natural level towards its natural level is discussed in paras. 35-8 below.

20. The main objection to equation (I) is the difficulty of computing *e*. It is supposed on general grounds to be less than 1. On the other hand, it would probably be wrong to suppose it *much less* than 1, since this would give an unrealistic decline in the marginal utility of income in the ranges of which we have experience. It would follow that the rate of interest ought to be above, but not much above, the growth rate *per caput*.

21. In *Towards a Dynamic Economics* (pp. 43-4) I suggested a method for measuring *e*. I proposed to take the eighth hour of work (or the sixtieth minute of the eighth hour) as a yardstick of constant disutility for a given individual. By appropriate conjoint variations in his basic rate of pay and his marginal rate (for the last hour or last minute thereof), and by allowing him freedom to vary the time worked, one could find out what

increase in the marginal rate sufficed to keep him working exactly eight hours, neither more nor less, as his total income rose owing to an increase in the basic rate. It has been objected to this that a rise in income might make him find more utility in leisure, so that the sixtieth minute of the eighth hour would cease to be a yardstick of unvarying disutility, but would conflate the actual toil of work with the disutility of foregoing leisure, the latter rising as income grew. This objection could readily be overcome by varying the conditions of the experiment. Let us suppose the length of the working day not subject to variation, so that the rising utility of leisure, with higher income, became irrelevant. Let us suppose a piece-rate superimposed upon a basic rate, both variable. The target output, say 100 pieces, should be fixed so that it was quite a considerable effort to achieve it. What increase in piece-rates would be required to induce the man to produce exactly 100 pieces, neither more nor less, as his income went up owing to successive rises in his basic rate? This seems to give an inexpugnable yardstick for cardinal measurement of the rate of decline in the utility of income as income rises.

22. I have suggested applying the experiment to one individual to avoid interpersonal comparison. It will be objected that a single individual's reactions to changes of income—not known to be permanent, if this is a mere experiment—would be quite unreliable. In practice, of course, one would make the experiment with a *large number* of different individuals, who were normally on different income scales owing to their position in the factory hierarchy, and would rely on the large number to overcome differences of personal temperament from man to man. This is the way in which things are commonly done in the natural sciences. Of course, no such measurement could be relied on to be 100% accurate. It is impossible to get measurements of *perfect* accuracy in physics—I am not speaking of quantum physics—or in chemistry. The practitioners of those sciences would not have done so well if they had decided in consequence from the beginning to use no cardinal numbers in the formulation of physical and chemical laws. This is true of economics also.

23. It is next necessary to draw the threads together. The "supply" equation, which should be regarded as determining the natural rate of interest, is

$$r_n = \frac{{}_{pc}G_n}{e} \qquad \ldots \ldots \ldots \text{(I)}$$

where G_n is taken to be an almost entirely independent variable, but possibly depending to a slight degree upon the rate of interest:

$$_{pc}G_n = f(r_n) \text{ (increasing or decreasing function)} \quad \ldots \ldots \text{(I}a\text{)}$$

The capital intensity of methods used for increments of production, and of the basketful of goods selected by consumers for their additional purchases, depends on the rate of interest:

$$C_r = f(r_n) \text{ (decreasing function)} \quad \ldots \ldots \text{(II)}$$

This equation should satisfy objectors who complain that I took no account of the substitutability of capital for other factors in my earlier equation. And finally, to repeat the equation from the earlier *Essay* in a somewhat different form,

$$s_r = C_r G_n \qquad \ldots \ldots \ldots \quad \text{(III)}$$

By this formulation the fraction of income to be saved becomes a *desideratum*, s_r.

24. Two points may be made in passing. In equation (III) the required amount of saving is stated as depending on the amount of capital required for the increment of output. But technical progress may alter, and often increase, the amount of replacement capital required per unit of output; it may also raise the required rate of replacements by rendering obsolete equipment hitherto expected to have a longer life. To take account of this it will be needful to re-work the theory that has been outlined in *gross* terms. This task is not attempted here.

25. This article is concerned with a steady shift of the "production function" outwards from the origin. It is not implied that the successive functions, moving outwards with time, are parallel to each other; the analysis has been consistent with innovations being neutral, labour saving or capital saving. Some students of growth have laid stress on the phenomenon of a movement *along* the productivity function in consequence, not of innovations, but of a rise in the ratio of capital to other factors due to the accrual of fresh saving. Such a movement implies a falling rate of interest (by Equation (II)). A falling natural rate of interest implies a falling natural rate of growth *per caput* (by Equation (I)), save in the event of e increasing, which seems improbable. Thus a shift along the production function, as distinct from a movement outwards of the production function, should occur only in periods when the rate of technical progress is falling. Such a shift may ensure that the rate of growth *per caput* does not fall as quickly as the rate of technical progress. None the less, it is essentially a phenomenon of a falling natural rate of growth.

26. To return to our main theme: it might be thought that, since e is a weighted average, s, the fraction of income actually saved would tend to approximate to s_r, the social requirement. There are a number of reasons why this may not be so, of which I will mention only the most outstanding. (i) T may be less, indeed much less, than 1, especially in developing societies. This would tend to depress saving. (ii) Individuals have their own youth–maturity–old-age patterns, which might cause them to save more or less than they would, if each was immortal and had an income continually growing at the same rate as the weighted average of incomes *per caput* for the economy. (iii) Companies save importantly. It would be wrong to suppose that these shape their policies to conform to the saving patterns required by the weighted average of their shareholders, or that the shareholders treat company savings as in effect their own, and save correspondingly less for themselves. Companies have their own motives,

some springing from the long run; they may desire to expand capacity without the forfeit of power or the expense involved in relying on the capital market for fresh funds. The shareholder, on his side, cannot be sure when the companies will distribute the profit on their ploughed-back savings, nor can those who determine current share values in the organised market for shares.

27. To revert to the terminology of the earlier *Essay*, the warranted rate of growth is above the natural growth rate, if actual saving (s) exceeds the required rate of saving (s_r), and conversely. While the natural rate of growth is determined almost entirely exogenously in relation to the variables of the equations and is therefore taken to *require* a specified amount of saving (s_r), the warranted rate of growth is taken to be determined by the actual rate of saving (s). Let us take the two cases, viz., an excess or deficiency of s compared with s_r, in turn.

28. If $s > s_r$, then we have the situation which Keynes diagnosed and about which he feared, along with other proponents of the "stagnation thesis." The warranted rate is then greater than the natural rate; but the actual rate cannot exceed the natural rate save for temporary phases. The natural rate is indeed the greatest that can be achieved on the long haul.[9] If the actual rate of growth is retarded by the full-employment ceiling, then it must fall below the warranted rate and a depression will set in.[10] Or a downturn can come, for reasons explained in an earlier article,[11] before the full-employment ceiling is reached, if producers correctly believe that demand cannot continue to expand indefinitely above the natural rate, viz., at its rate in the recent past. The special circumstances of the post-war period have caused us to think less about the dangers of "stagnation"; but they may still be lurking, especially if the maximum feasible rate of investment in developing countries proves to be disappointing.

29. A suggested recipe for the threat of stagnation, in addition to stimulating all kinds of public investment, or other investments the utility of which might be reckoned to exceed their monetary yields, is a Budget Deficit. As Political Economists we should not wish to discourage the propensity to save. It may be useful to have a high propensity to save deeply ingrained, in case times should change. Furthermore, the ownership of some capital funds gives a man a special kind of happiness and a sense of freedom. Without property we remain, although not in so severe a sense as Marx may have intended, wage slaves. Ownership promotes a spirit of independence. And so, if it happens that the sum total of citizens

---

[9] It has been suggested to me that this is not *necessarily* true, since, if the rate of interest were pushed and kept down *below* its natural level, a rate of growth above the natural level could in certain circumstances be sustained. This possibility must be recognised. It must be borne in mind, however, that a below-natural rate of interest may equally well be associated with a *lower*, as with a higher, rate of growth (cf. p. 591 *sup.*).

[10] This is in accordance with the instability principle, as described in the first *Essay*, and I need not revert to it in this one.

[11] "Domar and Dynamic Economics," *Economic Journal*, September 1959.

desire to hold, in the form of savings available for future use, a value greater than the sum total of the capital value of the land, buildings, equipment, work in progress, stock-in-trade, etc., that the community requires, the Government should provide reliable savings certificates. It is essential, of course, that in such a situation it should treat the proceeds of the sale of such certificates as income and remit taxation accordingly, with a view to sustaining the aggregate of demand for goods and services at a level conformable to the growth potential of the economy.

30. I made a cardinal mistake in *Towards a Dynamic Economics*, owing to still being sunk in static slumber. It occurred to me that, if saving were really so plentiful that the Government had to take a surplus off the market and plough it back into current expenditure, the logical corollary of such a state of affairs was that the rate of interest should be zero. If interest is the charge for a scarce factor, the economic function of which is to prevent capital being used for low-yielding projects and ensure that enough exists for all the higher-yielding projects, what need was there to have a positive rate of interest when revenue-yielding projects for capital outlay were so short that one had to plough saving back into public expenditure on current account? This point of view is plausible enough.

But in the light of equation (I) it is seen to be wrong. If $\dfrac{_{pc}G}{e} = 3$, it does not increase community welfare to plough savings into projects that yield less than 3%. We do not want by investment to transfer goods away from present consumption to consumption in subsequent years, if the investment increases the quantum of goods available in the subsequent years by no more than 2%. For the marginal utility of goods will in any case be down by 3% in the next year and by more later; therefore we do not want to give up the enjoyment of goods now unless we thereby get at least 3% more goods in subsequent years. Therefore the maintenance of a positive rate of interest is not inconsistent with the desirability of ploughing back some savings into current government expenditure, not merely in depression, but on the overall average year by year, providing that productivity per head is still growing. A positive rate of interest should be maintained, even when some savings are being made available to the general body of citizens for current expenditure, in order to prevent savings being ploughed into investments the yield of which is less than the current natural rate of interest, $\dfrac{_{pc}G_n}{e}$. The rate of interest should fall to zero only if output per head ceases to grow and $_{pc}G/e$ becomes zero.

31. If $s < s_r$ the economy may have a chronic tendency to inflation. This occurred for a number of years in mature countries after the Second World War, and it may explain the persistent tendency to inflation in some Latin American countries. For such inflation to occur there is no need for there to be any increase in banking credits; the excess investment, if it occurs, is automatically financed by the excess (inflationary) profits due to

the investment. This is a crucial point that divides anti-Keynesians from Keynesians, in the dwindling band of whom I would still align myself. None the less, I would not go so far as to hold that in these circumstances (viz. $s < s_r$) an inflationary tendency *necessarily* develops. The realisation of excess investment seems to imply, not indeed an increase in banking credit, but an accommodating spirit in the capital market. Developing countries may have a very narrow domestic capital market, or none, save for a tribe of "usurers" lending at exorbitant rates. In mature countries investors can usually pre-arrange finance, even if the total amount so arranged is running ahead of normal savings, *i.e.*, if there is excess of *ex ante* investment; if they do so and proceed on their business the aggregate of savings that they require will become available *en courant* through the inflationary process. But where capital markets are narrow or non-existent it may be impossible to make these pre-arrangements; the inflationary finance will not be generated and the investments will not be undertaken. Lack of saving will prevent the growth that would otherwise be possible.

32. It may be well to dwell a little longer on this point. The Keynesian scheme of thought had an attractive symmetry. If the propensity to save was excessive in relation to the propensity to invest, there would be a lapse into depression and unemployment. In the converse case there would be over-full demand and inflation; this second proposition seemed well confirmed by experiences in war-time and, to a lesser extent, during industrial investment booms. But somehow it has never seemed very plausible in relation to developing countries. There over-full demand does not usually arise in consequence of a deficiency of saving. In fact, the tendency of deficient saving to generate over-full demand must not be taken as a general law, but one dependent on the existence of an accommodating capital market, which allows the process by which excess investment generates the saving required for it (by the inflationary process) to get under weigh. Nor would the introduction of easy finance into developing countries be a satisfactory recipe, since inflation is something to be avoided and likely to militate against growth in the long run.[12] The true view surely is that, to obtain the optimum rate of growth, which is also in some sense a maximum, saving must be neither redundant nor deficient.

33. It is necessary to look closely at the equation, $s_r - C_r G_n$ when $s < s_r$. It might be thought that the dearth of savings would push the rate of interest up so high as to reduce C_r to a level at which G_n could be sustained. But this may not be so. C_r may not be very responsive, outside certain limits, to a high interest rate. Even if it is, there is no guarantee that it is sufficiently responsive and, more important, no guarantee that the brunt of the shortage of savings will be borne by C_r rather than by G, which can fall below G_n. If the actual growth (G) falls short of the natural growth (G_n), the demand for goods will be deficient and the shortage of savings

---

[12] See Ohlinschrift, *Inflation and Investment in Under-developed Countries*, by R. F. Harrod (1959).

will not be apparent. If, owing to the lack of demand for goods, producers do not expand orders, G will be low and there will not be inflation nor a felt shortage of savings nor any tendency for the rate of interest to rise.[13]

34. It is desirable to surround any remarks about developing countries by qualifications. The major obstacle to growth may well be lack of personnel or, to revert to a point mentioned earlier, graft. The concept of natural growth embodies not only technological progress but also the increase of personnel well adapted to enterprise and business management, and the increase of know-how, whether natural or artificially stimulated. Shortages in these respects may account for a low growth rate, rather than any deficiency of s, compared with s_r. If, on grounds of personnel and know-how, a rapid growth is not feasible, s_r will be low, and s, though low, may not fall short of it.

35. None the less, it is desirable to consider the case where s is below s_r and where inflation does not occur because the capital market is insufficiently accommodating. In such a case, to obtain the social optimum, it may be expedient to raise s towards the level of s_r by a budget surplus or compulsory levy. If such measures are introduced *for the first time*, or abruptly intensified, there will follow what we may call a "transitional period." If actual growth has been running below natural growth, solely by reason of the shortage of saving, this entails that there is some underemployment or mis-employment of general or special personnel; output may be low because the capital/output ratio is low owing to the time preference being high (T low). If it were decided to take some action to remedy this state of affairs by causing more saving, then the economy would proceed through a transitional period in which actual growth was above natural growth, owing to the harnessing of previously underemployed personnel and/or owing to the increase of the capital/output ratio in various sectors of the economy, through the reduction of the operative rate of interest towards r_n.

36. The features of such a transitional period lie for the most part outside the scope of the analysis of this paper. But some general remarks may be made. Since growth during the transitional period would be above the natural rate, which implies continuing full employment, the equilibrium rate of interest, assuming $T = 1$, during the transitional period (let us call it r_{tn}), would lie above r_n. Often the ruling rate of interest in developing countries, if there be such, is above r_n owing to the low value of T. Cf. equation (2) (p. 595). On the other hand, the equilibrium rate in such countries is kept down by the low rate of growth. Thus it might, in certain conditions, be expedient to establish, during the transitional period, a rate of interest above that previously obtaining. This may seem a paradoxical

---

[13] It will be evident to the judicious reader that this point, although entirely outside the ambit of Keynes' theories, is profoundly influenced by his mode of thought. It is analogous, within the realm of dynamics and in reverse, to Keynes' point that, if the *propensity* to save is excessive, causing depression, there will not be any felt excess of saving nor tendency for the rate of interest to fall.

accompaniment of the imposition of forced saving. But if the special measures taken raise the prospective growth rate, this will temporarily raise the natural rate of interest (r_{tn}) (equation (I)), and may raise it above the rate previously obtaining, except in economies where T is very low. In a developing economy there may be two rates, the high open-market rate, such as it is, largely governed by the low value of T, and a lower rate used to sieve official investment projects. It is important that the latter be kept high, to ensure the maximum rate of growth and prevent capital being deflected into low-yielding projects.

37. It is often stated that developing countries, which are short of capital, should concentrate on labour-intensive projects. This dictum can be accepted only with reserve. Its intellectual basis is presumably that, if $s < C_r G_n$, and if measures are taken to raise s, it is important that the accretion of s should benefit growth rather than C_r. All depends on how great the shortfall of s (by comparison with s_r) is in relation to available personnel and know-how. There is a danger of this shortage being exaggerated if constant attention is not paid to personnel and know-how. If the shortage is not great and if it is feasible within a relatively short term of years to bring capital disposal up to the level required, having regard to available resources of personnel and know-how, then the criterion for investment should be its *yield* and not whether it is capital-intensive or labour-intensive.

38. While it is true that the arrangement for extra saving in a developing country may give rise to a substantial "transitional" period, there is some danger of exaggerating its importance. If at a given point of time, t_o, growth is running below its natural rate through lack of saving, this implies that there is available personnel to implement improved methods of production, including those arising simply from an increase in the capital/output ratio. It is the process of bringing this personnel into fuller play that constitutes the "transitional" period. But there is not likely to be at t_o more than a limited fund of such personnel to spare; once that is taken up, "transitional" growth is merged into ordinary natural growth. It is quite true that, if in the country in question growth has been held back for a number of years owing to deficient saving, its current output at t_o may be far below the level, let us call it O_n, at which it would have been, if growth had been proceeding at its natural rate in the preceding years. It by no means follows that an arrangement for extra saving at and after t_o can raise output to O_n at once or during the "transitional" period. For natural growth *per caput* occurs through the cumulative accretion of experience and know-how and the improvement of personnel. *Lost years cannot be regained in full*. The very essence of growth (*per caput*) is education by practice and the gradual drawing out of the latent potentialities of personnel. *Vires acquirit eundo*. From t_o onwards it is to be expected that, with the provision of more saving, growth will be raised to a higher level, namely to its natural level, the height of which depends essentially on the capacity

of the population to improve itself.[14] The compulsory provision of extra saving should be regarded as releasing the growth potential of the community from bondage. It is important to avoid over-simplified ideas about the consequences of the mere provision of additional saving. This view might be regarded as pessimistic, in that it sets a limit to what can be done by one simple recipe (more saving); but it is optimistic in that it enables us to curb the impulses of those who believe that Utopia can be gained solely by the imposition of harsh austerity.

39. In mature economies also s may fall short of s_r, and this may generate demand inflation, as already noticed. But the authorities may and should seek to prevent demand inflation. Their problem is complicated by the superimposition of cycles on the trend. During the boom all available measures, monetary, fiscal and others, may be needed to damp demand. Monetary measures are probably quicker-working than fiscal. Similarly, all available measures may be needed to prevent a recession gathering momentum. What should be the trend of policy, taking bad times and good together, when actual saving is running below the required level?

40. Keynes and others have held the view that the current long-term rate of interest can be influenced by varying the quantity of money. This has been strikingly borne out by the British experience since the War. Keynes explicitly repudiated the idea of a natural rate of interest. Both Professor Hicks and Sir Dennis Robertson have reproached him for this, the former saying that he left the rate of interest hanging by its own bootstraps,[15] and the latter making a similar point in a brilliant passage—claiming that we have, after all, to give it an anchorage in the fundamental phenomena of Productivity and Thrift.[16] Despite Keynes' disclaimers, I have always held that there is a "natural" rate of interest implicit in the doctrines of the *General Theory of Employment, Interest and Money*, namely that required to sustain investment and aggregate demand at the full-employment, and at no more than the full-employment, level. If we ask what are the determinants of the value of that "natural" rate of interest in Keynesian theory, the answer must be the Propensity to Invest and the Propensity to Save, the latter determining the value of the "Multiplier." But these are only other names for Productivity and Thrift; so that it turns out that the classical doctrine finds its place in Keynesian doctrine. Keynes was, after all, bred up in that tradition.

41. But the natural rate of interest of the dynamic theory expounded in this article, and by that is simply meant the rate of interest that it is necessary to have if the economy is to advance at the optimum rate in accordance with its growth potential, is determined by the prospective growth of income and the elasticity of the community income utility

---

[14] This is subject to the limitation imposed on the analysis of this article, which relates to an insulated economy and thereby excludes the international flow of capital and know-how.

[15] *Value and Capital*, second edition, p. 164.

[16] *Essays in Monetary Theory*, p. 25.

curve (equation (I)). Thus this dynamic theory is in sharper conflict with Keynes than ever Keynes was with Robertson.

42. Let there be a situation in which s is less than s_r and it is desired to prevent a chronic tendency towards demand-inflation. Classical theory suggests that a rise in the interest rate would be desirable, so as to reduce investment demand and, possibly, encourage saving. But some voices can be heard from the wings suggesting that there is also something called a "fiscal" remedy—or is this allowable only to control the cycle? The voices may suggest that a Budget surplus would be better than a high interest rate, since a high interest rate bridges the gap mainly by lowering investment requirements, while the Budget surplus bridges the gap mainly by raising savings. And is it not better to raise savings than to reduce investment requirements? But is it better? Was there discernible, in the voices off, a note that would be condemned by Mr. Little, something persuasive, something emotive, possibly even a "value judgment" itself? Dynamic theory should enable us to resolve the issue on purely rational grounds.

43. Happily in that theory the natural rate of interest is determined independently of the demand for or supply of savings, present or prospective. If we can make approximate guesses about the growth potential per head (*i.e.*, $_{pc}G_n$) and the elasticity of income utility, then we can determine what rate of interest is consistent with that. I must not be supposed to be here deprecating such manipulation of the interest rate as may serve to iron out booms and slumps, *i.e.*, to prevent actual growth running away in either direction from a steady path. I am referring now to the average interest rate in both phases taken together. If the actual rate seems low by the criterion of the formula, then there is a case for raising it. (Raising the interest rate should be taken to include making borrowing difficult in imperfect markets.) This may indeed render some investment projects unpayable, but only those whose yield is so low that from the point of view of the social optimum they are undesirable. But if there is no reason to suppose that the rate is below its natural level as defined in equation (I), *then there should be resort to a Budget surplus.*

44. I may interject a topical observation. I deem it unlikely that Britain will be subject to chronic inflationary pressure on the demand side in the coming decade. But if I am wrong, the evil should be cured by a Budget surplus rather than by any further raising of the interest rate. And indeed, unless national income per head is destined to grow at a much greater rate in the coming period than it has done in the last decade, it would be surprising if 5% were not considerably too high.

45. What has been said is not inconsistent with the idea of easing a transition period by a high interest rate. Reference to such a period has already been made in relation to developing countries, where it may be a phenomenon of substantial magnitude. Big transitions are less likely in mature countries, but not impossible. Suppose a very large capital-requiring innovation. This will raise required saving by raising C_r. The innova-

tion may also affect the nature of replacement equipment and indeed raise the required rate of replacements (cf. p. 596 *sup.*). In fine, the change in a dynamic determinant will have considerably raised the requirement for saving (s_r). The rise in the requirement may be permanent or it may not be, that depending on the nature of future innovations. In the former event it might be expedient to ease the transition by allowing a temporary rise in the interest rate rather than by jacking up saving too suddenly and abruptly. But if the rate is raised above its natural level to ease a transition, the target should always be to reduce it again to that level at an early date.

34

What is Economic Growth?

and

The Costs of Economic Growth*

U.S. CHAMBER OF COMMERCE COMMITTEE ON ECONOMIC POLICY

Editors' Note

Fashions change in economics as they do in women's clothes. For example, in the 1930's secular stagnation was all the rage. In the mid-1950's, inflation became the main topic of concern. Now the word "growth" is on the lips of almost all economists and policy makers. We even judge economic systems by their growth rates.

What is growth? How fast should the economy grow? What can or should government do about growth? These are the concerns of the present article. Various measures of growth are discussed, in terms of: (1) "forced" industrialization of a country, as in the Soviet Union; (2) the aggregate or gross national product concept, which disregards the composition of output; (3) the productivity or national income per capita approach, which first subtracts the replacements required just to maintain the capital stock; (4) the welfare or consumption per capita definition, which the Chamber of Commerce believes is the most relevant to the current American scene.

Is more leisure to be preferred over more work? Should consumption be sacrificed at the expense of more investment? Should we favor the future rather than the present? How do we balance costs against the benefits of

* From the Report of the Committee on Economic Policy, U.S. Chamber of Commerce, *The Promise of Economic Growth* (Washington, D.C.: U.S. Chamber of Commerce, 1961), pp. 6-12; 13-21. © Chamber of Commerce of U.S.A. Reprinted by permission of publisher.

growth? This presentation should stimulate the student to think through his own answers to these provocative questions. He should keep in mind the possible conflict between sustaining a high growth rate and basic social values. In this respect, how much will society sacrifice to achieve rapid growth? How much choice does a nation really have among alternative possible growth rates? How can the developed countries help the under-developed ones to achieve a faster development and what happens to the latters' social structures in the process? These are among some of the most important problems facing the world community today.

WHAT IS ECONOMIC GROWTH?

❧ Economic growth has again joined the time-honored pantheon of God, country, motherhood, and full employment. Although all good men may pay them lip service, sincere and honorable men may disagree on how best to worship them, and even about the proper attributes of these objects of common worship. It is necessary, therefore, to discuss briefly some con-flicting concepts of economic growth and to indicate which definition will be employed in what follows. It is important to select a definition, because the methods of achieving growth, variously defined, may differ, and the pros and cons of growth depend upon the choice of definitions.

A. Structural Definition: Industrialization

The first definition of economic growth may be classed as structural. It is commonly applied to underdeveloped countries and may distinguish the concept of economic development from the concept of economic growth in the narrow sense, which applies just as properly to modern countries. Russia has, in the brief space of 40 years, reduced the proportion of its population engaged in agriculture from approximately 80% to roughly 50%. During the same period, it has at least doubled its urban population, who now constitute some 50% of the total. Over the same period of time, Russia has succeeded in increasing its output and capacity in steel many-fold; in creating industries which did not exist on Russian soil in 1917, in achieving self-sufficiency in a wide range of manufactured articles and mineral raw materials in which she was deficient in the past.

This process of structural development has characterized all nations on the move. Many backward nations are now at the stage achieved by Russia before 1917. The advanced nations went through the USSR stage of development in the 19th century.

This structural change, from agriculture to industry, from rural to urban residence, from a specialized and simple to a diversified economy, from traditional to modern technology, does not necessarily imply an increase in the standard of living and the level of income per capita. Such improvements in welfare have often, but not always, followed the structural development of an economy. There have been periods in the throes of industrialization, not only in Russia, but also in some western nations, when income and consumption per capita declined, rather than rose.

Within the context of economic growth through industrialization, it is possible to distinguish various stages with their appropriate indices. In the Soviet approach to industrialization, through buildup of heavy industry, steel is a relevant measure of economic growth; cement, coal and electric power are also important. Once the early stages of industrialization are completed, steel loses its relative relevance; the engineering industry (machinery, motor vehicles) and the chemical industry (petroleum products, sulfuric acid) become the significant indices, followed by electronics.

This approach, however, is an ideological one; it makes no allowance for consumer wants or needs. It is concerned with state power, not individual welfare. It is unfortunate, indeed, that many underdeveloped countries have felt their prestige required following this course, without realizing its political orientation. It is not a faster way to economic development; in general, it is just a less natural way. Industries are developed for whose products there is no internal market, so that the government must step in as a buyer and as a user of capital goods. Its advantages in growth rates have nothing to do with development priorities between capital and consumer goods industries and everything to do with the priority attached to development itself and the methods used to obtain and utilize development resources.

A special case of the structural criterion of growth emphasizes certain industries which are supposedly the backbone of military power. This consideration has been very important in Russian development plans and in Russian claims of progress achieved. The emphasis on steel, petroleum and similar items derives from their relevance for state power, rather than from their potential contribution to improved levels of living. This special definition must be discarded, since it is not applicable to most countries, which cannot entertain the prospect of military power or self-sufficiency in the munitions industry.

Proponents of structural change as the definition of growth may derive their enthusiasm in part from their expectation of its consequences for welfare. But many proponents would advocate structural change for its own sake. The factory, in particular the steel mill, is a symbol of status, the modern counterpart of ancient pyramids, both for the nation which acquires it and for the individual who works in it. It is the means of upward mobility for the individual and for the society, the method of breaking down the resistant structure of the traditional society, a school for urban life, the seed bed of new institutions and ways of thought and tangible evidence of national liberation.

B. Aggregate Definition: GNP

The second definition of economic growth may be called the aggregate or GNP concept. Growth is defined simply as an increase in the total output of goods and services as measured by available statistical techniques. It does not discriminate between industries and sectors, nor consider output divided by population or by working force. Aggregate growth, therefore, does not necessarily imply increased per capita income or increased output per worker. This concept has little to recommend it, other than its extreme simplicity. It may serve its purpose for propaganda among unlettered peoples, as a means of obtaining their consent and support for programs of development, imposed from above, which require popular discipline or individual sacrifices.

The GNP as a measure of increased output is, itself, subject to criticism, because it includes the costs of maintaining the nation's productive capacity intact. The national income, which omits these costs, is a more suitable measure of the net addition to a country's output, to a country's supply of goods and services. In a backward economy, the distinction may not be a very important one, because it may lack a large and rapidly depreciating stock of capital goods, human skills, and other productive resources whose maintenance and replacement would require the expenditure of a sizable proportion of the nation's efforts.

C. Productivity or GNP Per Capita

Thirdly, we come to the productivity definition of economic growth, which defines growth as increase in GNP or national income per capita. Strictly speaking, as a measure of productivity, growth should be expressed on a per worker, rather than a per capita, basis. Productivity is a complex concept which will be discussed later. In the long run, the labor force may remain in fairly constant proportion to the total population so that growth in output per capita and growth in output per worker proceed at the same rate. The distinction should be made, however, between man-year productivity and man-hour productivity, because of the secular trend toward shorter hours. Productivity per man-hour tends to increase at a rate substantially higher than the productivity per man-year. (Expression of productivity in terms of labor does not imply that output or increments in output are attributable exclusively to the efforts of labor. It is simply a convenient method of expressing gains in supply of goods and services available to individuals.)

Gains in productivity do not necessarily imply gains in levels of living. We must consider not only the increased output of goods and services, but also the nature of the increments in goods and services turned out and their distribution among the various ultimate consumers: individuals, institutions, and governments. The relationship between changes in output and changes in levels of living is also influenced by the distribution of output between consumption and investment, including defense, education and other services usually provided by the government.

D. Welfare or Consumption Per Capita

A fourth definition of economic growth is in terms of welfare or, specifically, in terms of per capita consumption and levels of living. This is the definition which is relevant to American interest in sustained and rapid economic growth. The other definitions are, at times, preferred in other countries, and, at times, considered in this country, as a response, for instance, to the psychological and military threat posed by rapid Soviet advance.

A continued increase in per capita consumption and levels of living requires continued increases in output per capita and, if population is not decreasing, in total output as well. But it implies more than this. It requires that increases in total output per capita be made available to individuals and be used mainly for the provision of additional goods and services in the consumer budget. The additional supplies provided must take into account consumer wants and demands. The easiest way to increase shoe production, as some Soviet bloc factories learned, is to turn out only left feet, all of the same size and style. But if the shoe doesn't fit, the consumer doesn't gain.

Economic growth as an increase in welfare can be considered as an increase in consumption per capita, or total consumption divided by total population, or it can additionally consider the distribution of consumption among the population; i.e., the relative equality or inequality in the distribution of income. Some would argue that welfare can be increased with a given total income for a given total population if this income is redistributed from the rich to the poor—if, in other words, luxuries are reduced in supply and the necessities provided for the poor are made more widely available. This is a very controversial subject; there is no agreement as to precisely how much redistribution would add most to welfare.

We can here ignore the question of income distribution, except insofar as it affects incentives and through incentives the rate of growth and output. As a goal of economic growth, we will treat consumption as an aggregate amount of goods and services divided by existing population, without regard to the manner of its distribution among individuals.

Per capita consumption includes much more than the supply of goods and services purchased on the market by individuals and households, plus such supplies as individuals and households provide for themselves. It includes the enormous range of goods and services provided by governments at all levels, and financed mainly by taxation. The allocation of production between the three great sectors of the economy—households, business firms and governments—is, in large part, dictated by the technical conditions of production, distribution and consumption. To a considerable extent, however, the choice is a matter of individual preferences. Each household makes its own choices on whether to provide certain goods and services for itself or to purchase them on the market. The choices between private enterprise and government provision, however, must be made through the political process. No two countries make the identical choice, and even within our country there are state and local differences in the respective roles of private and public enterprise.

If too large a role is assigned to government, the consequent burdens of taxation may dampen incentives and retard growth. If too small a role is permitted the public authorities, certain public services essential for the smooth functioning of the society and the economy may be neglected, and growth, likewise, retarded. Except for these possible consequences, the political choice between private and public production need not be further considered at this time.

In any economic or political system, economic growth ultimately means a diminishing share of effort and income allocated to obtain minimum needs of food, clothing and shelter, and an increasing share available for providing goods and services above subsistence needs, and therefore discretionary. Various economic and political systems differ in the composition of this share, in the proportion of this share going to the individual consumer, and in the discretion available to the consumer in guiding production and distribution.

It is meaningless to express economic growth as a percentage increase in some index. Five per cent of what? The composition of the increment is as important as its size. The appropriate yardstick of economic growth changes with the level of economic development. At very low levels of consumer income and welfare, per capita increases in agricultural output may be the most significant measure. They provide a more adequate minimum diet, itself contributing to rising labor productivity, and a margin of income and effort to devote to diversification of diet through the beginnings of trade and industry. Such beginnings contribute mightily to incentives for greater production by providing markets for agricultural output and by supplying goods which contribute directly to farm productivity or which widen the farmers' standard of consumption.

By the consumer welfare criterion of growth, after the grain and cloth standard come meat and shoes, which are succeeded by consumer durables. Only the United States and perhaps Canada have passed the automobile standard of welfare. In the very forefront of economic growth, in the flux of changing standards, who can venture to choose a yardstick of growth in the post-Detroit era? It may turn out to be travel and tourist expenditures, or children and college education, or a combination of these and other components of rising welfare in a consumer-guided economy. Certainly not wheat or steel.

Considering the varied and shifting composition of additional goods and services which growth provides, it is best not to think of growth in terms of specific commodities, but in terms of values; not in terms of output, but in terms of capacity. Thus, economic growth is the increase in capacity for providing whatever values have the highest priorities in a particular society: more goods, of whatever kind most desired, or more services, or even more leisure, if this is the "value" most desired for the price.

Unless a country has special advantages or disadvantages causing it to specialize and obtain much of its needs through trade, industrial development should advance from agricultural processing to textiles and shoes, then consumer durables, such as furniture and kitchen equipment, then through a progression of rising technical requirements and developing home markets, to production of radios, automobiles and the myriad components of an American standard of living, including a rising share of personal services. The transport and communications facilities, electric power, other capital goods and various elements of social overhead appropriate to each stage of economic growth would also be provided, but as by-products of rising welfare, not as the objectives of progress.

Considering the vast differences in objectives, methods, and priorities, it is as meaningless to assess the relative progress of the U. S. and the USSR in terms of their steel output or engineering graduates as it is to do so in terms of the number of passenger automobiles or private swimming pools. For the time being, at least, the two countries are not traveling the same road.

THE COSTS OF ECONOMIC GROWTH

Perhaps most of the best things in life are free, but economic growth is not. There are costs to pay, sacrifices to make, in order to maintain high rates of growth, or any growth at all. It is not possible to say, therefore, as many somewhat hysterical and unthinking publicists seem to be saying, that the more growth the better.

We must balance the benefits of growth against the costs of achieving various growth rates, and determine the point at which the increased benefits of more growth are just outweighed by the increased costs; this point represents the optimum rate of growth, which may be high or may be low, depending upon the value we place on its benefits and the efficiency with which we engineer growth in the economy.

Very definitely, the optimum rate of growth is not the maximum rate. We might, indeed, vastly accelerate growth, for a time, by housing the population in crowded barracks, placing them on minimum rations, extracting maximum effort by golden promises for future delivery or by force and terror and devoting all surplus thus obtained to research and investment.

A. Work versus Leisure

The rate of economic growth at any point in time depends largely upon the share of resources diverted from current consumption for investment purposes. Investment must be broadly interpreted to include any economic activity which increases the total supply of productive resources or improves their quality. Productive resources include managerial and labor supplies and skills, as well as plant, equipment, raw materials and the like. Investment, therefore, includes education and research as much as power plants and steel mills. Given the share of production devoted to investment, or to increasing future output, the actual amount of investment depends upon the level of current output. There are, then, two ways of increasing the rate of growth: raising the share of current income allocated to investment, and increasing current income itself.

Current income can be increased through more intensive utilization of existing productive resources. This is a one-shot approach to growth; once maximum utilization is achieved, no further gains in income can be wrested. But a permanently higher level of resource utilization means a larger pie to be divided at any time, and a larger amount available for investment without reduction in the amount, or share, of income devoted to consumption. In terms of labor, more intensive utilization may mean a higher level of employment, a larger labor force (higher labor force participation rates), longer hours, or a speed-up of work pace.

The cost of increased growth, then, is to be measured in terms of a sacrifice of leisure; the price we must pay for growth depends upon the value we attach to the leisure foregone. To the extent that the increased utilization of labor is a reduction in unemployment or idleness, rather than a sacrifice of leisure, growth, so far as the worker is concerned, is costless.

Leisure is a form of income. Idleness, on the other hand, is the deprivation of income. The distinction between the two, however subjective and difficult, must nevertheless be made, for it is at the core of the definition of employment and unemployment.

A rule of thumb measure of individual full employment is one's reaction to the opportunity to vary slightly one's hours of work *at the current wage rate*. If one chooses to work longer, he is underemployed. If one chooses to work less, he is overemployed.

Employment and leisure are the two alternative desirable uses of human time and effort. They are not to be measured in time alone. A worker may have a choice of distributing time between these two activities. He may also have the option of varying the degree of intensity with which he works (and with which he enjoys his leisure activities). A man may opt for more leisure, not by reducing his workweek, but by reducing his work pace. Or, he may reduce his workweek without reducing work effort by increasing his pace. Leisure and work have other dimensions. The different types of work between which a worker may choose once he is in mid-career may be extremely limited, but he always has a wide option in his choice of leisure activities.

Some leisure activities are complementary with work, because they require the expenditure of money earned by more work effort. Other leisure activities may be considered substitutes for work in that they either (1) produce some money income, or (2) provide goods and services directly which the man of leisure would otherwise have purchased on the market.

These possible income-yielding aspects of leisure activity raise thorny definitional problems. Would a man raise his own vegetables in his spare time, even if he did not save money as a result? Some would, and their gardening qualifies clearly as a leisure activity. Others may not, or may work less in their own kitchen gardens; their gardening is not, or not exclusively, a leisure-time activity. But what shall we call work performed for pay which is so enjoyable for the worker that he would choose to continue it, even if he were to receive substantially less remuneration?

Can we expect that, with the growth in labor force skills and reduction of tedium in many employments, the worker's preference for leisure will be weakened, his demands for shorter hours reduced? Can we anticipate that, if leisure-time activities develop a larger do-it-yourself component, the demand for work and its income will diminish? What if leisure-time activities are devoted more and more to education and other efforts which will widen occupational choice and increase the worker's market value?

In admitting the possibility that work may be enjoyable and that leisure may yield income, or may even be a kind of investment, we not only blur the distinction between work and leisure, but we also deny that either can be interpreted wholly in terms of a means-end relationship. Each is both end and means in varying degrees.

Idleness, by contrast, is neither a substitute nor a complement for work; it is involuntary, not a matter of choice. It yields no income; it has no uses.

If we consider leisure as one of our goals, one of the goods and services (real income) for which we work, we must place some value on it. Who can then say that a 5% rate of growth in output of goods and services is better than a 3% rate of growth? The latter, which provides more leisure, may indeed be preferable, and, for that matter, higher. Who can say that in all countries at all times growth as measured in national income statistics is better than no growth? For national income data which serve as bases for computing growth rates have two glaring omissions: the value of leisure, expressed in terms of income obtainable from alternative work uses of time, and the contribution which some leisure activities make to the total supply of goods and services. The loss of these values for the sake of more rapid growth must be counted among the costs of growth.

B. Consumption versus Investment

Any increase in output per capita, which is not the result of temporary increases in the intensity of resource utilization, requires some curtailment of current consumption. A part of current income must be saved and invested. Savings may be done by individuals, by corporations or other institutions, or by governments through taxation. The agencies and mechanisms differ greatly, but the essence is the same. Part of current income is withheld from consumption and the resources released are devoted to increasing the supply of consumer goods at future times.

An acceleration in the rate of growth in output and, therefore, in income available per capita, requires a reduction of current consumption. This consumption foregone (or consumption postponed) is, in part, a second major cost of growth. Its calculation is somewhat easier than the calculation of value of leisure foregone, because prices of consumer goods and services are daily determined on the market, whereas the price of leisure is not so easily estimated.

The relationship between an increase in investment and acceleration in the rate of growth is not a simple or necessarily a very rigid one. So-called capital/output ratios have been computed for a number of countries at various periods of time. These ratios express a relationship between investment in capital and increases in output which result from this investment. For a number of countries, the capital/output ratios have been estimated at about three to one; that is, increase in investment of $30 should yield an increase in annual income, once the investment is completed, of $10. The capital/output ratio varies from country to country and from time to time, and more important, it may vary considerably from industry to industry. The ratio which may be pertinent for the United States in the near future depends upon the kind of industry whose capacity and output would be expanded.

Investment is not restricted to production and use of tangible plant and equipment. It includes development of human resources and research into new materials, products, and techniques. The productivity of education is much more difficult to calculate than the productivity of investment in fixed plant and equipment. The relationship between time and money spent by a man in acquiring skills and increasing knowledge, and the increased income he may expect as a result over his working life (and, indeed, increase in his working life which he may anticipate) has not been accurately calculated. The return on college education may exceed the rate of return on investment in manufacturing equipment and plant, if subsidies to education are omitted, and fall slightly short of the productivity of investment in manufacturing plant and equipment, if private and public subsidies to education are included in its cost.[1]

The productivity of income and effort devoted to research is even more difficult to estimate than the productivity of investment in human skills. Investment in research, whatever its direct returns, is fundamental to economic growth in that it provides the long-run basis for the increased income to be obtained by investment, both in fixed capital and in human skills.

In considering the productivity of investment, it is not sufficient to think of it in the technical terms of capital/output ratios. Investment in education, for example, not only yields benefits in terms of greater produc-

---

[1] Solomon Fabricant, *The Study of Economic Growth*, National Bureau of Economic Research, Inc., 39th Annual Report, May 1959; p. 6.

tivity and higher income for the future; it can be undertaken entirely for its own sake. The individual, or many individuals, would be willing to undertake the effort and expense of acquiring an education, even if they expected no benefit in the form of higher income. Education for such people is a desirable form of consumption.

Some types of investment, although productive in the technical sense, may add little or nothing to welfare or income. Defense is the most important example. Although each American obtains some psychic income in terms of national security provided by our defense expenditures, it is not true that the degree or amount of security is, in any necessary way, related to the amount of defense spending. Increased defense spending, although it may raise GNP, may not increase security at all, since our security is relative to USSR defense efforts (and aggressive intentions), and not to our own efforts in isolation.

Another type of investment whose technical productivity may greatly overstate its contribution to welfare is that which implements the transfer of functions to business firms and governments which were formerly performed by individuals and households. Such investment adds to the GNP, but may or may not increase real incomes. Its effect on real incomes depends on the relative efficiency with which the functions are performed by institutions and by households and the relevant utilities and dis-utilities.

Lastly, investment, whatever the capital/output ratio, contributes to welfare only if the forthcoming goods and services are ultimately wanted and demanded by consumers. Investment creating large agricultural surpluses for which there are no markets may contribute nothing to our welfare; indeed, it may substract from welfare by wasting resources which might have been usefully employed in other ways.

C. Present versus Future

For the sake of growth, we must curtail our present consumption or present leisure, or in all probability, cut down the level of both. The greater the rate of growth, the greater the sacrifice we must make in leisure, in consumption, or in a combination of both. This sacrifice, however, is not a net cost of economic growth, for we are not giving up for all time the leisure and consumption which we forego today. We merely defer such leisure and consumption for the future, or, at least, we defer the opportunity to increase our consumption and our leisure on more favorable terms at some future time.

It does not follow that economic growth (defined as an increase in output per capita) is always a net gain, no matter what the rate of growth, simply because at some future date we will be able to enjoy all of the consumption and all of the leisure which we sacrifice in order to achieve growth. Future income or future consumption never has as great a value as the same income and consumption today. The depreciation or discounting in the value of income and consumption, as they are deferred into the more and more distant future, decreases the benefits of growth relative to the costs, until the point is reached where further increase in growth costs more than it is worth in terms of the increased future benefits.

The benefits of economic growth depend on (1) the size of the increments in future income and consumption which a given present sacrifice of consumption and leisure may provide (the capital/output ratio); (2) upon how long we must defer this increment in consumption, leisure and income; and (3) the rate at which we discount the future.

D. The Process of Creative Destruction[2]

In previous pages, we have discussed the relevance of the level of resource utilization to the rate of economic growth and to the cost of achieving this rate of growth. If resources are fully employed, a larger amount can be devoted to investment without reducing the amount or the share of consumption out of current income. There is, however, another side to this picture. The process of growth itself creates temporary underemployment or unemployment of productive resources, and the more rapid and pervasive the growth, the greater the amount of resource underemployment which is likely to occur.

Economic growth, by necessity, takes place in spurts. If a steel mill is under construction in a locality, large numbers of construction workers will be employed. Once the mill is completed, demand for construction labor, equipment, and materials will drop rather suddenly, very greatly, and perhaps permanently. On the other hand, once the steel mill is completed, demand may just as suddenly develop for steel workers to place this mill in operation. From the viewpoint of the locality alone, there has been sudden unemployment in the construction industry and sudden increase in the employment of steel workers who previously were unemployed in this locality or more likely had to be attracted from other localities by suitable wage offers. Such discontinuities in the investment process and in the associated demand for labor, materials, and equipment are typical. In a large and highly diversified economy, many of these sudden increases and decreases in demand cancel each other out. But in particular localities, in particular industries, in particular occupations, the fluctuations are often large and of serious implications for employment stability and income maintenance.

In the process of economic growth, old sources of supply may be gradually exhausted or new sources of supply quickly developed, leaving stranded mining communities. Old industries may change their location in pursuit of materials or in pursuit of markets which move with shifting population. New industries may arise which replace old; new materials

---

[2] See: J. A. Schumpeter, *Capitalism, Socialism, and Democracy:* 3rd edition; New York: Harper & Bros., 1950; Chapter VII.

may be developed, new products, new markets, all of which will create unemployment problems in some areas, industries and occupations. The more rapid the change in the location of economic activity, in the composition of products, in the nature of markets, in the choice of materials, the more numerous the depressed industry, depressed area, depressed occupation problems which will crop up in the wake of economic growth.

The problem of underemployed resources is only partly encompassed in terms of unemployed labor. Capital facilities of all kinds—mines, factories and the capital invested in highly specialized human skills—rapidly lose their value and may become permanently unemployed. The opportunities for converting a coal mine into an oil well are much more limited than those of converting a coal miner into a worker with another skill in greater demand. A revival in the demand for carriage makers, blacksmiths, and glass blowers could only be the result of economic catastrophe. Obsolete machines are replaced by newer, more efficient models long before they are worn out. Rapid obsolescence is a measure of economic growth. It entails no long-run cost to the community, however serious the loss to the owner.

Fluctuations in economic activity, frictional and technological unemployment, depressed areas, obsolete capital and skills, are not then necessarily a drag on growth; to some extent they are indices of growth, its unavoidable consequences. The argument that rapid growth is necessary to provide new job opportunities for workers displaced by technological change is entirely contradictory. Rapid technological change is practically the same thing as rapid growth in output per capita. If growth is slow, technological change is slow, and the number of technologically unemployed workers is small. Full employment is quite possible without growth in per capita output. Some economic insecurity, on the other hand, is inevitable in any dynamic economy. For maximum security we must turn to a static economy and a status society.

E. Balancing Costs and Benefits

The costs of economic growth, then, are three in number. First, we sacrifice current leisure for current work. Second, we sacrifice present consumption for present savings and investment. The burden of sacrifice may be borne exclusively in terms of present consumption, or in terms of present leisure (itself describable as a consumer good); more likely, however, we sacrifice some of each today for the sake of more of each in the future. The third sacrifice is stability of income and employment, security of the value of assets and skills, for more rapid growth in income and levels of living.

The costs are concentrated in the present; the benefits accrue indefinitely into the future. The costs, in terms of obsolescence of skills and capital, of unemployment are concentrated in particular regions, industries, and occupations; the benefits are broadly distributed.

The optimum rate of growth is determined ultimately by the Law of Value, which sets upper limits to the desirable rate of growth. The Law of Value states that the worth of any unit of a good or service to us is inversely related to the number of identical units in our possession. Thus, if our workweek is short, and our leisure long, we do not find a few more hours of work particularly irksome, nor miss much the loss of a few hours of leisure. If our work is long and our leisure short, however, we become extremely reluctant to cut down further on our leisure or to increase further our working week. The same relation applies to the relative values of consumption and savings (investment). We may willingly do without trifles and luxuries in order to save and invest, but hesitate to trim on near-necessities and essentials; likewise, we become increasingly averse to further increases in our savings and investment once they have reached respectable amounts. Only the miser regards a maximum amount of savings and investment as the optimum amount, and conversely with the maximum amount of consumption. Only the prodigal or wastrel gives no thought for the morrow but seeks to consume as much as he can today. Thus, most individuals achieve an optimum equilibrium somewhere between the extremes of all work and all play, and all consumption and all savings.

The equilibrium point further depends upon the rate at which the present value of future consumption and leisure decline as we postpone them further into time. For a second Law of Value states that the value of any unit of income or item of consumption depends upon the time of its availability; the more remote the future when the income or consumer good will be available, the lower its present value. The optimum rate of growth depends, in other words, on the rate of discounting the future relative to the present. It is not enough to say that a dollar invested today will be worth two dollars in ten years. Are two dollars ten years hence worth more, or worth less, than one dollar right now? How many birds in the bush are worth one bird in hand?

As an abstraction, we can say that the market rates of interest express the rate at which we discount the future. Of course, other factors influence interest rates, and no interest rate measures the discount functions of any one individual. For each of us has his own unique outlook; the relative weight we attach to the immediate, intermediate and remote future; to future within our lifetime and within the lifetime of our children. Each of us has various time horizons, for we are more reluctant to sow that which we shall not live to reap than to sow the seed whose fruits we expect to enjoy.

Knowing the efficiency of investment in adding to the future supply of goods and leisure, we can determine the optimum rate of growth. The greater the efficiency of investment, the higher the optimum rate of growth. The choice, however, requires complex valuation, not single measurement of tons of steel or housing starts.

FOR FURTHER READING

The experience of the depression of the 1930's, followed by extremely low levels of unemployment in World War II, started many economists here and abroad thinking about the question of full employment in the postwar economy. Perhaps the most famous of these is Lord Beveridge, whose book *Full Employment in a Free Society* (New York: W. W. Norton, 1945) is still widely influential. In this country, the Employment Act of 1946 has been passed and implemented. Ten years later, Gerhard Colm, himself a leading actor in this development of full employment policy in the early postwar years, edited a volume on *The Employment Act—Past and Future, a Tenth Anniversary Symposium* (Washington, D.C.: National Planning Association, 1956), which appraises the record of the machinery set up by the earlier Act and suggests ways in which it might be improved. Many recent developments in economic policy were foreshadowed in that volume. Naturally the student should read the various *Economic Reports of the President*, which are published each January, as well as the Joint Economic Committee's report on the same subject, which generally follows a few months later. Incidentally, the Joint Economic Committee carried out a major study in 1959—the largest since the monumental Temporary National Economic Committee study of the late 1930's— which was published as *Employment, Growth, and Price Levels*, along with more than twenty study papers. Since Arthur F. Burns played an important role as the chairman of President Eisenhower's first Council of Economic Advisors, his book on *Prosperity Without Inflation* (New York: Fordham University Press, 1957), is worth reading. It represents the considered thinking of a conservative economist of international reputation.

who experienced four years of policy formulation at the highest level. Of a more academic bent is the important volume published by the National Bureau of Economic Research on *Policies to Combat Depressions* (Princeton: Princeton University Press, 1956), which represents university thinking of a few years back. As to the longer-run problems of economic growth, the work by James S. Duesenberry on *Business Cycles and Economic Growth* (New York: McGraw-Hill, 1958) has not received the recognition it deserves as a major contribution. Similarly, the more theoretical book by D. Hamberg on *Economic Growth and Instability* (New York: Macmillan, 1956) has too long been overshadowed by the better-known work of Harrod and Domar. The work of Alvin Hansen, long a leading figure in formulating policies of the sort more likely to be adopted by Democratic than by Republican administrations, is brought up to date in his *Economic Issues of the 1960's* (New York: McGraw-Hill, 1961), which is stimulating and provocative. The Committee for Economic Development has had an important part in the education of businessmen as well as the community at large; its latest report on *Fiscal and Monetary Policy for High Employment*, Statement on National Policy by Research and Policy Committee (1962), is one of a long line of widely read and influential documents. The C.E.D. has also published a major work by Edward F. Dennison on *The Sources of Economic Growth in the U.S. and the Alternatives Before Us*, Supplementary Paper No. 13 (1962), which considers in a tough-minded way some of the basic problems of achieving and maintaining a rate of growth that seems essential for this country in the decade of the 1960's. An earlier book by George Terborgh, *The Bogey of Economic Maturity* (Washington, D.C.: Anderson House, 1945), considers the arguments put forward in the 1930's concerning the dismal future of the United States' economy. Since some voices are being heard along these lines as they were in the 1930's, the Terborgh book is worth reading for an understanding of some of the basic strengths inherent in the American enterprise system. Another best seller, Rostow's *Stages of Economic Growth* (London: Cambridge University Press, 1960), should be read for a broader perspective on the problem of growth in all types of societies, underdeveloped as well as advanced. Finally, the Rockefeller Panel Reports on the *Prospects for America* (New York: Doubleday, 1961), particularly Report No. 4, should be examined for a description of the glowing future that lies ahead.

BIBLIOGRAPHY

Books

Abbot, Charles C. *Management of the Federal Debt*. New York: McGraw-Hill, 1946.

Abramovitz, M. *The Role of Inventories in Business Cycles*. New York: National Bureau of Economic Research, 1948.

——. *Inventories and Business Cycles—With Reference to Manufacturers' Inventories*. Studies in Business Cycles No. 4. New York: National Bureau of Economic Research, 1950.

Abramson, Adolph G., and Mack, Russell H. *Business Forecasting in Practice: Principles and Cases*. New York: John Wiley and Sons, 1956.

Allen, J. S., and others. *The Economic Crisis and the Cold War*. New York: New Century Publishers, 1949.

Altman, G. T. *Invisible Barrier—A Tax Specialist's Analysis of the Business Cycle*. Los Angeles: De Vorss and Company, 1949.

The American Assembly. *United States Monetary Policy*. New York: Columbia University Press, 1958.

American Economic Association. *Readings in Business Cycle Theory*. Homewood, Ill.: Richard D. Irwin (The Blakiston Company), 1944.

American Institute of Economic Research, Research, Investment and Insurance Division. *What Will Deflation or More Deflation Mean to You?* New York: American Institute of Economic Research, 1955.

American Management Association. *The Economic Outlook and the Demand for Funds*. New York: American Management Association, 1948.

——. *Evaluating and Using Business Indicators, With Special Reference to Current Economic Outlook*. New York: American Management Association, 1959.

Anderson, H. D., and others. *Unemployment; It's Here, Let's Stop It Now!* Washington, D.C.: Public Affairs Institute, 1949.

Anderson, M. D. *Theory of Economic Aggregates—A Manual of General Business Forecasting.* Gainesville, Fla.: University of Florida Bookstore, 1945.
————. *Total Business Fluctuations.* Gainesville, Fla.: Kallman Publishing Company, 1949.
Arndt, H. W. *The Economic Lessons of the Nineteen-Thirties.* New York: Oxford University Press, 1944.
Auble, Arthur G. *The Depression of 1873 and 1882 in the United States.* Cambridge: Harvard University Library, 1949, Unpublished Doctoral Dissertation.
Ayres, Leonard P. *Turning Points in Business Cycles.* New York: Macmillan, 1939.
Babson, R. W. *If Further Inflation Comes.* Philadelphia: Lippincott, 1948.
Bach, G. L. *Inflation—A Study in Economics, Ethics, and Politics.* Providence: Brown University Press, 1958.
Backman, J. *How Real Are 1948 Profits?* New Wilmington, Pa.: Economic and Business Foundation, 1949.
Bailey, J. D. *Growth and Depression—Contrasts in the Australian and British Economies 1870–80.* Canberra: Australia National University, 1956.
Bakewell, P., Jr. *Inflation in the United States.* Caldwell, Ida.: Caxton, 1958.
Barber, C. L. *Inventories and the Business Cycle with Special Reference to Canada.* Canadian Study of Economics No. 10. Toronto: University of Toronto Press, 1958.
Barger, H. *Outlay and Income in the United States, 1921–1938.* New York: National Bureau of Economic Research, 1942.
Bassee, V. L. *Economic Forecasting.* New York: McGraw-Hill, 1958.
Beck, G. M. *A Survey of British Employment and Unemployment, 1927–45.* Oxford: Oxford University Institute of Statistics, 1951.
Bennett, S. V., Cowherd, H. S., Gibbons, C. C., and Taylor, H. C. *Full Employment in Your Community.* Chicago: Public Administration Service, 1947.
Berkovits, E., and Atkins, G. C. *The Key to Full Employment Without Regimentation.* Toronto: Longmans, Green, 1945.
————. *The Mechanics of Full Production and Full Employment—A Solution to Depressions.* Chicago: Wilcox and Follett, 1946.
Beveridge, Sir William H. *Unemployment, A Problem of Industry.* London: Longmans, Green, 1909.
————. *Full Employment in a Free Society.* New York: W. W. Norton, 1945.
Binns, K. J. *Social Credit in Alberta: Report Prepared for the Government of Tasmania.* Hobart, Australia: Government Printer, 1947.
Blaug, M. *Economic Theory in Retrospect.* Homewood, Ill.: Richard D. Irwin, 1962.
Bloomfield, Arthur. *Monetary Policy Under the International Gold Standard, 1880–1914.* New York: Federal Reserve Bank of New York, 1959.
Blough, R., and others. *A New Look at Inflation.* Chicago: University of Chicago Roundtable, 1948.
————. *What Do We Know About Economic Stability.* Chicago: University of Chicago Roundtable, 1949.
Bopp, Karl R., and others. *Federal Reserve Policy.* Postwar Economic Studies No. 8. Washington, D. C.: Board of Governors of the Federal Reserve System, 1947.
Borsodi, R. *Inflation is Coming! A Practical Postwar Plan.* Suffern, N. Y.: Bayard Lane, 1945.
Borts, G. H. *Regional Cycles of Manufacturing Employment in the United*

States, 1914–1953. Occasional Paper No. 73. New York: National Bureau of Economic Research, 1960.

Bowen, E. R. *Depressions—And How You Should Prepare for Them.* Chicago: Cooperative League of the U.S.A., 1949.

Bratt, E. C. *Business Forecasting.* New York: McGraw-Hill, 1958.

———. *Business Cycles and Forecasting.* Homewood, Ill.: Richard D. Irwin, 1961.

Brennan, Michael J., Jr. *Preface to Econometrics.* New York: South-Western Publishing Company, 1960.

British Institute of Management. *Business Forecasting.* Conference No. 3. London: British Institute of Management, 1949.

Budget Bureau. *Budget of the United States Government for Fiscal Year Ending June 30, 1946.* Washington, D.C.: U.S. Government Printing Office. (Issued annually from 1946 to 1962.)

Bureau of Labor Statistics. *Wholesale Prices, 1945.* Washington, D.C.: U.S. Government Printing Office, 1947.

———. *Retail Prices of Food, 1955–56—Indexes and Averages Prices.* Washington, D.C.: U.S. Government Printing Office, 1957.

———. *Frequency of Change in Wholesale Prices: A Study of Price Flexibility.* Washington, D.C.: U.S. Government Printing Office, 1959.

Burns, Arthur F. *Production Trends in the United States Since 1870.* New York: National Bureau of Economic Research, 1934.

———. *New Facts on Business Cycles.* Thirtieth Annual Report. New York: National Bureau of Economic Research, 1950.

———. *The Instability of Consumer Spending.* Thirty-second Annual Report. New York: National Bureau of Economic Research, 1952.

———. *Business Cycle Research and the Needs of Our Times.* Thirty-third Annual Report. New York: National Bureau of Economic Research, 1953.

———. *The Frontiers of Economic Knowledge.* Princeton: Princeton University Press, 1954.

———. *Prosperity Without Inflation.* New York: Fordham University Press, 1957.

———, and Mitchell, Wesley C. *Measuring Business Cycles.* New York: National Bureau of Economic Research, 1946.

Carney, J. J., Jr. *Institutional Change and the Level of Employment—A Study of British Unemployment 1918–1929.* Coral Gables, Fla.: University of Miami Press, 1956.

Carter, J. J., and Harwood, E. C. *Where Are We Going?* Great Barrington, Mass.: American Institute for Economic Research, 1948.

Caskey, W. F. *Freedom from Want After the War: A Postwar Program for the Reduction of Idleness and Want.* Alexandria: Virginia Printing Company, 1945.

Cassel, G. *The Theory of Social Economy.* 2 vols. London: Ernest Benn, 1932.

Casselman, P. H. *Economics of Employment and Unemployment.* Washington, D.C.: Public. Affairs Press, 1955.

Chambers, E. J. *Economic Fluctuations and Forecasting.* Englewood Cliffs, N.J.: Prentice-Hall, 1961.

Ciriacy-Wantrup, S. V. *Booms and Depressions, and the Farmer.* Berkeley: University of California Press, 1948.

Clark, Colin. *The Conditions of Economic Progress.* New York: Macmillan, 1951.

Clark, J. M. *Strategic Factors in Business Cycles.* New York: National Bureau of Economic Research, 1934.

————. *Social Control of Business*, chaps. xxvi, xxvii, xxviii. New York: McGraw-Hill, 1939.

Clay, H. *War and Unemployment*. London: Oxford University Press, 1945.

Clemence, Richard V. and Doody, Francis. *The Schumpeterian System*. Cambridge: Addison-Wesley Press, 1950.

Colean, M. L., and Newcomb, R. *Stabilizing Construction: The Record and Potential*. Committee for Economic Development Research Study. New York: McGraw-Hill, 1952.

Colm, G. *The Employment Act—Past and Future. A Tenth Anniversary Symposium*. Special Report No. 41. Washington, D. C.: National Planning Association, 1956.

Commission on Money and Credit. *Money and Credit: Their Influence on Jobs, Prices, and Growth*. New York: Prentice-Hall, 1961.

Committee for Economic Development. *Monetary and Fiscal Policy for Greater Economic Stability*. New York: Committee for Economic Development, 1948.

————. *How to Raise Real Wages*. New York: Committee for Economic Development, 1950.

————. *The Stabilizing Budget Policy*. New York: Committee for Economic Development, 1950.

————. *Defense Again Recession; Policy for Greater Economic Stability*. New York: Committee for Economic Development, 1954.

————. *Managing the Federal Debt*. New York: Committee for Economic Development, 1954.

————. *The Budget, The Economy, and Tax Reduction in 1956*. New York: Committee for Economic Development, 1956.

————. *Defense Against Inflation—Policies for Price Stability in a Growing Economy*. New York: Committee for Economic Development, 1958.

————. *Problems in Anti-Recession Policy*. New York: Committee for Economic Development, 1958.

————. *Fiscal and Monetary Policy for High Employment*. Statement on National Policy by Research and Policy Committee. New York: Committee for Economic Development, 1962.

Committee on Banking and Currency. *Inflation Control*. Hearings, 80th Congress, 2d Session, July 20–August 4, 1948, before the Senate Committee on Banking and Currency. Washington, D. C.: U. S. Government Printing Office, 1948.

————. *Area Assistance Act of 1956*. Hearings, 84th Congress, 2d Session, before the House Committee on Banking and Currency. Washington, D. C.: U. S. Government Printing Office, 1956.

————. *Redevelopment of Depressed Industrial and Rural Areas*. Washington, D. C.: U. S. Government Printing Office, 1956.

————. *Federal Assistance to Labor Surplus*. Washington, D. C.: U. S. Government Printing Office, 1957.

————. *Legislation to Relieve Unemployment*. Hearings, 85th Congress, 2d Session, before House Committee on Banking and Currency. Washington, D. C.: U. S. Government Printing Office, 1958.

————. *Area Redevelopment Act*. Hearings before a subcommittee of the Senate Committee on Banking and Currency. Washington, D. C.: U. S. Government Printing Office, 1959.

————. *Area Redevelopment Legislation*. Hearings, 86th Congress, 2d Session, August 18, 1960, before a subcommittee of the Senate Committee on

Banking and Currency. Washington, D. C.: U. S. Government Printing Office, 1960.

Committee on Government Operations. *Amending the Employment Act of 1946 to Include Recommendations on Monetary and Credit Policies and Proposed Price and Wage Increases.* Hearings, 85th Congress, 2d Session, July 21–22, 1958, before a subcommittee of the House Committee on Government Operations. Washington, D. C.: U. S. Government Printing Office, 1958.

———. *Amending the Employment Act of 1946 to Include Recommendations on Monetary and Credit Policies and Hearings on Proposed Price and Wage Increases.* Hearings, 86th Congress, 1st Session, March 25–26, and April 9, 1959, before a subcommittee of the House Committee on Government Operations. Washington, D. C.: U. S. Government Printing Office, 1959.

Committee on Labor and Public Welfare. *Area Development.* Hearings, 84th Congress, 2d Session, before the subcommittee on Labor of the Senate Committee on Labor and Public Welfare. Part I: January 4–February 24, 1956; Part II: February 24–April 26, 1956. Washington, D. C.: U. S. Government Printing Office, 1956.

Committee on Public Works. *Advance Planning of Public Hearings, House Committee on Public Works.* 81st Congress, 1st Session, July 19, 1949. Washington, D. C.: U. S. Government Printing Office, 1949.

———. *Acceleration of Public Works Program.* Hearings, 85th Congress, 1st Session, before the Senate Committee on Public Works. Washington, D. C.: U. S. Government Printing Office, 1958.

Conference on Economic Progress. *The Gaps in Our Prosperity and Needed Changes in National Economic Policies to Achieve Full Prosperity for All.* Washington, D. C.: Conference on Economic Progress, 1956.

———. *Inflation—Cause and Cure.* Washington, D. C.: Conference on Economic Progress, 1959.

Consultant Committee on Business Plant and Equipment Expenditure Expectations. *Statistics on Business Plant and Equipment Expenditure Expectations.* Washington, D. C.: Board of Governors of Federal Reserve System, 1955.

Consultant Committee on General Business Expectations. *An Appraisal of Data and Research on Businessmen's Expectations About Outlook and Operating Variables.* Washington, D. C.: Board of Governors of Federal Reserve System, 1955.

Copeland, D. B. *The Road to High Employment—Administrative Controls in a Free Economy.* Cambridge: Harvard University Press, 1945.

———, and Barback, R. H. *The Conflict of Expansion and Contraction. Documents Relating to Australian Economic Policy, 1945–1952.* Melbourne: Cheshire, 1957.

Copeland, M. A. *A Study of Money Flows in the United States.* New York: National Bureau of Economic Research, 1952.

Council of Economic Advisors. *Council of Economic Advisors. Third Annual Report to the President, December, 1948.* Washington, D. C.: U. S. Government Printing Office. (Issued annually 1947 to 1962.)

———. *Business and Government.* Washington, D. C.: U. S. Government Printing Office, 1949.

———. *Annual Economic Review.* Washington, D. C.: U. S. Government Printing Office, 1953.

Creamer, D., with assistance of Berstein, M. *Behavior of Wage Rates During*

Business Cycles. Occasional Paper No. 34. New York: National Bureau of Economic Research, 1950.

————. *Personal Income During Business Cycles*. Princeton: Princeton University Press, 1956.

Dauten, Carl A. *Investment and Business Activity, An Analysis and An Appraisal of the T.N.E.C. Hearings and Monographs on the Relationship of Savings to Investment and the Full Use of Productive Resources*. St. Louis: Washington University Publishers, 1944.

————. *Business Fluctuations and Forecasting*. New York: South-Western Publishing Company, 1954.

Delegation on Economic Depressions of the League of Nations. *Economic Stability in the Post War World—The Conditions of Prosperity After the Transition from War to Peace*. New York: Columbia University Press, 1945.

Dennison, Edward F. *The Source of Economic Growth in the United States and the Alternatives Before Us*. Supplementary Paper No. 13. New York: Committee for Economic Development, 1962.

Dewey, E. R., and Dakin, E. F. *Cycles: The Science of Prediction*. New York: Henry Holt, 1947.

Dillard, Dudley. *The Economics of John Maynard Keynes*. New York: Prentice-Hall, 1948.

Domar, Evsey D. *Essays in the Theory of Economic Growth*. New York: Oxford University Press, 1957.

Douglas, Clifford H. *Social Credit*. New York: W. W. Norton, 1933.

Douglas, Paul H. *Controlling Depressions*. New York: W. W. Norton, 1935.

————. *Memorandum to Members of the Joint Committee on the Economic Report*. On the Committee Report on the President's January 1952 Report. March 6, 1952. Washington, D. C.: U. S. Government Printing Office, 1952.

Duesenberry, J. S. *Income, Employment and Public Policy*. New York: W. W. Norton, 1948.

————. *Income, Saving, and Theory of Consumer Behavior*. Cambridge: Harvard University Press, 1952—Under the Title "The Consumption Function," the original version of this book was submitted as a doctoral dissertation at the University of Michigan, 1948.

————. *Business Cycles and Economic Growth*. New York: McGraw-Hill, 1958.

Eakin, F. *Price Problems—An Accounting Report*. Decatur, Ill.: Economic Accounting, 1948.

Economic Planning Agency of the Japanese Government. *Employment Structure and Business Fluctuations*. Tokyo: Economic Research Institute, 1959.

The Economic Report of the President Transmitted to the Congress January 8, 1947. Washington, D. C.: U. S. Government Printing Office. (Issued annually 1947 to 1962.)

————. *Hearings Before the Joint Committee on the Economic Report*. Washington, D. C.: U. S. Government Printing Office. (Issued annually 1947 to 1962.)

The Economics of Full Employment: Six Studies in Applied Economics Presented at the Oxford University Institute of Statistics. Oxford: Basil Blackwell, 1944.

Egle, W. P. *Economic Stabilization—Objectives, Rules and Mechanisms*. Princeton: Princeton University Press, 1952.

Eiteman, W. J. *Price Determination—Business Practice Versus Economic Theory.* Ann Arbor: University of Michigan, School of Business Administration, 1949.

Ellis, Howard S., Ed. *A Survey of Contemporary Economics.* Published for the American Economic Association. Philadelphia: Blakiston Company, 1948.

Empire Economic Union. *Post War Economic Policy.* London: Empire Economics Union, 1945.

Employment and Unemployment. *Initial Report of the Subcommittee on Unemployment.* Washington, D. C.: U. S. Government Printing Office, 1949.

Employment and Unemployment Statistics. Hearings, 84th Congress, 1st Session, November 7–8, 1955, before the Subcommittee on Economic Statistics of the Joint Committee on the Economic Report. Washington, D. C.: U. S. Government Printing Office, 1955.

Estey, J. A. *Business Cycles, Their Nature, Cause, and Control.* New York: Prentice-Hall, 1950.

Ezekiel, Mordecai. *Jobs for All Through Industrial Expansion.* New York; London: A. A. Knopf, 1939.

———. *Methods of Correlation Analysis.* New York: J. Wiley & Sons, Inc., London: Chapman & Hall, Ltd., 1941.

———, Ed. *Toward World Prosperity Through Industrial and Agricultural Development and Expansion.* New York and London: Harper & Bros., 1947.

———, (Co-author and Editor). *Use of Agricultural Surplus to Finance Economic Development in Underdeveloped Countries—A Pilot Study in India.* Washington, D. C.: Food and Agricultural Organizations of the United Nations, 1955 (F. A. O. Commodity Policy Study 6).

Fabian Society of New South Wales. *Fighting Inflation 1945–1949.* Pamphlet No. 5. Sydney: Fabian Society of New South Wales, 1949.

Fabricant, S. *The Output of Manufacturing Industries 1899–1937.* Cambridge: Harvard University Press, 1947.

———. *Economic Progress and Economic Change.* Thirty-fourth Annual Report. New York: National Bureau of Economic Research, 1954.

———, and others. *Relation of Production to Economic Stability.* New Wilmington, Pa.: Economic and Business Foundation, 1947.

Federal Works Agency. *Post-War Public Works, the Federal Works Administrator.* Washington, D. C.: U. S. Government Printing Office, 1944.

Fellner, William J. *A Treatise on War Inflation.* Berkeley: University of California Press, 1942.

———. *Monetary Policy and Full Employment,* rev. ed. Berkeley: University of California Press, 1947.

———. *Competition Among the Few; Oligopoly and Similar Market Conditions.* New York: A. A. Knopf, 1949.

———, and others. *Money, Trade, and Growth.* New York and London: Macmillan, 1951.

———. *Trends and Cycles in Economic Activity.* New York: Holt, 1956.

Fels, Rendigs. *American Business Cycles 1865–1897.* Chapel Hill: University of North Carolina Press, 1959.

Ferber, R. A. *A Study of Aggregate Consumption Functions.* New York: National Bureau of Economic Research, 1953.

Fisher, Irving. *The Purchasing Power of Money.* New York: Macmillan, 1913.

Fitch, Lyle, and Taylor, Horace, Eds. *Planning for Jobs.* Philadelphia: Blakiston Company, 1946.

Foster, William T., and Catchins, Waddill. *Profits*. Boston: Houghton Mifflin, 1925.

Frickey, Edwin. *Economic Fluctuations in the United States*. Cambridge: Harvard University Press, 1942.

――――. *Production in the United States, 1860–1914*. Cambridge: Harvard University Press, 1947.

Friedman, Milton. *Essays in Positive Economics*. Chicago: University of Chicago Press, 1953.

――――. *A Theory of the Consumption Function*. (Published for the National Bureau of Economic Research.) Princeton: Princeton University Press, 1957.

――――, and others. *Taxing to Prevent Inflation*. New York: Columbia University Press, 1943.

――――. *What Can Be Done About Inflation?* Chicago: University of Chicago Roundtable, 1946.

――――. *Sampling Inspection*. New York: McGraw-Hill, 1948.

――――. *A Program for Monetary Stability*. New York: Fordham University Press, 1959.

Fuller, C. A. *How to Produce Depressions*. Philadelphia: Dorrance and Company, 1949.

Galbraith, John Kenneth. *The Great Crash, 1929*. Boston: Houghton Mifflin, 1955.

――――. *The Affluent Society*. Boston: Houghton Mifflin, 1958.

Gaston, J. F. *Growth Patterns in Industry: A Reexamination*. New York: National Industrial Conference Board, 1961.

Gilbert, Milton, and Associates. *Comparative National Production and Price Levels*. Paris: OEEC, 1958.

Goodbar, J. E., and Bergeron, L. V. *A Creative Capitalism—Intended to Reveal Where Depressions Start, Where Lasting Cure Must Begin, and How Cure Can be Had Within the Capitalistic System of Private Enterprise*. Boston: Boston University Press, 1948.

Gordon, Robert Aaron. *Business Fluctuations*. New York: Harper & Bros., 1961.

Grebler, L. *Housing Issues in Economic Stabilization Policy*. Occasional Paper No. 72. New York: National Bureau of Economic Research, 1960.

――――, Blank, D. M., and Winnick, L. *Capital Formation in Residential Real Estate: Trends and Prospects*. Princeton: Princeton University Press, 1942.

Guttentag, J. M. *Some Studies of the Post-World War II Residential Construction and Mortgage Markets*. Unpublished Ph.D. Dissertation. New York: Columbia University Press, 1958.

Guyot, Yves. *Principles of Social Economy*. London: Swan Sonnenschein & Company; New York: Charles Scribner's Sons, 1892.

Haberler, Gottfried. *Prosperity and Depression*. Cambridge: Harvard University Press, 1958.

――――. *Inflation: Its Causes and Cures*. Washington, D. C.: American Enterprise Association, 1960.

Hald, E. C. *Business Cycles*. Boston: Houghton Mifflin, 1954.

Hamberg, D. *Business Cycles*. New York: Macmillan, 1951.

――――. *Economic Growth and Instability*. New York: Macmillan, 1956.

Hammond, C. *Prosperity Ahead*. Bradford, England: Author (Cliff St., Thornton), 1945.

Haney, Lewis H. *History of Economic Thought*. New York: Macmillan, 1949.

Hansen, Alvin H. *Fiscal Policy and Business Cycles*. New York: W. W. Norton, 1941.
———. *Economic Policy and Full Employment*. New York: McGraw-Hill, 1947.
———. *Monetary Theory and Fiscal Policy*. New York: McGraw-Hill, 1949.
———. *Business Cycles and National Income*. New York: W. W. Norton, 1951.
———. *Economic Issues of the 1960's*. New York: McGraw-Hill, 1961.
———, and Clemence, R. V. *Readings in Business Cycles and National Income*. New York: W. W. Norton, 1953.
Hardy, C. O., Williams, K. B., and Ellis, H. S. *Prices, Wages and Employment*. Washington, D. C.: Board of Governors of the Federal Reserve System, 1946.
Harris, Seymour E., Ed. *Postwar Economic Problems*. New York: McGraw-Hill, 1943.
———. *Inflation and the American Economy*. New York: McGraw-Hill, 1945.
———. *National Debt and the New Economics*. New York: McGraw-Hill, 1947.
Harrod, Sir Roy F. *The Trade Cycle*. Oxford: Clarendon Press, 1936.
———. *Are These Hardships Necessary?* London: R. Hart-Davis, 1947.
———. *Towards a Dynamic Economics*. London: Macmillan, 1948.
———. *The Life of John Maynard Keynes*. London: Macmillan, 1951.
———. *Economic Essays*. London: Macmillan, 1952.
———. *The Dollar*. London: Macmillan, 1953.
———. *Foundations of Inductive Logic*. New York: Harcourt, Brace, 1957.
———. *Policy Against Inflation*. New York: St. Martin's Press, Inc., 1958.
Hart, A. G. *Money, Debt and Economic Activity*. New York: Prentice-Hall, 1948.
Hauser, Philip M., and Leonard, William R., Eds. *Government Statistics for Business Use*. New York: John Wiley & Sons, 1956.
Hawtrey, Ralph G. *Good and Bad Trade; An Inquiry into the Causes of Trade Fluctuations*. London: Constable and Company, Ltd., 1913.
———. *Currency and Credit*. London: Longmans, Green, 1919.
———. *The Exchequer and the Control of Expenditure*. London; New York: Oxford University Press, 1921.
———. *The Economic Problem*. New York: Longmans, Green, 1925.
———. *Trade and Credit*. New York: Longmans, Green, 1928.
———. *The Gold Standard in Theory and Practice*. London: Longmans, Green, 1931.
———. *Trade Depression and the Way Out*. London: Longmans, Green, 1931.
———. *The Art of Central Banking*. London: Longmans, Green, 1932.
———. *Capital and Employment*. London: Longmans, Green, 1937.
———. *A Century of Bank Rate*. London: Longmans, Green, 1938.
———. *The Balance of Payments and the Standard of Living*. London; New York: Royal Institute of International Affairs, 1950.
Hayek, Friedrich A. *Prices and Production*. Vienna: J. Springer, 1931.
———. *Monetary Theory and the Trade Cycle*. London: J. Cape, 1933.
———. *Prices and Production*. London: G. Routledge and Sons, Ltd., 1935.
———. *Monetary Nationalism and International Stability*. London; New York: Longmans, Green, 1937.
———. *Profits, Interest, and Investment*. London: G. Routledge and Sons, Ltd., 1939.
———. *The Pure Theory of Capital*. London: Macmillan, 1941.

————. *The Road to Serfdom.* Chicago: University of Chicago Press, 1944.

————. *Individualism and Economic Order* (Essays). Chicago: University of Chicago Press, 1948.

Hayes, D. A. *Business Confidence and Business Activity—A Case Study of the Recession of 1937.* Michigan Business Studies, Vol. X, No. 5. Ann Arbor: University of Michigan School of Business Administration, 1951.

Hayes, H. G. *Saving, Spending and Employment.* New York: A. A. Knopf, 1945.

Hazlitt, H., and others. *Sixty Million Jobs.* Chicago: University of Chicago Roundtable, 1945.

————. *What You Should Know About Inflation.* Princeton: Van Nostrand, 1960.

Heimann, Eduard. *History of Economic Doctrines.* New York: Oxford University Press, 1959, Chap. vi.

Hickman, Bert G. *Growth and Stability of the Postwar Economy.* Washington, D. C.: Brookings Institution, 1960.

Hicks, J. R. *A Contribution to the Theory of the Trade Cycle.* Oxford: Clarendon Press, 1950.

Hobson, John A. *The Economics of Unemployment.* London: G. Allen & Unwin, Ltd., 1922.

————, and Mummery, A. F. *Physiology of Industry.* New York: Kelley & Millman, 1889.

————. *The Evolution of Modern Capitalism: A Study of Machine Production.* London: Walter Scott, Ltd., 1894.

————. *Rationalization and Unemployment.* London: G. Allen & Unwin, Ltd., 1930.

Hood, W. C., and Koopmans, T. C., Eds. *Studies in Econometric Method.* Cowles Commission for Research in Economics. Monograph No. 14. New York: Wiley, 1953.

Hopkins, E. *The High Crime of Inflation: How to Restore the Purchasing Power of the Dollar.* New York: Author (255 West 43d Street), 1948.

Houser, T. V. *The Cruelest Tax.* New York: Committee for Economic Development, 1958.

Hoyt, H. *One Hundred Years of Land Values in Chicago.* Chicago: University of Chicago Press, 1933.

Hudson, M. *Full Employment.* Boston: Christopher, 1946.

Hull, G. *Industrial Depressions.* New York: F. A. Stokes, 1911.

Hultgren, Thor. *Cyclical Diversities in the Fortunes of Industrial Corporations.* Occasional Paper No. 32. New York: National Bureau of Economic Research, 1950.

————. *Changes in Labor Costs During Cycles in Production and Business.* Occasional Paper No. 74. New York: National Bureau of Economic Research, 1960.

Hussey, M. *Foundry Activity as a Business Barometer—The Record: 1928–1949.* Philadelphia: Wharton School of Finance and Commerce, University of Pennsylvania, 1950.

Hyndman, H. M. *Commercial Crises of the Nineteenth Century.* London: Swan Sonnenschein & Company, 1902.

International Labor Office. *Public Investment and Full Employment.* Montreal: International Labor Office, 1946.

————. *Action Against Unemployment.* Geneva: International Labor Office, 1950.

Isard, Walter. *The Economic Dynamics of Transport Technology.* Cambridge: Harvard University Library, 1941. Unpublished Doctoral Dissertation.

Jacoby, N. H. *How Can We Avoid Economic Collapse?* Chicago: University of Chicago Roundtable, 1947.

————. *Can Prosperity Be Sustained? Policies for Full Employment and Full Production Without Price Inflation in a Free Economy.* New York: Holt, Rinehart & Winston, 1956.

————, and others. *The Murray Bill, A Means to Full Employment?* Chicago: University of Chicago Roundtable, 1945.

————, Roe, F., and Yntema, T. *Has a Business Recession Begun?* Chicago: University of Chicago Roundtable, 1947.

Jerome, Harry. *Migration and Business Cycles.* New York: National Bureau of Economic Research, 1926.

Johnston, E. A. *Steadier Jobs.* Washington, D. C.: U. S. Chamber of Commerce, 1944.

Joint Committee on the Economic Report. *Current Price Developments and the Problems of Economic Stabilization.* Washington, D. C.: U. S. Government Printing Office, 1947.

————. *Credit Policies.* Hearings, 80th Congress, 2d Session, April 13-May 27, 1948, before the Joint Committee on the Economic Report. Washington, D. C.: U. S. Government Printing Office, 1948.

————. *Corporate Profits.* Hearings, 80th Congress, 2d Session, Joint Committee on the Economic Report. Washington, D. C.: U. S. Government Printing Office, 1949.

————. *Federal Expenditure and Revenue Policies.* Washington, D. C.: U. S. Government Printing Office, 1949.

————. *Factors Affecting Volume and Stability of Private Investment.* Prepared by the Staff of the Subcommittee on Investment of the Joint Committee on the Economic Report, 81st Congress, 2d Session. Washington, D. C.: U. S. Government Printing Office, 1950.

————. *Monetary, Credit and Fiscal Policies.* Report of, and Hearings before the Subcommittee on Monetary, Credit and Fiscal Policies of the Joint Committee on the Economic Report, 81st Congress, 1st Session. Washington, D. C.: U. S. Government Printing Office, 1950.

————. *Monetary Policy and the Management of the Public Debt, Parts I and II.* 82d Congress, 2d Session. Washington, D. C.: U. S. Government Printing Office, 1952.

Joint Economic Committee. *Economic Indicators.* (Issued monthly by U. S. Government Printing Office.)

————. *Instrumentation and Automation.* Hearings, 84th Congress, 2d Session, before the Subcommittee on Economic Stabilization of the Joint Economic Committee. Washington, D. C.: U. S. Government Printing Office, 1957.

————. *Productivity, Prices and Incomes.* Material Prepared for the Joint Economic Committee. Washington, D. C.: U. S. Government Printing Office, 1957.

————. *Fiscal Policy Implications of the Current Economic Outlook.* Hearings, 85th Congress, 2d Session, before the Subcommittee on Fiscal Policy of the Joint Economic Committee. Washington, D. C.: U. S. Government Printing Office, 1958.

————. *The Relationship of Prices to Economic Stability and Growth.* Papers submitted by panelists and Hearings, 85th Congress, 2d Session, before the Joint Economic Committee. Washington, D. C.: U. S. Government Printing Office, 1958.

————. *Economic Policy Questionnaire.* Tabulation of Replies Submitted to the Subcommittee on Economic Stabilization of the Joint Economic Committee, 85th Congress, 2d Session, December 1958. Washington, D. C.: U. S. Government Printing Office, 1959.

————. *Employment, Growth, and Price Levels.* Part 1: The American Economy: Problems and Prospects; Part 2: Historical and Comparative Rates of Production, Productivity, and Prices; Part 4: The Influence of Prices of Changes in the Effective Supply of Money; Part 6A: The Government's Management of Its Monetary, Fiscal and Debt Operations. Washington, D. C.: U. S. Government Printing Office, 1959.

————. *Employment, Growth, and Price Levels.* 86th Congress, 1st and 2d Sessions. Washington, D. C.: U. S. Government Printing Office, 1959–60.

————. *Employment, Growth, and Price Levels.* Report of the Joint Economic Committee, 86th Congress, 2d Session, with Minority, Supplemental, and Additional Views. Washington, D. C.: U. S. Government Printing Office, 1960.

————. *Current Economic Situation and Short Run Outlook.* Hearings, 86th Congress, 2d Session, before the Joint Economic Committee. Washington, D. C.: U. S. Government Printing Office, 1961.

————. *Employment, Growth, and Price Levels.* Index to Hearings before Joint Economic Committee. Washington, D. C.: U. S. Government Printing Office, 1961.

Jones, R. C. *Effects of Price Level Changes on Business Income, Capital and Taxes.* Columbus: Ohio State University, American Accounting Association, 1948.

Jordan, S. *Inflation: What It Is, What It Does, and What to Do About It.* Asbury Park, N. J.: Enterprise Publishing Company, 1946.

Kalecki, Michal. *Essays in the Theory of Economic Fluctuations.* London: G. Allen & Unwin, Ltd., 1939.

————. *Studies in Economic Dynamics.* New York: Farrar and Rinehart, 1944.

Kasun, J. R. *Some Social Aspects of Business Cycles in the Los Angeles Area, 1920–1950.* Los Angeles: Haynes Foundation, 1954.

Katona, G. *Psychological Analysis of Economic Behavior.* New York: McGraw-Hill, 1951.

————, and Mueller, E. *Consumer Expectations 1953–1956.* Ann Arbor: University of Michigan Institute of Social Research, 1956.

Keynes, J. M. *The General Theory of Employment, Interest, and Money.* New York: Harcourt, Brace, 1936.

Keyserling, L. H., Clark, J. M., and Viner, J. *The President's Economic Program.* Current Business Study No. 3. New York: Trade and Industry Law Institute, 1949.

Kidner, F. L. *California Business Cycles.* Berkeley: University of California Press, 1946.

Klein, L. R. *The Keynesian Revolution.* New York: Macmillan, 1947.

————. *Economic Fluctuations in the United States 1921–1941.* Cowles Commission. New York: John Wiley & Sons, 1950.

————. *A Textbook of Econometrics.* Evanston, Ill.: Row, Peterson, 1953.

————, and Goldberger, A. S. *An Econometric Model of the United States, 1929–1952.* Amsterdam: North-Holland Publishing Company, 1955.

Koopmans, T. C., Ed. *Statistical Inferences in Dynamic Economic Models.* New York: J. Wiley & Sons, 1950.

Krooss, Herman E. *American Economic Development.* chap. ii. New York: Prentice-Hall, 1955.

Krout, J. A. *Prices, Wages and Inflation.* New York: Academy of Political Science, 1948.

Kurihara, K. K. *Monetary Theory and Public Policy.* New York: W. W. Norton, 1950.

Kuthe, H. C. *Prices and Business in 1947.* New York: Business Bourse, 1946.

Kuznets, Simon. *Seasonal Variations in Industry and Trade.* New York: National Bureau of Economic Research, 1933.

——. "Relation Between Capital Goods and Finished Products in the Business Cycle," in *Economic Essays in Honor of Wesley Clair Mitchell.* New York: Columbia University Press, 1935.

——. *National Income—A Summary of Findings.* New York: National Bureau of Economic Research, 1946.

——. *Shares of Upper Income Groups in Income and Savings.* New York: National Bureau of Economic Research, 1950.

Lange, O. *Price Flexibility and Employment.* Cowles Commission Monograph No. 8. Bloomington, Ind.: Principia Press, 1944.

Lauck, W. Jett. *The Causes of the Panic of 1893.* Boston: Houghton Mifflin, 1907.

League of Nations. *The Course and Control of Inflation: A Review of Monetary Experience in Europe After World War I.* New York: Columbia University Press, 1946.

League of Women Voters. *Fiscal Policy and Full Employment.* Washington, D. C.: League of Women Voters, 1949.

Lee, Maurice W. *Economic Fluctuations—Growth and Stability.* Homewood, Ill.: Richard D. Irwin, 1959.

Lerner, A. P., and Graham, F. P. *Planning and Paying for Full Employment.* Princeton: Princeton University Press, 1946.

Lewis, John P. *Business Conditions Analysis.* New York: McGraw-Hill, 1959.

Lintner, J. *Corporate Profits in Perspective.* New York: American Enterprise Association, 1949.

Loeb, H. *Full Production Without War.* Princeton: Princeton University Press, 1946.

Long, Clarence D., Jr. *Building Cycles and the Theory of Investment.* Princeton: Princeton University Press, 1940.

Luedicke, H. *How to Forecast Business Trends: A Special Report for Executives.* New York: Journal of Commerce, 1954.

Lundberg, Eric, Ed. *The Business Cycle in the Post-War World.* Proceedings of a Conference held by the International Economic Association, Oxford, September, 1952. New York: St. Martin's Press, 1955.

——. *Business Cycles and Economic Policy.* Cambridge: Harvard University Press, 1957.

Lunde, H. *Underwriting Prosperity—How We Have Stabilized a Growing Economy.* Bulletin No. 7. St. Paul, Minn.: Macalester College Bureau of Economic Studies, 1960.

Mack, Ruth P. *Consumption and Business Fluctuations—A Case Study of the Shoe, Leather, Hide Sequence.* Study in Business Cycles No. 7. Princeton: Princeton University Press, 1956.

Maisel, Sherman J. *Fluctuations, Growth, and Forecasting.* New York: John Wiley & Sons, 1957.

Malach, V. W. *International Cycles and Canada's Balance of Payments 1921–33.* Toronto: University of Toronto Press, 1954.

Malanos, G. J., and Thomassen, H. *An Econometric Model of the American Minor Cycle.* Atlanta: Bureau of Business and Economic Research, School of Business Administration, Georgia State College of Business Administration, 1960.

Marcus, E. *Canada and the International Business Cycle 1927–1939.* New York: Bookman Associates, 1954.

Martin, Robert F. *National Income in the United States, 1799–1938.* New York: National Industrial Conference Board, 1939.

Matthews, R. C. O. *The Business Cycle.* Chicago: University of Chicago Press, 1959.

Maxwell, J. A. *Federal Grants and the Business Cycle.* New York: National Bureau of Economic Research, 1952.

McCartney, Ernest R. *Crisis of 1873.* Minneapolis, 1935. A dissertation.

McConnell, John W. *The Basic Teachings of Great Economists.* New York: New Home Library, 1943.

McGrane, Reginald C. *The Panic of 1837.* Chicago: University of Chicago Press, 1924.

McKean, E. C., and Taylor, H. C. *Public Works and Employment from the Local Government Point of View.* Chicago: Public Administration Service, 1955.

Meade, J. E. *Planning and the Price Mechanism.* New York: Macmillan, 1949.

————. *The Control of Inflation—An Inaugural Lecture Delivered in Cambridge, March 4, 1958.* London: Cambridge University Press, 1958.

Mendershausen, Horst. *Changes in Income Distribution During the Great Depression.* New York: National Bureau of Economic Research, 1946.

Metzler, Lloyd, and others. *Income, Employment and Public Policy, Essays in Honor of Alvin Hansen.* New York: W. W. Norton, 1948.

Meyer, J. R., and Kuh, Edwin. *The Investment Decision.* Cambridge: Harvard University Press, 1957.

Millikan, M. F., Ed. *Income Stabilization for a Developing Democracy.* New Haven: Yale University Press, 1953.

Mills, Frederick C. *Price-Quantity Interactions in Business Cycles.* New York: National Bureau of Economic Research, 1946.

————. *The Structure of Post War Prices.* Occasional Paper No. 27. New York: National Bureau of Economic Research, 1948.

Mitchell, Broadus. *Depression Decade from New Era Through New Deal, 1929–1941.* New York: Rinehart, 1947.

Mitchell, Wesley C. *A History of the Greenbacks.* Chicago: University of Chicago Press, 1903.

————. *Business Cycles: The Problem and Its Setting.* New York: National Bureau of Economic Research, 1927.

————. *Business Cycles and Their Causes.* Berkeley: University of California Press, 1941.

————. *What Happens During Business Cycles.* New York: National Bureau of Economic Research, 1951.

Mooney, R. E., and Dale, E. L. *Inflation and Recession.* New York: Doubleday, 1958.

Moore, Geoffrey H. *Statistical Indicators of Cyclical Revivals and Recessions.* Occasional Paper No. 31. New York: National Bureau of Economic Research, 1950.

————. *Measuring Recessions.* Occasional Paper No. 61. New York: National Bureau of Economic Research, 1958.

————. *Business Cycle Indicators.* 2 vols. Princeton: Princeton University Press, 1961.

Morgan, E. V. *The Conquest of Unemployment*. London: Sampson Low, Marston & Company, 1947.

Morgan, T. *Income and Employment*. New York: Prentice-Hall, 1947.

Moulton, Harold G. *Controlling Factors in Economic Development*. chaps. ii, iii, and x. Washington, D. C.: Brookings Institution, 1949.

———. *Can Inflation Be Controlled?* Washington, D. C.: Anderson Kramer Association, 1958.

Muranjan, S. K. *Shadows of Hyper-Inflation*. Bombay: Hind Kitabs., 1949.

Murphy, Henry C. *National Debt in War and Transition*. New York: McGraw-Hill, 1950.

Musgrave, Richard A., and others. *Public Finance and Full Employment*. Postwar Economic Studies No. 3. Washington, D. C.: Board of Governors of the Federal Reserve System, 1945.

Myers, Charles A., Ed. *Wages, Prices, Profits and Productivity*. The American Assembly. New York: Columbia University Press, June, 1959.

Nathan Associates, R. R. *A National Economic Policy for 1949*. Washington, D. C.: Nathan Associates, 1949.

National Association of Manufacturers. *Program for Permanent Prosperity*. New York: National Association of Manufacturers, 1945.

———. *Employment Stabilization: Industry's Progress Toward Steady Work and Steady Pay*. New York: National Association of Manufacturers, 1948.

———. *Recent Economic Changes*. New York: National Association of Manufacturers, 1949.

National Bureau Committee for Economic Research. *Conference on Business Cycles Held Under the Auspices of Universities*. New York: National Bureau of Economic Research, 1951.

———. *Policies to Combat Depression. A Conference of Universities National Bureau Committee for Economic Research*. Princeton: Princeton University Press, 1956.

National Bureau of Commerce for Economic Research. *The Quality and Economic Significance of Anticipations Data*. Princeton: Princeton University Press, 1960.

National Bureau of Economic Research. *Basic Research and the Analysis of Current Business Conditions*. Thirty-sixth Annual Report—A Record of 1955 and Plans for 1956. New York: National Bureau of Economic Research, 1956.

———. *Policies to Combat Depression*. Princeton: Princeton University Press, 1956.

———. *The Quality and Economic Significance of Anticipations Data*. Princeton: Princeton University Press, 1960.

National Industrial Conference Board. *The Business Outlook 1949*. New York: National Industrial Conference Board. (Issued annually 1949 to 1962.)

———. *Economics of the President's Economists*. Study in Business Economics No. 20. New York: National Industrial Conference Board, 1949.

———. *Wages, Prices, Profits*. New York: National Industrial Conference Board, 1949.

———. *Economic Expansion—Patterns, Problems, Potentials*. New York: National Industrial Conference Board, 1950.

———. *Growth Patterns in Industry*. New York: National Industrial Conference Board, 1952.

———. *Progress Against Inflation*. New York: National Industrial Conference Board, 1960.

National Planning Association. *A Joint Statement on the Use of Chronic Unemployment.* Washington, D. C.: National Planning Association, 1961.

National Tax Association. *Budget Policy and Economic Outlook.* Washington, D. C.: National Tax Association, 1948.

Neff, P., and Weifenbach, A. *Business Cycles in Los Angeles.* Berkeley: University of California Press, 1949.

————. *Business Cycles in Selected Industrial Areas.* Berkeley: University of California Press, 1949.

Nemmers, E., and Janzen, C. *Dictionary of Economics.* Paterson, N. J.: Littlefield, Adams & Company, 1958.

Newbury, F. D. *Business Forecasting: A Survey of Practices and Methods.* New York: Controllership Foundation, 1950.

————. *Business Forecasting.* New York: McGraw-Hill, 1952.

Newman, Philip C., Gayer, Arthur D., and Spencer, Milton H. *Source Readings in Economic Thought.* New York: W. W. Norton, 1954.

Newman, William H. *The Building Industry and Business Cycles.* Chicago: University of Chicago Press, 1935.

Nourse, E. G. *Economics in the Public Service—The Intimate Story of the First Six Years of the Employment Act.* New York: Harcourt, Brace, 1953.

Nugent, R., Dewing, A. S., and Zahniser, B. *Stabilization of Production and Employment.* New Wilmington, Pa.: Economic and Business Foundation, 1947.

Ohlin, Bertel. *The Problem of Employment Stabilization.* New York: Columbia University Press, 1949.

O'Mahoney, J. C., and others. *Should Government Be Responsible for Continuing Full Employment?* Columbus: Reader's Digest, 1945.

Parker, R. S., Ed. *Economic Stability in New Zealand.* Wellington: New Zealand Institute of Public Administration, 1953.

Partington, John E. *Railroad Purchasing and the Business Cycle.* Washington, D. C.: The Brookings Institution, 1929.

Paul, Randolph. *Taxation for Prosperity.* New York: Bobbs-Merrill, 1947.

Payli, M. *An Inflation Primer.* Chicago: Henry Regnery, 1961.

Payne, Wilson F. *Business Behavior 1919–1922.* Chicago: University of Chicago Press, 1942.

Persoff, A. M. *Sabbatical Years with Pay—A Plan to Create and Maintain Full Employment.* Los Angeles: Charter Publishing Company, 1945.

Pierson, J. H. G. *Full Employment in Practice.* New York: New York University Institute on Post-War Reconstruction, 1946.

Pigou, A. C. *The Economics of Welfare.* London: Macmillan, 1920.

————. *Industrial Fluctuations.* London: Macmillan, 1927.

————. *The Theory of Unemployment.* London: Macmillan, 1933.

————. *Lapses from Full Employment.* New York: Macmillan, 1946.

————. *Employment and Equilibrium.* London: Macmillan, 1949.

————. *Keynes' General Theory.* London: Macmillan, 1951.

Platt, H. M. *Economic Indicators—Their Use in Business Forecasting.* Hanover, N. H.: Amos Tuck School, Dartmouth College, 1959.

Polanyi, M. *Full Employment and Free Trade.* New York: Macmillan, 1948.

Poole, Kenyon E., Ed. *Fiscal Policies and the American Economy.* New York: Prentice-Hall, 1951.

Private and Public Investment in Canada 1926–51. Ottawa: Department of Trade and Commerce, 1951.

Proposed Mid Year Economic Report. Hearings, 85th Congress, 2d Session, before the Senate Committee on Banking and Currency. Washington, D. C.: U. S. Government Printing Office, 1958.

The Quality and Economic Significance of Anticipations Data. Published for National Bureau of Economic Research. Princeton: Princeton University Press, 1960.

Rauch, Basil. *The History of the New Deal 1933–1938.* New York: Creative Age Press, 1944.

Ray, Delmar D. *Accounting and Business Fluctuations.* Gainesville: University of Florida Press, 1960.

Readings in Unemployment. Prepared for the Senate Special Committee on Unemployment Problems, 86th Congress, 1st Session. Washington, D. C.: U. S. Government Printing Office, 1960.

Regularization of Business Investment. A Conference of the Universities—National Bureau Committee for Economic Research. Princeton: Princeton University Press, 1954.

The Relationship of Prices to Economic Stability and Growth Commentaries. Submitted by Economists from Labor and Industry Appearing Before the Joint Economic Committee, 85th Congress, 2d Session, October 31, 1958. Washington, D. C.: U. S. Government Printing Office, 1958.

Reynolds, L. G. *Wage Rates, Inflation and Depression.* New Wilmington, Pa.: Economic and Business Foundation, 1948.

Robbins, Lionel. *An Essay on the Nature and Significance of Economic Science.* London: Macmillan, 1937.

Robertson, D. A. *Banking Policy and the Price Level—An Essay in the Theory of the Trade Cycle.* Reprint. New York: Augustus M. Kelley, 1949.

Robertson, D. H. *Banking Policy and the Price Level.* London: P. S. King & Son, 1926.

———. *A Study of Industrial Fluctuations (1915) with New Introduction by the Author.* London: London School of Economics and Political Science, 1948.

Robinson, Joan. *The Rate of Interest and Other Essays.* London: Macmillan, 1952.

———. *The Accumulation of Capital.* New York: Macmillan, 1957.

Rockefeller Brothers Fund. *The Challenge to America: Its Economic and Social Aspects.* Report of Panel IV of the Special Studies Project, "America at Mid-Century Series." New York: Doubleday, 1958.

Rockefeller Panel Reports. *Prospects for America.* New York: Doubleday, 1961.

Roosa, Robert V. *Federal Reserve Operations in the Money and Government Securities Markets.* New York: Federal Reserve Bank of New York, 1956.

Roose, Kenneth D. *The Economics of Recession and Revival—An Interpretation of 1937–38.* New Haven: Yale University Press, 1954.

Rostow, Walt W. *British Economy of the Nineteenth Century; Essays.* Oxford: Clarendon Press, 1948.

———. *The Process of Economic Growth.* New York: W. W. Norton, 1952.

———. *The Dynamics of Soviet Society.* New York: W. W. Norton, 1953.

———. *The Growth and Fluctuations of the British Economy 1790–1850.* Oxford: Clarendon Press, 1953.

———. *The Prospects for Communist China.* New York: Technology Press of Massachusetts Institute of Technology, 1954.

———. *Stages of Economic Growth.* Cambridge: Cambridge University Press, 1960.

Ruggles, Richard. *An Introduction to National Income and Income Analysis.* New York: McGraw-Hill, 1949.

Sayre, R. A. _Consumer Prices 1914–1948._ New York: National Industrial Conference Board, 1948.

Schields, M., and Woodward, D. B. _Prosperity: We Can Have It If We Want It._ New York: McGraw-Hill, 1945.

Schluter, W. C. _The Prewar Business Cycle, 1907–1914._ New York: Columbia University Press, 1923.

Schmidt, E. P. _Can Government Guarantee Full Employment._ Post War Readjustment Bill No. 13. Washington, D. C.: U. S. Chamber of Commerce, 1945.

——. _Mitigating Depression._ Washington, D. C.: U. S. Chamber of Commerce, 1945.

Schultze, C. L. _Recent Inflation in the United States, Study Paper No. 1. Study of Employment, Growth and Price Levels._ Joint Economic Committee. Washington, D. C.: Superintendent of Documents, 1959.

Schumpeter, Joseph A. _Epochen Der Dogmenund und Methodengeschichte._ Tubingen: J. C. B. Mohr, 1914.

——. _The Theory of Economic Development._ Cambridge: Harvard University Press, 1934.

——. _Business Cycles._ New York: McGraw-Hill, 1939.

——. _Capitalism, Socialism and Democracy._ New York: Harper and Brothers, 1950.

Shiskin, Julius. _Electronic Computers and Business Indicators._ Occasional Paper No. 57. New York: National Bureau of Economic Research, 1957.

Silberling, Norman J. _The Dynamics of Business._ New York: McGraw-Hill, 1943.

Simons, Henry C. _Economic Policy for a Free Society._ Chicago: University of Chicago Press, 1948.

Sinclair, W. A. _Economic Recovery in Victoria—1894–1899._ Canberra: Australian National University, 1948.

Singh, D. B. _Inflationary Price Trends in India Since 1939._ Bombay: Asia Publishing House, 1957.

Smith, Walter Buckingham, and Cole, Arthur Harrison. _Fluctuations in American Business, 1790–1860._ Cambridge: Harvard University Press, 1935.

Snyder, Carl. _Business Cycles and Business Measurement._ New York: Macmillan, 1927.

Snyder, Richard M. _Measuring Business Changes._ New York: John Wiley & Sons, 1955.

Social Action. _Roads to Full Employment._ New York: Social Action, 1945.

Soule, G. _Men, Wages and Employment in the Modern U. S. Economy._ New York: New American Library, 1954.

Sovani, N. V. _Post-War Inflation in India—A Survey._ Poona: Gokhale Institute of Politics and Economics, 1949.

Spencer, M. H., Clark, C. G., and Hoguet, P. W. _Business and Economic Forecasting—An Econometric Approach._ Homewood, Ill.: Richard D. Irwin, 1961.

Spiethoff, A. _Business Cycles._ International Economic Papers, No. 3. London; New York: Macmillan, 1953.

Sprague, Oliver M. W. _History of Crises Under the National Banking System,_ 61st Congress, 2d Session, Senate Document No. 538. Washington, D. C.: U. S. Government Printing Office, 1910.

Sprake, A. _Booms and Slumps._ New York: Pageant Press, 1959.

Staats, E. B. _Tools for Economic Forecasts._ Washington, D. C.: Council of State Governments, 1949.

Staff of the Subcommittee on Investment. _Factors Affecting Volume and_

Stability of Private Investment. Washington, D. C.: U. S. Government Printing Office, 1949.

Stewart, M. S. *There Can Be Jobs for All.* New York: Public Affairs Commission, 1945.

Stewart, W. W. *Monetary Policy and Economic Prosperity—Testimony Before the Macmillan Committee, July 3-4, 1930.* New York: American Enterprise Association, 1950.

Stigler, George J. *Trends in Output and Employment.* New York: National Bureau of Economic Research, 1947.

Strachey, John. *Contemporary Capitalism.* New York: Random House, 1956.

Subcommittee on Low Income Families, Joint Economic Committee on the Economic Report. *Low Income Families and Economic Stability.* 81st Congress, 1st Session. Washington, D. C.: U. S. Government Printing Office, 1950.

———. *Low Income Families and Economic Stability.* 81st Congress, 2d Session. Washington, D.C.: U. S. Government Printing Office, 1950.

Subcommittee on Monetary, Credit and Fiscal Policies. *Monetary, Credit and Fiscal Policies.* Washington, D. C.: U. S. Government Printing Office, 1950.

Subcommittee on Unemployment of the Joint Committee on the Economic Report. *Employment and Unemployment.* 81st Congress, 2d Session. Washington, D. C.: U. S. Government Printing Office, 1950.

Subcommittee on Unemployment of the Joint Committee on Low Income Families, Joint Economic Committee on the Economic Report. *Selected Government Programs Which Aid the Unemployed and Low-Income Families.* 81st Congress, 1st Session. Washington, D. C.: U. S. Government Printing Office, 1949.

Swanson, E. W., and Schmidt, E. P. *Economic Stagnation or Progress—A Critique of Recent Doctrines on the Mature Economy, Oversavings, and Deficit Spending.* New York; McGraw-Hill, 1946.

Terborgh, G. *The Bogey of Economic Maturity.* Chicago: Machinery and Allied Products Institute, 1945.

———. *Inflation and Postwar Profits.* Chicago: Machinery and Allied Products Institute, 1949.

Thomassen, H. *Business Planning for Economic Stability.* Washington, D. C.: Public Affairs Press, 1958.

Thorp, W. L., and Quandt, R. E. *The New Inflation.* New York: McGraw-Hill, 1959.

Tinbergen, Jan. *Statistical Testing of Business Cycle Theories: Vol. I—A Method and Its Application to Investment Activity; Vol. II—Business Cycles in the United States of America, 1919–1932.* Geneva: League of Nations, Economic Intelligence Service, 1939.

———. *Suggestions on Quantitative Business Cycle Theory.* Geneva: League of Nations, 1939.

———. *Business Cycles in the United Kingdom, 1870–1914.* New York: National Bureau of Economic Research, 1951.

———. *Econometrics.* New York: Blakiston, 1951.

———. *Reformation of Current Business Cycle Theories as Refutable Hypothesis.* New York: National Bureau of Economic Research, 1951.

———. *On the Theory of Economic Policy.* Amsterdam: North-Holland Publishing Company, 1952.

———. *Economic Policy; Principles and Design.* Amsterdam: North-Holland Publishing Company, 1956.

————, and Polak, J. J. *The Dynamics of Business Cycles—A Study in Economic Fluctuations.* Chicago: University of Chicago Press, 1950.

Toward Full Employment and Full Production: How to End Our National Economic Deficits. Washington, D. C.: Conference on Economic Progress, 1954.

Trade and Industry Law Institute. *The President's Economic Program.* New York: Trade and Industry Law Institute, June, 1949.

The Treasury and the Money Market. New York: Federal Reserve Bank of New York, 1954.

Tsiang, S. C. *The Variations of Real Wages and Profit Margins in Relation to the Trade Cycle.* London: Pitman and Sons, 1947.

Ulmer, M. J. *Trends and Cycles in Capital Formation by United States Railroads, 1870–1950.* New York: National Bureau of Economic Research, 1954.

Unemployment Problems. Hearings, 86th Congress, 1st Session and 2d Session, before Senate Special Committee on Unemployment Problems. Washington, D. C.: U. S. Government Printing Office, 1960.

Unemployment Situation and Outlook. Hearings, 87th Congress, 1st Session, before the Subcommittee on Employment and Manpower of the Senate Committee on Labor and Public Welfare. Washington, D. C.: U. S. Government Printing Office, 1961.

United Nations, Department of Economic Affairs. *Survey of Current Inflationary and Deflationary Tendencies.* New York: Columbia University Press, 1947.

U. S. Chamber of Commerce. *A Program for Sustaining Employment.* Washington, D. C.: U. S. Chamber of Commerce, 1947.

————. Economic Research Department. *Investment for Jobs.* Washington, D. C.: U. S. Chamber of Commerce, 1950.

————. Committee on Economic Policy. *Can We Depression-Proof Our Economy?* Washington, D. C.: U. S. Chamber of Commerce, 1955.

————. *The Mechanics of Inflation—An Analysis of Cost and Demand Pressures on the Price Level.* Washington, D. C.: U. S. Chamber of Commerce, 1957.

————. *Management Action to Promote Business Stability.* Committee on Economic Policy. Washington, D. C.: U. S. Chamber of Commerce, 1961.

————. *The Promise of Economic Growth (Report of the Committee on Economic Policy).* Washington, D. C.: U. S. Chamber of Commerce, 1961.

U. S. Department of Commerce. *U. S. Income and Output.* Supplement to *Survey of Current Business.* Washington, D. C.: U. S. Government Printing Office, 1958.

U. S. Department of Labor. *Economic Forces in the U. S. A. in Facts and Figures, Prepared by the U. S. Department of Labor.* Washington, D. C.: U. S. Government Printing Office, 1957.

University of Maryland Bureau of Business and Economic Research. *Inflation—Problems and Proposals.* College Park: University of Maryland Bureau of Business and Economic Research, 1948.

————. *Seasonal Fluctuations in Maryland Business: War and Postwar Adjustments; Industry and Area Differences.* College Park: University of Maryland Bureau of Business and Economic Research, 1949.

Vandermeulens, Alice, and Carlos, Daniel. *National Income: Analysis by Sector Accounts.* Englewood Cliffs, N. J.: Prentice-Hall, 1956.

Van Vleck, George W. *The Panic of 1857.* New York: Columbia University Press, 1943.

Volpe, P. A. *The International Financial and Banking Crisis, 1931–1933.* Washington, D. C.: Catholic University Press, 1945.

Waage, T. D. *Inflation: Causes and Cures.* New York: H. W. Wilson, 1949.

Warren, George F., and Pearson, Frank A. *Prices.* New York: J. Wiley and Sons; London: Chapman and Hall, 1933.

Weberg, Frank P. *The Background of the Panic of 1893.* Washington, D. C.: Catholic University Press, 1939.

Wecter, Dixon. *The Age of the Great Depression, 1929–1941.* New York: Macmillan, 1948.

Wernette, J. P. *The Future of American Prosperity.* New York: Macmillan, 1955.

———. *Growth and Prosperity Without Inflation.* New York: Ronald Press, 1961

Wicksteed, Philip H. *The Common Sense of Political Economy.* London: Macmillan, 1910.

Wilson, Thomas. *Fluctuations in Income and Employment.* New York: Pitman, 1948.

———. *Inflation.* Cambridge: Harvard University Press, 1961.

Wright, D. M. *The Economics of Disturbance.* New York: Macmillan, 1947.

Wright, Wilson. *Forecasting for Profit.* New York: John Wiley & Sons, 1947.

Young, M., and Prager, T. *There's Work for All.* London: Nicholson and Watson, 1945.

Articles

Abramovitz, Moses. "Influence of Inventory Investment in Business Cycles," *Conference on Business Cycles*, New York: National Bureau of Economic Research, 1951.

Ackley, Gardner A. "Inflation and Equality: Comment," *American Economic Review*, Vol. XXXIX, No. 4 (September, 1949).

———. "The Multiplier Time Period," *American Economic Review*, Vol. LXI, No. 3 (June, 1951).

———. "Inflation and Equality," *American Economic Review*, Vol. XXI, No. 3, (June, 1956).

Adams, W. "Accounting Practices and the Business Cycle," *Journal of Business* —University of Chicago (April, 1949).

Aftalion, A. "The Theory of Economic Cycles Based on the Capitalistic Techniques of Production," *Review of Economic Statistics*, Vol. IX, No. 4 (October, 1927).

Alexander, S. S. "The Accelerator as a Generator of Steady Growth," *Quarterly Journal of Economics*, Vol. LXIII, No. 2 (May, 1949).

———. "Issues of Business Cycle Theory Raised by Mr. Hicks," *American Economic Review*, Vol. XLI, No. 5 (December, 1951).

———. "Rate of Change Approaches to Forecasting: Diffusion Indexes and First Differences," *Economic Journal*, Vol. LXIX, No. 269 (June, 1958).

Allen, R. G. D. "Post-War Economic Policy in the U. S.," *Economic Journal*, Vol. LV, No. 217 (April, 1945).

———. "Wholesale Prices 1938–1948," *Economic Journal*, Vol. LIX, No. 234 (June, 1949).

———. "Movements in Retail Prices Since 1953," *Economica*, Vol. XXV, No. 98 (February, 1958).

Allen, S. G. "Inventory Fluctuations in Flaxseed and Linseed Oil, 1926–39," *Econometrica*, Vol., XXII, No. 3 (July, 1954).

Ames, E. "A Theoretical and Statistical Dilemma—The Contributions of Burns, Mitchell and Frickly to Business Cycle Theory," *Econometrica*, Vol. XVI, No. 4 (October, 1948).

———. "Trends, Cycles, and Stagnation in U. S. Manufacturing Since 1860," *Oxford Economic Papers* (October, 1959).

Apel, H. "Prices and Wages in Recession: Legal Versus Voluntary Restraints," *Social Research* (Summer, 1960).

Ascheim, J. "Price Level Stability at Full Employment: Recent American Experience," *Oxford Economic Papers* (October, 1955).

"Australian Full Employment Policy," *Monthly Labor Review* (August, 1945).

Bach, G. L. "Monetary-Fiscal Policy Reconsidered," *Journal of Political Economy*, Vol. LVII, No. 5 (October, 1949).

———. "Inflation in Perspective," *Harvard Business Review*, Vol. 36, No. 1 (January-February, 1958).

Backman, J. "Price Inflexibility—War and Post-War," *Journal of Political Economy*, Vol. LVI, No. 5 (October, 1948).

———. "Administered Prices: Their Nature and Behavior," *Current Economic Comment* (November, 1957).

Baker, J. G. "The Universal Discount as a Means of Economic Stabilization," *Econometrica*, Vol. XVI, No. 2 (April, 1948).

Ball, R. J., Hazlewood, A., and Klein, L. R. "Econometric Forecasts for 1959," *Bulletin of Oxford University Institute of Statistics* (February, 1959).

Barber, C. L. "Inventory Fluctuations in Canada, 1918–1950," *Canadian Journal of Economics and Political Science* (August, 1952).

Bassie, V. L. "Price Level Prospects," *Current Economic Comment* (February, 1949).

Bauer, P. T. "Lord Beveridge on Full Employment," *Kyklos*, Vol. I, No. 2 (1947).

Baumol, W. J., and Peston, M. H. "More on the Multiplier Effects of a Balanced Budget," *American Economic Review*, Vol. XLV, No. 1 (March, 1955).

Baxter, W. T. "The Accountants' Contribution to the Trade Cycle," *Economica*, Vol. XXII, No. 86 (May, 1955).

Bean, Louis H. "The Farmers' Response to Price," *Journal of Farm Economics*, Vol. XI (July, 1929).

———. "Some Limitations to the Control of Agricultural Production in the United States," *American Cooperation*, American Institute of Cooperation, 1932.

———. "Wholesale Prices and Industrial Stock Prices During and Immediately After the Two World Wars," *Review of Economic Statistics*, Vol. XXIX, No. 3 (August, 1947).

Beckerman, W. "The Recent United States Recession and the Strength of Primary Prices," *Bulletin of the Oxford University Institute of Statistics* (July–August, 1954).

Bell, E. V. "Hedging Against Inflation," *Conference Board Business Report Record* (April, 1946).

Bennion, E. G. "The Cowles Commission's Simultaneous Equation Approach," *Review of Economics and Statistics*, Vol. XXXIV, No. 1 (February, 1952).

Benoit-Smullyan, E. "Public Works in the Depression," *American Economic Review*, Vol. XXX, No. 1 (March, 1948).

———. "On the Meaning of Full-Employment," *Review of Economics and Statistics*, Vol. XXX, No. 2 (May, 1948).

Bernstein, E. M. "Latent Inflation: Problems and Policies," *International Monetary Fund Staff Papers* (February, 1950).

———. "Wage-Price Links in a Long Inflation," *International Monetary Fund Staff Papers* (November, 1958).

Berridge, W. A. "The World's Gold Supply," *Review of Economic Statistics*, Preliminary Volume II, No. 7 (July, 1920).

———. "Observations on Beveridge's 'Full Employment in a Free Society' and Some Related Matters," *Political Science Quarterly* (June, 1945).

Bezanson, A. "Inflation and Controls, Pennsylvania 1774–1779," *Journal of Economic History*, Supplement VIII (1948).

Bhattacharya, K. N. "Will India Face a Slump? An Aspect in Transition Economy," *Indian Journal of Economics* (January, 1945).

———. "Postwar Price Structure in India: Its Fundamental Disequilibrium," *Indian Journal of Commerce* (June, 1948).

Bieda, K. "Bankruptcies in Depression and Boom," *Economic Record*, Vol. XXXII, No. 65 (August, 1957).

Bishop, G. A. "A Note on the Overinvestment Theory of the Cycle and Its

Relation to the Keynesian Theory of Income," *American Economic Review*, Vol. XXXIII, No. 1 (March, 1951).

Blom, F. W. C. "Business Savings and Employment," *Oxford Economic Papers* (June, 1951).

Blyth, C. A. "The 1948–49 American Recession," *Economic Journal*, Vol. LXIV, No. 255 (September, 1954).

———. "The United States Cycle in Private Fixed Investment," *Review of Economics and Statistics*, Vol. XXXVIII, No. 1 (February, 1956).

Booker, H. S. "Have We a Full Employment Policy?" *Economica*, Vol. XIV, No. 53 (February, 1947).

Boulding, Kenneth E. "The Consumption Concept in Economic Theory," *American Economic Review*, Vol. XXXV, No. 2 (May, 1945).

Bowen, H. R. "Toward Economic Stability," *Current Economic Comment* (August, 1949).

Bowman, R. T., and Phillips, A. "The Capacity Concept and Induced Investment," *Canadian Journal of Economic and Political Science* (May, 1955).

Boyd, J. A., Jr. "1961: An Industrial and Stock Market Forecast for Canada and the United States," *Financial Analysts Journal* (January–February, 1961).

Bratt, E. C. "Business Cycle Forecasting," *Journal of Business—University of Chicago* (January, 1948).

———. "Data Needed to Forecast the Business Cycle," *Journal of Business—University of Chicago* (July, 1948).

———. "The Use of Behavior Classifications in Business Cycle Forecasting," *Journal of Business—University of Chicago* (October, 1949).

Braunthal, A. "Wage Policy and Full Employment," *International Postwar Problems* (January, 1946).

Brech, R. "The Role of Stocks in the British Economy," *Westminster Bank Review* (February, 1957).

Brems, H. "Business Cycles and Economic Policy," *Journal of Political Economy*, Vol. LXII, No. 3 (June, 1954).

Brinigar, G. K. "Income, Savings Balances, and Net Saving," *Review of Economic Statistics*, Vol. XXXV, No. 1 (February, 1953).

Brockie, M. D. "Theories of the 1937–38 Crisis and Depression," *Economic Journal*, Vol. LX, No. 238 (June, 1950).

Bronfenbrenner, M. "Postwar Political Economy: The President's Report," *Journal of Political Economy*, Vol. LVI, No. 5 (October, 1948).

Broude, H. W. "Bottleneck Phenomena and Cyclical Change: The Role of the Iron and Steel Industry," *Quarterly Journal of Economics*, Vol. LXVII, No. 3 (August, 1954).

Brown, A. J. "Inflation and the British Economy," *Economic Journal*, Vol. XLIX, No. 271 (September, 1958).

Brown, E. C. "Some Evidence on Business Expectations," *Review of Economics and Statistics*, Vol. XXXI, No. 3 (August, 1949).

———. "The Static Theory of Automatic Fiscal Stabilization," *Journal of Political Economy*, Vol. LXIII, No. 5 (October, 1955).

Brown, H. G. "Monetary and Fiscal Counter Depression Policy," *American Journal of the Economic Society* (July, 1959).

Brownlee, O. H. "The Theory of Employment and Stabilization Policy," *Journal of Political Economy*, Vol. LVIII, No. 5 (October, 1950).

Brozen, Yale. "Means for Maintaining Economic Stability," *Journal of Farm Economics, Canadian Journal of Agricultural Economics, Proceedings* (December, 1958).

Bruce, C., and Gibb, E. B. "The United States Recessions of 1948–49 and 1953–54," *Bulletin of the Oxford University Institute of Statistics* (July–August, 1954).

Burck, G., and Parker, S. S. "The Mighty Multiplier," *Fortune* (October, 1954).

Burck, G., and Silberman, C. "What Caused the Great Depression," *Fortune* (February, 1955).

Burgess, W. Randolph. "The National Debt," Statement Submitted to the Committee on Finance, United States Senate (85th Congress, 1st Session, July 29, 1957).

Burkhead, J. V. "Full Employment and Interest—Free Borrowing," *Southern Economic Journal* (July, 1947).

Burns, Arthur F. "Hicks and the Real Cycle," *Journal of Political Economy*, Vol. LX, No. 1 (February, 1952).

———. "Long Cycles in Residential Construction," *Frontiers of Economic Knowledge*, printed for the National Bureau of Economic Research by Princeton University Press (1954).

———. "New Facts on Business Cycles," *Frontiers of Economic Knowledge*, printed for the National Bureau of Economic Research by Princeton University Press (1954).

———. "The Current Business Recession," *Journal of Business* (April, 1958).

———. "Progress Toward Economic Stability," *American Economic Review*, Vol. L, No. 1 (March, 1960).

———. "Examining the New 'Stagnation' Theory," *Morgan Guaranty Survey* (May, 1961).

"Business Capital Investment in 1959," *Survey of Current Business* (December, 1958).

"Business Failures," *Federal Reserve Bank of Kansas City* (April, 1957).

Campbell, R. H. "Fluctuations in Stocks: A Nineteenth Century Case Study," *Oxford Economic Papers* (February, 1957).

"Canadian Program for Maintaining Employment and Income," *Monthly Labor Review* (July, 1945).

"Canadian White Paper on Employment and Income," *Federal Reserve Bulletin* (June, 1945).

Carver, T. N. "A Suggestion for a Theory of Industrial Depression," *Quarterly Journal of Economics*, Vol. XVII, No. 2 (May, 1903).

Chambers, E. J. "The 1937–38 Recession in Canada," *Canadian Journal of Economics and Political Science* (August, 1955).

———. "Canadian Business Cycle Since 1919," *Canadian Journal of Economics and Political Science* (May, 1958).

"Changing Demands in 1957," *Federal Reserve Bulletin* (November, 1957).

Chenery, H. B. "Overcapacity and the Acceleration Principle," *Econometrica*, Vol. XX, No. 1 (January, 1952).

Christ, C. F. "Aggregate Economic Models," *American Economic Review*, Vol. XLVI, No. 3 (June, 1956).

Churchill, B. C. "Rise in Business Population," *Survey of Current Business* (May, 1959).

Clague, E. "Interrelationship of Prices, Wages, and Productivity, 1946–57," *Monthly Labor Review* (January, 1958).

———. "The Consumer Price Index in the Business Cycle," *Monthly Labor Review* (June, 1958).

Clark, C. "A System of Equations Explaining the United States Trade Cycle, 1921–1941," *Econometrica*, Vol. XVII, No. 2 (April, 1949).

Clark, J. D. "Can Government Influence Business Stability," *Journal of Finance*, Vol. II, No. 1 (April, 1947).

Clark, J. G. "The Real Estate Cycle in San Diego, California, 1900–1932," *Journal of the American Institute of Real Estate Appraisers* (April, 1933).

Clark, J. M. "An Appraisal of the Workability of Compensatory Devices," *American Economic Review*, Vol. XXIX, No. 2 (May, 1939).

———. "Business Acceleration and the Law of Demand; A Technical Factor in Economic Cycles," *Quarterly Journal of Economics*, Vol. LIII, No. 4 (November, 1939).

———. "Employment Policy in a Divided World," *Social Research* (June, 1950).

Clemence, R. V., and Nixon, T. F. "Forecasting with Economic Indicators— The 1957–58 Recession," *Boston University Business Review* (Fall, 1959).

Clement, M. O. "The Concept of Automatic Stabilizers," *Southern Economic Journal* (January, 1959).

Cobren, G. M., and Liebenberg, M. "Inventories in Postwar Business Cycles," *Survey of Current Business* (April, 1959).

Cochrane, P. "The Austrian Economy," *Economic Record*, Vol. XXXIII, No. 68 (August, 1958).

Cohen, M., and Gainsbrugh, M. R. "The Capital Goods Market: A New Survey of Capital Appropriations," *Conference Board Business Record* (October, 1956).

Colm, G. "On the Road to Economic Stabilization," *Social Research* (September, 1948).

———. "Economic Barometers and Economic Models," *Review of Economics and Statistics*, Vol. XXXVII, No. 1 (February, 1955).

———. "Economic Outlook for 1956," *Looking Ahead* (December, 1955).

"Comparison of Price Movements, World War II—1950," *Monthly Labor Review* (September, 1950).

"Compass Points of Business," *Dun's Review* (May, 1949).

"Consumer Durable Goods in Recovery," *Federal Reserve Bulletin* (January, 1959).

"The Controversy Over Monetary Policy." Symposium by S. E. Harris, L. V. Chandler, M. Friedman, A. H. Hansen, A. P. Lerner, and J. Tobin. *Review of Economics and Statistics*, Vol. XXXIII, No. 3 (August, 1951).

Cooper, W. W. "Some Implications of a Program for Full Employment and Economic Stability," *Political Science Quarterly* (June, 1948).

Copeland, M. A. "Business Stabilization by Agreement," *American Economic Review*, Vol. XXXIV, No. 3 (June, 1944).

Coppock, J. D. "A Reconsideration of Hobson's Theory of Unemployment," *Manchester School: Economic and Social Studies* (January, 1953).

———. "Cushioning the Impact of United States Economic Fluctuations on the Rest of the World," *Journal of Finance*, Vol. XIV, No. 2 (May, 1959).

Cormier, G. H. "Movements in Commodity Prices Since 1951," *Monthly Labor Review* (December, 1954).

Coyle, D. C. "The Dilemma of Prosperity," *Yale Review* (Winter, 1947).

"The Current Inflation Problem—Causes and Controls," *Federal Reserve Bulletin* (December, 1947).

Cyert, R. M. "Oligopoly Price Behavior and the Business Cycle," *Journal of Political Economy*, Vol. LXIII, No. 1 (February, 1955).

Daly, D. J. "Seasonal Variations and Business Expectations," *Journal of Business—University of Chicago* (July, 1959).

Darling, P. G. "Manufacturers' Inventory Investment, 1947–1958," *American Economic Review*, Vol. XLIX, No. 5 (December, 1959).

Davis, T. E. "The Consumption Function as a Tool for Prediction," *Review of Economics and Statistics*, Vol. XXXIV, No. 3 (August, 1952).

Dawson, A. A. P. "The United Nations and Full Employment," *International Labor Review* (May, 1953).

De Chazeau, M. G. "Can We Avoid Depression in a Dynamic Economy?" *Harvard Business Review*, Vol. XXXII, No. 4 (July–August, 1954).

De Graff, A. "Price Disparity and Business Cycles," *Kyklos*, Vol. I, No. 4 (1947).

Derksen, J. B. D. "Long Cycles in Residential Building," *Econometrica*, Vol. VIII, No. 2 (April, 1940).

Dewey, D. J. "Crisis in Britain: A Note on the Stagnation Thesis," *Journal of Political Economy*, Vol. LIX, No. 3 (August, 1951).

Di Nardi, G. "Expenditure of the 'Lire Fund' for Anti-Cyclical Purposes," *Review of Economic Conditions in Italy* (November, 1948).

––––––. "Investment in Public Works for Economic Stability," *Review of Economic Conditions in Italy* (May, 1954).

Dobretsberger, J. A. "A Critical Review of the Discussions on Full Employment," *Kyklos*, Vol. I, No. 1 (1947).

Dobrovolsky, S. B. "Corporate Retained Earnings and Cyclical Fluctuations," *American Economic Review*, Vol. XXXV, No. 4 (September, 1945).

––––––. "The Effect of Replacement Investment on National Income and Employment," *Journal of Political Economy*, Vol. LV, No. 4 (August, 1947).

Domar, Evsey D. "Capital Expansion, Rate of Growth and Employment," *Econometrica*, Vol. XIV, No. 2 (April, 1946).

––––––. "Expansion and Employment," *American Economic Review*, Vol. XXXVII, No. 1 (March, 1947).

Douty, H. M. "Wages, Prices and Economic Policy in Great Britain, 1954–57," *Monthly Labor Review* (March, 1958).

Dow, J. C. R. "Fiscal Policy and Monetary Policy as Instruments of Economic Control," *Westminster Bank Review* (November, 1960).

––––––, and Dicks-Mireaux, L. A. "The Excess Demand for Labour. A Study of Conditions in Great Britatin, 1946–56," *Oxford Economic Papers* (February, 1958).

Duesenberry, James. "The Mechanics of Inflation," *Review of Economics and Statistics*, Vol. XXXII, No. 2 (May, 1950).

––––––. "Hicks on the Trade Cycle," *Quarterly Journal of Economics*, Vol. LXIV, No. 3 (August, 1950).

––––––, Eckstein, Otto, and Fromm, Gary. "A Simulation of the United States Economy in Recession," *Econometrica*, Vol. XXVIII, No. 4 (October, 1960).

Dye, H. S. "Certain Questions Raised by Hicks' Theory of the Trade Cycle," *Southern Economic Journal* (October, 1952).

Eckaus, R. S. "The Acceleration Principle Reconsidered," *Quarterly Journal of Economics*, Vol. LXVII, No. 2 (May, 1953).

Eckler, A. R. "A Measure of the Severity of Depressions, 1873–1932," *Review of Economic Statistics*, Vol. XV, No. 2 (1933).

"Economic Recovery Under Way," *Survey of Current Business* (February, 1959).

"The Economic Situation and Prospects," *National Institute of Economic Review* (January, 1959).

"The Economy in Recovery and Expansion—A Review of 1955," *Survey of Current Business* (February, 1956).

Egle, W. P. "The Problem of a Workable Program of Cooperation Between Private Enterprise and Government in Economic Stabilization," *Zeitschrift für Nationalökonomie* (1960).

Eisner, Robert. "A Distributed Lag Investment Function," *Econometrica*, Vol. XXVIII, No. 2 (January, 1960).

Ellis, Howard S. "Monetary Policy and Investment," *American Economic Review*, Vol. XXX, No. 2 (May, 1940).

"Employment and Income: Minister of Reconstruction Issues White Paper on Post-War Planning," *Labor Gazette* (May, 1945).

"Employment and Unemployment: Government Policies Since 1950," Parts I and II, *International Labor Review* (July and August, 1956).

"Employment Trends During the Past Two Decades," *Monthly Labor Review* (August, 1950).

Epstein, R. C. "Price Dispersion and Aggregative Analyses," *American Economic Review*, Vol. XXXVII, No. 3 (June, 1947).

Ewell, R. H. "The Roll of Research in Economic Growth," *Chemical Engineering News* (July 18, 1955).

Ezekiel, Mordecai. "Statistical Analysis and the Laws of Price," *Quarterly Journal of Economics*, Vol. XLII, No. 2 (February, 1928).

——. "The Cobweb Theorem," *Quarterly Journal of Economics*, Vol. LII, No. 1 (February, 1938).

"Federal Expenditure and Revenue Policy." From a Conference called by the National Planning Association. *American Economic Review*, Vol. XXXIX, No. 5 (December, 1949).

"Federal Reserve Board Committee Reports on Consumer Expectations and Savings Statistics," *Review of Economics and Statistics*, Vol. XXXIX, No. 1 (February, 1957).

Fellner, W. J. "Postscript on War Inflation," *American Economic Review*, Vol. XXXVII, No. 1 (March, 1947).

——. "The Robertsonian Evolution," *American Economic Review*, Vol. XLII, No. 3 (June, 1952).

——. "Rapid Growth as an Objective of Economic Policy," *American Economic Review*, Vol. L, No. 2 (May, 1960).

Fels, Rendigs. "The Long-Wave Depression, 1873–97," *Review of Economics and Statistics*, Vol. XXXI, No. 1 (February, 1949).

——. "Warburton vs. Hansen and Keynes," *American Economic Review*, Vol. XXXIX, No. 4 (September, 1949).

——. "Gold and International Equilibrium," *American Economic Review*, Vol. XXXIX, No. 6 (December, 1949).

——. "The Effects of Price and Wage Flexibility on Cyclical Contraction," *Quarterly Journal of Economics*, Vol. LXIV, No. 4 (November, 1950).

——. "American Business Cycles, 1865–79," *American Economic Review*, Vol. XLI, No. 3 (June, 1951).

——. "The American Business Cycle of 1879–85," *Journal of Political Economy*, Vol. LX, No. 1 (February, 1952).

——. "A Theory of Business Cycles," *Quarterly Journal of Economics*, Vol. LXVI, No. 1 (February, 1952).

Ferber, R. "The Accuracy and Structure of Industry Expectations in Relation to Those of Individual Firms," *Journal of the American Statistical Association* (June, 1958).

Fetter, F. W. "The Economic Reports of the President and the Problem of

Inflation," *Quarterly Journal of Economics*, Vol. LXIII, No. 2 (May, 1949).

Fforde, J. S. "Cyclical Fluctuations and the Growth of Discriminatory Alignments," *Economic Journal*, Vol. LXV, No. 257 (March, 1955).

"Financial Position and Buying Plans of Consumer, July 1949," *Federal Reserve Bulletin* (October, 1949).

"The Financial Position of Business," *Federal Reserve Bulletin* (June, 1959).

"Fiscal and Monetary Policy for High Employment," *Committee of the Committee for Economic Development* (December, 1961).

"Fiscal and Monetary Policies to Fight Inflation: Four Articles by B. V. Ratchford, H. S. Ellis, C. C. Balderston, B. W. Sprinkel," *Annals of American Academy of Political and Social Sciences*, Vol. CCCXXVI (November, 1959).

Fisher, A. G. B. "Less Stabilization: More Stability," *Kyklos*, Vol. I, No. 1 (1947).

Fisher, G. H. "Hicks' 'Elementary Case' Economic Model for the United States, 1929–1941," *Journal of American Statistical Association* (September, 1952).

———. "Endogenous and Exogenous Investment in Macro-Economic Models," *Review of Economics and Statistics*, Vol. XXXV, No. 3 (August, 1953).

Fisher, Irving. "Our Unstable Dollar and the So-Called Business Cycle," *Journal of the American Statistical Association* (June, 1925).

Fishman, L., and Fishman, B. G. "Price Stability as a Goal of Public Policy," *Current Economic Comment* (February, 1959).

Forchheimer, K. "The 'Short Cycle' in Its International Aspects," *Oxford Economic Papers* (March, 1945).

Ford, A. G. "Argentina and the Baring Crisis of 1890," *Oxford Economic Papers* (June, 1956).

Friedman, Milton. "A Monetary and Fiscal Framework for Economic Stability," *American Economic Review*, Vol. XXXVIII, No. 3 (June, 1948).

———. "Federal Reserve Policy and 100 Percent Money," *Monetary Policy and the Management of the Public Debt*. Hearings, 82nd Congress, 2d Session, before the Subcommittee on General Credit Control and Debt Management of the Joint Committee on the Economic Report. Washington, D. C.: U. S. Government Printing Office (1952).

———. "The Demand for Money: Some Theoretical and Empirical Results," *Journal of Political Economy*, Vol. LXVII, No. 4 (August, 1959).

Frisch, Ragnar. "The Inter-Relation Between Capital Production and Consumer Taking," *Journal of Political Economy*, Vol. XXXIX, No. 5 (October, 1931).

———. "Propagation Problems and Impulse Problems in Dynamic Economics," In *Economic Essays in Honor of Gustav Cassel*. London: G. Allen & Unwin, Ltd., 1933.

"Full Employment in the Transition Period," *International Labor Review* (December, 1945).

Galbraith, John Kenneth. "Does Monetary Policy Work?" *Congressional Record* (April, 1958).

Garland, J. M. "Some Aspects of Full Employment I," *Economic Record*, Vol. XX, No. 2 (December, 1944).

———. "Some Aspects of Full Employment II," *Economic Record*, Vol. XXI, No. 13 (June, 1945).

Garvy, G. "Kondratieff's Theory of Long Cycles," *Review of Economic Statistics*, Vol. XVI, No. 4 (November, 1943).

Gehrels, F. "Inflationary Effects of a Balanced Budget Under Full Employment," *American Economic Review*, Vol. XXXIX, No. 5 (December, 1949).

George, E. B. "Should Full Employment Be Guaranteed," Parts I-III, *Dun's Review* (October, November, December, 1947).

——. "Harnessing the Economic Cycle," *Dun's Review* (March, 1950).

Gibson, J. D. "Business Prospects in Canada," *Canadian Journal of Economics and Political Science* (August, 1949).

Gilbert, Donald W. "Business Cycles and Municipal Expenditures," *Review of Economic Statistics*, Vol. XV, No. 3 (August, 1933).

Goldenweiser, E. A. "Post-War Problems and Policies," *Federal Reserve Bulletin* (February, 1945).

——. "Douglas Committee Report," *American Economic Review*, Vol. XL, No. 3 (June, 1950).

Goodwin, Richard. "Innovations and the Irregularity of Economic Cycles," *Review of Economic Statistics*, Vol. XXVIII, No. 2 (May, 1946).

——. "A Non-Linear Theory of the Cycle," *Review of Economics and Statistics*, Vol. XXXII, No. 4 (November, 1950).

——. "The Non-Linear Accelerator and the Persistence of Business Cycles," *Econometrica*, Vol. XIX, No. 1 (January, 1951).

——. "A Model of Cyclical Growth," in Erik Lundberg, Ed., *The Business Cycle in the Post-War World*. New York: St. Martin's Press, 1955.

Gordon, Robert Aaron. "Price Adjustments in the Reconversion Period," *Proceedings of the 21st Conference of the Pacific Coast Economic Association* (December, 1946).

——. "Business Cycles in the Interwar Period: The 'Quantitative-Historical' Approach," *American Economic Review*, Vol. XL, No. 2 (May, 1949).

——. "Cyclical Experience in the Interwar Period: The Investment Boom of the Twenties," Unpublished Paper Presented to the Universities—National Bureau Conference on Business Cycle Research, November 25–27, 1949.

——. "Wesley Mitchell and the Study of Business Cycles," *Journal of Business—University of Chicago* (April, 1952).

——. "Investment Behavior and Business Cycles," *Review of Economics and Statistics*, Vol. XXXVII, No. 1 (February, 1955).

——. "Types of Depression and Programs to Combat Them," *Policies to Combat Depression*, A Conference of the Universities—National Bureau Committee for Economic Research, Princeton: Princeton University Press, 1956.

Gragg, C. I., and Teele, S. F. "The Proposed Full Employment Act," *Harvard Business Review*, Vol. XXIII, No. 3 (Summer, 1945).

Graham, Frank D. "International Trade Under Depreciated Paper. The United States 1862–79," *Quarterly Journal of Economics*, Vol. XXXVI, No. 2 (February, 1922).

——. "Full Employment Without Public Works, Without Taxation, Without Public Debt, and Without Inflation," *International Postwar Problems* (October, 1945).

Granie, J. "The Budgetary Equilibrium, A Wrong Guarantee Against Inflation," *Openbare Financien*, Vol. IV, No. 3 (1949).

Grant, J. McB., and Mathews, R. L. "Accounting Conventions, Pricing Policies and the Trade Cycle," *Accounting Research* (April, 1957).

Grebler, L. "Stabilizing Residential Construction—A Review of the Post-War Test," *American Economic Review*, Vol. XXXIX, No. 4 (September, 1949).

———. "The Role of Residential Capital Formation in Post War Business Cycles," *Conference on Savings and Residential Financing*. Proceedings, U. S. Savings and Loan League, 1959.

Gross, B. M., and Lewis, J. P. "The President's Economic Staff During the Truman Administration," *American Political Science Review* (March, 1954).

Guttentag, J. M. "Credit Availability, Interest Rates and Monetary Policy," *Southern Economic Journal* (January, 1960).

———. "The Short Cycle in Residential Construction, 1946–59," *American Economic Review*, Vol. LI, No. 3 (June, 1961).

Haas, G. C., and Ezekiel, Mordecai. "Factors Affecting the Price of Hogs," *U. S. Department of Agriculture Bulletin 1440* (1926).

Haavelmo, T. "Statistical Testing of Business-Cycle Theories," *Review of Economic Statistics*, Vol. XXV, No. 1 (February, 1943).

Haberler, Gottfried. "Mr. Keynes' Theory of the 'Multiplier': A Methodological Criticism," *Zeitschrift für Nationalökonomie* (1936).

———. "Some Observations on the Murray Full Employment Bill," *Review of Economic Statistics*, Vol. XXXVII, No. 3 (August, 1945).

———. "The Pigou Effect Once More," *Journal of Political Economy*, Vol. LX, No. 3 (June, 1952).

———, Harris, S. E., Duesenberry, J. S., and Meyer, J. R. "Brief Comments on the Recession," *Review of Economics and Statistics*, Vol. XL, No. 4 (November, 1958).

Hagen, E. E., and Kirkpatrick, N. D. "The National Output and Full Employment in 1950," *American Economic Review*, Vol. XXXIV, No. 4 (September, 1944).

Hahn, L. A. "Compensatory Reactions to Compensatory Spending," *American Economic Review*, Vol. XXXV, No. 1 (March, 1945).

———. "Wage Flexibility Upwards," *Social Research* (June, 1947).

Halasi, A. "The Contribution of the Bretton Woods Agreement to Full Employment," *International Postwar Problems* (January, 1945).

———. "Toward a Full Employment Program," *International Postwar Problems* (October, 1945).

Halm, G. N. "International Measures for Full Employment," *Review of Economics and Statistics*, Vol. XXXII, No. 3 (August, 1950).

Hamberg, D. "The Recession of 1948–49 in the U. S. A.," *Economic Journal*, Vol. LXII, No. 245 (March, 1952).

———. "Steady Growth and Theories of Cyclical Crisis," Parts I-II, *Metroeconomica* (April and August, 1954).

Hamilton, D. "Keynes, Cooperation, and Economic Stability," *American Journal of the Economic Society* (October, 1954).

Hansen, Alvin H. "Mr. Keynes on Underemployment Equilibrium," *Journal of Political Economy*, Vol. XLIV, No. 5 (October, 1936).

———. "A New Goal of National Policy: Full Employment," *Review of Economic Statistics*, Vol. XXVII, No. 3 (August, 1945).

———. "Some Notes on Terborgh's—The Bogey of Economic Maturity," *Review of Economic Statistics*, Vol. XXVIII, No. 1 (February, 1946).

———. "The First Reports Under the Employment Act of 1946," *Review of Economic Statistics*, Vol. XXIX, No. 2 (May, 1947).

————. "Cost Functions and Employment," *American Economic Review*, Vol. XXXVII, No. 4 (September, 1947).

————. "Needed: A Cycle Policy," *Industrial and Labor Relations Review* (October, 1947).

Harberger, A. C. "The Economics of the President's Economic Reports," *Journal of American Statistical Association* (September, 1956).

Harris, Seymour E. "Some Aspects of the Murray Full Employment Bill," *Review of Economic Statistics*, Vol. XXVII, No. 3 (August, 1945).

————. "Effectiveness and Coordination of Monetary, Credit, and Fiscal Policies," *Metroeconomica* (October, 1949).

————, Ellis, H. S., Colm, G., Hansen, A. H., and Bronfenbrenner, M. A. "A Symposium on the Economic Report of the President and Related Documents," *Review of Economics and Statistics*, Vol. XXXVI, No. 3 (August, 1954).

Harrod, Sir Roy F. "An Essay in Dynamic Theory," *Economic Journal*, Vol. XLIX, No. 193 (March, 1939).

————. "Measures to Prevent a Slump," *Foreign Affairs* (July, 1949).

————. "Notes on Trade Cycle Theory," *Economic Journal*, Vol. LXI, No. 242 (June, 1951).

————. "Domar and Dynamic Economics," *Economic Journal*, Vol. LXX, No. 273 (September, 1959).

————. "Second Essay in Dynamic Economics," *Economic Journal*, Vol. LXXI, No. 278 (June, 1960).

Hawkins, D., and Simon, H. A. "Note: Some Conditions of Macroeconomic Stability," *Econometrica*, Vol. XVII, Nos. 3 & 4 (July-October, 1949).

Hawtrey, R. "Mr. Harrod On the British Boom" *Economic Journal*, Vol. LXVII, No. 264 (December, 1956).

Hayek, Friedrich A. "Capital and Industrial Fluctuations," *Econometrica*, Vol. II, No. 2 (April, 1934).

————. "The Maintenance of Capital," *Economica*, Vol. II, New Series, No. 7 (August, 1935).

————. "Economics and Knowledge," *Economica*, Vol. IV, New Series, No. 13 (February, 1937).

Hayes, S. P., Jr. "The Business Cycle Needs a Brake," *Dun's Review* (February, 1948).

————. "The Business Cycle; Psychological Approaches," *Political Science Quarterly* (March, 1948).

Hazelett, R. "Public Management of Private Employment," *American Economic Review*, Vol. XLVII, No. 1 (March, 1957).

Henderson, P. D., Holland, D. G., and Seers, D. "The Crisis of 1951," *Bulletin of Oxford University Institute of Statistics* (October, 1951).

Hermens, F. A. "Domestic Post War Problems," *Review of Social Economics* (December, 1942).

————, and Wallace, G. S. "Inflation and Anti-Inflation Policies in the United States, 1939–1949," *Zeitschrift für die gesammelte Stratswissenschaft*, Vol. CV, No. 4 (1949).

Herrick, L. "Employment and Post War Prosperity," *Yale Review* (December, 1944).

Hickman, Bert G. "Federal Spending and the Stability of the Post-War Economy," *Federal Expenditure Policy for Economic Growth and Stability, Papers Submitted by Panelists Appearing Before the Subcommittee on Fiscal Policy*, Joint Economic Committee, 85th Congress, 1st Session (November 5, 1957).

————. "The Contraction of 1953–54," *Review of Economics and Statistics,* Vol. XL, No. 1 (February, 1958).

————. "An Experiment With Weighted Indexes of Cyclical Diffusion," *Journal of American Statistical Association* (March, 1958).

————. "Postwar Cyclical Experience and Economic Stability," *American Economic Review,* Vol. XLVIII, No. 2 (May, 1958).

————. "Diffusion, Acceleration, and Business Cycles," *American Economic Review,* Vol. XLIX, No. 4 (September, 1959).

Hicks, J. R. "A Suggestion for Simplifying the Theory of Money," *Economica,* Vol. II, New Series, No. 5 (February, 1935).

————. "The World Inflation," *Irish Banking Review* (September, 1958).

Higgins, B. "The Optimum Wage Rate," *Review of Economics and Statistics,* Vol. XXXI, No. 2 (May, 1949).

————. "Reder on Wage Price Policy," *Canadian Journal of Economics and Political Science* (May, 1949).

————. "The Concept of Secular Stagnation," *American Economic Review,* Vol. XL, No. 1 (March, 1950).

————. "Interactions of Cycles and Trends," *Economic Journal,* Vol. LXV, No. 260 (December, 1955).

Hirst, R. R. "Inflation—Its Impact on Enterprises," *Economic Record,* Vol. XXV, No. 49 (December, 1949).

Holland, M. "The Influence of Business Cycles on Industrial Research," *Dun's Review* (December, 1946).

Holmans, A. E. "The Eisenhower Administration and the Recession 1953–55," *Oxford Economic Papers* (February, 1958).

Holzman, F. D. "Income Determination in Open Inflation," *Review of Economics and Statistics,* Vol. XXXII, No. 2 (May, 1950).

————. "Inflation: Cost Push and Demand Pull," *American Economic Review,* Vol. I, No. 2 (March, 1960).

Hood, R. C. "Reorganizing the Council of Economic Advisors," *Political Science Quarterly* (September, 1954).

Hooton, F. G. "Risk and Cobweb Theorem," *Economic Journal,* Vol. LXXI, No. 277 (March, 1960).

Hoover, E. D. "Wholesale and Retail Prices in the Nineteenth Century," *Journal of Economic History* (September, 1958).

Horsefield, J. K. "The Measurement of Inflation," *International Monetary Fund Staff Papers* (February, 1950).

————. "Inflation and Deflation in 1694–1696," *Economica,* Vol. XXIII, No. 91 (August, 1956).

Howenstine, E. J. "Some Principles of Compensatory Action," *Quarterly Journal of Economics,* Vol. LX, No. 4 (November, 1946).

————. "Public Works Policy in the Twenties," *Social Research* (December, 1946).

————. "Compensatory Public Work Programmes and Full Employment: A Study of the Mobility of Resources in the Construction Industry," *International Labor Review* (February, 1956).

"How Much Unemployment?" A Symposium. *Review of Economics and Statistics,* Vol. XXXII, No. 1 (February, 1950).

Hoyt, H. "The Effect of Cyclical Fluctuations upon Real Estate Finance," *Journal of Finance,* Vol. II, No. 1 (April, 1947).

Hubbard, Joseph B. "Business Declines and Recoveries, 1873–1932," *Review of Economic Statistics,* Vol. XV, No. 2 (May, 1933).

————. "Business Declines and Recoveries," *Review of Economic Statistics,* Vol. XVIII, No. 1 (February, 1936).

Hughes, J. R. "The Commercial Crisis of 1857," *Oxford Economic Papers* (June, 1956).

Hultgren, T. "Costs and Profits in Changing Times," *Dun's Review* (August, 1950).

Ichimura, S. A. "A Tentative Non-Linear Theory of Economic Fluctuations in the Purely Competitive Economic System I," *Kyoto University Economic Review* (October, 1953).

————. "A Tentative Non-Linear Theory of Economic Fluctuations in the Purely Competitive Economic System II," *Kyoto University Economic Review* (April, 1954).

"Inflation Problems at Home and Abroad," *Monthly Labor Review* (January, 1947).

Iochi, R. "The Role of Price Dispersion," *Annals Hitotsubashi Academy* (April, 1955).

"Is Another Major Contraction Likely." Papers by A. Achinstein and B. G. Hickman, *American Economic Review Proceedings,* Vol. XLVIII, No. 2 (May, 1958).

Isard, Walter. "A Neglected Cycle: The Transport-Building Cycle," *Review of Economic Statistics,* Vol. XXIV, No. 4 (November, 1942).

Jack, D. T. "Full Employment in Retrospect," *Economic Journal,* Vol. LXII, No. 248 (December, 1952).

Jacobsson, P. "Problems of Employment," *Skandinavian Bankers Quarterly Review* (July, 1952).

————. "Problems of Employment," *Skandinavian Bankers Quarterly Review* (October, 1952).

————. "Predictability in Economics," *Skandinavian Bankers Quarterly Review* (April, 1955).

————. "The Problems of Moderating the Present Boom," *Skandinavian Bankers Quarterly Review* (January, 1956).

Jaffe, A. J., and Wolfbein, S. L. "International Migration and Full Employment in the U.S.," *Journal of American Statistical Association* (September, 1945).

"The January 1949 Report of the President," *Review of Economics and Statistics,* Vol. XXXI, No. 3 (August, 1949).

Jenkins, S. "Australia Plans Full Employment," *Far East Survey* (August 29, 1945).

Johnston, J. "Econometric Models and the Average Duration of Business Cycles," *Manchester School of Economic and Social Studies* (September, 1955).

Jones, H. "Some Aspects of Demand for Consumer Durable Goods," *Journal of Finance,* Vol. IX, No. 2 (May, 1954).

Jones, R. C. "Effect of Inflation on Capital and Profits: Record of Nine Steel Companies," *Journal of Accountancy* (January, 1949).

Joseph, M. F. W. "The British White Paper on Employment Policy," *American Economic Review,* Vol. XXXIV, No. 4 (September, 1944).

————. "Principles of Full Employment," *International Postwar Problems* (October, 1945).

Jung, C. "Investment Decisions and Non-Linear Cycle," *Journal of Industrial Economics* (October, 1955).

Kahn, R. F. "The Relation of Home Investment to Unemployment," *Economic Journal,* Vol. XLI, No. 162 (June, 1931).

Kaldor, Nicholas. "A Classificatory Note on Determinateness of Equilibrium," *Review of Economic Studies*, Vol. 1 (February, 1934).

———. "Mr. Hicks on the Trade Cycle," *Economic Journal*, Vol. LXI, No. 244 (December, 1951).

———. "The Relation of Economic Growth and Cyclical Fluctuations," *Economic Journal*, Vol. LXIV, No. 253 (March, 1954).

———. "A Model of Economic Growth," *Economic Journal*, Vol. LXVIII, No. 268 (December, 1957).

Kalecki, M. "Full Employment by Stimulating Private Investment?" *Oxford Economic Papers* (March, 1945).

———. "The Maintenance of Full Employment After the Transition Period: A Comparison of the Problem in the United States and United Kingdom," *International Labor Review* (November, 1945).

———. "Full Employment After a Transition Period: A Rejoinder," *American Economic Review*, Vol. XXXVII, No. 3 (June, 1947).

———. "A New Approach to the Problem of the Business Cycle," *Review of Economic Studies*, Vol. XVI (2), No. 40 (1949–50).

Keiser, N. F. "The Development of the Concept of 'Automatic Stabilizers'," *Journal of Finance*, Vol. XI, No. 4 (December, 1956).

Keizer, D. M. "The Short Run Outlook for Business Investment in New Plant and Equipment," *Journal of Business—University of Chicago* (July, 1955).

Keyserling, L. H. "Housing and Inflation: A Reply to Professor Ellis," *American Economic Review*, Vol. XL, No. 1 (March, 1950).

Kirty, U. S. R. "The Beginnings of Monetary Explanations of the Trade Cycle," *Indian Journal of Economics* (April, 1945).

Kisselgoff, Avram, and Modigliani, Francis. "Private Investment in the Electric Power Industry and the Acceleration Principle," *Review of Economics and Statistics*, Vol. XXXIX, No. 4 (November, 1957).

Kitchin, J. "Cycle and Trends in Economic Factors," *Review of Economic Statistics*, Vol. V, No. 1 (January, 1923).

Klein, L. R. "A Post-Mortem on Transition Predictions of National Product," *Journal of Political Economy*, Vol. LIV, No. 4 (August, 1946).

———. "The Use of Econometric Models as a Guide to Economic Policy," *Econometrica*, Vol. XV, No. 2 (April, 1947).

———. "Statistical Testing of Business Cycle Theory: The Econometric Method," in Erik Lundberg, Ed., *The Business Cycle in the Post-War World*. New York: St. Martin's Press, 1955.

Klopstock, F. H. "Western Europe's Attack on Inflation," *Harvard Business Review* (September, 1948).

Knox, A. D. "On a Theory of the Trade Cycle," *Economica*, Vol. XVII, No. 67 (August, 1950).

———. "The Acceleration Principle and the Theory of Investment: A Survey," *Economica*, Vol. XIX, No. 75 (August, 1952).

Kondratieff, N. D. "The Long Waves in Economic Life," *Review of Economic Statistics*, Vol. XVII, No. 4 (November, 1935).

Koopmans, T. C. "The Econometric Approach to Business Fluctuations," *American Economic Review*, Vol. XXIX, No. 2 (May, 1939).

Korpelainen, L. "Trends in Cyclical Movements in Industrial Employment in Finland 1885–1952," *Scandinavian Economic History Review*, Vol. V (1957).

Kravis, I. B., and Ritter, A. S. "World Prices, 1948 Compared with 1939," *Monthly Labor Review* (November, 1948).

Krishna, V. S. "International Cooperation for Controlling Trade Cycles," *Indian Journal of Economics* (January, 1945).

Kubinski, Z. M. "The Great Depression in an Export Economy: A Case Study of the Sudan," *Financial Publiques*, Vol. XIII, No. 1 (1953).

Kuznets, Simon. "Relations Between Capital Goods and Finished Products in the Business Cycle," *Economic Essays in Honor of Wesley Clair Mitchell*. New York: Columbia University Press, 1935.

Lacey, K. "Profit Measurement and the Trade Cycle," *Economic Journal*, Vol. LVII, No. 228 (December, 1947).

Lange, Oskar. "The Rate of Interest and the Optimum Propensity to Consume," *Economica*, Vol. V, No. 17 (February, 1938).

Lebergott, Stanley. "Forecasting the National Product," *American Economic Review*, Vol. XXXV, No. 1 (March, 1945).

———. "Annual Estimates of Unemployment in the United States, 1900–1954," *The Measurement and Behavior of Unemployment*, A Conference of the Universities—National Bureau Committee for Economic Research, Princeton: Princeton University Press, 1957.

Leontief, W. "Econometrics," in Howard S. Ellis, Ed., A *Survey of Contemporary Economics*, Published for the American Economic Association by Blakiston, Co., 1948.

Lerner, Abba A. "Saving and Investment: Definitions, Assumptions, Objectives," *Quarterly Journal of Economics*, Vol. LIII, No. 4 (August, 1938).

Lerner, A. P. "An Integrated Full Employment Policy," *International Postwar Problems* (January, 1946).

———. "The Inflationary Process: Some Theoretical Aspects," *Review of Economics and Statistics*, Vol. XXXI, No. 3 (August, 1949).

Levitt, T. "Investment, Depression, and the Assurance of Prosperity," *Journal of Finance*, Vol. IX, No. 3 (September, 1954).

Lewis, J. P. "The Lull That Came to Stay," *Journal of Political Economy*, Vol. LXIII, No. 1 (February, 1955).

———. "The Problem of Price Stabilization: A Progress Report," *American Economic Review Proceedings*, Vol. XLIX, No. 2 (May, 1959).

———. "Building Cycles: A Regional Model and Its National Setting," *Economic Journal*, Vol. LXXI, No. 279 (September, 1960).

Lindsay, R. "The Stability of Business Capital Outlays," *Review of Economics and Statistics*, Vol. XL, No. 2 (May, 1958).

Lipton, M. "Construction Boom in the Making," *Conference Board Business Record* (February, 1955).

Livingston, S. M. "Expansionary Force of Inventory Outlays," *Survey of Current Business* (May, 1947).

Lovasy, G. "Prices of Raw Materials in the 1953–54 Recession," *International Monetary Fund Staff Papers* (February, 1956).

———, and Zassenhaus, H. K. "Short Run Fluctuations in U. S. Imports of Raw Materials, 1928–39 and 1947–52," *International Monetary Fund Staff Papers* (October, 1953).

Lundberg, E. "Business Cycles—Past and Present Experiences," *Skandinavian Bankers Quarterly Review* (October, 1958).

———. "How Successful Has the Swedish Stabilization Policy Been?" *Skandinavian Bankers Quarterly Review* (April, 1960).

Lunde, Harold I. "Underwriting Prosperity: How We Stabilized A Growing Economy," in *How to Be Your Own Economist*. St. Paul, Minn.: Macalester College Bureau of Economic Studies, 1960.

Lutz, Friedrich A. "The Outcome of the Saving-Investment Discussion," *Quarterly Journal of Economics*, Vol. LII, No. 4 (August, 1938).

Lutz, V. "Multiplier and Velocity Analysis: A Marriage," *Economica*, Vol. XXII, No. 85 (February, 1955).

Machlup, Fritz. "Period Analysis and Multiplier Theory," *Quarterly Journal of Economics*, Vol. LIV, No. 1 (November, 1939).

MacGowan, T. G. "Can Business Men Forecast Business Activity?" Part I, *Dun's Review* (October, 1949).

Mack, Ruth. "The Direction of Change in Income and the Consumption Function," *Review of Economics and Statistics*, Vol. XXX, No. 4 (November, 1948).

———. "The Process of Capital Formation in Inventories and the Vertical Propagation of Business Cycles," *Review of Economics and Statistics*, Vol. XXXV, No. 3 (August, 1953).

———. "Notes on Subcycles in Theory and Practice," *American Economic Review Proceedings*, Vol. XLVII, No. 2 (May, 1957).

Mack, R. P., and Zarnowitz, V. "Cause and Consequence of Changes in Retailers' Buying," *American Economic Review*, Vol. XLVIII, No. 1 (March, 1958).

Maher, J. E. "Forecasting Industrial Production," *Journal of Political Economy*, Vol. LXV, No. 2 (April, 1957).

Maisel, S. J. "Timing and Flexibility of a Public Works Program," *Review of Economics and Statistics*, Vol. XXXI, No. 2 (May, 1949).

Malack, V. W. "Internal Determinants of the Canadian Upswing, 1921–29," *Canadian Journal of Economics and Political Science* (May, 1950).

Marcus, E. "The Cyclical Adjustment Pattern of an 'Open Economy': Canada, 1927–1939," *Economic Journal*, Vol. LXII, No. 246 (June, 1952).

———. "Cyclical Turning Points: Canada, 1927–1939," *American Economic Review*, Vol. XLIII, No. 4 (September, 1953).

———. "Countercyclical Weapons for the Open Economy," *Journal of Political Economy*, Vol. LXII, No. 6 (September, 1954).

Margolis, J. "Public Works and Economic Stability," *Journal of Political Economy*, Vol. LVII, No. 4 (August, 1949).

Marrama, V. "Short Notes on a Model of the Trade Cycle," *Review of Economic Studies*, Vol. XIV (1), No. 35 (1946–47).

Marschak, J. A. "A Cross Section of Business Cycle Discussion," *American Economic Review*, Vol. XXXV, No. 3 (June, 1945).

Martin, William McChesney. "The Battle Against Recession," *Federal Reserve Bulletin* (May, 1958).

Marx, F. M. "Maintaining High Level Production and Employment: A Symposium," *American Political Science Review* (December, 1945).

Massel, J. "Price Trends in the 1959 Economy and the Outlook," *Monthly Labor Review* (February, 1960).

Matthews, R. C. "The Effect of Wage-Cuts on Employment," *Economic Journal*, Vol. LXI, No. 243 (September, 1951).

Maynard, G. W. "Impact Prices and Inflation: The Experience of the United Kingdom, 1950–52," *Oxford Economic Papers* (October, 1955).

McCarthy, P. J. "Employment Policies and the Employment Act," *Review of Social Economics* (September, 1949).

McEvoy, R. H. "The Federal Reserve-Treasury Controversy," *Current Economic Comment* (November, 1950).

McNair, M. P. "Some Practical Questions About the Murray Bill," *Review of Economic Statistics*, Vol. XXVII, No. 3 (August, 1945).

————. "The Full Employment Problem," *Harvard Business Review*, Vol. XXIV, No. 1 (Autumn, 1945).

"The Measure of Underemployment," *International Labor Review* (October, 1957).

Mendelssohn, R. C. "Three B. L. S. Series as Business Cycle Turn Signals," *Monthly Labor Review* (September, 1959).

Merry, D. H., and Burns, G. R. "Full Employment—The British, Canadian and Australian White Papers," *Economic Record* (December, 1945).

Metzler, Lloyd A. "The Nature and Stability of Inventory Cycles," *Review of Economic Statistics*, Vol. XXIII, No. 3 (August, 1941).

————. "Business Cycles and the Modern Theory of Employment," *American Economic Review*, Vol. XXXVI, No. 3 (June, 1946).

————. "Factors Governing the Length of Inventory Cycles," *Review of Economic Statistics*, Vol. XXIX, No. 1 (February, 1947).

————. "The Theory of International Trade," in Ellis, Howard S., Ed. *A Survey of Contemporary Economics*, published for the American Economic Association, Philadelphia: Blakiston Company, 1948.

Meyer, J., and Kuh, E. "Acceleration and Related Theories of Investment: An Empirical Inquiry," *Review of Economics and Statistics*, Vol. XXXVII, No. 3 (August, 1955).

Meyers, A. L. "Some Implications of Full Employment Policy," *Journal of Political Economy*, Vol. LIV, No. 3 (June, 1946).

Michaely, M. "Domestic Effects of Devaluation Under Repressed Inflation," *Journal of Political Economy*, Vol. LXIII, No. 6 (December, 1955).

Miconi, G. "Recession in Italy During the Last Fifteen Years," *Review of Economic Conditions in Italy* (November, 1960).

Mikesell, R. F. "Gold Sales as an Anti-Inflationary Device," *Review of Economic Statistics*, Vol. XXVIII, No. 2 (May, 1946).

Mills, E. S. "Expectations, Uncertainty and Inventory Fluctuations," *Review of Economic Studies*, Vol. XXII (1) (1954–55).

Mills, F. C. "Elasticity of Physical Quantities and Flexibility of Unit Prices in the Dimension of Time," *Journal of the American Statistical Association* (December, 1946).

Millspaugh, M. "Problems and Opportunities of Relocation," *Law and Contemporary Problems* (Winter, 1961).

Mitchell, Wesley C. "The Role of Money in Economic History," *Journal of Economic History*, Supplement IV (December, 1944).

————, and Burns, Arthur F. "Production During the American Business Cycle of 1927–33," *National Bureau of Economic Research Bulletin 61* (November, 1936).

Modigliani, F. "Fluctuations in the Saving Ratio—A Problem in Economic Forecasting," *Social Research* (December, 1947).

Montgomery, A. "Economic Fluctuations in Sweden in 1919–1921," *Scandinavian Economic History Review*, Vol. III (1955).

Moore, Geoffrey H. "Business Cycles and the Labor Market," *Monthly Labor Review* (March, 1955).

————. "The Diffusion of Business Cycles," in Solow, Robert A., Ed., *Economics and the Public Interest*. New Brunswick, N. J.: Rutgers University Press, 1955.

————. "Measuring Recessions," *Journal of the American Statistical Association* (June, 1958).

————. "The 1957–58 Business Contraction: New Model or Old?" *American Economic Review Proceedings*, Vol. XLIX, No. 2 (May, 1959).

Moret, M. "Stocks and Entrepreneurial Strategy During Business Cycles," *Économique Appliquée* (July-September, 1956).

Morton, W. A. "Trade Unionism, Full Employment and Inflation," *American Economic Review*, Vol. XL, No. 1 (March, 1950).

———. "Keynesianism and Inflation," *Journal of Political Economy*, Vol. LIX, No. 3 (June, 1951).

Mosak, J. L., and Salant, W. S. "Income Money and Prices in Wartime," *American Economic Review*, Vol. XXXIV, No. 3 (December, 1944).

Murty, G. V. R. "The Benefits of Price Instability," *Indian Journal of Economics* (April, 1954).

Musson, A. E. "The Great Depression in Britain, 1873–1896," *Journal of Economic History* (June, 1959).

Muth, J. F. "Optimal Properties of Exponentially Weighted Forecast," *Journal of the American Statistical Association* (June, 1960).

Nagashima, K. "A Survey of Business Cycles in Post War Japan," *Bulletin of the University of Osaka Prefecture* (1958).

Nassimbene, R., and Wooden, D. G. "Growth of Business Capital Equipment 1929–53," *Survey of Current Business* (December, 1954).

Neff, P. "Professor Friedman's Proposal: Comment," *American Economic Review*, Vol. XXXIX, No. 4 (September, 1949).

Neisser, H. "Realism and Speculation in Employment Programs," *International Postwar Problems* (October, 1945).

———. "The Economic State of the Nation," *Social Research* (September, 1949).

———. "Critical Notes on the Acceleration Principle," *Quarterly Journal of Economics*, Vol. LXVIII, No. 2 (May, 1954).

Newbury, F. D. "A Forecast of Business Prospects," *Harvard Business Review*, Vol. XXV, No. 2 (Spring, 1947).

Newman, H. E. "Full Employment as a Goal of Public Policy," *American Journal of Economic Society* (April, 1958).

Newman, P. K. "A Note on 'Risk and the Cobweb Theorem'," *Economic Journal*, Vol. LXI, No. 242 (June, 1951).

Nourse, E. G. "The Employment Act and Act of Employment," *Dun's Review* (November, 1947).

———. "Why I Had to Step Aside," *Collier's* (February 18, 1950).

———. "Ideal and Working Concepts of the Employment Act," *Monthly Labor Review* (February, 1957).

———. "Some Questions Emerging Under the Employment Act," *American Economic Review*, Vol. I, No. 2 (May, 1960).

———, Gordon, R. A., and others. "The Employment Act in the Entire Thinking of our Time: A Symposium," *American Economic Review Proceedings*, Vol. XLVII, No. 2 (May, 1957).

Novick, P., and Fisher, G. H. "The Federal Budget as a Business Indicator," *Harvard Business Review*, Vol. XXXVIII, No. 3 (May-June, 1960).

Nurkse, R. "The Cyclical Pattern of Inventory Investment," *Quarterly Journal of Economics*, Vol. LXVII, No. 3 (August, 1952).

———. "Period Analysis and Inventory Cycles," *Oxford Economic Papers* (September, 1954).

Ohlin, Bertil. "Some Notes on the Stockholm Theory of Saving and Investment," *Economic Journal*, Vol. XLVII, Nos. 1 and 2 (1937).

Okerman, J. "Political Economic Cycles," *Kyklos*, Vol. I, No. 2 (1947).

Okun, A. M. "Review of Some Economic Forecasts for 1955–57," *Journal of Business—University of Chicago* (July, 1959).

———. "On Appraisal of Cyclical Turning Point Predictors," *Journal of Business—University of Chicago* (April, 1960).

O'Leary, J. J. "The Effects of Monetary Policies on the Mortgage Market," *Journal of Finance*, Vol. XIII, No. 2 (May, 1958).

Oshborne, H. D. "National Income and Product—A Review of the 1957–58 Decline and Recovery," *Survey of Current Business* (November, 1958).

Paish, F. W. "Savings and Investment," *Westminster Bank Review* (November, 1948).

———. "Inflation in the United Kingdom, 1948–1957," *Economica*, Vol. XXV, No. 98 (May, 1958).

Palmer, G. F. D. "The Rate of Interest in the Trade Cycle Theories of Professor Hayek," *South African Journal of Economics* (March, 1955).

Paradiso, L. J., and Smith, M. A. "Consumer Purchasing and Income Patterns," *Survey of Current Business* (March, 1959).

Paton, W. A. "Measuring Profits Under Inflation Conditions: A Serious Problem for Accountants," *Journal of Accountancy* (January, 1950).

Pearson, F. A., and Paarlberg, D. "Sixty Million Jobs and Six Million Farmers," *Journal of Farm Economics* (February, 1946).

Pedersen, J. "Interest Rates, Employment and Changes in Population," *Kyklos*, Vol. II, No. 1 (1948).

Persons, Warren M., Tuttle, Pierson M., and Frickey, Edwin. "Business and Financial Conditions Following the Civil War in the United States," *Review of Economic Statistics Supplement*, Preliminary Vol. II, Supplement 2 (July, 1920).

Pesek, B. P. "A Comparison of the Distributional Effects of Inflation and Taxation," *American Economic Review*, Vol. I, No. 1 (March, 1960).

Pesmazoglu, J. S. "Some International Aspects of British Cyclical Fluctuations, 1870–1913," *Review of Economic Studies*, Vol. XVI (3), No. 41 (1948–49).

———. "Some International Aspects of German Cyclical Fluctuations," *Weltwirtschaftliche Archive*, Vol. LXIV, No. 1 (1950).

———. "A Note on the Cyclical Fluctuations of British Home Investment, 1870–1913," *Oxford Economic Papers* (February, 1951).

Phillips, A. W. "Stabilization Policy in a Closed Economy," *Economic Journal*, Vol. LXIV, No. 254 (June, 1954).

———. "Stabilization Policy and the Time-Form of Lagged Responses," *Economic Journal*, Vol. LXVIII, No. 266 (June, 1957).

Pierson, J. H. G. "A Full Employment Program," *American Federal* (August, 1945).

———. "The Underwriting Approach to Unemployment: A Further Explanation," *Review of Economics and Statistics*, Vol. XXXI, No. 3 (August, 1949).

———. "On Underwriting Consumption and Employment," *American Economic Review*, Vol. XLV, No. 4 (September, 1955).

Pigou, A. C. "Some Considerations on Stability Conditions, Employment and Real Wage Rates," *Economic Journal*, Vol. LV, No. 220 (December, 1945).

———. "Over-Employment," *Economica*, Vol. XVII, No. 66 (May, 1950).

Please, S. "The Counter-Cyclical Behavior of Public Investment in the United Kingdom During the War," *Financial Publiques* (1959).

Porter, R. S. "Buffer Stocks and Economic Stability," *Oxford Economic Papers* (January, 1950).

"Prices During the Economic Expansion," *Federal Reserve Bulletin* (January, 1956).

"Prices in the Second Quarter of 1947," *Monthly Labor Review* (September, 1947).

"Primary Markets and Consumer Prices in 1947," *Monthly Labor Review* (March, 1948).

"The Problem of Economic Instability," A Report by a Subcommittee of the Committee on Public Issues of the American Economic Association. *American Economic Review*, Vol. XL, No. 4 (September, 1950).

"Production and Prices in the Latter Part of 1949," *Federal Reserve Bulletin* (January, 1950).

Ramsey, F. P. "A Mathematical Theory of Saving," *Economic Journal*, Vol. XXXVIII, No. 152 (December, 1928).

Rao, V. K. R. V. "Full Employment and Economic Development," *Indian Economic Review* (August, 1952).

"Recent Changes in Production and Prices," *Federal Reserve Bulletin* (July, 1949).

"Recent Price Trends," *Federal Reserve Bulletin* (April, 1958).

"Recent Unemployment Trends: Part I—Early Postwar Years," *Monthly Labor Review* (May, 1950).

"Recent Unemployment Trends: Part II—Early Postwar Years," *Monthly Labor Review* (September, 1950).

Reder, M. W. "The Theoretical Problems of a National Wage-Price Policy," *Canadian Journal of Economics and Political Science* (February, 1948).

Reedman, J. N. "Some Reflection on the Teaching of Business Cycle Theory," *South African Journal of Economics* (March, 1945).

Reid, Margaret G. "Capital Formation in Residential Real Estate," *Journal of Political Economy*, Vol. LXVI, No. 2 (April, 1958).

"Report of the Royal Commission on Prices," *Labor Gazette* (June, 1949).

"A Review of Economic Conditions in 30 Countries," *Die Weltwirtschaft* (December, 1956).

Riggleman, John R. "Building Cycles in U. S., 1875–1932," *Journal of American Statistical Association* (June, 1933).

Riley, H. E. "Recent Trend and Outlook in the Price Situation," *Monthly Labor Review* (January, 1957).

Robbins, L. "Thoughts on the Crisis," *Lloyds Bank Review* (April, 1958).

Robertson, D. H. "A Survey of Modern Monetary Controversy," *Manchester School of Economic and Social Studies* (1938).

Robertson, W. "Unemployment in Belgium and Full Employment Policy," *Economica*, Vol. XIX, No. 74 (May, 1952).

Robinson, Joan. "Mr. Harrod's Dynamics," *Economic Journal*, Vol. LIX, No. 233 (March, 1949).

Robinson, N. Y. "The Acceleration Principle: Department Store Inventories, 1920–1956," *American Economic Review*, Vol. XLVI, No. 3 (June, 1956).

Robinson, R. "Employment, Growth and Price Levels: The Joint Economic Committee Report," *American Economic Review*, Vol. L, No. 5 (December, 1960).

Robinson, S. A. "Sir William Beveridge on Full Employment," *Economic Journal*, Vol. LV, No. 217 (April, 1945).

Rohrlick, G. F. "Measuring the Impact of V. A. Benefit Payments in a Recession," *Labor Market* (July, 1958).

Roose, Kenneth D. "The Recession of 1937–38," *Journal of Political Economy*, Vol. LVI, No. 3 (June, 1948).

———. "Federal Reserve Policy and the Recession of 1937–38," *Review of Economics and Statistics*, Vol. XXXII, No. 2 (May, 1950).

————. "The Role of Net Government Contribution to Income in the Recession and Revival of 1937–38," *Journal of Finance*, Vol. VI, No. 1 (March, 1951).

————. "The Empirical Status of Business Cycle Theory," *Journal of Political Economy*, Vol. LX, No. 5 (October, 1952).

————. "The Production Ceiling and the Turning Point of 1920," *American Economic Review*, Vol. XLVIII, No. 3 (June, 1958).

Ropke, W. "Repressed Inflation," *Kyklos*, Vol. I, No. 3 (1947).

Rosa, R. V. "Use of Consumption Function in Short Run Forecasting," *Review of Economics and Statistics*, Vol. XXX, No. 2 (May, 1948).

Rosen, S. "The Post-World War II Economic Forecasts," *Delaware Notes* (1954).

————. "Two Post War Recessions," *Delaware Notes* (1956).

Rosenbluth, G. "Changing Structural Factors in Canada's Cyclical Sensitivity, 1903–54," *Canadian Journal of Economics and Political Science* (February, 1958).

Ross, C. R. "Price Stability in the United Kingdom," *Bulletin of the Oxford University Institute of Statistics* (August, 1958).

"Rostow on Growth," *The Economist* (August 15, 1959).

Rostow, Walt W. "The United Nations' Report on Full Employment," *Economic Journal*, Vol. LX, No. 238 (June, 1950).

————. "Some Notes on Mr. Hicks and History," *American Economic Review*, Vol. XLI, No. 3 (June, 1951).

————. "The Stages of Growth," *Economic History*, Vol. XII, No. 1 (August, 1959).

————. "The Problem of Achieving and Maintaining a High Rate of Economic Growth: An Historian's View," *American Economic Review*, Vol. L, No. 2 (May, 1960).

Ruth, N. "Full Employment in New Zealand," *Economic Record*, Vol. XXVI, No. 50 (June, 1950).

Sadie, J. L. "A Note on the Business Cycle in South Africa 1937–40." *South African Journal of Economics* (March, 1946).

Salant, W. A. "Saving, Investment, and Stability," *American Economic Review Proceedings*, Vol. XLVI, No. 2 (May, 1956).

Samuelson, Paul A. "Interactions Between the Multiplier Analysis and the Principle of Acceleration," *Review of Economic Statistics*, Vol. XXI, No. 2 (May, 1939).

————. "Built-In Stabilizer of Our Economy," *The Reporter* (February 17, 1953).

Saville, L. "Cyclical Fluctuations in Foundry Activity," *Journal of American Statistical Association* (December, 1954).

Sayers, R. S. "The Instability of the American Economy," *Westminster Bank Review* (August, 1949).

Schendstok, B., Simons, D., Tinbergen, J., and Dalmulder, F. J. "The Situation of the Public Finance as Affected by and Affecting Business Cycles in the Netherlands Before 1939," *Openbare Financien*, No. 2 (1948).

Schultze, C. L. "Creeping Inflation: Causes and Consequences," *Business Horizons* (Summer, 1960).

Schumann, C. G. W. "Aspects of the Problem of Full Employment in South Africa," *South African Journal of Economics* (June, 1948).

————. "Three Analogies in Business Cycle Theory," *South African Journal of Economics* (March, 1954).

Schumpeter, Joseph A. "The Explanation of the Business Cycle," *Economica*, No. 21 (December, 1927).

——. "The Analysis of Economic Change," *Review of Economic Statistics*, Vol. XVII, No. 2 (May, 1935).

——. "The Decade of the Twenties," *American Economic Review*, Vol. XXXVI, No. 2 (May, 1946).

Schweitzer, Arthur. "Spiethoff's Theory of the Business Cycle," *University of Wyoming Publications*, Vol. VIII, (April, 1941).

Scott, I. O., Jr. "A Comparison of Production During the Depressions of 1873 and 1929," *American Economic Review*, Vol. XLII, No. 4 (September, 1952).

Seers, D. "The Post-War Cost of Living," *Bulletin of Oxford University Institute of Statistics* (June, 1950).

——. "The Summer Recession in 1952," *Bulletin of Oxford University Institute of Statistics* (February-March, 1953).

Shaw, E. S. "Burns and Mitchell on Business Cycles," *Journal of Political Economy*, Vol. LV, No. 4 (August, 1947).

Shinohara, M. "Real and Money Income Multiplier," *Annals Hitatsubashi Academy* (April, 1953).

Shiskin, J. "Electronic Computers and Business Indicators," *Journal of Business* (October, 1957).

Shubik, M. "A Business Cycle with Organized Labor Considered," *Econometrica*, Vol. X, No. 2 (April, 1952).

Silberling, N. J. "British Financial Experience 1790–1830," *Review of Economic Statistics*, Preliminary Vol. 1, No. 4 (October, 1919).

Simler, N. J. "Rigid Prices, the Inflationary Bias and the Goal of Economic Policy," *Review of Social Economics* (September, 1954).

Simmons, E. C. "The Uses and Limitations of Monetary-Fiscal Policy in Economic Stabilization," *Southern Economic Journal* (April, 1952).

Simons, H. C. "The Beveridge Program: An Unsympathetic Interpretation," *Journal of Political Economy*, Vol. LIII, No. 4 (September, 1945).

Simpson, P. B., and Anderson, P. S. "Liabilities of Business Failures as a Business Indicator," *Review of Economics and Statistics*, Vol. XXXIX, No. 2 (May, 1957).

Singer, M. "Inflation Without Full Employment: Study," *Social Research* (Spring, 1959).

Slichter, Sumner H. "The Period 1919–1936 in the United States: Its Significance for Business Cycle Theory," *Review of Economic Statistics*, Vol. XIX, No. 1 February, 1937).

——. "Comments on the Murray Bill," *Review of Economic Statistics*, Vol. XXVII, No. 3 (August, 1945).

——. "Is a Recession Necessary?" *Dun's Review* (August, 1947).

——. "What Is America's Short Term Business Outlook?" *Dun's Review* (January, 1950).

——. "How Stable Is the American Economy?" *Yale Review* (June, 1950).

——. "How Stable Is the Economy?" *Commercial and Financial Chronicle* (October 23, 1952).

——. "Thinking Ahead: On the Side of Inflation," *Harvard Business Review*, Vol. XXXVII, No. 5 (September-October, 1959).

"The Slump and What to Do About It," *Fortune* (June, 1949).

Slutzky, Eugen. "The Summation of Random Causes As the Source of Cyclic Processes," *Econometrica*, Vol. V, No. 2 (April, 1937).

Smith, Henry. "Marx and the Trade Cycle," *Review of Economic Studies,* Vol. IV (June, 1937).

Smithies, A. "Full Employment in a Free Society," *American Economic Review,* Vol. XXXV, No. 3 (June, 1945).

———. "The Control of Inflation," *Review of Economics and Statistics,* Vol. XXXIX, No. 3 (August, 1957).

Smullyan, E. B. "Net Investment, Consumption and Full Employment," *American Economic Review,* Vol. XXXIV, No. 5 (December, 1944).

———. "Rejoinder [to A. R. Sweezy]," *American Economic Review,* Vol. XXXIV, No. 5 (December, 1944).

———. "Seventeen Post-War Plans—The Pabst Post-War Employment Award," *American Economic Review,* Vol. XXXV, No. 1 (March, 1945).

Snider, D. A. "French Monetary and Fiscal Policies Since the Liberation," *American Economic Review,* Vol. XXXVIII, No. 3 (June, 1948).

Snider, J. L. "What's Ahead for Prices and Business," *Harvard Business Review,* Vol. XXVI, No. 6 (November, 1948).

———. "Business Prospects and Problems in the 1950's," *Harvard Business Review,* Vol. XXVIII, No. 1 (January, 1950).

Solomon, E. "The Current Recovery: An Analysis," *Journal of Business—University of Chicago* (April, 1955).

Solow, Robert. "A Contribution to the Theory of Economic Growth," *Quarterly Journal of Economics,* Vol. LXX, No. 1 (February, 1956).

Sommers, A. T. "Business Highlights: Review and Outlook," *Conference Board Business Record* (December, 1957).

Spear, H. M. "Dividend Policies Under Changing Price Levels," *Harvard Business Review,* Vol. XXVII, No. 5 (September, 1949).

Spengler, J. J. "The Future of Prices," *Southern Economic Journal* (July, 1946).

Sproul, A. "Why We Can't Afford Deflation," *American Affairs* (April, 1948).

Stanback, T. M., Jr. "The Textile Cycle: Characteristics and Contributing Factors," *Southern Economic Journal* (October, 1958).

Stein, H. "Price Flexibility and Full Employment," *American Economic Review,* Vol. XXXIX, No. 3 (June, 1949).

Stekler, H. O. "Diffusion Index and First Difference Forecasting," *Review of Economics and Statistics,* Vol. XLIII, No. 2 (May, 1961).

Stern, Ernest H. "Capital Requirements in Progressive Economies," *Economica,* Vol. XII, No. 47 (August, 1945).

Straus, E. M. "Prices, Income Flow and Employment," *Quarterly Journal of Economics,* Vol. LX, No. 3 (August, 1946).

Strayer, P. J. "Stabilization of Personal Incomes—A Limited Fiscal Policy," *American Economic Review,* Vol. XL, No. 5 (December, 1950).

———. "Full Employment—1954 Model: A Review Article," *American Economic Review,* Vol. XLIV, No. 5 (December, 1954).

Strotz, R. H., McAnulty, J. C., and Naines, J. B., Jr. "Goodwin's Nonlinear Theory of the Business Cycle: An Electro-Analog Solution," *Econometrica,* Vol. XXI, No. 3 (July, 1953).

Sufrin, S. C. "Recession and Its Cure 1958–59," *Business Review—University of Washington* (May, 1959).

Swan, T. W. "Progress Report on the Trade Cycle," *Economic Record,* Vol. XXVI, No. 2 (December, 1950).

Sweezy, A. R. "Reply [to E. B. Smullyan]," *American Economic Review,* Vol. XXXIV, No. 5 (December, 1944).

Tait, D. C. "Development Works and Full Employment," *International Labor Review* (November-December, 1946).

Talamona, M. "Building Fluctuations and Business Cycles in Italy: 1863–1945," *Review of Economic Conditions in Italy* (May, 1959).

Tangri, S. S. A. "A Reconsideration of the Sun-Spot Theory of Business Cycles," *Indian Journal of Economics* (January, 1954).

"Ten Economists on Inflation," *Review of Economics and Statistics*, Vol. XXX, No. 2 (February, 1948).

Thomas, Margaret E. "The Predictive Value of Consumer Expenditure Data as a Method of Forecasting Economic Fluctuations." Paper presented at 1954 meeting of the American Statistical Association (1954).

Tinbergen, Jan. "Suggestions on Quantitative Business Cycle Theory," *Econometrica*, Vol. III, No. 3 (July, 1935).

———. "Econometric Business Cycle Research," *Review of Economic Studies*, Vol. VII, No. 2 (February, 1940).

———. "Critical Remarks on Some Business Cycle Theories," *Econometrica*, Vol. X, No. 2 (April, 1942).

———. "Reformation of Current Business Cycle Theories as Refutable Hypothesis," in *Conference on Business Cycles*, New York: National Bureau of Economic Research, 1951.

———. "The Analysis of Unemployment Figures and the Alleged Correspondence Between Causes and Cures," *Metroeconomica* (August, 1953).

Tintner, G. "The 'Simple' Theory of Business Fluctuations: A Tentative Verification," *Review of Economic Statistics*, Vol. XXVI, No. 3 (August, 1944).

Tobin, J. "Taxes, Saving, and Inflation," *American Economic Review*, Vol. XXXIX, No. 5 (December, 1949).

Towle, H. L. "Economic Maturity: An Industrial View," *Journal of Business— University of Chicago* (October, 1946).

Tress, R. C. "The Contribution of Economic Theory to Economic Prognostication," *Economica*, Vol. XXVI, No. 103 (August, 1959).

Triffen, R. "The Return to Convertibility: 1926–33 and 1958– ," *Banca Nazionale of Lavoro Quarterly Review*, No. 48 (March, 1959).

———. "Tomorrow's Convertibility: Aims and Means of the International Monetary Policy," *Banca Nazionale Del Lavoro Quarterly Review*, No. 49 (June, 1959).

Tsiang, S. C. "Accelerator Theory of the Firm, and the Business Cycle," *Quarterly Journal of Economics*, Vol. LXV, No. 3 (August, 1951).

Tsuru, S. "Business Cycle and Capitalism, Schumpeter vs. Marx," *Annals Hitatsubashi Academy* (April, 1952).

Turvey, R. "Some Notes on Multiplier Theory," *American Economic Review*, Vol. XLIII, No. 3 (June, 1953).

"Two Views on Basic Economic Questions," *The Morgan Guaranty Survey* (August, 1961).

Tyndall, D. G. "A Suggestion for the Control of Peacetime Inflation," *Journal of Finance*, Vol. IV, No. 4 (December, 1949).

Uhr, C. G. "Knut Wicksell—A Centennial Evaluation," *American Economic Review*, Vol. XLI, No. 5 (December, 1951).

Ulmer, M. J. "Autonomous and Induced Investment," *American Economic Review*, Vol. XLII, No. 4 (September, 1952).

United Nations. "Consumption Trends in Western Europe," *Economic Survey of Europe in 1958*, Geneva, 1959.

U. S. Department of Commerce. *Business Cycle Developments*, Washington, D. C.: U. S. Government Printing Office (October, 1961, *seriatim*).

Van Waasdijk, T. V. "Some Notes on Price Inflation in South Africa 1938–1948," Parts I-II, *South African Journal of Economics* (September and December, 1949).

Vawter, J. "End of the Post-War Bull Market?" *Financial Analyst Journal* (January-February, 1961).

Villard, H. H. "The Council of Economic Advisors and Depression Policy," *American Economic Review*, Vol, XL, No. 4 (September, 1950).

Vinci, F. "The Curbing of Inflationary Processes," *Review of Economic Conditions in Italy* (September, 1956).

Viner, J. "The Employment Act of 1946 in Operation," *Review of Economic Statistics*, Vol. XXIX, No. 2 (May, 1947).

———. "Can We Check Inflation," *Yale Review* (December, 1947).

Vining, R. "Regional Variation in Cyclical Fluctuation Viewed as a Frequency Distribution," *Econometrica*, Vol. XIII, No. 3 (July, 1945).

———. "The Region as a Concept in Business-Cycle Analysis," *Econometrica*, Vol. XIV, No. 3 (July, 1946).

———. "Measuring State and Regional Business Cycles," *Journal of Political Economy*, Vol. LV, No. 3 (August, 1947).

Wald, H. P. "Fiscal Policy, Military Preparedness, and Postwar Inflation," *National Tax Journal*, Vol. LV, No. 2 (March, 1949).

Walker, G. R. "Postwar Jobs—A New Approach," *International Postwar Problems* (July, 1945).

Walker, K. F. "A Preliminary Study of Some Aspects of Australian Business Cycles," *Sociological Review* (January-October, 1946).

Walker, R. "A Note on Secular Savings Around Alternative Trends," *Manchester School of Economics and Social Studies* (September, 1957).

Wallace, H. A. "The Use of Statistics in the Formation of National Full Employment Policy," *Journal of American Statistical Association* (March, 1945).

Wantrup, S. V. C. "Resource Conservation and Economic Stability," *Quarterly Journal of Economics*, Vol. LX, No. 2 (May, 1946).

Warburton, C. "Normal Production, Income Production, Income and Employment 1945–1965," *Southern Economic Journal* (January, 1945).

———. "Monetary Theory, Full Employment and the Great Depression," *Econometrica*, Vol. XIII, No. 2 (April, 1945).

———. "The Misplaced Emphasis in Contemporary Business—Fluctuation Theory," *Journal of Business—University of Chicago* (October, 1946).

———. "Volume of Savings, Quantity of Money and Business Instability," *Journal of Political Economy*, Vol. LV, No. 3 (June 1947).

———. "Hansen and Fellner on Full Employment Policies," *American Economic Review*, Vol. XXXVIII, No. 3 (June, 1948).

———. "Bank Reserves and Business Fluctuations," *Journal of American Statistical Association* (December, 1948).

———. "Monetary Policy and Business Forecasting, I," *Journal of Business—University of Chicago* (April, 1949).

———. "The Theory of Turning Points in Business Fluctuations," *Quarterly Journal of Economics*, Vol. LXIV, No. 4 (November, 1950).

———. "How Much Variation in the Quantity of Money Is Needed?" *Southern Economic Journal* (April, 1952).

———. "Money and Business Fluctuations in the Schumpeterian System," *Journal of Political Economy*, Vol. LXI, No. 6 (December, 1953).

Wasson, R. G. "Beveridge's 'Full Employment' in a Free Society," *Harvard Business Review*, Vol. XXIII, No. 3 (Summer, 1945).

Waugh, F. V. "Excise Taxes and Economic Stability," *Journal of Farm Economics* (August, 1948).

Welcker, J. W. "Divergent Views on Corporate Profits," *Harvard Business Review*, Vol. XXVII, No. 2 (March, 1949).

Wenzlick, D. S. "What About Rents," *Journal of the American Institute of Real Estate Appraisers* (January, 1933).

Wenzlick, R. "The Problem of Analyzing Local Real Estate Cycles," *Proceedings of the American Statistical Association* (March, 1933).

Williams, John H. "Deficit Spending," *American Economic Review*, Supplement, Vol. XXXI, No. 2 (May, 1941).

Wilson, E. B. "Measuring Business Cycles," *Quarterly Journal of Economics*, Vol. LXIV, No. 2 (May, 1950).

Wilson, Thomas. "Some International Aspects of Employment Policy," *Oxford Economic Papers* (February, 1951).

———. "Cyclical and Autonomous Inducements to Investment," *Oxford Economic Papers*, New Series, V (March, 1953).

Winkle, F. F. "Some Aspects of the Recent Inflation and Stabilization of the Hungarian Currency," *South African Journal of Economics* (September, 1947).

Wood, E. "Recent Monetary Policies," *Journal of Finance*, Vol. X, No. 3 (September, 1955).

Worcester, D. A., Jr. "Monetary Versus Fiscal Policy at Full Employment," *Journal of Finance*, Vol. XII, No. 1 (March, 1957).

Working, Holbrook. "Factors Determining the Price of Potatoes in St. Paul and Minneapolis," University of Minnesota, Agricultural Experiment Station, Technical Bulletin 10 (1922).

Worsley, T. B. "Economic Stabilization," *Annals American Academy of Political and Social Science* (November, 1951).

Worswick, G. D. N., and Martin, K. "Prices and Wage Policy," *Bulletin of the Oxford University Institute of Statistics* (March, 1948).

Wray, M. "Seasonal Demand and Uncertainty in Consumer Goods Industries —Some Case Studies," *Journal of Industrial Economics* (October, 1958).

Wright, A. H. "The Interaction of the Multiplier and Price Mechanisms," *Economica*, Vol. XXII, No. 88 (November, 1955).

Wright, D. McC. "Hopes and Fears—The Shape of Things to Come," *Review of Economic Statistics*, Vol. XXVI, No. 4 (November, 1944).

———. "Inflation and Equality," *American Economic Review*, Vol. XXXVIII, No. 5 (December, 1948).

———. "The Budget, the Business Cycle and Russia," *Commercial and Financial Chronicle* (July 14, 1949).

———. "The Great Guessing Game—Terborgh vs. Hansen," *Review of Economics and Statistics*, Vol XXXVIII, No. 1 (February, 1956).

Youngson, A. J. "Investment Decisions, Trade Cycle and Trend," *Oxford Economic Papers* (September, 1954).

Yule, G. V. "Why do We Sometimes Get Nonsense Correlations? A Study of Sampling and the Nature of Time Series," *Journal of the Royal Statistical Society*, Vol. LXXXIX, Part I (January, 1926).

INDEX

ABOUT THE EDITORS

JOHN J. CLARK, currently Assistant Dean and Director of the Graduate Division at St. John's University College of Business Administration, has also taught at the Polytechnic Institute of Brooklyn. He received his B.B.A. from St. John's University, and did his graduate work at the City College of New York (M.B.A., 1950) and at New York University (Ph.D., 1959). Professor Clark is co-editor of *Thought Patterns: Business and Liberal Arts*, Volume X, and is a contributor to many scholarly and business publications, among them the *Atlanta Economic Review*, *Thought Patterns*, *Personnel*, the *Long Island Commercial Review*, the *Annual Financial Review* of the New York *World Telegram*, and the *Proceedings* of the U. S. Naval Institute. In addition to his activities in business and economics, he has been concerned with education in his field, having served on the Middle States Accrediting Committee of the College of Business Administration, and co-authored *New Concepts in Business Education*, published by the St. John's University Press in 1961.

MORRIS COHEN, Associate Editor and Associate Economist at *Fortune* since 1960, is also a Professorial Lecturer in Economics at the Graduate School of Business, St. John's University. He received his B.A. from the University of Pennsylvania and his M.A. from Pennsylvania State College, and continued his graduate studies at Harvard University, where he was awarded his M.P.A. and Ph.D. Before joining the staff of *Fortune*, he served as Senior Economist of the National Industrial Conference Board for seven years, and spent four years with the Office of Business Economics of the U. S. Department of Commerce. He has lectured at the Baruch School of Business, Fairleigh Dickinson University, the Massachusetts Institute of Technology, and Pennsylvania State College. In 1952–3 he was Harvard's Sheldon Travelling Fellow in Economics at the University of Cambridge. Professor Cohen has frequently contributed articles to such publications as *Thought Patterns*, *Review of Economics and Statistics*,

Journal of the American Statistical Association, and the *American Economic Review.* He has presented several papers to the American Marketing Association and the American Statistical Association which have subsequently appeared in their published proceedings, and is the author of "The NICB Appropriations Survey" in *The Quality and Economic Significance of Anticipation Data* (1959), and of "The Income Side: A Business User's Viewpoint" in *A Critique of the United States National Income and Product Accounts* (1958), both published by the Princeton University Press.

A NOTE ON THE TYPE

This book is set in Electra, a Linotype face designed by W. A. Dwiggins. This face cannot be classified as either modern or old-style. It is not based on any historical model, nor does it echo any particular period or style. It avoids the extreme contrasts between thick and thin elements that mark most modern faces, and attempts to give a feeling of fluidity, power, and speed.

DATE

1/13 2:30
11/22/9:30
2-16 1:00